From Adam to Us

Part 2: Castles to Computers

Ray and Charlene Notgrass

Activities by Bethany Poore
Maps by Nate McCurdy

From Adam to Us Part 2
Ray and Charlene Notgrass
Activities by Bethany Poore
Maps by Nate McCurdy

ISBN 978-1-60999-085-5

Copyright © 2016 Notgrass History. All rights reserved.
Printed in 2022.
No part of this material may be reproduced without permission from the publisher.

Cover Photo Credits
Front Cover: Carcassonne, France (leoks/Shutterstock.com), Ship (Pixabay)
St. Basil's Cathedral in Moscow, Russia (Marina99/Shutterstock.com)
Llama in Machu Picchu, Peru (Alexandra Copley/Shutterstock.com)
Singapore (Patrick Foto/Shutterstock.com), Space Walk (NASA)
Back Cover: Eiffel Tower in Paris, France (Pixabay), Author Photo (Mev McCurdy)

All product names, brands, and other trademarks mentioned or pictured
in this book are used for educational purposes only.
No association with or endorsement by the owners of the trademarks is intended.
Each trademark remains the property of its respective owner.

Unless otherwise noted, Scripture quotations taken from the
New American Standard Bible, Copyright 1960, 1962, 1963, 1971, 1972, 1973, 1975, 1977, 1995
by the Lockman Foundation. Used by permission.

Cover design by Mary Evelyn McCurdy
Interior design by Charlene Notgrass

Printed in the United States of America

Notgrass History • 975 Roaring River Road • Gainesboro, TN 38562
1-800-211-8793 • notgrass.com

Table of Contents

Unit 16 – Chivalry, Trade, and New Freedoms 509

    Lesson 76 – World Biography: Mansa Musa of the Mali Empire 511

    Lesson 77 – Our World Story: The Hundred Years War 516

    Lesson 78 – God's Wonder: God Created the Salzkammergut 525

    Lesson 79 – World Landmark: Lubeck and the Hanseatic League 530

    Lesson 80 – Daily Life: Beginnings of Change in Church and Government 536

Unit 17 – The Early Renaissance 541

    Lesson 81 – God's Wonder: The Voyages of Zheng He 543

    Lesson 82 – World Landmark : The Forbidden City 551

    Lesson 83 – World Biography: Prince Henry the Navigator 556

    Lesson 84 – Our World Story: The Fall of Constantinople 562

    Lesson 85 – Daily Life: The Italian Renaissance 568

Unit 18 – The Late 1400s 575

    Lesson 86 – God's Wonder: Venice, Italy 577

    Lesson 87 – World Biography: Ivan the Great 583

    Lesson 88 – Our World Story: Printing in Renaissance Europe 589

    Lesson 89 – World Landmark: Machu Picchu of the Inca 596

    Lesson 90 – Daily Life: Making Porcelain in the Ming Dynasty 603

Unit 19 – The Early 1500s 609

- Lesson 91 – World Landmark: Florence, Italy 611
- Lesson 92 – God's Wonder: Columbus Discovers the Caribbean and the New World 619
- Lesson 93 – Daily Life: Sailing with Brave Explorers 627
- Lesson 94 – World Biography: Nicolaus Copernicus 633
- Lesson 95 – Our World Story: Martin Luther and the Reformation 638

Unit 20 – The Late 1500s 643

- Lesson 96 – Our World Story: Kings and Queens of England 645
- Lesson 97 – World Landmark: The Jewish Community in Lublin, Poland 652
- Lesson 98 – God's Wonder: Potosi Silver Mine in the Andes Mountains 658
- Lesson 99 – World Biography: Suleyman I and the Ottoman Empire 665
- Lesson 100 – Daily Life: The People of Southeast Asia 669

Unit 21 – The Early 1600s 679

- Lesson 101 – Our World Story: The Beginnings of the British Empire 681
- Lesson 102 – World Biography: William Shakespeare 690
- Lesson 103 – God's Wonder: God Created the Food Grown Around the World 695
- Lesson 104 – World Landmark: Sweden and the Thirty Years War 704
- Lesson 105 – Daily Life: The Rule of the Shoguns in Japan 710

Unit 22 – The Late 1600s 715

- Lesson 106 – Our World Story: The Dutch Golden Age 717
- Lesson 107 – Daily Life: The Mughal Empire 723
- Lesson 108 – World Biography: Louis XIV of France 730
- Lesson 109 – God's Wonder: God Created Tibet 737
- Lesson 110 – World Landmark: London, England 743

Unit 23 – The Early 1700s 749

- Lesson 111 – God's Wonder: God Created the Island of Mauritius 751
- Lesson 112 – Our World Story: The Reign of Peter the Great of Russia 757
- Lesson 113 – World Biography: Johann Sebastian Bach 763
- Lesson 114 – World Landmark: Easter Island 769
- Lesson 115 – Daily Life: The Moravians 775

Unit 24 – Age of Revolutions 781

Lesson 116 – World Biography: Frederick the Great of Prussia 783

Lesson 117 – Daily Life: The Industrial Revolution 790

Lesson 118 – World Landmark: Paris, France 799

Lesson 119 – Our World Story: The American and French Revolutions 805

Lesson 120 – God's Wonder: God Created the Cape of Good Hope 813

Unit 25 – Quest for Freedom 819

Lesson 121 – Our World Story: Napoleon and the Congress of Vienna 821

Lesson 122 – World Landmark: Singapore 827

Lesson 123 – Daily Life: Independence in Haiti and South America 834

Lesson 124 – God's Wonder: All Things Are Possible with God 842

Lesson 125 – World Biography: Hans Christian Andersen 849

Unit 26 – The Victorian Era 855

Lesson 126 – World Biography: Queen Victoria 857

Lesson 127 – Our World Story: The Crimean War 866

Lesson 128 – Daily Life: Japan's Open Door 871

Lesson 129 – World Landmark: The Eiffel Tower 877

Lesson 130 – God's Wonder: God Created Gold 883

Unit 27 – The Early 1900s 889

Lesson 131 – World Biography: Sun Yat-sen 891

Lesson 132 – God's Wonder: God Created the North and South Poles 898

Lesson 133 – Daily Life: Inventions Around the World 904

Lesson 134 – Our World Story: The Great War 911

Lesson 135 – World Landmark: Christ the Redeemer, Rio de Janeiro 918

Unit 28 – The Mid-Twentieth Century 923

Lesson 136 – Our World Story: World War II 925

Lesson 137 – World Landmark: Berlin and the Cold War 938

Lesson 138 – God's Wonder: God Created the Land of India 949

Lesson 139 – Daily Life: Television Around the World 957

Lesson 140 – World Biography: C. S. Lewis 965

Unit 29 – The End of the Twentieth Century ... 971
  Lesson 141 – World Biography: Douglas Nicholls, an Aboriginal Australian ... 973
  Lesson 142 – God's Wonder: God Created Space ... 980
  Lesson 143 – Our World Story: Nikolaikirche and the End of Communism in Europe ... 988
  Lesson 144 – World Landmark: Building Up ... 995
  Lesson 145 – Daily Life: People Groups Around the World ... 1001

Unit 30 – Us ... 1009
  Lesson 146 – World Biography: Queen Elizabeth II ... 1011
  Lesson 147 – Our World Story: Turmoil in the Middle East ... 1019
  Lesson 148 – World Landmark: Sports Bring Us Together ... 1026
  Lesson 149 – God's Wonder: God's World Still Supports Human Life ... 1033
  Lesson 150 – Daily Life: Our Interconnected World ... 1040

Family Activities ... FA-33

Credits and Sources ... CS-15

Index ... I-1

16 Chivalry, Trade, and New Freedoms

Old Town of Tallinn, Estonia

Lessons
76 - World Biography: Mansa Musa of the Mali Empire
77 - Our World Story: The Hundred Years War
78 - God's Wonder: God Created the Salzkammergut
79 - World Landmark: Lubeck and the Hanseatic League
80 - Daily Life: Beginnings of Change in Church and Government

Literature *Otto of the Silver Hand*

1301-1400

Mansa Musa, emperor of the Mali Empire in West Africa, became one of the richest men in the history of the world. The French and English fought a war that lasted over one hundred years. Prince archbishops ruled in the region of Salzburg in the Salzkammergut, home to the world's oldest salt mine. In the northern part of the Holy Roman Empire, Lubeck became the leading city of the Hanseatic League, an organization of merchants and cities that generated great wealth through trade on the Baltic Sea. Men such as Peter Waldo in France, John Wycliffe in England, and Jan Hus in Bohemia began to preach against flaws they saw in the Roman Catholic Church at the same time that English barons were challenging the authority of the king of England.

Mansa Musa
of the Mali Empire

Lesson 76　　　　　　　　　　　　　　　　　　　　World Biography

Religion and government continued to be intertwined in kingdom after kingdom in the late Middle Ages. After the death of Muhammad, Muslims spread their caliphates (see page 421) to more and more places in the Middle East and as far east as Iran and Mesopotamia. However, when Genghis Khan led his Mongols into Muslim areas, many Muslims escaped onto the Anatolian Peninsula and established caliphates there.

By the 1300s Muslims had conquered much of northern Africa and moved south of the Sahara Desert into an area in West Africa called the Sudan. Though a modern country of Sudan exists in East Africa, the geographical region called the Sudan extends across Africa south of the Sahara Desert from the Atlantic Ocean in the west to the Red Sea in the east. See map on page 513.

West Africa became a trading center where merchants sold gold from the Sudan and salt brought in by Muslim traders from North Africa. West Africans traded with various foreign countries, especially with countries in Europe.

Founding the Mali Empire

Africans have long passed down their histories through poems, songs, and oral storytelling. The epic poem "Sundiata" tells about the life of Sundiata Keita of West Africa. In the 1200s, he founded the Mali Kingdom in a savannah along the upper Niger River. Residents of a savannah experience a long rainy season and an even longer

Boys wash a goat in the Niger River in Mopti, Mali.

dry season each year. Through wars with neighboring peoples, Sundiata expanded the kingdom of Mali into an empire.

Mansa Musa became ruler in 1307. Musa was a member of Sundiata's family, perhaps his grandson or maybe his great-nephew. Mansa Musa expanded the empire even more until it reached the size shown in the map on page 513. At its peak, the Mali Empire may have had a population of from forty to fifty million people. Mali became rich by trading in gold, salt, and copper. During the lifetime of Mansa Musa, Mali used cowrie shells as currency, both for trade and for the payment of taxes.

Pilgrimage to Mecca

Mansa Musa was a Muslim. In 1324 he made a pilgrimage to Mecca. He traveled west through what is now Mauritania, then north through what is now Algeria. His caravan included 60,000 people, of whom 12,000 were his personal slaves. All of his retinue wore Persian silk and a rich fabric called brocade, woven with patterns in gold and silver. Five hundred slaves, each with a gold-covered staff, went before him as he rode on horseback. His baggage train included eighty

Above: Djenne merchants in 2011 carry goods to market by boat across the Niger River and by cart. Below: A camel caravan hauls salt in the Sahara Desert near Timbuktu in modern Mali.

Lesson 76 - Mansa Musa of the Mali Empire

camels, each of which carried 300 pounds of gold. That was 24,000 pounds of gold! Based on the value of gold today, Mansa Musa left home with about $400 million worth of gold. The camel caravan on page 512 carries salt.

Mansa Musa and his caravan stopped in Cairo, Egypt. The event was a sensation. People in this city of one million talked about it for years. He spent so much gold there that the price of gold in Cairo fell for over ten years. The reputation of Mansa Musa's wealth spread throughout North Africa and into Europe.

Djenne

Mali was home to the city of Djenne, which is considered to be the oldest city in Africa south of the Sahara Desert. Merchants began using it as a trading post between 850 and 1200. See modern Djenne merchants at left.

A large number of terra-cotta sculptures produced between the time when Jesus was born through the 1400s has been discovered in Djenne. The world's largest mud building is the Djenne Mosque, built in 1907 and pictured at right. It stands on the site of the mosque built there during the time of the Mali Empire.

Djenne Mosque

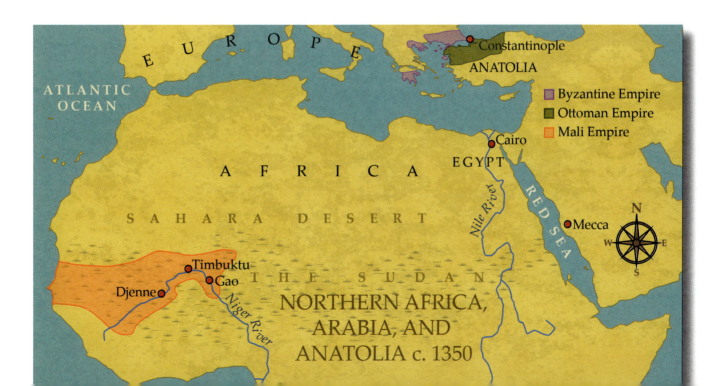

NORTHERN AFRICA, ARABIA, AND ANATOLIA c. 1350

Timbuktu

Around 1100 a herding people called the Tuareg established a stopping place on the southern edge of the Sahara Desert about eight miles away from the Niger River. Two Tuareg men and the Sahara Desert are pictured on page 515. Called Timbuktu, the city served nomads of the Sahara and traders who moved along the river. Here they traded salt, dates, kola nuts, and gold dust.

Mansa Musa made Timbuktu part of the Mali Empire. It became a key trading site and a center for Islamic education and art. From Timbuktu, Muslims spread Islam further into Africa. Mansa Musa built a palace there. Timbuktu is home to three of West Africa's oldest mosques, including the Djinguereber Mosque, constructed around 1325.

Gao of the Songhay

During Mansa Musa's pilgrimage to Mecca, one of his generals captured Gao, yet another trading city. Gao was the capital of the Songhay Empire. Mansa Musa stopped in Gao while on his pilgrimage and took two sons of the king of Songhay home with him as hostages. Capturing Gao and the Songhay Empire increased the Mali Empire considerably because the Songhay realm stretched for 1,000 miles along the Middle Niger River. Ibn Battuta, mentioned on page 506, visited Mali in the 1350s. He said that traveling through the Mali Empire from north to south required about four months.

While Islam spread in Mali, Christians in Ethiopia in eastern Africa created beautiful copies of the Scriptures and beautiful art, as seen in the photos below.

Left: Painting of St. Luke Created by an Ethiopian Artist in the Lake Tana Region of Ethiopia, Late 1300s;
Center: Leaf from the Ethiopian Gospels, Copied by the Scribe Matre Krestos in the Language Ge-ez, Early 1300s;
Right: Bronze Cross Used in Church Services, Ethiopia, c. 1400s

Lesson 76 - Mansa Musa of the Mali Empire

Tuareg Men in Their Camp at Timbuktu

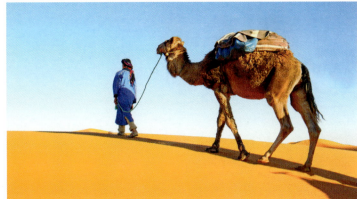
Sahara Desert, North Africa

Mansa Musa died in 1337. In the early 1400s, the Mali Empire began to decline. Outside armies invaded, and the Empire experienced a civil war. Mansa Musa was one of the richest men who has ever lived. However, his kingdom did not last. Jesus told us where we can find true riches that will last.

> *Do not store up for yourselves treasures on earth,*
> *where moth and rust destroy, and where thieves break in and steal.*
> *But store up for yourselves treasures in heaven,*
> *where neither moth nor rust destroys,*
> *and where thieves do not break in or steal;*
> *for where your treasure is, there your heart will be also.*
> *Matthew 6:19-21*

Assignments for Lesson 76

Our Creative World — Read the excerpts from *The Rihla* on pages 55-57.

Map Book — Complete the activities for Lesson 76 on Map 22 "Northern Africa, Arabia, and Anatolia."

Timeline Book — In the box for Lesson 76 on page 18, write "Mansa Musa makes a pilgrimage to Mecca."

Student Workbook or Lesson Review — If you are using one of these optional books, complete the assignment for Lesson 76.

Thinking Biblically — Write the words of Matthew 6:19-21 in the center of a piece of paper. Around the verse, draw some earthly "treasures" that people have acquired both now and in history.

Literature — Read chapters VIII-IX in *Otto of the Silver Hand*.

Family Activity — Make "Mansa Musa's Caravan." See page FA-33 for instructions.

The Hundred Years War

Lesson 77   Our World Story

During the Late Middle Ages, Europeans created new inventions that had a positive impact on others. The spinning wheel improved manufacturing. The windmill and water mill improved both farming and manufacturing. The compass improved navigation. Riders benefited from the horseshoe, stirrups, and high-backed saddle.

Europeans cleared forest lands for farming and to provide living space for their growing population. Farmers took advantage of the newly-invented iron plowshare. They also began to use the three-field farming method. They planted a third of the land in grain—wheat, barley, or rye—in the autumn; and another third in oats, peas, beans, barley, and lentils in the spring. The legumes added nitrogen to the soil, which made the crops more nutritious. The other third of the fields lay fallow (resting while not being planted with any crop) for a year.

People opened universities in several cities across Europe. Artists created beautiful paintings that showed everyday life. Great authors, such as Thomas Aquinas who wrote about theology, Roger Bacon who wrote about science, and Dante Alighieri who wrote literature, produced writings that had a **profound** influence on the way people in Europe thought. Architects and craftsmen created elaborate cathedrals that have stood for centuries.

The Middle Ages have been described as the Dark Ages. Though this is simply not accurate, Europeans of the Middle Ages experienced great tragedies, and warfare was almost constant.

Castles

Since warfare was a common occurrence, many families of the nobility in Europe built castles as their dwelling places. Some nobles built castles to show their power. For instance,

Thomas Aquinas and Augustine

if a king captured a new area, he might demonstrate his strength and intimidate any opposition by having a noble construct a castle there. More obviously, a castle provided defense against enemies. Armies used castles to defend an area, a river, or a road from an enemy attack.

Location was important. Many nobles built their castles on hills. Others constructed a moat to surround the castle and make it harder for enemies to get inside. As seen in the photo above, a moat was a wide ditch filled with water. A castle that used a moat for

Top: In 1385 Sir Edward Dallingridge built Bodiam Castle near Robertsbridge in East Sussex, England, to defend the area during the Hundred Years War. Notice the moat surrounding the castle. Left: Drawbridge of Scaliger Castle, Built in the 1200s, in Sirmione Scaligero, Italy; Right: Portcullis of Malbork Castle in Poland, Built in the 1200s and Expanded after 1309

defense would also have a drawbridge that could be lowered to allow people to enter the castle and raised to keep enemies out. A portcullis, such as the one at right above, also protected the entrance into the castle. This was a heavy gate made of either iron or wood covered with iron. Like the drawbridge, a portcullis could be raised and lowered. A gatehouse or towers on either side of the gateway provided a place for lookouts to watch for an enemy's approach.

Unit 16 - Chivalry, Trade, and New Freedoms

Round Towers of Conwy Castle in Conwy, Wales

Battlements and Towers of Guimarães Castle in Northern Portugal

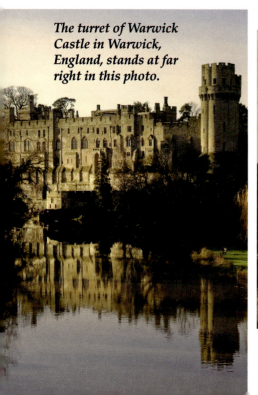

The turret of Warwick Castle in Warwick, England, stands at far right in this photo.

Castles had common features. They had thick walls. A battlement usually topped the outer wall. Defenders attacked an approaching army from an interior walkway behind the battlement. The battlement of the castle at center left stands between its square towers.

If a castle had two walls, the enclosed area between the walls was called a bailey or ward. Towers on the exterior walls, such as those at left, enabled defenders to see great distances in all directions across the surrounding countryside. A turret, such as the one at lower left, provided an even better lookout position.

The most fortified and best-defended part of a castle was the keep. The keep often included the rooms where the owners of the castle lived. In many castles the largest of these rooms was the great hall. Castles were stately and **romantic**, but since they were made of stone they usually were also cold and damp and not very comfortable. Straw covered the floors until rugs became common. Wall tapestries, such as the one in the keep below, served two purposes: they were beautiful but they also had the **practical** benefit of making rooms warmer. A castle was a busy place, with work areas for carpenters, blacksmiths, craftsmen, cooks, and many other workers. Many castles also included a chapel.

The residents of a castle had to be able to endure a siege. A siege was not a direct attack. During a siege, enemy forces

Wall Tapestry Inside the Keep at Château de Chaumont in Chaumont-sur-Loire, France

Lesson 77 - The Hundred Years War

surrounded the castle to cut it off from other people. A castle under siege could receive neither supplies nor additional soldiers to help fight the enemy.

Corvin Castle (also known as Hunyad Castle) in Hunedoara, Romania

Castles required a well or other water source, large areas for food storage, and some type of waste disposal system. Usually a village grew up around the castle, where workers, their families, and other people lived. During a siege, the townspeople took refuge inside the castle, so the supplies inside had to be sufficient for the townspeople as well as the noble and his household.

Castles might seem invincible, but armies invented several ways to attack them. Catapults launched heavy stones or other objects into a castle. Battering rams could break down a gate or part of a wall. Siege towers protected soldiers as they approached a castle. See these war machines below. Sometimes soldiers called sappers dug a tunnel underneath a castle wall to weaken it. Sometimes they accomplished this by starting a fire in the tunnel. Until the invention of the cannon, a castle was an effective defense against enemies. However, cannon shot fired again and again could eventually damage castle walls to the point that they no longer kept out the enemy.

Left: Wooden Catapult in the Tsarevets Fortress in Veliko Tarnovo, Bulgaria; Center: Battering Ram and Cart for Carrying Projectiles in Shumeg, Hungary; Right: Siege Tower in Morocco

Knights

A medieval army had hundreds or thousands of foot soldiers and archers, plus men assigned to the catapults and other weapons. Knights formed the horse-mounted part of the military called the cavalry. In the feudal system, a knight was bound to serve a particular lord on whose land he lived.

The son of a knight, or another young man who sought to become a knight, often began serving his father or another knight as a page around age seven. He learned about caring for horses and equipment. Around age twelve, he became a squire, also called an esquire or a

Armored Knights

valet. During this period the squire taught pages while he learned about combat and about how to conduct himself in society. A squire accompanied his knight into battle as his armor-bearer. A knight's armor could weigh as much as fifty-five pounds, and sometimes his horse was armored as well. When a squire was judged ready for battle and when he had the money needed to purchase his equipment, a ceremony pronounced him a knight.

Over time, knights came to follow a code of conduct called chivalry. This included respecting the Catholic Church, assisting the poor and weak, obeying one's superiors, and defending women. Orders or groups of knights were common, such as the Most Noble Order of the Garter and the Order of the Golden Fleece. When warfare became less common in the later Middle Ages, knights began to hold tournaments or mock battles as a form of entertainment. Tournaments gave knights practice in the skills they would need when true conflict arose.

The Start of the Hundred Years War

As we described in Lesson 70, the nobility and royalty of England and France became intertwined in a complicated way through marriage. French and English nobles and royal families wanted to control the same places. This began before the Norman Conquest of 1066 and continued into the 1300s. Normans from France controlled England. England controlled large

Lesson 77 - The Hundred Years War

areas of France. Some nobles in France were loyal to England. Other nobles and the royalty in France opposed some of their own countrymen. The continuing **rivalry** and **suspicion** often erupted in battles.

A war over who would inherit the throne of France began in 1337. The French king Charles IV died in 1328. King Edward III of England was his closest male relative and claimed the right to become king of France. A French assembly, however, declared that Philip, Count of Valois in France and first cousin to Charles IV, should become King Philip VI of France.

Edward III was also Duke of Aquitaine, a region in southwestern France. He accepted the assembly's decision, but changed his mind when Philip VI began to meddle in the affairs of Aquitaine. In 1337, Philip claimed Aquitaine as part of his dominion. As a result, Edward III declared himself king of France in 1340 and began trying to overthrow Philip VI.

The conflict continued for over one hundred years. The two sides fought battles occasionally, but more often the army of one side laid siege for several months to a town or castle controlled by their enemy. Sometimes a siege was successful, sometimes an opposing army attacked the besiegers, and sometimes the besieging army simply gave up and left. The places of conflict were so numerous and widespread that generations came and went and still the conflict continued.

The Battle of Crecy

In 1346 Edward III landed with an army in northern France and moved toward Calais. Philip VI took up a defensive position with his forces against the English at Crecy-en-Ponthieu, which lay between Calais and Paris, both of which are seen on the map on page 534. Italian crossbowmen made up part of the French army. Edward III defeated the French through the use of the newly-invented longbow and cannon and by using effective battlefield tactics. Edward III did not pursue Philip VI but instead moved on to besiege and capture the port of Calais on the English Channel, a location of great importance to the English.

The Battle of Crecy is significant for a number of reasons. Edward III came to be recognized as the most powerful ruler in Europe. The battle changed European warfare because the longbow could be reloaded and fired much faster than the crossbow. Making use of an early cannon also made a difference for the English. Inventions such as the longbow and the cannon made the military purpose of knights obsolete. Kings also became more powerful and less dependent on the feudal system for a supply of soldiers for their armies. See a French castle which changed hands seven times during the Hundred Years War at right and an English castle built for defense during the war on page 517.

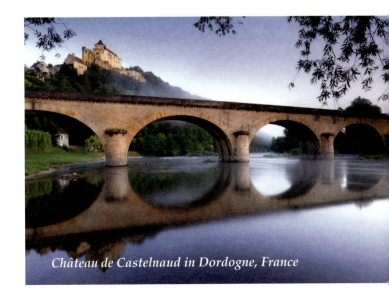
Château de Castelnaud in Dordogne, France

The Black Plague

In 1347, just one year after the Battle of Crecy, a disaster befell Europe. People in port cities began falling ill to a plague. The plague spread throughout the continent of Europe. Sufferers developed black swellings in their armpits and on other parts of their bodies, and they often died suddenly. We now understand that the disease was the bubonic plague, spread by fleas from infested rats on trading ships from Asia.

The rate of infection varied from place to place, although in many cities the death toll was enormous. At the time, people did not understand contagious diseases. The disease spread because people lived close together and had poor sanitation practices. The plague spread much more quickly in cities. Not as many people died in rural areas.

People tried all manner of ways to stop the illness, including magic. Some people attacked Jews because they wrongly blamed the Jews for the plague. The plague continued for four years. However, shorter and less severe outbreaks occurred every few years after that.

We have no way of knowing the exact number of people who died, but a fairly good estimate is that twenty-five million people, or about one-third of the population of Europe, perished. England suffered even more. Historians believe that the population of England in 1400 was about one-half what it had been in 1300. The population of Europe probably did not regain the level it was before the plague until the early 1500s. Beyond the devastating fear and grief, many fighting men and millions of farmers and artisans died. Not as much food was available for those who survived because there weren't enough farmers to work the land. Prices for goods and services rose because these things were scarce and thus highly valued. Life in Europe did eventually recover, but the recovery took many years.

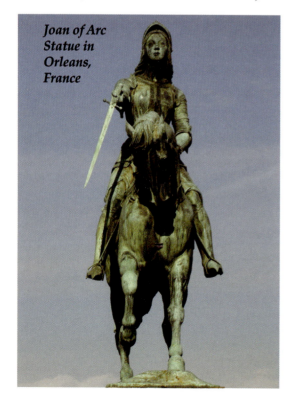

Joan of Arc Statue in Orleans, France

Joan of Arc

The plague slowed down the Hundred Years War, but it did not stop it. Despite the English victory at Crecy, the long-term trend was favorable for the French. The English had to carry on their efforts far from home, which made it hard to keep their army supplied with what they needed to live and succeed. The turning point came in 1429 when a young French girl became the inspiring leader of French forces.

Joan was born the daughter of a tenant farmer in 1412. When she was sixteen, she claimed to begin hearing voices and seeing visions that told her she was to lead the French to victory over the English. She went to the castle where Charles, the heir to the

Lesson 77 - The Hundred Years War

French throne, lived at the time. Charles was fighting again against England's King Henry VI over who would become the next king of France. Joan told Charles that she wanted to lead an army against the English and that she would see him crowned as king. She said that the decisive confrontation would take place at Orleans, a French city that had been under siege by English forces for months. It is seen on the map on page 534.

At first the French did not know what to do with this young girl who claimed to hear divine voices, dressed in men's clothes, and said she would lead French fighting forces to victory. Theologians of the Church questioned her and then advised Charles to allow her to help. In May of 1429 Joan led the French army as they broke the siege of Orleans. The French defeated and scattered the English forces. They continued to be victorious over the English in other places. Charles was crowned as King Charles VII of France on July 29, 1429. Joan was in attendance and acknowledged him as her king. She then continued to lead troops.

French allies of the English captured Joan on May 23, 1430. A Church court official who was friendly to the English king put her on trial in early 1431. She was found guilty of being a heretic because she claimed to have direct communication with God. Joan confessed that she was loyal to the Church, but she was burned at the stake on May 30, 1432, when she was around nineteen years of age. Joan of Arc continues to be a hero to the French and a symbol of French national pride.

The English became distracted by their own conflict at home when two families, the House of York and the House of Lancaster, fought the War of the Roses to determine who would become the next king of England. Lesson 96 describes this war. Meanwhile, French King Charles VII conquered Normandy and Aquitaine. By 1453 Calais was the only place in France that England still controlled. A century later England gave up its claim to Calais.

England and France never signed a peace treaty to end the Hundred Years War. Fighting over who would control the throne of France simply ended. English kings gave up their efforts to control France and concentrated on matters within their own borders. The French monarchy ruled over an increasingly unified nation that became the strongest in Europe for many years.

Joan of Arc Window in the Chapel of St. Benedict Monastery, Bristow, Virginia

The one who desires life, to love and see good days,
Must keep his tongue from evil and his lips from speaking deceit.
He must turn away from evil and do good;
He must seek peace and pursue it.

1 Peter 3:10-11

Assignments for Lesson 77

Our Creative World — Read the excerpt from "The Song of Joan of Arc" on page 58.

Timeline Book — In the box for Lesson 77 on page 18, write "English and French fight at Crecy." In the box for Lesson 77 on page 19, write "Joan of Arc leads the French at the Siege of Orleans."

Student Workbook or Lesson Review — If you are using one of these optional books, complete the assignment for Lesson 77.

Vocabulary — Copy the following sentences, placing the correct vocabulary word in the blank: profound (516), romantic (518), practical (518), rivalry (521), suspicion (521).

1. Alissa eyed her dog with _____ when she saw slobber on her tablet.

2. I decided to spend some of my birthday money on _____ needs.

3. Dr. Wilson's lecture on the role of the church in the Middle Ages had many _____ points.

4. Christy loves to write _____ poems about knights and fair ladies.

5. Our coaches try to make sure that we keep the _____ friendly among the soccer teams.

Creative Writing — Write a short story that takes place in a castle. Your story should be at least one page.

Literature — Read chapters X-XI in *Otto of the Silver Hand*.

Kokorin Castle near Prague in the Czech Republic

God Created the Salzkammergut

Lesson 78 God's Wonder

Pass the salt, please! The salt (sodium chloride) in the shaker on your kitchen table is a tremendously valuable and important **element** for life in our world. Production of salt around the world today totals 150 to 200 million tons each year. From ancient times, people have recognized the importance of salt and have placed a high value on it. As we learned in Lesson 76, the salt trade was one of the sources of Mansa Musa's great wealth.

Supplying salt for mankind is one of the many ways that God has provided for His Creation. He has placed salt in the oceans of the world and also in certain places in the dry ground. Salt is vital to the proper functioning of our bodies. In the ancient world, salt had two main uses: preserving meat and flavoring food. Before the invention of refrigeration, people rubbed meat with large amounts of salt, after which it could last a long time. People also valued salt for its ability to make food taste better. As the ancient patriarch Job said: "Can something tasteless be eaten without salt?" (Job 6:6).

Salt has given us some familiar sayings. A person who is "worth his salt" is someone who does his job well. The origin of the phrase dates to Roman times when Rome paid soldiers in salt. A good worker was worth the salt that he was paid. The Latin word *sal*, meaning salt, is the origin of our word salary, which is what someone is paid for his work. To take a statement "with a grain of salt" means that the statement itself might not be true or good. It might need "a grain of salt" for you to be able to swallow (or accept) it.

Salt in the Bible

Sometimes the Bible expresses the cleansing or **antiseptic** value of salt. Elisha threw salt into a spring and declared that the Lord had purified the water (2 Kings 2:19-21). People caring for newborn babies commonly rubbed them with salt as an antiseptic (Ezekiel 16:4). Jesus called His followers "the salt of the earth" (Matthew 5:13). In other words, Christians are to be a life-enhancing and preserving influence in a corrupt and dying world. In the same verse, Jesus goes on to say that salt that has become tasteless is good for nothing. Salt becomes useless when it is contaminated with other materials.

The Salt of the Salzkammergut

The Alps, seen in the satellite image below, are the tallest mountain range in Europe and one of the largest and tallest mountain ranges in the world. This mountain chain lies between northern and southern Europe. The Salzkammergut region lies in the eastern Alps in what is now Austria. It is home to red deer, European bison, wolves, lynxes, and brown bears. Salzkammergut means "Salt Chamber Estate" in German. Beneath this beautiful area of Alpine mountains and lakes are rich salt deposits. The city of Salzburg, made famous by the movie *The Sound of Music*, lies on the edge of the Salzkammergut. Salzburg means "Salt Castle."

Near Salzburg is the village of Hallstatt, the oldest city in the Salzkammergut. Hallstatt means "Salt Settlement." Celtic people once lived in this area and hall is the Celtic word for salt. Hallstatt is home to the world's oldest known salt mine. Historians believe that salt mining began in this area before 1000 BC. These miners left bronze pickaxes, ladders, and **whetstones** (used to sharpen metal tools). They left evidence that they bundled chips of pinewood together to make torches which they positioned in rock **crevices** to give off light. A miner could produce enough salt in one year for about 1,000 families. After a period of decline of salt production there, it resumed in the early Renaissance.

In addition to the rich salt **deposits** beneath the Salzkammergut, God also created many caves, including the Dachstein ice cave and the over-fifty-mile-long Hirlatzhöhle cave. He made the limestone Dachstein Mountains, which reach almost 10,000 feet in height. Among the more than seventy lakes in the area are the Attersee, Mondsee, Traunsee, and Wolfgangsee. Landscapes and native wildlife of the Salzkammergut are pictured at right.

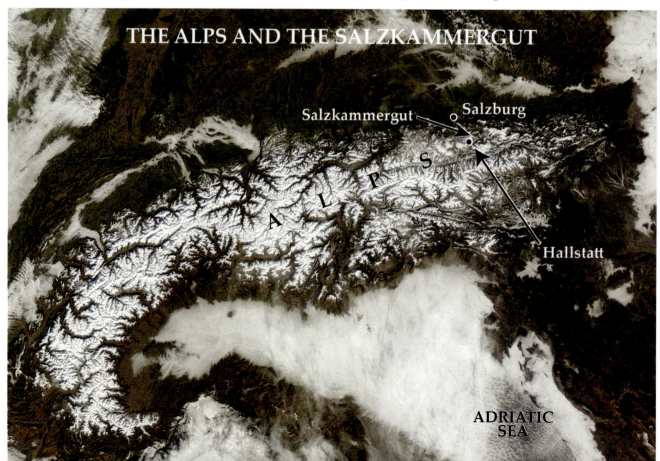

Clockwise from Top Left: Brown Bear at Alpenzoo in Innsbruck, Austria; Lake Hallstatt with Swan; View of the Alps with Lake Mondsee; Berchtesgaden Salt Mine at Hallstat, Austria; Wolf at Alpenzoo; Lynx at Alpenzoo; Town of Hallstatt; Dachstein Cave; European Bison at Alpenzoo; Center: Waterfall at Hallstat

Unit 16 - Chivalry, Trade, and New Freedoms

The Archbishopric of Salzburg

The Holy Roman Empire was a federation of independent cities and regions; it never had a capital city. Salzburg and the Salzkammergut were part of the Holy Roman Empire, which dated back to the days of Charlemagne.

Rupert, a Roman Catholic missionary, came to the Salzkammergut region in 696. There he founded a monastery and a convent. Charlemagne requested that Pope Leo III make Salzburg an archbishopric in 798. An archbishopric is an area led by an archbishop.

Hohensalzburg Fortress sits on Mönchsberg Mountain and Festungsberg Mountain. Archbishop Gebhard ordered that construction begin in 1077. Construction continued through the 1300s and also in later centuries.

Hohensalzburg in Salzburg

By the 1200s the archbishops of Salzburg had taken the title of prince archbishops. Salzburg became an independent state in 1292. These prince archbishops ruled Salzburg from the Salzburg Residenz Palace, pictured on page 529. A cathedral chapter consisting of twenty-four men assisted the prince archbishop. Men serving as representatives from the Salzburg area met in a body called a *diet* (German for congress or assembly). This diet also helped the prince archbishops govern Salzburg. The first Salzburg diet met in 1327.

Rupert brought the message of the gospel to the people of "Salt Castle." Paul told the Christians in Colossae that a Christian's speech should have the positive, preserving impact on others symbolized by salt, instead of a corrupting influence. Paul said:

Let your speech always be with grace, as though seasoned with salt, so that you will know how you should respond to each person.
Colossians 4:6

Statue of Rupert, Salzburg Cathedral

Assignments for Lesson 78

Timeline Book — In the box for Lesson 78 on page 19, write "Salt mining operations expand in Salzburg area."

Student Workbook or Lesson Review — If you are using one of these optional books, complete the assignment for Lesson 78.

Thinking Biblically — Read Matthew 5:1-14 to see the context of Jesus telling His followers that they were the salt of the Earth.

Vocabulary — Write a paragraph that uses all of these words. Consult a dictionary if you need help with their definitions: element (525), antiseptic (525), whetstone (526), deposit (526), crevice (526).

Literature — Read chapter XII in *Otto of the Silver Hand*.

Salzburg Residenz Palace

Lubeck
and the Hanseatic League

Lesson 79 World Landmark

The northern boundaries of the Holy Roman Empire were the North Sea to the west and the Baltic Sea to the east. See map on page 534. During the late Middle Ages, cities along the coast of the Baltic became centers of international trade. The city of Lubeck sat on an island in the Trave River, just nine miles from where the Trave emptied into the Baltic. See photo at right. Because of this location near the Baltic and near major cities of Europe, Lubeck became the most important European port for international trade.

The national boundaries that exist on a map of Europe today still did not exist. However, Franks were living in what is now France, Hungarians were living in what is now Hungary, Germans were living in what is now Germany, and so forth. The Holy Roman Empire was mainly a German empire. Lubeck was a German city.

Founding the Hansa

In the late Middle Ages, people working in city governments supported local businesses because they realized how much those businesses benefited the cities, especially those which bought from and sold to other nations. Lubeck and other cities along with the businesses in them organized a *hansa* (German word for guild or association). This group of cities was called the Hanseatic League. League members worked together to help businesses be more successful.

Kingdoms often placed taxes, called tariffs, on items traders brought into their ports. Sometimes kingdoms required ship owners to pay fees before they would allow the ships to stop at their ports. Tariffs and fees raised money for the kingdom. They also made it easier for

Lubeck, Germany, Along the Trave River with St. Mary's Church at Left and St. Peter's Church at Right

530

Lesson 79 - Lubeck and the Hanseatic League

local businesses that produced the same items to make a profit. Local people could buy locally-made items cheaper because the cost did not include money to cover the price of tariffs and fees. By working together, the Hanseatic League sometimes was able to negotiate with kingdoms in order to lower tariffs or fees.

The map on page 534 shows some of the major cities that were part of the League. Over the years cities joined and dropped out. The maximum number of cities involved was about 200, but some 70 or 80 of them were the heart of the League for many years. Lubeck became the most important city in the League and was known as the Queen of the Hansa.

Many cities in northern Germany were working together by the late 1200s, but historians believe that the League officially began in 1356 when a diet of representatives from various towns and businesses met in Lubeck. The diet did not always meet in Lubeck, and it did not meet every year; but it became an important way for League members to communicate with each other. At each meeting the diet considered various resolutions and policies, but cities did not have to follow them.

Shipping Goods on the Baltic Sea

League members worked together to transport goods. They contributed to the cost of building a fleet of ships. See historic ships and a ship pulley below. The League paid for the training of pilots for ships. They also built lighthouses so that ships could make it into and out of port more safely.

The lighthouse called Alter Leuchtturm at right was constructed in 1539. The Zuraw port crane in Gdansk, Poland, was built between 1422 and 1444. It lifted heavy cargo from ships and positioned ship masts. It is pictured on the next page.

The Lubeck lighthouse called Alter Leuchtturm dates from 1539.

Historic ships sail on the Baltic Sea near the German shore in 2015.

Ship Pulley in Lubeck

Hanseatic League Trading Activities

Zuraw Crane in Gdansk, Poland

Businesses in Lubeck handled such items as spices, fruit, wheat, rye, flax, timber, honey, leather, copper, iron, fish, and amber (a tree resin used for perfume, jewelry, and medicine). After the League encouraged the development of industry in northern Germany, traders also sold metal and wood products, woolen fabrics, linen fabrics, and even silk. The League grew so large and successful that it was able to insist on agreements that gave it a monopoly on trade in certain places.

Cities in the League became the richest and most powerful traders on the Baltic Sea. As a result, money from the profits in trade made many people wealthy and made it possible to build grand buildings in those cities. The League established businesses in many places, including Gdansk, Poland, pictured at top left (the city's German name is Danzig); Tallinn, Estonia, pictured on page 509; and Visby, a former Viking settlement on an island in Sweden; Brugge in what became Belgium; Riga, in what is now Latvia; London and Boston, England; and Novgorod, Russia.

Novgorod, Russia • Visby, Sweden • Boston, England

Top: Transfiguration Church Begun in 1345, Novgorod, Russia; Two Views of City Wall of Visby, Sweden; Bottom: Novgorod Kremlin, Novgorod, Russia; St. Botolph's Church, Constructed Between 1309 and 1390, Boston, England,

London, England • Brugge, Belgium • Riga, Latvia

Top Left: Guildhall in London was built between 1411 and 1440. Center: Construction of the town hall of Brugge, Belgium, began in the late 1300s. It includes a vaulted oak ceiling with scenes from the New Testament. Top Right: This statue near the Brugge Town Hall honors Jan Breydel of a butcher guild and Pieter De Coninck of a weaver guild. Together they led a revolt in 1302. The tower is the Belfry of Brugge. Construction began in 1282. Left: These landmarks of Riga, Latvia, include St. Peter's Church, first mentioned in documents in 1209; a statue of Roland, nephew of Charlemagne; and the House of the Blackheads, originally constructed by the city of Riga and rented to merchants. It was first mentioned in documents in 1334.

Buyers and Sellers Help Each Other

Of course, people have to be able to buy the goods that a business offers if the business is going to be successful. League businesses could sell goods to kings and nobles, but they had more success when more people could buy what they were selling. As European workers produced more goods and traders sold more goods, the income of many people increased and those who were not wealthy began to be able to afford goods made in other countries. This benefited both the people and the Hanseatic League.

Trade Wars

Since the German people of the Holy Roman Empire were divided into a number of small kingdoms, the Hanseatic League could not depend on a strong government to provide police and military protection for traders. Therefore, the League created military forces of their own to provide protection against pirates.

The Hanseatic League became so powerful that it was difficult for cities and kingdoms which were not a part of the League to buy, sell, and make a profit in international trading. When kingdoms opposed the growing power of the Hanseatic League, the League's military sometimes fought against the armies of those kingdoms.

In the 1300s, the Kingdom of Denmark was one of the most powerful kingdoms in Europe. In the 1360s Danish King Valdemar IV tried to stop the League's power in the Baltic Sea. However, the League's military force defeated the Danish. In 1370 Denmark agreed to a treaty called the Peace of Stralsund which recognized the League's power of trading along the Baltic Sea.

Decline of the Hanseatic League

As nation-states grew more unified and powerful, they were able to resist the League's demands for control of trade. When nations such as the Netherlands grew in economic power, they found their own markets to buy and sell and stopped depending on the Hanseatic League. The Dutch, who are the people of the Netherlands, defeated the Hanseatic army in a war that lasted from 1438 to 1441. The Treaty of Copenhagen gave Dutch traders the right to trade grain along the Baltic. The League gradually weakened and was no longer the most powerful group of traders in northern Europe. The last meeting of the diet of the Hanseatic League took place in 1669.

The City of Lubeck

Two main streets ran north and south in the middle of Lubeck. These streets enabled people and vehicles to move easily. The streets also marked the dividing line between the city's social classes. Rich merchants lived in their splendid houses on the western side of the island, while small businessmen and artisans lived in more humble dwellings on the eastern side. The city eventually outgrew the island and spread to surrounding land.

Lesson 79 - Lubeck and the Hanseatic League

By the time the last diet met in 1669, money earned in trade had helped to build grand buildings in the city of Lubeck. Perhaps the best known landmark is the brick Holsten Gate (or Holstentor), begun in 1464. This gate, pictured at right, marks the entrance to Old Town. The Burgtor or Fortress Gate was built in 1444. The towers of the Lubeck Cathedral, St. Mary's Church, and St. Peter's Church mark the city's skyline. St. Mary's is pictured at right below. Both St. Mary's and St. Peter's can be seen in the photo on page 530. The Salzspeicher, pictured at right below, has six storehouses built to hold salt mined in Luneburg, about forty-five miles from Lubeck.

In one way or another, we are all involved in buying and selling the goods people grow and make. Jesus compared seeking the Kingdom of God to a merchant engaged in the pearl trade. Finding His kingdom is worth more than everything else we might acquire:

Holsten Gate

Burgtor or Fortress Gate

St. Mary's Church

Salzspeicher Salt Storehouses

*Again, the kingdom of heaven
is like a merchant seeking fine pearls,
and upon finding one pearl of great value,
he went and sold all that he had and bought it.
Matthew 13:45-46*

Assignments for Lesson 79

Our Creative World — Read the "Letter to the Aldermen of Culm" on pages 59-60.

Map Book — Complete the activities for Lesson 79 on Map 23 "Selected Cities of Europe 1300-1400."

Timeline Book — In the box for Lesson 79 on page 18, write "Hanseatic League is established."

Student Workbook or Lesson Review — If you are using one of these optional books, complete the assignment for Lesson 79.

Creative Writing — Make a list of ways that the Hanseatic League impacted trade and daily life in Europe. Your list should include at least seven items.

Literature — Read chapter XIII in *Otto of the Silver Hand*.

Beginnings of Change in Church and Government

Lesson 80 — Daily Life

Nothing is more important for a person than his or her relationship with God through Jesus Christ. This relationship is to guide a person every day in his every word, thought, and action. For a Christian, everyday life is centered in and based upon Jesus Christ.

A Christian does not live his life on his own. He has fellowship with other Christians, who are members of the Lord's church. This fellowship provides encouragement, guidance, and sometimes correction.

Peter Waldo and the Waldensians

During the Middle Ages, almost all believers in western Europe were members of the Roman Catholic Church. The Roman Catholic Church hierarchy was powerful and controlled Church practices. From time to time, individuals and groups worked to correct what they saw as errors in what the Church taught and practiced. One such individual was Peter Waldo. In the late 1100s, Waldo's teachings spread from his home area in southeastern France into other parts of Europe. His followers came to be called Waldensians.

Peter Waldo Statue, Worms, Germany

Waldo believed that the Church had left many of the teachings of the New Testament. However, he did not want to tear down the Roman Catholic Church or start a new church. His purpose was to **reform** the Church. Peter Waldo preached in public even though he was not an ordained priest. This violated Catholic practice. Waldo used a translation of Scripture that was in his own language and not in Latin. This also was a violation of Catholic practice. Waldo taught that the pope and other members of the Roman Catholic hierarchy (see chart on page 430) did not have authority over persons' individual lives before God.

The Roman Catholic Church taught that after a Christian dies, he goes to purgatory, a place of punishment where they believed a person atones for his sins before going to heaven. Waldo taught against the belief in purgatory. Peter Waldo opposed baptizing infants, believing instead that people should be baptized after they are able to repent and to confess their own faith in Jesus. He taught against giving special honor to people whom the Church called saints and against the belief that the Church could bestow forgiving grace on people through confession to priests and through acts of penance (see page 471).

Roman Catholic leaders saw Waldo as a **heretic**, a teacher of error. In 1215 the Church began working to stop his preaching and to stop people from following him. First, the Church excommunicated Waldo and others in the movement. When this did not stop them, the Church began to persecute Waldensians. This persecution reduced but did not completely eliminate the Waldensian movement.

The Inquisition

The Roman Catholic Church strongly opposed people who believed and taught things different from their official doctrines. They began the Inquisition to eliminate what the leaders saw as heresy within the Church. Individual bishops oversaw districts called dioceses. In 1184 Pope Lucius III authorized bishops to search for heresy in their dioceses. Some bishops were strict in obeying the pope's instructions and others were more lenient, so the pope took over the process. In 1227 Pope Gregory IX appointed judges to hear cases. In 1248 the Church issued a handbook of acceptable procedures for identifying and judging heretics. Four years later, Pope Innocent IV approved the use of torture on suspected heretics.

Church officials usually began dealing with an accused heretic by offering minor punishment if the person admitted his error. If this did not happen, authorities (sometimes from the Church and other times from the local government) conducted a trial. Few people were allowed to be present, and no one served as a defense attorney for the accused because people were afraid of being branded heretics themselves. Punishment for heresy included such things as making a pilgrimage, wearing a yellow cross, or going to prison. The Church intended these punishments to lead the accused to repent of the accusation against him. Those who admitted their actions but did not recant (admit their wrong and take it back) were usually burned at the stake. Some Waldensians were convicted of heresy in Inquisition trials and executed as a result.

The Magna Carta and the Rights of Individual Citizens

While some people were challenging the authority of the Roman Catholic Church, others were claiming rights as citizens. Governments throughout history have made choices about what rights to grant to their citizens. Male citizens in Athens could take part in making laws. Citizens of the Roman Empire, such as the apostle Paul (see page 314), had certain rights, as did people living under the **feudal** system. Nobles in Germanic tribes in the Holy Roman Empire had the right to select their kings.

Still, in general a king claimed that all governmental authority belonged to him. English kings after William the Conqueror began the practice of issuing a charter or guarantee of liberties for the nobles (also called barons). However, King John did not issue such a charter when he became king of England in 1199. During his reign English barons began to resent John's actions and his increased taxes. On June 15, 1215, a group of barons met with John and demanded that he put his seal of approval on the Magna Carta (Latin for Great Charter, called such because it was a large-sized document). The document listed actions forbidden to the king and guarantees of rights for the barons according to the laws of England. In other words, the king could not do whatever he wanted with someone he didn't like. If the king wanted to take action against someone, he had to follow the same laws that applied to everyone. The king could not make up the law; instead, the king obeyed the law just like everyone else. To learn about one right guaranteed in the Magna Carta, read Clause 39 of the Magna Carta in the box below. King John approved the Magna Carta, a copy of which is in the chapter house of Salisbury Cathedral, pictured below.

King John did not keep his end of the agreement, and the barons began a war against him in the months that followed. John died the year after he signed the Magna Carta, and his son Henry III reached an agreement with the barons that brought about peace. The Magna Carta helped establish a foundation of personal rights of citizens and the rule of law, instead of the power of individual leaders. This principle has inspired political freedom in nation after nation.

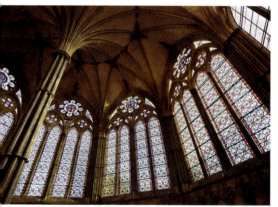

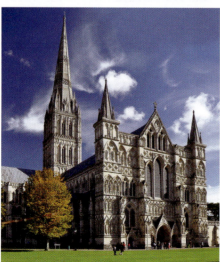

Magna Carta, Clause 39

No free man shall be arrested or imprisoned or disseised [removed from property on which he is lawfully living] or outlawed or exiled or in any way victimised, neither will we [the king] attack him or send anyone to attack him, except by the lawful judgment of his peers or by the law of the land.

Above Left: Salisbury Cathedral Chapter House;
Left: Salisbury Cathedral

New Questions

The English barons and the Waldensians were asking a question others began asking: What rights do individuals have with regard to the authorities to whom they answer? The Waldensians did not want to end the Roman Catholic Church; they wanted to correct the practices that they believed were unscriptural. Did they have the right to raise their objections? If their objections were not answered, did they have the right to worship separately and follow their consciences? Were they subject to the Roman Catholic Church for their salvation? With regard to political rights, the English barons did not want to end the monarchy and begin a democracy. They were beginning to wrestle with a basic question: What was the ultimate authority in a nation: the king and whatever he said, or the laws of a nation, to which even the king was subject? Did people have the right to certain freedoms and the right to be protected from unfair treatment?

John Wycliffe, Morning Star of the Reformation

John Wycliffe, born in the early 1300s, studied at Oxford University in his home country of England. He later became a Roman Catholic priest and a scholar at Oxford, which was his alma mater. Wycliffe began speaking and writing against what he saw as **erroneous** teachings and practices in the Church. He said that the hierarchy of the church was not in keeping with Scripture.

Wycliffe Window in Wycliffe College Chapel, University of Toronto, Toronto, Canada

Wycliffe opposed the Church accumulating wealth. He also objected to the Church selling indulgences. Church officials sold indulgences to individuals who wanted to help a deceased loved one get out of purgatory and go to heaven. The Catholic Church taught that Jesus and the people who had been named saints had built up a surplus of good works. The Church taught that the purchase of an indulgence would transfer the merit of the good works of Jesus and the saints to their loved one, thus enabling him or her to go to heaven.

Wycliffe believed that people should have Bibles in their own languages. He thought that this would help people know and obey God's teachings. The Roman Catholic Church only allowed the Bible to be written in Latin. Since only educated people knew Latin at this time, this meant that most people could not read the Bible for themselves. Wycliffe and a few fellow scholars produced a handwritten translation of the Bible in English. A quote attributed to Wycliffe states: "This Bible is for the government of the People, by the People, and for the People." Wycliffe encouraged men to go out and preach the simple truth of the Bible and to teach his ideas about reform. He called these men Poor Preachers. Their critics called them Lollards, from a Dutch word meaning mumbler.

The Roman Catholic Church condemned Wycliffe's teaching, banned his writings, and excommunicated him. Church officials did not execute Wycliffe, but some of the Poor Preachers were killed because of their beliefs and teachings. Wycliffe died in 1384. He is often called the Morning Star of the Reformation. In a letter to the Duke of Lancaster in 1381, Wycliffe said: "I believe that in the end the truth will conquer."

Jan Hus, Bohemian Reformer

Jan Hus, who was born in 1370, was a reformer in Bohemia, which is now part of the Czech Republic. Hus learned of Wycliffe's ideas and began to teach them. He was especially critical of the Church's wealth. The Church owned about half the property of Bohemia and imposed heavy taxes. Hus also expressed disapproval of the sale of indulgences. Hus was arrested, put in jail, placed on trial, and convicted of heresy. When he was burned at the stake in 1415, his last words were: "O holy **simplicity**."

The Meaning for Everyday Life

The power of the Roman Catholic Church and the power of kings had remained fairly constant in Europe for about a thousand years. At this point in history, however, a few people expressed different ideas on both Church and government. Because of what a few people such as English barons, Peter Waldo, John Wycliffe, and Jan Hus were willing to do, life would eventually change for everyone in Europe.

Jan Hus Memorial, Prague, Czech Republic

*It was for freedom that Christ set us free;
therefore keep standing firm and do not be subject again to a yoke of slavery.
Galatians 5:1*

Assignments for Lesson 80

Our Creative World — Read John 1:1-9 from the Wycliffe translation on page 61.

Timeline Book — In the box for Lesson 80 on page 19, write "Wycliffe and followers translate the Bible into English."

Student Workbook or Lesson Review — If you are using one of these optional books, complete the assignment for Lesson 80 and take the test for Unit 16.

Thinking Biblically — Write a paragraph about the advantages of people being able to read the Bible in their own language.

Vocabulary — Copy these words, each on a separate line: reform (536), heretic (537), feudal (537), erroneous (539), simplicity (540). Look up each word in the dictionary. Next to each word, write what part of speech it is according to the way the word is used in the lesson.

Literature — Read chapter XIV and the Afterword in *Otto of the Silver Hand*. If you are using the Student Workbook or Lesson Review, answer the literature review questions on *Otto of the Silver Hand*.

17   The Early Renaissance

Cathedral of Florence, Italy, with Bell Tower Designed by Giotto and Dome Designed by Brunelleschi

Lessons
81 - God's Wonder: The Voyages of Zheng He
82 - World Landmark: The Forbidden City
83 - World Biography: Prince Henry the Navigator
84 - Our World Story: The Fall of Constantinople
85 - Daily Life: The Italian Renaissance

1401-1453

In 1405 the Chinese Yongle Emperor sent Admiral Zheng He on the first of seven voyages. The Yongle Emperor's greatest achievement at home was the construction of his massive palace complex, which came to be called the Forbidden City. Prince Henry the Navigator sent Portuguese ships on explorations along the coast of West Africa. Eleven hundred years after its founding, the Byzantine Empire's capital city of Constantinople fell to the Muslim Ottoman Turks in 1452. Scholars from Constantinople fled to Italy, bringing with them treasured manuscripts and helping to ignite the Italian Renaissance.

The Voyages of Zheng He

Lesson 81 — God's Wonder

The Chinese developed excellent skills in shipbuilding and navigation, especially during the Song Dynasty and the Yuan Dynasty, established by Kublai Khan of Mongolia. While the ships of the Hanseatic League were trading on the Baltic Sea, the Chinese were sailing ships to nations to their south for the same purpose. Chinese ships sailed in the China Sea and some ventured into the Indian Ocean.

The China Sea

Both the East China Sea and the South China Sea are arms of the Pacific Ocean along the coast of East Asia. The Taiwan Strait separates the East China and South China Seas. The East China Sea is relatively shallow, averaging a depth of only 1,100 feet or one-fifth of a mile. The South China Sea is much deeper, averaging 3,976 feet or three-fourths of a mile. Both seas teem with sea creatures. Researchers have identified 1,787 species of fish in the South China Sea alone. Among the edible species in the China Sea are shrimp, tuna, mackerel, and sardines. The China Sea has hundreds of islands, atolls, cays, banks, reefs, and rocks, such as those below. A few of the many creatures that are at home in the South China Sea are pictured on the next page.

Rocks in the South China Sea Off the Coast of Vietnam

Creatures at Home in the South China Sea

Coral Reef

Hawksbill Turtle

Chinese White Dolphins

Sea Cucumber

The Indian Ocean

The Indian Ocean stretches from Africa in the west to Australia in the east. In the north it is bounded by Arabia, the Indian subcontinent, the Bay of Bengal, and the Andaman Sea. People differ about the sea's exact southern border. Some say it reaches to Antarctica, while others call the waters north of Antarctica the Southern Ocean. The Indian Ocean is about one-fifth of the world's ocean area. Its average depth is 12,990 feet, or almost two and a half miles. The Indian Ocean also has many coral reefs and islands, including the island country of Seychelles. See picture at right. These reefs and islands are home to brittle stars, crabs, mollusks, sea urchins, sponges, starfish, worms, and beautiful reef fish.

Albatrosses and frigate birds are common along the coastlines of the Indian Ocean and many penguin species live on its southern

Anse Source d'Argent Beach, La Digue Island, Seychelles

islands. More than 100 species of minute copepods live in the Indian Ocean, as do jellyfish, polyps, and the Portuguese man-of-war. Fish living there include coral groupers, flying fish, the humphead or Napoleon wrasse, lantern fish, luminous anchovies, sailfish, and sharks. God placed sea turtles in the Indian Ocean, as well as marine mammals such as dolphins, seals, and whales.

Creatures at Home in and over the Indian Ocean

Albatross over the Indian Ocean

Blacktip Reef Shark with Reef Fish and Coral Near the Modern Island Nation of Maldives

Hermit Crab in the Indian Ocean

China Becomes a Naval Superpower

In 1368 the Ming family began to overthrow Kublai Khan's Yuan Dynasty. This began the Ming Dynasty (see chart of Chinese dynasties in Lesson 131). In 1381 the Mings conquered the last area ruled by the Mongols. In 1402 Zhu Di became the third Ming emperor of China. Zhu Di took the title Yongle, which means Perpetual Happiness. Like the two Ming emperors before him, Zhu Di wanted to demonstrate the great power of China to the nations around him. He wanted those nations to pay him tribute and to recognize him as "lord of all under heaven."

For this purpose, the Yongle Emperor sent a fleet of ships over thousands of miles to the "western oceans." Though this was impressive, China had sent ships to many of these same ports before. What was most spectacular about these voyages was the combination of the size of the fleet, the distances covered, and the individual ships themselves. The emperor chose Zheng He, whom he had known since his youth, to lead these voyages. Zheng He had been born in southwest China. When he was ten years old, the emperor at the time captured him and brought him to the capital for military training. Zheng He became a strong military leader. He was an imposing figure, standing over six feet tall with a chest measurement of sixty inches (the average man today measures about forty inches).

Scroll with Mustard Plant and Butterflies Painted on Silk, Ming Dynasty

The First Voyage, 1405-1407

Though China already built the best ships in the world, the Yongle Emperor ordered that new awe-inspiring ships be built for the first voyage. The fleet consisted of over three hundred ships, including about sixty huge treasure ships. The largest ships were over 400 feet long and 160 feet wide, with nine masts and twelve sails. These treasure ships were somewhat like modern cruise ships. They were four decks high and included beautiful staterooms with balconies overlooking the sea. The fleet also included supply ships. Some carried fresh water for the soldiers and crews. Others carried gifts of Chinese silk, brocades, porcelain, lacquerware, tea, and objects of iron. Still others carried soldiers, horses, or cannons which showed military strength. See illustrations of Zheng He and his ships on page 547. The crew of 27,800 men included sailors, construction workers, repairmen, soldiers, diplomats, doctors, astronomers, and scholars.

Zheng He and his fleet departed from China, sailing first into the East China Sea and then into the South China Sea. They visited ports in what are now Vietnam, Thailand, the Malay Peninsula portion of Malaysia, and the Indonesian island of Java before leaving the South China Sea and sailing into the Indian Ocean.

Zheng He and his fleet crossed the Indian Ocean to the island of Ceylon (now called Sri Lanka), just southeast of the southern tip of India. From there they traveled into the Arabian Sea to the port of Calicut (sometimes spelled Kalikut; the modern city is called Kozhikode) on the western side of the tip of the Indian subcontinent. Calicut was the source of the fabric we know as calico. See his route on page 549. The numbers on this map indicate the farthest port reached on each of Zheng He's seven voyages.

This statue of the Yongle Emperor is in his tomb in the Ming Tombs in Beijing, China.

The Second Voyage, 1408-1409, and the Third Voyage, 1409-1411

Apparently Zheng He organized the second trip but did not go himself. On this voyage, the Chinese took sixty-eight ships to Calicut to attend a ceremony to inaugurate its new king.

On the third voyage, Zheng He himself led a fleet of forty-eight large ships and an army of 30,000 to some of the same places the first two excursions had visited. They also went to Malacca on the Malay Peninsula. There Zheng He traded for ebony, aloe, and dammar (a substance used in caulking, an important part of shipbuilding). The Chinese built a stockade where they could store merchandise before sending it back to China.

The fleet also went to the northern tip of the Indonesian island of Sumatra and then sailed again to Ceylon. On Ceylon, Zheng He became involved in a conflict with the king of one part of Ceylon. The Chinese defeated the local force, and Zheng He took the king back to China as a captive. The Chinese eventually released him and allowed him to go home.

The Fourth Voyage, 1413-1415

Zheng He led more than 28,000 men and sixty-three ships on the fourth voyage. He revisited Southeast Asia and India. Some ships in the fleet ventured to Bengal, on the northern coast of the Bay of Bengal where Bangladesh is today.

These Chinese stamps and the one on page 550 commemorate the 600th anniversary of Zheng He's first voyage.

Then Zheng He sailed to Hormuz on the Persian Gulf, where the Chinese traded for sapphires, rubies, topaz, pearls, coral beads, amber, woolen goods, and carpets. Because Zheng He traveled to Muslim lands on the fourth voyage, twenty-five year-old Ma Huan, a Chinese Muslim, served as translator. On this voyage, the Chinese became involved in a local conflict on Sumatra.

The Fifth Voyage, 1417-1419, and the Sixth Voyage, 1421-1422

As a result of Zheng He's voyages, representatives of many countries traveled to China to pay their respects (and their tribute) to the emperor. Some of these traveled with Zheng He, while others made the journey by other means. A major mission of the fifth voyage was to take seventeen representatives back home to their respective countries. The fleet visited Java, Sumatra, the Malay Peninsula, Maldives (an island group in the Indian Ocean), Ceylon, Cochin, and Calicut.

Zheng He and his fleet ventured even further west, going beyond Hormuz to Aden on the southern Arabian coast. Zheng He met with the sultan of Aden. The Chinese traded their gold, silver, porcelain, sandalwood, and pepper for precious jewels, pieces of coral as much as two feet long, and other items. Apparently on this trip the Chinese received lions, zebras, leopards, ostriches, white pigeons, and a giraffe to deliver as gifts to the emperor. Continuing west, the fleet reached the East African coast, visiting Mogadishu and Brawa in modern Somalia and Malindi in today's Kenya (see photo at left). Again some officials from nations that Zheng He and his crew visited traveled back to China with the fleet.

The city of Gedi, located near Malindi, Kenya, was at its peak during this period.

On the sixth voyage, the fleet followed a familiar route, visiting Southeast Asia, India, the Persian Gulf, the Red Sea, and the east coast of Africa. The main purpose of this voyage was to take nineteen emissaries home after they completed visits to China. This time the fleet might have gone as far south as Mozambique on the East African coast.

The Seventh Voyage, 1431-1433

The Yongle Emperor died in 1424. His son, Zhu Gaozhi, did not send out any voyages. However, Zhu Gaozhi lived only a short time after assuming the throne. His son and successor, Zhu Zhanji ordered another voyage. Zheng He led 100 large ships with more than 27,000 men on his final voyage. Again they visited Southeast Asia, India, the Persian Gulf, and the Red Sea. Part of the fleet may have visited Malindi. Zheng He never returned to China. He either remained at Calicut because of poor health or died on the return trip and was buried at sea.

VOYAGES OF ZHENG HE

China Turns Inward

China was the superpower of Asia and the Indian Ocean rim in the early 1400s. They had the best and largest ships and most advanced navigation techniques and equipment in the world. However, their status as a superpower did not last. Within a few decades, the Chinese stopped sending out trade vessels. Less than a century after Zheng He's death, the emperor ordered the destruction of all large ships.

Ming emperors began focusing on needs and projects within China. Some advisers to the emperor believed that the voyages were not worth the expense. In addition, a common perception among the Chinese was that they were the center of the world. They called themselves the Middle Kingdom, meaning the middle of the Earth. They believed that other peoples were only primitive barbarians.

The voyages of Zheng He were an amazing accomplishment. He devoted the last twenty-eight years of his life to making trip after trip to the western seas. These journeys connected one part of the world with other parts. Despite the "Middle Kingdom" viewpoint, there was much to see and acquire through contacts with other people. The trips he commanded demonstrated what people could do on this huge planet where God has put us all.

There are three things
which are too wonderful for me,
Four which I do not understand:
The way of an eagle in the sky,
The way of a serpent on a rock,
The way of a ship in the middle of the sea,
And the way of a man with a maid.
Proverbs 30:18-19

Assignments for Lesson 81

Our Creative World — Look at the photos of Architecture in the 1400s on page 62.

Map Book — Complete the assignments for Lesson 81 on Map 24 "Voyages of Zheng He."

Timeline Book — In the box for Lesson 81 on page 19, write "Voyages of Zheng He."

Student Workbook or Lesson Review — If you are using one of these optional books, complete the assignment for Lesson 81.

Creative Writing — Imagine that you are writing an application letter to Zheng He as he is recruiting for one of his voyages. Explain why you are interested in traveling with him and how you would be of benefit to the expedition. Make your letter at least three paragraphs.

Family Activity — Make "Coral Reef Art." Instructions begin on page FA-34.

The Forbidden City

Lesson 82 — World Landmark

The grandest project Zhu Di, the Yongle Emperor, undertook during his reign was his huge palace complex in Beijing, the Ming capital city. The complex included residences for the royal family, shrines for worship, and great halls for ceremonies. Other emperors expanded it until some sources say that it had 9,999 rooms. Today we know of at least 8,886 rooms in 980 buildings, plus courtyards, marble terraces, and formal gardens. It is the world's largest palace complex and the largest collection of preserved ancient wooden structures in the world. See photo below and diagram on page 554.

Palace Complex with Modern Beijing in the Distance

Symbols in the Architecture of the Forbidden City

The Chinese thought of the North Star as the center of heaven. They called it the Purple Star. Since they believed that China was the Middle Kingdom of the world, they called the emperor's home the Purple Palace. No one could enter the palace complex without his permission. Therefore the Chinese people called it the Purple Forbidden City or, more commonly, the Forbidden City. The Forbidden City served as the palace of the emperor of China for centuries.

During the earliest years of the Forbidden City, the Meridian Gate was the formal entrance to the place complex.

Those who designed the Forbidden City positioned and **aligned** its buildings according to the Chinese art of placement called *feng shui*. The Chinese believed that proper placement created balance and harmony in the environment and contributed to a positive attitude among the people living and working there. To the Chinese, the north was the source of cold winds and enemies. Therefore, they built the complex to face south.

Every element of the project, including the colors used and the number of doors, bridges, statues, and **ornaments** on the roof, had meaning. The library of the Forbidden City was constructed with a black roof, which symbolized water to protect the books from fire. During the Ming Dynasty, only the emperor used the color yellow. The yellow roofs of the buildings symbolized his power, as did the golden brick floors which **paved** its halls.

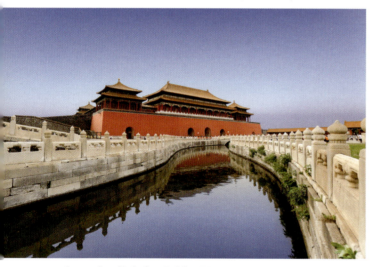
A canal called the Golden Water River passes through the Forbidden City. Five wooden bridges crossed it in the time of the Yongle Emperor. They were later replaced with five bridges made of marble.

The Outer Court and the Inner Court

The Forbidden City includes an outer court at the front (south) and an inner court in the rear (north). From south to north, in the outer court are three large halls called the

Moat and Lookout Tower

Lesson 82 - The Forbidden City

Hall of Supreme Harmony (the largest hall, which contained the royal throne), the Hall of Middle (or Central) Harmony, and the Hall of Preserving Harmony.

The Gate of Heavenly Purity separates the Outer Court and the Inner Court. In the Inner Court were the residences for the imperial family. The main buildings of the Inner Court were the Palace of Heavenly Purity (containing the emperor's quarters), the Hall of Union, and the Palace of Earthly Tranquility (residence of the empress). Other living quarters for the royal household stood nearby. At the north of the Inner Court is the Gate of Divine Might. The eastern and western gates of the palace complex are called the East Glorious Gate and the West Glorious Gate.

Defense of the Palace Complex

To protect the emperor from enemies, workers built a moat 175 feet wide and a wall more than thirty feet tall. The wall is about twenty-eight feet thick at the bottom and about twenty-one and a half feet at the top. The slant of the wall made it difficult for invaders to climb. A lookout tower stands at each corner of the outer wall.

Building the World's Largest Palace Complex

One hundred thousand skilled craftsmen and one million laborers worked from 1407 to 1421 building the Forbidden City. Historians and scientists today can learn about the techniques used to build the palace complex by studying the written records, drawings, and models that the Ming Dynasty preserved.

A pair of bronze lions guard the Gate of Heavenly Purity, separating the Outer Court from the Inner Court.

The Gate of Divine Might stands at the northern boundary of the Forbidden City.

Because the Forbidden City is constructed of wood, servants filled the many cauldrons placed throughout the city so that water was quickly available in case of fire. This one is covered with gold.

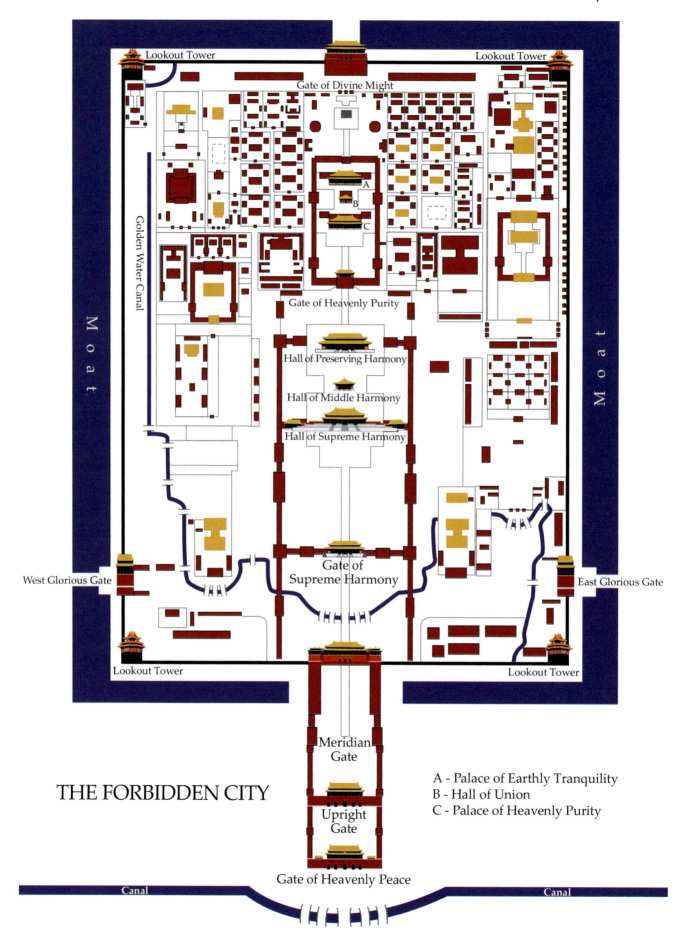

Lesson 82 - The Forbidden City

The palace and grounds of the Forbidden City are lavish. Workers made the golden bricks that pave its halls. The pillars of the Forbidden City are whole logs of Phoebe zhennan trees, native only to China. The wood of the Phoebe zhennan is sometimes called golden silk. The trees can grow to a height of about one hundred feet. Torrential rains aided workers in getting the **felled** logs into a nearby river. From there workers steered the logs into the Grand Canal to Beijing and then towed them to the construction site.

Stone for giant carvings such as the one at right came from a quarry near Beijing. To move the huge pieces of rock, workers poured water on roads in cold weather to form ice and then pulled the stones along on **sledges**.

Chinese emperors and their subjects used the word heaven to describe their grand constructions. However, it is the Lord God who rules the true heaven.

Stone carvings of Nine Dragons on staircase behind the Hall of Preserved Harmony

*The Lord is in His holy temple;
the Lord's throne is in heaven;
His eyes behold, His eyelids test the sons of men.
Psalm 11:4*

Assignments for Lesson 82

Timeline Book — In the box for Lesson 82 on page 19, write "Forbidden City opens as a Ming palace."

Student Workbook or Lesson Review — If you are using one of these optional books, complete the assignment for Lesson 82.

Thinking Biblically — What happens when a person puts faith in an earthly ruler and an earthly palace? What happens when a person trusts in God and delights in His heaven? Answer these questions in one or two paragraphs.

Vocabulary — Make a drawing for each of these words that illustrates what it means: align (552), ornament (552), pave (552), fell (555), sledge (555). Write the word under the drawing. Check in a dictionary if you need help with their definitions.

Prince Henry the Navigator

Lesson 83 — World Biography

With Muslims controlling the Middle East and North Africa, European traders who traveled overland through those regions had to pay local **middlemen** for permission to pass through their land. Europeans longed for an easier way to get direct access to Asia. They wanted a way to get back and forth between Europe and Asia by sea. Europeans also had other motivations for sea exploration beyond finding better trade routes.

Desire to Share Jesus with Africans and Asians

Leaders in the Roman Catholic Church and some national kings wanted to take the gospel to people who had never heard it. The prospect of evangelizing central Africa and parts of Asia motivated them.

A man stands ready to search for gold at the Koupela mine in Burkina Faso, Africa.

Gold, Power, and Glory

Europeans learned that Africa south of the Sahara contained large deposits of gold. Nations in that day measured their wealth by the amount of gold they possessed, so Europeans wanted to have access to African gold. Since increased trade, greater access to gold, and the discovery of other treasures were possible, some European rulers wanted their share. Their imaginations could scarcely begin to grasp what they might obtain if daring attempts at exploration proved successful.

A Letter from a Mythical Kingdom

Europeans saw the Muslim religion as a challenge to Christianity. Muslim armies threatened European leaders. The Europeans wanted to be victorious over the Muslims in battle. If they couldn't be victorious, then they hoped to avoid fighting with them at all.

Lesson 83 - Prince Henry the Navigator

Europeans heard stories about a Christian kingdom on the fringes of the Muslim world, either in Asia or northeast Africa. They were intrigued. The leader of this kingdom was reported to be a powerful king called Prester John (or Presbyter John). Around 1165 a letter supposedly from Prester John passed from one European ruler to another. When Europeans had contact with Christians in Ethiopia, some believed that they had found the kingdom of Prester John. Rulers of some European countries wanted to join with Prester John and do battle against the Muslims. However, Prester John proved to be a **myth**. No one ever found such a kingdom, and the idea died out.

A Desire to Learn About the Unknown

Europeans did not have extensive knowledge about the whole world and were curious about what was beyond the places that they knew. Just as rumors arose about Prester John, Europeans wondered about what they might find in the unexplored oceans. Would they find monsters and **whirlpools** that would consume any ships that ventured near them? Europeans had long wondered what was beyond the oceans near their shores. Now European **naval** technology was just then reaching the level that made sea exploration a possibility.

Portugal Becomes a Nation

The modern country of Portugal is the westernmost country on the European continent. Muslim invaders took control of most of the Iberian Peninsula (where Spain and Portugal are located) in the 700s. Christians slowly fought back.

A nobleman from France, Henry of Burgundy, helped Christians on the peninsula fight the Muslims and push them out. The Iberian Peninsula was divided into small kingdoms. In 1094 the king of Castile (which was then one of the most powerful kingdoms on the peninsula and which is now part of Spain) rewarded Henry with the northern area of what would become Portugal and named him the Count of Portugal. Henry's son, Afonso Henriques, won many victories over the Muslims. In 1140 Afonso, depicted in the statue at right, declared himself to be king of Portugal. The king of Castile recognized his claim, and Portugal became a separate country.

More than two centuries later, King John I was ruling Portugal when his third son, Henry, was born in 1394. Henry grew up to be a devout believer in Jesus Christ.

Prince Henry had a strong desire to oust Muslims from North Africa. In 1415 at the age of 21, Henry led an expedition

Statue of King Afonso Henriques in Guimaraes, Portugal

that captured the Islamic-controlled port of Ceuta on the coast of Morocco in northern Africa, on the southern shore of the Strait of Gibraltar. His father made him the governor of the Order of Christ, a group of military monks whose purpose was to fight Muslims.

A School at Sagres

Prince Henry soon founded a school at or near Sagres at right, the most extreme southwestern point of the Iberian Peninsula and therefore the most southwestern point in Europe. Here he assembled geographers, astronomers, shipbuilders, and mapmakers to share information, improve Portuguese shipbuilding **techniques**, and develop new sailing technology. Henry's stated goals were to send out expeditions and to evangelize the nations.

Exploring the Coast of Africa

The Portuguese hoped that controlling Ceuta would help them become wealthy from the gold that came from central Africa. When this did not happen, Henry ordered Portuguese ports that lay on the western coast of Africa to gain control of that gold. Over several years Portuguese vessels pushed further and further south along the African coast. Wind and weather were crucial factors for a ship to be able to arrive at its destination.

Lighthouse at Sagres, Portugal

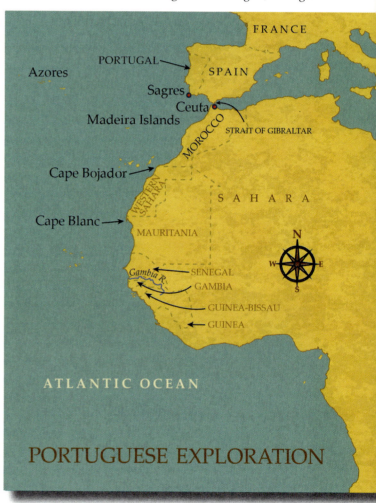

The ships sailed as close to land as they safely could. However, they could not get too close to shore for fear of a shipwreck caused by hitting a reef or sandbar. The Portuguese were sailing into literally uncharted waters, so they had to advance carefully.

One specific obstacle was Cape Bojador, a promontory on the coast of what is now Western Sahara. European sailors feared whatever was beyond the cape, which they thought included monsters and untold difficulties. Between 1424 and 1434 Prince Henry sent out fifteen expeditions with the goal of sailing beyond the cape, but each one returned with the captain saying he was too afraid to do so. Finally in 1434 Captain Gil Eannes tricked his crew. He sailed west before

West African Coast From Morocco to Guinea

reaching the cape, went out of sight of land, and then headed back east after they had passed the cape. In this way the crew did not know when they reached Cape Bojador and did not know to fear what lay ahead.

Little by little, Portuguese sailors ventured further and further south along the African coast. In 1441 they reached Cape Blanc, at the border of what is now Western Sahara and Mauritania. Five years later, the Portuguese arrived at the mouth of the Gambia River, the location of the modern country of Gambia. By 1460, the year Prince Henry died, Portuguese explorers reached Guinea. Because of their explorations, the Portuguese began to control the buying and selling of gold in Africa, which made the country prosperous. See places where the Portuguese explored along the coast of Africa in the map and photos at left.

The Portuguese also learned about numerous islands off the African coast. Though many Africans likely already knew about them, they were new discoveries for the people of Europe.

European maps of the 1300s showed a chain of islands called the Azores about 800 miles to the west of Portugal. A Portuguese explorer arrived there in 1427, and Portuguese settlers came in 1439. The Portuguese also settled the Madeira Islands in the same region of the Atlantic. The settlers there began sugar plantations, which were highly profitable.

Henry the Navigator, Infante of the Kingdom of Portugal. Created by Droz after Old Miniature, published in Magasin Pittoresque, *Paris, 1843*

The Navigator

Henry authorized about fifty explorations. Though Henry never went on any of the journeys of exploration he organized, his encouragement of ever further ventures gave him the title of Prince Henry the Navigator. He had a considerable impact in Portugal, on navigation, and on Portugal's resulting influence on Europe.

The Portuguese Sell African Slaves

One terrible consequence of Portuguese exploration along the coast of Africa was that many Africans became slaves. To provide labor for the sugar production on the Madeira Islands, the Portuguese began buying slaves from African kings and traders. The Portuguese also took some slaves to Portugal and sold them to other countries.

Portuguese trade became like trade in the Roman Empire many centuries before. The book of Revelation describes this trade in a passage in which God prophesies the destruction of Rome.

*. . . cargoes of gold and silver and precious stones and pearls
and fine linen and purple and silk and scarlet,
and every kind of citron wood and every article of ivory and
every article made from very costly wood and bronze and iron and marble,
and cinnamon and spice and incense and perfume and frankincense
and wine and olive oil and fine flour and wheat and cattle and sheep,
and cargoes of horses and chariots and slaves and human lives.*
Revelation 18:12-13

Lesson 83 - Prince Henry the Navigator

Stamps Honoring Prince Henry the Navigator from the Republic of the Congo, Cuba, and Rwanda

Assignments for Lesson 83

Our Creative World — Read about Great Zimbabwe and look at the photos on page 63.

Map Book — Complete the assignments for Lesson 83 on Map 25 "Portuguese Exploration."

Timeline Book — In the box for Lesson 83 on page 19, write "Prince Henry begins sending expeditions to Africa."

Student Workbook or Lesson Review — If you are using one of these optional books, complete the assignment for Lesson 83.

Vocabulary — Write a paragraph that uses all of these words: middleman (556), myth (557), whirlpool (557), naval (557), technique (558). Consult a dictionary if you need help with their definitions.

Monument of the Discoveries at Lisbon, Portugal

The Fall of Constantinople

Lesson 84   Our World Story

Constantinople, capital of the Byzantine Empire, was on the far eastern edge of Europe. The city sat at the southern end of the Bosphorus Strait just south of an inlet called the Golden Horn. Across the Bosphorus from Constantinople was the Anatolian Peninsula on the continent of Asia.

In the Bosphorus Strait

The nineteen-mile-long Bosphorus Strait, pictured at right, is the only water route leading out of the Black Sea. Trading ships going from cities along the Black Sea to the Mediterranean must travel first through the Bosphorus and then into the Sea of Marmara. From the Sea of Marmara, they travel through another strait, the thirty-eight-mile-long Dardanelles, pictured below, before reaching the Aegean Sea and then the Mediterranean.

Rise of the Ottoman Turks

The Turks are an ethnic group that came from Central Asia near the Caspian Sea. They moved west when the Mongols invaded their territory in the 1200s and 1300s. Most Turks adopted Islam as their religion. One of the many Turkish tribes that moved into the Anatolian Peninsula was the Kayi tribe. One leader of the Kayi was Osman I, who reigned from 1299 to 1326. When Osman's caliphate grew in power, Muslims from other regions migrated to the Anatolian Peninsula as well. The name Osman is the origin of the name Ottoman. Osman's kingdom grew into the Ottoman Empire, centered in Anatolia. While the

The Dardanelles at Gallipoli

Lesson 84 - The Fall of Constantinople

power of the Ottoman Empire grew, the power of the Byzantine Empire based in Constantinople was declining.

Osman I captured the city of Bursa, just south of the Sea of Marmara in 1326. See a waterfall near Bursa below. The Ottoman Turks continued to enlarge their empire until they ruled the portion of the Balkan region of southeastern Europe around Constantinople. In 1354 they established a base in Europe at Gallipoli, pictured on page 562. In 1360 the Ottomans captured the Byzantine city of Adrianople, about 150 miles northwest of Constantinople, and made it their European capital. By 1365, the Ottoman Empire surrounded Constantinople. Traders from Venice in Italy sailed through the Dardanelles and the Sea of Marmara to bring supplies to the city.

The Ottomans experienced a brief setback in 1402 when Timur (or Tamerlane), who claimed to be a Mongol, defeated them in a battle. However, the Ottomans soon recovered and continued to expand their boundaries.

Saitabat Waterfall Near Bursa

As the Ottoman Empire expanded, the area controlled by Constantinople became smaller and smaller. As of the early 1400s, the only other lands held by the Byzantines beyond Constantinople were a few small outposts on the Greek Peninsula.

The Ottoman Turks, like many other people groups in history, wanted to expand their power. One special target was the city of Constantinople itself. Muslims had first attacked the city from 674 to 678 but had failed to capture it. The city had a triple wall around it, so a direct assault was difficult and costly for any attacking army. Nevertheless, the Ottomans wanted Constantinople because of its strategic location along the Bosphorus and at the boundary between Europe and Asia. They also wanted the great wealth the city contained.

Mehmet II (his name is a form of Muhammad) was born in 1432. He became sultan or ruler of the Ottoman Turks when he was twelve years old. A rival deposed him, but he regained the title in 1451 at the age of nineteen. Mehmet dedicated himself to the goal of capturing Constantinople.

Constantine XI Appeals to Europe for Help

Byzantine Emperor Constantine XI, born in 1404, appealed to Christians in Europe for help to defend the city against the Ottomans. See statue of Constantine XI below. Pope Eugene IV had organized a small army in 1444, but the Ottomans crushed it at Varna in Bulgaria, and the soldiers never reached Constantinople. In 1452, one year after Mehmet II came to power, Pope Nicholas V paid a group of about 200 archers to help defend Constantinople. A few hundred men from the cities of Venice and Genoa in Italy also came to fight the invaders.

In general, however, Europeans turned a deaf ear to pleas for Constantinople's defense. Defending Constantinople was not a goal that many Europeans held. Calls for help in defending it had been too frequent, and efforts to do so had not helped Europe. Most Europeans did not see a need for keeping Constantinople as a stronghold of Christianity. They did not think that the loss of the city would threaten their security.

In addition, the division between Roman Catholics and Orthodox Christians was deep and bitter. Leaders of the Roman Catholic Church and the Orthodox Church attempted to unite in 1438-1439, but most of the clergy in both groups did not support it. In 1452 Constantine XI agreed for Isidore, Catholic cardinal of Kiev and a former leader in the Orthodox Church, to announce a union between the two groups on December 12 in the Cathedral of Hagia Sophia. The announcement was unpopular in Constantinople, and Orthodox leaders rejected the agreement a few years later.

Constantine XI Statue, Athens, Greece

Lesson 84 - The Fall of Constantinople

The Siege of Constantinople

In 1453 Constantinople had a population of about 50,000 and a defense force of about 8,000. The Ottoman Turk army numbered about 80,000 (some estimates by historians are even higher). In addition, the Ottomans had over one hundred warships.

In April 1453, Mehmet II, below, began a fifty-day siege of the city. Defenders of Constantinople had erected an iron chain across the mouth of a water inlet called the Golden Horn to prevent ships from entering it and attacking the city. See map inset on page 563. Mehmet II avoided the obstacle by moving his ships overland across greased runners to enter the Golden Horn. Twice Mehmet II offered for residents to leave if the city surrendered, but the emperor refused.

Ottoman sappers dug tunnels underneath the walls of the city, but defenders from Constantinople entered the tunnels to fight the invading warriors and then destroyed the tunnels. When the Ottomans erected siege towers against the walls of the city, the Byzantine defenders cast a burning substance called Greek fire on them. We don't know the precise formula for Greek fire, but it probably included petroleum and sulfur. The Greek fire caused significant damage.

One of the defenders of Constantinople was Nestor, a young man who had been captured by the Turks in Moldavia and forced to convert to Islam. He was a member of Mehmet's army when it approached Constantinople, but he ran away and joined the army defending the city. He later said that he ran away so that he would not die a Muslim. Nestor survived the assault and became a monk in an Orthodox monastery.

Probably the deciding factor in the confrontation was the relatively new weapon of the cannon. In 1451 Constantine XI had hired a Hungarian engineer named Urban to develop artillery for the city's defense. When Constantine did not pay him as much money as he wanted, Urban offered his services to the Muslims, whose payment pleased him. Urban produced a 29-foot cannon that could fire stones weighing 1,200 pounds. It required sixty oxen to move it, and a crew could only fire it seven times in one day because it became so hot. The much smaller cannons of the Byzantine defenders were largely ineffective.

Constantinople Falls to the Ottoman Turks

Before dawn on May 29, 1453, the Ottomans began an all-out assault on Constantinople. Cannon fire demolished sections of the walls. The Turks entered the city and caused great destruction and death. Among those the Turks killed in the battle was Emperor Constantine XI. The battle ended by noon. After over 1,100 years, Constantinople had fallen and the Byzantine Empire was no more. In addition to killing many people, the Ottomans captured thousands and made them slaves.

The Sultan Mehmet II by Gentile Bellini, who visited the court of Mehmet II in Istanbul. The painting is dated November 25, 1480.

In 1452, the year before he captured nearby Constantinople, Sultan Mehmet II ordered the construction of the Rumeli Hisari Fortress along the narrowest point of the Bosphorus Strait.

Constantinople is now called Istanbul. Some think this name is from the phrase "Islam City." More likely it is from the Greek phrase *eis tin polis*, which means "in the city." The Turks changed the Cathedral of Hagia Sophia into a mosque. The Ottomans either changed or demolished other church buildings in the city. However, the sultan allowed the Orthodox Church to remain in the city if they accepted his rule. Istanbul remained the center of the Orthodox faith. Mehmet II appointed a new Orthodox leader, who was given the title of patriarch. The pope called for a crusade to liberate the city, but nothing came of this appeal.

As a result of the fall of Constantinople, many scholars fled the city and went to Italy. There they helped advance the Renaissance, which we will discuss in the next lesson. European traders continued to do business with Muslims in the Middle East, but the new reality that Istanbul was now ruled by Muslims led many Europeans to seek a new route for trading in Asia.

In a similar situation to what happened to Constantinople, the prophet Jeremiah had lamented the fall of Jerusalem to the Babylonians many centuries earlier:

How lonely sits the city
That was full of people!
She has become like a widow
Who was once great among the nations!
She who was a princess among the provinces
Has become a forced laborer!
Lamentations 1:1

Assignments for Lesson 84

Our Creative World — Read about the Fall of Constantinople on page 64.

Map Book — Complete the assignments for Lesson 84 on Map 26 "Ottoman Empire, 1453."

Timeline Book — In the box for Lesson 84 on page 20, write "Ottoman Turks capture Constantinople."

Student Workbook or Lesson Review — If you are using one of these optional books, complete the assignment for Lesson 84.

Creative Writing — Write at least one paragraph describing the photograph of the Rumeli Hasari Fortress on page 566.

The Italian Renaissance

Lesson 85 — Daily Life

Renaissance comes from the French word for **rebirth**. The Renaissance in Europe was a time of rebirth and renewal in learning about our world and discovering new ways of doing things. It lasted from about 1300 to 1600.

During the Renaissance, many people encouraged learning. Professors and students studied ancient languages and documents. Artists tried new techniques in the arts. These changes did not take place all at once, nor did they happen everywhere at once. The European Renaissance began in Italy, especially in the city of Florence.

Looking Backward, Looking Forward

During the Renaissance, Europeans took a renewed interest in ancient Greek and Roman civilizations. Many Renaissance scholars believed that those peoples had accomplished great things in art, science, government, and warfare, and that they could be a model for people in their own day.

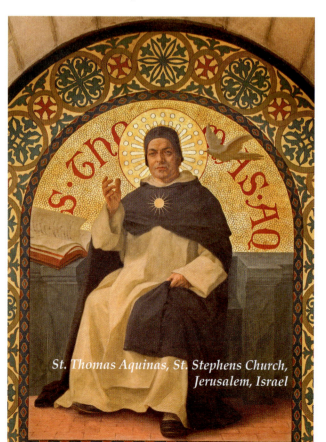
St. Thomas Aquinas, St. Stephens Church, Jerusalem, Israel

As you will remember from our study of those civilizations in *From Adam to Us*, the Greeks and Romans did accomplish amazing things, but they were not perfect. Their pagan belief systems affected their view of human life, and they had the same human failings as any person or civilization has. Renaissance thinking did not emphasize the negative aspects of those civilizations.

Renaissance thinkers did not just look backward into history. They also looked forward to see what new accomplishments would be possible in the future.

Studying God and Studying Man

Catholic scholar Thomas Aquinas, pictured on page 568, lived from 1225 to 1274. He wrote about his search to understand and explain God more fully. European universities began as places to study theology, which is the study of God and His relation to the world. During the Renaissance, many Europeans stopped thinking about the world the way people had in the centuries before. They developed a new worldview. The basic change was from being focused on God to being focused on man. Study in monasteries had focused on God. Before the Renaissance, scholars had emphasized the importance of preparing for the everlasting life that came after life in this world ended.

Renaissance thinking, by contrast, focused on man in this world: his language, competing philosophies, how he was portrayed in art, what he had accomplished in the past, and other areas of human endeavor. One term for this emphasis is humanism. Humanism was strongest in Italy, while scholars in northern Europe remained more interested in spiritual matters.

Petrarch, Language, and Literature

Francesco Petrarca, who lived from 1304 to 1374, was a leader in the early Renaissance. He was better known as Petrarch. Petrarch was born in Italy but spent many years living in France with his father, who had been forced out of Italy because of his views about government. While studying law, Petrarch came upon some writings of the Roman orator Cicero and became enamored with classic literature. Petrarch searched through libraries at monasteries and found many long-lost manuscripts of works by ancient writers. Monks from previous centuries had copied the manuscripts, which they then stored away and forgot. Petrarch developed a personal library that became a model for others in the Renaissance.

Petrarch encouraged other people to study ancient writers. Up until this time, Aristotle had been the accepted authority in universities. Petrarch especially wanted to see the people of his day become familiar with Plato, whose writings he found more interesting than those of Aristotle. Petrarch believed that Plato's works, which mentioned the ideas of the world being created by an all-powerful God and the immortality of the soul, would strengthen a person's Christian faith.

Petrarch studied classical Latin. He also studied philology, the science of the meanings and histories of words. He encouraged the study of history, which to him conveyed the stories of what wise and courageous men of antiquity had done. See statue of Petrarch at right.

Statue of Francesco Petrarca (Petrarch), Florence, Italy

Unit 17 - The Early Renaissance

Statue of Giovanni Boccaccio, Florence, Italy

Petrarch was a mentor to Giovanni Boccaccio who lived from about 1313 to 1375. Boccaccio also rummaged through monasteries looking for manuscripts. In doing so he discovered a book by the Roman historian Tacitus, who lived in the late first and early second centuries AD. Boccaccio was one of the first Europeans of modern times to study Greek. He had his tutor translate Homer's *Iliad* and *Odyssey* into Latin. The translations were poorly done, but Boccaccio was one of the first people in a long time that we know about who even attempted to read these classics. See statue of Boccaccio at left.

Better Tools for Studying the Bible

One reason that Italians became interested in the study of Greek was the arrival from Constantinople of Greek scholars, some of whom left the city in the late 1300s and early 1400s out of fear of an impending Ottoman attack. They brought thousands of manuscripts of ancient documents with them to be kept safe in libraries in Italy. During the same period, Islamic scholars came to Italy and brought ancient Arabic, Greek, and Hebrew texts. The presence of these scholars also encouraged learning during the Renaissance.

The greater knowledge of ancient languages helped in practical ways in church life. The New Testament was written in Greek, but the Bible that the Roman Catholic Church used was the Latin translation called the Vulgate. Jerome had completed this translation around 405. This was the only Bible that the Catholic Church accepted. A better knowledge of Greek manuscripts enabled the scholar Erasmus, depicted in the stamp at right, to publish a Greek New Testament in 1516. This Greek New Testament helped later Bible translators.

Dutch Stamp Honoring Erasmus, 1969

Renaissance Artists

The art of the Middle Ages used bright colors and portrayed Biblical subjects, but the scenes were flat with no depth. Renaissance artists developed techniques that made their work much more lifelike. A pioneer of the new style was Giotto di Bondone, who lived from 1267 to 1337. Giotto was born in a village near Florence, Italy. His scenes looked as if they had been painted by an **eyewitness**. He used light and shadow to show depth. He used perspective when he painted persons or objects, making them seem more real. One outstanding example of his work are the thirty-five scenes from the life of Jesus that he painted on the walls of the Scrovegni Chapel in Padua, Italy. His work had a great influence on painters of the 1400s. Giotti designed the bell tower pictured on pages 541 and 572.

Lesson 85 - The Italian Renaissance

Tribute Money *by Masaccio*

Donato di Niccolo di Betto Bardi, known as Donatello, who lived from 1386 to 1466, was born in Florence and became an influential sculptor. His statue of St. George, below, shows the influence of ancient Greek sculpture.

Tommaso Cassai, called Masaccio, who lived from 1401 to 1428, was born near Florence. His portrayals of Biblical scenes at the church of Santa Maria Novella in Florence feature people in natural, **lifelike** poses. Masaccio's painting above is called *Tribute Money*. It tells the story of three moments in Peter's life. While Jesus stands in the center with His disciples, He tells Peter what to do to pay their taxes. At left, Peter takes the coins from a fish's mouth. At right, Peter pays the tax collector.

Filippo Brunelleschi, who lived from 1377 to 1446, was also from Florence. After serving as a goldsmith's apprentice, he spent ten years in Rome where he was fascinated by Roman architecture. His interest in mathematics helped him develop precise formulas in order to portray perspective. He designed the dome of the Cathedral of Florence as well as the means for workers to lift it into place. Brunelleschi's dome is pictured on pages 541 and 572, along with a bell tower designed by Giotto.

In northern Europe, Jan van Eyck (1380?-1441) of Flanders (a region now divided between France and Belgium) excelled in the portrayal of realistic detail. He also was one of the first artists to use oil-based paint. Previous artists used tempera, made by mixing pigments with a binder such as egg whites, or fresco, which is water-based pigments painted on fresh plaster. See a painting by Jan van Eyck on page 573.

Statue of St. George *by Donatello, Church of San Michele, Florence, Italy*

Cathedral of Florence, with Bell Tower Designed by Giotto and Dome Designed by Brunelleschi

Moving Away from Feudalism

The local manor and town began to connect to the other communities, and feudalism started to disappear. Local guilds could no longer control activity in their trades. Businessmen began more and more to hire workers and pay them **wages**. Instead of simply farming land and receiving part of the produce, men could work and earn money. Kings began to receive taxes instead of receiving part of the profits from farms or businesses.

Some businessmen did not own companies that produced things to sell; instead, they owned businesses that invested money or loaned money to other businessmen. These investment businesses were banks, which began in Italy but spread throughout Europe.

Christian Humanism

As Renaissance leaders changed from a focus on God to a focus on man, they emphasized religion and faith less than scholars did during the Middle Ages. Still, most Renaissance scholars believed in God. Many began to wonder if they could practice what they called "Christian humanism." Like other Renaissance thinkers, people who practiced Christian humanism shifted their focus from exclusively studying God and His will for people to studying people. However, they did this from the perspective of faith in God.

Lesson 85 – The Italian Renaissance

The Roman Catholic Church and its traditions and beliefs had dominated life in Europe for centuries. The increased interest in ancient languages and manuscripts, however, meant that scholars looked anew at the original meaning of the Scriptures and at ancient writers such as Augustine and others from the early church. This study raised the possibility in some minds that Christians could—and perhaps even should—live and function as a church in ways different from the ways they had known all their lives.

Church teaching in the Middle Ages did not emphasize building wealth. Instead, the Church emphasized poverty and humility. Monasteries and religious orders were the prime examples of this. Some people living during the Renaissance began to wonder how the Church should respond to the increase in wealth and higher status of merchants, businessmen, and bankers. Were these people wrong to make life better for themselves and their customers? Could a person live above **dire** poverty and be faithful to God?

Much of the art from the Renaissance honored God and portrayed Biblical scenes and characters in lifelike and effective ways. Artists had the opportunity to use new techniques to depict humans well but still to glorify God. However, some of what artists and authors produced did not honor God but merely focused on man.

People who came to Italy as traders or students learned about this new Renaissance way of thinking and took the ideas back to their homelands. Two areas where people took a special interest in these new ideas were Flanders and some of the German states. The Renaissance would come to rock the very foundations of life for Europeans in ways they could not imagine.

The Man in a Turban *by Jan Van Eyck may be a self-portrait.*

These stamps with paintings of the Madonna and Child and Madonna and Child with St. Anne by Renaissance artist Albrecht Dürer were printed in the United Arab Emirates in 1970.

Because God made people in His image, we can do amazing things. However, in every age, we must remember who made us and honor Him. In his letter to the Romans centuries before, Paul wrote about God's judgment on people who did not recognize His divine power or honor Him as they should.

*For even though they knew God,
they did not honor Him as God or give thanks,
but they became futile in their speculations,
and their foolish heart was darkened.*
Romans 1:21

Assignments for Lesson 85

Timeline Book — In the box for Lesson 85 on page 20, write "Ghiberti completes the Gates of Paradise."

Student Workbook or Lesson Review — If you are using one of these optional books, complete the assignment for Lesson 85 and take the test for Unit 17.

Thinking Biblically — Make a list of at least five ways that people in our world today practice humanism (the focus on man and what he does and has done).

Vocabulary — Write your own definition for each of these words: rebirth (568), eyewitness (570), lifelike (571), wage (572), dire (573). Look in the lesson for clues for the meaning of the words. When you are finished writing your definitions, look in a dictionary for comparison.

18　The Late 1400s

Copy of the Gutenberg Bible in Washington, D.C.

Lessons	86 - God's Wonder: Venice, Italy
	87 - World Biography: Ivan the Great
	88 - Our World Story: Printing in Renaissance Europe
	89 - World Landmark: Machu Picchu of the Inca
	90 - Daily Life: Making Porcelain in the Ming Dynasty
Literature	In *The King's Fifth* by Scott O'Dell, a young Spanish mapmaker travels with a band of conquistadors in Central America seeking gold. (See "Notes to Parents on the Literature" in the back of the Answer Key.)

1454-1491

A settlement on islands off the northeastern coast of Italy became the powerful trading city of Venice. Ivan the Great spread out into what is now northern Russia from the small kingdom of Moscow and refused to pay tribute to the Golden Horde of the Mongols and Tatars. Johann Gutenberg and the printers who followed him changed the way that people learned by making it possible for many people to have books. On the other side of the world, the Inca were expanding into what was probably the world's largest empire during the late 1400s, while they amassed amazing wealth in gold. In China craftsmen were refining the craft of making porcelain and shipping it far beyond their borders.

Venice
Italy

Lesson 86 — God's Wonder

In 452 Attila had led the Huns into northern Italy and attacked the city of Aquileia, one of the richest Roman cities, as well as several other towns. Most residents either died or became prisoners. The rest fled to a cluster of islands two miles away, where a few fishermen lived.

The coast of northeastern Italy nearby was marshy and swampy. Beyond the islands are a row of sandbars with gaps in between them. Beyond the sandbars is the Adriatic Sea. In the midst of the sandbars is a lagoon, which is a shallow body of water separated by sandbars from a larger body of water. The Po and Plave Rivers flow into the lagoon. To the north on the mainland are the beautiful Italian Alps. See photos at right.

Wanting to find refuge from future attacks, the displaced people decided to build a new city on the islands where the shallow waters of the muddy lagoon and the unstable currents discouraged potential invaders from the sea.

The new residents drove wooden **piles** through the mud of the islands and into the hard clay beneath. Most piles were of alder trees from Slovenia. The alder is a member of the birch family, and its wood resists decay when it is under water. The people laid oak timbers and limestone slabs on the piles as foundations, and then they began to construct buildings. See map on page 578.

Alpine Ibex in Gran Paradiso National Park in the Italian Alps

Po River

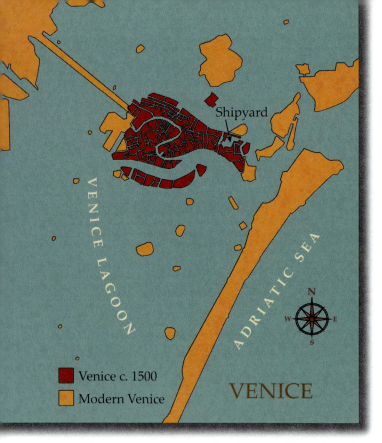

Unit 18 - The Late 1400s

When Goths and Lombards invaded Italy in later centuries, more Italians escaped to the new city on the islands. The name of the region in Italy was Veneto, for the Veneti people who lived there. We know the city as Venice.

The people who came to the islands formed communities with others from their homelands. In 466 the communities on the islands chose representatives to serve on a council to govern their new city. As more people came and new communities formed, their representatives joined the council. In 697 the council of representatives declared Venice to be a republic. They formed a **parliament** and chose a single head of state. The title for this leader was *dux*, the Latin word for leader, which became *doge* in Venice and is the source of the title of duke used in other parts of Europe.

The Growth of Venice

Venetians took advantage of their location and became expert traders. They caught and sold fish. They bought oil, wine, and grain from growers on the **mainland** and shipped these goods to cities along the Adriatic coast. The gaps between the sandbars allowed skilled captains of trading ships to sail to and from the city by way of the Adriatic.

By the 800s, Venice engaged in trade with Constantinople and cities in North Africa. Venice continued to grow more powerful and influential through the centuries. Eventually Venetians established colonies or trading posts on the Dalmatian coast of the Balkans (see photo below) and on Crete and Cyprus. They also established colonies or posts on the Anatolian Peninsula; in Alexandria, Egypt; at Tyre and Sidon in Palestine; and along the Black Sea and the Indian Ocean.

As we learned in Lesson 71, merchants of Venice helped to fund the Fourth Crusade. In Lesson 75, we learned that Marco Polo was from Venice.

Venice reached the height of its power and wealth in the 1400s. At that time the city had the largest fleet of trading ships in Europe, protected by the largest navy. One estimate places the number at 300 seagoing vessels, 3,000 smaller ships, and 45 galleons (large armed trading vessels later used for war), with crews that totaled over 30,000 men. The shipyard at Venice could build or repair one hundred vessels at a time with its labor force of 15,000. Merchants could acquire just about

Aerial View of Kotor, Montenegro, from its fortress. Venetians ruled this area from 1420 to 1797.

Lesson 86 - Venice, Italy

anything at Venice or from Venetian traders, including gold, copper, tin, jewels, **ebony**, ivory, paintings, mosaics, silk, spices, animals, hides, and slaves.

Venice's aggressive pursuit of trade led to conflict with other cities, especially Genoa in northwestern Italy. Venice defeated Genoa in a war in 1380, gained control over trade in the eastern Mediterranean, and grew to become one of the largest cities in Europe. Venetian artists and architects became leaders in the Renaissance. See examples of art below.

Left: The Embriachi family of Venice created this triptych in the early 1400s. Right: This painting of the Madonna and Child was created in Venice in the workshop of Bartolomeo Vivarini in 1477.

Venice

San Giorgio Maggiore Island, Venice, Italy

The Setting of the Jewel

The city of Venice, called the Jewel of the Adriatic, sits on about 120 islands in the Venetian lagoon. See an aerial view of one of its many islands above. Some 400 canals run between the islands and are used as "streets." About 400 bridges, such as the ones at left and at right, connect the islands. The largest canal is the Grand Canal, pictured at top right. The Grand Canal winds through the center of the islands. People traveled in Venice not by horse and cart but by boat. Traditionally, the boats in the Venetian canals were gondolas. Tides come into and out of the canals each day helping to keep them clean. Today a **causeway** connects the city to the mainland.

Venice is home to many works of art and to striking architecture and beautiful plazas. Perhaps the most famous architectural

Canal in Venice

Lesson 86 - Venice, Italy

Gondolas on the Grand Canal with the Basilica di Santa Maria della Salute in the Background

Canals and Bridges of Venice

landmark is the Basilica of St. Mark, pictured on page 582. One of the longest lasting industries in the city creates world-famous Venetian glass. As a seacoast town near sandbars, Venetians had plenty of sand to use in glass.

Sometimes called the Queen of the Adriatic, Venice is a beautiful city in a dramatic and unusual setting. This community is a remarkable example of how man's ingenuity applied to God's Creation has produced amazing results.

Behold, the nations are like a drop from a bucket, and are regarded as a speck of dust on the scales; behold, He lifts up the islands like fine dust.
Isaiah 40:15

Assignments for Lesson 86

Our Creative World — Look at the photos about International Trade and Coins on pages 65-66.

Timeline Book — In the box for Lesson 86 on page 20, write "Venice takes control of the island of Cyprus."

Student Workbook or Lesson Review — If you are using one of these optional books, complete the assignment for Lesson 86.

Vocabulary — Copy the list of vocabulary words, then write the correct definition beside each word: pile (577), parliament (578), mainland (578), ebony (579), causeway (580).
  a. the central part of a body of land not including islands
  b. a long thin column (such as wood or steel) driven into the ground to bear a load vertically
  c. the hard, black-toned wood from a tropical tree
  d. a raised road that is laid across marshy ground or water
  e. a body formed for the making of laws

Creative Writing — How would life in Venice, a city so closely surrounded and impacted by water, be different from life where you live? Make a list of at least seven ways.

Literature — *The King's Fifth* moves back and forth between journal entries (organized by date) and narrative (organized by chapter numbers). Your reading assignments will include these in the order they appear in the book. Read the September 23 journal entry and chapter 1.

Dome of the Basilica of St. Mark

Ivan the Great

Lesson 87 **World Biography**

In the mid-1400s, Russia was not a unified country. The land was a collection of scattered domains, each with its own ruler, called a grand duke or grand prince, and a capital city. The Mongol Golden Horde claimed to rule all of the land, but its power over the area was weak. All they were able to do was to collect annual tribute from the Russian people, which Russian dukes and princes took to the Mongol capital in Sarai Batu. See artifacts and architecture of the Golden Horde at right. When the Mongols had come west, the Tatar people from central Asia had joined with them to conquer Eastern Europe. The Tatars spoke Turkic, and many had become Muslim. Many Russians and other Europeans referred to the invaders, including the Mongols, as Tatars. Tatar is sometimes written Tartar, which is how some Europeans pronounced it.

Ivan III

Ivan III was born in 1440 to Vasily II, the grand duke of Moscow. At the time Vasily

Artifacts and Architecture of the Golden Horde

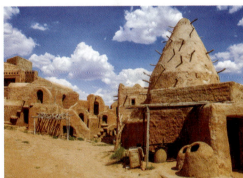

Left Column: Silver Cup from the 1200s or 1300s Carried by a Warrior of the Golden Horde; Mausoleum of Djanike Khanum, Daughter of Golden Horde Khan Tokhtamysh in Chufut Kale, Near Russia in the Crimea of Ukraine
Right Column: Two Views of a Replica of Sarai Batu; Dirham Coins of the Golden Horde

was fighting a civil war against his brothers. When Ivan was six years old, Vasily declared him to be his successor in order to ensure that Ivan would inherit the throne. Vasily also announced that Ivan was engaged to Maria, the daughter of the grand prince of Tver. They were officially (but only formally) married when Ivan was twelve. Tver became part of Moscow's domain and was thus no longer a rival power. That year Ivan also began serving in his father's army. Over the next ten years Ivan learned about leading military expeditions and handling diplomatic relations.

When Vasily died in 1462, Ivan became grand duke of Moscow at the age of 22 and began taking over other Russian dukedoms. He did this through conducting bold military conquests, having other rulers sign treaties that recognized Moscow's sovereignty, and simply declaring that he was annexing other lands to Moscow. In this way he acquired all of northern Russia between what is now Finland and the Ural Mountains, including the important trading city of Novgorod. Ivan also gained authority over several cities that had been part of Lithuania and Poland. In all, Ivan tripled the amount of land that Moscow controlled. In 1480 Ivan refused to pay tribute to Ahmed, the khan of the Tatars. The Tatars did not attempt to collect it, and their rule over Russia ended.

Millennium of Russia, Novgorod, Russia

Millennium of Russia

The bronze monument at left is called the Millennium of Russia. Erected in Novgorod in 1862, it commemorates 1,000 years of Russian history. The monument weighs one hundred tons. The earliest historic figure, who is standing at the center of the dome, is a warrior prince named Rurik. His figure celebrates the arrival of the Varangians in 862. On his shield is the number 6370, which represents the number of years since God created the world according to a Byzantine calculation.

Lesson 87 - Ivan the Great

Dome of the Millennium of Russia, Novgorod, Russia

The figure holding the cross on the left side of the dome, as pictured on page 584, is Vladimir the Great, who made the decision that Russia would be a Christian kingdom. Among the relief statues at the bottom of the monument are Olga, grandmother of Vladimir; Yaroslav the Wise, son of Vladimir, who continued to promote Christianity in Russia; the monk Anthony, who founded the Monastery of the Caves; and Methodius and Cyril, missionaries to the Slavs (see Lessons 68 and 69). In the center of the close-up of the dome above is Ivan III.

Influence of the Byzantine Empire

Ivan's wife Maria died in 1467. Five years later he married Zoe, the niece of Constantine XI, the last Byzantine emperor. Zoe took the name of Sophia. Moscow was the largest remaining Orthodox city. Since people had called Constantinople the new Rome, Ivan came to see Moscow as the third Rome. Ivan began calling himself the tsar (sometimes spelled czar), which is the Russian form of the name Caesar. In the eyes of Ivan, Moscow and the Russians were beginning to achieve the greatness of a new empire.

Ivan copied the Byzantine Empire when he adopted the double-headed eagle as the symbol of his authority. Ivan's government compiled a law code in 1497. This was the first time that anyone had written down the laws of Moscow in a single place.

Russian Double-Headed Eagle

The Kremlin

Because of Sophia's influence, Ivan III employed Russian and Italian Renaissance architects and craftsmen to build up and beautify Moscow. One of the most important and lasting projects was the expansion of the Kremlin.

The Russian word *kremlin* means fortress. Many major cities in Russia had a kremlin as a government headquarters and a place where people could go if the city were attacked. The first Kremlin in Moscow was a wooden structure begun in 1156. Grand Duke Dmitri Donskoi put stone walls in place in the 1300s. Ivan ordered new walls of red brick, which stand today.

The Moscow Kremlin is a ninety-acre complex on the Moscow River. It is roughly the shape of a triangle with one corner cut off. The outside wall is 1.4 miles long. It has five gates and twenty-nine towers. The Kremlin was the headquarters of both the government and the Russian Orthodox Church. It contains numerous cathedrals, palaces, an arsenal, an armory, and gardens.

On Cathedral Square inside the Kremlin stand the Cathedral of the Assumption, where rulers were crowned; the Annunciation Cathedral, the church of the tsars; and Archangel Cathedral, the burial place of the tsars. The Ivan the Great Bell Tower, completed after Ivan's death, rises 266 feet. The Grand Kremlin Palace contains the beautiful throne hall, pictured at right.

Ivan III died in 1505. His son, Vasily III, then became grand duke. The son of Vasily III, Ivan IV, was grand duke from 1530 to 1584. This later Ivan was a cruel man who was given to outbursts of anger. He earned the title of Ivan the Terrible.

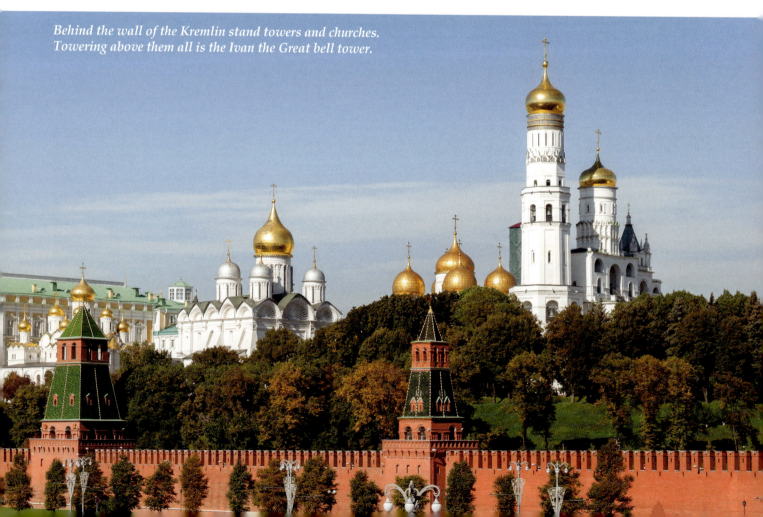

Behind the wall of the Kremlin stand towers and churches. Towering above them all is the Ivan the Great bell tower.

Lesson 87 - Ivan the Great

Grand Kremlin Palace

Top Row: Kremlin Exterior; Doors in Georgievsky Hall; Center Row: Throne Hall; Throne; Royal Suite; Bottom Row: The Palace of Facets; Georgievsky Hall

Ruler of All Russia

The strong leadership of Ivan III put Russia on the road to becoming a powerful nation. He began unifying Russian lands and the Russian people under the authority of Moscow. Ivan III was the first to use the title "Ruler of All Russia." A later diplomat to Russia gave him the title "Ivan the Great."

Proverbs reminds us that wisdom is essential for a ruler to be successful:

Detail of Ivan the Great on the Millennium of Russia Monument in Novgorod

*I, wisdom, dwell with prudence,
And I find knowledge
and discretion.
By me kings reign,
And rulers decree justice.
By me princes rule, and nobles,
All who judge rightly.
Proverbs 8:12, 15-16*

This 1967 stamp from the U.S.S.R. depicts the Cathedral of the Annunciation in the Kremlin.

Assignments for Lesson 87

Timeline Book — In the box for Lesson 87 on page 20, write "Ivan III frees Russia from Tatar control."

Student Workbook or Lesson Review — If you are using one of these optional books, complete the assignment for Lesson 87.

Thinking Biblically — Read Proverbs 8 regarding wisdom.

Creative Writing — Write one paragraph describing one of the photographs of the Grand Kremlin Palace on page 587.

Literature — Read chapters 2-4 in *The King's Fifth*.

Printing
in Renaissance Europe

Lesson 88   **Our World Story**

Europeans produced books by hand-copying text and drawing and painting illustrations on parchment. Parchment refers to a writing sheet made from animal skin, usually sheep, calf, or goat. See example at right. Vellum is a term for high quality parchment. This form of copying was beautiful (as with the Lindisfarne Gospels, for example), but writing carefully using elaborately illustrated text by hand on sheets of animal skin was slow and expensive. A wealthy local church or nobleman might own a copy of the Scriptures. A university would have a few copies of standard, classic works. A book was a rare item, and the vast majority of people could not read.

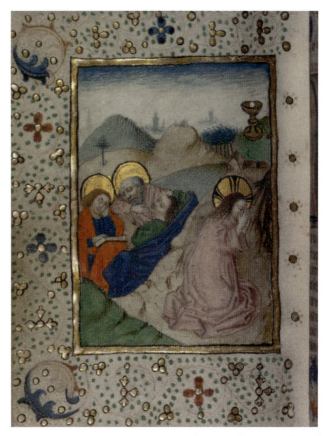

Hand-Painted Illustration on Parchment of the Garden of Gethsemane from the Zwolle Bible, Zwolle, Netherlands, 1470

Printing in China

In Lesson 75 we discussed the development of printing in China. We described block printing, which involved carving an entire page from wood in reverse, putting ink on it, and pressing it against paper or parchment to produce the printed page. We also described movable printing, in which a printer placed individually carved characters in a mold, pressed the mold against paper, then reused the characters to make other pages.

Traders brought to Europe knowledge of the technology that the Chinese developed, but some significant difficulties still remained. First, wooden print blocks did not last long in the printing process. The wooden characters wore down and the print quality decreased fairly rapidly. Second, printers needed less expensive surfaces on which to print. Printing on parchment was costly. A single handwritten copy of the Bible, for instance, required about 170 calfskins or about 300 sheepskins.

The Chinese invented paper around the same time that Jesus came to Earth. A papermaker put **hemp** waste in water, soaked it, and beat it to a pulp with a wooden mallet. Then he spread the pulp on wire mesh in a frame for it to dry in a sheet, and then a worker cut it to the desired size. The Chinese later used other plant fibers, such as tree bark and bamboo.

Paper Comes to Europe

Arab traders brought the technology for making paper to Europe, but many people did not trust the new material. In fact, sometime between 1221 and 1231, Holy Roman Emperor Frederick II issued a decree that said any documents written on paper were **invalid**. Historians have offered several possible reasons for this decree. Perhaps it was because of the hold of tradition. Perhaps paper seemed quite fragile compared to parchment. The emperor might have been influenced by wealthy sheep and cattle owners who feared losing the market for parchment.

The Story of Gutenberg

People in several different cities in Europe worked on a way to print using movable type, but one man led the effort that made printing a reality. Johann Gutenberg was born around 1400 in the city of Mainz in what would become Germany. He served as an apprentice to a goldsmith and learned how to cut gemstones. While Gutenberg lived in Strasbourg, France, he worked on ideas for printing. He returned to Mainz in 1438. Gutenberg used his training in working with gold to cut **dies** to form individual metal letters. He put the letters in a mold or frame to create a page. He developed a press that pressed sheets of paper onto the mold. He learned this technology from winemaking and papermaking. Metal letters lasted longer than wooden ones, but Gutenberg needed ink that would adhere to metal. Artists in Flanders had begun using oil-based paint (see page 571). Gutenberg adapted that idea by mixing powdered charcoal called lampblack in linseed oil varnish to create an ink that would stay on the metal letters and transfer smoothly and without smudges to paper.

Papermakers in Europe began to create paper from cotton or linen rags that were cleaned, bleached, and made into a pulp. A grid of wire mesh held the sheet of pulp while it dried. Then the sheet was pressed and hung up to dry. To help the paper not absorb so much ink, workers coated it with animal **gelatin**. Paper became fairly common in Europe in the early 1400s. The cost was about one-sixth that of parchment.

Johannes Gutenberg by Pierre-Jean David d'Angers, France, 1839

Lesson 88 - Printing in Renaissance Europe

The Gutenberg Bible

The first book that Gutenberg printed was the Bible in 1455. This was the Latin Vulgate translation that Jerome had completed in 405. See painting of Jerome below. Gutenberg's Bible took 641 sheets of paper or 1,282 pages in two volumes. A written account from 1474 of this first book said that Gutenberg printed 300 sheets per day using six presses. After he printed one side of a sheet, he had to let it dry before he printed the other side. When he had enough copies of one sheet printed, he pulled the type out of the forms, set type for another page, and printed those copies. See engraving above. After all of the pages were printed, workers bound them together. Gutenberg printed about 200 copies of the Bible. Twenty-three complete copies are known to exist today, along with portions or fragments of several others. See pages from one of the first copies on page 575.

Johann Gutenberg (at Right) in an Engraving from 1881

This first printed book was beautifully done. The technology was amazing. The printed letters looked like handwritten letters, which is the look that the first printers wanted to reproduce. At first the desires and financial resources of the Church determined what was printed: prayer books, the writings of Thomas Aquinas, and other Church-related materials. Soon, however, many others saw the benefit of printed books. Schools wanted grammar books, mathematics books, dictionaries, and encyclopedias. Demand grew for medical books, legal books, histories, and Latin classic literature. Most of those who lived on farms were **illiterate** and had no use for books. However, merchants, artisans, lawyers, and government officials who lived in towns saw the need for education, acquiring the ability to read, and owning books.

Two other people closely associated with Gutenberg's printing business were Johann Fust, who invested money in it, and Peter Schöffer, Fust's son-in-law. See photos on the next page.

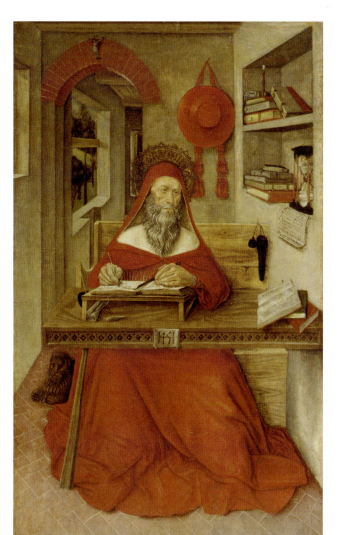

Italian artist Antonio da Fabriano II created this painting of Jerome just four years before Gutenberg printed his first Bible.

Gutenberg had to spend a great deal of money to begin his printing business, and he was not able to pay back the money Fust had invested. Fust sued him and got ownership of the equipment. Either Gutenberg or Fust and Schöffer printed an edition of the Psalms in 1457. All of the copies known to exist are on vellum. The Psalms used three colors of ink.

The Gutenberg Bible

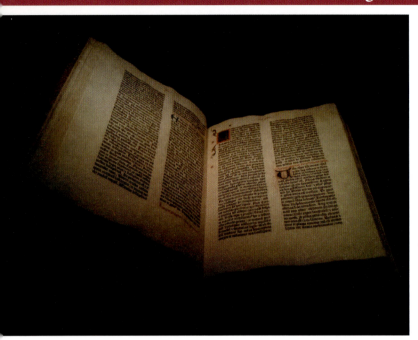

Above: Gutenberg Bible; Top Right: This type has been set up just as the type was set up to print the Gutenberg Bible. At Right: This detail of the Gutenberg Bible shows color that was added by hand.

Left: The Johann Gutenberg Monument erected in 1852 in Frankfurt am Main, Germany, honors Johann Gutenberg (at Top of Pedestal in Center) and Other Printing Pioneers, including Johann Fust (Center Photo), and Peter Schöffer (at Right in the Photo at Right)

Lesson 88 - Printing in Renaissance Europe

The Spread of Printing

Printing technology spread throughout Europe quickly. Once Gutenberg and those working with him figured out how to do it, others could reproduce the technology. By 1500 an estimated one thousand printers had established businesses. By this time printers had produced thousands, perhaps millions, of printed items.

Although printing with movable type was easier and faster than hand-copying, it was still not easy. The process involved several steps, as we have indicated: molding the metal letters (backward!), making a frame to hold the letters, putting the letters in place (backward!), inking the letters, applying the paper and pressing it on the letters (after making the paper and cutting it to the desired size), printing the other side of the paper, and assembling the book. Still, printing was much more efficient than hand-copying.

Even so, hand-copying did not suddenly disappear. Printers did not want to go to the trouble of printing a very small number of copies of a book. In addition, owning a hand-copied book gave a person a certain amount of social status. Other people knew that such beautiful books were very expensive.

The first book printed in English was *The Recuyell of the Historyes of Troye*, a collection of stories about the Trojan War. William Caxton printed it about 1471 after he learned the printing trade in Cologne, Germany. See the picture at right. Caxton's second book was *The Game and Playe of the Chesse* (which is an antiquated way to spell chess), an English translation that Caxton made from two French translations of a book written in 1275 by an Italian Dominican friar. Caxton printed this book in 1474 in Brugge. Both of these books had an appeal to nobles and people in royal courts, who were likely to be able to read. The first offered stories of bravery in battle, and the second compared a chess game to courtly life with its kings, queens, bishops, knights, castles, and pawns.

William Caxton holds a printed page from The Recuyell of the Historyes of Troye. *Art by Louis Rhead*

The Impact of Printing

Movable printing in Europe had a revolutionary effect on many aspects of life. It enabled information to circulate more easily and quickly. Learning became easier as more books became available. Previously, even university classes involved a professor reading out of a book and students copying down the words. Learning to read became easier as the forms of letters became standardized. A wider range of books became available. The process of hand-copying resulted in numerous errors that only increased in number as copyists produced more copies. Printed materials contained fewer errors than hand-copied ones.

Printing changed the process of memorization: people no longer had to memorize as much information because they could simply look it up in their books. Printing also gave birth to related industries and technologies, such as the building of paper mills and the making of metal letters.

To say that Gutenberg invented printing does not do justice to all of the people who played a part in the development of this technology, such as the Chinese who developed wooden print characters and paper, on whose shoulders Gutenberg stood; the Europeans who worked on the metal letters, printing press, and paper he used; and the people who were involved with Gutenberg in his printing business.

Gutenberg apparently started over after the legal battle with Fust and printed other books later in his life. He received a pension and other benefits from the bishop of Mainz. Gutenberg died in 1468, but he was not at all a wealthy man as a result of his work that changed the world.

Paul placed a great value on the written documents he owned:

When you come bring the cloak which I left at Troas with Carpus, and the books, especially the parchments.
2 Timothy 4:13

Belarusian, Russian, Ukrainian, and American Printing

Left: This statue honors Francis Skaryna, the first Belarusian printer, who published several books of the Bible in Belarusian, beginning in 1571. Top Right: This stamp honors Ivan Fyodorov, the first book printer in Russia and Ukraine. He published the first Church Slavonic Bible in 1580-1581. Bottom Right: This stamp commemorates the first book printed in America, the 1639 Bay Psalm Book.

Lesson 88 - Printing in Renaissance Europe

Assignments for Lesson 88

Timeline Book — In the box for Lesson 88 on page 20, write "Gutenberg Bibles are printed."

Student Workbook or Lesson Review — If you are using one of these optional books, complete the assignment for Lesson 88.

Thinking Biblically — Why do you think that Gutenberg chose the Bible as the first book to print? List at least five reasons.

Vocabulary — Look up each of these words in a dictionary and read their definitions: hemp (590), invalid (590), die (590), gelatin (590), illiterate (591).

Literature — Read chapter 5 and the September 24 journal entry in *The King's Fifth*.

Family Activity — Complete the "Making Paper" activity. Instructions begin on page FA-36.

Stamps Honoring Gutenberg

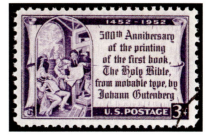

From Top to Bottom: United States, 1952; Hungary, 1962; Germany, 2000; and Cambodia, 2001

Machu Picchu of the Inca

Lesson 89   World Landmark

In the last half of the 1400s, Europeans were developing a culture of the printed word. The printing press rapidly expanded the importance of writing. Europeans had practiced this skill for centuries, but it was now changing because of Gutenberg's invention. Writing allowed Europeans to study and share God-given Scripture, keep historical records, maintain business accounts, develop literature, and follow a reliable standard of laws. For example, when we study an historic building in Europe, we know the architectural planning that went into it, how much workers received for their labor, often the names of the architect and foremen who worked on the project, and many other details about the endeavor because of the written records that people kept.

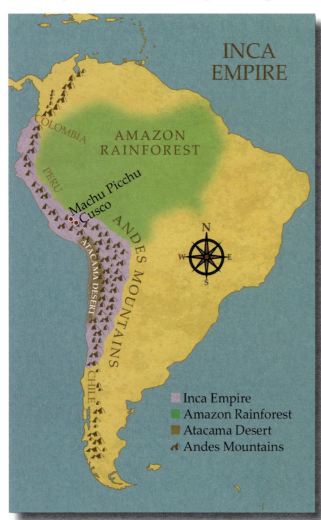

During the same period halfway around the world, in the mountains of what would become Peru, people engaged in another amazing building project over seven thousand feet above sea level. These people were the Inca. Their work was sound in terms of architecture and engineering, and it still stands today. However, they had, as far as we know, no iron, no steel, no wheels, and no written language.

The Inca of South America

A noble family called Inca ruled what is now Cusco, Peru, around 1200. From Cusco, Emperor Pachacuti, a descendant of the Inca, began to conquer the people groups in the

Lesson 89 - Machu Picchu of the Inca

surrounding area in 1438. By some estimates, the empire, which they called "Land of Four Quarters," became the largest on Earth by the late 1400s, with a population of as many as ten million people.

Though technically "Inca" refers to the first Inca royal family and the descendants of that family, today the term Inca is used to refer to all of the people who became part of the empire. The Inca Empire spread out over 2,500 miles from modern Colombia to Chile and from the Atacama Desert to the Amazon Rainforest. The Inca built temples, fortresses, and 14,000 miles of roads, including two main highways and the many roads that joined them. They dug irrigation canals and farmed on terraces they built on mountainsides.

The Inca capital at Cusco became a center of indescribable wealth with roads and temples made of gold. It even had a sculpture garden with soil, a crop of maize, llamas and their babies, and shepherds all made of gold!

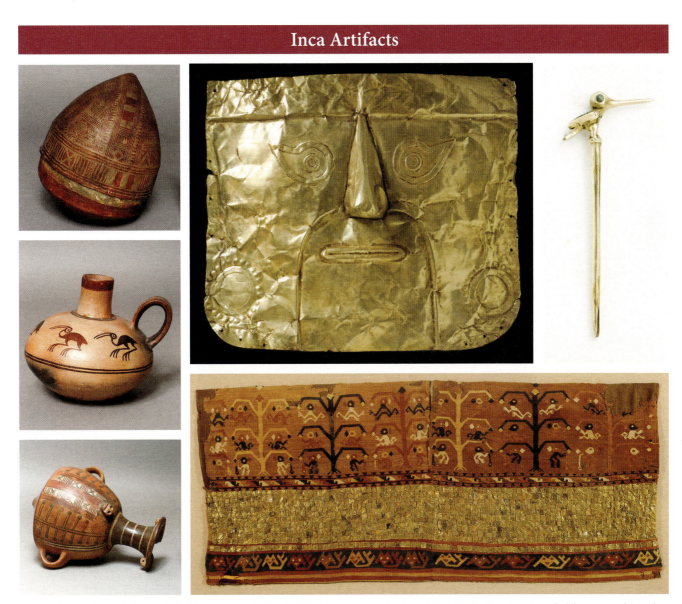

Inca Artifacts

Left Column: Gourd Box, 1430-1560; Ceramic Jar, 1430-1532; Ceramic Urn, 1438-1532; Top Center: Gold Repoussé Mask; Top Right: Gold Spoon in the Form of a Hummingbird, 1250-1470; Bottom Right: Tunic Made of Cotton with Gilded Silver

A Mountain Complex

The Inca built a mountaintop complex 7,875 feet above sea level, located fifty miles northwest of Cusco. The name of the mountain is Machu Picchu, so that is what historians have come to call the complex. The mountaintop stands about 2,000 feet above the Urubamba River Valley, which surrounds the mountain on three sides. See photo at right.

Urubamba River Valley

Animals Native to Machu Picchu

Top Row: Vicuña, Alpaca, Guanaco; Second Row: Spectacled Bear, Dwarf Brocket, Neotropical Otter; Third Row: Ocelot, Llama at Machu Picchu; Left: Andean Cock-of-the-Rock

Lesson 89 - Machu Picchu of the Inca

Machu Picchu

Machu Picchu sits between two other steep peaks on the eastern slope of the heavily forested Andes Mountains. Machu Picchu, which means "Old Peak" in Quechua, is the center of several Inca sites. The Quechua people are modern descendants of the Inca.

The surrounding countryside includes grasslands, polylepis thickets, and cloud forests. Polylepis is a family of trees and shrubs that grow in the Andes. They have thick, multi-layered bark with evergreen leaves. A cloud forest is a high-altitude forest that has almost continual mist and cloud cover and 100 percent humidity. Because of the abundance of moisture, a cloud forest has a rich diversity of plant life.

Structures at Machu Picchu

The complex of Machu Picchu, seen above, covers a total of about five square miles. Some 3,000 stone steps lead up to the summit. The site includes about 200 structures, mostly made of white granite and which researchers

Cloud Forest Seen from Machu Picchu

Clockwise from Top Left: Trapezoid Window; Stonework, Building with Reconstructed Thatched Roof, Three Views of Terraces, Hitching Post of the Sun; Center: Temple of the Sun

believe originally had thick thatched roofs. One evidence of the amazing skills of the Inca builders is that the cut stones used in the buildings do not have mortar holding them together, but a person cannot insert a knife between the stones because they fit together so well.

The site also includes about 700 terraces, which were used for farming. Researchers have called the large carved stone, seen at left, the Intihuatana (which means "Hitching Post of the Sun" in Quechua).

The Inca dug a canal about 2,500 feet long that led from a mountain spring and fed fountains at the site. Machu Picchu also had a drainage system that took water away from the structures. The mountaintop receives about seventy-six inches of rainfall per year. This is higher than the average rainfall in any city in the lower forty-eight United States. Machu Picchu needed a good drainage system because the construction work changed the lay of the land. The 700 terraces made the slopes stable so they would not wash away with all the rainwater flowing down them. See terraces at lower left of page 600.

The Purpose of Machu Picchu

The Inca did not leave records about the purpose of Machu Picchu. Their descendants have no legends explaining it. Ideas about its use and the names that researchers have given to certain structures are guesses—educated guesses by people who have studied the Inca, but still guesses.

Scholars have offered several suggestions. One common idea is that it was an estate for the royal family, perhaps a retreat from the nearby capital city. Another common suggestion is that it was a place for religious observances, likely centering on the worship of the sun. A third idea is that the Inca used it for an astronomical observatory. The site, especially the Intihuatana, appears to be aligned with astronomical events such as the solar solstice and equinox (thus the name that researchers gave the Intihuatana). Another idea is that it was a military stronghold. Perhaps the site served more than one purpose.

Archaeologists believe one part of Machu Picchu was the sacred area for religious ceremonies. What scholars now call the royal district includes what may have been palaces for the royal family, the Zone of the Princesses, and housing for workers in the royal household. Another section of Machu Picchu was perhaps a farming zone with houses for farm workers. A residential neighborhood provided housing for other workers. Researchers have named other structures the Temple of the Sun, the Room of the Three Windows, and the Residence of Wise Persons. Scholars generally believe that fewer than one thousand people stayed at Machu Picchu.

Experts believe that the Inca began building Machu Picchu around 1438, after the Inca ruler Pachacuti defeated enemy tribes. They believe the Inca abandoned the site around 1532. The site was covered with dense vegetation and unknown to the outside world until Hiram Bingham, an archaeologist and professor at Yale University, went there in 1911 as he was trying to find another Inca site. Local natives told him about something being on the top of the mountain they called Machu Picchu, and a young boy led him to the site.

Shout for joy, O heavens! And rejoice, O earth!
Break forth into joyful shouting, O mountains!
For the Lord has comforted His people
And will have compassion on His afflicted.
Isaiah 49:13

Assignments for Lesson 89

Our Creative World — Read the excerpt from the *Royal Commentaries of the Inca* on pages 67-68.

Map Book — Complete the assignments for Lesson 89 on Map 27 "Inca Empire."

Timeline Book — In the box for Lesson 89 on page 19, write "Inca begin building Machu Picchu."

Student Workbook or Lesson Review — If you are using one of these optional books, complete the assignment for Lesson 89.

Creative Writing — Write a poem of at least eight lines about the Inca.

Literature — Read chapters 6-7 in *The King's Fifth*.

Making Porcelain in the Ming Dynasty

Lesson 90   **Daily Life**

In Lesson 81 we learned about the beginnings of the Ming Dynasty and the Yongle Emperor who sent Zheng He on grand voyages and built the Forbidden City. The Yongle Emperor's grandfather Zhu Yuanzhang was born in 1328 to a poor tenant-farming family in Anhui Province in China. A tenant farmer worked land that was owned by someone else. He lived on the land and received a small share of the crop as payment for his work. Zhu's parents died when he was in his teens. He became a Buddhist monk and lived in a monastery.

Soldiers of the Mongol Yuan Dynasty destroyed the monastery while stopping a local rebellion. Zhu joined a rebel army to fight the Mongols. He became a leader in the rebellion and called his faction *Ming*, meaning bright. The rebellion grew and spread. The Mongols lost control of province after province, and in 1368 they abandoned their capital of Beijing. The Chinese rebels took control of the country, and Zhu declared himself to be Emperor. Zhu called the new dynasty Ming and took the throne name of Hung-wu, which means great military power. See a traditional portrait of the Hung-wu Emperor above. The Ming was the last native Chinese dynasty to rule China. It followed the Mongols and lasted until an army of Manchu warriors from Manchuria overthrew it in 1644.

1962 Stamp with Painting of Hung-Wu

Hung-wu and later Ming emperors encouraged traditional Chinese ways, but Hung-wu was a harsh ruler toward those who did not accept his ideas. During the Ming Dynasty, Mongolia, Korea, and countries in Southeast Asia recognized the power of China and paid tribute to the Ming emperor.

Bronze Coins from the Time of Hung-Wu

Kaolin

The top bowl was made in China between 1368 and 1644. The lower bowl was made in Jingdezhen, China, between 1700 and 1800.

Ming Porcelain Production

Chinese craftsmen had begun to produce porcelain objects during the Han Dynasty (206 BC-220 AD). Much of what they made went out of the country through international trade. In the Song Dynasty, emperors began to build royal factories to make items for use in the imperial palace. In 1004 the Song emperor Zhenzong selected the town of Jingdezhen in Jiangxi Province as the center for imperial porcelain production. By the 1300s, most porcelain pieces came from this city. The appeal of Jingdezhen was the presence of a high hill that contained a large amount of a mineral known as kaolin. The name of this mineral came from the Chinese words for tall (*kow*) and hill (*ling*).

Ceramics are objects that are made of clay. Ceramics include brick, tile, clay pipe, and pottery. One kind of pottery is porcelain. Craftsmen make porcelain by heating the objects to about 2,200 to 2,600 degrees, which hardens them. Porcelain is the hardest ceramic product. It is made up of kaolin, which is a pure white clay that forms when the mineral feldspar breaks down, and petuntse, which is a kind of feldspar found only in China. To create porcelain, a craftsman makes a powder of petuntse and mixes it with the kaolin. Notice artifacts at left.

As you can see in the white bowl at left, porcelain is translucent, which means that some light can pass through. The word porcelain comes from *porcellana*, the Italian

Lesson 90 - Making Porcelain in the Ming Dynasty

word for cowrie shell, an object that is also translucent. People often call porcelain items china or fine china because the production of them first took place in China. True porcelain has a bell-like sound when a person gently strikes it. People place a high value on porcelain because of its beauty and its strength.

How Porcelain Is Made

A craftsman forms a porcelain object either on a potter's wheel, as seen at right, or in a mold. If he wants to change the surface of the piece, he does so through carving on it, as seen at right below, or by **perforating** it with small holes or embossing raised designs on the surface. As seen in the photo below, he then heats it (this is called firing) in a **kiln** to make it hard. At the 2,200 to 2,600 degree temperature range, the petuntse vitrifies or melts and forms a glass. Kaolin resists heat, so it does not melt. This enables the object to maintain its shape. The petuntse **fuses** to the kaolin.

At first Chinese porcelain was white, like the examples on page 604. Then artists began painting it with a mixture that included cobalt. Cobalt is a silver-white metallic element with properties similar to those of iron and nickel. Its main use is in alloys with other metals. Cobalt oxides (compounds with cobalt and oxygen) add a deep blue color to pottery or paint. Blue and white porcelain first appeared during the Yuan Dynasty. Craftsmen perfected the process during the Ming period.

Turning Porcelain on a Potter's Wheel Before Firing

Firing Porcelain in a Kiln

Carving Porcelain Before Firing

Modern Porcelain Production in China

Porcelain Created at Jingdezhen During the Ming Dynasty

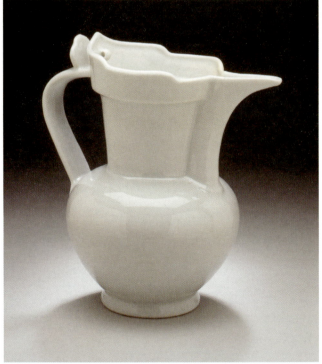

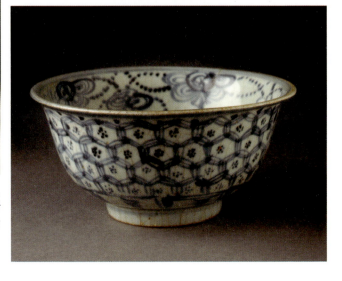

Left Column: Two Views of a Dish with Gardenia Spray, Lotus, Pomegranates, Peaches, and Grapes, 1488-1505; Right Column: Pitcher (Called a Ewer or Sengmaohu), 1403-1424; Bowl with Flowers and Festoons, Late 1400s or Early 1500s

Lesson 90 - Making Porcelain in the Ming Dynasty

Ming porcelain has elaborate designs. These designs changed from time to time as new emperors came to the throne and wanted distinctive new patterns. Each emperor also had his own unique reign mark, which craftsmen placed on items that they produced during the emperor's reign.

After a craftsman shapes, fires, and paints an object, he then coats it with a clear glaze called celadon. See example at right. If he fires an object at a relatively low temperature, it is called earthenware. Glazing earthenware makes the object waterproof. Firing at a high temperature creates what is called stoneware. Stoneware is very hard and is waterproof without glaze.

A craftsman will sometimes apply enamel over the glaze. This enamel coating requires a second firing to make it permanent. An innovation that Ming craftsmen developed was adding manganese to the cobalt to keep it from bleeding during firing and thus **distorting** the artwork.

During the Ming Dynasty, the best porcelain, made from the best raw materials and reflecting the greatest skill, went to the emperor's palace. The emperor also wanted top-quality pieces to present as diplomatic gifts to representatives of other nations. Most of the rest went in trade to other countries, usually to royal or noble households. Muslims made up the largest market to the west for Ming porcelain, which the Chinese exported as far as Turkey. Few common people, either in China or other countries, owned a piece of Ming porcelain.

Porcelain with a Celadon Glaze, c. 1300

Craftsmen decorated this blue and white covered jar with a cloud and a dragon. It was produced between 1522 and 1566 during the Ming Dynasty. It is part of the collection at the Palace Museum in Beijing, China. The Palace Museum is in the Forbidden City.

These Chinese stamps from 1991 celebrated the chinaware industry in Jingdezhen.

Porcelain production reached its **pinnacle** during the Ming Dynasty. The restoration of Chinese culture after the period of Mongol rule caused a burst of creative energy among Chinese artisans.

The Lord equips people made in His image with the skills they need to create amazing works. The opportunity for each of us is to use the skills He gives us to bless others and glorify Him.

*As each one has received a special gift,
employ it in serving one another
as good stewards of the manifold grace of God.
Whoever speaks, is to do so as one
who is speaking the utterances of God;
whoever serves is to do so as one
who is serving by the strength which God supplies;
so that in all things God may be glorified
through Jesus Christ, to whom belongs
the glory and dominion forever and ever. Amen.*
1 Peter 4:10-11

Assignments for Lesson 90

Our Creative World — Read the Chinese Poetry from the Ming Dynasty on page 69.

Timeline Book — In the box for Lesson 90 on page 20, write "The Ming Dynasty rebuilds the Great Wall."

Student Workbook or Lesson Review — If you are using one of these optional books, complete the assignment for Lesson 90 and take the test for Unit 18.

Thinking Biblically — What gifts and talents do you have that you can use for the glory of God? Make a list of at least five things.

Vocabulary — Copy these words, each on a separate line: perforate (605), kiln (605), fuse (605), distort (607), pinnacle (608). Look up each word in the dictionary. Next to each word, write what part of speech it is according to the way the word is used in the lesson.

Literature — Read chapters 8-9 in *The King's Fifth*.

19　The Early 1500s

Columbus Monument, Barcelona, Spain

Lessons	91 - World Landmark: Florence, Italy
	92 - God's Wonder: Columbus Discovers the Caribbean and the New World
	93 - Daily Life: Sailing with Brave Explorers
	94 - World Biography: Nicolaus Copernicus
	95 - Our World Story: Martin Luther and the Reformation
Literature	*The King's Fifth*

1492-1550

The city of Florence, Italy, continued to be the epicenter of the Renaissance with artists such as Leonardo da Vinci and Michelangelo. Christopher Columbus and his crew set sail from Spain in three small ships and accidentally came upon a New World, unknown to Europeans. Other explorers from various European nations continued to search the world. In less than half a century, sailors had gone east to Asia around the Cape of Good Hope in Africa, explored coastlands of North and South America, and sailed around the world. Scientists such as Nicolaus Copernicus began to discover new ways to think about the universe beyond the Earth. Martin Luther and others worked to reform the Roman Catholic Church.

Florence
Italy

Lesson 91 — World Landmark

We have already learned about some of the people from Florence, Italy, who influenced the extraordinary period called the Renaissance. Today we examine people and places in the city that is often called the birthplace of the Renaissance.

History of Florence

The city of Florence is in north-central Italy in the region of Tuscany. As seen in the photo below, it sits on both banks of the Arno River at the foot of the Apennine Mountains (also pictured on page 254). The Etruscans founded the first settlement at the site. After a civil war in the Roman Republic destroyed the city, Julius Caesar established a colony there in 59 BC. He named it *Florentia*, Latin for blossoming. In Italian the city is called Firenze.

The population of Florence was about 5,000 in the year 900. Around the year 1000 the city began to grow rapidly, and it became an independent city-state. The population reached 30,000 in 1200 and grew to about 100,000 in the early 1300s. The discovery of a new way to refine wool caused the Florence woolen textile industry to expand quickly. The city also grew as a result of Florentine bankers who made financial investments in industry and trade. Citizens of Florence suffered from the Black Plague and from wars with other city-states in Italy in the 1300s and 1400s, causing the

Florence, Italy, with the Arno River and the Apennine Mountains

population to shrink. However, over the long term Florence continued to grow in size and importance.

Florence was the home of the wealthy and powerful Medici family. Members of the family ruled the city pretty much as dictators, except for brief periods when others successfully challenged their power. However, the Medicis helped to make Florence the home of beautiful works of art through their encouragement of art in the city.

Leonardo da Vinci

Leonardo da Vinci was a great painter, but he was also an **observant** student of the world around him. His wide interests in art and science cause many people to see him as a prime example of what is called the "Renaissance man."

Da Vinci was born in 1452 near the village of Vinci, outside of Florence. His name, da Vinci, simply means "of Vinci." In the late 1460s he became an apprentice to Andrea del Verrocchio, a leading painter and sculptor in Florence. Leonardo soon became well-known as an excellent artist.

Leonardo da Vinci left Florence in 1482 to become court artist for the duke of Milan, where he lived until 1499. Da Vinci served the duke as military engineer, civil engineer, sculptor, and painter. He painted *The Last Supper* on a wall of the dining room in a monastery in Milan. In 1499 an invading French army forced the duke of Milan out of office. Da Vinci left the city and returned to Florence. By then he had built a large following and had begun to inspire the next generation of artists, including Sandro Boticcelli, Raphael, and Michelangelo. In 1503 he began painting the *Mona Lisa*, which took three or four years to complete. The subject of the portrait was probably the wife of Francesco del Giocondo, a Florence silk merchant. Mona Lisa is a shortened form of Madonna Lisa, which means "My lady, Lisa." See copies of *The Last Supper* and *Mona Lisa* on page 613.

Flag of Florence

Leonardo da Vinci Statue, Milan, Italy

The Florence government asked both Leonardo and Michelangelo to produce paintings for the walls of the Palazzo Vecchio, which means Old Palace and served as the city hall. Da Vinci tried a new approach to painting but it did not work, so he abandoned the project.

In 1515 Pope Leo X gave Leonardo rooms at the Vatican, which is the headquarters of the Roman Catholic Church. Da Vinci completed few paintings during this time. The next year, the king of France, Francis I, invited Leonardo to become court artist, engineer, and architect. Da Vinci moved into quarters connected to a royal palace near Tours. He died in 1519.

Left: Depiction of The Last Supper *on a 1981 Stamp from Cyprus; Right: Depiction of* Mona Lisa *on a 1972 Stamp from Togo*

Leonardo da Vinci had an active mind and great talents. He was one of the first artists to use **sketches** to plan his paintings. He also used drawings to record his architectural and engineering ideas, such as one concept for a helicopter and another for a parachute. Da Vinci studied such subjects as mechanics, anatomy, and the flight of birds. He recorded many thoughts in notebooks, often writing backwards from right to left using what some call mirror writing because one can read it by holding it up to a mirror. We do not know for sure why he did this. Perhaps it was to make it harder for others to read his notes, perhaps it was because he was left-handed and it came more naturally, or perhaps he learned differently from the way that most people do.

Michelangelo

Michelangelo Buonarroti is one of the most famous artists and sculptors in history. His work endures as a pinnacle of the Renaissance.

Michelangelo was born in 1475 into a respected family of Florence. He was born in the village of Caprese, where his father was a government official. Michelangelo became an apprentice at the age of twelve to a popular artist in Florence, Domenico Ghirlandajo. Before completing his apprenticeship, Michelangelo started working on being a sculptor, studying under a student of Donatello. Lorenzo de Medici, who was then the ruler of Florence, invited Michelangelo to live at his palace and continue his studies.

David *by Michelangelo*

The Medicis temporarily lost their position of power in Florence in 1494, so Michelangelo traveled to other cities. He lived in Rome from 1496 to 1501 and continued to work as a sculptor. His most famous work from this period is the *Pieta*, pictured on page 614. It is a portrayal of Mary holding the body of Jesus after He had been crucified.

The Pieta by Michelangelo

    Michelangelo returned to Florence in 1501 and lived there until 1505. During this period he completed his famous statue of David, seen on page 613. We only know of some sketches for his proposed work at the Palazzo Vecchio in Florence. Some researchers believe he did work on it and his work was later covered up.

    From this point Michelangelo took on huge projects. Pope Julius II commissioned him to carve statues for his tomb. The tomb is pictured on page 646. He began to create a fresco on the ceiling of the Sistine Chapel and worked on the project from 1508 until 1512. He worked on a **scaffold**, standing up and not lying down as many have thought. Michelangelo worked for the Medici family in Florence again from 1515 to 1534. Then he left Florence, never to return. From 1536 to 1541, Michelangelo worked at the Vatican, creating *The Last Judgment* for the altar wall in the Sistine Chapel.

    Michelangelo produced his last paintings when he was about 75. He also wrote poetry in his later years. Michelangelo died in 1564.

Cathedral of Santa Maria del Fiore

Florence is home to many beautiful and historic churches. The Cathedral of Santa Maria del Fiore (Cathedral of St. Mary of the Flower) is also called the Cathedral of Florence. This classic Italian Gothic cathedral is pictured on pages 541 and 572. Arnolfo di Cambio designed it. Work began in 1296. Arnolfo died in 1302. Giotto (mentioned in Lesson 85) began overseeing the work in 1334 when he was 67 years old. He concentrated on the bell tower, also seen on pages 541 and 572, until his death three years later. Completed in 1359, the tower contains seven bells and stands 278 feet tall. Work on the cathedral continued until 1418. The exterior is pink, white, and green marble.

Above the main entrance on the inside is the large clock seen below. Florence artist Paolo Uccello painted the clock face in 1443. It shows four men's faces in the four corners of the frame. Most people believe these are Matthew, Mark, Luke, and John; but some believe they are four prophets. The clock shows 24 hours using Roman numerals. The numbers begin at the bottom and proceed in counterclockwise direction around the face of the clock. In that day, "Italian time" was 24 hours, and the 24th hour was the hour just before sunset. The clock has a single hand to indicate the hour (again common in that day). The clock still works.

In 1418 only one major component of the cathedral was missing: the dome. Workers had built the cathedral but had left a 150-foot-wide hole. Since workers needed to build the dome on top of the building, they could not approach the project using the typical scaffolding from the ground. Florentines believed that God would eventually send someone to build the dome. In 1418 the overseeing committee announced a competition to determine a plan. Filippo Brunelleschi (mentioned on page 571) won the competition, but the committee named his rival, Ghiberti, to be co-supervisor.

The plan of Brunelleschi involved first building an interior dome of brick with a **herringbone** pattern, held together with horizontal stone rings that distributed the weight evenly. This interior dome provided support for the exterior dome, although there was enough room between them for a staircase leading up to

Clock by Paolo Uccello at the Cathedral of Santa Maria del Fiore

the lantern on top. Despite some personal conflicts between the two supervisors, workers finished the dome in 1463. It is the largest masonry dome ever built. The interior of the inner dome features the painting *The Last Judgment* by Giorgio Vasari and his student, Frederico Zuccari. They accomplished the project between 1572 and 1579. The Cathedral of Florence is commonly called Il Duomo, meaning The Dome.

Baptistery of San Giovanni

Baptistery of San Giovanni

The Cathedral of Florence stands on one side of the Piazza del Duomo. On the opposite side stands the Baptistery of San Giovanni (Italian for St. John), pictured above. It is an eight-sided structure that predates the cathedral. Christians built an eight-sided baptistery on this site as early as the 400s. They built the current structure around 1059. A Christian tradition holds that the sides represent the eighth day, meaning the resurrection of Christ on the first day of the week. The baptistery features three sets of bronze doors showing people from the Bible, scenes from the life of John the Baptist and the life of Christ, and the **personification** of Christian virtues. These entrances stand on the east, north, and south sides. Andrea Pisano designed the south doors, which were created in 1336. Ghiberti completed the north door panels in 1424. He finished the east doors in 1452. The east doors, which Michelangelo called the Gates of Paradise because of their intricate beauty, are pictured on page 141.

Annunciation *by Fra Angelico*

The Church of San Marco

The Church of San Marco (Italian for St. Mark) opened in 1443. It once had a convent that has been converted into a museum. The former convent has paintings by several artists, including Guido di Pietro. Di Pietro was born near Florence around 1400. He became a Dominican monk in 1418. He was known for his deep devotion to God and came to be called Fra Angelico (Angelic Brother). Some of his works that are housed at this location are the *Altarpiece*, the *Annunciation* (pictured at left), the *Crucifixion*, the *Deportation* (depicting people removing the body of Jesus from the cross), and the *Last Judgment*. Fra Angelico died in 1455.

Lesson 91 - Florence, Italy

Left: Basilica of San Lorenzo and the Arno River; Right: Staircase Designed by Michelangelo

The Basilica of San Lorenzo

The Basilica of San Lorenzo (St. Lawrence), pictured above, was the parish church of the Medici family. Brunelleschi oversaw this building project from its beginning around 1419 until his death in 1446. Work was largely completed by 1459. The interior features white walls and arcades (walkways) with gray columns. Michelangelo designed a beautiful facade for the building, but it was never constructed. The Biblioteca Laurenziana (Italian for Lawrence Library) contains about 11,000 manuscripts and about 4,500 copies of very early books. Michelangelo designed the library staircase, pictured at right above, and the benches in the reading room. The building contains the tombs of several of the Medici family, and Michelangelo carved statues which stand on the tombs. The structure also houses paintings by other artists.

Side View of the Basilica of Santa Croce

Basilica of Santa Croce

The Basilica of Santa Croce (Italian for Basilica of the Holy Cross) is the largest Franciscan church in the world. It has sixteen separate chapels. Construction began in 1294, and the structure was completed in 1442. The basilica has several frescoes by Giotto. It houses the tombs of several famous Florentines, including Michelangelo and the artist Lorenzo Ghiberti.

The Palazzo Vecchio

The Palazzo Vecchio is located in the heart of the city. Arnolfo di Cambio, the architect of the Cathedral of Florence, designed this structure as well. Begun in 1299, it was finished in 1322. It features a 311-foot-tall bell tower that the city government once used to warn citizens of emergencies.

Monogram of Christ on the Entrance of the Palazzo Vecchio, Florence, Italy

The entrance to the Palazzo Vecchio honors Jesus with the letters YHS, which stand for Jesus in Greek. Beneath this monogram is the Latin phrase "King of Kings and Lord of Lords." The book of Revelation portrays the triumphant Christ coming in judgment against His enemies:

> *And on His robe and on His thigh He has a name written,*
> *"KING OF KINGS, AND LORD OF LORDS."*
> *Revelation 19:16*

Assignments for Lesson 91

Our Creative World — Read the "Letter from Michelangelo to His Father" on page 70.

Timeline Book — In the box for Lesson 91 on page 20, write "Lorenzo de Medici takes control in Florence."

Student Workbook or Lesson Review — If you are using one of these optional books, complete the assignment for Lesson 91.

Vocabulary — Make a drawing for each of these words that illustrates what it means: observant (612), sketch (613), scaffold (614), herringbone (615), personification (616). Write the word under the drawing. Check in a dictionary if you need help with their definitions.

Creative Writing — Do you think that religious art, such as paintings of Biblical scenes and sculptures of people from the Bible and Christian history, are effective in encouraging people in their faith? Write one or two paragraphs explaining your answer.

Literature — Read the September 27 journal entry and chapter 10 in *The King's Fifth*.

Columbus Discovers
The Caribbean
and the New World

Lesson 92 — God's Wonder

The Caribbean Sea is an arm of the Atlantic Ocean. It is the world's largest marginal sea. A marginal sea is separated from a major ocean by surrounding landmasses. In the case of the Caribbean, the separating landmasses are Cuba and Hispaniola on the north and the Lesser Antilles on the east.

The Caribbean is connected to the Gulf of Mexico by the Yucatan Channel and to the Atlantic Ocean by many straits that flow between islands. The largest of these straits are the Windward Passage, which runs between Cuba and Hispaniola, and the Mona Passage between Hispaniola and Puerto Rico. Refer to the map on page 620.

Covering about one million square miles, the Caribbean measures 1,700 miles from east to west, which is almost as far as the distance between New York City and Denver, Colorado. The sea varies from 500 to 800 miles from north to south. The Caribbean contains about twice the water volume of the Mediterranean. The Magdalena River in Colombia, South America, is the largest river that flows into the Caribbean. Lake Maricaibo in Venezuela, South America, is the largest bay off the Caribbean.

The waters of the Caribbean are clear and warm, averaging about 75°. They are less salty than the Atlantic, and the range of tides is very small, rising only to about one foot. Caribbean currents run clockwise. Water comes into the sea from the Atlantic through straits that run between the Lesser Antilles. The waters

Top: Trunk Bay on St. John Island, U.S. Virgin Islands
Bottom: These mangrove islands and shallow coral reefs are part of the Bocas Del Toro Archipelago in the Caribbean Sea and are part of the nation of Panama.

become warm and flow out of the sea through the Yucatan Channel into the Gulf of Mexico. In the gulf those waters form the Gulf Stream, which flows back into the Atlantic.

The floor of the Caribbean has several deep trenches separated by undersea plateaus and mountain ranges. The deepest point in the sea, 24,720 feet below sea level, is in the Cayman Trench, which lies between Cuba and Jamaica.

The Caribbean Islands

The Caribbean is named for the Carib natives, who lived on the Lesser Antilles. The sea includes about 7,000 islands. Thirteen of them are independent countries, and others are territories claimed by other nations. Many of the islands in the Caribbean are the tops of volcanic mountains. Volcanoes and earthquakes are fairly common in the Caribbean region. Many of the islands are small islets, while others are coral reefs (a few of which are inhabited).

Mapmakers divide the Caribbean Islands into two main groups, the Greater Antilles and the Lesser Antilles. The Greater Antilles include the larger islands of Cuba, Jamaica, Hispaniola (which is divided into Haiti and the Dominican Republic), Puerto Rico, and the Cayman Islands. The Lesser Antilles are a long arc of islands at the eastern edge of the Caribbean Sea. At the north end of this chain are the Leeward Islands. South of the Leeward Islands are the Windward Islands. The Lesser Antilles islands that curve westward north of the coast of Venezuela are called the Leeward Antilles. Three of the Leeward Antilles are sometimes called the ABC islands. They are Aruba, Bonaire, and Curacao. The Caribbean also has other islands outside of these groups, such as the Bocas Del Toro Archipelago, pictured on page 619. The Bahama Islands are north of the Greater Antilles and are islands in the Atlantic, not the Caribbean.

The Caribbean Islands have lush tropical vegetation and rich marine life but no large wild animals. Some unusual or unique species live here. For instance, dozens of species of butterflies

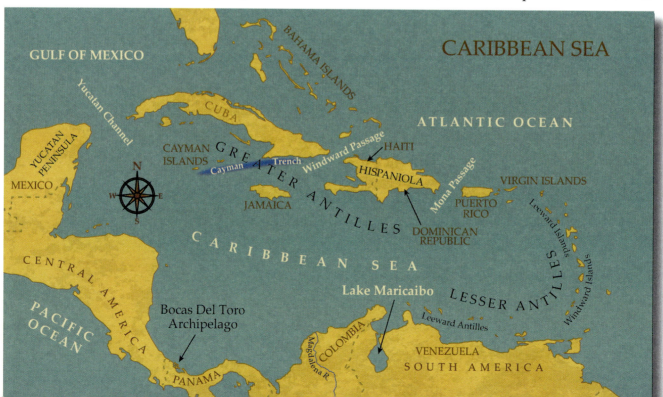

are unique to Hispaniola. The islands are on the migration path for birds between North and South America. Temperatures average about 80 degrees in summer and 75 degrees in winter. Rainfall varies widely throughout the region.

The origin of the name *Antilles* is not clear. It might come from the Portuguese words *anti*, which means before, and *ilha*, which is a very old word that means island. Some believe it was a name for a mythological land or island that people expected to find somewhere between Europe and India.

The people of Europe and Asia did not know that the Caribbean Sea and the Caribbean Islands existed until 1492 when an Italian sea captain, who had spent several years in Portugal, and who sailed for the king and queen of Spain, came upon them by accident while trying to find a water route to Asia.

Searching for a Water Route to Asia

Christopher Columbus was born in 1451 in the seaport city of Genoa in northwestern Italy. A monument to Columbus in his birth city is pictured below. When he was fourteen, he became a sailor on ships that sailed in the Mediterranean Sea. By the age of twenty-five, Columbus had moved to Portugal, the home of Prince Henry the Navigator, who had encouraged Portuguese sea exploration. Columbus continued to work as a sailor, sailing in the Atlantic Ocean.

European traders and navigators wanted to find a water route to Asia, specifically India, China, and the Spice Islands in Southeast Asia. Besides wanting to trade with people in those places, they also believed that they could find riches there. Because Muslim officials often made it difficult for European traders to travel on the Silk Road, the Portuguese in particular hoped to find a way around Africa to get to the East; but they had not yet accomplished this.

A few people, including Christopher Columbus, wondered if it would be possible to reach the Far East by sailing west from Europe. Most educated people knew that the Earth was round, so they did not fear falling off the edge. However, their understanding was limited or incorrect in other ways. In the 100s AD, Ptolemy, a mathematician and geographer in Alexandria, Egypt, estimated the size of the Earth, but his estimate was only about three-fourths of its actual size. Ptolemy also thought that the Eurasian landmass was much larger than it really is. These two errors led Columbus to think that Europe and Asia were closer than they are. In addition, Marco Polo in the 1200s had estimated that Japan was about 1,500 miles east of China, when in fact it is only about 500 miles east at its closest point. This also led Columbus to think that the Atlantic was smaller than it really is. He estimated that Japan was about 3,000 miles west of Portugal, when in fact it is about 12,000 miles west. Columbus

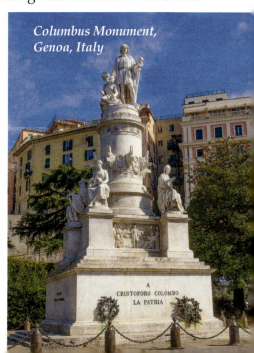

Columbus Monument, Genoa, Italy

also had no idea that a large landmass lay between Europe and Asia. On the basis of these faulty estimates, Columbus believed that he could successfully sail west to reach Asia.

Columbus Seeks a Sponsor

Columbus wanted to find a king who would pay for a voyage west in search of Asia. His idea was that the king could then claim the lands he reached as colonies. The monarch could also share the wealth that Columbus expected to discover.

This 1992 stamp from Vietnam illustrates Columbus with King Ferdinand and Queen Isabella.

Columbus hoped to get the support of the king of Portugal, but the king's advisers encouraged him to invest in sailing around Africa instead. In 1485 he rejected Columbus' request.

Columbus appealed to King Ferdinand and Queen Isabella of Spain the next year, but they also refused him. Nevertheless, Columbus lived in Spain for several years while the king and queen supported him. In 1492 Ferdinand and Isabella reconsidered and agreed to provide the money that Columbus requested. They are illustrated in the stamp above.

The First Voyage of Christopher Columbus

Columbus acquired three ships and had a total crew of 90 men. Two brothers, Martin Alonso Pinzon and Vicente Yanez Pinzon, captained the *Niña* and the *Pinta*, while Columbus was captain of the *Santa Maria*. The three ships left the port of Palos in southwest Spain on August 3, 1492. Among the few books Columbus had on board was *The Travels of Marco Polo*.

God created air, temperature, and the rotation of the Earth in such a way that near the equator, the wind blows almost constantly toward the west. We call these winds trade winds because trading ships with sails depended on wind to be able to move. Columbus sailed south to the Canary Islands off the western coast of Africa because from there he believed he could use the trade winds to travel west more quickly. Pictured on page 623 is a tower on La Gomera Island. The tower is from the oldest military fort in the Canary Islands. The fort was constructed in the mid-1400s. While Columbus and his crew were in the Canary Islands, the *Santa Maria* required repairs that took about one month to complete. Finally on September 6 they left the Canaries and headed west.

A replica of the Santa Maria *sails off the coast of Portugal.*

Columbus had very simple navigational equipment. He had a compass, an hourglass to tell time, and a quadrant to determine his position, which was often not accurate. He determined his latitude by the North Star. He simply guessed the ship's speed.

FIRST VOYAGE OF CHRISTOPHER COLUMBUS

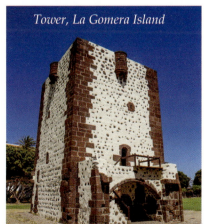

Tower, La Gomera Island

As the ships continued west into unknown territory, fear and suspicion grew among crew members. After forty-one days on the open ocean, they sighted land on October 12.

Columbus believed they had reached the East Indies. As a result, he called the people living there Indians. He named the island San Salvador. Most people believe he landed on what later became known as Watling Island in the Bahamas, but we don't know for sure.

Compare the route of Columbus on the previous page to the route of Zheng He on page 549. While exploring the Caribbean, Columbus sailed to Cuba, where native guides led him along the northern coast, which he thought was part of China. He also explored another island which he named Hispaniola, which means "the Spanish isle." Columbus established a settlement on Hispaniola and left thirty-nine crew members there. The *Santa Maria* had been damaged beyond repair while they were in the Caribbean, so the crew used the lumber from it to build a fort. The remaining crew returned to Spain in the two other ships, taking back objects and also some island natives that Columbus had captured and forced to come with him. The people, objects, and reports he brought back caused great excitement and interest in Europe.

The Second Voyage

Ferdinand and Isabella were eager to sponsor a second voyage, which began in September of 1493. This time Columbus had seventeen ships and a crew of 1,200 men, including Catholic friars, whose mission was to teach Christianity to the natives. After another stop in the Canaries, the fleet accomplished the journey in twenty-one days. They made landfall near Dominica in the Lesser Antilles. They returned to Hispaniola but found that the crew had vanished and the settlement had been destroyed. Columbus never learned with certainty what had happened. The Spanish established another settlement elsewhere on the island. During this visit, the crew saw several islands, including Puerto Rico, Jamaica, and the southern coast of Cuba.

However, many of the men who came did not want to work, and Columbus was not an effective leader. Some returned to Spain and reported their complaints. A court official came to the Caribbean in 1495, and Columbus returned to Spain the next year to defend himself.

The Third Voyage

Columbus organized a third voyage, which departed Spain in 1498. He went further south this time, sailing past Trinidad and the northern coast of South America. He saw the mouth of the Orinoco River in what is now Venezuela and realized that he might be seeing a continent that Europeans had not known about previously.

Spaniards on Hispaniola again rebelled against Columbus' rule. Some crew members returned to Spain and informed Ferdinand and Isabella about the rebellion. The monarchs sent Francisco de Bobadilla to investigate and take charge of the entire mission. He arrived in 1500, arrested Columbus, and returned him to Spain in chains. The captain of the ship offered to remove the chains, but Columbus said he wanted the monarchs to free him. They did release him after he arrived, but they sent Nicolas di Ovando to serve as governor on Hispaniola.

Replica of the Santa Maria *in a Park in Columbus, Ohio*

Lesson 92 - Columbus Discovers the Caribbean and the New World

The Fourth Voyage

In 1502 Columbus, now over fifty years old and in poor health, wanted to sail again; and again Ferdinand and Isabella agreed to sponsor him. Columbus visited Martinique and Hispaniola. Then he headed further west and sailed along the coast of Central America. However, he made no contact with the Maya, whom we discussed in Lesson 64. Though natives told him about it, Columbus decided not to cross the Isthmus of Panama to see the great ocean on the other side. During their travels, his ships became unseaworthy, and Columbus became stranded on Jamaica. He was able to send for help to Ovando on Hispaniola and was finally able to return to Spain in 1504. Columbus died in 1506.

New World Stamps Honoring Columbus

What Did Columbus Accomplish?

Christopher Columbus set out on his voyages with erroneous information about the size of the Earth. He had no knowledge of the American continents or the islands in the Caribbean. He was mistaken about where he thought he landed. He was often unpopular with his men, and the rulers and people of Spain did not always respect him. He did not obtain riches and status as a result of his exploits.

Yet Christopher Columbus changed the world. He did not "discover America" in one sense, since people had been living there for many centuries. However, he did enable Europeans to know about the Americas. When Europeans realized that these were different islands from the East Indies, they called the Caribbean Islands the West Indies. Many explorers undertook voyages in the years to come on behalf of several European countries. They went to establish colonies and to search for a fountain of youth, for gold, and for any other sources of wealth they might find.

Columbus expressed a desire to bring the gospel to people living in these lands previously unknown to Europeans. However, he and other Europeans did not treat the indigenous Americans with the justice, respect, and kindness that God commanded. They also claimed these newly-discovered lands as their own even though people already lived there.

The people of every nation matter to God, who sent His Son to die for them as it is written in the book of Revelation:

And they sang a new song, saying,
"Worthy are You to take the book and to break its seals;
for You were slain, and purchased for God with Your blood
men from every tribe and tongue and people and nation."
Revelation 5:9

Assignments for Lesson 92

Our Creative World — Read the excerpt from *The Destruction of the Indies* on page 71.

Map Book — Complete the assignments for Lesson 92 on Map 28 "Caribbean Sea."

Timeline Book — In the box for Lesson 92 on page 21, write "Columbus sails to the Caribbean."

Student Workbook or Lesson Review — If you are using one of these optional books, complete the assignment for Lesson 92.

Creative Writing — What traits does an explorer need to have to be successful? Write a paragraph answering this question, including at least three traits.

Literature — Read chapters 11-12 in *The King's Fifth*.

Sailing with Brave Explorers

Lesson 93 — Daily Life

The first voyage of Christopher Columbus in 1492-1493 did more than just reveal a New World to Europe in terms of geography. It also created a new world of possibilities in people's minds. In the Renaissance, people were thinking new thoughts and trying new endeavors in such fields as art, architecture, and science. Now people were learning about new places and new ways of getting to other parts of the world. The world they had thought they knew was not the world that really existed. Notice the statue of Columbus in Barcelona, Spain, on page 609. It is as if he is pointing the way not only for himself but for others.

Leif Ericsson and Zheng He had sailed to lands new to them many years before Columbus. But news of Ericsson's journey had not transformed Europe, and China followed Zheng He's voyages with a long period of withdrawal. By contrast, people reported Columbus' journey widely, and explorers from many nations followed the example of Columbus. Meanwhile, Portugal continued to try to reach the Far East by going around Africa.

Both Spain and Portugal claimed ownership of lands they discovered. In 1493 Pope Alexander VI tried to settle the competition between the two countries by dividing the world between them. He decreed that the world would be divided along an imaginary north-south line. The pope said that Portugal could explore to the east and Spain to the west. In 1494 the two countries signed a treaty agreeing to this. Though the treaty eased the conflict between Spain and Portugal, other nations ignored the decree and explored where they wished.

The Life of a Sailor

Journeys of exploration were possible because of the thousands of men who worked as sailors. The life of a sailor around 1500 was hard. He was out at sea for months, sometimes even years, at a time. He performed hard work every day. He cleaned. He repaired. He handled sails and heavy ropes. When

Sailors on a Replica of the Santa Maria

Unit 19 - The Early 1500s

Sailors on a Replica of the Santa Maria

waves or storms brought water into the ship's hold, he pumped it out. A sailor faced frequent dangers from storms, hidden reefs, pirates, and getting lost due to miscalculation. Often he had to deal with filthy living conditions and low rations.

Why would a man become a sailor? Some sailors did not choose their work but were forced into it. Sometimes a ship took on prisoners as part of the crew. The captain could offer freedom in return for the man's service. Some countries practiced impressment. Impressment allowed for a captain and crew to force a man to serve on a ship, something like his being drafted into the army. Other men became sailors to seek adventure and riches.

For some, the life of a sailor was almost all he had ever known. Boys as young as eight might work on a ship, doing simple tasks such as swabbing (cleaning) the decks. A boy in his late teens could do other jobs such as serving as a lookout or pumping water from the hold.

Adult sailors worked with the sails and ropes. The pilot was in charge of navigation. The boatswain oversaw the adjusting of sails and made sure that men carried out the captain's orders. Other specific roles included the gunner (who kept the guns and ammunition in working order), the cooper (who made and repaired barrels), the carpenter, and the barber (who often was also the ship's dentist and surgeon).

Ships made frequent stops at ports to make trades. In addition to his responsibilities to get his ship where it was supposed to go, the captain had to make sure that his ship had everything the men needed, including water, food, and medicine. They also carried parts and supplies that might be needed to repair the ship.

When they had fuel, sailors cooked on portable wood stoves. Their main meal was often a stew made from salted meat or fish. They often ate a hard biscuit called hardtack. Sometimes they had some cheese. They might drink a watery ale or wine. Food deteriorated rapidly because of a lack of ventilation, poor drainage in the hold, or infestations by rats, mice, and worms.

Only a few of the highest ranking officers had cabins and bunks. Most sailors simply found a spot to sleep on the deck or below deck during a storm. The men alternated keeping three watches during the night. Sailors generally received low wages, especially when compared to workers on shore. However, they did have a chance at profiting by trade.

Sailor pastimes included carving, drawing, singing and dancing, playing instruments, and playing card and dice games.

Sailors didn't always do what they were supposed to do. A ship's captain had to enforce discipline because chaos and rebellion could be disastrous—even deadly—on a ship. A captain couldn't simply fire a rebellious seaman and tell him to go find another job. Captains disciplined their sailors for wrongs. This not only punished the sailor who was insubordinate; it also served as a warning to others. Punishment for a serious offense often took the form of a beating on a sailor's bare back with a cat-o'-nine-tails. This was a whip that had nine strands of rope or leather, often with each one having a bit of metal or bone attached to it. The punishment for the most serious crimes, such as mutiny (rebellion) or murder, was death by hanging.

Bartholomew Diaz

As we discussed in Lesson 83, explorers from Portugal pushed further and further south along the western coast of Africa in the mid-1400s. However, they didn't know how long the continent of Africa was or even if it had a southern tip they could sail around.

In 1481 and 1482, Bartholomew Diaz, who had been born around 1450, commanded an expedition down the West African coast to look for gold. He traveled as far as what became Ghana. In 1487 Portugal's King John II ordered Diaz to sail to the southern end of Africa. On this voyage, Diaz commanded a fleet of three ships with a total crew of 170 men. After the expedition passed the mouth of the Orange River in southern Africa, a storm blew them out to sea. They did not see land for thirteen days. Diaz realized that the storm had blown them around the southern tip of Africa and began to explore the southeastern coast of Africa. However, the ships were getting low on supplies, and his exhausted sailors convinced him to return to Portugal. On their way back, Diaz identified the Cape of Good Hope, which is on the southwestern coast of Africa. Some say he named it the Cape of Good Hope because he hoped it would lead to the discovery of a route to India. Others say King John II named it later. The expedition returned to Lisbon in 1488.

This South African stamp from 1988 celebrates the 500th Anniversary of Diaz sailing around the Cape of Good Hope.

Vasco da Gama

In 1494 Diaz began to oversee construction of a fleet intended to sail to India. King Manuel I of Portugal asked the father of Vasco da Gama to lead the expedition, but the elder

This stamp from Portugal celebrates the 500th anniversary of the birth of Vasco da Gama.

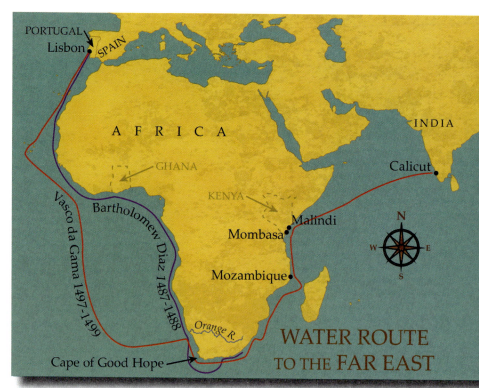

da Gama died before it could take place. The king then asked Vasco to lead it. The fleet departed Lisbon on July 8, 1497, and reached the Cape of Good Hope on November 22. They stopped at several ports along the East African coast. Muslim traders tried to seize the Portuguese ships in Mozambique and Mombasa. However, people in Malindi gave them a friendlier welcome. There da Gama arranged for a guide to lead them to India. On May 20, 1498, da Gama and crew arrived in Calicut, India, where Zheng He had landed almost a century earlier (see Lesson 81).

Da Gama's visit to India was not successful. The Indian ruler was insulted at the small gifts that he brought, and Muslim traders did not want to let the Europeans become involved in any trade there. The Portuguese left India in August of 1498. See water routes above.

Over one hundred of da Gama's 170 men died of scurvy on the trip. His small crew arrived back in Portugal in September of 1499. Scurvy is a disease which sailors often contracted on long voyages. Men with scurvy became weak and developed sore gums and joints, had their teeth fall out, became anemic, and often died. While they were at sea, sailors rarely were able to eat vegetables and citrus fruits, which supply necessary Vitamin C. It wasn't until 1753 that Scottish physician James Lind proved that sailors could avoid scurvy by eating oranges, limes, and lemons.

Another expedition from Portugal in 1500 established good relations with the rulers and traders at Calicut, so da Gama made another voyage in 1502 and returned home in 1503. He then retired from making sea voyages. The king of Portugal named da Gama viceroy (governor) of India in 1524. He sailed to India but died there on December 25 of that year.

1934 Canadian Stamp Honoring Jacques Cartier

Lesson 93 - Sailing with Brave Explorers

An Age of Exploration and Discovery

The end of the 1400s and first half of the 1500s was an age of exploration and discovery. Many explorers gathered crews to sail to far away places on the globe and literally around the world in the coming years. They included:

- John Cabot of Italy, who sailed for England in 1497 and explored the eastern coast of what became Canada. Cabot was the first European to venture to this area since the Vikings did so around 1000.

- Amerigo Vespucci of Italy, who claimed to have discovered a "New World" on a voyage to South America in 1497. A German mapmaker, Martin Waldseemuller, believed that Vespucci was the first European to reach the new region. In 1507 Waldseemuller proposed calling the region America in honor of Vespucci.

- Pedro Cabral of Portugal, who sailed to Brazil in 1500 and claimed the land for his country.

- Ferdinand Magellan, who led an expedition that sailed around the world from 1519 to 1522. Magellan was a Portuguese who sailed for Spain. Magellan died in a conflict in the Philippines, but a few of his men made the entire trip around the world.

- Giovanni da Verrazzano of Italy, who explored the Atlantic coast of North America in 1524. Verrazzano was an Italian who sailed for France.

- French explorer Jacques Cartier, who explored the coast of Canada and the St. Lawrence River in North America in 1534-1535. He is pictured at left.

Honoring Explorers

Left Column: Amerigo Vespucci Statue, Florence, Italy; Portuguese Stamp Honoring Pedro Cabral; Right Column: John Cabot Statue, Bristol, England; Giovanni da Verrazzano Statue, Greve in Chianti, Italy

Relatively small ships, with relatively small crews of men, sailed over the huge seas of our world and changed how people lived. James compared the power of the human tongue to the power of a small rudder, which guides the path of a ship wherever the pilot decides:

Look at the ships also, though they are so great and are driven by strong winds, are still directed by a very small rudder wherever the inclination of the pilot desires. So also the tongue is a small part of the body, and yet it boasts of great things. See how great a forest is set aflame by such a small fire!
James 3:4-5

Assignments for Lesson 93

Our Creative World — Read the "Letter to the King and Queen of Castille" on page 72.

Map Book — Complete the assignments for Lesson 93 on Map 29 "Water Route to the Far East."

Timeline Book — In the box for Lesson 93 on page 21, write "Da Gama brings Ming porcelain to Portugal."

Replica of the Ship of Ferdinand Magellan

Student Workbook or Lesson Review — If you are using one of these optional books, complete the assignment for Lesson 93.

Thinking Biblically — Copy James 3:4-5 at the top of a piece of paper. Under the words, draw a picture of a ship. Use one of the ships shown in the drawings and photographs in this unit as a model.

Literature — Read the October 6 journal entry and chapter 13 in *The King's Fifth*.

This French map from about 1547 shows portions of the Americas explored by Europeans in the early 1500s.

Nicolaus Copernicus

Lesson 94 — World Biography

New ways to create art and architecture.
New places to explore and new lands to discover.
And a new way to see the universe!

The new way of seeing the universe that came about during the Renaissance resulted primarily from the work of a few men. The first was Nicolaus Copernicus.

How Most People Viewed the Universe

Around 1500 most people believed that the Earth sat motionless at the center of the universe and that all heavenly bodies moved around it. Aristotle had promoted this idea, and the astronomer Ptolemy of Alexandria had also written about it in the 100s AD. Scientists believed that the heavenly bodies moved around the Earth in perfectly circular orbits and were encased within a series of clear, hard shells. These shells of progressively greater size supposedly surrounded the Earth, with the heavenly bodies always at constant distances from the Earth. This theory supported the belief that the universe was relatively small.

A View of the Milky Way from the Phu Soi Dao Mountains of Thailand

Aristotle said that beyond the stars lay a **sphere** that rotated from west to east and that the motion of this sphere drove the other spheres or shells in the opposite direction, from east to west. He believed that these actions produced the movement of the heavenly bodies that we see from Earth. Aristotle believed that beyond this sphere was the highest heaven. Scientists did not explain where the spheres got their motion. They simply believed that superior laws of motion governed the heavens, laws that were not the same as those that governed motion on Earth.

Although this was the basic idea that most people thought, it did not explain apparent slight irregularities in the orbits of the planets. Planets sometimes even appeared to move backward. Ptolemy believed that the circles in which the planets moved were slightly irregular or off-center.

A few astronomers throughout history had disagreed with Aristotle and Ptolemy. Pythagoras was a Greek scientist and mathematician who lived in the 500s BC. In the century after his death, the followers of Pythagoras developed the theory that a central fire sat at the center of the universe and that the Earth, the sun, the planets, and the stars all rotated around the fire. Aristarchus of Lamos, who lived from 310 to 230 BC, apparently believed that the sun was the center of the universe. We do not have the writing of Aristarchus on this subject, but a later scientist, Archimedes, said that Aristarchus believed this. Aristarchus also thought that the fact that the Earth rotates on its **axis** causes the heavenly bodies to appear to move. Ptolemy rejected the ideas of Aristarchus because in his mind they didn't fit his observations as well as the theory that the Earth was at the center of the universe.

The Life of Copernicus

Nicolaus Copernicus was born in 1473 in Thorn (now called Torun), Poland, on the Vistula River south of the Baltic port city of Gdansk. Find Gdansk on the map on page 534. His father was financially successful, and his mother was the daughter of a successful merchant. Her brother, Nicolaus' uncle, became a bishop in the Roman Catholic Church.

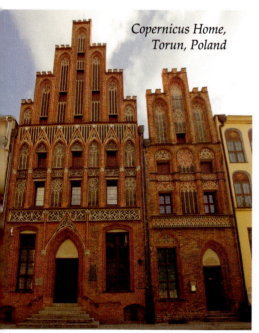
Copernicus Home, Torun, Poland

Nicolaus was taught at home as a boy. After his father died, his uncle looked after his education and helped him in his career. Nicolaus enrolled in the University of Krakow in Poland in 1491 and studied there for four years. He then studied church law (also called canon law) at the University of Bologna in Italy from 1496 to 1500. He pursued astronomy as a hobby beginning in 1497. In Bologna Copernicus lived in the same house with the main astronomer at the university, Dominic Novarra.

With his uncle's assistance, Copernicus received an appointment as church canon at the cathedral in Frauenburg (now Frombork), Poland, about 100 miles from his birthplace. Copernicus then studied medicine at the University of Padua, also in Italy, from 1501 to 1503. He received a degree in canon law from the University of Ferrara, Italy, in 1503. During his studies, Copernicus learned painting skills and produced a self-portrait which still exists. After receiving his degree, Copernicus returned to Poland and resumed his career as church canon.

In this position, Copernicus had several church administration responsibilities, such as collecting rents on church properties. During this time he apparently practiced medicine, and he wrote a paper about reforming the monetary system. He also made observations about the heavens.

In 1514, the Catholic Church asked for his assistance in creating a more accurate calendar. The calendar then in use was not very accurate, with the result that special days and the seasons did not always occur at **logical** times in the year. We do not know if Copernicus ever attended any meetings about the calendar, but he did write a paper in which he presented some of his ideas about the motions of the sun and planets.

Throughout his life, Copernicus continued to make observations and calculations about the movement of the heavenly bodies. He was familiar with the ideas of Aristarchus. Copernicus was reluctant to publish more detailed ideas beyond what he had written in 1514, but he finally decided to do so in 1543, shortly before he died. His book was called *On the Revolution of the Heavenly Bodies*. A popular story says that friends placed the finished book in his hands as he lay on his deathbed.

Nicolaus Copernicus

The Copernican Theory of the Universe

Copernicus wanted to identify the simplest explanation for the movement of the heavenly bodies. He believed that Ptolemy's idea of irregular circular orbits to explain the movements was too complicated. Copernicus proposed that the Earth and other planets revolved in perfectly circular orbits around the motionless sun, which sat at the center of the universe. He also believed that the Earth rotated on its axis and that a slow wobble of the axis occurred continuously. Copernicus thought that this theory provided the best explanation for how the movement of the heavenly bodies appeared from Earth.

Ways that Copernicus Was Mistaken

Copernicus differed in some ways from how we understand the universe to work today. He believed that the sun is the center of the universe and that it is motionless, but we now understand that the sun is one star that moves through the universe and that it rotates on its axis.

Like astronomers before him, Copernicus continued to believe in spheres of motion in which the heavenly bodies move. Modern astronomers no longer believe that these exist.

Copernicus also believed that the orbits of the planets are circular, but later astronomer Johannes Kepler in 1609 demonstrated that planets move in **elliptical** orbits. Despite all of these differences, Copernicus was essentially correct in his thinking about the relationships between the sun and the planets. In the early 1600s, Galileo used a telescope to confirm the findings of Copernicus.

The Impact of Copernican Theory

The insights of Copernicus were amazing, given the established understanding of his day and especially since he made his observations without a telescope or modern equipment. His theory helped people understand that the universe is much larger than they had previously believed. Copernicus challenged the common thinking that the Earth is the center of the universe. Scientists and historians consider the work of Copernicus to be the beginning of the scientific revolution. He is seen as the father of modern astronomy.

The ideas of Copernicus differed from the accepted Roman Catholic doctrine that the Earth was the center of the universe. Many religious leaders believed that the idea of the sun being at the center of the universe went against the teaching of Scripture. They pointed to such passages as Joshua 10:12-14, which describes the sun not going down for a whole day, and Ecclesiastes 1:5, which describes the sun rising and setting. Copernicus caused people to reconsider how we should understand those passages in the Bible. We now understand that those verses describe how we see heavenly bodies from Earth, not that those bodies move around a **stationary** Earth at the center of the universe.

Copernicus approached his studies with a deep faith in God as the Creator of the universe which he studied. In the introduction to *On the Revolution of the Heavenly Bodies*, Copernicus spoke of "the grace of God, without whom we can accomplish nothing." Copernicus thought of himself as a philosopher. He wrote: "It is [the philosopher's] endeavor to seek the truth in all things, to the extent permitted to human reason by God."

Copernicus also said: "For when a man is occupied with things which he sees established in the finest order and directed by divine management, will not the unremitting contemplation of them and a certain familiarity with them stimulate him to the best and to admiration for the Maker of everything, in whom are all happiness and every good?"

Copernicus Statue, Montreal, Canada

Like David so many centuries before, Copernicus considered the skies and felt amazed at the workings of God.

*The heavens are telling of the glory of God;
And their expanse is declaring
the work of His hands.
Psalm 19:1*

Assignments for Lesson 94

Timeline Book — In the box for Lesson 94 on page 22, write "Copernicus publishes his scientific theories."

Student Workbook or Lesson Review — If you are using one of these optional books, complete the assignment for Lesson 94.

Thinking Biblically — Read Psalm 19:1-6.

Vocabulary — Write five sentences, using one of these words in each: sphere (634), logical (635), axis (635), elliptical (636), stationary (636). Check in a dictionary if you need help with their definitions.

Literature — Read chapters 14-15 in *The King's Fifth*.

Family Activity — Make a "Creation Collage." Instructions begin on page FA-38.

Copernicus Statue, Torun, Poland

Martin Luther and The Reformation

Lesson 95 — Our World Story

The Roman Catholic Church had carried the banner of the Christian faith in Western Europe for over one thousand years. Its servants had taught pagans about Jesus, served the sick and the poor, and opposed those who taught contrary to truths about God and Jesus.

And yet the Catholic Church had failings. It had acquired vast material wealth and in some ways had become worldly. Some of its leaders were corrupt and **immoral**. The Church often used the way it practiced **Communion** and **confession** as a tool to control its members. The emphasis on good works as the means of salvation differed with the New Testament emphasis on faith and grace. Some practices, such as the monastic movement and the role of priests, were not found in the New Testament. One particularly troublesome practice was the selling of indulgences (see page 539).

Was there a way to have faith, selfless service, and commitment to the truth without worldliness, corruption, and departure from Scripture? One man who thought so was Martin Luther.

The Story of Martin Luther

Martin Luther was born in 1483. As he grew up, he developed a deep passion to serve God. Once when Luther was caught in a violent thunderstorm, he committed himself to becoming a monk. When he visited Rome in 1510, however, he was shocked at the worldliness and corruption he saw at the center of the Church. Luther earnestly wanted peace with God, but he didn't believe he could find it within the practices of the Catholic Church that he saw.

When Luther received the opportunity to teach theology at the University of Wittenberg in Germany, he decided to read the Bible for himself, which was unusual at that time. He was amazed at what he read. The most central thing he saw was an

A U.S. stamp honors the 500th anniversary of the birth of Luther.

emphasis on faith and grace and not on works to earn salvation. To Luther, the worst error of the Church was the selling of indulgences.

Luther wrote a list of ninety-five points (or theses) about Church doctrine. On October 31, 1517, he nailed the list to the door of the Castle Church in Wittenberg, seen below. People often posted their thoughts in this way to generate discussion on particular issues. Luther's list was unusually long and especially pointed in its criticism of the Catholic Church. Both those who agreed with Luther and those who disagreed reacted strongly. People did indeed debate and discuss his ideas. Luther published tracts or small booklets which spread his teachings further.

The pope condemned Luther as a heretic in 1520. Luther showed that he rejected the pope's authority by burning a copy of the pope's decree against him. The next year, the diet (or parliament) of the city of Worms made a government decision by condemning Luther as a heretic and banishing him from all of the Holy Roman Empire. A noble who was friendly toward Luther took him into protective custody and kept him at Wartburg Castle for about a year. Luther worked to spread and defend his ideas. Luther did not intend to create another Church; he wanted to reform the only Church he had ever known by encouraging it to go back to the teachings of Scripture.

The Catholic Church responded by excommunicating Luther and his followers. Afterward, those who were excommunicated became a separate fellowship. Since Luther and others like him were protesting Catholic practices with the purpose of reforming those practices, the movement they created is called the Protestant Reformation.

The Impact of Luther

Throughout the Holy Roman Empire, which was primarily made up of German kingdoms, congregations and princes decided whether they wanted to be loyal to Rome or align with Luther's movement. This was a period of great unrest. Violence erupted in several cities. Charles V, a Catholic serving as emperor of the Holy Roman Empire, engaged in military action to try to force Lutheran churches and provinces to become Catholic again. By the time of Luther's death in 1546, about half of the princes in the empire had decided to side with Luther.

Castle Church, Wittenberg, Germany

In 1555 a government council produced the Peace of Augsburg, a document which stated that each local prince could decide whether the official religion in his territory would be Catholic or Lutheran. Some Lutheran territories tolerated Catholics and some Catholic places tolerated Lutherans. In the places that would not tolerate people of a non-official religion, people either had to move or face persecution or limited rights.

The re-thinking of Christian doctrine that Luther began spread far and wide. One central idea of his teaching was that salvation was by faith in Christ alone and did not depend on works of merit that a person performed (such as taking a pilgrimage, making a contribution, or saying a certain number of prayers). Another key idea of Luther's was his dependence on Scripture alone as spiritual authority and not on traditional Church practices. As a result, Luther rejected the authority of the pope, monasticism, the requirement for priests to be unmarried, and other Catholic doctrines.

Also, Luther taught that the individual believer could have a relationship with God through Jesus Christ and did not need a priest or saints or others to **intercede** for him. Luther believed that every Christian could and should read the Bible. To encourage this, he translated Scripture into German. Luther also composed hymns in German and compiled a German hymnbook so that every member and

Martin Luther Statue, Dresden, Germany

not just a choir could sing praise to God. Lutheran congregations used German instead of Latin in their services. The Martin Luther monument above stands in Dresden, Germany.

Like every person who has ever lived besides Jesus, Luther had his failings. He could be intolerant of people who disagreed with him. He harshly criticized a revolt by poor people against the taxes that German lords imposed on them, even supporting the peasants being put to death. Luther also spoke unkindly about Jews and endorsed persecuting them. Another practice that Luther did not see the need to change was the close tie between the Church and the state. He did not believe that the Church could or should exist apart from the active support and involvement of the political leader of a country.

Why Luther's Reformation Took Hold

Luther was not the first person to differ from Catholic doctrine and practice. As we learned in Lesson 80, the Waldensian movement had tried to reform the Church centuries before. John Wycliffe and Jan Hus had spoken out against Catholic practices, but their efforts did not result in a great reform movement. Others had expressed criticism from time to time but had not brought about significant changes in the Church.

Lesson 95 - Martin Luther and the Reformation

The reform movement of Martin Luther took hold for several reasons. A large number of people agreed with him and supported his calls for change, both because they wanted a meaningful faith and because they did not agree with Catholic teaching and practices. Also, a number of German princes were willing to reject the authority of the pope in Rome. This gave political support to the movement. People in various places were developing a sense of national **identity**, so they were willing to separate from the pope in Italy. The changes that came about in the Renaissance encouraged people to think anew about this most important aspect of their lives—their relationship with God. The availability of the printing press allowed Luther to spread his ideas quickly over a wide area.

Other Reformers

When Luther opened the door of Church reformation, it could not be closed. Lutherans became the Christian majority in the Scandinavian countries. Ulrich Zwingli preached religious reform in Switzerland about the time that Luther did. He became the political leader in Zurich, Switzerland. He was killed in a religious conflict in 1531. Notice the Zwingli monument above right. A generation after Luther, John Calvin became the most influential voice for change in Europe and influenced millions. The Reformation Wall at right was erected in 1909 to commemorate the 400th anniversary of the birth of John Calvin.

People in other countries also formed churches based on Reformation principles and teachings. Huguenots were Calvinist

Reformers

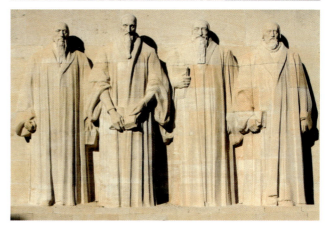

Top: Zwingli Monument, Zurich, Switzerland; Center: The Reformation Wall in Geneva, Switzerland, includes relief sculptures of four reformers who worked in Geneva, plus one reformer each from France, the Netherlands, Germany, America, Britain, and Hungary. Bottom: The second relief statue from the left represents John Calvin.

Several popes of the Roman Catholic Church oversaw construction of St. Peter's Basilica in the 1500s. Located in what is now Vatican City, the headquarters of the Roman Catholic Church, St. Peter's is the largest church building in the world.

Protestants in France. In the Netherlands, the Dutch Reformed movement took hold. Presbyterians became dominant in Scotland. The Anabaptists became a large movement in various countries. England also experienced a reformation, which we discuss in Unit 20.

The Catholic Church admitted the need for reforms and made some changes in its practices. All of these developments took place within a relatively few years after Luther's life. It was a time of great upheaval for Christians in Europe, and those changes spread to other parts of the world as explorers and settlers ventured into new lands.

For by grace you have been saved through faith;
and that not of yourselves,
it is the gift of God;
not as a result of works, so that no one may boast.
Ephesians 2:8-9

Assignments for Lesson 95

Our Creative World — Read the "Letter to Katherine Luther" on page 73.

Timeline Book — In the box for Lesson 95 on page 21, write "Martin Luther posts his Ninety-Five Theses."

Student Workbook or Lesson Review — If you are using one of these optional books, complete the assignment for Lesson 95 and take the test for Unit 19.

Thinking Biblically — Read Ephesians 2:1-10.

Vocabulary — Find each of these words in a dictionary, then find the definition that corresponds to the way the word is used in this lesson. Copy the words and definitions: immoral (638), Communion (638), confession (638), intercede (640), identity (641).

Literature — Read chapters 16-17 in *The King's Fifth*.

20 The Late 1500s

The Tower of London

Lessons
96 - Our World Story: Kings and Queens of England
97 - World Landmark: The Jewish Community in Lublin, Poland
98 - God's Wonder: Potosi Silver Mine in the Andes Mountains
99 - World Biography: Suleyman I and the Ottoman Empire
100 - Daily Life: The People of Southeast Asia

Literature *The King's Fifth*

1551-1600

In England the Tudor family came to the throne as the result of a civil war. One Tudor king, Henry VIII, brought about the English Reformation that created the Anglican Church. Henry's daughter, Elizabeth I, led England in its first steps toward becoming a world power. In Europe, Jews endured prejudice and hatred and founded a remarkable community and university in Lublin, Poland. Spanish explorers in South America developed an amazingly rich silver mine that became "the treasury of the world." Suleyman I led the Ottoman Empire in becoming a major power in the Middle East. The people of Southeast Asia endured and adapted to numerous invasions by people from other lands.

Kings and Queens of England

Lesson 96　　　　　　　　　　　　　　　　　　　　　　　　　　Our World Story

The Protestant Reformation began in Germany with a man in the Roman Catholic Church, Martin Luther. It became a political revolution as local rulers decided whether their domains would be Catholic or Lutheran. The English Reformation began with a decision by a government ruler, which had an impact on the churches of the realm.

Background: The War of the Roses

In Lesson 70 we learned how people battled for control of the English throne before the Norman Conquest. Such battles occurred again later. The English house of Plantagenet began when Henry II came to the throne in 1154. As the family grew over time, the two main branches were the Lancasters and the Yorks. Henry IV, Henry V, and Henry VI from the house of Lancaster ruled from 1399 to 1461. Henry VI was a weak ruler, and the house of York began a civil war in 1455 to take control of the government. This conflict came to be called the War of the Roses because the York family symbol was a white rose and the symbol of the house of Lancaster was a red rose. The house of York gained control and ruled from 1461 to 1485.

A replica of the royal banner flies overhead, and a reenactor in Tudor clothing plays medieval songs on a wooden flute at a reenactment of the Battle of Tewkesbury, which took place during the War of the Roses.

The Lancasters at left and the Yorkists at right approach the battle line in a 2012 reenactment of the Battle of Tewkesbury.

The decisive Battle of Bosworth in 1485 took the life of Yorkish King Richard III and ended the York Dynasty. The leader of the Lancasters was Henry Tudor. He became Henry VII and began the house of Tudor. In 1486 Henry married Elizabeth of York, thus uniting the two families who had previously been at war with one another.

Henry VIII

Arthur, son of Henry VII, married Catherine of Aragon. She was the daughter of Ferdinand and Isabella of Spain, the rulers who had funded Christopher Columbus when he sailed to the Caribbean. Arthur died before his father Henry VII died in 1509, so his brother Henry VIII became king. Henry VIII wanted to marry his brother's wife, Catherine, in order to continue England's alliance with Spain. This marriage violated Church law, so Henry asked Pope Julius II for special permission, and the pope granted it. See Julius' tomb at left. Henry and Catherine married and had six children, but only one, Mary, lived to adulthood.

The Catholic Church was strong in England, and Henry was a strong defender of Catholic doctrine. He wrote a booklet against Luther's ideas in 1521. For this Pope Leo X gave him the title Defender of the Faith.

Michelangelo created this tomb for Pope Julius II. At lower center is his well-known statue of Moses.

English Reformer William Tyndale

William Tyndale was born in 1494, possibly at North Nibley in Gloucestershire, England. He studied at Oxford and Cambridge Universities and became a Roman Catholic priest. The ideas of Martin Luther had a great influence on Tyndale. Tyndale wanted to make the Scriptures available to the English people in their own language. He started work on an English translation of the New Testament. Making an English translation violated the Catholic tradition of using only a Latin translation, and Church officials disapproved of Tyndale's Lutheran leanings. The English government was so strongly aligned with the Catholic Church that it forbade Tyndale from publishing his translation of the Bible. Tyndale went to Germany and completed the

Tyndale Monument at North Nibley, Gloucestershire, England

translation in 1525. He had it printed there and smuggled copies into England. Catholic officials saw this as heresy. They captured Tyndale in Belgium in 1534 and executed him as a heretic in 1536. His last words were, "Lord, open the king of England's eyes."

Pope Clement VII

Seeking an Heir to the Throne

Henry VIII wanted a son to be his **heir** to the English throne. After the difficulties of the War of the Roses, England had many potential rivals wanting the throne. Henry didn't think a queen would be a strong enough ruler for the Tudor Dynasty to maintain its hold on the throne. When it became apparent that Catherine was not likely to give birth to a son, Henry wanted to **annul** their marriage. An annulment is a pronouncement that a marriage is invalid and is to be treated as though it never happened.

Henry was not only concerned with having a son. He also wanted to marry Anne Boleyn, who was an attendant to Catherine. When Henry asked Pope Clement VII (pictured above left) for an annulment, the pope refused. However, the Archbishop of Canterbury, who was head of the Catholic Church in England, did issue the annulment. Henry married Anne in 1533. A daughter was born to them, whom they named Elizabeth. The pope responded by excommunicating Henry VIII.

The next year, in 1534, Henry had Parliament pass the Act of Supremacy, which declared the English monarch to be the head of the Church in England and stated that the English monarch was not subject to any other authority. The Catholic Church in England came to be called the Church of England or Anglican Church, but it changed very few of its practices. The law named the Archbishop of Canterbury as the leading official of the Church under the monarch's headship. One major change that did take place was that Henry **abolished** monasteries in England. The monasteries were a source of pro-Catholic influence, and they also owned considerable wealth. Henry took over this wealth and used it to pay for government expenses. He also gave some of the money to individuals in order to gain their support. Henry executed a few of the leading officials who opposed his break with the pope in Rome.

In 1536 Henry accused Anne of adultery and treason and had her executed. He then married Jane Seymour. Jane gave birth to a son, Edward. She died a few days later. Henry's fourth marriage was to Anne of Cleves, but the Church of England annulled the marriage after only a few months. He then married Catherine Howard but had her executed for treason. His sixth wife, Catherine Parr, who had twice been widowed before marrying Henry, outlived him. Henry died in 1547. Pictured below are United Kingdom stamps portraying Henry VIII and his six wives.

In 1997 the United Kingdom issued this series of stamps of King Henry VIII and his wives. On the top row are Catherine of Aragon, Anne Boleyn, and Jane Seymour. On the bottom row are Anne of Cleves, Catherine Howard, and Catherine Parr.

Edward VI, Mary I, and Elizabeth I

All three surviving children of Henry VIII became monarchs of England. Edward VI assumed the throne when his father died. Edward was nine years old. Two regents or protectors, who served one after the other, actually ran the government before Edward died in 1553 after only six years as king. The second regent, the Protestant Duke of Northumberland, wanted to prevent Mary, who was Henry's daughter from his first wife, Catherine, from becoming queen, because she had continued in the faith of the Roman Catholic Church. The duke proclaimed Lady Jane Grey, who was the sixteen-year-old great-granddaughter of Henry VII, to be queen. She reigned for only nine days. Mary had her arrested and had herself crowned queen. Lady Jane was later executed.

Mary I came to the throne in 1553. She set about to restore the Catholic Church as the official religion of England. Mary married the Catholic Prince Philip II of Spain, **reconciled** England with the pope, and had Protestant leaders, including the Archbishop of Canterbury, executed.

Lesson 96 - Kings and Queens of England

In 1556, Philip II became king of Spain. He left England and never returned. Mary died in 1558 without any children.

Upon Mary's death, Henry's other daughter, Elizabeth I, daughter of Anne Boleyn, became queen. She ruled for 45 years and was the strong monarch that Henry had doubted any woman could be. Parliament passed laws that reestablished the Church of England and made the monarch its head once again.

The Church of England changed to become more Lutheran and Calvinist in its doctrine. It also allowed its priests to marry. In addition to her efforts in England, Elizabeth gave assistance to Protestant Huguenots in their battle against the Catholic French authorities. She also helped Dutch Protestants in their conflict with Catholic Spain, which ruled the Netherlands at the time.

Elizabeth encouraged overseas explorations. During her reign, Sir Francis Drake, Sir Walter Raleigh, and others explored under the British flag. The English also made their first attempts to establish colonies in America.

The Defeat of the Spanish Armada

A turning point that affected political and religious history in Europe and other parts of the world took place in 1588.

Pope Pius V excommunicated Elizabeth I in 1570 and declared that she was not a **legitimate** monarch. English Catholics hoped that they could reclaim the throne through Mary Stuart. She had become queen of Scotland when she was just six days old. Mary, whose birthplace is pictured on page 650, was a granddaughter of the sister of Henry VIII. Known as the Queen of Scots, she was next in line for the throne of England after Elizabeth. However, Mary had to flee Scotland in 1568 because of Protestant opposition there. When she came to England, Elizabeth put her under house arrest. At times Mary supported plots to remove Elizabeth. Elizabeth ordered her execution in 1587.

Philip II of Spain wanted to reassert the Catholic claim to the English throne. In 1588 he sent his mighty fleet, called the Armada, to attack England. See the replica of a Spanish

Engraving of Edward VI by H. T. Ryall

Mary I, on a 1984 stamp from the Democratic People's Republic of Korea.

Elizabeth I is depicted on this 2009 stamp from the United Kingdom.

Left Column: Linlithgow Loch and Linlithgow Palace, Birthplace of Mary Queen of Scots, at West Lothian, Scotland; View from the Palace Wall; Right Column: Replica of a Spanish Galleon from the 1600s at Grand Harbour, Malta; Cannon on this Ship

galleon and cannon at right above. His plan was for the ships to ferry Catholic troops from the Netherlands to England. Philip expected Catholics in England to rise up in support and overthrow Elizabeth. However, the English fleet inflicted great losses on the Spanish naval force. Bad weather finished off the Spanish Armada.

As a result of this loss, Spain was no longer the dominant world power that it had been. Other nations recognized England's new status as one of the leading countries of the world and ruler of the seas.

In just a few years, England went from being a Catholic nation that forbade an English translation of the Scriptures to a Protestant nation with its own Church that gave official approval to an English translation. Henry VIII authorized the Great Bible, published in 1539, to be placed in every church in England. See the page from the Great Bible at far right. The immediate motivation for the Protestant Reformation in England was the desire of Henry VIII to divorce one wife and marry another. The impact of this change spread throughout England and, as the English planted colonies on foreign soil, throughout the world.

Ironically, the strong female Tudor Elizabeth I was the last of that house to rule. Elizabeth never married and had no children. She is sometimes called the Virgin Queen or Good Queen Bess. Upon her death, the English throne passed to the Stuart family when James I became king in 1603.

Lesson 96 - Kings and Queens of England

It is not God's will that Christians be at odds with one another. In all things, Christians should be "diligent to preserve the unity of the Spirit in the bond of peace" (Ephesians 4:3) while remembering the desire of Jesus:

I do not ask on behalf of these alone,
but for those also who believe in Me through
their word; that they may all be one;
even as You, Father, are in Me and I in You,
that they also may be in Us, so that
the world may believe that You sent Me.
John 17:20-21

Title Page from the 1539 Great Bible

Assignments for Lesson 96

Our Creative World — Read the "Advice to a Servant" on page 74 and Queen Elizabeth's "Speech to the Troops at Tilbury" on page 75.

Timeline Book — In the box for Lesson 96 on page 22, write "English navy defeats the Spanish Armada."

Student Workbook or Lesson Review — If you are using one of these optional books, complete the assignment for Lesson 96.

Vocabulary — Copy the following sentences, placing the correct vocabulary word in the blank: heir (647), annul (647), abolish (647), reconcile (648), legitimate (649).
  1. The nation's parliament held a special meeting to determine the _____ winner of the election.
  2. I heard that our neighbor Mr. Pello is _____ to a large fortune.
  3. We hope that the opposing parties will be able to _____ their differences.
  4. Some would question the church's right to _____ a marriage.
  5. Would it be better to _____ the monarchy in favor of democracy?

Creative Writing — If you could meet one person mentioned in this lesson, who would it be? Write one paragraph explaining your answer.

Literature — Read chapter 18 and the October 7 journal entry in *The King's Fifth*.

The Jewish Community in Lublin, Poland

Lesson 97 — World Landmark

The descendants of Abraham have for a long time found it difficult to find a safe place to live. Israel became a nation before it had a homeland. God led the Israelites out of slavery in Egypt and called them to be His people when He gave them the Law on Mt. Sinai in the wilderness. God then led the Israelites into the Promised Land.

The Diaspora

After the Israelites lived in their God-given homeland for centuries, Assyria carried the tribes of the Northern Kingdom away from their land and into captivity. Babylon later carried Judah (also called the Southern Kingdom) into captivity. Cyrus of Persia allowed the people of Judah, called Jews, to return. Not all the Jews returned, however. Some remained in Babylon, while others moved elsewhere.

By the first century AD, significant Jewish populations existed in many cities, including Alexandria, Egypt; Rome, Italy; Damascus, Syria; and Ephesus on the Anatolian Peninsula. The scattered people of Israel are called the Diaspora, a Greek word meaning dispersed.

In many of the places where Jews lived, the Gentile population on the whole did not like them. The Jews were different: they followed different customs, they ate only certain foods, and they practiced a different and exclusive religion.

Jews generally lived in their own section of a town. Often laws required them to do this in order to keep them away from the rest of the people. However, this separateness gave Jews protection from attacks and helped them maintain their culture and religion.

Jews in the Holy Land rebelled against Roman authority in 132 AD under the **dynamic** leader Simon Bar Kochba, but the Romans crushed the revolt in 135. Emperor Hadrian expelled the Jews from the Holy Land. The Jews dispersed into other cities of the Roman Empire. In the late 300s, Emperor Theodosius I, who declared Christianity to be the official religion of the empire, extended toleration to the Jews and said that they could live in the empire. Some Jews returned to the Holy Land, but when the Muslims conquered the area in the 600s, many Jews left.

Lesson 97 - The Jewish Community in Lublin, Poland

The Middle Ages

Jews settled in many cities of Europe. Look at the photos and captions on this page. In some places people continued to treat the Jews badly because of **prejudice** against them. Though centuries had passed since the death, burial, and resurrection of Jesus, some Christians saw Jews as the people who killed Christ. As a result they treated the Jews with hatred and suspicion. Lesson 71 referred to the attacks on Jews during the first Crusade. People spread tales about Jews engaging in evil practices (see Lesson 77). Many people blamed the Jews for the Black Plague.

Jews left many of the cities of Italy in the 900s, sometimes because they were forced to do so and sometimes in an effort to be safe. When they left, many moved to cities further north. Sometimes entire countries forced Jews to leave. England expelled all Jews in 1290. France did likewise in 1394. King Ferdinand and Queen Isabella of Spain ordered them out in 1492, and Portugal did so in 1497. Many exiled Jews moved into the German states.

Some Jews went to Venice. In the 1500s, officials in Venice required Jews to live in an area called the **ghetto**. This word, which originated in Venice, became the term used for a section of a city where a particular ethnic or religious population lived. In some places, authorities locked the Jews inside their ghettos at certain times of day.

This water pitcher (also called an aquamanilia) bears this inscription in Hebrew: "Blessed be the King of the Universe, who has instructed us to wash our hands." Scholars believe it was created by a German or Dutch artist, c. late 1200s or early 1300s.

Left: A Street in the Jewish Quarter of Girona, Spain; Right: Doors of the Spanish Synagogue in Venice, Italy

Yiddish

Jews from Spain, Portugal, and the Middle East were called Sephardim. Those from other European countries were called Ashkenazim. The Ashkenazi Jews who lived in Germany developed the language and culture that is known as Yiddish. See postcard at right. The Yiddish language is largely based on German, with influences from Hebrew, Slavic, and other languages where Jews lived. It is written with Hebrew letters from right to left, as Hebrew is. *Yiddish* is simply the word for Jewish in the Yiddish language. The word Yiddish is also used as a term to describe European Jewish culture. Yiddish literature emphasized stories about Jewish life in Europe.

In the box at right are some Yiddish words, written with English letters, with their original meanings and meanings that have developed over time.

The Movement to Poland

During the Middle Ages, in many places Jews were not allowed to own property. They had once worked their own land as farmers, but now they could not do this. Jewish men had to provide for their families in some way, so they turned to trades such as making crafts and peddling goods from wagons. One profession that some Jews adopted was moneylending.

Catholic doctrine forbade church members from charging interest on loans to other members. However, businessmen wanted to borrow money to expand their businesses, and Jews were willing to make these loans. Residents of many cities wanted the goods and services that Jews provided, but they didn't want Jews living among them.

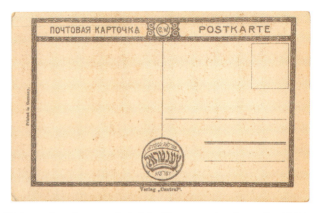

This postcard was printed in Germany in the early 1900s. At top left is the word postcard in Yiddish and at right the word is written in German.

Yiddish Words Used in English

bagel—small round bread with a hole in the middle, which is boiled before it is baked

chutzpah—nerve, boldness, or gall

glitch—a slip; came to mean a slight error or problem

klutz—a block of wood; came to refer to a clumsy person

mazel tov—good luck or best wishes; often used as a toast or to say congratulations

nosh—light snack

shlep—to carry around something you don't really need

shmaltz—chicken fat or grease; shmaltzy when used to describe literature or a play means excessively sentimental or corny

Lesson 97 - The Jewish Community in Lublin, Poland

When the Ashkenazim faced persecution in Western Europe, many headed east and settled in Eastern Europe. The photo at right shows the traditional Eastern European Ashkenazi clothing for a married woman.

In the 1100s, Jews began to settle in Poland, which was much more **tolerant** toward Jews than other places in Europe. Some scholars have estimated that by the 1550s, over three-fourths of all Jews in the world lived in Poland.

Lublin and the Jewish School

Though it had the third largest Jewish population of any city in Poland, the city of Lublin in southeastern Poland became the most important cultural, business, and educational center for Jews in Poland and throughout Europe. The earliest evidence of Jews in Lublin dates from the early 1300s. In 1385, the Polish king became the ruler of Lithuania to the east as well. This made Lublin an even more important location for people in that area, including Jews. The marketplace in Lublin offered a wide variety of goods from many lands. The city hosted two fairs every year, one at the end of summer in September and one in midwinter around the first of February.

In response to a Tatar attack (see Lesson 87), King Casimir III (also called Casimir the Great) built a castle on a hill in Lublin in 1341 and encircled the city with walls. At first Jews were not allowed to live within the city, but King Casimir allowed them to establish their own community at the base of the castle hill. By the mid-1400s, Jews in Lublin could set up shops in the marketplace to sell their wares and the city had given Jews land for their own cemetery, seen below.

Traditional Eastern European Ashkenazi Clothing

This gate was part of the wall Casimir built to defend the city of Lublin.

Around 1515 Jewish scholars established a school in Lublin, the Jeshybot Yeshiva, which became the world center for the teaching of the Talmud. The Talmud is a collection of commentaries and interpretations of the Law of Moses, which is called the Torah. Jewish teachers called **rabbis** provided the commentaries and interpretations found in the Talmud. The Talmud has two parts:

- The Mishnah is a collection of oral teachings by rabbis and Jewish scholars. The oldest Mishnah writings date from the 200s AD, but some of them are based on teachings that are much older.

- The Gemara contains commentary on the Mishnah and dates from the 500s AD.

The Jeshybot Yeshiva became the largest Talmudic school in the world. Jewish students from many countries came to study there. The Torah and the Talmud guided Jews' lives, but written copies were not readily available. Students could come to Lublin, read the texts, and hear scholars discuss their meaning. Lublin came to be called the Jewish Oxford, referring to the city in England known for its university. Lublin was also called the Jerusalem of the Polish Kingdom. Another Talmudic school, pictured below, opened in Lublin in 1930. Founders chose Lublin as the location of this school because of the history of Jewish scholarship in the city.

In 1547 the world's first Hebrew printing press began operation in Lublin. In 1567 the king of Poland granted the head of the Jeshybot Yeshiva the status and rights equal to those of the heads of Christian universities in Poland. Also in 1567, Jews built the Maharshal Shul synagogue in Lublin. In 1569 Poland and Lithuania signed the Union of Lublin, which brought the two nations already ruled by the same king under a single government. See stamp at right.

In 1602 the Jews of Lublin numbered about 2,000, which was about one-fourth of the city's population. Jews in Lublin and many other cities lived under the authority of the government,

The Yeshivat Chachmei opened in Lublin in 1930. Today it serves as a Jewish community center.

but they also had a chief rabbi and Jewish elders from wealthy and prominent families. In 1580 Jewish representatives from Greater Poland (the central and western sections of the country), Lesser Poland (the eastern part), Lithuania, and Russia came together for the first meeting of a Jewish council called the Council of Four Lands. The council met twice each year during the Lublin fairs. The council collected taxes and passed laws for Jews. Here and elsewhere, Jews were not allowed to participate in city or national government, so the Jews of this region established this Council, which was the only one among the Jews that governed such a large area.

This stamp printed in Poland in 1938 commemorates the union of Poland and Lithuania in 1569.

In Poland, and especially in Lublin, Jews had a place where they could live, study, and worship in relative safety. Long ago, their ancestor Abraham had wandered in Canaan before God brought his descendants out of Egypt into the Promised Land. In Lublin a community of Jews enjoyed a respite from their people's long history of wandering from place to place, as the psalmist says:

> *. . . they wandered about from nation to nation,*
> *From one kingdom to another people.*
> *Psalm 105:13*

Assignments for Lesson 97

Our Creative World — Read about the Jewish synagogue and cemetery on page 76.

Timeline Book — In the box for Lesson 97 on page 21, write "Jewish yeshiva in Lublin, Poland, is founded."

Student Workbook or Lesson Review — If you are using one of these optional books, complete the assignment for Lesson 97.

Thinking Biblically — What is the proper attitude for a Christian to have toward a person who practices the Jewish faith? Write one paragraph answering this question.

Vocabulary — Write your own definition for each of these words: dynamic (652), prejudice (653), ghetto (653), tolerant (655), rabbi (656). Look in the lesson for clues for the meaning of the words. When you are finished writing your definitions, look in a dictionary for comparison.

Literature — Read chapters 19-20 and the October 8 journal entry in *The King's Fifth*.

Potosi Silver Mine in the Andes Mountains

Lesson 98 — God's Wonder

After Columbus came to the Caribbean region on behalf of Spain, Spanish explorers and *conquistadors* (Spanish for conquerors) ventured onto the American continents to claim land, to conquer the people they found living there, and to take whatever riches they found back to Spain. As you read about these men, find their pictures below.

In 1513 Vasco Núñez de Balboa led his men across the Isthmus of Panama. They became the first Europeans to see the Pacific Ocean from the east. That same year, Ponce de Leon, who had sailed with Christopher Columbus on his second voyage to the New World, landed in what became Florida. He searched for a fountain of youth, which he had heard about but did not find.

The Aztecs of Mexico

By the early 1400s, a people who called themselves Culhua-Mexica ruled an empire in what would later become central Mexico (the word Mexico comes from *Mexica*). Historians refer to them as Aztecs. By 1519 the Aztec Empire included five to six million people. The center

Spanish Explorers in the New World

Clockwise from Top Left: 1948 Spanish Stamp Honoring Hernando Cortés; Statue of Ponce de Leon in Puerto Rico; 1963 Panamanian Stamp Honoring Vasco Núñez de Balboa; Equestrian Statue of Francisco Pizarro in His Birthplace of Trujillo, Spain

of the empire was Tenochtitlán, which was home to some 140,000 or perhaps even 200,000, making it the largest city ever built in North or South America before Europeans came to those continents. Tenochtitlán was an impressive city with pyramids painted red and blue. It had streets and canals where people traveled on canoes. Inside the Sacred Precinct were a ball court, homes of Aztec priests, and schools where nobles trained to become priests. Kings and nobles lived in white palaces nearby where they enjoyed gardens and zoos.

The Aztec were excellent farmers who planted all available land, including swampland which they reclaimed. Craftsmen worked as potters, weavers, sculptors, featherworkers, and gemworkers.

Hernando Cortés began exploring Central America in 1519. He led an army into Aztec territory and captured their ruler Montezuma II, who later died while in their custody. The empire ended in 1521, when Cortés and his army defeated them. The last Aztec emperor was Cuauhtémoc, whose bust in Mexico City is pictured below.

Aztec Artifacts

Cuauhtémoc Bust in Mexico City

Left Column: Aztec Mirror Made of Obsidian, c. 1400-1521; This female idol, made from volcanic stone, holds two objects which probably represent maize cobs, c. 1400-1521. Right Column: Another idol made from volcanic stone, c. 1400-1521; Basalt Sculpture of a Knotted Rattlesnake, 1100-1520

Unit 20 - The Late 1500s

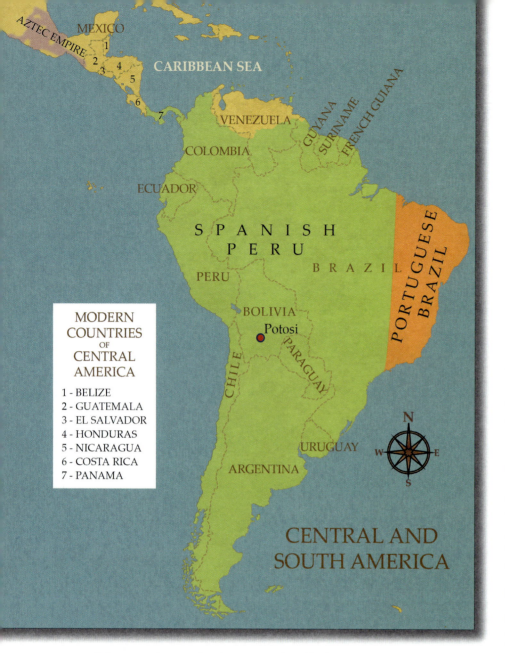

Hernando de Soto of Spain led an expedition to explore what became the southeastern United States from 1539 until he died there in 1542.

Like the Aztecs to their north, the wealthy and vast Inca Empire we learned about in Lesson 89 soon fell to the Spanish. Between 1530 and 1535, Francisco Pizarro led his army into Inca territory and conquered them (see map on page 596).

As we learned in Lesson 93, Portugal and Spain had agreed to divide the world between them at a certain line of longitude. Because of this, Portugal claimed the far eastern part of the continent, as seen on the map at left. Pizarro claimed the western part of the continent for Spain and called the entire region Peru. What a Native American found in the Andes Mountains of Peru turned out to provide more riches for Spain than they could possibly have imagined.

Silver Discovered at Potosi

After Pizarro conquered the Inca Empire, the Spanish forced many of the Inca to become slaves. The Inca had been active in mining for some time. Diego Huallpa was an Inca miner who worked at Porco, which had been the main Inca silver mine. Huallpa's Spanish overseer ordered him to climb a nearby red mountain to look for an Inca shrine. As Huallpa came down the mountain, a gust of wind caused him to fall. His arm dug into the dirt, revealing a huge vein of silver in the mountain. As word got out about the find, thousands of Spanish and Inca prospectors rushed to the "Cerro Rico" or Rich Hill of Potosi. They discovered other silver veins and deposits of tin, zinc, lead, and copper. Mining experts consider the Potosi silver deposit to be the richest silver mine in the world. Miners continue to extract silver from the mine.

Left Column: Red Entrance to the Potosi Mine and a Piece of Silver Ore; Above: Cerro Rico and the City of Potosi

Potosi is located in the Andes Mountains in what is now the country of Bolivia. The summit of Cerro Rico is about 15,800 feet above sea level. The city of Potosi, seen above, sits at the foot of the mountain and is about 13,400 feet above sea level, making it one of the highest cities in the world. By the early 1600s as many as 120,000 to 160,000 people lived in Potosi. It was one of the largest cities in the world, and by far the largest in the New World at that time.

Silver Mining

The first silver mines at Potosi were open pits, in which workers dug out silver ore using iron bars. Workers then heated the ore in smelting ovens made of stone and clay called *huayras*, from the Quechua word for wind. Refiners built a fire in an oven, and the wind blowing through it heated the ore and separated the silver from other materials. One early record told of some 6,000 huayras glowing through the night on the landscape around the mountain. Most huayras burned dense moss or llama dung for fuel.

In 1554 Bartolome de Medina in Mexico developed a technique called patio refining that he used at Potosi. He combined crushed silver ore with salt, water, copper sulfate, and mercury in a thick mixture that workers spread onto a flat surface called a patio. As refiners stirred the combination, the mercury amalgamated with or joined to the silver and drew it away from the other parts. Workers then washed and heated the mixture, which drove off the mercury, leaving almost pure silver that they formed into ingots. The process required that workers build dams on mountain streams, which formed reservoirs that supplied water to power the 140 mills that crushed the ore into powder.

When miners exhausted the silver ore that was close to the surface, they dug tunnels that bored deep into the mountain to bring up silver. The miners carried candles to light their work below the surface. They broke up the deposits with hammers and carried twenty-five-pound sacks of silver-laden dirt and rocks up ladders to the surface. The high water table in the mountain required constant pumping until workers dug drainage tunnels beginning in 1556. The mining of huge silver deposits led to many related occupations, such as drivers for pack animals and suppliers of needed materials. Historians believe that the Potosi area was the largest industrial complex in the world in the 1500s.

Modern Workers in the Potosi Mine

When you see a beautiful piece of silver, remember that the first people who handled it may have been men in Bolivia who put on their work boots, dug it out of the earth, pushed it in a cart or carried it up a steep incline—either many years ago or just in the last few years.

Treasury of the World

By 1650 workers had brought out thousands of tons of silver from the mountain. The Spanish built the Royal Mint at Potosi in 1575. Records indicate that by 1640 the mint annually produced five million peso coins, each weighing one ounce.

The mining and minting at Potosi greatly increased Spain's wealth. The Spanish government received one-fifth of the money created there. This money paid for Spain's explorations and other activities around the world. As the Spanish purchased foreign goods, a great deal of silver from Potosi ended up in China and India. People referred to Potosi as the "treasury of the world." The Spanish began to use the phrase "vale un Potosi" (worth a Potosi) to refer to something of great value.

The wealth produced at Potosi had its costs. For instance, the large quantity of mercury that the workers used there did serious damage to people and the environment. Providing fuel for the refining process resulted in the deforestation of the landscape.

The National Mint of Bolivia in Potosi has a museum showing historic artifacts. See exterior and interior photos on the next page.

National Mint of Bolivia

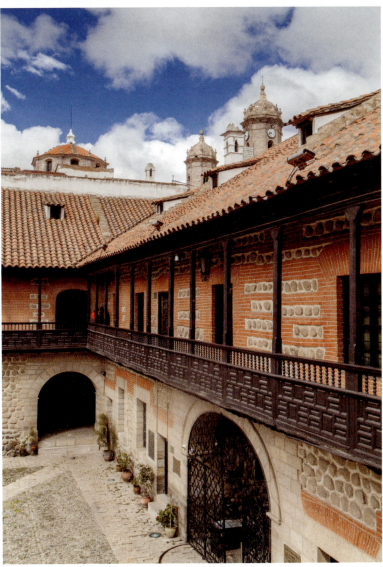

Labor at Potosi

Mining is often hard, dangerous work. Some free laborers and some slaves from Africa worked in the mines, in the refining process, and in the mint; but much of the labor came through a required labor system called *mita*, which was Quechua for turn. The Inca had used a system of labor that required Inca men to build roads and to work on other community projects. They were assigned to work a certain number of days each year on such projects.

The Spanish who operated the mines at Potosi also required Inca men to work, usually for many more days than the Inca themselves had required. These men often brought their families with them, which explains why the population in Potosi increased so much in so short a time. Inca miners had a great fear of what they believed was the spirit that ruled the underworld, which they called El Tio. They made sacrifices to El Tio to keep him from becoming angry at them for removing minerals from his realm. The Inca people themselves benefited from the

This silver Spanish coin dates from the time of King Philip V who reigned from 1700 to 1746.

public works projects that they had completed through the earlier mita system, but the benefits from the Potosi mine flowed to the Spanish, not the Inca.

The wisdom and understanding God offers to people is so valuable that God compares it to gold and silver.

*How much better it is
to get wisdom than gold!
And to get understanding
is to be chosen above silver.
Proverbs 16:16*

Assignments for Lesson 98

Our Creative World — Read the excerpt from *The True History of the Conquest of New Spain* on pages 77-78.

Map Book — Complete the assignments for Lesson 98 on Map 30 "Central and South America."

Timeline Book — In the box for Lesson 98 on page 22, write "Silver mint founded in Potosi (modern Bolivia)."

Student Workbook or Lesson Review — If you are using one of these optional books, complete the assignment for Lesson 98.

Thinking Biblically — Copy Proverbs 16:16 in the center of a piece of paper. Around the words, draw objects made of silver.

Literature — Read chapters 21-22 in *The King's Fifth*.

Family Activity — Make "Silver Coins of Potosi." Instructions begin on page FA-40.

Suleyman I
and the Ottoman Empire

Lesson 99 World Biography

Europeans called him the Magnificent. He was the strongest ruler of his day in Europe and the Middle East in terms of lands ruled, wealth, and accomplishments. The tenth sultan of the Ottoman Empire, Suleyman I, was born in 1494 and came to power in 1520 at the death of his father, Selim I. Selim had built a large and powerful kingdom. Suleyman, whose name is the Arabic form of Solomon, possessed the abilities not only to maintain the kingdom but to increase it.

Suleyman sent or led conquering armies to the east and to the west. He eventually controlled lands on three continents. He organized the laws of his empire, authorized large and beautiful building projects, and encouraged the arts.

Lawgiver

Muslims refer to Suleyman as the Lawgiver. He organized the ways in which the Ottoman Empire had applied basic Muslim laws, called Shariah laws, to **contemporary** situations. Suleyman put the laws into final form, and no later sultan sought a further revision.

Statue of Suleyman the Magnificent, Istanbul, Turkey

Conqueror

Kingdoms who followed Islam had been major military forces in the Mediterranean region since the religion began and spread in the 600s. In the 1400s European nations pushed back. Prince Henry of Portugal had set out to take Muslim ports along the West African coast (see Lesson 83). In the late 1400s Ferdinand and Isabella fought Muslims living on the Iberian Peninsula.

Suleyman saw himself as the **rightful** ruler of the world. His efforts at expanding Ottoman control were, in his mind, simply efforts to put his rightful role in the world into practice.

In Lesson 71, we learned about the Hospitallers of St. John of Jerusalem. In the early 1500s, the Hospitallers held the islands of Rhodes and Malta. In 1522 Suleyman and his armies seized control of Rhodes. However, he was unable to take Malta when he tried to do so in 1526.

Also in 1526, Suleyman defeated Hungarian forces at the Battle of Mohacs and put that country under his control. He supported John I as his **puppet** ruler there. Suleyman had a continuing struggle with the Habsburg Dynasty based in Austria, which had governed Hungary (Lesson 104 explains the Habsburg Dynasty, also spelled Hapsburg). Habsburg archduke Ferdinand took back part of Hungary and claimed it all. At this, Suleyman and his forces returned. Not only did the Muslims retake all of Hungary but they also laid siege to Vienna, the capital of Austria. The siege was not successful, but Ottoman control of Hungary became secure. In all, Suleyman conducted seven campaigns in Hungary.

Statue of Barbarossa, Antalya, Turkey

The Ottomans built a powerful **fleet** of fighting ships on the Mediterranean. Led by naval commander Barbarossa, in 1538 the Ottoman fleet defeated a combined fleet from the pope, Spain, Venice, and Genoa at the Battle of Preveza off the western coast of Greece. The Ottoman navy took over Tunisia and Algeria on the coast of northern Africa; raided the coasts of Spain, France, and Italy; and captured much of Greece. While the Ottoman navy ruled the Mediterranean, their eastern fleet was active on the Red Sea and in the Persian Gulf.

The Arts

Suleyman supported the arts. He encouraged music, calligraphy, manuscript painting, and the production of textiles, ceramics, and glazed tiles, as seen above right. He also encouraged the study of philosophy. His fellow Muslims considered him to be one of the greatest Muslim poets.

Suleyman sponsored building projects such as bridges, mosques, and palaces in Istanbul and elsewhere. He refurbished the Dome of the Rock in Jerusalem and authorized projects in Mecca and Medina in Arabia (Muslim cities discussed in Lesson 63).

Interior of the Suleymaniye Mosque, Istanbul, Turkey

His chief architect, Sinan, oversaw many projects including the Suleymaniye Mosque complex in Istanbul, constructed from 1550 until 1558. See its interior above and its exterior at right.

Lesson 99 - Suleyman I and the Ottoman Empire

Tile Panels from Iznik, Turkey, Late 1500s

Decline of the Ottoman Empire Begins

The reign of Suleyman I was the high point of Ottoman power, accomplishment, and influence. After his rule, the empire began to **unravel**.

In his last years, Suleyman largely withdrew from active leadership. He left matters in the hands of three sons, who fought each other for control of the empire. Suleyman died in 1566 when he was once more in Hungary, leading a siege of the city of Szigetvar. The Ottoman army won the battle after the death of Suleyman, but the victory came at great cost of life for both sides. The Austrian emperor and Selim II agreed to a truce in 1568.

Suleyman's son Selim II was able to gain control over his two brothers and succeeded his father. The Ottoman Empire lasted for about 350 more years, but it never regained the status it had under Suleyman.

Though Sultan Suleyman I achieved great things in the eyes of the world, his life ended as does the life of every person, and his empire slowly unraveled. The psalmist reflected on greatness as God sees it:

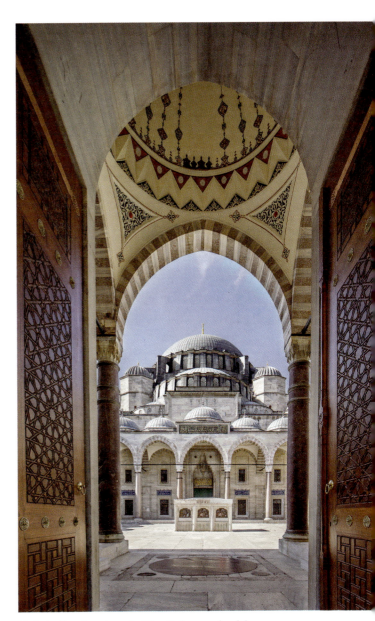

Gate to the Courtyard of the Suleymaniye Mosque, Istanbul, Turkey

The Lord looks from heaven;
He sees all the sons of men;
From His dwelling place He looks out
On all the inhabitants of the earth,
He who fashions the hearts of them all,
He who understands all their works.
The king is not saved by a mighty army;
A warrior is not delivered by great strength.
A horse is a false hope for victory;
Nor does it deliver anyone by its great strength.
Behold, the eye of the Lord is on those who fear Him,
On those who hope for His lovingkindness.
Psalm 33:13-18

Assignments for Lesson 99

Our Creative World — Read "A Visit to the Wife of Suleyman" on pages 79-80.

Timeline Book — In the box for Lesson 99 on page 22, write "Istanbul has an extensive water supply system."

Student Workbook or Lesson Review — If you are using one of these optional books, complete the assignment for Lesson 99.

Thinking Biblically — Read Psalm 33.

Vocabulary — Find each of these words in a dictionary, then find the definition that corresponds to the way the word is used in this lesson: contemporary (665), rightful (665), puppet (666), fleet (666), unravel (667). Copy the words and definitions.

Literature — Read chapters 23-24 in *The King's Fifth*.

The People of Southeast Asia

Lesson 100 — Daily Life

Imagine that you are living with your family and helping to farm the small patch of land on which you live. One day new people appear who do not look like anyone you have seen before. They are wearing a different kind of clothes. Their skin is a different color from yours. They speak a language you have never heard and do not understand.

One of your tribe who does understand their language speaks to your village and says, "These people say that they have come from far away over the waters. They say that they are your new masters. They say you must do the work they tell you to do. If you do not obey them, they say that they have weapons that they will use on you and your family, weapons that can hurt you and send you to the world down under."

Then he looks sad and says, "They say that we have a new king, one who lives a long way away. We are no longer our own people; we are his people."

What would you do? What would your parents do?

This is what happened time and again in the part of the world we call Southeast Asia.

Top Left: Man from the Island of Bali in Indonesia; Bottom Left: Traditional Fishing Basket in Malaysia; Above: Fisherman at Lake Inle in Myanmar

669

Southeast Asia

Southeast Asia includes the Indochinese Peninsula, the Malay Peninsula, and the Malay Archipelago, which is the largest group of islands in the world. The Malay Archipelago includes the more than 17,000 islands of Indonesia and the 7,000 or so islands of the Philippines. Indonesia contains Borneo, which is the third largest island in the world. Only the islands of Greenland and New Guinea (which lies just outside the archipelago) are larger. Southeast Asia is home to the modern countries of Thailand, Laos, Cambodia, Vietnam, Myanmar (Burma), Singapore, Indonesia, Malaysia, Timor-Leste (East Timor), Brunei Darussalam, and the Philippines. A few islands in the region are the possessions of other countries. The modern names of several Southeast Asian countries derive from the larger people groups who once lived there, including the Thai, Khmer, Lao, Viet, Burmese, and Malay. See map at right.

We do not know when the first people arrived in Southeast Asia. The evidence we have indicates that these people were or became animists. Animism is the belief that the world is filled with both good and bad spirits. Animists believe that these spirits affect every aspect of people's lives. Animists wear charms, burn incense, and conduct other rituals in an effort to honor good spirits, guard against evil spirits, and appease spirits that might turn against them if offended. Apparently most of the people of Southeast Asia also believed that the spirits of their deceased ancestors influenced their lives and that the people would suffer negative consequences if they failed to respect and even worship the spirits of these ancestors.

The people living in Southeast Asia in the 1500s built many structures from bamboo. They commonly built their houses above ground, raised on piles, with center and corner posts, woven or plank walls, and tall gabled roofs made of thatch or palm fronds. The designs of their houses and many objects in their houses reflected their beliefs. Bronze was widely used to make statues, gongs, and drums. Bronzeworks were especially numerous in Vietnam.

For many people, growing rice was their main occupation. Generally people understood that the ruler owned all of the land; everyday people simply farmed it to support their families. However, Vietnam developed a tradition of private ownership of land. Some Southeast Asians who lived on coastlands or along rivers were fishermen. Everyday people usually lived in the same village their entire lives, unless they had to move because of war or famine. The people of Southeast Asia practiced slavery. Slaves were usually people captured by slave traders or who were prisoners of war. The peoples of Southeast Asia often fought each other.

Mekong Delta, Vietnam

Lesson 100 - The People of Southeast Asia

A huge factor of everyday life for many in Southeast Asia is the 2,703-mile-long Mekong River, pictured at left. The Mekong is the second-most biodiverse river in the world after the Amazon. The Mekong starts in Tibet and flows south through China, Myanmar, Laos, Thailand, Cambodia, and Vietnam. Many people get their livelihood from the Mekong, especially the fishermen who fish its waters. Tonle Sap Lake in southern Cambodia is the source of the Tonle Sap River, which flows southeast into the Mekong at Phnom Penh, the modern capital of Cambodia. However, during the rainy season the Mekong has so much water that it pushes into the Tonle Sap River, forcing it to flow in the opposite direction.

Scenes of Southeast Asia

Oriental Dwarf Kingfisher, Thailand

The earless monitor lizard is native only to the northern part of Borneo which is home to the sultanate of Brunei.

Near Bodgaya Island, Sabah, Malaysia

Cormorant Fisherman in Phangnga, Thailand

Long-Tailed Macaque, Indonesia

Vang Vieng, Laos

Stilt Houses Near Kratie, Cambodia

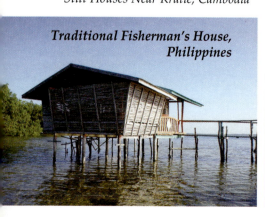
Traditional Fisherman's House, Philippines

Rice Field in Thailand

Lesson 100 - The People of Southeast Asia

The Peoples and Past Empires of Southeast Asia

Many national identities and languages existed in Southeast Asia by the 1500s. See photos at left and on pages 674 and 677. No one kingdom or empire was very powerful when European explorers began to arrive, but the region had been home to powerful empires in the centuries before.

The Khmer people, centered in what is now Cambodia, had built the Khmer Empire beginning in the 800s. The Khmer Empire was the largest and most powerful of these former empires. At times the Khmer ruled large areas of Southeast Asia.

The Khmer people built Angkor, an intricately-designed capital city, which included a complex system of moats, canals, and reservoirs fed by water from the nearby Phnom Kalen hills. These waterways supplied the needs of the city and of the surrounding farms. Though the area has a six-month rainy season and is dry the other six months, this water system enabled them to have two or three rice crops each year. Feeding many people was important because, at a time when London had a population of about 25,000, Angkor and nearby villages had an estimated population of about one million. Thai invaders captured Angkor in 1431, and the Khmer abandoned the city.

The Lao people of Laos were once part of the Khmer, but they became a distinct nationality. The people who lived in what is now Laos around 500 BC carved large stone jars in which they placed the ashes of their dead. This area became known as the Plain of Jars. A portion is pictured at right.

The Champa people lived along the coast of what became central and southern Vietnam and gradually became part of the Vietnamese people.

Traditional Khmer Cambodian Dancer

Boy in Traditional Dress of Myanmar

Ethnic Orang Asli people of Malay wear traditional clothes at a Malaysia Wedding Exhibition in Kuala Lumpur.

Plain of Jars, Laos

The sea-going Srivijaya Empire came to power in the late 600s. Raiders from India weakened it in 1025, and its power lessened as other kingdoms grew. By the late 1200s the Srivijaya Empire was almost gone.

Dance Drama in Thailand

The Funan Kingdom became powerful around 100 AD in what is now southern Cambodia, but it had lost power by 600. The Chenla people came to power to the north of Funan, but the Chenla Kingdom dissolved in the 700s.

Zheng He visited Southeast Asia during his voyages in the early 1400s. See map on page 549. By the 1500s, the various ethnic groups of Southeast Asia had subdivided into local peoples, each of whom generally had their own language. Experts have identified about a dozen main language families, but they have also identified about 1,000 distinct languages and dialects which those outside each language group could not understand. Only the major national languages had writing and literature.

Invaders from China and India

China has had a major influence in Southeast Asia. The Han Dynasty took control of Vietnam in the 100s AD. The Vietnamese overthrew their Chinese masters in 939. The Chinese regained control in 1407, but the Vietnamese rose up against China again in 1428. When the Vietnamese were able to govern themselves, the leaders generally came from two families, the Trinh in the north and the Nguyen in the south of Vietnam. The Chinese taught the Vietnamese farming, fine arts, and Confucian philosophy. The Chinese moved into other areas of Southeast Asia as well. The Mongol Yuan Dynasty which we studied in Lessons 74 and 75 conquered the city of Pagan in Myanmar in 1287.

A Malay couple wears traditional Malacca Malay wedding clothes, which have been influenced by both Malay and Chinese styles.

India also had a major influence in Southeast Asia. First merchants and then settlers came from India and dominated life in the region, especially from about 20 AD until about 1200. People from India brought their styles of art and architecture to Southeast Asia. They also brought their Hindu and Buddhist religions. Southeast Asia never developed a caste system of social classes like that in India. The statues of Buddha created in Southeast Asia looked different from the statues in India. The nuclear family was relatively more important in Southeast Asia, while the extended family was more important in India. The Chinese had much more influence than did Indians. The people of Southeast Asia maintained many of their traditional ways while

Lesson 100 - The People of Southeast Asia

Hindu Temple in Singapore

they adopted some of the ways of the Chinese and Indian invaders. See Hindu temple in Singapore at left.

Temples, Stupas, and Pagodas

Buddhism became the predominant religion in the region, but some people held on to animist beliefs as well. Southeast Asians constructed huge Buddhist temples.

The Khmer spent about forty years building the Angkor Wat, which means Angkor Temple, in the 1100s. It was dedicated to the Hindu god Vishnu. It is the largest religious building in the world, covering an area of about 500 acres. A moat that is 590 feet wide surrounds it. The city of Angkor has several temples. These are multi-layered, intricately carved structures. Buddhist and Hindu beliefs influenced their layout, statues, and relief carvings. There is some evidence that Angkor Wat once served as an astronomical observatory.

Angkor Wat

Stupas are a common sight throughout Southeast Asia. Stupas are large, tall structures which Buddhists use for meditation. Large temples commonly have a stupa at their center. Pagodas, which are multi-storied towers that get smaller toward the pointed top, originated in India and spread as a form of stupa to China, Japan, and Southeast Asia. The construction of all of these buildings required the labor of many persons over several years.

Invaders from Other Lands

Muslim traders from the Middle East came to Southeast Asia in the 1300s, seeking spices and teaching Islam. Large numbers of people in Malaysia and Indonesia converted to Islam, while a much smaller number converted in the southern Philippines. After Vasco da Gama proved that Europeans could get to Southeast Asia by way of the Cape of Good Hope, the Portuguese began to have more contact with people in the region. They fought Muslims to take over the city of Malacca in Malaysia in 1511.

Pagodas of the Taman Ayun Temple on the Island of Bali in Indonesia

Europeans at various times established colonies in portions of Southeast Asia. Only Thailand was never a European colony. Britain chartered the British East India Company in 1600, but it became powerful mainly in India and not in Southeast Asia.

The Dutch established the Dutch East India Company in 1602. They pushed out the Portuguese and fought off the British to establish a colony in Malacca, Malaysia.

The French created the French East India Company in 1604, but the French did not become as powerful in the region.

This 1992 stamp from Brunei Darussalam depicts the Asian Paradise Flycatcher.

Lesson 100 - The People of Southeast Asia

Top Left: A member of the Ifugao tribe who are native to the Philippines plays a bamboo nose flute in Kota Kinabalu, Malaysia. At Left and Above: These Ifugao women wear their national dress in Banaue, Philippines.

The Spanish in the Philippines

The Spanish came to Southeast Asia, not by way of the Cape of Good Hope, but by way of the Strait of Magellan. First they came to the islands that became the Philippines. The first Spanish representatives to arrive were Portuguese ship captain Ferdinand Magellan and his crew. Though Magellan was Portuguese, he sailed for Spain. After crossing the Atlantic and passing through the Strait of Magellan near the tip of South America, Magellan and his crew sailed for over three months across the Pacific, stopping briefly on Guam. In March of 1521, they landed on islands which Magellan claimed for Spain. Magellan converted some of the islanders to Christianity, but he was killed on April 27, 1521, during a battle between warring native groups in the islands. In 1543 Ruy Lopez de Villalobos sailed to these islands from Mexico on behalf of Spain. Villalobos gave them the name Philippines in honor of the Spanish Prince Philip, who later became King Philip II. Manila became the capital of the Spanish East Indies in 1571. It remains the capital of the Philippines today.

Before the Spanish arrived, the Philippines did not have a national ruler. After they came, Filipinos continued to lead their villages, but the Spanish controlled regional and national governments. Many Filipinos began working for the Spanish.

Roman Catholic priests taught Spanish language and culture to people on the islands. Spanish became the official language. Priests also taught the Filipinos about Jesus. In the Philippines, a majority of the people became believers in Jesus Christ.

*For I am not ashamed of the gospel,
for it is the power of God for salvation to everyone who believes . . . .
Romans 1:16*

Assignments for Lesson 100

Map Book — Complete the assignments for Lesson 100 on Map 31 "Southeast Asia."

Timeline Book — In the box for Lesson 100 on page 22, write "Manila is capital of the Spanish East Indies."

Student Workbook or Lesson Review — If you are using one of these optional books, complete the assignment for Lesson 100 and take the test for Unit 20.

Creative Writing — Reread the first three paragraphs on page 669. Write two or three paragraphs answering the questions, "What would you do? What would your parents do?"

Literature — Read chapter 25 and the October 10 journal entry in *The King's Fifth*.

Above: Eighty-Eight-Foot-Tall Statue, Christ the King of Dili at Dili, Timor-Leste

21 The Early 1600s

Marian Column Erected to Celebrate the End of Swedish Occupation During the Thirty Years War, Munich, Germany

Lessons
- 101 - Our World Story: The Beginnings of the British Empire
- 102 - World Biography: William Shakespeare
- 103 - God's Wonder: God Created the Food Grown Around the World
- 104 - World Landmark: Sweden and the Thirty Years War
- 105 - Daily Life: The Rule of the Shoguns in Japan

Literature *The King's Fifth*

1601-1650

The government based on the island of Great Britain eventually built colonies all around the world. In the first half of the 1600s, it founded some of its first colonies in the Caribbean and in North America. At the same time, William Shakespeare retired to his birthplace in Stratford-upon-Avon, England, after a career as an actor and playwright in London. Shakespeare created a body of literature many believe to be the best ever produced in the English language. The exchange of foods created by God between the Old World and the New World changed the way people ate around the globe. Sweden was a major world power involved with many other European countries in the Thirty Years War. At the same time, shoguns ruled Japan, assisted by the samurai class.

Note: Lesson 103 is about many places around the world.

The Beginnings of the British Empire

Lesson 101   Our World Story

In the 1500s, Spain and Portugal competed to see who would gain more wealth from overseas exploration and trade. While both Spain and Portugal claimed land in South America, Spain conquered more and more areas in the New World, and Portugal focused more on the Far East. Both countries became wealthy. Other countries sent out explorers, too.

At first European explorers wanted to get whatever wealth they could and bring it home, whether by mining deposits of precious metals, such as those found at Potosi, or by establishing trading posts in faraway places. But then people began to think about other reasons to venture to new lands. They realized that they could build colonies in these other lands. Then they could sell goods produced in the home country to the people who went to live in those colonies. Unlike explorers just passing through, colonists could search thoroughly for resources available in new lands. Kings dreamed of ruling **vast** empires that stretched around the world.

Some Christians felt another motivation. They realized that the people who lived in the New World and in Southeast Asia needed to know Christ. They wanted to go there to teach them.

Several countries began colonies around the world at the same time. They competed to get to a place first and benefit from the natural resources God had placed there. Sometimes countries fought each other about who had the right to be in a particular location and who could buy and sell there. As you read this lesson, find the colonies on the map on pages 686-687.

Building a colony in a new land required months and sometimes years of preparation. Organizers had to gather money and supplies and find people who would commit to such an endeavor. At first only small numbers of settlers moved to the New World and Southeast Asia, and they built only a few colonies.

Oldest Church in the Americas, Begun in 1512: Cathedral of St. Mary of the Incarnation, Santo Domingo, Dominican Republic

681

Portuguese Colonies

The Portuguese defeated Muslim traders in India in 1498 and began to build their own trading settlements. From there they traveled to the Spice Islands in Indonesia and to China and Japan to trade there. The Portuguese began to establish their first settlements in Brazil in 1533, thirty-three years after Pedro Cabral had claimed the area for Portugal (see page 631). They also had trading colonies along the eastern coast of Africa and at the Strait of Hormuz, the entrance to the Persian Gulf.

Dutch Colonies

As mentioned in Lesson 100, Dutch businessmen formed the Dutch East India Company in 1602. They had considerable business success in Southeast Asia.

In 1609 English explorer Henry Hudson, sailing for the Netherlands but actually working for the Dutch East India Company, entered the mouth of what later became known as the Hudson River on the eastern coast of North America. Many explorers believed they would find a "northwest passage" through North America that would enable them to travel on to Asia where they could do business. Henry Hudson hoped that the Hudson River was this northwest passage. It was not, but Hudson noticed the possibility for developing a fur trade with indigenous Americans. See the Hudson plaque at right below. In 1614 a map published in the Netherlands labeled the area New Netherlands. Dutch businessmen founded the Dutch West Indies Company in 1621 to develop settlements there. Dutch settlers moved into New Netherlands around the mouth of the Hudson in 1624, and the settlement was named New Amsterdam the next year.

French Colonies

Jacques Cartier sailed up the St. Lawrence River to the present location of Montreal, in what became Canada (see page 631). Over fifty years later, Samuel de Champlain made several trips to the Caribbean on behalf of his native France. In 1605 he and other Frenchmen established the Port Royal settlement in Nova Scotia, seen below. Champlain founded Quebec in 1608, the first permanent settlement in what was called New France.

Left: Reconstruction of 1605 Settlement at Port Royal National Historic Site, Canada; Right: This plaque in Henry Hudson Memorial Park in New York City illustrates the Dutch East India Company giving a Commission to Henry Hudson.

At that time, New France consisted of the area along the St. Lawrence River. French businessmen formed the Company of New France in 1627. The French government gave the company the rights to conduct fur trading in New France in return for helping 200-300 settlers come there from France each year.

English Explorers and Pirates During the Reigns of Mary I and Elizabeth I

Like many European countries, England wanted to find a better way to reach Asia and participate in the spice trade. From 1553 to 1559, during the reign of Mary I and the first year of the reign of Elizabeth I, London merchants paid for efforts to sail northeast from England around Scandinavia and Russia. In 1577 Sir Humphrey Gilbert proposed sailing northwest from England to go around North America to get to Asia. Both plans failed because the icy waters of the Arctic Sea were **impassable**.

This ship in Brixham, England, is a replica of the Golden Hind *in which Drake and his crew sailed around the world.*

Queen Elizabeth encouraged English ships to raid Spanish ships carrying treasure from the New World to Spain. Sir Francis Drake and other "sea dogs" carried out this piracy. Though this brought income to the English treasury, it created tension in the relationship between England and Spain. Drake also brought slaves from Africa to the Caribbean and sold them to Spanish businessmen who had built plantations there.

From 1577 to 1580, Drake and his men became only the second crew to sail around the world. The English proclaimed him a hero when he returned. Drake fought against the Spanish for several years and was second-in-command when the English defeated the Spanish Armada in 1588 (see pages 649-650).

England Tries to Plant Colonies in North America

In 1583 Sir Humphrey Gilbert sailed to North America and claimed Newfoundland in what became Canada for Queen Elizabeth I. Gilbert and his crew did not establish a colony. On their return voyage, he and his men were lost at sea near the Azores. Nevertheless, historians credit Sir Humphrey Gilbert with beginning the British Empire.

Sir Richard Grenville led an expedition in 1585 to plant a colony on Roanoke Island in what is now North Carolina, but the effort failed. Grenville's cousin, Sir Walter Raleigh (half-brother of Sir Humphrey Gilbert), sponsored but did not participate in another attempt, which also did not last. In 1587 Raleigh again sponsored an attempt to begin a colony at Roanoke. The governor of the colony returned to England for supplies. When he returned to Roanoke in 1590, the people of the colony had vanished.

Raleigh also participated in the defeat of the Spanish Armada. He led an expedition in 1595 up the Orinoco River in the region of Guyana in South America (the map on pages 686 and 687 uses the original spelling of Guiana). He was searching for a **reputed** city of gold, but he did not find one. Raleigh continued to raid and battle with the Spanish for several years. Despite all of their efforts, by 1600 the English did not have any functioning colonies in the New World.

The First Successful English Colony in North America

The first permanent English colony in the New World began in 1607 at Jamestown, Virginia, with about one hundred men. Virginia was named for Queen Elizabeth I, the Virgin Queen, who had died four years before. Jamestown was named for King James I. When he succeeded Elizabeth as monarch, James was already serving as king of Scotland. He became King James I of England.

The chief stated purposes for the Jamestown colony were to spread the gospel and to make a profit for investors. Another stated purpose was to send social outcasts away from England, including poor people and criminals. The men who settled in Jamestown did not have the skills needed to make the colony work well. Many of the first settlers died from illness or a lack of food.

John Smith helped to save the colony. He encouraged the settlers to stop seeking gold and to grow profitable crops. The colony became successful when they began to grow tobacco and ship it back to England.

The colonists in Jamestown were the first people in North America to use the labor of slaves from Africa. These first slaves may not have lived a permanent life of slavery as later slaves did; it is possible that they were indentured servants who were only committed to working for a certain number of years.

Jamestown Colony, Virginia

Left: Reconstruction of Jamestown Settlement in Virginia; Center: Queen Elizabeth II of England greets members of the Powhatan tribe at the 400th Anniversary of the Jamestown Colony; Right: English Soldier Reenactors at the 400th Anniversary

Lesson 101 - The Beginnings of the British Empire

Colonists Seeking Religious Freedom

Meeting House at Plimoth Plantation, Plymouth, Massachusetts

Over the next several decades, the English planted a series of successful colonies on the Atlantic coast of North America. Three were founded by English men and women seeking religious freedom. Just thirteen years after the founding of Jamestown, Christians settled in the area that became Massachusetts. Some Christians in England, including Roman Catholics and groups called Separatists and Puritans, did not have the same beliefs as the Church of England. Puritans wanted to purify the Anglican Church of what they believed to be unbiblical practices, while Separatists wanted to leave the Church of England altogether and be a completely separate group. Separatists settled in Plymouth in 1620 (see photo above). Puritans established the Massachusetts Bay Colony in 1630. Maryland began in 1634 as a haven for Roman Catholics, who were persecuted in England. In these new colonies, Separatists, Puritans, and Catholics had the opportunity to practice their faith as they wished away from the direct oversight of the Church of England.

When people from the Massachusetts Bay Colony disagreed with religious practices there, one group founded Rhode Island in 1636 and another group founded Connecticut in 1638. The Carolina colony, which later divided into North Carolina and South Carolina, began in 1663 primarily as an attempt to profit from agriculture.

English Colonies in the Atlantic, the Caribbean, and South America

English men and women also began colonies on islands in the Atlantic and the Caribbean Sea and in South America. A colony in Guyana in South America only lasted two years. Attempted colonies on the islands of St. Lucia in 1605 and Grenada in 1606 also failed quickly.

In 1609 Sir George Somers was leading a fleet of supply ships to Jamestown, Virginia, when a storm blew Somers' ship off course. Somers grounded the ship on a reef at Bermuda, and the emergency settlement the men built on the island was the beginning of an English colony. Bermuda is an island in the Atlantic Ocean near the Bahamas.

Fort St. Catherine in St. George, Bermuda, was completed in 1609 and was later extensively renovated.

During the 1620s and 1630s, the English built successful colonies on the islands of St. Kitts, Nevis, Dominica, Barbados, Barbuda, Antigua, and Montserrat in the Caribbean. In 1655 England took the island of Jamaica from Spain. The English established colonies in the Bahamas in 1666.

Between 1620 and 1640, more English colonists went to the Caribbean than went to North America. About 40,000 settled in the Caribbean Islands and in Bermuda. Almost 20,000 of these settled in Barbados. By contrast, during the same period about 30,000 English settlers went

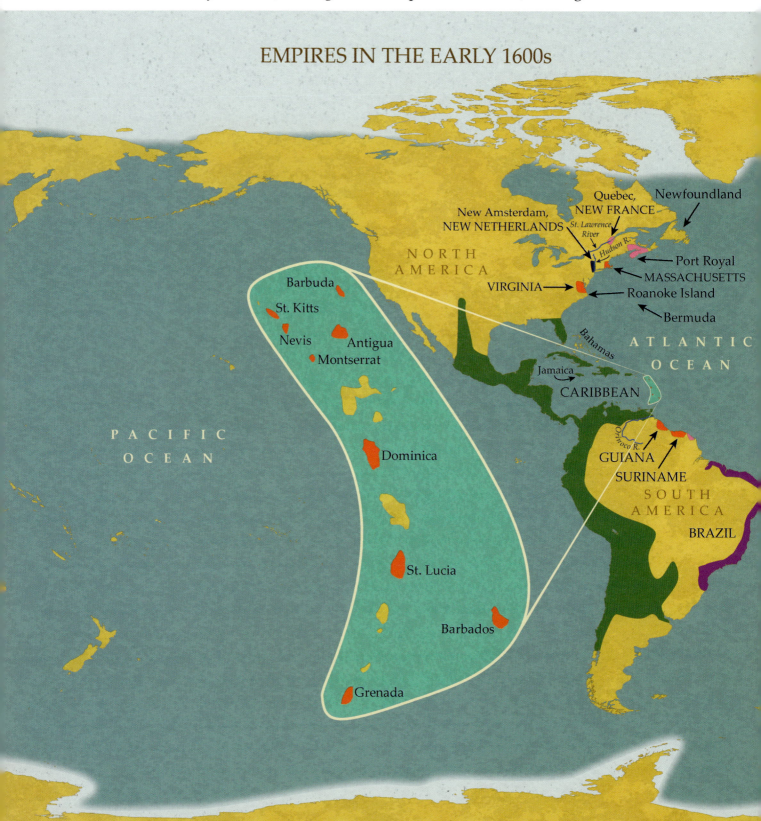

EMPIRES IN THE EARLY 1600s

to England's colonies on the North American continent. About half of those settlers went to Massachusetts.

For many years, England's colonies in the Caribbean were more financially successful than their colonies in North America. However, North America had more land and a more temperate climate, which meant that over time a greater number of English colonists settled on the continent.

England Fights Other European Countries

The English fought a series of wars with countries which also wanted colonies in the New World, including the war in which England defeated the Spanish Armada in 1588.

Most of the major countries of Europe fought a series of wars between 1618 and 1648. These conflicts are known as the Thirty Years War. England and France fought between 1627 and 1629 as a part of that war. The conflict between these two countries involved religion and disputes over trade. During the war the French colonies of Port Royal and Quebec in what is now Canada surrendered to the English, but the English gave them back to France in a treaty signed in 1632.

Trees in the Matapica Swamps, Suriname, South America

In 1651 England began passing the Navigation Acts. These laws restricted how the colonies could do business. For instance, one law required that all goods imported into England from America, Asia, and Africa had to come on ships in which Englishmen made up more than half of the crew. Another **provision** said that goods from Europe had to come into England on ships from England or from the country where the goods originated. England passed the Navigation Acts to keep the Dutch from making any profit from trade with England. The result was a war between England and the Netherlands that began in 1652. It ended with a treaty in 1654, but the two countries fought several times again in later years.

In 1664 the English attacked New Amsterdam, and the Dutch surrendered. The English took over the city and renamed it New York. The Dutch had seized Suriname on the northern coast of South America that year, but the English accepted that the Dutch would continue to rule Suriname. See photo of Suriname above.

English Plantations in Ireland

In addition to building colonies far from home, the English government also built in Ireland, its island neighbor next door. It seized lands in Ireland and made them into plantations. The English also brought in English citizens to live there. England pursued this plantation policy from the last half of the 1500s until the mid-1600s. By that time, in a country where Catholics had been the majority, English Protestants had come to control the northern part of Ireland, plus large areas of the south.

Lesson 101 - The Beginnings of the British Empire

Queen Elizabeth I commanded the Earl of Leicester to take possession of Blarney Castle, but he was unable to do so. Blarney Castle is the home of the famous Blarney Stone, which visitors kiss because of the superstition that doing so will give them eloquent speech. A portion of Blarney House, which is the castle's keep, and a portion of the castle wall are pictured at right.

Plantations in Ireland and colonies in the New World were the first **conquests** in what would later become the British Empire.

Many seek the ruler's favor,
But justice for man
comes from the Lord.
Proverbs 29:26

Assignments for Lesson 101

Timeline Book — In the box for Lesson 101 on page 23, write "English colonize the island of Barbados."

Student Workbook or Lesson Review — If you are using one of these optional books, complete the assignment for Lesson 101.

Vocabulary — Look up each of these words in a dictionary and read their definitions: vast (681), impassable (683), reputed (684), provision (688), conquest (689).

Creative Writing — Imagine that you are a settler in a colony in North or South America. Write a letter of at least one page to a relative in your home country, trying to persuade him or her to join the colony.

Literature — Read chapters 26-27 in *The King's Fifth*.

Blarney House and a Portion of a Wall at Blarney Castle,
County Cork, Ireland

William Shakespeare

Lesson 102 — World Biography

William Shakespeare was born to John and Mary Arden Shakespeare on April 23, 1564, in Stratford-upon-Avon, England, about seventy-five miles northwest of London (the date is uncertain). The name of the town means "Stratford on the banks of the River Avon." John was a successful merchant, glove-maker, and farmer. He held several positions in city government.

We have little information about William's life. People rarely kept the information that we would like to have, and no one knew that William would become famous one day. He probably attended the free grammar school in Stratford, where he concentrated on learning Latin and reading Latin literature. Stratford was an important market town, which meant that on holidays actors performed pageants and plays, often about the famous Robin Hood. We know that by 1569 traveling companies of actors put on plays there. Although William lived in a small town, he probably had many opportunities to see people and hear stories from other places.

Birthplace of William Shakespeare

William married Anne Hathaway in 1583. Their children were Susanna and twins Hamnet and Judith. Hamnet died in 1596 at age eleven.

Home of Anne Hathaway

Shakespeare Acts and Writes in London

At some point, William went to London to work as an actor. We know from comments by other writers that Shakespeare was performing in London by 1592. It is possible that Shakespeare wrote plays which premiered in 1592 at the Rose, pictured below. Because crowded facilities tended to help spread disease, London officials closed theaters in the city from 1592 until 1594, because of an outbreak of the plague. During this time, Shakespeare published two long, narrative poems that were well liked.

By 1594 Shakespeare was a member of Lord Chamberlain's Company (also called the Chamberlain's Men). Companies of actors had patrons or sponsors to give them credibility to help their ticket sales. Lord Chamberlain was an advisor to Queen Elizabeth I. Shakespeare wrote plays for the group to perform, usually two per year. Because he invested money in the company, he was able to share the profits it earned. Shakespeare also earned income from writing plays and acting in them. The Chamberlain's Men played at the Swan, pictured below.

Apparently Shakespeare enjoyed financial success from his endeavors. In 1597 he bought the second-largest house in Stratford. We assume that his family continued to live in Stratford while Shakespeare stayed in London for much of the year with his work.

The Chamberlain's Men usually performed in a theater called the Theatre, which stood on a piece of land they leased. After a disagreement with the landlord, the owners of the Theatre took the structure apart and built the Globe. The Globe opened in 1599 and had a capacity of 3,000 spectators.

These 1995 stamps from the United Kingdom feature theaters from Shakespeare's day: the Rose, the Swan, the Globe (built in 1599), and the Globe (rebuilt in 1614).

It was an outdoor theater where performances took place in the afternoons in good weather, using natural light. See picture above. The Globe burned down in 1613 during a performance of Shakespeare's *Henry VIII*, and the owners rebuilt and reopened it the next year. The 1614 globe is pictured above at lower right.

When King James I came to power in 1603, he also became a sponsor of Lord Chamberlain's Company and they came to be called the King's Men. From 1609, the company also performed in the Blackfriars Theatre, which was indoor, used candlelight, and could host performances year-round. Also in 1609, a London publisher printed a collection of sonnets written by Shakespeare called *Shakespeare's Sonnets*. A sonnet is a sixteen-line poem that has a particular rhyming pattern.

Shakespeare Retires

Shakespeare entered retirement or semiretirement around 1611 or 1612 when he moved back to Stratford. His daughter Susanna had married in 1607, and Judith married in early 1616. William Shakespeare died on April 23, 1616. He was fifty-two. He was buried beneath the floor of Holy Trinity Church in Stratford-upon-Avon, pictured on page 693.

Shakespeare did not publish his plays during his lifetime, although about eighteen of them appeared individually in print form. Copyright laws such as those we know today did not exist then, so his plays were probably written down by others during performances and later published. In 1623, seven years after his death, two of his former associates published the First Folio, which was a collection of thirty-six plays by Shakespeare, half of which had not been published before.

The Globe was reconstructed in the late 1900s. Queen Elizabeth II opened it in June 1997.

Actors perform inside the reconstructed Globe, 2010.

Theaters in Shakespeare's Day

Several theaters operated in London during Shakespeare's day, of which the Globe was typical. It was twenty-sided and open-air, with three levels of covered balcony seats. The cheapest and least desirable ticket locations were on the floor in front of the stage. Here the audience stood to watch a play from ground level, where there was no seating. Tickets for the bench seats in the balconies cost more.

The stage extended several feet into the ground-floor level. A canopy covered the stage. Actors came onto the stage through curtains hanging at the back of the stage. A trap door in the stage floor and one in the balcony provided the entrance for a ghost or a divine figure. The stage had no front curtain and no props. The actors usually wore elaborate costumes. Women rarely attended theatrical performances. See the exterior and interior of the 1997 reconstruction of the Globe at left.

The Influence of Shakespeare

William Shakespeare wrote a total of thirty-six plays, 154 sonnets, and two long narrative poems. Scholars put his plays into three categories: histories (about real historical figures such as kings of England, for which Shakespeare did research in history books), tragedies (which tell sad stories, sometimes about historical figures), and comedies (which tell lighthearted stories). Shakespeare produced the most widely-admired body of literature in the English language. His work helped

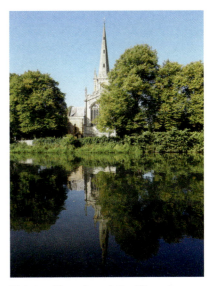

Trinity Church and the River Avon

to shape English literature for centuries. People have translated Shakespeare's plays into many languages, and actors still perform them all over the world.

The plays of Shakespeare continue to be popular for many reasons. He created vivid, memorable characters. He told stories that capture the audience's attention and heart. Shakespeare effectively portrayed the human experience, including love, ambition, jealousy, and many other human traits.

One of the most striking features of Shakespeare's plays is how he used the English language. While most people have a vocabulary of a few thousand words at most, Shakespeare used about 20,000 different words in his writings. An estimated ten percent of those words Shakespeare created himself. Many of these words we still use today, including **fashionable**, **lackluster**, **softhearted**, and gloomy. He created memorable phrases such as the green-eyed monster (referring to jealousy), fair play, a **foregone** conclusion, the be-all and end-all, and heart of gold. He created striking word pictures in his descriptions. In the play *Julius Caesar*, the character Cassius describes Roman emperor Julius Caesar in this way:

> Why, man, he doth bestride the narrow world
> Like a Colossus, and we **petty** men
> Walk under his huge legs and peep about
> To find ourselves dishonorable graves.

People use his lines, such as "Parting is such sweet sorrow" and "A rose by any other name would smell as sweet," so often that they may not even realize they are quoting Shakespeare.

Bust of Shakespeare outside of Guildhall Art Gallery, London

Shakespeare wrote at the same time that the King James Bible, named for King James I, was published in 1611. See a copy of the first edition below.

Shakespeare's plays include some elements that reflect common beliefs of his day, such as ghosts and witches. But he also taught many lessons about good and evil, the fact that we all will face judgment someday, and the dangers of hatred and jealousy. Scholars of Shakespeare have counted in his writings some 2,000 references to people, events, or ideas in the Bible. Shakespeare's works show the power of words.

First Edition of the King James Bible, Published in 1611

Like apples of gold in settings of silver
Is a word spoken in right circumstances.
Proverbs 25:11

Assignments for Lesson 102

Our Creative World — Read the speech by Polonius from *Hamlet* on page 81.

Timeline Book — In the box for Lesson 102 on page 23, write "Shakespeare's company builds the Globe Theatre." In the box for Lesson 102 on page 31, write "A new Globe Theatre is built in London."

Student Workbook or Lesson Review — If you are using one of these optional books, complete the assignment for Lesson 102.

Thinking Biblically — Copy Proverbs 25:11 in the center of a piece of paper. Divide the rest of the page into four sections. In each section, draw a small cartoon that illustrates the verse.

Vocabulary — Write five sentences, using one of these words in each: fashionable (693), lackluster (693), softhearted (693), foregone (693), petty (693). Check in a dictionary if you need help with their definitions.

Literature — Read chapters 28-29 in *The King's Fifth*.

God Created the Food Grown Around the World

Lesson 103   God's Wonder

By the time God created animals and people on the sixth day of the Creation week, He had already created their food on the third day.

Then God said, "Let the earth sprout vegetation, plants yielding seed, and fruit trees on the earth bearing fruit after their kind with seed in them"; and it was so. Genesis 1:11

After the flood, God also gave people meat to eat (Genesis 9:3). While God provided many wild foods for them to gather, He also gave them the job of caring for animals and growing crops. The first child born to Adam and Eve was Cain, who was a "tiller of the ground." The second child, Abel, was a "keeper of flocks" (Genesis 4:2).

Though God provided food for people in every land where they lived, many foods varied from place to place. When explorers began coming to the New World, they found new foods they had not known in the Old World and took them back home. Beginning with the second voyage of Columbus in 1493, they brought Old World foods to eat while they settled in the New. On that voyage, Columbus brought hogs, cattle, sheep, goats, and chickens for meat. He brought wheat seed, grapevine cuttings, chickpeas, melons, olives, onions, lettuce, radishes, sugarcane, and fruit stones (the part of the fruit that grows into a fruit tree). In this lesson, we concentrate on the exchange of crops between the Old and New Worlds. See a New World settlement at right.

Columbus' men built the La Isabela settlement in the Dominican Republic in 1493.

Potatoes from the Andes

No one in the Old World knew about potatoes before explorers brought them there from South America. In Offenburg, Germany, in 1853, a sculptor erected a statue of Sir Francis Drake. The statue stood looking into the horizon, holding a potato. The inscription read: "Sir Francis Drake, disseminator of the potato in Europe in the year of Our Lord 1586. Millions of people who cultivate the earth bless his immortal memory." Nazis tore down the statue in 1939 due to anti-foreign sentiments. Though historians don't know for certain that Drake brought the potato to Europe, someone did, and it changed the history of the continent.

Before the time of Christ, the peoples living in the Andes were growing potatoes. When the Spanish came, the varieties they grew varied from village to village. Today almost 5,000 varieties grow in the Andes. See photo at left.

Quechua woman peels potatoes at a market in Puno, Peru.

The Spanish conquistadors learned about potatoes from the Inca and took them back to Europe. By the 1560s, Spanish farmers in the Canary Islands were exporting potatoes to France and the Netherlands. Monarchs of Europe began enjoying potatoes as a novelty food in their courts and sailors began eating potatoes because they prevented scurvy. However, it took many years for potatoes to become a staple. When they did, potatoes became an extremely important food source for Europeans and helped them to survive crop failures and famines.

New World Sweet Potatoes and African Yams

When Columbus came to the New World, sweet potatoes were growing in many places in Central and South America and the Caribbean. Columbus brought them back to Spain. A history of plants published in 1597 in England has an illustration of the sweet potato and mentions them being eaten roasted or boiled with prunes. Shakespeare mentioned sweet potatoes in *The Merry Wives of Windsor*.

Above: Wheelbarrow with Yams in Nigeria; Below: Yam Field in Nigeria

In the United States, sweet potatoes are often called yams, but actually the yam is a completely different plant that originated in Africa and Asia. Americans started calling the softer varieties of sweet potatoes yams because African slaves called them yams. Slaves called these tubers yams because they reminded them of the yams they ate in Africa. Yams are much larger than sweet potatoes and can grow as long as five feet! See Nigerian yams and yam field on page 696.

Cassava from the New World

By the 1400s, native peoples in the Caribbean and in Central and South America were growing cassava. Other names for cassava are yuca and manioc. They had learned how to prepare this root crop so that it is not toxic, as it is in its natural state. Natives served cassava bread to Christopher Columbus. You may have eaten cassava in tapioca pudding. The Portuguese took the vegetable to the Congo Basin of Africa around 1558. Cassava has become one of the most important food sources in Africa. Cassava also became an important food in Southeast Asia. It is now grown in more than ninety countries worldwide.

Growing Cassava in South America and Southeast Asia

Women cut cassava in Ecuador at left and in Thailand at right.

Rice from Asia

Archaeologists have found evidence of rice being grown in China and India long before the birth of Christ. Rice continues to be the most important food available to much of the population of Asia.

At a much later date, but still before the birth of Jesus, Africans of the Niger River Valley began to raise a different species of rice. Muslims brought rice to Spain about 700 AD. Then farmers began to grow rice in Italy and later in southeastern Europe.

The Spanish brought rice to the Caribbean and South America beginning in the late 1400s. English colonists began to grow rice in the 1600s. It became an important export crop in the Carolina colony in the late 1600s.

Growing Rice in Central America and Southeast Asia

Left: A 1983 stamp from Nicaragua illustrates Nicaraguans working in a rice paddy.
Right: A 1985 stamp from Indonesia illustrates Indonesians working in a rice paddy.

Wheat from the Middle East

Farmers grew wheat in the Middle East by the time of Abraham's grandson Jacob. Long before Jesus' birth, farmers were growing the crop in Asia, Europe, and North Africa. Wheat was a major crop in Europe by the time explorers began coming to the New World. Columbus brought wheat to the Caribbean on his second voyage in 1493. The Spanish brought it to Mexico, Argentina, and the southwestern United States in the 1500s.

In the early 1600s, the French brought wheat to Nova Scotia. The English brought it to Jamestown and Plymouth. The Dutch and Swedes brought it to what became New York, New Jersey, Delaware, and Pennsylvania.

Growing Wheat in the Old World and the New World

Top Row: Old World Stamps - Israel, 1958; Cyprus, 1967; France, 1957
New World Stamps - Brazil, 1951; Canada, 1988
Bottom Row: Old World Stamps - Ireland, 1963; Portugal, 1963; Germany, 1946

Corn from the Americas

Corn was unknown anywhere in the Old World before Columbus brought the first Europeans to the New World. Natives of the Americas grew corn on the islands of the Caribbean, on the plains of North America, in Mexico, and in the high mountains of the Andes. The cornbelt stretched as far north as southern North Dakota and as far south as northern Argentina and Chile. Growing corn was important to many native groups in the New World, but it was especially important to the Aztecs, the Maya, the Incas, and the Pueblo peoples of what became the southwestern United States.

After bringing animals and seeds to the Americas on his second voyage, Columbus took corn seeds back with him to Europe. Native Americans later taught English colonists how to raise corn. Today corn is an important crop on every continent in the world except Antarctica.

Growing Corn in America and Africa

Left: Corn Dance at Santa Clara Pueblo in New Mexico; Right: Maasai Warrior in Cornfield in Tanzania, Africa

Coffee from Africa and Tea from China

The first known coffee plants grew in the forests of Ethiopia. An Ethiopian goatherd named Kaldi is given credit for discovering the plant when he noticed that after his goats ate coffee leaves and coffee berries, they didn't want to sleep at night. He shared his discovery with a monk at a local monastery, who appreciated that coffee helped him stay awake during evening prayer. The monk shared it with other monks at the monastery.

The first coffee cultivation occurred in Arabia. From there it spread to Persia, Egypt, Syria, and the Anatolian Peninsula, where people drank it in coffeehouses. Coffee drinking became popular in Europe in the 1600s, but some people thought it might be an evil drink. When coffee arrived in Venice in 1615, local clergymen opposed it. Pope Clement VIII tried it and gave it his approval. Coffee became popular in Austria, England, France, Germany, and Holland, especially for breakfast and in coffeehouses.

Arabs tried to keep other nations from raising coffee, but the Dutch took seedlings to India in the late 1600s. When coffee failed to grow there, they took it to the islands of Indonesia, where they were successful in growing coffee trees. The Dutch brought coffee to New Amsterdam in the mid-1600s, though tea was the more popular drink.

In the 1700s, the mayor of Amsterdam in the Netherlands gave a coffee plant to King Louis XIV of France. A young officer in the French navy took a seedling from that tree to the New World island of Martinique. From there people took coffee seeds and seedlings to other islands and to Brazil. Coffee eventually became one of the most valuable crops in the world.

The history of tea goes much further back than coffee. According to Chinese legend, Emperor Shen Nung was sitting beneath a tree. As his servant boiled water, leaves from the tree fell into the water, and the emperor decided to try it. The Chinese placed tea containers in tombs during the Han Dynasty (206 BC-220 AD). The drink became popular in China during the Tang Dynasty (618-906). Japanese monks studying in China brought the drink back to Japan. People in India have also enjoyed tea since before the birth of Jesus.

Portuguese traders and missionaries in the Far East began drinking tea in the 1500s. The first Europeans who brought tea to Europe to sell were Dutch traders who brought Chinese tea to the Netherlands in 1606. From there it spread to other parts of Europe.

The first reference to tea in England was in a coffeehouse advertisement in a London newspaper in 1658. The drink became popular in England after King Charles II married a Portuguese princess who enjoyed drinking tea. Tea's popularity in England spread to its colonies in North America.

Growing Tea in Asia and Coffee in Brazil and Southeast Asia

Left: Tea Plantation at Munnar, India; Top Row: Tea Pickers in Assam, India, and at Hangzhou, China; Bottom Row: Coffee Farmer in Vangyawn Village, Lao Ngam, Salavan, Laos; Coffee Harvester in Vila Mariana, Brazil

Sugarcane from the South Pacific and India

Honey was a common sweetener in the ancient world. The first mention of honey in the Bible is in Genesis 43, when Jacob told his sons to take honey as a gift to the Egyptians who were selling grain during the famine they were suffering. Honeybees were not native to North America. The first honeybees in North America were likely those English colonists brought to Virginia in 1622.

Sugarcane also provided sweeteners for ancient peoples. People make both sugar and molasses from sugarcane. Farmers in the islands of the South Pacific and in India grew this crop before the birth of Jesus. Alexander the Great found sugarcane in Pakistan in 326 BC. The Chinese began to grow the crop about 100 BC and Europeans about 636 AD. In the 1400s, Europeans grew sugarcane on islands in the Atlantic as well as in North Africa. However, sugar was very expensive in Europe. Only the wealthy could afford it, and then only in small amounts.

Cuttings from sugarcane plants were among the many plants Columbus brought to the Caribbean Islands on his second voyage. The climate was ideal for growing the crop. The Spanish, including Columbus' son Diego, worked to establish sugarcane plantations, but it was the English who were finally successful. The British began a system of sugarcane plantations, bringing in thousands of slaves from Africa to work on them.

Sorghum from Africa

Sorghum is indigenous to Africa. People eat sorghum grain in many different ways: boiled like rice, cracked for making a porridge similar to oatmeal, baked into a flatbread, and popped like popcorn. The stems of some types of sorghum can be used to make a sweet syrup. Farmers grew it in India and Assyria before the birth of Christ. Chinese farmers grew sorghum during the 1200s. Seeds came to North America in the early 1600s. In North and South America, it has been grown mainly as feed for animals. The sweet variety is popular in the southern United States for making syrup.

Growing Sugarcane in India and the Caribbean

Worker makes sugar out of sugarcane in Jasso Majara, India.

Sugarcane Plantation, Maharashtra, India

Sugar Mill, Betty's Hope Sugar Plantation, Antigua

Sugarcane Field, Cuba

Growing Sorghum in Africa and South America

Left: Woman of the Hamer ethnic group prepares Sorghum in Omo Valley, Ethiopia. Center: Stamp depicts women threshing sorghum in the Transkei region of South Africa. Right: Sorghum grows in Mato Grosso, Brazil.

Chocolate of Central and South America

The Aztecs and Maya made a drink from the beans found inside the fruit of the wild cacao tree. Anything made from the cacao bean is called chocolate, which in its powdered form is called cocoa. According to legend, the Aztec emperor Montezuma hosted the Spanish explorer Hernando Cortés at a banquet that included a chocolate drink. The drink was unsweetened. The Spanish had the idea of adding honey or sugar and took it back to Spain where a sweetened chocolate drink became popular. From Spain, the popularity of chocolate slowly spread to other countries in Europe, especially among royalty.

After explorers came to the New World, the Spanish started raising cacao in Ecuador about 1635. By the end of the century, the Dutch were growing cacao on the island of Curaçao; the English on the island of Jamaica; and the French on the islands of Martinique, St. Lucia, and the Dominican Republic and in Brazil, Guyana, and Grenada. Today cacao is grown in lands that lie ten degrees of latitude above and below the equator.

Growing Chocolate in Central America and the Caribbean

Left: Cacao Tree in Costa Rica; Right: Cacao Tree in the Dominican Republic

In God's wisdom He provides man food in the seeds of rice, corn, wheat, and sorghum; the roots of potatoes, cassava, and sweet potatoes; the beans of cacao and coffee trees; the stems of sorghum and sugarcane; and the leaves of tea.

Cacao Beans Inside a Cacao Pod

He causes the grass to grow for the cattle,
And vegetation for the labor of man,
So that he may bring forth food from the earth,
And wine which makes man's heart glad,
So that he may make his face glisten with oil,
And food which sustains man's heart.
Psalm 104:14-15

Assignments for Lesson 103

Our Creative World — Read the recipes from *A Daily Exercise for Ladies and Gentlewomen* on pages 82-83.

Timeline Book — In the box for Lesson 103 on page 23, write "The British East India Company opens a post in Madras."

Student Workbook or Lesson Review — If you are using one of these optional books, complete the assignment for Lesson 103.

Thinking Biblically — Write a paragraph answering the question, "Why do you think God created people to need food?"

Creative Writing — Make a list of at least fifteen foods and drinks that you enjoy that include one or more of the following ingredients: rice, corn, wheat, sorghum, potatoes, cassava (tapioca), sweet potatoes, chocolate, coffee, sugar, and tea.

Literature — Read the October 12 journal entry in *The King's Fifth*.

Family Activity — Make an "Old World New World Cookbook." Instructions begin on page FA-43.

Sweden
and the Thirty Years War

Lesson 104　　　　　　　　　　　　　　　　　　　World Landmark

Svaneholm Castle by Svaneholmssjön Lake, Skurup, Sweden

Sweden is the third largest country in the European Union after France and Spain. It is slightly larger than the state of California. See map on page 707. However, Sweden has one of the smallest populations in Europe. Germany has about 81 million people and France has about 67 million, while Sweden has a population of just under 10 million. Some 97 percent of Sweden's land area is uninhabited.

Sweden shares a similar language and culture with Denmark and Norway, the other two Scandinavian countries. Sweden covers the eastern part of the Scandinavian Peninsula, with Norway to its west. Denmark is a peninsula jutting north from the European continent and lies to the south. The term *Scandinavia* comes from Scandia, the province at the southern tip of Sweden, which Denmark once controlled.

Water and islands are important to Sweden's geography. Its east, south, and southwest borders are a long coastline. The Gulf of Bothnia lies to the east of Sweden and the Baltic Sea to its south and southwest. Sweden's land area includes tens of thousands of islands. Stockholm, the capital and largest city, sits partly on the eastern shore of the Scandinavian Peninsula and partly on fourteen islands nearby. About fifty bridges connect the various parts of the city. Sweden is home to over 95,000 lakes, including the one pictured above. Lakes cover about 9 percent of the total area of Sweden.

The country has three geographic regions. Gotaland, with its plains and low hills, is the southern part. It has relatively mild weather as a result of the influence of the Gulf Stream (see Lesson 59). Snow is rare on the southern coast. Svealand is the middle section, with taller hills, cooler temperatures, and more winter snow. The northern part is the Norrland. This mountainous region is cold, with long winters and short, mild summers. Much of the Norrland is above the Arctic Circle. Mountains in this section lie along the border with Norway. The few residents here usually experience snow from mid-October to mid-April. Temperatures in Sweden can range from -63° in the far north during winter to an occasional 100° in summer in the south.

The Swedish people are descendants of Germanic tribes from Europe who migrated across the Baltic. The Finns and the Lapps are the largest ethnic minorities in the country.

Two of the largest industries in Sweden are mining the rich iron **ore** deposits and producing lumber and other wood products. About 69 percent of the land area is covered with forests. Only 7 percent of the land is suitable for farming.

The northern section of Sweden includes part of Lappland, a region north of the Scandinavian Peninsula. Lappland from the northern coast of Norway. This region is home to the Lapp or Sami people, who are known for herding reindeer. This northernmost part of Sweden, the "Land of the Midnight Sun," has fifty-six days of continuous daylight in summer. However, it also experiences thirty-two days of pure darkness in the winter.

Lappland

Top Row: Reindeer Camp Along the Baltic Sea; 1972 Finnish Stamp with Sami in Winter Clothing; Reindeer breeder wears traditional Sami clothing while leading a white reindeer which is pulling a sleigh. Bottom Row: Traditional Sami Turf Hut; Traditional Sami Reindeer Skin Yurts

The Gospel Comes to Sweden

The Catholic monk Ansgar brought the gospel to Sweden in the mid-800s. Ansgar was born in France about 801. After becoming a monk, he taught in Westphalia in northwestern Germany and then evangelized first in Denmark and later in Sweden. As the first known teacher of the gospel in the region, Ansgar is often called the Apostle of the North. The first Christian king

Unit 21 - The Early 1600s

St. Ansgar Statue, Hamburg, Germany

of Sweden was Olof Skötkonung, who became a believer about the year 1000. However, paganism did not completely disappear for many years. By the mid-1100s the majority of Swedish people were Roman Catholic.

From King Ladulås to King Gustav I

We usually think of Swedish Vikings exploring to the west, but they actually traveled more to the east, going to the Baltic coast and Russia and to the Black Sea and Caspian Sea. Swedish traders traveled as far as the Byzantine Empire and even to Baghdad.

The Swedish city of Visby was a key port in the Hanseatic League (see Lesson 79). In 1280 King Magnus Ladulås established a nobility and a feudal system for the country. In the 1300s, Sweden suffered from the Black Plague, as did the rest of Europe.

After many years of conflict among the Scandinavian countries and conflicts among their royal families, in 1389 Denmark, Norway, and Sweden accepted Queen Margaret I of Denmark as their common ruler. A meeting of representatives in Kalmar, Sweden, in 1397 officially created the Kalmar Union of the countries, which lasted until 1523. In that year, following a period of conflict and division in the Union, Gustav I Vasa of Sweden rebelled, and the Swedish nobles elected him as their king. In 1527, only ten years after Martin Luther began his break with Rome, Gustav I declared that the Lutheran Church would be the official church of Sweden.

King Gustav II Adolph and the Thirty Years War

We don't think of Sweden as a major military power today, but in the first half of the 1600s it was one of the **dominant** forces in Europe. Swedes took on this role during one of the saddest chapters in European history, which we know as the Thirty Years War.

Statue of King Gustav II Adolph, Goteborg, Sweden

After Martin Luther and those who agreed with him broke with the Roman Catholic Church, kings and princes throughout Europe began deciding if they were going to remain Catholic or become Lutheran. This led to military conflicts as leaders led armies against those who disagreed with them. After many years marked by warfare from time to time, European leaders adopted the Peace of Augsburg (in Bohemia and seen on the map at right) in 1555, which largely halted religious conflict in Europe for over sixty years.

This situation changed in 1618. Bohemia (now part of the Czech Republic) was then part of the Holy Roman Empire. The capital of Bohemia was Prague. Catholics and Protestants lived in Bohemia in an **uneasy** coexistence. Ferdinand, the

king of Bohemia, was an ardent Catholic. Protestants began building churches on land that the Catholics claimed but which the Protestants believed was legally available to them. In 1618 the Catholic Archbishop of Prague ordered the destruction of a Protestant church building. Protestant representatives in Prague put two Catholic officials on trial for violating their freedom of religion. The Protestants threw the two officials and their secretary out of a window. All three were unhurt, but this event **sparked** armed conflict between Protestants and Catholics all over Europe.

The Thirty Years War began with battles between Catholic and Protestant rulers and their armies. Other conflicts erupted over territorial and political issues, sometimes involving Catholic versus Catholic rulers, such as when Catholic France waged war against the Catholic Habsburg Dynasty, which ruled Austria and Spain. Over the three decades, the war involved most of the nations of Europe. The majority of the fighting took place in what became Germany, but it extended into other areas of Europe. Because European nations had founded colonies in other parts of the world, fighting also took place in the Caribbean, India, Africa, and South America and affected colonies in North America (see page 688).

When Gustav II Adolph, seen in the statue at left, came to the throne after the death of his father in 1611, Sweden was fighting Denmark, Russia, and Poland. Gustav ended the war with Denmark, made a truce with Poland, and kept fighting Russia. Gustav began building an empire

This 1936 Swedish stamp depicts Count Axel Oxenstierna.

that included Finland, Estonia, Latvia, and Lithuania, which lie north of Poland. He renewed the fighting against Poland in 1620 and concluded another truce with the Poles in 1629.

Gustav also worked on issues within Sweden. He strengthened the Swedish parliament, called the Riksdag; made government more efficient; and reorganized high school education for young men. Count Axel Oxenstierna, pictured at left, served as the king's chancellor or chief adviser.

In the 1630s, King Gustav II Adolph led his army into the Thirty Years War on the side of German Protestants. Gustav supported other Protestant rulers in the battle against the Catholics, especially against the Catholic Habsburg Dynasty of Austria, mentioned on page 666.

The Habsburg Dynasty was a large royal family whose members ruled many countries in Europe. The dynasty had begun in 1273 when Rudolf I became the first of nineteen Habsburg rulers of the Holy Roman Empire. Armies serving the Habsburg rulers added to the territory of the Holy Roman Empire by conquering other lands. The power of the Habsburg family grew stronger in Europe when members of the family married the kings and queens of other European countries.

In 1631 Gustav and the Swedes won the Battle of Breitenfeld, near Leipzig in the German district of Saxony. Gustav became in practical terms the master of Germany and one of the most powerful leaders in Europe. He led another army against a Catholic force in the Battle of Lutzen, also near Leipzig, in 1632. The Swedish army was again victorious, but Gustav was killed in the battle. His daughter Christina, seen below, succeeded him to the throne of Sweden, and Count Oxenstierna continued to serve in her government.

The Peace of Westphalia

In 1648, after five years of negotiations, the warring countries agreed to a series of treaties. The treaties were made in the Westphalia region of Germany. These treaties together comprise the Peace of Westphalia. See stamps below. The outcome was similar to the Treaty of Augsburg in that each ruler could decide the official state church for his region. This could be Catholic, Lutheran, or, for the first time, Calvinist. Calvinists follow the teachings of John Calvin. Another change was that a person who did not want to practice the state religion could practice his own religion without interference and without having to move. Some of the nations that had

Left: 1998 German stamp celebrates the Peace of Westphalia; Right: 1997 stamp from Sweden celebrates the Peace of Westphalia with a likeness of Queen Christina.

Lesson 104 - Sweden and the Thirty Years War

been involved in the fighting, including Sweden, received additional lands.

Thirty years of fighting, however, had devastated much of Europe, especially the German lands. The physical destruction was immense, but even worse was the human **toll** from warfare, famine, and disease. The common people of Europe suffered the greatest losses. Scholars estimate that the population of the German states fell by about 30 percent, or almost one-third. In some locations in Europe perhaps half the residents died. Notice the column on page 679 which celebrates the end of Swedish occupation of Germany during the Thirty Years War.

Stockholm Cathedral, Begun in 1306

The outcome of the war ended the pope's control over European nations and increased the number of independent countries. The treaties all but eliminated any power of the Holy Roman Empire. France replaced Spain as the main power in Western Europe. Some fighting continued in places from time to time, but it caused nowhere near the devastation of the Thirty Years War.

The rulers of Europe recognized Sweden as the leading power in the Baltic region. Sweden continued to colonize even during the war. A group of Swedish settlers established a colony in Delaware and New Jersey in 1638 called New Sweden. The Dutch took it over in 1655. Sweden reached the greatest extent of its empire between 1654 and 1660 under Charles X Gustav.

It is tragic that the rulers of Europe did not come to the agreement reached in the Peace of Westphalia before the bloodshed and destruction of war. When Peter got out his sword to defend Jesus in the Garden of Gethsemane:

> *Jesus said to him, "Put your sword back into its place;*
> *for all those who take up the sword shall perish by the sword."*
> *Matthew 26:52*

Assignments for Lesson 104

Map Book — Complete the assignments for Lesson 104 on Map 32 "Scandinavia."

Timeline Book — In the box for Lesson 104 on page 23, write "Gustav II becomes king of Sweden."

Student Workbook or Lesson Review — If you are using one of these optional books, complete the assignment for Lesson 104.

Vocabulary — Copy these words, each on a separate line: ore (705), dominant (706), uneasy (706), spark (707), toll (709). Look up each word in a dictionary. Next to each word, write what part of speech it is according to the way the word is used in the lesson.

Literature — Read chapters 30-31 in *The King's Fifth*.

The Rule of the Shoguns in Japan

Lesson 105   Daily Life

During the Middle Ages in Europe, Japan was divided into small provinces. Though a series of emperors led Japan, a clan ruled each province, and a clan leader ruled the clan. These provincial leaders usually were not interested in maintaining peace and governing their provinces in a way that helped the people who lived there. Instead, they often fought each other to be able to control more land. Sometimes a provincial leader or group of provincial leaders challenged the authority of the emperor. This competition meant that continuing warfare characterized the daily life of people in Japan, sometimes in one region, sometimes in another, and sometimes in many places at once.

The Shogun and the Samurai

Around 800 the Emishi clan of northern Japan rebelled against Emperor Kammu. General Sakanoue no Tamuramaro defeated the Emishi in 801, and the emperor gave Sakanoue the title of Seii-Tai-Shogun, which means "Barbarian-Conquering General." Historians usually shorten this title to *shogun*, which is usually translated "general."

During this period, a class of warriors developed who were called *samurai*, from the Japanese word for servant. Fathers passed down the title of samurai to their sons. For many years the samurai's main job was to defend the large estates of wealthy aristocrats or lords in the provinces. In this way they were similar to the knights of Europe.

In the 1000s and 1100s, the samurai developed a code of conduct called *bushido* or "the way of the warrior." They honored horsemanship and the ability to use a bow and arrow. Even more important were the personal characteristics of bravery, self-discipline, personal honor, and absolute obedience and loyalty to the *daimyo*, Japanese for "lord." The samurai wore bulky, elaborate clothing that included protective armor and a helmet. They carried a long curved sword and a short one. See samurai objects at right.

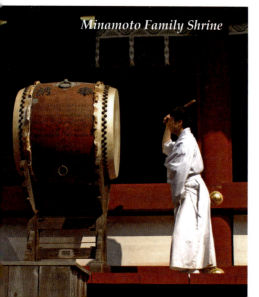
Minamoto Family Shrine

Lesson 105 - The Rule of the Shoguns in Japan

Samurai Objects

Left Column: Samurai Formal Inner Robe (top) and Surcoat (Bottom), Worn 1615-1868; Right Column: Stirrup for Samurai Horseman, Mid-1800s; Samurai Armor, 1700s; Bottom: Samurai Sword Reproduction

Shogun Rule Begins

In 1185 the samurai warrior Minamoto Yoritomo led an army that defeated all others and gained authority over all Japan. He had even more power than the emperor. In 1192 the emperor (who really had no choice in the matter) gave him the title of shogun. The emperor ruled from the capital of Kyoto, but Minamoto established his headquarters in the city of Kamakura. See a family shrine on page 710.

For most of the next seven hundred years, the shoguns were the real rulers of Japan. Historians call a government led by a shogun a shogunate. A shogun passed his position on to his son, as would a king. A series of three clans or dynasties held the position of shogun. The first is called the Kamakura shogunate. Though Japan continued to have an emperor during these centuries, the emperor did not have any real power and was only a figurehead who symbolized national unity. The emperor appointed the shogun, but everyone knew whom he would appoint. In Japan, the emperor was rarely even seen in public.

Minamoto Yoritomo appointed his own governors and tax collectors. A governor ruled a province; a tax collector ruled over estates within provinces. Minamoto and later shoguns maintained their power through the loyalty of the samurai, who served as military officers and administrators. In other words, the shogun had power because he had the army on his side. This arrangement, called the *bakufu*, meaning camp office, remained the pattern of shogun rule. From time to time someone would challenge the rule of a shogun, or two daimyos would have a conflict with each other, but there were more periods of peace under the shoguns than there had been before.

A samurai and his wife and daughter leave a bathhouse, followed by their servant, in this painting on mulberry paper by Mizuno Toshikata, who lived from 1866 to 1908.

Daily Life in the Time of the Shoguns

Japanese society had four main classes under the emperor, shogun, and daimyos. Of these four classes, the one with the highest prestige was made up of samurai warriors. See a samurai and his family at left. The second highest social class were the peasants, the everyday farmers. Japanese society saw these people as more important to the life of the nation than the third class, which were the artisans. After all, if the farmers did not grow food, the artisans could not produce their wares. The fourth and lowest class were the merchants. As a rule the Japanese did not respect merchants because they did not actually produce anything, but the Japanese used the work of merchants to gain wealth in trade. Below the fourth class were people who were untouchable, who were not even considered to be in a class.

The times of peace during the centuries of shogun rule encouraged the development of cultural interests. At times during the rule of the shoguns, dance and drama flourished. Such peaceful artistic pursuits as flower arranging and landscape gardening, which were not practical in times of war, became popular. Since the military was so important, the craft of making beautiful swords became highly honored. When the economy could grow, when farmers and artisans could work, and when leaders did not spend the nation's wealth on making war, the number of poor people decreased and many cities grew.

Missionaries and Traders from Europe During the Second Shogunate

During the Ashikaga shogunate, Portuguese traders came to Japan. They were actually blown there in a shipwreck in 1543, but this opened the door to trade between Japan and Europe. Within a century, Dutch, Spanish, and British traders arrived and competed with each other.

Lesson 105 - The Rule of the Shoguns in Japan

Seven men had formed the Society of Jesus in Paris in 1537. Members of the Society are called Jesuits. In 1549 Jesuit priest Francis Xavier, who was one of the original seven, brought the message of Christ to Japan. Xavier preached in India before coming to Japan. He was in Japan only two years but converted many to Roman Catholicism. Many other Jesuits as well as other Catholics also came to evangelize Japan. It is estimated that by 1581 Japan was home to about 200 churches and 150,000 believers. This changed the face of Japanese religion and society. Jesuits became some of the leading advisers to the emperor.

The Third Shogunate

After the Ashikaga shogunate fell in 1573, another period of turmoil followed. In 1600 Tokugawa Ieyasu gained control. Three years later the emperor declared him to be the shogun, and the Tokugawa shogunate began. Tokugawa relocated the shogunate capital to Edo, which became the city of Tokyo.

Himeji Castle in Himeji, Japan, was remodeled into its present form during the reign of Tokugawa Ieyasu.

Tokugawa wanted to strengthen his rule and remove the emperor even further from day-to-day involvement, so his government promoted the idea that the emperor was divine and that no one should see his face. As a result, the emperor lived inside his palace and no one outside of his family ever saw him. The Tokugawa shogunate ruled over an increasingly peaceful period. As a result, over time samurai warriors had little real fighting to do. They enjoyed the prestige of their position without having to engage in warfare. Notice the castle from the time of Tokugawa above.

At first, Tokugawa maintained contact with the rest of the world. For instance, he exchanged gifts with King James I of England and other European rulers. However, within a few years the Tokugawa shoguns became suspicious of contact with the West. They saw Christianity as a threat to their Buddhist religion and to the loyalties of the feudal system, and they saw becoming a Christian as treason. In 1614 Tokugawa ordered all foreign priests expelled and all church buildings destroyed. He told Japanese Christians to renounce their faith or be put to death. Some evangelists and believers refused to submit to these decrees, and they lost their lives. The Japanese authorities did not fully enforce these orders until 1638, when the believers were all but wiped out. Only a few Christians remained in remote areas of the country.

In 1639 the Tokugawa shoguns prohibited any further trade with Western nations to prevent any Western influence. They prohibited Japanese people from going to other countries. The only exceptions were that the shoguns reaffirmed their loyalty to China, and they allowed Dutch traders to continue doing limited business in Japan from a post on a small island.

Japan continued in this self-isolation until the middle of the 1800s, when the country renewed contact with the rest of the world. In addition, in 1868 the imperial family reasserted its authority over the country and ended shogunate rule. The emperor once again became the real ruler of Japan.

At many times in history, unbelievers have forced Christian missionaries out of their countries. When the Jewish leaders commanded Peter and John not to speak or teach at all in the name of Jesus:

> *Peter and John answered and said to them,*
> *"Whether it is right in the sight of God*
> *to give heed to you rather than to God,*
> *you be the judge;*
> *for we cannot stop speaking*
> *about what we have seen and heard."*
> *Acts 4:19-20*

Assignments for Lesson 105

Our Creative World — Read the excerpts from "Letter from William Adams" on pages 84-85.

Timeline Book — In the box for Lesson 105 on page 22, write "The first Catholic missionaries reach Japan."

Student Workbook or Lesson Review — If you are using one of these optional books, complete the assignment for Lesson 105 and take the test for Unit 21.

Thinking Biblically — Read Acts 4:1-22 concerning Peter and John's meeting with the Jewish leaders.

Creative Writing — Write a short story of at least one page about the people in the painting of a samurai and his family on page 712. The story can be from the perspective of the samurai, his wife, his daughter, or the servant.

Literature — Read the October 13 journal entry in *The King's Fifth*. If you are using the Student Workbook or Lesson Review, answer the literature review questions on *The King's Fifth*.

22

The Late 1600s

Dutch Delft Tiles from the 1600s

Lessons
106 - Our World Story: The Dutch Golden Age
107 - Daily Life: The Mughal Empire
108 - World Biography: Louis XIV of France
109 - God's Wonder: God Created Tibet
110 - World Landmark: London, England

Literature
Madeleine Takes Command by Ethel C. Brill is set in Canada. With her parents away, Madeleine must take charge in defending the fort against an attack by the Iroquois. (See "Notes to Parents on the Literature" in the back of the Answer Key.)

1651-1700

The Netherlands was a major European power with great naval strength in the late 1600s as they enjoyed a Golden Age of art and architecture. The Mughal Empire in India, which had flourished for more than a century, was beginning to shrink. King Louis XIV built France into a mighty kingdom while his opulent lifestyle set a standard for royal living that other European kings tried to copy. In the high mountains that God created in Tibet, the fifth Dalai Lama, leader of the Tibetan Buddhist religion, had the grand Potala Palace constructed in the capital city of Lhasa. Architect Christopher Wren helped to rebuild the city of London, England, after its Great Fire of 1666.

The Dutch Golden Age

Lesson 106   Our World Story

Nations rise and fall in their power and influence in the world. The small country of the Netherlands was once a major political and economic power in Europe, and its people have had **significant** impact in many places.

The Netherlands

The word Netherlands means low lands. Much of the land of the country is near or below sea level. The Netherlands, Belgium, and Luxembourg are often called the Low Countries. The Netherlands is also called Holland. As seen in the map at right, Holland is actually only one province. The capital city, Amsterdam, is located in the Holland province. A common name for the people and language of the Netherlands is Dutch. This word is related to the term that Germans use for themselves and their language: Deutsche.

German tribes lived in the area we now know as the Netherlands before the Romans came. The Rhine River, pictured at right, runs through the Netherlands. The area south of the Rhine was part of the Roman Empire until about 300 AD.

Frankish and Saxon tribes moved there in the 400s. Charlemagne later made it part of his empire. Even later the area became one of the independent states in the Holy Roman

Rhine River in the Netherlands

Empire. The Netherlands became part of the Habsburg Empire through royal marriages and other political arrangements. First, the Habsburg monarch of Austria ruled the Netherlands, and later the Habsburg Spanish king ruled there.

The Eighty Years War

After the Protestant Reformation began, many Dutch became Protestants. This displeased the Catholic Habsburgs. In 1568 the Dutch people rebelled against Spain. This began the Eighty Years War between the Netherlands and Spain. The seven northern provinces of the Netherlands declared their independence in 1588 and became the Republic of the Netherlands. Spain only recognized their independence in 1648 in the Peace of Westphalia, which ended both the Eighty Years War and the Thirty Years War we discussed in Lesson 104. The southern provinces remained loyal to the Habsburgs. The southern provinces were first called the Spanish Netherlands, as seen on the map on page 717. Later, when Austria took them over, they were called the Austrian Netherlands. The Austrian Netherlands became most of the modern country of Belgium.

The 1600s

The high point of Dutch wealth, accomplishment, and influence was during the 1600s. This period is often called the Dutch Golden Age.

Several factors contributed to the accomplishments of this period. The Dutch had shown themselves to be a hardworking people in many ways, most notably in how they carved out their country. Because much of the Netherlands is close to the sea and below sea level, the "low lands" on which they lived were wet and marshy. The Dutch reclaimed the land by pumping water out and building **dikes** and canals, such as those pictured at left, to contain the ocean waters. Their land became some of the most fertile farmland in Europe.

In addition, the Dutch republic believed in political and economic freedom. Therefore, they encouraged trade, industry, craft and textile production, and creation of art. Many people went to the republic as refugees to escape war in other parts of Europe. Protestants also went there to practice their faith in freedom. When these immigrants arrived, they used their talents to support themselves and in so doing they contributed to the wealth of the country.

This aerial view shows the protective dike and green fields of Ameland Frisian Island in the North Sea.

A Dutch Canal

Top Left: Tulips in the Netherlands; Right: Windmill in Zeddam, Netherlands
Left: This girl in traditional Dutch folk costume and wooden shoes is at the Goudse Kaasmarkt, a Gouda cheese market which has been in operation for more than three hundred years.

Two symbols of the Netherlands are windmills and tulips. Windmills were built to pump water and to grind grain. The Zeddam windmill pictured above was constructed sometime before 1454. The famous Dutch tulip industry began in the late 1500s when a **horticulturist** brought to the Netherlands bulbs of the tulip, a flower which had originated in Turkey. By the early 1600s, people were already buying and selling Dutch tulips. The Dutch were also wearing wooden shoes by this time.

Dutch Sea Power

The Netherlands are located in a strategic position for trade. In northern Europe, on the coast of the North Sea, where the Rhine River enters the sea from its course through Germany, the Netherlands became a center for fishing as well as for trade going in all directions. Dutch shipbuilders constructed merchant ships that were larger than those built elsewhere so that they could transport more goods. See photos at right.

The Netherlands became a leading sea power during the 1600s. The number of Dutch merchant ships tripled between 1600 and 1650. At one point Dutch ships carried about half of the goods that European merchants shipped. Banks based in the Netherlands grew. Amsterdam became one of Europe's leading business centers.

Reproduction of the 1600s Dutch Ship Indiaman *and the Reproduction of a Ship's Hold at the National Maritime Museum*

Dutch Colonies and Settlements

Dutch traders and adventurers established colonies in Ceylon, Indonesia, the Caribbean Islands, South America, and South Africa. Jan Van Riebeeck founded the first European colony in South Africa when he established a Dutch settlement at what is now Cape Town. Van Riebeeck had begun working with the Dutch East India Company when he was twenty years old. He worked in Japan, Indonesia, and Indochina. As he returned from one trip to the Far East, his ship stopped at the Cape of Good Hope in South Africa, seen on the map on page 630. After spending eighteen days there, Van Riebeeck decided that the Dutch could grow fresh produce on the cape and supply crews of passing ships. Van Riebeeck and his wife arrived in South Africa in 1652, where for ten years he led the first Dutch settlement on the cape. He oversaw planting crops, building a fort, and trading cattle with natives. From this base, some Dutch families left the Dutch East India Company and established farms in South Africa. They were called *free burghers* (which means citizens) or *Boers* (which means farmers).

Delft Blue Tile, 1600s

Art and Architecture

Painting flourished in the Netherlands during the 1600s. Dutch artists had a strong art tradition in their own country, and they also learned from Flemish (Belgian) and Italian artists. Unlike Renaissance artists, Dutch artists did not receive their main financial support from a royal family (since the country had no king) or from aristocratic families. Since it was a Protestant country, the Catholic Church did not support them. The Dutch Reformed Church did not support artists either, because it opposed the use of images in their buildings. Instead, middle-class merchants supported Dutch artists. These merchants with successful businesses could commission and purchase paintings that reflected the life they knew in the Netherlands and the settings around them.

Some of the greatest artists in history worked during this period. Frans Hals was a leading portrait painter, painting both individuals and large groups of soldiers and businessmen. Jan Vermeer and Pieter de Hooch were known for their indoor scenes. Jacob van Ruisdael's specialty was landscapes that featured the fields and canals, clouds and sunlight of the Netherlands. Paintings by these four artists are pictured at right.

The greatest of the Dutch masters was Rembrandt Harmenszoon van Rijn, usually called Rembrandt. He was a brilliant artist who captured and effectively portrayed what he saw around him. He used dark colors and shadows to emphasize the inner persons of the people in his works, which he revealed in their facial expressions and body language. Rembrandt painted portraits, landscapes, scenes from everyday life and from history, and some 100 self-portraits. One of his best known works is *The Night Watch*, which presents the Amsterdam militia assembling on a mission. In his later career he produced paintings of many Biblical scenes and stories. One favorite is *The Return of the Prodigal Son*, seen at right. Popular and respected during his lifetime, Rembrandt attracted many students who wanted to learn his techniques. Rembrandt was **prolific**. Art scholars estimate that he produced between 2,000 and 3,000 paintings, prints, and drawings. The exact number is uncertain, because art scholars are not sure whether or not some works attributed to Rembrandt were actually produced by his students.

Lesson 106 - The Dutch Golden Age

Art of the Dutch Masters

Top Row: 1999 Dutch Stamp with View of Haarlem *by Jacob van Ruisdael; 1982 French Stamp with* The Lacemaker *by Jan Vermeer; Bottom Row: Reproduction of* Storeroom *by Pieter de Hooch from an Illustrated Encyclopedia of Art Galleries in Europe, Published in Russia, 1901; 1971 Union of Soviet Socialist Republics (U.S.S.R.) Stamp with* Portrait of a Young Man with a Glove *by Frans Hals; 1970 U.S.S.R. Stamp with* The Return of the Prodigal Son *by Rembrandt*

Dutch architects produced many beautiful buildings. The Dutch also created beautiful **ceramic** pieces at Delft and other Dutch cities. See examples on pages 715 and 720.

The End of the Dutch Golden Age

Between 1652 and 1674, England fought a series of wars with the Dutch because the English wanted to take the lead in international shipping and trading. Though they failed to defeat the Dutch at this time, the wars drained money from the Dutch economy. Resources that had formerly gone to building business endeavors had to be spent on equipment and supplies needed to fight the wars. In addition, other nations grew in their business activities and competed with the Dutch in trade. In the 1700s the Dutch became a less powerful nation.

Rembrandt studied the Bible and based about a third of his paintings on Scripture. In *The Raising of the Cross*, he portrayed himself in an artist's beret as one of the men raising the crucified Jesus into position. Rembrandt knew that his sins and the sins of others had placed Jesus on the cross.

He Himself bore our sins in His body on the cross, so that we might die to sin and live to righteousness; for by His wounds you were healed.
1 Peter 2:24

1960 New Zealand Christmas Stamp with Adoration of the Shepherds *by Rembrandt*

Assignments for Lesson 106

Timeline Book — In the box for Lesson 106 on page 24, write "Vietnamese and Cambodians resist the Dutch."

Student Workbook or Lesson Review — If you are using one of these optional books, complete the assignment for Lesson 106.

Vocabulary — Copy the list of vocabulary words, then write the correct definition beside each word: significant (717), dike (718), horticulturist (719), prolific (720), ceramic (721)
  a. a scientist in the field of growing flowers, fruits, and vegetables
  b. producing a large amount
  c. a bank built to control water
  d. a product made of clay that has been hardened by heating
  e. important; noticeable

Creative Writing — Write one paragraph describing one of the paintings in this lesson.

Literature — Read the foreword and chapters I and II in *Madeleine Takes Command*.

The Mughal Empire

Lesson 107 — Daily Life

Hinduism is a religion that began to develop in India centuries before Christ. It has no single authority or book, and groups within Hinduism hold many different doctrines on such subjects as deities, life after death, and how to live.

The main activities of Hinduism involve worship at a shrine in the home, although Hindu temples do exist. Part of Hindu teaching involves the recognition of social castes or classes, and the belief that people are not supposed to change out of the caste into which they were born.

Most people in India around 1500 believed in Hinduism and accepted their position in life, although some Muslims lived there also. This worldview and lifestyle encountered a huge change when the Muslim Mughal Dynasty began to rule most of India and nearby areas starting in 1526.

The Mughal (sometimes called Mogul) Empire dominated India during the 1500s and 1600s. Only the southern tip of India and the island of Ceylon were outside of the empire. Daily life in the empire became a blend of Persian and Indian cultures.

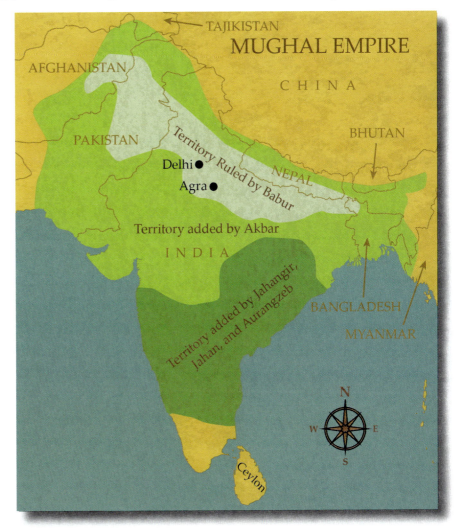

Early Mughal Rulers

Zahiruddin Muhammad claimed to be descended from Timur (or Tamerlane, mentioned on page 563) and Genghis Khan (see Lesson 74). He succeeded his father on the throne of Farghana in Turkestan, Central Asia. He was twelve years old and became known as Babur. When older relatives who did not want him to rule them deposed Babur, he fled the country. He first moved to Afghanistan and then went to India. He later captured the area around Delhi in 1526. There Babur founded the Mughal Kingdom, which he ruled until 1530. See map on page 723. The name *Mughal* or *Mogul* is a corruption of the word Mongol. The local residents did not know what to expect at first, but Babur allowed Hinduism to continue and even permitted the construction of new Hindu temples. See painting of Babur in a battle at right.

Babur's son, Humayun, ruled in his father's place until 1540. Humayun was a poor leader who lost control of his kingdom to rebels from Afghanistan. Humayun regained power in 1555, but he died the next year. See his tomb below.

Akbar, son of Humayun, became an able leader. He became ruler when he was thirteen and reigned for forty-nine years. Akbar recaptured much of his grandfather's empire that Humayun had lost. He brought under his control the areas that are now northern and central India, Pakistan, Nepal, and Bangladesh, plus portions of Tajikistan, Afghanistan, China, Bhutan, and Myanmar.

Akbar brought stability to the realm. He established the structure of government that remained in place for the duration of the Mughal Dynasty. Akbar combined smaller kingdoms

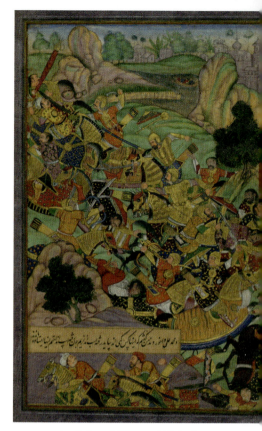

An Ink and Pigment Painting of Babur Confronting His Enemies, c. 1500s

Left: Tomb of Humayun, New Delhi, India; Above: Tomb of Akbar, Agra, India

In this manuscript, an old Sufi (a follower of a particular branch of Islam from that time period) laments his lost youth. The ink and pigment illustration portrays a typical formal garden from the time of Akbar, 1597-1598.

and made the central government much stronger (see map on page 723). At the same time, he named governors for the provinces and depended on them to rule those areas effectively under the authority of the central government. Akbar was also tolerant of religions other than Islam. He employed Hindus in his government and ended the tax that his predecessors had imposed on non-Muslims. This was a popular move among Hindus and others.

Akbar oversaw great building projects and commissioned many illustrated manuscripts. The manuscript at left was created during his reign. Akbar came to be called Akbar the Great. His tomb is pictured on page 724.

Akbar's son Jahangir, whose portrait is below, ruled from 1605 until 1627. He began a huge building program, which included many palaces, monuments, and gardens. Jahangir especially appreciated Persian culture. His rule promoted the use of the Urdu language as the official language of the empire. Urdu blended the cultures in the kingdom by using Arabic and Persian script and vocabulary with Sanskrit (ancient Indian) grammatical structure. Jahangir also continued to commission illustrated manuscripts, including an illustrated history of his reign.

Notice the illustrations of daily life in the Mughal art on pages 726 and 727. Among them, a prince and two companions play musical instruments, a superior and his attendant ride on a white elephant, and a prince takes part in falconry.

Archers in this period used thumb rings, and people also wore archer's thumb rings as decorative jewelry. People made beautiful, useful items such as mirrors. Artisans created objects from a variety of materials: silk textiles, ivory and jade thumb rings, and gold coins.

Notice the portrait of a ram. This piece was created during the reign of Jahangir, who encouraged artists to paint studies of plants and animals.

Drawing of Emperor Jahangir, by Manohar and Abu'l Hasan, 1620-1625

Art of the Mughal Empire

Left Column: *The Musical Mode, c. 1700; Two Young Men Riding a White Elephant, 1600s*

Right Column: *Portrait of a Ram, 1625-1650; Prince with a Falcon, c. 1600-1605*

Art of the Mughal Empire

Top Left and Center: Archer's Thumb Rings. The left ring is made of walrus ivory, the right ring of nephrite jade, gold, and gems. The center ring was probably only decorative. Right: Leaf-Shaped Mirror Made of Nephrite Jade and Rock Crystal with Traces of Gilding, c. 1675-1700; Second Row: Gold Mohur (Coin) of Akbar, 1556-1605; Gold Mohur of Jahan, 1628-1658; Left: Textile Panel Made of Cut Silk Velvet

The Taj Mahal

Jahan became the fifth Mughal emperor and ruled until 1658. Like his grandfather Akbar and his father Jahangir, Jahan was a patron of architecture and the arts. When his favorite wife, Mumtaz, died in 1629, Jahan decided to build a tomb for her in Agra in northern India. He wanted the tomb to be a tremendous monument to her and to their love.

The tomb, which we know as the Taj Mahal (which means "Crown of Palaces"), took twenty years to build and employed 20,000 workers. Jahan used an architect and also craftsmen from other parts of the world. He chose to build the monument of white marble on a base of red sandstone. The building sits in a beautiful garden and is 186 feet square. The central dome is seventy feet in diameter and rises 120 feet in height. The structure has elaborate carvings and monuments in and around it. Mumtaz and Jahan both are buried in its vault. Jahan also built the Great Mosque of Delhi and other large public structures.

The Reign of Aurangzeb

The son of Jahan, Aurangzeb, seized the throne from his father in 1658. An aggressive leader, Aurangzeb tried to expand the empire while fighting rebellions within it at the same time. Aurangzeb was strongly pro-Islam. He enforced Muslim Sharia law. Aurangzeb invaded Hindu regions in central and southern India. He conquered a great deal of territory and captured many people and made them slaves.

Aurangzeb excluded Hindus from serving in the government, reestablished a tax on non-Muslims, and destroyed many Hindu temples and schools. Aurangzeb persecuted the Sikh ethnic group. As a result of his

Taj Mahal, Agra, India

policies, the Sikhs rebelled against him, as did Hindu warriors called Marathas in western India. Landowners, called Rajputs, in what became central and northern India and eastern Pakistan, also rebelled.

The actions of Aurangzeb weakened the unity of the empire. Soon after he died in 1707, the empire began to break up. The Mughals continued to reign, but the area they controlled shrank.

Daily life in the Mughal Empire saw many changes over its years of existence, including the change from acceptance of religious diversity to rejection of such diversity, changes in language, and changes in the outlook of the ruler, which affected whether people could live in peace or had to live in uncertainty and oppression.

Lesson 107 - The Mughal Empire

The poor man and the oppressor have this in common:
The Lord gives light to the eyes of both.
Proverbs 29:13

Assignments for Lesson 107

Our Creative World — Read "The Tiger, the Brâhman, and the Jackal" on pages 86-87.

Map Book — Complete the assignments for Lesson 107 on Map 33 "Mughal Empire."

Timeline Book — In the box for Lesson 107 on page 24, write "The Taj Mahal is completed."

Student Workbook or Lesson Review — If you are using one of these optional books, complete the assignment for Lesson 107.

Thinking Biblically — Write one paragraph answering this question: What happens when people try to force others to follow a certain religion?

Literature — Read chapters III and IV in *Madeleine Takes Command*.

Left: Emperor Aurangzeb Portrait, c. 1752; Right: Emperor Aurangzeb Carried on a Palanquin, c. 1775

Louis XIV of France

Lesson 108 — World Biography

Louis XIV, king of France, set the standard for royal power in Europe in the 1600s. He increased the authority of the French monarchy and involved his country in greater international trade, numerous European wars, and far-reaching colonial settlement. During his reign France became the most powerful nation in Europe.

Background: Louis XIII and Cardinal Richelieu

The monarchy of France had been growing stronger for some time before Huguenots and nobles threatened its authority and stability in the 1500s and early 1600s. As the Reformation spread into France, most French Protestants aligned themselves with the teachings of John Calvin. They were called Huguenots after the Swiss reformer Besançon Hugues. As the Huguenots increased in number in France, the Catholic monarchy grew harsher in its persecution in an effort to stamp them out. Finally, in 1598 French King Henry IV issued the Edict of Nantes, illustrated below. It gave Protestants the right to worship freely and to build church buildings in certain specific areas of the country (though not in Paris).

1969 French Stamp of Henry IV and the Edict of Nantes; 1974 French Stamp of Cardinal Richelieu

French nobles also threatened the king of France when they expressed a desire to share in the decision-making authority of government. France did not have a representative assembly to make laws. However, it did have an institution called the Estates-General, a body of representatives of the clergy, the nobility, and the general public, which made recommendations to the king. The assembly only met when the king called it into session. Louis XIII became king of France in 1610 when he was eight years old. In 1614 Louis called for the Estates-General to meet, but he quickly dismissed them when he (and his advisers who were really running the country) didn't like the proposals the assembly made.

Catholic Cardinal Richelieu, pictured at left, was the real power during the reign of Louis XIII. Richelieu took several steps to increase the authority of the French king. Cardinal Richelieu again limited the rights of Huguenots. He also took several steps to limit the power of nobles. Richelieu encouraged international trade to bring in more wealth to the king. He also let newly-rich merchants buy titles of nobility, which meant that the king would have nobles who were loyal to him. Richelieu died in 1642. His successor was Cardinal Mazarin.

The Sun King

Louis XIII died in 1643, when his son, also named Louis, was only four years old. The child's mother served as regent until the young man became an adult. Cardinal Mazarin helped to guide the government.

When Mazarin died in 1661, Louis XIV surprised France and the rest of Europe when he declared that he would rule without a prime minister and make all decisions himself.

Louis XIV never doubted his own ability and importance. He chose the sun as the symbol for his monarchy and so became known as the Sun King. In his mind, he was as important to France as the sun is to the world. Expressing his belief in his importance to the French government, he reportedly once said, "L'etat, c'est moi" ("The state, it is me"). He believed that his authority as king came from God and therefore no one was to question his decisions. Louis increased the size of the army, in part to defend against an attack by another country but also to maintain order should any rebellion arise within France.

Though Louis did not have a prime minister, he did appoint Jean Baptiste Colbert to serve as his finance minister. Colbert increased taxes and appointed agents throughout the country to collect those taxes. However, the nobles, the clergy, and some businessmen did not have to pay taxes. The merchants and workers, who did have to pay them, resented the increase.

The French government actively supported business activity under the approach known as mercantilism. European government officials had long helped private business, but they did this locally through organizations such as guilds or the Hanseatic League of cities. Under mercantilism, the national government encouraged and gave financial help to industry. Then the government taxed industries to make back some of the money it had given to them. The government encouraged foreign trade but also collected import tariffs. These tariffs helped industries within the country. Products from other countries were more expensive, because buyers had to pay both the price and the added tariff. The French government also financially supported people who founded foreign colonies.

Exploration in North America

We have discussed French colonies in previous lessons. Beginning in the 1660s, France became even more active in exploring and settling North America. Louis wanted French explorers to obtain furs and mineral ores from the New World to bring back to France. He also hoped they would find a northwest passage through North America to the Pacific Ocean and thus to China. Louis also wanted French colonists to take the gospel to Native Americans.

In 1668 French settlers founded Sault Sainte Marie in what would become Michigan. Five years later, French explorers

Top: 1986 Canadian Stamp of Joliet and Marquette; Bottom: 1968 U.S. Stamp of Joliet and Marquette

Louis Joliet and Jacques Marquette explored the Mississippi River from its origin to a point south of what became Memphis, Tennessee. In 1675, Marquette founded a mission at Kaskaskia in what would become Illinois. The stamps above from Canada and the United States commemorate their voyage.

In 1682 explorer Robert de La Salle led a group who built a fort near the site of Memphis. Soon thereafter they reached the mouth of the Mississippi River on the Gulf of Mexico. La Salle claimed the entire Mississippi River Valley for France and called it *Louisiane* (in English, Louisiana) in honor of Louis XIV. In 1718 the French founded the city of New Orleans.

1970 French Stamp with King Louis XIV and His Palace

The Arts and Versailles

Louis established academies for students to study painting, sculpture, architecture, science, music, and other disciplines in France. He also funded the Paris Observatory. The pinnacle of Louis' artistic endeavors was the building of the Palace of Versailles. He completely revamped a hunting lodge built by Louis XIII about twelve miles outside of Paris. The palace is a quarter-mile long and contains 1,300 rooms. Reconstruction began in 1661, took twenty-seven years, and required the labor of some 20,000 workers. The palace was built on 20,000 acres of cultivated grounds including 250 acres of gardens. The palace provided Louis and his court with

Lesson 108 - Louis XIV of France

the ultimate in luxury. It also got the king out of Paris, which was sometimes unstable. The royal residence at Versailles provided another way for the king to exercise control over the nobles. Louis made the nobles his personal officers, and many of them lived at Versailles. The elaborate palace was a model of luxury that other European monarchs tried to imitate, although none could match it. King Louis also led Europe in fashion. French culture became the standard that many other nations in Europe sought to follow.

Scenes from the Palace of Versailles

Above: Royal Chapel; Below: Symbol of the Sun King; Bottom Left; The Orangery; Bottom Right: Hall of Mirrors

Huguenot Refugees

As a Catholic monarch, Louis wanted to limit the influence of the Huguenots. He believed that they were a threat to the stability of the country as well as being in error theologically. In 1685 Louis repealed the Edict of Nantes. As a result, some 200,000 to 400,000 Huguenots fled the country and scattered to many places. Besides creating a hardship for many believers, Louis' move cost France the wealth and services of thousands of productive workers and craftsmen.

Huguenots in America and Germany

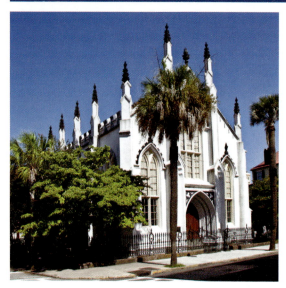 

*Left: Huguenot Church, Charleston, South Carolina;
Right: Huguenots and other Separatists lived near the Jerusalem gate in the old city wall of Buedingen, Germany.*

The Wars of Louis XIV

Louis led his armies into four major wars, which expanded the power of France in Europe but also cost the country dearly in terms of men and money.

The War of Devolution of 1667-1668. Although the kings of France and Spain were Catholic, they were of different families. The French king belonged to the Bourbon Dynasty, while the Spanish monarch was a member of the Habsburg family. France and Spain competed with each other for power and prominence in Europe and in the world during this time. In 1667 and 1668 France and Spain fought the War of Devolution over which country would control the Spanish Netherlands. Louis believed that the rule of the Spanish Netherlands had "devolved" onto his wife (and therefore himself) through royal intermarriages in Europe, instead of onto her half-brother, who was the king of Spain. As a result of the war, France gained some towns in the area of Flanders in the Spanish Netherlands.

The Third Anglo-Dutch War of 1672-1678. France became involved in one of the wars between England and the Netherlands. France entered the war on the side of England, even though the two countries were usually bitter rivals. France still wanted the Spanish Netherlands and

Lesson 108 - Louis XIV of France

invaded the Netherlands to take control of Dutch trade. Louis also wanted to punish the Dutch for opposing France during the War of Devolution. The British navy helped the French army. The Dutch were able to stop the French so that France only gained a small amount of territory.

The War of the Grand Alliance of 1689-1697. In the late 1600s, after Louis built up the French army and navy, England, Spain, the Netherlands, the Holy

Roman Empire, and the tiny country of Savoy on the French and Italian border joined forces to stop French aggression. This war focused on who would rule Spain and was another conflict between the French Bourbons and the Spanish Habsburgs. The war was inconclusive, but France did not gain power over Spain.

The War of Spanish Succession of 1701-1713. By 1701 Philip V, a grandson of Louis XIV, had become king of Spain. When other countries came together against France out of fear that a French-Spanish combination would become a European superpower ruled by a single monarch, French troops guarded the Spanish Netherlands in support of Philip's rule. The war dragged on for several years until the countries involved signed the Treaty of Utrecht in 1713. The treaty guaranteed that a single monarch would not rule the two countries.

The End of the Reign of Louis XIV

When the Peace of Westphalia ended the Thirty Years War in 1648, France was the leading power in Europe. However, the wars and extravagant building programs Louis undertook left France weaker and in poor financial shape when he died in 1715. In addition, Louis had not achieved his dreams of conquest.

One of Four Gates from the City of Brugge in Flanders

Louis reigned for a total of seventy-two years. Louis' great-grandson followed him as Louis XV. By the end of the 1700s, the French people were exasperated by the arrogance and greed of Louis XIV and his successors. This exasperation led to rebellion.

A king, and any person in a position of authority, has the opportunity to do great good or great harm. Such a person should use that position wisely and justly.

*The king's wrath
is like the roaring of a lion,
But his favor
is like dew on the grass.
Proverbs 19:12*

Statue of Louis XIV at Versailles Palace

Assignments for Lesson 108

Our Creative World — Read the excerpt from *The Voyage of François Leguat* on pages 88-89.

Timeline Book — In the first box for Lesson 108 (1682) on page 24, write "La Salle claims the Louisiana Territory for France." In the second box for Lesson 108 (1688), write "Huguenots seek freedom in South Africa."

Student Workbook or Lesson Review — If you are using one of these optional books, complete the assignment for Lesson 108.

Thinking Biblically — Copy Proverbs 19:12 onto a piece of paper and illustrate the verse. You may choose to illustrate the similes given in the verse or to illustrate the verse another way.

Creative Writing — If you were a monarch, what would you want your symbol to be (as Louis XIV's symbol was the sun)? Design the symbol on a piece of paper and write a paragraph below the design about what the symbol means.

Literature — Read chapters V and VI in *Madeleine Takes Command*.

God Created Tibet

Lesson 109 — God's Wonder

Because of its high elevation, Tibet has been called the Roof of the World. Tibet lies to the north of India, Nepal, Myanmar, and Bhutan, which are pictured at right. It is about the same size as South Africa, or about one-eighth the size of the United States. The Tibetan Plateau (mentioned on pages 88, 111, and 494) lies in central Tibet. It is the highest and largest plateau in the world. Most of the land that people are able to farm lies in the valleys in the eastern and southeastern parts of the country, where the plateau is below 12,000 feet. Most of the Tibetan people live in these valleys.

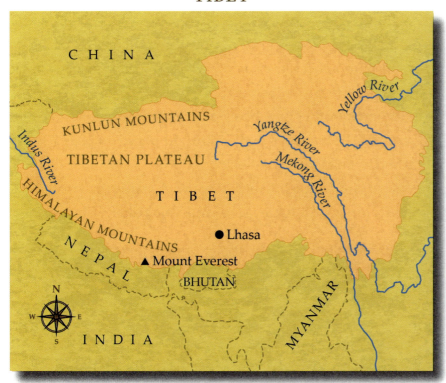

At Right from Top to Bottom: Tibet's Neighbors India, Nepal, Myanmar, Bhutan

Unit 22 - The Late 1600s

Top to Bottom: Tibetan Plateau; Kunlun Mountains; Mountain Village; Lake Namtso; Below: Views of Mount Everest (Center View is at Sunrise, Right View is at Sunset)

Though it has forests and **grasslands**, much of Tibet is covered with wastelands of gravel, rock, and sand. Many of its lakes and rivers have **barren** shores and a high salt content. The Kunlun Mountains, the highest peaks of which rise over 20,000 feet, are on the northern border. Along the southern border are the Himalayan Mountains, the tallest mountain range in the world. Among the Himalayas is Mount Everest, the tallest mountain in the world at 29,035 feet. These geographic features are pictured at left and below. The Himalayan range is the source of some of the great rivers of Asia, including the Indus, Mekong, Yangtze, and Yellow Rivers.

The Himalayas block the monsoon winds from the south, so Tibet only receives about ten inches of rainfall per year. However, blizzards and strong winds are common. The average January temperature is 24°, and the average July temperature is 58°.

Farming in Tibet

Only a small portion of the land of Tibet is suitable for raising crops, so Tibetan farmers concentrate on raising livestock, including camels, cattle, donkeys, goats, horses, sheep, and yaks (a hairy type of ox). The yak is particularly important to the traditional way of life in Tibet. It provides transportation and serves as a beast of **burden**. It gives milk and eventually provides meat. Tibetans use the hide of the yak for shoe leather and boats and its hair for cloth and tent coverings. The cowbells in the top right photo on page 739 are attached to belts made of yak wool.

The primary crop in Tibet is barley. A **staple** dish is tsampa, made from ground barley, tea, and yak butter. Tibetans also

Lesson 109 - God Created Tibet

eat animal products, including meat (yak, beef, and mutton) and dairy (milk **curd** and yogurt). They enjoy drinking sweet tea made with sugar and butter tea made with butter and salt. They often serve tsampa and butter tea together.

Yaks, Barley Farming, and Cooking Tsampa

Tibetan Wildlife

God has created over 5,000 different kinds of plants to live in Tibet. Several of Tibet's many species of wild animals are pictured below.

*Left Column: Clouded Leopard; Bar Headed Goose; Blue Sheep; Golden Takin; Tibetan Snow Cock;
Center Column: Yunan Snub-Nosed Monkey; Oriental Small-Clawed Otter; Malayan Sun Bear;
Right Column: Kiang; Himalayan Marmot; Himalayan Tahr; Tibetan Eared Pheasant; Pere David's Deer*

The Potala Palace

Most Tibetans are Buddhists. Lamaism is the particular kind of Buddhism that Tibetans practice. The spiritual leader of Lamaism is the Dalai Lama.

The Potala Palace, which is the traditional home of the Dalai Lama, is the highest ancient palace in the world. It is made of rammed earth, wood, and stone and sits 12,300 feet above sea level atop a high mountain in the capital city of Lhasa. King Songtsen Gampo, who founded the Tibetan Empire, built a palace on the site in the 600s. It later burned. The fifth Dalai Lama had a new structure built in the same location starting about 1645 to serve as his residence, the center of Lamaist religion, and the headquarters of Tibet's government (the Dalai Lama was at that time also head of the government).

The structure was built in phases until its completion in 1694. Construction took the efforts of 7,000 laborers and 1,500 artists and craftsmen. Its walls average about ten feet thick. The complex covers 32 acres. It houses almost 700 wall murals as well as statues and other works of art. To enter the palace a person must climb about 300 feet of steps, or the length of a football field.

Tibet and China

Tibet has historically been an independent country, but at various times throughout history China has taken it over. Tibet paid tribute to Genghis Khan in the 1200s. Then the Mongol Yuan Dynasty of China ruled it. Tibet later reclaimed its independence, but the Qing Dynasty of China, which began in 1644, asserted control of Tibet.

Top and Center: Views of Potala Palace; Bottom: These two women are circling the Potala Palace, believing it will bring them good luck.

The one true God loves the Tibetan people, though many do not know Him. The majestic mountains of their country are testimony to His power.

By awesome deeds You answer us in righteousness,
O God of our salvation,
You who are the trust of all the ends of the earth and of the farthest sea;
Who establishes the mountains by His strength,
Being girded with might;
Who stills the roaring of the seas,
The roaring of their waves,
And the tumult of the peoples.
Psalm 65:5-7

Assignments for Lesson 109

Our Creative World — Read the excerpt from *With the Tibetans in Tent and Temple* on pages 90-92.

Timeline Book — In the box for Lesson 109 on page 24, write "The Dalai Lama begins building the Potala Palace."

Student Workbook or Lesson Review — If you are using one of these optional books, complete the assignment for Lesson 109.

Vocabulary — Write a paragraph that uses all of these words: grassland (738), barren (738), burden (738), staple (738), curd (739). Consult a dictionary if you need help with their definitions.

Literature — Read chapters VII and VIII in *Madeleine Takes Command*.

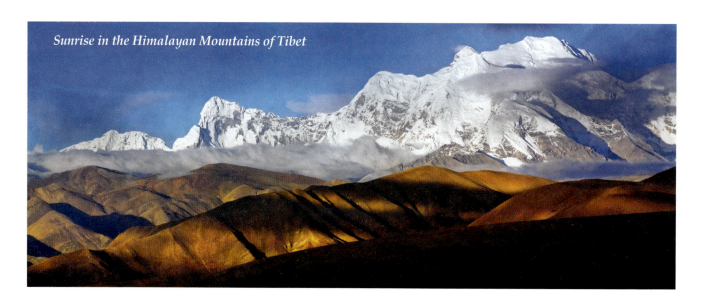
Sunrise in the Himalayan Mountains of Tibet

London, England

Lesson 110 — World Landmark

During the 1600s, London, England, experienced two political revolutions, a plague, and a devastating fire that almost destroyed the entire city. London recovered, however, and became a larger, busier, and more important city than before.

History of London

When the Romans occupied Britain, they built an army camp along the Thames River in the approximate location of the future City of Westminster, just west of London. They also built a trading post to the east of the camp and called it Londinium. By 250 the Romans had built a protective wall around Londinium. This wall defined the city for centuries. See ruins below.

After Roman troops left Britain in the early 400s, the city (which later came to be called London) declined, and many people moved away. After the Angles, Saxons, and Jutes began to invade the island, the Saxons built a new city they called Lundenwic outside of the walls of London. When Alfred the Great united the Saxons, he reestablished London within the walls, and the people abandoned Lundenwic.

King Ethelbert of Kent had a wooden cathedral built in London in 604 to honor the apostle Paul and Mellitus, the first bishop of East Saxon. This structure, called St. Paul's Cathedral, burned a few years later. Workers built a replacement from 675 to 685. Vikings burned this second church. A third cathedral burned in 1087 and a fourth in the Great Fire of London, discussed later in this lesson.

Ruins of Roman Wall in London

In the mid-1000s, King Edward III (called the Confessor) built a palace and church on the Thames west of London, near the site of the Roman camp. This "west minster" (so called to distinguish it from St. Paul's, the east minster) was the start of Westminster Abbey and the town of Westminster. The palace of Westminster became the **seat** of English government. William the Conqueror was crowned king of England there in 1066. Construction of the current church, pictured below, began in 1245 during the reign of King Henry III.

Left: Westminster Abbey and Choir School; Right: View of London Bridge *by Claude de Jongh, c. 1632*

William the Conqueror built a castle just outside the walls of the city. Today it is known as the Tower of London. It is pictured on page 643. The first stone bridge to **span** the Thames was London Bridge, completed in 1209. It replaced a wooden bridge, which the Romans had first built and which had been replaced several times. Notice the painting of London Bridge above.

In the 1500s and early 1600s, London was a busy, growing city. The king built palaces in and to the west of London. Wealthy merchants also built large homes outside of the city walls. Drama companies built theaters such as the Globe on the south side of the Thames because the city forbade them within the walls. London became a world trading center during the reign of Queen Elizabeth I. By the mid-1600s, London's population was an estimated half-million people, most of whom lived outside the walls. The cities of London and Westminster grew together to become one **metropolis**.

Oliver Cromwell and the English Civil War

In the early 1600s, conflict grew between the king, who claimed absolute power, and Parliament, the elected body of representatives whose members wanted more power in government. The king was a traditional Anglican (Church of England), while Parliament had a majority of Puritans, who wanted to purify the Church of England. The conflict between the king and Parliament erupted into civil war in 1642. King Charles I and his army opposed a Puritan force led by Oliver Cromwell, a member of Parliament.

Cromwell Statue at Westminster

Lesson 110 - London, England

The Puritans defeated the king's army. Charles I was captured, tried, and executed in 1649. Charles' son, also named Charles, fled the country to France. Parliament abolished the monarchy and created a republic with Cromwell in an office called Lord Protector. Cromwell died in 1658, and his son then ruled for a short time. However, the Puritan government was unpopular with the people, so in 1660 Parliament invited Charles II, son of the executed Charles I, to return from exile in France and resume the Stuart Dynasty. We will return to this political story later in this lesson.

1992 United Kingdom Stamp, 350th Anniversary of the English Civil War

English Civil War Reenactors

Trouble in London

By the 1660s London was crowded. Its buildings were unsafe. Most of the structures stood close together and were built of wood and pitch with thatch roofs. Streets were very narrow. Warehouses near the docks held combustible items that merchants traded, such as oil, rope, and candle tallow. Observers had warned of the danger of fire for many years. A blaze in 1633 destroyed part of London Bridge and a small section of the city.

Then in 1665 the Black Plague struck the city. Tens of thousands of people died in the crowded and **unsanitary** conditions. The worst of the plague passed by mid-1666.

The Great Fire

The summer of 1666 was hot and dry. On Sunday, September 2, a fire started in the home of the royal baker, Thomas Farynor, who lived in Pudding Lane. The baker's family escaped by crawling out of a window and crossing neighboring roofs to safety. The fire spread to surrounding buildings. A strong east wind was blowing, and fire rapidly **engulfed** more and more of the city. London had no organized fire department, and the efforts of volunteers using leather buckets did little good. When the mayor of London first heard about the fire, he doubted that it was a real problem and delayed taking action.

Thousands of people fled London, either on land or by boat on the River Thames. Smoke was visible in Oxford, about sixty miles away. Londoners tore down buildings that were not on fire, hoping the blaze would not jump over the gaps they created. These fire breaks proved an effective way to help stop the spread of the fire.

The Monument: Great Fire of London, 1666, Designed by Christopher Wren

By the following Thursday the fire was under control. Approximately eighty percent of the city had been destroyed, including St. Paul's Cathedral, about 84 other church buildings, and 44 guild halls. The lead roof of St. Paul's melted and ran into the street. Thirteen thousand homes were lost. London Bridge was about one-third destroyed. Amazingly, fewer than twenty people died in the fire. However, about 100,000 were left homeless. Many who left the city never returned to live there again.

Rebuilding London

Sir Christopher Wren, a mathematician, scientist, and architect, received the commission to rebuild St. Paul's. He also designed or helped with the reconstruction of about 55 other churches and several other buildings. A man of great faith, Wren closely guided the reconstruction of St. Paul's. This process took thirty-five years, from 1675 until 1710.

The new St. Paul's is in the baroque style of architecture, which has intricate and elaborate features. The cathedral also has elements of classical Greek and Roman styles. Two elaborate towers stand above the main entrance. The cathedral features a dome that rises to 365 feet above the ground. Eight arches support the dome. Mosaics and fresco paintings decorate the interior of the dome. A wall that slopes inward supports the inner shell of the dome. This wall

St. Paul's Cathedral, London

creates a "whispering gallery," which means that a listener on one side of the gallery can hear a whisperer on the other side of the gallery almost 138 feet away. Flying buttresses that extend outside the building support low domes over interior spaces. These buttresses are similar to the flying buttresses of medieval Gothic cathedrals. The interior of the cathedral is made of light-colored limestone and marble and has many gold elements and works of art. The effect is a much brighter interior than those found in medieval cathedrals.

Sir Christopher Wren is buried beneath the floor of the cathedral. His epitaph on the floor under the dome says in Latin, "Beneath lies buried the founder of this church and city Christopher Wren, who lived more than ninety years not for himself but for the public good. Reader, if you seek his monument, look around you."

Rebuilding the city of London took about fifty years. A new tax on coal helped to pay for the work. Some 9,000 homes were rebuilt. New laws required that buildings have brick or stone exteriors. Citizens organized firefighting departments and made other improvements in city life. The tradition developed that no building in London was to be taller than the dome of St. Paul's. This tradition continued for almost 250 years, until 1962.

The Glorious Revolution

While Londoners were rebuilding after the fire, another royal revolution took place. Charles II was secretly a Catholic who wanted to restore the Catholic Church as the state religion of England. He died in 1685 before he was able to fulfill his plans. Charles' brother, James II, inherited the throne when Charles died.

James II was openly Catholic, but his daughter Mary of the Netherlands, pictured at right, was a Protestant. The English expected Mary to succeed her father, so they tolerated James' rule. However, in 1688 James' wife gave birth to a son, a male heir to the throne, whom James had christened in the Catholic Church.

It appeared that the predominately Protestant people of England would continue to have a Catholic monarch. Parliament invited Mary's husband, the Protestant William of Orange of the Netherlands, along with Mary, to invade England with an army. James II fled the country rather than force a confrontation, and Parliament offered the throne to William and Mary. Parliament passed a Bill of Rights in 1689 limiting

2010 United Kingdom Stamp wth Portrait of Mary

the powers of the monarch and guaranteeing certain individual liberties for British citizens. This change is called the Glorious or Bloodless Revolution. It is significant because no battles took place to bring about this revolution and because the monarch now ruled with Parliament's permission instead of Parliament needing the king's permission to meet. In 1701 Parliament passed a law forbidding a Catholic from holding the throne of Britain.

For centuries believers have praised God in St. Paul's Cathedral in London.

Silver Coin Depicting William of Orange, 1695

But let all who take refuge in You be glad, let them ever sing for joy;
And may You shelter them,
That those who love Your name may exult in You.
Psalm 5:11

Assignments for Lesson 110

Our Creative World — Read the excerpt from *The Diary of Samuel Pepys* on pages 93-94.

Timeline Book — In the box for Lesson 110 on page 24, write "A large fire consumes much of London."

Student Workbook or Lesson Review — If you are using one of these optional books, complete the assignment for Lesson 110 and take the test for Unit 22.

Thinking Biblically — Sir Christopher Wren used his talents for the glory of God and to help others. Write one or two paragraphs about someone you know who uses his or her talents for the glory of God and to help others.

Vocabulary — Copy the following sentences, placing the correct vocabulary word in the blank: seat (744), span (744), metropolis (744), unsanitary (746), engulf (746)
1. Flood waters sometimes _____ the roads near the river.
2. Sao Paulo is a sprawling _____ in Brazil.
3. Cape Town is the _____ of South Africa's parliament.
4. The time period covered in the museum's new exhibit will _____ native tribes to modern cities.
5. The spread of disease can often be blamed on _____ practices or conditions.

Literature — Read chapters IX and X in *Madeleine Takes Command*.

Family Activity — Make and play the "Let's Go To London Game." Instructions begin on page FA-45.

23 The Early 1700s

Sunrise at Ahu Tongariki on Easter Island, Chile

Lessons
111 - God's Wonder: God Created the Island of Mauritius
112 - Our World Story: The Reign of Peter the Great of Russia
113 - World Biography: Johann Sebastian Bach
114 - World Landmark: Easter Island
115 - Daily Life: The Moravians

Literature *Madeleine Takes Command*

1701-1750

In the early 1700s, first the Dutch and later the French built colonies on the island of Mauritius, five hundred miles east of the African island of Madagascar. When the century began, Peter the Great was bringing European culture into Russia. In 1703 he established St. Petersburg as the new capital city, naming it for the apostle Peter. In Germany Johann Sebastian Bach was composing music to the glory of God. In 1722 Dutch sailors came upon Easter Island far off the coast of South America in the Pacific Ocean and were amazed at the hundreds of giant statues the Rapanui people had created there. In Germany Pietists such as the Moravians were trying to live pious lives that honored God. They began to share the gospel with people in various places in the Old and New Worlds.

God Created the Island of Mauritius

Lesson 111 — God's Wonder

Mauritius Coastline Along the Indian Ocean

God placed the three Mascarene Islands in the Indian Ocean five hundred miles east of the African island of Madagascar and 2,450 miles southwest of India. The Mascarenes include the island of Réunion, which is governed by France, and the islands of Mauritius and Rodrigues, which are both part of the tiny nation of Mauritius. The distance between the islands of Mauritius and Réunion is 140 miles. The much smaller Rodrigues is almost 384 miles from Mauritius. The islands of Mauritius and Réunion combined are less than two-thirds the size of the state of Rhode Island.

Coral reefs surround the Mauritius coastline on all sides except the south. See a section of the Mauritius coast above and a coral reef scene at right.

Much of the beautiful rainforest of Mauritius lies in Black River Gorges National Park in the southwestern part of the island. Nearby is Valley of the Colors Nature

Coral Reef off Mauritius

Park. Within the park are beautiful waterfalls and an area of dunes made of red, brown, yellow, green, blue, purple, and violet sand. See photos below.

At Left and Below: Waterfalls in Southwestern Mauritius
Above: Black River Gorges National Park;
Bottom Row: Two Views of Sand Dunes in Valley of the Colors Nature Park

Lesson 111 - God Created the Island of Mauritius

The maps of Mauritius at lower right show both the island and its location in relation to Africa. The island is warm all year. The average summer temperature is 79 degrees, and the average temperature in winter is 72 degrees. The island's central plateau receives up to 200 inches of rainfall each year.

Mauritius is home to an amazing diversity of plants and animals. Ebony trees with their hard and dense wood grow there, as do ferns and wild orchids.

Many endemic species live on the island. An endemic species is a species that lives only in a certain region. The ornate day gecko, pictured at right, is a reptile endemic to Mauritius.

As far as we know, the island of Mauritius was uninhabited before the late 1500s. Sometimes endemic species are threatened when people bring in new plants or animals. This happened in Mauritius. The island was once the home of the dodo, a large member of the pigeon family that did not fly and was about the size of a wild turkey. Early residents killed dodos for food and sport, and animals they brought in were enemies of the bird. The dodo became extinct about 1681. See an illustration of the dodo below.

Ornate Day Gecko

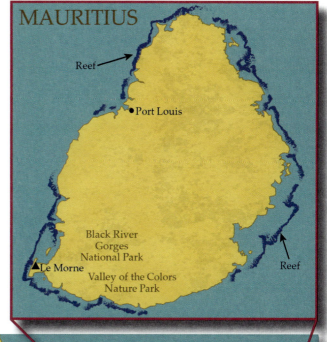

1974 Cuban Stamp with Dodo

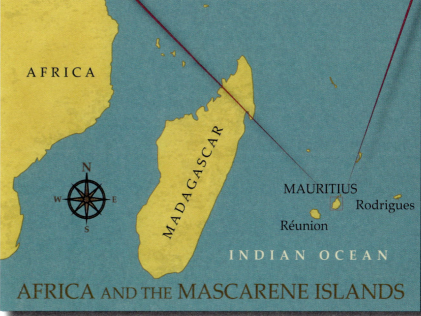

Flying Creatures of Mauritius

Endemic Creatures on Top Row: Cuckoo Shrike; Mauritius Parakeet, Pink Pigeon

Left Column: Utetheisa Cruentata Moth, Whimbrel, Ruddy Turnstone, Common Waxbill; Second Column: Baby White-tailed Tropicbird, Plains Cupid Butterflies, Violet Dropwing Dragonfly, Common Moorhen; Third Column: Red-whiskered Bulbul, Madagascar Fody, Malagasy Grass Yellow Butterflies; Right Column: Mauritian Flying Fox (Endemic), Black Percher Dragonfly, Striated Heron

Lesson 111 - God Created the Island of Mauritius

History

Arab sailors visited the island of Mauritius as early as the 900s, as did sailors from the Malay Peninsula and the African Swahili tribe. Mauritius was unknown to European explorers when the Portuguese came upon it in 1498. They began using the island, which

Mauritian Sugar Plantations

they called Cirné, as a port of call, but they did not establish permanent settlements there.

Mauritius remained uninhabited until the Netherlands claimed it as a territory in 1598 and established a colony there in 1638. The Dutch renamed it for Prince Maurice of Nassau (a region in the Netherlands). Maurice later became ruler of the Netherlands.

Dutch colonists started sugar plantations on Mauritius (see photo above). They brought African slaves to the island to cut forests and to work on these plantations. However, the Dutch were not able to make a profit from their efforts, so they abandoned the island in 1710. After that, pirates lived there.

French explorers claimed the island in 1715 and named it Ile de France (Island of France). French colonists settled there in 1721 and once more brought in slaves to work. The French governor founded the city of Port Louis in 1736. He named the city for King Louis XV of France. See French cannon below.

Mauritius became an important stop in the trade routes that passed through the Indian Ocean. Because of the island's history, modern residents are descendants of European settlers, African slaves, Chinese traders, and Asian Indian laborers and traders. About two-thirds of the population is considered Indian, one-fourth is called Creole (European-African or European-Indian), and the rest are either Chinese or European. Most of the Europeans are of French descent.

Le Morne

Slavery is a sad part of human history. It began long before the coming of Christ. The apostle Paul urged Christian slaves and slave owners to see each other as brothers. This new perspective on slavery helped lead to an end of slavery in Europe in the early Middle Ages. However, traders and explorers renewed the practice of slavery after Europeans began to plant colonies in various parts of the world. We learn more about the history of slavery in Lesson 124.

French Cannon on Mauritius

Le Morne Mountain

Le Morne, pictured above, is a rugged, isolated mountain that stands on a peninsula on the southwestern tip of Mauritius. Runaway slaves, called maroons, used caves and crevices in the mountain as well as the surrounding forest as places to hide when slave traders brought them to the island from Africa, Madagascar, India, or Southeast Asia.

God created an amazing, beautiful world. He created people in His image who are capable of doing wonderful things. But human beings are sinners, and they often fail in how they treat other people and God's amazing world. We see these truths on the tiny island of Mauritius.

Bless the Lord, all you works of His,
In all places of His dominion;
Bless the Lord, O my soul!
Psalm 103:22

Assignments for Lesson 111

Our Creative World — Look at the illustrations of the dodo on pages 95-96.

Timeline Book — In the box for Lesson 111 on page 25, write "French settlers arrive in Mauritius."

Student Workbook or Lesson Review — If you are using one of these optional books, complete the assignment for Lesson 111.

Thinking Biblically — Read Psalm 103.

Creative Writing — Write a short story of at least one page that relates to slaves and the mountain of Le Morne.

Literature — Read chapters XI and XII in *Madeleine Takes Command*.

The Reign of Peter the Great of Russia

Lesson 112   Our World Story

As Europe experienced the Reformation and Renaissance, Russia was mired in the past. The Rurik Dynasty had begun in 862 with Prince Rurik (mentioned on page 584). This dynasty fell in 1598. The new dynasty of the Romanov family began in 1613. Between those two dates, Russia experienced what is now called the Time of Troubles. A famine took the lives of one-third of the population. The country fought a long war with Poland. Many Russians were struggling and expressed their anger and frustration in protests.

The vast majority of Russians were serfs, who were little more than slaves on the estates where they lived and worked. A series of laws issued in 1649 gave new rights to the upper classes but made life harder for the serfs.

Peter Becomes Czar

Peter of the Romanov family was born in 1672, the son of Czar Alexis by the czar's second wife. Alexis died in 1676, and he was succeeded by his oldest son, Fedor. Fedor died in 1682. Peter, who had not expected to rule at all, found himself co-czar at the age of ten with his half-brother Ivan V, who had severe mental and physical limitations. Ivan's sister Sophia actually ruled the country as regent for seven years. In 1689 Peter's supporters forced Sophia to retire. Because of Ivan's disabilities, the nobles, the military, and the people recognized Peter as the real czar of Russia. Ivan died in 1696.

When Peter began his reign, he ruled the largest country on Earth in terms of land area.

Illustration of Peter the Great Created in 1718

See map above. However, the country was sparsely populated, with only about eight million people. This was about the same number of people as Poland and much fewer than the nineteen million in France. Both of those nations had much less territory.

Peter Leads the Military

Peter grew up with the freedom to study and investigate whatever he wished. He was an **inquisitive** and eager learner. From childhood Peter loved the military. In 1695 at age twenty-three, he led his army against the Ottoman Empire. The next year the Russians captured from the Ottomans the port city of Azov on the Sea of Azov (pictured on page 387 and shown on the map above). Russia's northern ports were iced over in the winter. Capturing Azov gave the Russians a warm water port. Because the Sea of Azov empties into the Black Sea, this new port provided greater opportunities for Russian traders and for the Russian military.

Around 1700 several countries in northern Europe wanted to limit Sweden's power. In 1700 Russia entered the Great Northern War when it joined an alliance with other countries against Sweden. In order to be able to carry on the war, Peter improved the Russian army and created a navy. He established a military draft that required men to serve in the army. To build **artillery**, Peter ordered men to work in iron mines, to build **forges**, and to establish transport lines to run between the mines and forges. Peter ordered the construction of shipyards to build a fleet for trade and warfare on the Baltic Sea.

Peter lost Azov to the Ottomans in 1711. However, Russia gained territory from Sweden during the Great Northern War. It gained ports on the Baltic Sea that Russians could use to

Lesson 112 - The Reign of Peter the Great of Russia

reach Europe. A treaty signed in 1721 ended the war. In 1722-23, Russian forces captured more territory when they took land along the Caspian Sea from Persia.

Peter Makes Changes Inside Russia

In 1697 and 1698, before Russia entered the Great Northern War, Peter toured Europe with about 250 other Russians in what was called the Grand Embassy. For part of the time Peter traveled in disguise under the name Sergeant Peter Mikhaylov. He worked in shipyards in the Netherlands and Great Britain. When he was not in disguise, Peter tried to get European monarchs to join him as allies who would help him fight against the Ottoman Empire. During these travels, Peter also learned European customs. He recruited experts to help Russia in engineering, architecture, art, and science. After eighteen months, Peter's royal guards at home in Russia revolted, so he cut his trip short and returned to Russia, where he put an end to the revolt.

During his reign, Peter modernized Russian government and society. In 1703 he founded the city of St. Petersburg on land Russia had won from Sweden. He made the city the new capital of Russia. Among the grand buildings he had built there is his palace Peterhof. Peter's goal was to make St. Petersburg the heart of his reforms and of the new Russia he hoped to create.

The monument at top left was erected in Moscow in 1997. It honors Peter the Great for forming the Russian navy 300 years before. At left is a close-up of Peter on the monument. Above: This 2014 Russian stamp commemorates the Battle of Gangut, fought during the Great Northern War.

Peterhof Palace in St. Petersburg

Left Column: Two Views of the Palace's Chapel; Above: Fountain and Pool, Sitting Room; Below: The Palace

Peter made government more honest and efficient. He encouraged education and created the Russian Academy of Science. He also established a museum, a library, and an art gallery. Peter modernized the Russian calendar and alphabet. He started the first Russian newspaper. The first newspaper in Europe had begun publication in 1605, and others had quickly followed. Peter required nobles to adopt European customs, obtain an education, and devote their lives to **civil** or military service. He encouraged Russians to wear the clothing styles of Europe. Peter built new roads and canals and helped to build more industry. Through these changes, he increased trade with Europe and raised the stature of Russia in the minds of Europeans.

Not all of Peter's changes were positive. Leaders of the Russian Orthodox Church, fearing a loss of their power because of change, opposed the reforms that Peter made. As a result, Peter made the Church a department of the government that answered to the czar. This put the Church under the czar's control and made its considerable financial resources available to him for his plans.

Peter raised taxes to pay for wars and for projects. The new taxes fell hardest on the poor. A "soul tax" enacted in 1718 required a certain amount to be paid by every person (every "soul") in Russia. This required a new census to get an accurate count. He ordered men to work in mines and factories against their will. Peter strengthened the manorial system that tied serfs even more firmly to the estates. A 1722 law said that a serf could not leave the land where he lived without written permission. A later addition to the law required a serf to get written permission from the military as well before he could leave an estate. Peter treated harshly those who did not approve of his reforms and building projects.

Landowners had the responsibility for collecting taxes, for controlling the movement of the serfs, for deciding what work the serfs did, and for punishing people who violated the law. In other words, the landowners served as heads of little governments on their estates. After Europe had left serfdom behind, Russia became even more dependent on it. In Peter's day an estimated 95 percent of Russians were serfs, who were bound either to the land, the mines, or the factories where they worked.

The Impact of Peter's Reign

Peter stood an imposing six feet seven inches tall. He inspired deep loyalty from many of those who served him, but he was not able to overcome the **corruption** that existed in Russia. He was not able to change the desire for the old ways that many Russians felt.

Peter's rule as emperor of Russia brought great changes to his country and helped to bring Russia into the modern age. However, his failure to make life better for the serfs remained a serious problem in Russia. Peter died in 1725. A series of weak rulers followed him until Catherine II, often called Catherine the Great, became empress in 1762.

Catherine honored Peter the Great by commissioning the statue at right, which depicts the czar as "The Bronze Horseman." The statue is perched on a single piece of red granite. The horse stands on a snake, which represents Peter's enemies, including those who opposed his reforms.

Peter the Great chose to name his new capital city after the man who wrote down these words in his first epistle, words from God which instruct us in how to treat all people:

*To sum up, all of you
be harmonious, sympathetic,
brotherly, kindhearted, and humble in spirit;
not returning evil for evil or insult for insult,
but giving a blessing instead;
for you were called for the very purpose
that you might inherit a blessing.*
1 Peter 3:8-9

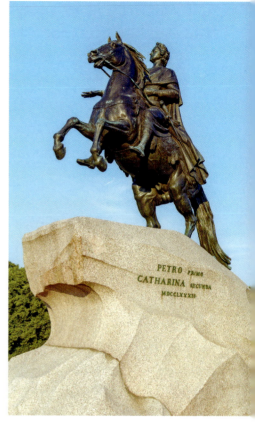

"The Bronze Horseman" in St. Petersburg, Russia

Assignments for Lesson 112

Our Creative World — Read about Russian games on page 97.

Map Book — Complete the assignments for Lesson 112 on Map 34 "Russia of Peter the Great."

Timeline Book — In the box for Lesson 112 on page 25, write "St. Petersburg is founded in Russia."

Student Workbook or Lesson Review — If you are using one of these optional books, complete the assignment for Lesson 112.

Thinking Biblically — Copy 1 Peter 3:8-9.

Vocabulary — Look up each of these words in a dictionary and read their definitions: inquisitive (758), artillery (758), forge (758), civil (761), corruption (761).

Literature — Read chapters XIII and XIV in *Madeleine Takes Command*.

Johann Sebastian Bach

Lesson 113   World Biography

Johann Sebastian Bach was a musical genius. He was an accomplished organist and music instructor, and he was one of the most prolific and creative composers of all time. He wrote many different kinds of works. Musicians still perform and audiences still enjoy his compositions today. Most importantly, Bach composed music to the glory of God.

Music in European Life

In the late 1600s and early 1700s, local churches played an important part in village, town, and city life in Europe. Most people attended church services. Ministers were well educated and townspeople generally respected them. Those who attended church services appreciated music for singing and music for instruments. Singers and musicians who performed such works were often local celebrities.

Music was also a big part of social life in individual homes and citywide events. Families who could afford it often gave their children music lessons. Royal and noble families often hired court musicians to compose works and to perform at social gatherings. Town festivals featured music, and sometimes composers premiered original works that they had written especially for the occasion. Composers wrote the first operas during this time period. These operas told stories through vocal and instrumental songs with elaborate presentations on stage.

Above: 1982 Stamp from the German Democratic Republic with Painting, Music Making at Home, *by Frans van Mieris; Left: Illustration of a Home Concert in the 1700s by Saint-Aubin, Published 1844*

The Baroque Era

Historians call the period from 1600 to 1750 the Baroque Era. The word *baroque* comes from the Portuguese word *barroco*, which means an irregularly shaped pearl. Baroque art, architecture, and music were elaborate and included complicated details. On page 746 we mentioned that St. Paul's Cathedral in London was an example of baroque architecture.

Baroque music has multiple lines which are played at the same time and which interweave and play off of each other. This results in an intricate composition that appeals to the emotions of the listener. Music experts consider the work of Johann Sebastian Bach to be the high point of baroque music.

St. George's Church, Eisenach, Germany

Bach's Life

Johann Sebastian Bach was born in 1685 in the German city of Eisenach. A church in his birth city is pictured above. Bach was born into a family that produced fifty-three prominent musicians over seven generations. The extended Bach family was close and scheduled annual gatherings, which continued even when the family became quite large and spread out. This family of Protestants began their get-togethers by singing a Christian chorale. Afterward, they enjoyed improvising music and laughing together.

Bach's father had an identical twin brother. Both became musicians. They were so alike in almost every way that even their wives had difficulty telling them apart. Bach's father, Johann Ambrosius Bach, probably gave Sebastian his first music lessons, but both his parents died before Sebastian was ten years old. Bach and a younger brother then lived with an older brother who was an organist and who continued their music lessons.

When Bach was fifteen years old, he became part of the choir at St. Michael's School in Lüneburg and later a violinist in its orchestra. He then became the organist at the Church of St. Boniface, called the New Church, in Arnstadt, Germany, home to many members of the Bach family.

In Arnstadt Bach began to compose music for the organ. He worked in this position until 1707. During his time at New Church, Bach traveled 200 miles to Lubeck (tradition says that he walked) to hear the great organist and composer Dietrich Buxtehude. Bach stayed in Lubeck for many weeks to be near Buxtehude. His employers in Arnstadt were displeased that he was gone so long. Bach was frustrated that his superiors did not appreciate his compositions. He soon left Arnstadt and took a position as organist at the Church of St. Blaise in Muhlhausen.

Portrait of Johann Sebastian Bach by Elias Gottlieb Haussmann, c. 1746

Lesson 113 - Johann Sebastian Bach

Bach had similar problems while working in Muhlhausen. In 1708 Bach took the position of church organist and chamber musician for the Duke of Saxe-Weimar. He remained in this job for nine years. Here he composed religious music. For a time, Bach composed a new cantata each week. A cantata is a composition that includes several songs. During the same time, he was composing works for organ. Though he very much wanted the position of *kapellmeister* (musical director), he never received this position for the Duke.

In 1717 Bach became kapellmeister for Prince Leopold of Anhalt-Cothen, Germany. Here he wrote some church compositions and many nonreligious pieces.

In 1723 Bach moved to Leipzig, in the German state of Saxony. Here he lived for the rest of his life. Bach was kapellmeister for Thomaskirche (German for St. Thomas Church) and for the Thomaskirche School. This church provided the music for other churches in the city, so Bach became in a sense music director for all of Leipzig. Bach created some of his greatest works in Leipzig.

Thomaskirche, Leipzig, Germany

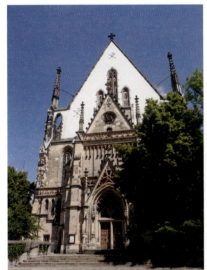

These views of Thomaskirche include the Bach stained glass window inside and the Bach statue outside the church.

Bach's Music

Bach's intricate work appealed to people's intellect and also to their senses. In each of his compositions or movements within a composition, Bach conveyed one emotion and used one rhythm. In a composition, Bach would usually establish a theme and then restate it in a slightly different way in a higher or lower voice. Writing music this way became a common practice among composers of classical music.

We have over 1,000 compositions by Bach, and scholars believe that many more were lost. Bach wrote a variety of music, but he wrote about three-fourths of his works for use in worship. He wrote various organ and choral works for church services, including:

- **Cantatas.** A cantata presents a story (usually from the Bible) by means of songs, which singers and a small orchestra perform. Bach also wrote some cantatas for local festivals with nonreligious themes. These were sometimes based on a poem. About 200 Bach cantatas are known, although he probably composed many others.

- **Oratorios.** An oratorio is a long musical composition that presents a story through songs. Oratorios are different from operas in that oratorios do not include action and are performed without scenery. Probably the most famous oratorio is *Messiah* by George F. Handel, which was first performed in 1741. Bach wrote several oratorios for Christmas and Easter. He apparently wrote five oratorios about the suffering and crucifixion (called the Passion) of Christ, although the only ones that survive today are those he wrote based on the accounts in the books of Matthew and John. Bach included the older hymn "O Sacred Head, Now Wounded" in his *Passion According to St. Matthew*. The premier performance of *St. John Passion* was performed in Leipzig's Nikolaikirche (translated St. Nicholas Church). The interior of the Nikolaikirche and its organ are pictured below.

- **Motets.** A motet is a musical composition based on Scripture that includes lyrics for singers. Sometimes performers sing motets a cappella.

Ceiling of the Nikolaikirche and Its Organ

Bach's compositions for non-church settings included:

- **Works for Individual Instruments.** Bach wrote for the organ, cello, flute, violin, and viola.

- **Chamber Orchestra Suites.** During this time in history, a chamber orchestra was a small ensemble that often performed for an invited group in a large room in a private home. Today chamber orchestras, such as the one pictured at right, often perform in public.

Four Seasons Chamber Orchestra performs music by Bach in Dnepropetrovsk, Ukraine.

- **Concertos.** A concerto is a work with three movements or parts. A concerto often features a particular instrument such as a harpsichord or violin. Some of Bach's most famous works are his six Brandenburg Concertos.

- **Coffeehouse Music.** This type of music served as entertainment at public coffeehouses. Both well-known and up-and-coming musicians performed at coffeehouses. One Bach work is a humorous composition called the "Coffee Cantata."

- **Music for Harpsichord Instruction.** In addition to writing music and performing it, Bach also taught others how to play music.

- **Experimental Music.** Bach experimented with music to see what was possible. Musicians did not perform these pieces during his lifetime, but today musicians appreciate them as demonstrations of Bach's genius.

Today musicians and listeners alike consider Bach's music to be some of the most beautiful and important musical compositions ever written.

Bach's Family

In 1707 Bach married his second cousin, Maria Barbara Bach, with whom he had seven children. She died in 1720. The following year he married a professional singer, Anna Magdalena Wilchen, with whom he had thirteen children. Bach was a devoted father. Sadly, nine of his twenty children died before their father. The happiest times of Bach's life were the years when all of his children were still around him. He also enjoyed being a grandfather. Bach died in Leipzig in 1750.

Bach's Faith

Bach was a devout Lutheran. He sought to express and reflect his faith in all of his compositions. He once wrote, "The aim and final end of all music should be none other than the glory of God and the refreshment of the soul." At the end of his musical scores, even ones that were "nonreligious," Bach usually wrote "S.D.G." These are the initials of the Latin words *Soli Deo Gloria*, which means "Glory to God Alone."

Praise the Lord!
Sing to the Lord a new song,
And His praise in the congregation of the godly ones.
Psalm 149:1

Assignments for Lesson 113

Our Creative World — Read the "Letter to Georg Erdmann" by J. S. Bach on pages 98-99.

Timeline Book — In the box for Lesson 113 on page 25, write "Bach becomes a musical director in Leipzig."

Student Workbook or Lesson Review — If you are using one of these optional books, complete the assignment for Lesson 113.

Thinking Biblically — How can music bring glory to God and refreshment to the soul? Write a paragraph answering this question.

Literature — Read chapters XV and XVI in *Madeleine Takes Command*.

Family Activity — Hold "A Musical Evening." Instructions begin on page FA-46.

Easter Island

Lesson 114   **World Landmark**

Easter Island, which is now part of the country of Chile, South America, is an isolated place in the Pacific Ocean. The people who live there are far away from any other people. The nearest other inhabited island is Pitcairn Island, which is over 1,000 miles away. The nearest point of land on a continent is in Chile, over 2,000 miles away.

The native inhabitants of Easter Island call it Rapa Nui. The people are known as the Rapanui. Our best understanding is that their ancestors were some of the Polynesian people who spread over the islands of the Pacific. Those Polynesians likely first came to Easter Island around the time of the Crusades, between 1000 and 1200 AD.

Rano Kau Volcano, Easter Island

Easter Island has a triangular shape formed by three volcanoes rising from the ocean. The middle of the island has high plateaus and **craters**, and much of the coastline consists of cliffs. Some of the craters, such as Rano Kau, pictured at right, contain lakes of collected rainwater.

When humans arrived, the island was probably covered with millions of palm trees, some perhaps 100 feet tall (as tall as a ten-story building). Birds such as rails, parrots, herons, and owls lived on the island, along with lizards and geckos. Migratory seabirds nested there. Many types of sea creatures swam around the island, including nanue, poopó, mahi-mahi, tuna, and lobsters. Turtles occasionally came ashore.

The Moai

According to local legend, the chief of the original settlers was named Hoto-Matua. As generations passed, the people divided into several clans. The clans generally recognized one chief who was king over all of the clans. Honoring their ancestors was an important part of Rapanui culture.

Along the shoreline of Easter Island are stone platforms of varying sizes called *ahu*. The ahu usually include a ramp paved with pebbles leading up to a raised rectangular platform. Archaeologists believe that the Rapanui used the ahu as places to **mourn** islanders who had died. The islanders also erected *moai* (large stone statues) on the platforms.

The most recognizable artifacts on Easter Island are oversized moai heads, such as the one pictured at right. Actually, artists carved the statues down to the waist including arms and hands, but many of these are buried. Some of the statues also have carvings on their backs, which match tattoos that some islanders had on their backs.

The average height of the statues is thirteen feet, over twice as tall as the average adult. The average weight is thirteen tons, which is about the same as seven minivans. Many of the statues are much larger. The largest moai erected on the island was thirty feet tall and weighed eighty-two tons.

Moai on Easter Island

Most of the nearly 900 statues found on the island were carved at Rano Raraku, a volcanic crater. The sides of the crater are composed of **compacted** volcanic ash, known as tuff. The islanders carved the moai in the sides of the crater using stone tools.

They started by cutting the general outline of the figure and making spaces in the rock wall for several people to work on the statue. As illustrated in the photo on page 771, workers left many statues unfinished. This helped archaeologists understand the process of creating the moai.

Unfinished Moai at the Top of Rano Raraku Volcano

Once they had finished the main carving, they pulled a statue out of the crater. According to local tradition, the statues then "walked" to their appointed locations on the ahu. Modern experiments have attempted to discover how islanders could have moved the statues over long distances. Using multiple ropes, a group of people can rock the statues back and forth in such a way that they appear to walk as they move forward. Other experimenters have successfully rolled the statues on logs. Even with this method, the islanders might have moved the statues as they stood upright. Several roads connecting various parts of the island provided paths on which islanders could move the moai. Islanders placed some of the statues along the roads.

Islanders polished carved statues with pieces of pumice to give them a smooth exterior. They inserted eyes made of coral with obsidian or scoria stone pupils into the eye sockets. Some of the moai, such as the one at right, had *pukao* on top of their heads. These were **cylindrical** hats or topknots.

A small number of wooden objects from Easter Island feature symbols known as *rongorongo*, pictured on page 772. In the Rapanui language, this means "to recite or to chant." Apparently only a small number of people on the island knew how to create and interpret the symbols, and their meaning is not known today. Rapanui also carved petroglyphs on rock walls and caves around the island, as seen at right.

Center: Moai with Red Hat
Bottom: Petroglyph

Moai on Easter Island

Changes on Easter Island

The people of Easter Island carved the moai over a period of several centuries, from perhaps 1200 to 1600 AD. After this time, the island society apparently suffered a collapse. The island lost many of its trees. Perhaps islanders cut them down, but the reason is unclear. This led to soil erosion, which made farming more difficult. The lack of trees limited the number and size of boats that could be constructed for fishing. The land birds that had lived on the island became extinct.

A Rapanui tradition took place each year when members of each clan chose one male member to represent the clan in a competition. These men swam from Easter Island to the small, rocky island of Motu Nui. The goal was to be the first one to collect an egg laid by a sooty tern, swim back to Easter Island, and climb a cliff to the ceremonial site called Orongo. The winner was called the *tangata manu* (bird-man) and his clan received special privileges until the next year's competition. The contest was very dangerous because of sharks and the steep cliff. See pictures at right.

During the 1600s, the islanders began to have serious conflicts with each other. According to local tradition, a civil war took place about 1680 and many of the inhabitants died.

Rongorongo

Motu Nui as Seen from the Ruins of Orongo

Sooty Tern

Lesson 114 - Easter Island

Moai with Elongated Ears

Contact with Europeans

Jacob Roggeveen was the leader of a Dutch expedition with three ships and 223 men. They left the Netherlands on August 1, 1721. After sailing around the tip of South America, they set out across the Pacific.

The expedition came upon a remote island on Easter Sunday, April 5, 1722. Since the island was not on their maps and charts, Roggeveen named it Paasch Eyland, which is Dutch for Easter Island. The natives came out to meet the ship, some in canoes and some swimming. Several of the Dutch went ashore and visited briefly with the natives.

The Dutch noted that the islanders were tall and strong. They also had strong teeth—one of them cracked a large, hard nut with his teeth. Some of the men had short hair while others had long hair that was braided and coiled on top of their heads. Another **striking** feature of the islanders was their stretched earlobes. From childhood, they gradually widened a slit in their earlobes until they could wear large ear ornaments in the enlarged lobes. The Dutch noticed that if the islanders were doing something active, they would take out their ear ornaments and hang their earlobes on the tops of their ears.

The Dutch saw the "remarkably tall stone figures" on the island. They could not understand how the statues had been erected. After a quick inspection, they incorrectly guessed that the statues had been molded in place out of clay.

During the visit, some of the Dutch soldiers felt threatened by the Rapanui and opened fire, killing several of them. Nearly 50 years passed before another outside ship came to the island. A Spanish expedition visited in 1770, an English one in 1774, and a French one in 1786. In the 1700s and 1800s, islanders knocked down all of the standing moai during conflict between the clans. The ones that are standing today were set back up beginning in the 1950s.

A View of the Monuments of Easter Island, Rapanui, c. 1775-1776, by British painter William Hodges, is the earliest known painting of the monuments.

The people of Rapa Nui provide further evidence of the creativity of people made in God's image. Their ancestors figured out how to travel across a wide ocean, and they established their own society far away from any other people. The Rapanui used art to express their understanding of the world.

For He looks to the ends of the earth
And sees everything under the heavens.
Job 28:24

Assignments for Lesson 114

Timeline Book — In the box for Lesson 114 on page 25, write "Dutch sailors reach Easter Island."

Student Workbook or Lesson Review — If you are using one of these optional books, complete the assignment for Lesson 114.

Vocabulary — Find each of these words in a dictionary, then find the definition that corresponds to the way the word is used in this lesson: crater (769), mourn (770), compacted (770), cylindrical (771), striking (773). Copy the words and definitions.

Creative Writing — Imagine that you are one of Jacob Roggeveen's men. Write a journal entry of about one page about the day your party visited Easter Island.

Literature — Read chapters XVII and XVIII in *Madeleine Takes Command*.

The Moravians

Lesson 115 — Daily Life

In the Lord's church, teaching what is right is essential. It is vital that the church teaches the truth. Jesus said that He is the truth (John 14:6). Therefore the truth matters. Paul, depicted in the statue at right, warned about those whose teaching was not in agreement with the **sound** words of Jesus Christ (1 Timothy 6:3-5). If the church does not stand firm in the truth, people might teach anything, and their listeners might believe false teaching.

In the Lord's church, right living is also essential. The New Testament is clear that Christians are to live in a way that is "worthy of the calling" they have received (Ephesians 4:1). Christ died for our sins, and when we accept that truth we are to live differently. Peter told his readers to be holy in their behavior because God is holy (1 Peter 1:15-16).

In the early days of the Protestant Reformation, both Protestants and Catholics sometimes focused on topics such as the authority of the Church and the pope and doctrines such as the role of Mary, the idea of purgatory, and the practice of selling indulgences, although they condemned ungodly lifestyles as well.

This statue of Paul stands in Basílica de Nuestra Señora de Las Angustias in Granada, Spain. Pedro Duque Cornejo created the statue in 1718.

Pietism

A few years after the death of Jan Hus (see page 540), some of the followers of Hus in Bohemia organized themselves into a fellowship of believers. These Hussites emphasized the sole authority of Scripture, simple worship as described in the New Testament, participating in Communion simply as a memorial of Christ and not as a way to obtain forgiveness, and right Christian living. Catholics and Hussites fought each other during the Thirty Years War, which lasted from 1618 to 1648. We discussed this war on page 688 and in Lesson 104. Catholics drove many of the Hussites from Bohemia, and they scattered to live in various places.

During the 1600s, some leaders in the Dutch Reformed Church placed special emphasis on the need for believers to live lives that honored the gospel. Some German Lutherans learned about these teachings. Philip Jacob Spener (born in 1635) was a Lutheran minister in Frankfurt, Germany. He spoke and wrote about the need for a heart religion instead of just a head religion. Spener held meetings in his home for believers to share Bible reading, prayer, and their life experiences with the goal of deepening their devotion to Christ. This probably doesn't sound very **radical** today, but in that day, it simply wasn't done. Spener is considered the father of German Pietism. Pietists emphasized the piety or spiritual devotion of individuals, though they also taught the importance of correct doctrine. Spener also taught in Dresden and Berlin. Two of the men whom Spener greatly influenced were August Francke and Nicholas Zinzendorf.

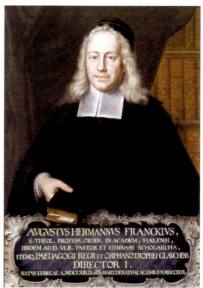

Top: Portrait of August Hermann Francke; Bottom: Bronze Statue of Francke with Two Orphans, Halle, Germany, by Sculptor Christian Daniel Rauch

August Hermann Francke, pictured at right, was a Lutheran professor who taught the Hebrew language at the University of Leipzig. There he started a Bible school that led to a spiritual awakening among undergraduate students and children in the city. Francke moved to Halle in 1692 to teach at an elementary school. There he encouraged godly living among his young students. He founded a school for poor children and also the orphanage at left.

Francke's Orphanage: Waisenhaus der Franckeschen Stiftungen, Halle, Germany

Lesson 115 - The Moravians

Count Nicholas Zinzendorf

Count Nicholas Ludwig Zinzendorf of Saxony, pictured at right, was born in 1700. Philip Jacob Spener was his godfather. Nicholas' father died when the boy was only six weeks old. Nicholas' grandmother, who was a Pietist and a friend of Spener, reared him.

Count Nicholas Zinzendorf

From an early age Nicholas had a deep devotion to Christ. When he was ten, Nicholas began attending Francke's school. He and five other boys formed the Order of the Grain of Mustard Seed, pledging themselves to love all people and to spread the gospel. When he was nineteen, Zinzendorf visited an art gallery in Dusseldorf. There he saw a painting of Christ wearing the crown of thorns. An inscription read, "All this I did for you. What are you doing for me?" From that time forward, Zinzendorf deepened his commitment to Christian service. Though Nicholas thought about becoming a Lutheran minister, he decided to become a lawyer and worked for a time for the government of Saxony.

In the early 1700s, Hussites in Moravia were suffering persecution. Some became **refugees** in Saxony. In 1722 Zinzendorf welcomed many of them to his estate. They created a town on Zinzendorf's estate, naming it Herrnhut, which means "The Lord's Watch." Other religious refugees came also. In 1727 the group established rules for living in their community. They committed themselves to a strong fellowship and to a godly lifestyle.

During the 1700s, these Christians came to be called either Herrnhutters or, because many had come from Moravia, Moravians. They called themselves Brethren. Zinzendorf became their leader. In addition to guiding their devotion to the Lord and their community life, he also wrote many hymns and helped the Moravians develop meaningful worship services.

The 1762 engraving at right depicts Moravians at an Easter memorial service at the Herrnhut cemetery. Notice that the men are all on the left and the women are all on the right.

Easter Memorial Service at the Herrnhut Cemetery

Moravian Mission Work

From their earliest days, the group placed great importance on mission work. They carried the gospel to other places in Europe and to other parts of the world. Their mission efforts had a profound impact on Anglican minister John Wesley. When Wesley traveled to the American colony of Georgia in 1734, he

Moravian immigrants built this tannery in Bethlehem, Pennsylvania, in 1761.

met a group of Brethren missionaries on the ship. He was impressed with the Moravians' faith and deep devotion to God. In 1738, when Wesley was back in England, he had a profound religious experience that changed the direction of his life and ministry. He became much more concerned with Christian lifestyle and devotion and began to teach a specific method of devotion to God. His followers became known as the Methodist Church. Wesley visited Herrnhut later that year.

In 1740 Moravians established four settlements in the Pennsylvania colony in America, naming them Bethlehem, Nazareth, Lititz, and Hope. They also established a settlement in Salem (now Winston-Salem), North Carolina. See a tannery in Bethlehem above and scenes from Salem at right. At this time many people in the American colonies were experiencing a time of Christian revival, now known as the Great Awakening.

Moravians taught the Inuit peoples in Greenland and Labrador, slaves on sugar plantations in the Caribbean, Native Americans in North America (the Delaware and the Cherokee in particular), and native peoples in South Africa and in Suriname and Guyana in South America.

The Moravians faced bitter opposition and harsh persecution, even from other Lutherans. In fact, in 1727 the government of Saxony **expelled** Zinzendorf for ten years because they saw him as teaching heresy and organizing a strange **sect**. He used this time to travel and to do evangelism elsewhere. The Moravians, sometimes by direct teaching and sometimes just by their lifestyle, challenged the practices and lifestyles of existing churches and the ministers who served there. As the Moravians continued to trust the Lord and lived to serve Him, the Lutheran Church eventually came to accept them as fellow brethren in Christ.

In addition to the work of Zinzendorf in Germany and Wesley in England, the Great Awakening in America, and the missionary efforts of the Moravians, other believers also encouraged people to be more devoted to Jesus. Learn about one of these in the box at left.

Finnish Pietists

Paavo Ruotsalainen, the son of Finnish farmers, became a lay preacher and led Pietists among the Finnish people. In 1977 the country honored the life of Ruotsalainen with this stamp celebrating his birth in 1777.

Scenes of Old Salem in North Carolina

The Pietist Movement had Hussite, Reformed, and Lutheran influences. The history of the movement teaches an important lesson about daily life for Christians. In addition to holding correct doctrinal beliefs, Christians must live out their faith in Jesus in their daily lives. Pietists made an important emphasis in their teaching about lifestyle. However, we must remember that neither being in a particular church nor following a man-made list of rules is sufficient to save. Salvation is only through Jesus Christ.

> *Who is there to harm you if you prove zealous for what is good?*
> *But even if you should suffer for the sake of righteousness, you are blessed.*
> *And do not fear their intimidation, and do not be troubled,*
> *but sanctify Christ as Lord in your hearts,*
> *always being ready to make a defense*
> *to everyone who asks you to give an account*
> *for the hope that is in you, yet with gentleness and reverence;*
> *and keep a good conscience so that in the thing in which you are slandered,*
> *those who revile your good behavior in Christ will be put to shame.*
> *1 Peter 3:13-16*

Assignments for Lesson 115

Our Creative World — Read about the Moravian missionaries on page 100.

Timeline Book — In the box for Lesson 115 on page 25, write "Moravians go to the West Indies and Greenland."

Student Workbook or Lesson Review — If you are using one of these optional books, complete the assignment for Lesson 115 and take the test for Unit 23.

Vocabulary — Write a paragraph that uses all of these words: sound (775), radical (776), refugee (777), expel (778), sect (778). Consult a dictionary if you need help with their definitions.

Creative Writing — Write down the names of five people mentioned in this lesson. Next to each name, write an adjective that describes that person based on what you read about them in the lesson.

Literature — Read chapters XIX and XX and the epilogue in *Madeleine Takes Command*. If you are using the Student Workbook or Lesson Review, answer the literature review questions on *Madeleine Takes Command*.

24

Age of Revolutions

Portion of the 1783 Treaty of Paris with Signatures of Three of America's Founding Fathers

Lessons
- 116 - World Biography: Frederick the Great of Prussia
- 117 - Daily Life: The Industrial Revolution
- 118 - World Landmark: Paris, France
- 119 - Our World Story: The American and French Revolutions
- 120 - God's Wonder: God Created the Cape of Good Hope

Literature
In *The Switherby Pilgrims* by Eleanor Spence, an English spinster takes ten orphans to Australia to make a living on a land grant. (See "Notes to Parents on the Literature" in the back of the Answer Key.)

1751-1800

In 1740 Frederick II began his reign in Prussia. By his death in 1786, he had greatly expanded his kingdom and become, in the hearts of his subjects, Frederick the Great. The Industrial Revolution began in England as inventors created increasingly better machines to produce goods in newly-built factories. Paris, France, grew as an intellectual and artistic center. In the late 1800s, new philosophies of the Enlightenment inspired a war for independence in the English colonies in America and a revolution to overthrow the monarchy in France. The European wars that resulted from the French Revolution changed who ruled the beautiful Cape of Good Hope at the southwestern tip of Africa.

Frederick the Great
of Prussia

Lesson 116   World Biography

In the 1700s, the area we know as Germany was a patchwork of independent German states lying northwest of Austria and Poland. These states included kingdoms ruled by kings, principalities ruled by princes, duchies ruled by dukes, and so forth. Many of these German rulers attempted to take lands beyond their own as a way to gain power and wealth. Prussia was a duchy on the southeastern coast of the Baltic Sea.

The Hohenzollern Dynasty

The Hohenzollern family ruled a region called the electorate of Brandenburg. The family had become nobility in the 1000s when other nobles recognized them as the counts of the region of Zollern. *Hohen* is the German word for high. The family took their name from their beautiful mountaintop castle. They were thus the "High Zollern" or Hohenzollern family. Their first castle called Hohenzollern House dated from before 1061. This complex was mentioned in a document from 1267. That castle was destroyed in 1423. Another was begun in 1454. In 1850 a member of the Hohenzollern family began to restore the dilapidated castle. See the restored castle below.

Hohenzollern Castle Above the Clouds in Burg Hohenzollern, Germany

Unit 24 - Age of Revolutions

Charlottenburg Palace, Berlin

The Hohenzollern family was originally Roman Catholic, but after the Reformation a branch of the family became Protestant. As time went on, the Hohenzollerns competed with the Habsburg family of Austria to be the most powerful family in the German-speaking regions of Europe. Protestant Hohenzollerns ruled Brandenburg, then they added Prussia to their domain. Frederick Wilhelm of the Hohenzollern family served as Prince Elector of Brandenburg from 1640 to 1688.

The emperor of the Holy Roman Empire continued to claim authority over a large region of central Europe. See map on page 787. In 1701 Holy Roman Emperor Leopold I gave Frederick Wilhelm's son permission to declare himself King Frederick I in Prussia. Frederick made Berlin the Prussian capital and built the Charlottenburg Palace, pictured at left.

The Birth and Childhood of Charles Frederick, the Future Frederick the Great

Frederick Wilhelm, son of King Frederick I, married Sophia Dorothea of Hanover, who was the daughter of British King George I. She is pictured at right. In 1712 Sophia gave birth to a son. King Frederick I rejoiced that he now had a grandson who could become king after his son Frederick Wilhelm.

The entire city of Berlin rejoiced at the birth of the future heir to the throne of Prussia. One week later amid great pomp and beating drums and cannon fire, the baby boy, dressed in cloth-of-silver (a cloth wholly or partly made of silver) and a little crown, was christened Charles Frederick. The Charles was quickly dropped and the little prince came to be called Frederick or his nickname Fritz.

Rulers of the Hohenzollern Dynasty and Their Relation to Frederick the Great

Great-Grandfather — Frederick Wilhelm, Prince Elector of Brandenburg (1640-1688)
Grandfather — Frederick I, King of Prussia (1688-1713)
Father — Frederick Wilhelm I, King of Prussia (1713-1740)
Frederick II (the Great), King of Prussia (1740-1786)
Nephew — Frederick Wilhelm II, King of Prussia (1786-1797)

Lesson 116 - Frederick the Great of Prussia

Frederick I died in 1713. His son Frederick Wilhelm was twenty-five years old and his grandson Fritz was one. Frederick Wilhelm became Frederick Wilhelm I, King of Prussia.

Governesses took care of Fritz until he was seven years old. Afterward male tutors provided his education. Frederick Wilhelm I was a devoted father to his son, taking him hunting and on yearly inspections of the Prussian army, but he was also demanding. The king wrote instructions about what he wanted his son's tutors to teach. Following is an excerpt of those instructions:

> ### Frederick Wilhelm I's Instructions for His Son's Education
>
> 1. Must impress my Son with a proper love and fear of God, as the foundation and sole pillar of our temporal and eternal welfare. . . . For we are Protestant to the bone in this country. . . . But the grand thing will be, To impress on him the true religion, which consists essentially in this, That Christ died for all men, and generally that the Almighty's justice is eternal and omnipresent . . . .
>
> 2. He is to learn no Latin; . . . . Let the Prince learn French and German, so as to write and speak, with brevity and propriety, in these two languages, which may be useful to him in life. That will suffice for languages,—provided he have anything effectually rational to say in them.
>
> 3. Let him learn Arithmetic, Mathematics, Artillery,—Economy to the very bottom. And, in short, useful knowledge generally . . . . History in particular;—Ancient History only slightly;—but the History of the last hundred and fifty Years to the exactest pitch . . . . by way of hand-lamp to History, he must be completely master of; as also of Geography, whatever is remarkable in each Country . . . .
>
> 4. With increasing years, you will more and more, to a most especial degree, go upon Fortification,—mark you!—the Formation of a Camp, and the other War-Sciences; that the Prince may, from youth upwards, be trained to act as Officer and General, and to seek all his glory in the soldier profession.
>
> *These instructions and the quote below are excerpted from the twenty-two volume* History of Freidrich II of Prussia: Frederick the Great *by Thomas Carlyle.*

King Frederick Wilhelm also gave specific instructions about what little Fritz must do each morning.

> . . . he is to rise at 7; and as soon as he has got his slippers on,
> shall kneel down at his bedside, and pray to God,
> so as all in the room may hear it . . . , in these words:
> "Lord God, blessed Father, I thank thee from my heart
> that thou hast so graciously preserved me through this night.
> Fit me for what thy holy will is; and grant that I do nothing this day,
> nor all the days of my life, which can divide me from thee.
> For the Lord Jesus my Redeemer's sake. Amen."

Frederick Wilhelm was a strong ruler who built an efficient government and a powerful army. By the time Fritz was ten

The original portrait of Sophia Dorothea by Antoine Pesne is housed at Charlottenburg Palace.

years old, his father had made arrangements for his son to have his own little company of soldiers—110 boys about his age chosen from noble families. Rentsel, a soldier who was seventeen years old, drilled all of the boys, thus teaching Fritz the beginning lessons of being a military leader.

Fritz, pictured at right when he was fourteen years old, was more interested in literature and music than in military matters when he was young. However, he decided to follow his father's example. He learned all he could about politics and war. In return, Frederick Wilhelm agreed for his son to use his free time playing the flute, writing poetry and music, and exchanging letters with well-known writers and teachers to discuss philosophy and ideas.

The original Antoine Pesne portrait of Frederick as the Crown Prince, painted in 1736, is housed at Hohenzollern Castle.

Frederick II Becomes King of Prussia

Frederick Wilhelm died in 1740. His son Frederick became king of Prussia. He was kind to his widowed mother, building her a palace and giving her a new title, not the customary Queen Dowager, but Her Majesty the Queen Mother. As king, Frederick was first called Frederick II. After winning the hearts of his subjects, he came to be called Frederick the Great.

War of Austrian Succession, the Seven Years War, and Conquering Poland

A few months after becoming king, Frederick became involved in the question of who would be the next ruler of the large and complex Habsburg domain after the death of Charles VI. Charles VI, who was a member of the Habsburg family, had been the Holy Roman Emperor and the emperor of the Habsburg Empire, also called the Austrian Empire. The oldest child of Charles VI was Maria Theresa. No woman had ever led the Holy Roman Empire. Maria Theresa proposed that she lead the Habsburg Empire and that her husband lead the Holy Roman Empire.

Some European rulers supported her plan, but others opposed it. Those who opposed her wanted to weaken the Habsburg Dynasty. To try to diminish Maria Theresa's power, Frederick II led an army that invaded and captured the region of Silesia, which lay between Austria and Prussia and which Austria claimed. Silesia was rich in minerals and other natural resources. This began what historians call the War of Austrian Succession. When the war ended in 1748, the treaty recognized Maria Theresa as archduchess of Austria but allowed Prussia to keep Silesia.

This painted enamel and copper gilt box was created in St. Petersburg, Russia, to commemorate a Russian victory against Prussia during the Seven Years War.

Frederick II also became involved in the Seven Years War (1756-1763) between France and Great Britain and the allies of each. Prussia sided with Great Britain and Austria sided with

Lesson 116 - Frederick the Great of Prussia

Military Uniforms from the Time of Frederick the Great

France. The war involved conflict in several places around the world. The French and Indian War between France and Great Britain, which took place in North America from 1754 to 1763, became part of this global conflict.

Frederick proved to be an excellent military leader. His military campaigns and his leadership at home enabled Prussia to become a major power in Europe. See map below. After 1763 Frederick pursued more peaceful policies, but he still had an interest in expanding Prussian control. In 1772 Prussia, Austria, and Russia divided up a large part of Poland to claim as their own. Prussia took over most of western Poland. Poles resisted being treated this way, but their efforts were unsuccessful.

HOLY ROMAN EMPIRE - GERMAN STATES

Frederick Improves Life Within Prussia

Frederick reformed several areas of government and society. He established impartial court procedures and abolished the use of torture as punishment for all but the most serious crimes. Frederick permitted a degree of freedom of speech and of the press. He had a policy of religious toleration. He was Protestant, but he permitted Jesuits to come to Prussia. He even constructed St. Hedwig's Cathedral, pictured below, for Catholics in Berlin. However, Frederick was not progressive in every area. He severely limited the rights of Jews. He also preserved social ranks and classes, and he did not improve the lives of serfs.

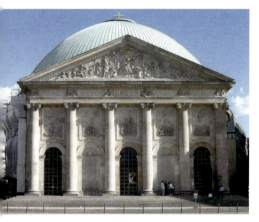

St. Hedwig's Cathedral, Berlin

Frederick gave assistance to certain industries. He introduced better cattle breeding and the crop rotation system, both of which were already used in Western Europe. His government drained swamps in river valleys for use as farmland, reforested areas that had been heavily cut, and resettled 300,000 immigrants as farmers on sparsely settled lands.

Frederick usually started his workday by 6:00 a.m. He wanted to make almost all major decisions himself. He required written reports from the heads of government departments and frequently inspected government operations personally.

Frederick the Musician

As king, Frederick continued to love music. As seen in the painting at right, he also performed as a flutist. He wrote more than one hundred flute sonatas, plus other compositions. He employed many singers and musicians to perform at his court. Among them for a time was one of the sons of Johann Sebastian Bach. Frederick built a grand opera house in Berlin, the Konzerthaus Berlin. The original was destroyed during World War II (1939-1945). However, from 1952 to 1955, it was rebuilt according to the design of Frederick's original architect and is pictured below.

When Frederick the Great died in 1786, he left an efficient government that was financially strong. Frederick and his queen, Elisabeth Christine of Brunswick-Wolfenbüttel-Bevern, had no children. Frederick Wilhelm, son of Frederick the Great's brother Augustus Wilhelm, succeeded his uncle as Frederick Wilhelm II.

A ruler can order soldiers into battle, give people justice before the law, and take steps to provide financial opportunities. Someone in such a role should take the responsibility seriously and work to bless as many lives as he can.

Konzerthaus, Berlin

This painting, Flute Concert with Frederick the Great in Sanssouci *by Adolph Menzel, 1850-1852, is fifty-five inches tall and eighty inches wide. Sanssouci was Frederick the Great's beloved summer palace.*

*In the light of a king's face is life,
And his favor is like a cloud with the spring rain.
Proverbs 16:15*

Assignments for Lesson 116

Our Creative World — Read Frederick's "Military Instructions to His Generals" on pages 101-102.

Map Book — Complete the assignments for Lesson 116 on Map 35 "Holy Roman Empire - German States."

Timeline Book — In the box for Lesson 116 on page 26, write "Frederick the Great meets J. S. Bach."

Student Workbook or Lesson Review — If you are using one of these optional books, complete the assignment for Lesson 116.

Thinking Biblically — Make a list of at least five attributes needed by a Christian leader of government.

Literature — Read chapters 1-2 in *The Switherby Pilgrims*.

The Industrial Revolution

Lesson 117 — Daily Life

The Industrial Revolution was the start of a huge change from a farming-based society in which people made goods by hand at home to an **industry**-based society in which people made goods by operating machines in factories. This revolution began in England in the 1700s and spread to other parts of the world. The English historian Arnold Toynbee first used the term "Industrial Revolution" in the mid-1800s to describe the change that took place in England between 1760 and 1840.

The revolution began in Britain for several reasons. Great Britain had large deposits of coal and iron ore, which were important resources for early industries. British society and government encouraged individuals to engage in scientific research, develop inventions, and pursue business ideas. In addition, Britain was free of many of the problems that other nations had. For instance, many of the German states were not unified; this kept them from combining the resources they needed to develop industry. A revolution followed by a controlling ruler kept the French from developing industry until many years later (we learn more about that revolution in Lesson 119).

Spinning, Boiling, and Reeling Flax, County Down, Ireland

The Industrial Revolution Changed How People Worked

Throughout history, most families lived on farms and made what they needed in their own homes or workshops. The illustration at left shows women spinning, boiling, and reeling thread.

A relatively few people made items such as pottery and iron goods to sell to others. Most people performed all of the tasks necessary to create such items. Sons usually went into the same work that their fathers had done.

A few changes in the way people made things took place in the centuries before the Industrial Revolution. Members of a guild came together to produce such items as jewelry, silverware, leather goods, and weapons. Merchants sometimes hired individuals to produce items in their homes for merchants to sell. A merchant might bring fibers to a home, where the wife or daughter spun thread. A merchant sometimes owned the spinning wheel or loom the woman used, and sometimes he even owned the house where the family lived.

In the Industrial Revolution, manufacturers built large mills and factories where many laborers worked together to make goods to sell. **Craftsmen** had often used their own tools; in factories workers used machines that belonged to the factory owner. Manufacturers built the first textile mill in the 1740s. Inventors created machines that could make textiles faster. Around 1738, larger spinning machines began to replace home spinning wheels.

Englishman James Hargreaves invented the spinning jenny in 1764. Richard Arkwright patented his water frame in 1769. Arkwright had been a wigmaker and barber before teaming up with clockmaker John Kay to make a machine that could spin ninety-six strands of yarn at one time. People called the machine a water frame because a waterwheel powered it. Arkwright and Kay patented a carding machine in 1775. Arkwright built many factories in England and Scotland, including his Masson Mills factory below. In 1779 Samuel Crompton invented the spinning mule, seen at right.

Spinning Mule

Sir Richard Arkwright and His Masson Mills Factory

In 1784 minister Edmund Cartwright, who had no experience in industry, visited an Arkwright mill and decided he wanted to invent a weaving machine. Despite **scorn** by others, he went on to invent the steam-powered loom, which helped to expand the weaving industry.

In 1803 John Horrocks invented an all-metal loom, the parts of which would not wear out or break as easily as wooden parts. By 1835 workers in Britain were using about 120,000 power looms. Most wove cotton fabric. Compare the factory illustrations from 1782 and 1835 on pages 792 and 793 to see how technology changed.

Scenes at Irish Linen Mills, 1782

Top: Men wind, warp, and weave yarn. At left is a warping mill. Center: Three men and a woman wash, rub, glaze, and boil the linen fabric. Bottom: In the lapping room, men measure and fold the linen and then tie it into bolts to prepare it for shipping to market. Illustrations by William Hincks.

Each worker in a factory did not perform every task needed to create a finished product. Instead each individual performed only one or a very few tasks. This is called specialization, which made it possible to make things faster and to make many more products.

The new factories that produced more goods meant that some people who had worked at home for merchants lost their jobs. However, many of these people went to work in the factories or found other jobs, including helping to make the machines that factories used. The overall effect in the long run was that more people were able to work.

Workers went from spending their days with their families in and near their homes to spending them in factories with dozens or hundred of individuals from many families.

The length of the typical workweek did not change at first, even though work moved from the farm to the factory. The typical worker in both places worked twelve to fourteen hours per day six days per week. However, factory work was usually more physically demanding, was more continuous throughout the day, and was more **monotonous** than farm work, as each worker did the same thing over and over all day long.

The Industrial Revolution Affected Where People Lived

Society started changing from being based in small towns and farms to being based in cities where large industries operated. Before the Industrial Revolution began, no more than ten percent of the population of Europe lived in cities. The rest lived in small towns, in villages, and on farms. As businessmen built factories, workers and their families moved to live nearby. Factory towns appeared; small towns and cities grew larger.

In England people called certain lands commons. The common people could use the commons as pasture for raising livestock. About this time, British Parliament began to pass enclosure laws. Enclosure laws permitted wealthy landowners to enclose or fence off property that was once the commons and to charge rent for using the land. Many people lost their way of life. Many displaced persons moved to cities, where they became laborers for factories. Some emigrated to the colonies.

For many years, cities could not keep up with the growing need for sanitation, clean water, **sufficient** decent housing, and good streets. Pollution increased as factories burned coal and the smoke filled the air. Crime increased as those who did not work tried to take advantage of those who did.

Though fewer people lived on farms, the growing city populations depended on the food grown by the smaller rural population. Over time growth in industry and technology helped farmers. Inventors and engineers created better farm equipment that could produce larger crops with less work. The English population as a whole became healthier when they had more food to eat, and people began to live longer on average. The population of Britain grew from 6.5 million in 1750 to fourteen million in 1830.

Scenes at English Cotton Mills, c. 1835

The Swainson Birley and Company Cotton Mill in Preston, Lancashire, England, c. 1835, was seven stories high and had 660 windows.

A power loom weaves cotton, c. 1835.

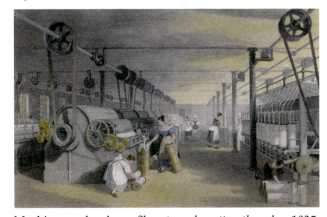

Machines card and rove fibers to make cotton thread, c. 1835.

Of course, people had to buy the goods that factories produced; otherwise, the factories would go out of business. In other words, a market had to exist for these goods. Eventually the workers themselves had greater incomes and were able to buy more items made in factories. The phrase standard of living refers to the material circumstances that people have, including the food they eat, their health and health care, and the material goods they own. The Industrial Revolution raised the standard of living of many people.

However, along with the increase in material goods came problems such as pollution and separation of families. Spiritual lives suffered because cities offered new temptations people had not known in the country.

The Industrial Revolution Caused a Need for More Natural Resources

Before the Industrial Revolution, most energy used in human work came from the humans themselves or from animals such as horses and mules. Machinery in factories required much more energy than humans or animals could provide.

Inventors had created the first steam engines around 1700, but for many years steam engines required considerable fuel and were not efficient in producing power. By 1776 James Watt, a Scottish engineer, invented a better steam engine that used less fuel and was more efficient in producing power for machinery. The statue below honors Watt, along with William Murdoch who invented gas lighting, and Matthew Boulton, a businessman who built industries using their inventions.

Gilded Bronze Statue of Boulton, Watt, and Murdoch, Birmingham, England

The use of machinery meant that workers used more natural resources than they had before. Companies imported more cotton from England's colonies to make cloth goods. Coal mining increased to provide more coal for fuel. Iron mining increased as the demand grew for iron to make machines, tools, and bridges.

The Industrial Revolution Changed Transportation

For centuries, people and goods moved by foot and on horse-drawn vehicles and in wind-powered ships. The English began to build turnpikes in the mid-1700s. A person wanting to travel on a turnpike paid a toll, and the toll-taker turned a pike or pole to open a gate and allow the traveler onto the road. The tolls paid for road construction and maintenance. The new roads made travel easier, but by the end of the 1700s many of them badly needed repair. Dirt roads developed deep ruts as wagons traveled over them and became muddy in wet weather. Scottish engineers John McAdam and Thomas Telford developed better ways to prepare road surfaces. McAdam figured out how to lay down tightly-packed crushed rock in layers. Telford used large flat stones as a foundation for road surfaces. People used their techniques to build hard-surface roads, which replaced dirt roads.

In 1803 Englishman Richard Trevithick produced the first steam locomotive, illustrated at right. Workers built railroads on which these locomotives could move. People improved railroads over the following decades. The new locomotives hauled coal and iron more rapidly than had been possible before. The number of trains hauling people and goods began to grow in the 1830s.

To improve water transporation, governments widened and deepened rivers. They also built new canals and lighthouses and updated old ones. In 1807 American Robert Fulton invented the first successful steamboat. Now water transportation no longer depended on wind or the direction of a river's flow.

1976 Polish Stamp Honors Trevithick

The Industrial Revolution Changed How People Paid for Things

When each family made just about everything they needed for themselves, they only had to come up with the money to buy their home and farm, some tools, and a few extras that they could not produce. To build a factory, however, someone had to purchase land, build a building, purchase machinery, and start paying workers. This required a great deal of money up front, before workers could make much to sell.

Money became more important than it had been in the days of self-sufficiency. Only a few wealthy individuals and small groups who put their resources together had the money necessary to build a factory. People who had acquired large fortunes, such as those who had money from an inheritance or from trade, often wanted a way to invest their money. At the same time, businessmen wanted to find people who could provide the money for them to use to implement their ideas. Capital is the money needed to start a business. Capitalists are the people who invest the money. Capitalism is the economic system in which individuals invest money to start and grow businesses. Capitalism began to grow rapidly during the Industrial Revolution.

Another way that people could invest in businesses was by putting their money in a bank. Banks make loans to businesses and serve other purposes, including providing a safe place for people to keep their money. Banks also gave people the ability to make purchases by writing checks instead of paying with cash. Having an account at a bank kept people from having to carry cash when they traveled long distances. The number of banks in London grew from twenty in 1750 to seventy in 1800.

The Industrial Revolution Changed Government

Before the Industrial Revolution, only men with a certain amount of wealth could vote in elections for members of the English Parliament. Many citizens had no say in government. Merchants and traders provided much economic growth during the Industrial Revolution. They wanted a say in the laws that Parliament passed which directly affected their businesses. Over time Parliament passed laws that changed voting qualifications, but this was a slow process. English women did not receive the right to vote until the 1900s.

Slater Mill in Rhode Island

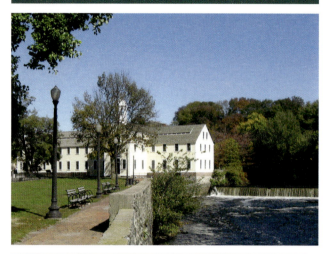

Views of Slater Mill and the Dam Which Powered Its Machines and an Historic Interpreter with a Machine

Exporting Industrial Technology

As industry grew in Great Britain, the government tried to keep knowledge and technology on the island. It was against the law for people who had knowledge of industrial technology to leave the country or to send machinery or information out of the country. However, these laws proved unreasonable. They couldn't be enforced.

In 1750 John Holker went to France and helped to develop spinning techniques for textiles there. In 1789 Samuel Slater moved to Rhode Island in the new United States and built from memory the first water-powered spinning mill there. See photos at left. In 1799, Englishman William Cockerill built textile machinery in Belgium.

Some people from other countries came to Great Britain to learn about industry. From 1810 to 1812, Francis Cabot Lowell from the United States visited textile mills in England. He later built a factory in Waltham, Massachusetts. He built it so that the entire process of making cotton cloth could be accomplished under one roof. In 1838 German businessman Alfred Krupp went to Sheffield, England, and learned about making steel. Krupp returned to Germany and became a leader in steel production there.

Large-scale industries started first in Great Britain, then in Britain's American colonies, and then in Belgium, France, and Germany. Shipbuilding was one of the first large American industries. In 1776 Americans built about one-third of all British ships. In the early 1800s American Eli Whitney figured out how to make standard, interchangeable parts so that workers could assemble items more quickly. The first product he created this way was a rifle. Most of the earliest American industries developed in New England.

People Who Opposed the Industrial Revolution

Not everybody welcomed the Industrial Revolution. Some people did not like the disruption it caused to family and small-town life. Often children in families had to work long hours in factories to contribute to the family income. Also, for many years workers received low wages because factory owners tried to keep their costs to a minimum. Workers eventually organized into unions to present their demands to owners as a group instead of as individuals.

For a short time, individuals who feared what industrialization meant for their jobs tried to stop change by destroying machines in factories. A group called the Luddites in England began doing this in 1811. Their inspiration was a man named Ned Ludd, but historians are not sure whether he was a real person or only a mythical figure. The Luddites, illustrated below, continued to destroy machines until 1816. They acted out of fear and without the understanding that change is part of any economic system. Changes that cost jobs in the short run create jobs in the long run as people begin new industries and as workers retrain to get new skills. The government treated these vandals harshly.

The Industrial Revolution affected empire-building. As we have seen in earlier lessons, many countries established overseas colonies in order to obtain wealth from those places. With the Industrial Revolution, colonies became even more important as sources for natural resources and as markets for goods produced in factories in the home country.

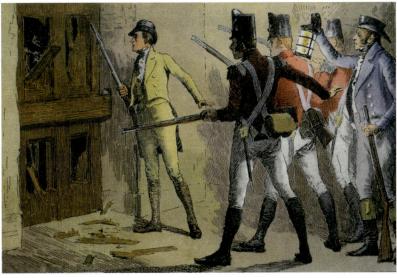

The colored engraving at left illustrates a factory owner confronting Luddites who want to destroy his loom. At right soldiers and factory owners stand inside a textile factory while Luddites attempt to break down a door.

The Industrial Revolution affected education. For many years England had only two universities, Oxford and Cambridge. People founded many more universities during the Industrial Revolution because industries needed engineers and other professionals.

The changes brought on by the Industrial Revolution did not all happen at once, nor did they happen everywhere at the same time. Once the changes started and began to spread, however, they did not stop. Our daily lives continue to change because of industrialization.

Come now, you who say, "Today or tomorrow we will go to such and such a city, and spend a year there and engage in business and make a profit." Yet you do not know what your life will be like tomorrow. You are just a vapor that appears for a little while and then vanishes away. Instead, you ought to say, "If the Lord wills, we will live and also do this or that."
James 4:13-15

Assignments for Lesson 117

Timeline Book — In the box for Lesson 117 on page 26, write "James Watt's steam engine goes into production."

Student Workbook or Lesson Review — If you are using one of these optional books, complete the assignment for Lesson 117.

Thinking Biblically — Copy James 4:13-15.

Vocabulary — Copy the list of vocabulary words, then write the correct definition beside each word: industry (790), craftsman (791), scorn (791), monotonous (792), sufficient (793).
  a. derision, disrespect
  b. adequate, meeting a given need
  c. the making of products by machines in factories
  d. tedious, without variety
  e. a skilled worker in a handicraft or certain trade

Literature — Read chapters 3-4 in *The Switherby Pilgrims*.

Family Activity — Make "The Industrial Revolution: Before and After" Book. Instructions begin on page FA-48.

Paris, France

Lesson 118   World Landmark

As the capital of France for over 1,000 years, Paris has been home to many dramatic events. As we learn in Lesson 119, Paris experienced one of its most dramatic events during the late 1700s.

Paris is located on a fertile plain on either side of the Seine River in northern France. From Paris, the Seine continues to flow about 100 miles to the north before emptying into the English Channel. Merchants from France and from all over central Europe brought goods to Paris. With access to the Channel, these goods could go all over the world. As a result, Paris became a major economic center.

The Pont Neuf bridge, built from 1578 to 1607, connects portions of Paris that lie on either side of the Seine River. The bridge crosses the Ile de la Cité.

The city has also become an intellectual and artistic center. Writers, scholars, and artists have gathered there for centuries.

The Gauls and the Romans in Paris

People began living in the area that became Paris over two thousand years ago. The first known inhabitants were the Parisii tribe of Gauls. About 250 to 200 BC, the Parisii built a fishing village there on the largest of several islands in the Seine. The island is now called *Ile de la Cité*, which means Island of the City. The island is pictured on page 799.

In 52 BC Julius Caesar led an invading Roman army that conquered the area that became Paris. Caesar described his campaigns there in a book called *Gallic Wars*. The Romans established a colony they called Lutetia. This settlement continued to grow until the 200s AD, when barbarians began to make repeated invasions. Around 300 AD, the name of the town became Paris for the Parisii.

Stained Glass Window Honoring Dionysius in St. Vincent de Paul Church in Paris

Missionaries Bring the Gospel to Paris

In the mid 200s, Dionysius (usually called Denis) went from Italy to the Roman colony of Lutetia to teach the gospel. Two companions, Rusticus and Eleutherius, accompanied him. These three **evangelists** saw numerous Roman structures and pagan temples there. The evangelists converted many people. This concerned the pagan priests. Roman authorities arrested the three and put them to death during a persecution that took place under Emperor Decius.

Genevieve was a Gallic Christian in the 400s who became a nun at the age of 15. When her parents died, she went to live in Paris. In 451, when the army of Attila the Hun threatened the city, Genevieve organized a huge prayer effort. God heard their prayers and saved the city. Attila directed his forces toward Orleans instead. Genevieve also helped with another confrontation a few years later. In 464 Childeric I, the leader of a group of Franks (another European tribe), **besieged** Paris. Genevieve was a contact between the city and Childeric. She obtained food for the city and convinced Childeric to release the prisoners he had captured. The Roman Catholic Church considers Genevieve to be the patron saint of Paris.

The Frankish leader Childeric was the father of Clovis. Clovis inherited his father's kingdom in 481. In 486 Clovis defeated the last large Roman force in Gaul. Over the next few years he defeated other Gallic armies and conquered much of present-day France. Clovis was converted to faith in Jesus in 496. By 507 Clovis stood alone as ruler of the Franks. Clovis captured Paris in 507 and made it his capital. He died in 511.

Lesson 118 - Paris, France

By 600 the Roman Catholic Church had an estimated 238 monasteries in the land of the Franks. Between the years 500 and 700, believers built about 83 churches in Frankish lands. The Catholic Church became even stronger in France during the reign of Charlemagne, whom we studied in Lesson 66.

As they did in many cities, Catholics in Paris established the *Hotel-Dieu* (which means Inn of God) in 651 and provided care for travelers and the poor. It was the first hospital in Paris and continued to serve patients until 2013.

Statues of John the Baptist, Stephen, and Genevieve at the Cathedral of Notre Dame

Viking Invasions and the Capets

In the 800s Vikings from Scandinavia began invading Frankish lands. They captured and burned Paris in 845 and caused much other destruction in the area during that century.

Hugh Capet, count of Paris, became king of the Franks in 987. He made Paris his capital. Hugh encouraged culture, the arts, and learning. Paris grew in size and influence under Hugh and his successors.

Hugh's son, Robert the Pious, ordered the construction of fourteen monasteries and seven churches, as well as a new palace and the Hall of Justice. In 1163 Pope Alexander III laid the cornerstone for a new cathedral on the site of two older churches on the Ile de la Cité. Workers spent two years digging the foundation, and construction work continued for about one hundred years more. The new Gothic cathedral, the Cathedral of Notre Dame of Paris, pictured at right, was one of the first to use flying buttresses. Historians believe that Gothic architecture began in France.

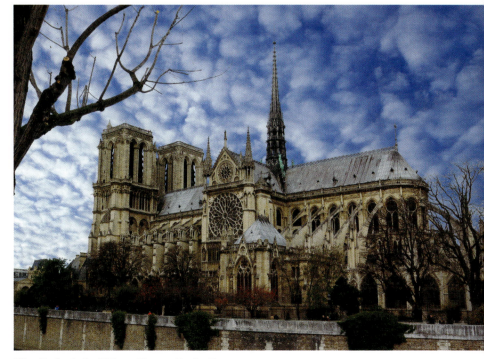

The Cathedral of Notre Dame, Paris, France

Stained Glass Window of Louis IX at Notre Dame de Clignancourt Church, Paris

Louis IX of the Capets, who became king in 1226 at the age of twelve with his mother as regent, grew up to be a popular and respected monarch known for his piety. He arranged peace with Henry III of England, who was his brother-in-law, and oversaw the construction of several important buildings in Paris. Louis led a crusade to Egypt from 1248 to 1250 that had mixed results. Louis was not able to defeat the Egyptians, but he did help Christian forces in Syria. Louis then led a campaign against the Muslims in northern Africa. He died in Tunisia in 1270. Later generations know Louis IX as St. Louis. See his image at left.

Paris Becomes a Center for Education

After the founding of the University of Paris, discussed on page 481, other schools operated in Paris as well. Estimates are that Paris had about forty colleges by 1400, fifty by 1500, and sixty-five during the 1600s. Most were located on the southern side of the Seine, which Parisians call the Left Bank. The area became known as the Latin Quarter because students and faculty usually spoke to one another in Latin. The northern or Right Bank was the home of the business district, the theater district, and many government buildings.

King Philip II, who reigned from 1180 to 1223, encouraged culture and learning in Paris, which became the focal point of learning for Europe during the Middle Ages. Such well-known teachers as Albertus Magnus, Thomas Aquinas, Duns Scotus, and Roger Bacon all taught in Paris during the 1200s. In 1349 approximately 502 professors were teaching in the city. By 1403 that number had increased to 709.

Improvements and Conflicts in Paris

Around 1200 King Philip II began the work of paving the streets of Paris. He also built walls and towers around the city. As the city grew, workers built larger circles of walls around it.

In 1302 King Philip IV (called the Fair) became involved in a conflict with Pope Boniface VIII over what influence the pope could have in the secular decisions of the French government. Philip summoned the Estates-General to Paris (see page 731) in order to gain their support against the pope. The assembly agreed with the king in this matter.

Paris did not escape difficulties during the conflicts between France and England. During the Hundred Years War, the English occupied Paris for about 15 years, from 1431 to 1446.

Paris was a key city in the Renaissance. The city continued to be active in art and learning. During the Renaissance, city planners designed new **boulevards**, palaces, and squares. They took as their models the architecture of the ancient Greek and Roman civilizations.

Printing came to Paris in 1470. In 1463 Gutenberg's partners, Fust and Schoffer, brought some printed books to Paris. However, local guilds of scribes and booksellers, who had a monopoly at the Sorbonne (a college of the University of Paris) on the sale of books in the city, opposed the two men. Paris officials seized the books and drove the Germans out of the city. Eleven years later Louis XI paid Schoffer a compensation for the books that had been taken. In 1470 a group of men set up a printing press at the Sorbonne to produce books. Another group set up a second press in 1473. Many French printers were in business by 1500.

Famous Paris Buildings

Paris is home to many beautiful and historic buildings. The Louvre, pictured at right, began as a fortress that Philip II built about 1200 on the Right Bank of the Seine. In the mid-1300s Charles V remodeled it into a country house with fortifications. When Francis I decided in 1546 to remake it once again, he wanted to create a palace that would **rival** the grandest buildings in Italy. French sculptor Jean Goujon carved statues inspired by Greek and Roman sculpture for the palace and grounds. Later kings added additional courts and wings until the building was a half-mile long and covered about forty acres. The last king to occupy the Louvre was Louis XIV, who moved from there to his new palace at Versailles. The Louvre now houses a museum.

The Louvre along the Seine River

Bourbon Palace

In 1370 Charles V began to build the Bastille (the French word for a strongly fortified structure, similar to the English word **bastion**), on the Right Bank. He intended for it to be a fortress to strengthen the city's defenses. By the 1600s, officials were using it as a prison. They kept there hundreds of people who disagreed with the king and let their disagreements be known. The Bastille became a symbol of royal authority, which was sometimes brutal and unfair.

The Bourbon Palace, pictured above, was completed in 1728 for the daughter of Louis XIV. It now houses the National Assembly (part of the modern French Parliament). The Place de la Concorde, which means Square of Peace, is a public square built between 1754 and 1763 across the Seine from the Bourbon Palace. Luxembourg Palace was built in the early 1600s. The French Senate meets there today.

Louis XV promised to build a new church in the abbey of St. Genevieve if he recovered from an illness. He did, and the new Church of St. Genevieve was built from 1758 to 1790. It stands in the Latin Quarter.

Luxembourg Palace

Unless the Lord builds the house, They labor in vain who build it; Unless the Lord guards the city, The watchman keeps awake in vain.
Psalm 127:1

Assignments for Lesson 118

Our Creative World — Read the excerpt from *Memoirs of the Court of Marie Antoinette, Queen of France* on page 103.

Timeline Book — In the box for Lesson 118 on page 26, write "Louis and Marie Antoinette marry at Versailles."

Student Workbook or Lesson Review — If you are using one of these optional books, complete the assignment for Lesson 118.

Vocabulary — Copy these words, each on a separate line: evangelist (800), besiege (800), boulevard (803), rival (803) bastion (803). Look up each word in the dictionary. Next to each word, write what part of speech it is according to the way the word is used in the lesson.

Creative Writing — Look in the lesson for five adjectives and the nouns they modify. Copy them and next to them write a phrase that has the same or nearly the same meaning. A thesaurus might help you. Here is an example: respected monarch = honored king.

Literature — Read chapters 5-6 in *The Switherby Pilgrims*.

The American and French Revolutions

Lesson 119 | **Our World Story**

The years 1776 and 1789 were landmark years in world history. The thirteen British colonies along the coast of America declared their independence from Great Britain in 1776, and a revolution began in France in 1789. These events had profound impact both where they occurred and around the world. Both events resulted in new ways of thinking about society and government. Each one was the result of an immediate series of events that led up to it, but each was also the result of a broad new way of thinking about the world that influenced both Europeans and Americans, a way of thinking called the Enlightenment.

For centuries before 1687, people in Europe had lived with many assumptions about religion, government, and society.

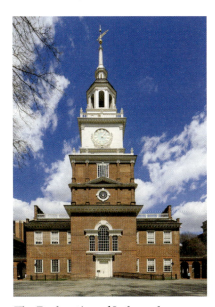

The Declaration of Independence was signed in the Pennsylvania State House, now called Independence Hall, in Philadelphia, Pennsylvania.

- Many people believed that the church and the government should support each other. Typically the leader of a nation chose one church to be the official state church. That church received money from the government, which collected taxes to support the church. That church's officials had special status in the eyes of the government. The government provided protection for the church.

- Many monarchs came to believe that it was wrong to differ with a king or queen about anything because God had chosen him or her to be monarch and that was the end of the discussion. Most people also assumed that a monarch's oldest child was the correct person to inherit the throne and become the country's next ruler.

- Most people believed that God planned for society to follow a permanent arrangement. European societies had royalty (a royal family), nobility (families with considerable wealth and power), and common people (workers, shopkeepers, farmers, serfs, slaves; in

An Evening with Madam Geoffrin, by Anicet Charles Gabriel Lemonnier

other words, everybody who wasn't royalty or nobility). People believed that this was the way things were supposed to be and that this arrangement could not change.

The Enlightenment

During the 1600s and 1700s, some philosophers, writers, and scientists began proposing a new way to look at the world. We have learned how Copernicus gave people a different way to look at the physical universe by suggesting that the Earth was not at its center (see Lesson 94). In the centuries before, people had believed that God operated the universe in a way that people could not understand. Now many believed that God operated the universe by laws that people could figure out.

In 1687 Isaac Newton published *Mathematical Principles,* in which he showed how the universe operated on the basis of reliable laws of nature. Gravity, for instance, worked the same way and had the same effect everywhere. Newton also taught a standard way to determine these laws using human logic or reason. Philosophers, writers, and scientists believed that they were becoming enlightened by a new awareness about how the world worked. Therefore, this movement that emphasized reason as the way to study and improve the world came to be called the Enlightenment. Many scholars see the Enlightenment as beginning with Newton's publication. One of the philosophers who expressed Enlightenment ideas was Voltaire, who was a major influence on Frederick the Great of Prussia. The painting above illustrates an actor reading a Voltaire play to a group of French nobles.

Enlightenment thinking lay behind the political and social events that brought about revolutions in America and France.

Conflicts Between England and Her American Colonies

The English had begun establishing colonies along the coast of North America in 1607. English and Scots-Irish settlers from Great Britain moved to America and created a new society. The colonists saw themselves as British. The colonies were like Britain in some ways but different in others. One major difference was that commoners who had not owned property and who had limited opportunity for using their talents in Great Britain had become property owners and influential persons in the colonies.

For many years the British government did not try to control what happened in the colonies. In America colonists were able to run their own government to a large degree while still being a part of the British Empire. By allowing British citizens to move there and develop the land, Great Britain gained more wealth. Colonists bought goods made in Britain, and they sent American goods to Britain.

Lesson 119 - The American and French Revolutions

After Britain defeated France in the French and Indian War, Britain became more active in ruling the American colonies. British King George III declared in 1763 that English subjects could not move west of the Appalachian Mountains to settle the land that France had ceded to England at the end of the war. This frustrated many colonists. They had fought in the war as British citizens, and the king's declaration seemed unfair. In addition, Britain imposed new taxes on the colonies to pay for debts from the war and to pay for the expenses of British troops who were stationed in the colonies. The king said the troops were there for the colonies' defense, but colonists knew that the king might use the British army as a police force against the Americans if he chose to do so.

Conflict between the American colonists and the British government grew worse in the late 1760s. Britain passed the Sugar Act, the Stamp Act, and the Townshend Acts, all of which imposed new taxes. Many Americans **resented** the taxes because the colonists had no vote in selecting members of Parliament, who created the taxes. The colonists also resented the Quartering Act, which required them to house British troops in their homes.

The conflict became more than words when British troops fired on a gathering of colonists in 1770 in an incident we call the Boston Massacre. In 1773, because of a change in the tax on tea, colonists dumped hundreds of crates of tea into Boston harbor in the Boston Tea Party, illustrated below. The British Parliament closed Boston Harbor and passed laws creating other restrictions on the colonists. Americans called these the Intolerable Acts. Colonists began collecting rifles and storing ammunition. Representatives from the colonies began meeting together in what they called the Continental Congress. Residents and governments in the thirteen colonies had not been unified before, but the common threat of British oppression brought the American colonists together. The British government sent more troops to America to quell the unrest.

1973 U.S. Stamps Commemorating the 200th Anniversary of the Boston Tea Party

The American Revolutionary War Begins

American colonists and British troops fought at Lexington and Concord in Massachusetts in April of 1775, thus beginning the American Revolutionary War. In July of 1776 the Continental Congress adopted a Declaration of Independence, which announced that the colonies were a separate and independent nation. The Declaration included Enlightenment ideas. It stated certain self-evident truths that justified the separation on the basis of human reason. These self-evident or obvious truths were that all men are created equal, that the Creator gives men rights that cannot be taken away, and that people have the right to alter or abolish their government when it threatens those rights.

Not all American colonists agreed with the Declaration. Many who did not want to fight against the mother country moved to Canada, the British West Indies, or Great Britain.

The Continental Army of the new United States of America seemed like a David going against the Goliath of the well-trained British force, which was the strongest army in the world. The British won several battles. Americans, however, fought on their homeland and in defense of their homeland. In contrast, the British had to travel across the ocean and depend on getting supplies sent to them.

Top Left: Reenactors at Freehold, New Jersey, portray British soldiers at the Battle of Monmouth in 1780. Above and at Left: Reenactors at McConnells, South Carolina, portray American Continental soldiers at the Battle of Huck's Defeat. Right: Statue of General George Washington on Boston Common, Boston, Massachusetts

American leaders such as Benjamin Franklin and John Adams went to France to seek assistance in fighting the British. The French helped the United States by providing financial assistance and by providing military leaders such as the Marquis de Lafayette. Prussian and Polish military officers also went to America to offer assistance.

George Washington, commander of the American force, wisely chose his battles. He was an inspiring leader for his often poorly-fed and poorly-clothed troops. British commanders did not always provide good leadership. The Americans fought better than the British did and won several important battles. Americans defeated the English in the Southern colonies and in battles

Above: Reenactors portray Washington's Continental Army marching to receive the British surrender at Yorktown, Virginia.

in the West (the region between the Appalachians and the Mississippi River). The main British army surrendered at Yorktown, Virginia, on October 19, 1781. See reenactment at left.

The United States and Great Britain concluded the Treaty of Paris in 1783, which recognized American independence. The first page of that treaty is pictured below. Notice that it begins with these words: "In the Name of the most Holy & undivided Trinity." A portion of the signature page is pictured on page 781. The signatures include David Hartley, a British Member of Parliament, and these American Founding Fathers: John Adams, who later became the second President of the United States; Benjamin Franklin, inventor, printer, and America's first diplomat; and John Jay, first Chief Justice of the Supreme Court.

Notice the statue of Benjamin Franklin below. As America's ambassador to France, he became a celebrity there in the late 1700s.

Left: First Page of the Treaty of Paris; Above: The Benjamin West painting depicted on this 1983 U.S. Stamp commemorates the 200th anniversary of the signing of the Treaty of Paris; Right: This small terra-cotta figure of Benjamin Franklin stands 15 1/2 inches tall on a gilded base. Artist François Marie Suzanne created it in 1793. The French bought many such likenesses of Franklin in many sizes and made from materials as costly as marble and as inexpensive as a cheap paper print.

Trouble in France

In the 1770s France was a nation in crisis. Farmers had suffered poor harvests for several years. The government was deeply in debt because of money it had spent to fight the French and Indian War and to assist the United States in its war for independence. Millions of Frenchmen lived in **abject** poverty.

In 1789 King Louis XVI called a meeting of the Estates-General to obtain their approval for an increase in taxes. This was their first meeting since 1614 during the reign of Louis XIII. However, after a dispute with the king over how the Estates-General would vote, the Third Estate, made up of the representatives of the general public, walked out. These representatives defiantly declared themselves to be the one true National Assembly and began working on a constitution to create a new form of government with limited powers for the king.

This 1971 French stamp commemorates the opening of the Estates-General with a cardinal, a nobleman, and a lawyer.

The French Revolution

Louis XVI began gathering troops at Versailles. Citizens of Paris began to arm themselves. On July 14, 1789, Frenchmen stormed the Bastille (the prison mentioned in Lesson 118), because they saw it as the symbol of the uncaring and tyrannical rule of the king. The revolutionaries wanted to seize weapons stored in the Bastille and release the political prisoners held there. The revolutionaries found only seven men **incarcerated** there, and they destroyed the Bastille. Historians see this act as the beginning of the French Revolution.

The new self-declared National Assembly issued a Declaration of the Rights of Man and Citizen, which stated the principles for which they were fighting. Leaders of the French Revolution were outspoken in their belief in Enlightenment ideas. They believed that they were creating a new kind of government and society based exclusively on reason, and they hoped that people around the world would respond to their example and initiate similar revolutions in their own countries. The revolutionaries created a new calendar, with 1792 being proclaimed Year I. The calendar had newly-named months, and each month had three weeks of ten days each. The new government put an early form of the metric system of measurement into use.

What followed, however, was not based on reason. Turmoil followed turmoil. This new, supposedly enlightened government acted in many cruel ways. Because of this, historians generally agree that the Age of Enlightenment ended in 1789. Many leaders of the French Revolution mixed hatred and their personal desires with their supposed reason.

In 1792 revolutionaries arrested Louis and his wife, Marie Antoinette, pictured on page 811. They called French leaders together to conduct a constitutional convention which voted to abolish the monarchy and establish a republic. Leaders were divided on what to do with the king.

In this painting, Franklin's Reception at the Court of France, 1778, *by Anton Hohenstein, Benjamin Franklin stands near the center in a brown suit and is receiving a laurel wreath from a woman. Louis XVI and his wife, Marie Antoinette, are seated.*

When some leaders began to talk about executing him, some other leaders withdrew from the government. The representatives who remained voted to execute the king. The revolutionaries beheaded the king early in 1793 and his wife in October, both by the guillotine.

Even more radical leaders gained control of the government, and the French experienced the Reign of Terror from 1793 to 1794. Revolutionary Maximilien Robespierre and his "Committee of Public Safety" ordered tens of thousands of executions. Other leaders later executed him.

More chaos followed, but one army officer, Napoleon Bonaparte, helped to stop the **anarchy**. After France tried one form of government after the other, in 1799 Napoleon seized power for himself. At first he pretended to cooperate with others. In 1804 he declared himself emperor and began the Napoleonic Empire. During these years of turmoil, monarchs of other European countries fought wars against the French because they feared that their own subjects would follow the example of the French Revolution.

At the end of the period of revolution, after all that France had suffered to bring about greater rights and freedoms, the country once again had a government with an absolute ruler. However, even with a dictator, citizens enjoyed more rights than they had under the French king.

The Significance of the Revolutions

Leaders of both the American and the French Revolutions acted on the basis of such Enlightenment ideas as the rejection of absolute monarchy and a desire for greater rights and freedoms for individuals. They believed that human society could improve by using reason and science to solve problems. They separated the connection between church and state. However, the two revolutions were also different in several important ways.

Most importantly, the leaders of the American Revolution believed in God and in the working of "the great Governor of the Universe," as they described Him in the Articles of Confederation, the document that formed America's first national government. The French revolutionaries, on the other hand, rejected belief in God. They tried to establish a heaven on Earth on the basis of human reason alone.

The American Revolution resulted in greater freedom and more citizens having the right to participate in government; the French Revolution resulted in unrestrained violence, **repression**, and a return to monarchy, though France did move toward greater democracy later in the 1800s. The American Revolution inspired patriots in other countries to seek freedom and greater human rights. The French Revolution also inspired some people, even though it stands as an example of a bad solution to a bad problem.

People made in God's image can do great things as they use reason. However, there is only One who truly enlightens mankind.

In Him was life, and the life was the Light of men.
The Light shines in the darkness, and the darkness did not comprehend it.
John 1:4-5

Assignments for Lesson 119

Our Creative World — Read the excerpt from *A Calm Address to Our American Colonies* by John Wesley on page 104.

Timeline Book — In the first box for Lesson 119 on page 26 (1783), write "Treaty of Paris ends the American Revolution." In the second box for Lesson 119 (1789), write "Attack on the Bastille prison in Paris."

Student Workbook or Lesson Review — If you are using one of these optional books, complete the assignment for Lesson 119.

Vocabulary — Write five sentences, using one of these words in each: resent (807), abject (810), incarcerate (810), anarchy (811), repression (812). Check in a dictionary if you need help with their definitions.

Literature — Read chapter 7 in *The Switherby Pilgrims*.

God Created the Cape of Good Hope

Lesson 120   God's Wonder

The Cape of Good Hope is not the southernmost point of Africa. It is the southwesternmost point of the continent and is about 93 miles west of Cape Agulhas, which is the southernmost point of the continent. The Cape of Good Hope does not mark the dividing line between the Atlantic and Indian Oceans. That division is also marked by Cape Agulhas. See satellite image below.

The significance of the Cape of Good Hope in ship travel is that, when a ship is sailing down the western coast of Africa, the Cape is the point at which the ship begins sailing more east than south. Finding the Cape of Good Hope gave the Portuguese hope that they could sail around Africa to India and the East Indies.

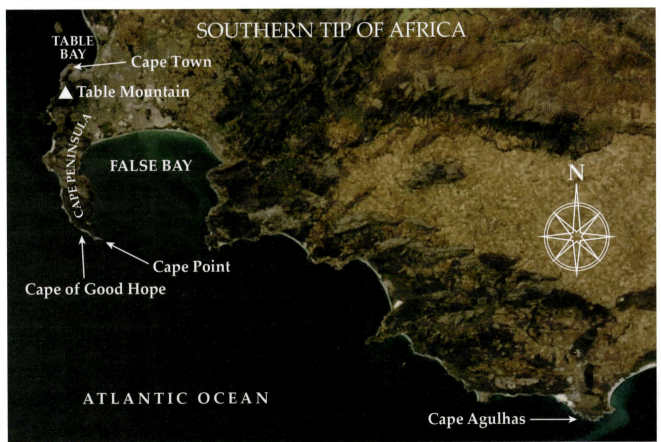

Above: Two Views of the Cape of Good Hope; Top Right: False Bay

The Geography of the Cape of Good Hope

A cape is a body of land that extends into a lake, a sea, or an ocean. It is also sometimes called a promontory, a point, or a headland. A cape is similar to a peninsula, although a peninsula is usually larger than a cape.

The Cape of Good Hope extends to the southwest from a larger peninsula called Cape Peninsula. Another cape, Cape Point, seen below, lies a little over a mile to the east and extends from the southeast of Cape Peninsula. The cold Benguela Current meets the warm Agulhas Current near the Cape of Good Hope. God created breathtaking beauty here. English navigator Sir Francis Drake, who sailed around the globe from 1577 to 1580, called it "the fairest cape in the entire circumference of the world." Even though the weather at the Cape of Good Hope can be beautiful, it also has violent storms that cause grave danger to ships. The Cape of Good Hope is about 2600 miles from the nearest coast of Antarctica.

Two Views of Table Mountain, One with Tablecloth Cloud and One at Sunset

The Cape Peninsula is about thirty miles long. At its northern end is Cape Town. Look at the image at left. It shows the topography of a portion of the image shown on page 813. Notice that the compass orientation is unusual. Cape Town is situated on Table Bay, at the foot of Table Mountain. Cape Peninsula forms the western coast of False Bay, pictured at top right. False Bay got its name because hopeful Portuguese sailors returning from the east thought that this bay was Table Bay.

Lesson 120 - God Created the Cape of Good Hope

Table Mountain is a large, fairly flat mountain about two miles wide. Its highest point is about 3,563 feet above sea level. A remarkable weather feature occurs here when southeastern winds push up the slope into colder air. Moisture in the atmosphere condenses to form a cloud that sometimes moves swiftly and envelops the top of the mountain. This cloud is called the tablecloth cloud. See Table Mountain and the tablecloth cloud at left.

Plants on Cape Peninsula

Botanists have divided the world into six floral kingdoms. These areas are defined by the kind of plants that grow there. Five of these kingdoms are 1) the United States, Canada, Europe, most of Asia, and northern Africa; 2) Central and South America; 3) Most of Africa, the Middle East, India, and Southeast Asia; 4) Australia and New Zealand; and 5) Antarctica.

The sixth and smallest of the floral kingdoms, but the one with the richest diversity in comparison to its land area, is the southern tip of Africa. The Cape Floral Kingdom makes up only one half of one percent of the land area of Africa, but 20 percent of the different kinds of plants found in Africa grow here. The Cape Peninsula has about 1,100 species of plants, and many are found nowhere else on Earth.

Plants of the Cape Floral Kingdom

Left Column: Mandela Gold Bird of Paradise, King Protea, Erica, Restios; Right Column: Sugarbush, Pelargonium, Tree Pincushion, Orange Flame

Animal Life On and Near Cape Peninsula

Many mammals live on Cape Peninsula, including several species of antelope. A few hundred Chacma baboons live there. The peninsula is home to about 250 species of birds, including one of only two colonies of African penguins. Varying water temperatures to the east and to the west attract diverse marine life near Cape Peninsula, including the Cape fur seal and Dusky Dolphins.

Above: African Penguin, Dusky Dolphin, Far Left: Colony of Cape Fur Seals; Center: Cape fur seals swim in False Bay.

Antelope and Baboons of Cape Peninsula

Antelope Clockwise from Top Left: Common Duiker, Grey Rhebok, Steenbok, Eland, Klipspringer, Red Hartebeest, Bontebok, Grysbok

Bottom Row: Chacma Baboons at a Waterhole (left), at Cape Point (center), and near the Cape of Good Hope (right)

Lesson 120 - God Created the Cape of Good Hope

More Mammals of Cape Peninsula

Clockwise from Left: Cape Clawless Otter, Cape Mountain Zebra, Cape Ground Squirrel, Cape Foxes, Cape Porcupine, Rock Hyraxes or Dassies

A Brief History

The first people known to have lived on the Cape Peninsula were the Khoikhoi people. The Portuguese were the first Europeans to visit there, but they did not establish settlements. Both Bartholomew Diaz and Vasco da Gama erected Christian crosses on the Cape of Good Hope. The crosses at right stand where those earlier wooden crosses stood.

The Cape of Good Hope was in a strategic location to provide rest and supplies for sailors traveling between Europe and the Far East. The camp that Jan van Riebeeck established on Table Bay in 1652 (see pages 719-720) eventually became Cape Town.

During the wars that revolutionary France fought against other European countries, the French army occupied the Netherlands. Since the British and French were enemies, this French occupation made the Dutch an enemy of Britain also. The British used this situation as an excuse to attack the Cape colony and gain control of this important outpost in 1795. Great Britain returned the colony to the Netherlands in 1803, reoccupied it in 1806, and finally gained permanent control through a treaty with the Netherlands in 1814.

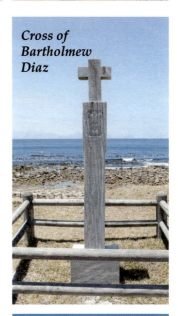

Cross of Bartholmew Diaz

Cross of Vasco da Gama

The beautiful and intriguing natural wonder God created on the southwestern tip of Africa has played an important role in world history for centuries.

Praise the Lord from the earth,
Sea monsters and all deeps;
Fire and hail, snow and clouds;
Stormy wind, fulfilling His word;
Mountains and all hills;
Fruit trees and all cedars;
Beasts and all cattle;
Creeping things and winged fowl.
Psalm 148:7-10

Left Column: Orange-Breasted Sunbird, Cape Sugar Bird on a King Protea; Above: African Wood Owl; Below: African Black Oystercatchers

Assignments for Lesson 120

Timeline Book — In the box for Lesson 120 on page 27, write "British seize the Dutch Cape Colony in South Africa."

Student Workbook or Lesson Review — If you are using one of these optional books, complete the assignment for Lesson 120 and take the test for Unit 24.

Thinking Biblically — Copy Psalm 148:7-10 in the center of a piece of paper. Around the words, illustrate the verse.

Creative Writing — Choose five of the photos in this lesson. Write a brief description of each photo. Under each description write three adjectives that describe the photo. Example:

Picture of Vasco de Gama cross on page 817
tall, erect, lonely

Literature — Read chapter 8 in *The Switherby Pilgrims*.

25 Quest for Freedom

Portrait of William Wilberforce, Esq. M.P. - The Abolitionist, *Lithograph by Endicott & Swette*

Lessons	121 - Our World Story: Napoleon and the Congress of Vienna
	122 - World Landmark: Singapore
	123 - Daily Life: Independence in Haiti and South America
	124 - God's Wonder: All Things Are Possible with God
	125 - World Biography: Hans Christian Andersen
Literature	*The Switherby Pilgrims*

1801-1850

Fifteen years after the French Revolution of 1789, Napoleon Bonaparte declared himself to be Emperor of the French and soon set out to extend his empire in Europe and in the New World. In 1819 Sir Stamford Raffles established a trading post in Singapore. It grew rapidly from the beginning, and today the nation of Singapore is one of the most densely populated in the world. Inspired by the American war for independence from England, leaders in Haiti and in South America fought for and won independence from France, Spain, and Portugal. In England William Wilberforce fought a battle for freedom for slaves. In Denmark Hans Christian Andersen wrote stories that continue to entertain and teach people around the world.

Napoleon and the Congress of Vienna

Lesson 121   Our World Story

Napoleon Bonaparte was born in 1769 on the French-held island of Corsica. Corsica lies in the Mediterranean Sea off the northwest coast of Italy. Napoleon studied at the Ecole Militaire (Military School) in Paris. He graduated as a second lieutenant in the artillery.

In 1791 Napoleon became a lieutenant colonel in the Corsican National Guard. When Corsica declared its independence from France in 1793, Napoleon moved to France and began developing a reputation as an effective leader in the French military. He worked to maintain order during the chaos of the French Revolution, and he successfully led troops in battle during France's conflicts with other European nations. Napoleon also led French forces in Egypt.

Rise to Power

In 1799 Napoleon took part in a *coup d'etat* (literally "blow of the state," or revolt) against the revolutionary government that was in place at the time. He became first consul or leader of a three-man Consulate. In 1802 the government declared him to be first consul for life, a declaration that the voters of France overwhelmingly approved. Two years later, Napoleon declared himself to be Emperor of the French. In a ceremony in the Cathedral of Notre Dame in Paris, as illustrated in the engraving at right, Napoleon took the crown from Pope Pius VII and crowned himself. The new emperor wanted to make it clear that he answered to no one.

Napoleon crowns himself.

Amid the wreckage of the Revolution, Napoleon wanted to exercise power, and the people of France wanted the order that Napoleon appeared able to provide. His goals were to bring stability to France, defeat the enemies of France, and build an empire that recaptured the glory of Rome. Napoleon was willing to keep some of the republican reforms the Revolution had put in place, but he left no question that he held all power.

Revolutionary leaders had removed the Roman Catholic Church as the state religion. They replaced it with what was called the Cult of Reason, a "religion" focused on people rather than a deity. Napoleon ousted the Cult and brought back the Catholic Church, but in a relationship that clearly placed it under his control. He appointed the people he wanted to be Catholic bishops, and the bishops then answered to the pope concerning their work in the Church. He allowed freedom of religion. Napoleon himself was an unbeliever.

Napoleon Statue on His Birth Island of Corsica

The Emperor built a more efficient government and made taxes more fair. He abolished serfdom. All adult males could vote, but they only voted to indicate whom they wanted as candidates. Napoleon decided who actually served. He appointed people to work in government on the basis of their ability and not on the basis of their family connections.

Inspired by the new Bank of the United States in America, Napoleon created the Bank of France to bring stability to the nation's economy. The empire established a system of public education. Perhaps the most significant reform that Napoleon put in place was organizing a code of laws and enabling the legal system to operate more effectively. The Code of Napoleon was the basis for the legal system that France uses today.

Statue of Napoleon at Versailles Palace

The Napoleonic Wars

The rulers of other nations in Europe had feared that France would export the Revolution into their countries. As mentioned on page 811, conflicts had begun between France and some of those countries before Napoleon came to power. The threat from France continued under Napoleon but for a different reason. Napoleon wanted to extend his power as far as he could. He hoped to extend his empire beyond Europe to North and South America. When that proved to be unworkable, he decided to sell the Louisiana Territory to the United States.

Lesson 121 - Napoleon and the Congress of Vienna

As the result of his invasions into and seizures of other countries, by 1810 Napoleon ruled France, Spain, most of the German states, the kingdoms of Italy and Naples, and the Duchy of Warsaw, as seen on the map at right. Napoleon fought the armies of Prussia, Austria, and Portugal. Denmark, which controlled Norway, became a reluctant ally by signing a treaty. Napoleon often put his relatives in place as rulers of the conquered territories.

Napoleon did suffer some significant losses. In 1805 the British fleet under Admiral Horatio Nelson defeated the French and Spanish navies at the Battle of Trafalgar off southern Spain. Nelson himself died in the battle. See statue at right. This defeat ended any threat of the French Empire expanding into Britain or other countries by sea.

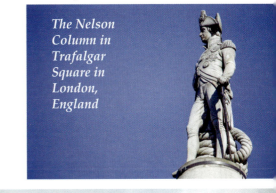

The Nelson Column in Trafalgar Square in London, England

Napoleon's most significant loss came at the hands of the Russian army. In 1812 the French began an invasion of Russia with 400,000 soldiers plus thousands of additional support personnel. The Russians fought with determination, and a bitter Russian winter finished off the French. Napoleon retreated to France with a fraction of his original army.

Reenactment of the Battle of Borodino Between the Russian and French Armies on the 200th Anniversary of the Battle

In 1814 the forces of Europe were arrayed against Napoleon, and his exhausted officers refused to continue the fight. Napoleon abdicated (gave up) his role as emperor. He went into exile on the island of Elba in the Mediterranean, a few miles from the coast of Italy. But Napoleon wasn't finished trying to rule. In 1815 he returned to France. Amid the cheers of adoring Frenchmen, he made his way to Paris, building a new army as he went.

1977 stamp from Equatorial Guinea shows Napoleon departing for Elba.

Napoleon's troops advanced into Belgium, where a combined force of British, Dutch, and Prussian soldiers, led by the Duke of Wellington of Great Britain, met and defeated the French army at the Battle of Waterloo in Waterloo, Belgium. Lacking the support of the French government, Napoleon surrendered to the British, who exiled him to the island of St. Helena in the South Atlantic far off the coast of Africa. There he lived out his days and died in 1821.

Reenactment of the Battle of Waterloo

In 2009 history enthusiasts from twenty-four countries reenacted the Battle of Waterloo at Waterloo, Belgium.

The Congress of Vienna

After Napoleon abdicated for the first time in 1814, the Austrian foreign minister (an official similar to the U.S. Secretary of State) called a meeting in Vienna of the leaders of European nations to rebuild the continent on the basis of how matters had stood before Napoleon came to power. Nine kings, dozens of princes, and hundreds of diplomats spent ten months in Vienna sorting out who should rule in the various countries affected by Napoleon. They also discussed what should happen with the colonies that European nations held. Napoleon's return interrupted their discussions for a time, but after Waterloo they returned to Vienna to finish their work.

Lesson 121 - Napoleon and the Congress of Vienna

Maurice de Tallyrand, the French representative, had been Napoleon's foreign minister. When Napoleon was nearing his fall from power, Tallyrand made secret deals with some of the enemies of France. He promised to work for a restoration of the Bourbon Dynasty in France. As a result, the leaders of the other countries were not harsh in their treatment of France.

Drawing of the Congress of Vienna by Jean-Baptiste Isabey

The participants in the Congress of Vienna wanted to resist the spread of revolutionary ideas, restore monarchies to their positions of authority, and create a balance of power so that no single country in Europe could dominate the others.

The majestic Schönbrunn Palace in Vienna, remodeled in the 1750s, was a residence of the Habsburg Dynasty. Napoleon used it briefly as his headquarters during a military campaign in Austria. It was the scene of many social events during the Congress of Vienna. The palace has over 1,400 rooms.

The Congress of Vienna recognized the brother of the late Louis XVI as Louis XVIII, the rightful king of France (the son of Louis XVI had died from illness in 1795 at the age of ten). The royal families of Spain and Portugal were restored to power. The Dutch and Austrian Netherlands came together under the Dutch king. Austria led a new German confederation of thirty-nine German states. Switzerland became an independent country. Great Britain gained control of several overseas territories, which expanded the British Empire. Powerful nations entered into alliances that were designed to prevent problems from developing into war. The leaders of these nations declared that they would hold meetings to resolve differences instead of rushing to build up their armies.

Napoleon was a brilliant administrator and an able military leader, but his self-focused lust for power led to his downfall. The leaders of Europe who met in the Congress of Vienna believed that they could decide the fate of millions of people in Europe and around the world and bring back rule by monarchs. They did not allow the people in those countries to have a say in their own governments.

It is an abomination for kings to commit wicked acts,
For a throne is established on righteousness.
Proverbs 16:12

Assignments for Lesson 121

Our Creative World — Look at the examples of French art on pages 105-107.

Map Book — Complete the activities for Lesson 121 on Map 36 "Europe, 1810."

Timeline Book — In the box for Lesson 121 on page 27, write "Napoleon is exiled to Saint Helena."

Student Workbook or Lesson Review — If you are using one of these optional books, complete the assignment for Lesson 121.

Creative Writing — Make a list of the key events in Napoleon's rise to power and fall from power. List at least seven events.

Literature — Read chapter 9 in *The Switherby Pilgrims*.

Singapore

Lesson 122 World Landmark

The small country of Singapore lies at the southern tip of the Malay Peninsula. Singapore is just north of the island of Sumatra, which is part of Indonesia. Find Singapore on the map on page 671 and the maps below. The major portion of the country of Singapore is the island of Singapore, on which is located the city of Singapore.

Located about 110 miles north of the equator, Singapore has a hot and humid climate. The average annual temperature is 80 degrees, although it rarely gets warmer than 94 degrees. The country receives about 95 inches of rainfall each year. The wet season is November through March, while the dry season runs from June through October.

The island of Singapore is about one-fourth the size of Rhode Island. Sixty-three small islands are also part of the country. Today Singapore is one of the most densely populated countries

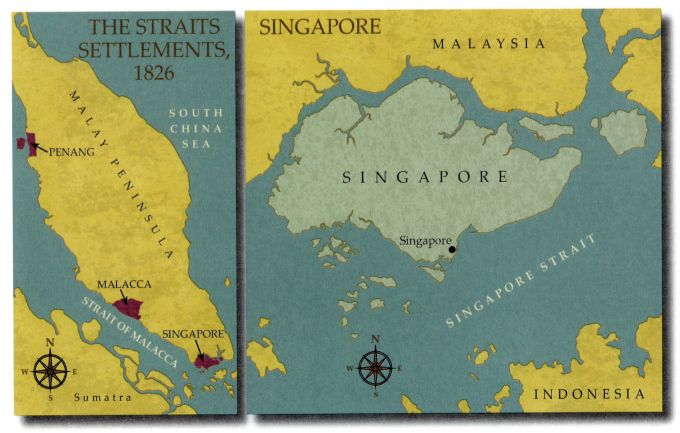

827

in the world. It is home to about 5.5 million people, or an average of almost 20,000 people per square mile.

God has created a beautiful **tropical** environment in Singapore. Even with its dense population, it is still home to over 40,000 species of wildlife, including 384 species of birds and 1,416 species of plants. See a few examples below.

Native Animals of Singapore

Rhinoceros Frog, Earless Agamid, Great Orange Tip Butterfly, Blue-Crowned Hanging Parrot, Cream-Coloured Giant Squirrel

Singapore Rainforest with Orchid and Lizard

Much of Singapore is at sea level. The highest point, which is in the middle of the island, is only about 581 feet above sea level. Much of the island was once covered by **rainforest**, but most of that has been cut for development and farming. The only rainforest remaining is also in the central part of the island. See photos of the Singapore rainforest at left.

Lesson 122 - Singapore

Only about two percent of the land is used for farming today, which means that the people must import much of their food. However, Singapore is one of the leading countries in the world in trade, manufacturing, and business investments. The shortest water route from India to China cuts through the Indian Ocean and the South China Sea. Since this route goes by Singapore, the island has been part of international trade for centuries.

Pirates, Traders, and the Orang Laut

Though written histories going back as far as the 100s AD mention towns that may have been on Singapore Island, the earliest reliable mention of the island in written history dates from 1349. A Chinese traveler recorded that two groups lived on different parts of the island: a group of pirates who attacked trading vessels, and a group of peaceful Malay and Chinese traders. Another group, the Orang Laut (meaning Sea People) from Malaysia, fished from houseboats offshore.

The Parameswara Sultanate and the Portuguese

Around 1300 a prince named Parameswara from Sumatra founded a trading city that he called Singapura, which means "Lion City" in Sanskrit. His reason for naming it this is unclear. Singapore Island has no lions. In just a few years, Thai invaders drove him out. Parameswara fled to the Malay Peninsula and established a sultanate.

As we learned on page 676, the Portuguese entered the East Indies in the early 1500s and captured the Malaysian port of Malacca on the Malay Peninsula in 1511. The Parameswara sultanate claimed to control Singapore, but in 1613 the Portuguese destroyed it.

An Asian child model is wearing the traditional dress of the Bugis people.

The Bugis and the Gambier Plantations

Trade continued to increase in the region, however. In the years that followed, the Bugis people on the island of Sumatra and nearby islands developed an active trade that included growing pepper and gambier. People use gambier, pictured at right, to produce medicines. They also use it as an agent for tanning hides. The Bugis used gambier waste to fertilize pepper plants. By 1784 growers had brought in some 10,000 laborers from China to work on gambier plantations. Some gambier growing spread to Singapore Island. The Bugis continue to be one of the largest ethnic groups in Indonesia.

Gambier

The Dutch and the English in the East Indies

As we have learned before, Dutch and English traders were entering the East Indies by the early 1600s, but the English decided to pull out of the East Indies and concentrate on building trade in India. In 1641 the Dutch captured Malacca and replaced the Portuguese as the leading European power in the region. As time went on, however, Dutch control weakened. By 1795 the Netherlands were at war with France, just as other countries were during the French Revolution. The king of the Netherlands fled to Britain and temporarily placed all Dutch overseas territories under British control so that France would not be able to capture them.

In the late 1700s the British established two small outposts on the western coast of Sumatra. The British had extensive trade in India and China, and they wanted a good base somewhere between. In the Congress of Vienna, Great Britain agreed to return Java (the island southeast of Sumatra) and the port of Malacca to the Dutch. The Dutch returned to the East Indies and soon placed heavy taxes on British ships coming into the ports they controlled. The British government in London, along with the British East India Company, again discussed whether they should leave the East Indies in order to avoid conflict with the Dutch.

The British Begin a Trading Center in Singapore

Sir Stamford Raffles (born in 1781) began his career as a **clerk** for the British East India Company in London and later served the company in India. For five years (1811-1816) he was British governor general of Java. Raffles disagreed with the idea of Britain withdrawing from the East Indies. He sailed to India and convinced Governor General Lord Francis Hastings of the need for a strong British position in the East Indies. With Hastings' approval, in early 1819 Raffles and a friend, Colonel William Farquhar, claimed a spot at the mouth of the Singapore River, the location of the present city of Singapore. Perhaps one thousand people lived on the island at that time. The British concluded a treaty with the reigning sultan, Hussein Mohammed Shah, who allowed the British to establish a port on Singapore Island in return for an annual payment and land set aside for his family. See the family palace on page 832.

Sir Stamford Raffles Statue in Singapore

Raffles decided that the British would charge no duties for ships to land and trade at Singapore. This was an important step. The Dutch charged high fees, and charging such fees was common at ports. Charging no fees encouraged trading ships to land at Singapore instead. Raffles hoped the British would make money by engaging in business that went through their port and from other purchases that traders made there. The British East India Company hoped to make a profit and send revenue to the government in London.

The plan for duty-free trade at Singapore worked. Within six weeks, over one hundred ships were anchored at Singapore. In a few months, the population of Singapore had grown to 5,000 and included Malays, Chinese, Bugis, Arabs, Indians, and Europeans. In eighteen months, what had once been a fishing village numbered 10,000 residents. The free trade arrangement continued to attract settlers and traders from many different places. Items exchanged in Singapore included coffee, spices, edible bird's nests, gold dust, ivory, rice, exotic birds, silk, tea, and porcelain.

Raffles on 1954 Singapore Stamp

A City Plan and Government for Singapore

Raffles laid out a plan for the town that called for each ethnic group to have its own section. The Chinese were the fastest growing group, so they had the largest section. The Chinese district was further subdivided into areas where people spoke the same Chinese **dialect**. Other ethnic neighborhoods still in existence today are Little India and Kampong Gelam, which was set aside in 1822 for Malays, Bugis, and Arabs.

Scenes from Chinatown, Little India, and Kampong Gelam

As the population grew in the limited space of the city, one of the more common building plans was the shophouse. See examples below. This was a narrow and deep structure that had a shop or other business on the first floor and living quarters on the second floor.

Raffles also established a law code and guidelines for how the British would govern the city. He left Singapore in 1823 and never returned. In 1824 Britain and the Netherlands signed a treaty that recognized each country's area of influence. The Dutch accepted British control of Singapore. Raffles died in London in 1826.

Shophouses in Singapore

Two years later, the British East India Company grouped together several East Indies colonies, including Singapore, calling them the Straits Settlements. See map on page 827. The British East India Company oversaw these colonies from its offices in India. In 1867 Great Britain declared Singapore to be a crown colony, which meant that the British monarch would appoint a governor who would oversee the colony instead of the private British East India Company.

Singapore Immigrants

With trade growing rapidly in the early 1800s, Singapore was a rough-and-tumble place. Some Indians who came to Singapore were businessmen. Many others were prisoners. Britain used Singapore as a **penal** colony for Indian prisoners for many years. These Indians had to work hard, but they gained skills in brick making, carpentry, and road and building construction. With these skills, they were able to find work when they had served their prison sentences.

The Malay Heritage Center was once a palace belonging to the Sultan's family.

The British brought thousands of poor workers from China. Some signed up for free passage to Singapore, but others were tricked or kidnapped. The Chinese traveled on crowded ships in terrible conditions, much like the slave ships that carried Africans to North America and the Caribbean. When they arrived, employers paid the passage for healthy workers. Others had to work for up to a year to pay for their transport. By 1878 the Chinese population on the island reached 34,000. Not many Malays moved to Singapore, even though Malaysia is the country nearest to Singapore. Today, the population of Singapore is seventy-eight percent Chinese, fourteen percent Malay, seven percent Indian or Pakistani, and one percent European, American, or other Asian.

In the first half of the 1800s, Singapore faced continuing problems with pirates on the sea and lawlessness on the land. In 1843 Britain appointed the city's first superintendent of police, and matters improved considerably. Because Singapore was such a dangerous place, few women and children came in the early years. Education was not a high priority. Raffles had suggested the construction of a public school, but this did not take place until 1835. Charities and missionaries also established schools for the relatively few children there.

In the first fifty years of British occupation of Singapore, the population increased to 85,000. In 1867 sixty European companies did business in Singapore. The opening of the Suez Canal in

Lesson 122 - Singapore

1869, which connected the Mediterranean Sea with the Red Sea, encouraged even more traffic between Europe and Asia. Singapore became even more important to British and international trade.

In the story of Singapore, we see once again how geographic location and people from different parts of the world combined to create an important historical landmark. The God who created the beauties of Singapore loves all the people from the many nations who live there.

> *By common confession, great is the mystery of godliness:*
> *He who was revealed in the flesh,*
> *Was vindicated in the Spirit,*
> *Seen by angels,*
> *Proclaimed among the nations,*
> *Believed on in the world,*
> *Taken up in glory.*
> *1 Timothy 3:16*

Assignments for Lesson 122

Our Creative World — Read the excerpt from *Trade and Travel in the Far East* on pages 108-109.

Timeline Book — In the box for Lesson 122 on page 27, write "The British establish a port at Singapore."

Student Workbook or Lesson Review — If you are using one of these optional books, complete the assignment for Lesson 122.

Vocabulary — Make a drawing for each of these words that illustrates what it means: tropical (828), rainforest (828), clerk (830), dialect (831), penal (832). Write the word under the drawing. Check in a dictionary if you need help with their definitions.

Creative Writing — If you could be the founder of a city, where would it be? What would you name it? What major buildings would you build first? What industries would you encourage to come there? Write one or two paragraphs answering these questions and adding any other ideas you have.

Literature — Read chapter 10 in *The Switherby Pilgrims*.

Independence in Haiti and South America

Lesson 123 — Daily Life

What if you lived in a country where your family had to pay taxes, your older brothers had to serve in the military, and your father had to work on a government project a certain number of days each year—but no one in your family was able to vote? What if your family had no say in who would be mayor, governor, or president?

This was the situation in which most of the people in most places in the world lived for most of world history. Our situation today, in which adult men and women can vote and hold office in most countries of the world, is the result of a long, slow process that is not finished yet.

From Absolute Monarchy to Elected Governments

We have discussed before how from earliest times a people group or a nation usually identified a wealthy individual or a powerful military leader to be their ruler. For much of world history, these rulers acted as absolute monarchs, meaning that they had absolute power over their nations and their people.

Occasionally in history a relatively larger part of a nation's population has participated in their government. As we mentioned in Lesson 119, the new ideas of the Enlightenment raised the possibility of people voting to elect their government. This idea of the value of the individual in determining government came from Christian teaching, which said that every person was worth the death of Christ on the cross.

For the grace of God has appeared, bringing salvation to all men. Titus 2:11

Opening his mouth, Peter said: "I most certainly understand now that God is not one to show partiality, but in every nation the man who fears Him and does what is right is welcome to Him." Acts 10:34-35

Governments began to change in a few places in the 1600s. When colonists in Virginia first elected the House of Burgesses in 1619, it became the first representative legislative body in the New World. In the Glorious Revolution of 1688, discussed on page 747, the English Parliament chose a king. Both of these events were major changes in the way countries functioned.

Election Day in Philadelphia *by John Lewis Krimmel, 1815*

After the American Revolution, the United States showed the world a kind of government far different from most others that had existed around the world throughout history. Everyday American citizens, who fought for and paid taxes for their government, actually determined who would serve in their government on the national, state, and local levels.

People began to see that if the individual mattered enough to be able to vote, he also mattered in many other ways that society needed to protect. As more citizens gained the right to vote in a few countries, their citizens gained other rights as well. These included the right to own property, the right to a fair trial, and the right to avoid unreasonable search of their homes.

The beacon of freedom that shone forth from the United States enlightened other parts of the Western Hemisphere. We will look at the fight for independence in Haiti and Brazil and at the efforts of Simón Bolívar and José de San Martín in several countries in South America.

Independence for Haiti

Christopher Columbus claimed the island of Hispaniola in the Caribbean for Spain. Spanish settlers later brought Africans to work there as slaves. When the Spanish left, French, English, and Dutch settlers came. Enough French people came that Spain recognized French control of the western third of the island, an area which the French called Saint-Domingue. French settlers brought in more Africans to work on their coffee and spice plantations. By 1788 there were eight times more slaves than French colonists in Saint-Domingue.

In 1791, during the French Revolution, the slaves in Saint-Domingue rebelled, destroying towns and plantations. A former slave, Toussaint L'Ouverture, took control and restored order. Napoleon sent an army that captured L'Ouverture, and he died in prison. Nevertheless, the rebel slaves defeated the French army. On January 1, 1804, General Jean-Jacques Dessalines, a rebel leader, proclaimed the independent country of Haiti. He became its first ruler and is considered the founding father of Haiti. Haiti experienced further turmoil, but this was the first successful revolution in the New World following the American Revolution.

Left and Center: Toussaint L'Ouverture; Above: This 1977 Haitian stamp shows Jean-Jacques Dessalines.

Independence for Brazil

Portuguese settlers enslaved native peoples to work on their plantations in Brazil. When many of the native slaves died, the Portuguese brought over Africans to work as slaves. By 1800 the population of Brazil was about 3.5 million, and over half of them were slaves.

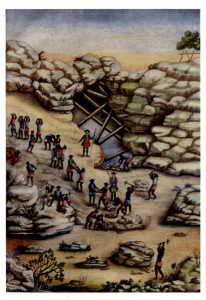

Slaves are at work in this illustration of diamond mining by Brazilian artist Carlos Julião, c. 1770s.

France invaded Portugal in 1807 because Portugal had helped Britain in a war against Napoleon. The Portuguese royal family fled to their colony of Brazil. Most members of the royal family returned to Europe in 1821, but Prince Pedro remained to oversee the colony. The Portuguese who had been born in Brazil offered to make Pedro their ruler if he would help them become independent. On September 7, 1822, Pedro declared Brazil to be an independent nation. Pedro I became emperor and established a constitutional monarchy. In the illustration on the top left of page 837, he takes an oath of obedience to the constitution. However, Pedro was a poor leader. Because many in Brazil opposed him, he resigned in 1831. He left the throne to his five-year-old son Pedro II. Pedro II began to rule in 1840 at the age of fourteen and guided a period of progress and growth.

Lesson 123 - Independence in Haiti and South America

Top Left: In this illustration by Félix Taunay, Prince Pedro I takes the oath of obedience to the constitution of Brazil. Bottom Left: Independence Monument and Burial Place of Pedro I in São Paulo, Brazil; Top Right: Oil Painting of Emperor Pedro II, Age Twelve, by Felix Taunay; Bottom Right: Simón Bolívar by Arturo Michelena

The Leadership of Simón Bolívar

Simón Bolívar was born in Venezuela in South America in 1783 to wealthy Spanish parents who had also been born in America. His parents died when he was young, and a series of tutors educated him. One tutor, Simón Rodríguez, taught Enlightenment ideas to the young Bolívar. Bolívar went to Europe to complete his education. He was a witness to the last days of the French Revolution, which he viewed as an inspirational struggle for freedom from oppression. On a later trip to Europe, he witnessed the coronation of Napoleon, which he said filled him with disgust. Bolívar also visited the new United States, and he resolved to use his life to liberate South Americans from Spain.

Bolívar fought battles of liberation in many parts of South America. Venezuela declared independence in 1811. During the conflict Bolívar spent time in Haiti, where the Haitian president encouraged him to outlaw slavery wherever his crusade for liberty was successful. Bolívar committed himself to doing this. Bolívar's armies suffered many setbacks, but in 1819 he declared the Republic of Grand Colombia, which included Venezuela, Columbia, Panama, and Ecuador. The Spanish still held most of the territory in question, but Bolívar led his followers to a brilliant military victory, and by the end of 1819 a constitution was in place and Bolívar was president.

Bolívar left Grand Colombia to join the battle for independence in Peru, which José de San Martín was leading. San Martín declared Peru free in 1821. Part of Peru became the country of Bolivia, which was named in Bolívar's honor. Bolívar helped write the constitution for Bolivia. Bolívar then returned to Grand Columbia, where he wanted more power and assumed the role of dictator. This cost him popular support. Venezuela and Ecuador broke away from Colombia, and Bolívar resigned in 1830. By this time, his health was declining. He died later that year.

Simón Bolívar was an eloquent spokesman and effective military leader in the cause of freedom. He freed his own slaves in 1821 and worked against slavery wherever he could. Bolívar believed that the most

San Martín Proclaims the Independence of Peru *by Juan Lepiani*

able people should run a government until the public was able to participate in it. He worked for strong central governments. Even though Bolívar did not have much experience running a government, and he had serious differences with other leaders, he accomplished much. Many in South America remember Bolívar as a hero of independence.

The Leadership of José de San Martín

José de San Martín also led many South Americans in their quest for independence. San Martín was born in Argentina in 1778 to Spanish parents. His family returned to Spain when José was about eight. San Martín became a Spanish army officer. He served for twenty-two years in the Spanish army and fought with Spain against Napoleon from 1808 to 1811. San Martín then returned to Argentina to help his birth country gain independence from Spain. They succeeded in 1816. He helped Chile secure its independence in 1818 and led the fight in Peru in 1825. The statues below honor San Martín. The map at left shows the year of independence for each South American country.

Left and Center: San Martín Monuments in Cordoba and Ushuaia, Argentina; Right: Unveiling of the Monument to General José de San Martín at the Argentina Embassy in Washington, D.C., in October 1925

The Monroe Doctrine

While the revolutions in South America were taking place, Spain requested assistance from its allies to help it recapture its colonies. Great Britain and the United States opposed Spain's desire to do this. Britain was stronger than the United States, but both countries wanted to increase their trade in Central and South America. In addition, the United States wanted to help other people gain the freedom it enjoyed.

In 1823 President James Monroe announced what came to be known as the Monroe Doctrine. This doctrine stated that European powers should no longer see the Western Hemisphere as a place to establish colonies. Monroe implied that the United States (backed with the strength of the British navy) would oppose such colonization with military force if necessary.

European countries accepted this stance and did not try to establish any further colonies in the Americas. Spanish colonialism in the Western Hemisphere ended completely when the United States defeated Spain in the Spanish-American War of 1898.

Movements for freedom have enabled many more people to live in greater peace, safety, and prosperity, conditions which in turn help to further the gospel of Christ.

This illustration of President Monroe establishing the Monroe Doctrine is in the United States Capital.

Lesson 123 - Independence in Haiti and South America

First of all, then, I urge that entreaties and prayers,
petitions and thanksgivings, be made on behalf of all men,
for kings and all who are in authority,
so that we may lead a tranquil and quiet life in all godliness and dignity.
This is good and acceptable in the sight of God our Savior,
who desires all men to be saved
and to come to the knowledge of the truth.
1 Timothy 2:1-4

Assignments for Lesson 123

Our Creative World — Read the excerpt from the Constitution of Hayti on pages 110-111.

Map Book — Complete the activities for Lesson 123 on Map 37 "Independence."

Timeline Book — In the box for Lesson 123 on page 27, write "Brazil declares independence from Portugal."

Student Workbook or Lesson Review — If you are using one of these optional books, complete the assignment for Lesson 123.

Thinking Biblically — Write down the name of at least one person who is in authority over you in your local, state, and national governments and one thing you could pray about for each person.

Literature — Read chapter 11 in *The Switherby Pilgrims*.

All Things Are Possible With God

Lesson 124 — God's Wonder

The God's Wonder lesson today is not about a place but about an idea, a man who believed in that idea, and the way God used that man to make what seemed like an impossible idea a reality.

Slavery in the Ancient World

Slavery is the practice of one person owning another person as property and having complete control over that person's life. People have practiced slavery all over the world from ancient times to the present.

Historical records indicate that the Sumerians practiced slavery many centuries before Christ. Assyrians, Egyptians, Persians, Chinese, Indians, Africans, and indigenous Americans all had slaves. A person usually did not become a slave because of his skin color but because his people were defeated in battle. A criminal or someone who owed another person a great deal of money might also have to work as a slave. Some slaves were well educated and highly skilled. Some held positions of responsibility but still were not free. One example is Joseph, son of Jacob and great-grandson of Abraham whose brothers sold him into slavery in Egypt.

The Law of Moses regulated how the Israelites were supposed to treat their slaves. See, for instance, Leviticus 25:44-55. The Israelites were not supposed to enslave their fellow Israelites, and the Law told how the Israelites could release the slaves they did own.

Slavery was common in Greece and Rome. In the 400s BC, perhaps one-third of the population of Athens were slaves. A large portion of the population of Rome were slaves. In the fresco from Pompeii at left, a couple has a conversation with their slave. We don't know as much detail about slavery in ancient China or Africa, but we know it existed in many parts

Fresco of Slave and His Owners from Pompeii, Italy

of the world for centuries. Most people in the ancient world believed that slavery was simply part of human society and that it was something that might happen to anybody. Few ancient writers believed it to be wrong or unjust.

A slave usually had no or very few rights. Usually they could not marry, testify in court, or own property. A slave was property. His owner had almost absolute authority to do whatever he wished with his own property. Owners generally found that slaves who were treated well were more productive workers. Though harsh treatment did not usually make a slave work harder, most owners were willing to punish slaves harshly and even in some cases put them to death.

Slaves performed much physical labor in ancient societies, including making handcrafts, farming, mining, and doing household chores. A **gang** of slaves at work in a field or in a mine controlled by an overseer was common, and the work was hard.

Some slaves were able to gain their freedom. An owner sometimes granted freedom to a slave for exceptional service or freed him in his will. Some slaves were able to save up money to purchase their freedom. Records from the temple of Artemis in Ephesus indicate that a slave could obtain his freedom by making a large enough gift to the temple.

The gospel profoundly changed the slave-master relationship. Paul taught masters how to treat their slaves:

Masters, grant to your slaves justice and fairness,
knowing that you too have a Master in heaven. Colossians 4:1

Paul also encouraged slaves to obtain their freedom if they could (1 Corinthians 7:21).

Slavery and Serfdom in the Middle Ages

After the fall of Rome, slavery in Europe declined. When fewer wars took place, the number of slaves who were prisoners of war decreased also. During the Middle Ages, wealthy landowners did not practice slavery. They did keep serfs on their land, a practice which was similar to slavery in some ways.

Conflicts between Christians and Muslims resulted in slavery. Arabs had practiced slavery before Islam appeared. When Christians and Muslims fought in the Middle East, Northern Africa, and southern Europe, both groups made slaves of their prisoners.

Plantation Slavery

Following the Crusades, Italian merchants established sugar-growing plantations on islands in the Mediterranean, and they bought slaves to work on these plantations. Some slaves came from Russia and other parts of Europe, but by 1300 Africans had begun to work as slaves on these plantations. North African Muslims bought these slaves from other Africans and sold them to European slave traders. This was not a new idea in the region, since the various nations and tribes of Africa had long practiced slavery.

Dutch Painting of a Boy with a Slave Collar, 1600s

As Portuguese traders and explorers ventured down the western coast of Africa, they purchased Africans and sold them as slaves to other Europeans. When the Portuguese established sugar plantations on islands off the coast of Africa, they used slaves to work the crops. Spanish and Portuguese colonists in the New World enslaved native peoples and also purchased African slaves, most of whom had been captured by other Africans and sold to European traders. French, English, and Dutch colonists purchased African slaves to work their cotton, sugar, and tobacco plantations.

Between the 1500s and 1800s, slave traders carried millions of Africans to the New World in horrible conditions on slave ships. Many Africans died making the voyage across the Atlantic. Of those who arrived safely, historians estimate that four out of ten of these slaves went to Brazil. Most of the rest went to Cuba, Jamaica, Saint-Domingue (which later became Haiti), and other Caribbean plantation colonies. Only about five percent came to colonies in North America, but all of the original thirteen British colonies in what became the United States practiced slavery.

Debate About Slavery

During the 1700s, some writers in Europe began to **condemn** slavery. They said that the practice was a violation of human rights. American leaders writing the U.S. Constitution in the U.S. Constitutional Convention in 1787 had heated debates over slavery. By that time, northern states had outlawed slavery while the southern states continued the practice. Some people began to see that the nation that stood for "life, liberty, and the pursuit of happiness," as the Declaration of Independence expressed it, was being **inconsistent** in allowing slavery.

Slave Funeral at Plantation, a colored lithograph by Théodore Bray, was created c. 1840-1850. It illustrates a funeral in Suriname in South America.

Lesson 124 - All Things Are Possible with God

The Constitution included some compromises in an attempt to please both defenders and opponents of slavery. The document did not use the word "slave." It allowed the practice to continue, but it said that Congress could outlaw the slave trade twenty years after the Constitution went into effect.

Those who defended slavery in America believed that Southern plantation owners had to have slaves to provide the labor for their cotton, tobacco, and sugar plantations. They also feared that freeing the slaves would cause huge social problems. They had the prejudiced idea that people with different skin colors could not live together peacefully. Southern states had strict laws called slave codes, which forbade slaves from having such basic rights as the right to travel freely and the right to obtain an education.

Two slaves in São Paulo, Brazil, stand beside the litter in which they carried this woman c. 1860.

William Wilberforce

William Wilberforce was born in England in 1759, the son of a wealthy merchant. He lived a carefree, worldly life. Wilberforce was elected to the House of Commons (the lower house of Parliament, something like the U.S. House of Representatives) in 1780. About 1785 he was convicted of the Lordship of Jesus Christ and of his need to live for a greater purpose than his own pleasure.

Wilberforce dedicated himself to two great causes. One cause was an effort to improve the morals of the English people. Wilberforce gave one-fourth of his income to charities. He helped to start such organizations as the Society for Bettering the Cause of the Poor, the British and Foreign Bible Society, and the Church Missionary Society. He helped single mothers and young people who were in trouble with the law. In all, Wilberforce gave some form of assistance to sixty-nine charitable causes. In 1797 he published a book with a long title that expressed his passion: *A Practical View of the Prevailing Religious System of Professed Christians in the Higher and Middle Classes of This Country Contrasted with Real Christianity*.

The other cause to which Wilberforce devoted his life was the **abolition** of slavery. Thomas Clarkson, who was about the same age and was a passionate opponent of slavery and the slave trade, had a profound influence on Wilberforce.

Wilberforce's Friendship with John Newton

Wilberforce was also deeply affected by the life of John Newton. Newton, born in 1725, first went to sea when he was eleven years old. By 1745 he was involved in the slave trade and living an immoral life. During a storm in 1748, Newton was convicted of his need to devote himself to God. He continued in the slave trade for a few years but retired from the sea in 1754. He began studies that led to his becoming an Anglican minister in 1764. Newton wrote many hymns, but his most famous was "Amazing Grace."

Portrait of William Wilberforce by Stephen C. Dickson, Based on a Painting by John Rising

In 1787 Newton broke his silence on the subject of the slave trade with a book, *Thoughts Upon the African Slave Trade*, which described in detail the horrible, **inhuman** conditions that existed on slave ships. Newton was 34 years older than Wilberforce, and he encouraged the younger man in his abolitionist crusade. For a time Wilberforce thought about becoming a minister, but Newton urged him to use his talents to work for abolition as a Member of Parliament.

Wilberforce's Fight in the House of Commons

As Wilberforce spoke and wrote against slavery, he was the target of harsh verbal attacks, campaigns of lies about him, and even threats and physical assaults by those who had a financial investment in the slave trade. The practice of slavery was such an accepted part of British society and of the economics of the empire that most people believed his campaign to end slavery was a foolish idea that would never succeed.

In 1789 Wilberforce introduced the first of many resolutions in the House of Commons that called for a gradual end either to slavery or to the slave trade. His resolution failed to pass. Wilberforce continued to introduce such bills in many of the years that followed. They all failed. Many members of the House did not attend when votes were taken on bills related to slavery so that they would not have to vote.

The Slave Trade Ends in the British Empire

Wilberforce and his allies did not give up. They continued to speak about the issue and to educate the public. Gradually God softened people's hearts and the tide turned. By 1807 many Members of Parliament were making speeches opposing the slave trade and supporting Wilberforce. On February 23, 1807, the House of Commons voted 283 to 16 to end the slave trade throughout the British Empire. Wilberforce bowed his head and wept. John Newton, blind and in failing health, heard the news with joy. He died in December of that year. The United States outlawed the slave trade as of January 1, 1808.

Slavery Ends in the British Empire

Never in good health, Wilberforce retired from Parliament in 1825 but continued to do what he could for the abolitionist cause. Though people could no longer import slaves from other countries, people could continue to own the slaves they already had. In 1833, as his health was failing, Wilberforce learned that the Members of Parliament had agreed to clear the path of parliamentary procedures in a way that guaranteed that Parliament would pass a law to make slavery illegal throughout the empire. Wilberforce died three days later after giving his life to the struggle to end slavery out of his deep Christian convictions.

The law that Parliament passed changed the lives of millions of people within the empire. Because the British Empire was the largest and most powerful empire in the world, the example that Parliament set in ending the age-old practice of slavery influenced governments in other parts of the world.

Ending slavery elsewhere was a slow process. Haiti had abolished slavery when it declared its independence in 1804. Most of the newly independent countries of South America, which we discussed in Lesson 123, did away with slavery when they became free. France ended the practice in 1848. The United States, after a bitter civil war, ended slavery when the Thirteenth Amendment to the Constitution passed in 1865. Spain ended slavery in its territories of Puerto Rico in 1873 and Cuba in 1886. Brazil abolished slavery in 1888.

Slavery was once an accepted part of human society and practiced around the world. Today slavery is not legal anywhere in the world; however, it continues illegally in many places. It is usually called human trafficking today, and many charitable groups and government organizations are working to end it.

This statue of William Wilberforce stands in the garden of the house where he was born which is now the Wilberforce House Museum.

Moving from slavery to freedom is an event worthy of great rejoicing. Christ offers each person true spiritual freedom, regardless of his or her station in life.

There is neither Jew nor Greek, there is neither slave nor free man, there is neither male nor female; for you are all one in Christ Jesus.
Galatians 3:28

Assignments for Lesson 124

Our Creative World — Read the lyrics of "Amazing Grace" on page 112.

Timeline Book — In the box for Lesson 124 on page 27, write "Slavery is abolished in the British Empire."

Student Workbook or Lesson Review — If you are using one of these optional books, complete the assignment for Lesson 124.

Thinking Biblically — Read Leviticus 25:44-55, a portion of the Law of Moses concerning the treatment of slaves.

Vocabulary — Write your own definition for each of these words: gang (843), condemn (844), inconsistent (844), abolition (845), inhuman (846). Look in the lesson for clues for the meaning of the words. When you are finished writing your definitions, look in a dictionary for comparison.

Literature — Read chapters 12-13 in *The Switherby Pilgrims*.

This 2007 United Kingdom stamp commemorates the 200th anniversary of the abolition of the slave trade with a portrait of William Wilberforce.

Hans Christian Andersen

Lesson 125　　　　　　　　　　　　　　　　　　　　　　　**World Biography**

Once upon a time in a land far away, there lived a man who loved to tell stories. He wrote down his stories and published them in books. Children loved to hear and to read his stories, and adults loved them, too. People all over the world loved his stories so much that, even though he came from a poor family and had many disappointments in life, he became his country's most famous author.

Stories about people who overcome difficulties inspire us. They remind us that we can do great things ourselves, even if we go through hard times. This man's story is like that.

Andersen as a Child and Young Adult

Hans Christian Andersen was born in Odense, Denmark, in 1805. Odense is a city on Funen Island. Hans' father was a shoemaker, and his mother was a washerwoman who apparently was not able to read. His Lutheran parents were poor but loving.

When Hans was very young, his parents took him to see a play. Hans loved the theater and decided that he wanted to be an actor. His father died when Hans was eleven years old. Hans went to the school for poor children in Odense and worked as an **apprentice** for a weaver and then for a tailor. When Hans was fourteen, he left school and went to Copenhagen, the capital of Denmark. He hoped that he could become famous by singing and acting in theaters. This did not happen. Hans earned very little from the occasional acting work he was able to get and almost starved.

When someone is having a difficult time, often a friend can provide just the right boost to help him. That is what happened

*Top: Statue of Andersen in Odense;
Center: Andersen's Childhood Home;
Bottom: Funen Island*

to Hans. An older benefactor, Jonas Collin, believed in Hans and paid for him to go back to school. Jonas also convinced the king of Denmark to help Hans with a scholarship.

Hans loved to write. He wrote poems and novels, and in 1829 he published his first play.

Folk Tales

In many places in Europe in the early 1800s, people told what are called folk tales. These are stories about made-up people who do amazing things, go to strange places, and learn important lessons about life. Some of these stories tell about children who have to learn important lessons by going through difficult experiences. Some tell about such things as trees and animals that talk. Stories that include talking animals or **imaginary** little people such as gnomes, dwarfs, and elves are called fairy tales. A fairy tale does not necessarily tell about a fairy, but it often will have imaginary creatures or talking animals who have human characteristics, such as being wise or foolish or impatient.

Adults in the early 1800s entertained one another by telling stories, just as their ancestors had done for centuries. They also entertained and taught their children by telling them fairy tales. If a story tells about a rabbit who learns a lesson the hard way, or about a prince who learns that he is really no better than anyone else, that story can teach children important lessons about life.

Two brothers in Germany, Jacob and Wilhelm Grimm, were literature and language scholars. The brothers collected fairy tales. In 1812 and 1815, they published collections of German fairy tales. The Grimm Brothers did this not so much to sell books as to preserve in written form the stories that people passed down from one generation to another. People often call the stories that these brothers collected *Grimms' Fairy Tales*, or *Fairy Tales from the Brothers Grimm*.

Top: 1985 German Stamp of Brothers Wilhelm and Jacob Grimm; Left Column: 2005 Jersey Stamp of Rumpelstiltskin; 1985 Hungarian Stamp of Little Red Riding Hood and the Wolf; Right Column: 1976 Comoros Stamp of Hansel and Gretel; 1965 German Federal Republic Stamp of Snow White and the Seven Dwarfs

The Stories of Hans Christian Andersen

In 1835 Hans Christian Andersen published his first stories. Three of them were his versions of popular folk tales or fairy tales, but another was a story he made up. His stories were very popular, so he kept writing them. Usually he would publish **booklets** with four stories, but eventually a publisher collected his stories into a single volume. Some of Andersen's stories were based on his own life experiences. "The Ugly Duckling" is about a plain, homely duckling who is rejected by others but who grows up to be a beautiful swan. Many people believe that this is really a story about Andersen himself.

He made several trips throughout Europe. He published **accounts** of his travels, and people enjoyed reading about his experiences because he was such a good storyteller. When Andersen was in England, he met the famous author Charles Dickens.

When we face disappointments in life, we have to go on living and working and helping people. This is what Andersen had to do. He loved three different ladies, but none of them ever agreed to marry him. He was heartbroken, but he kept writing stories and enjoying the pleasure that his stories brought to people.

Andersen used some of his stories to teach spiritual lessons, especially about the reality of heaven. He wrote a story of faith called "God Can Never Die." He sometimes told people that when they were facing a difficult time they needed to say the Lord's Prayer. He once told about praying, "God, my God, I have never doubted." Modern publishers have **edited** out much of the faith in Andersen's work, so that aspect of his writing is not as well known today.

Andersen became a famous author in his lifetime, and today he continues to be well known. He wrote poetry, novels, plays, and travel sketches, but what became popular all over the world were the 156 tales or stories he published. Some of his most popular stories, in addition to "The Ugly Duckling," include "The Princess and the Pea," "The Emperor's New Clothes," "The Little Mermaid," "The Snow Queen," and "Thumbelina."

Left to Right: Illustrated page from "The Ugly Duckling," 1893; 1987 Hungarian Stamp with "The Ugly Duckling;" Floral Depiction of "The Princess and the Pea" in Jesperhus Holiday Park in Denmark

Celebrating and Remembering Hans Christian Andersen

Clockwise from Top Left: Andersen Statue and the Ugly Duckling in Central Park, New York City; Andersen Statue in Slovakia; Andersen Actor with 1869 Photo of Andersen by Thora Hallager; Copy of the Last Page of "The Little Mermaid" in Andersen's Handwriting; A Girl Signing the Register Below Andersen's Signature at the Hans Christian Andersen Museum in Odense; An Illustration of "The Fir Tree," by Vilhelm Pedersen, the First Artist to Illustrate Andersen's Tales; Andersen Statue in Copenhagen; Center: Silhouette of "The Shepherdess and the Chimney Sweep" Cut by Andersen Himself; 2005 Stamp from Belarus Honoring Andersen

Lesson 125 - Hans Christian Andersen

Why Stories Are Important

People love to hear stories. They take us to faraway places, show us how foolish we can be, and illustrate human relationships and experiences that we all know. Stories often help us learn important lessons more effectively than if we just heard an idea or a statement of truth. This is why Jesus told the stories that we call parables. He could have just said, "People respond to the gospel differently," but instead He told the parable of the sower (Matthew 13), which vividly describes those differences. Jesus could have just said, "God is happy when a lost person is saved," but His stories about a lost sheep, a lost coin, and a lost boy help us feel the joy that God has (Luke 15).

Once in the Old Testament, Jotham told a story about when the trees wanted to anoint a king for themselves. The trees got into trouble when they asked the bramble to be their king, just like Jotham believed the Israelites were getting into trouble by making Abimelech their king (Judges 9:7-21).

God gave people the ability to think about how things might be different from the way they are. This is one way that we learn and grow. When a young man reads a story about someone who shows courage, he thinks about how he ought to be courageous and not just live for himself. When a young woman reads a story about a princess waiting for the right man to come along, she learns how important it is to be patient about getting married, and she envisions a happy home. Reading a story about someone who has a bad habit, gets into trouble, learns an important lesson, and changes his ways can help someone who has a bad habit to believe that he can be different and also help him see what might happen if he doesn't change. If you can't imagine being different, you won't be different, however much you say you believe that people can be different.

Everybody knows that animals can't talk and that little people such as dwarfs and gnomes don't exist, but stories about such things illustrate important truths in an entertaining way. We don't believe in goblins, but we do need to understand that evil is real and that the devil's temptations are serious.

If we can imagine, then we can imagine ourselves being more like Jesus. Paul said, "Consider yourselves to be dead to sin, but alive to God in Christ Jesus" (Romans 6:11). A person dies to sin when he becomes a Christian (Romans 6:3-4). God will change the way that person thinks so that he is able to put off the old ways and put on the new person in Christ, as Paul teaches in Colossians 3:9-10. The gospel is not a fairy tale, of course; it is the truth. The story of Jesus is God's true story that serves as our guide and model for becoming more like Him.

Stories such as those that Hans Christian Andersen told teach important lessons about right and wrong. They teach problem-solving skills and the truth that actions have consequences. They show how the good guys win by doing the right thing. "The Princess and the Pea" teaches us not to be deceived by appearances. "The Emperor's New Clothes" reminds us how foolish it is to be prideful and how important it is to do the right thing even when no one around us is doing so.

Seeing What Is Possible

Hans Christian Andersen published an autobiography in 1855. He called it *The Fairy Tale of My Life*. Andersen died in 1875.

Hans Christian Andersen understood the power of stories. Because he did, he helped many people around the world to live more happily ever after.

Artist Elisabeth Jerichau-Baumann painted this picture of Hans Christian Andersen reading to her children in 1862.

In Matthew 13, a large crowd stood on a beach, and Jesus "spoke many things to them in parables," including this one about the kingdom of heaven being worth everything:

The kingdom of heaven is like a treasure hidden in the field, which a man found and hid again; and from joy over it he goes and sells all that he has and buys that field.
Matthew 13:44

Assignments for Lesson 125

Timeline Book — In the box for Lesson 125 on page 27, write "Andersen publishes a collection of fairy tales."

Student Workbook or Lesson Review — If you are using one of these optional books, complete the assignment for Lesson 125 and take the test for Unit 25.

Thinking Biblically — Read Matthew 13:44-50, which includes three of the parables of Jesus.

Vocabulary — Copy the following sentences, placing the correct vocabulary word in the blank: apprentice (849), imaginary (850), booklet (851), account (851), edit (851).

1. The politician agreed to an interview with the promise that the network would not _____ any of her answers.
2. Sara brought home a _____ on endangered marine life from the environmental fair.
3. I am interested in being an _____ to a carpenter.
4. We never get bored when Mr. and Mrs. Thomas give us an _____ of their most recent trip.
5. Lily paints wonderful pictures of fairies, elves, and other _____ creatures.

Creative Writing — Write a fairy tale of at least one page.

Literature — Read chapter 14 in *The Switherby Pilgrims*. If you are using the Student Workbook or Lesson Review, answer the literature review questions on *The Switherby Pilgrims*.

Family Activity — Read stories by Hans Christian Andersen. See page FA-50 for instructions.

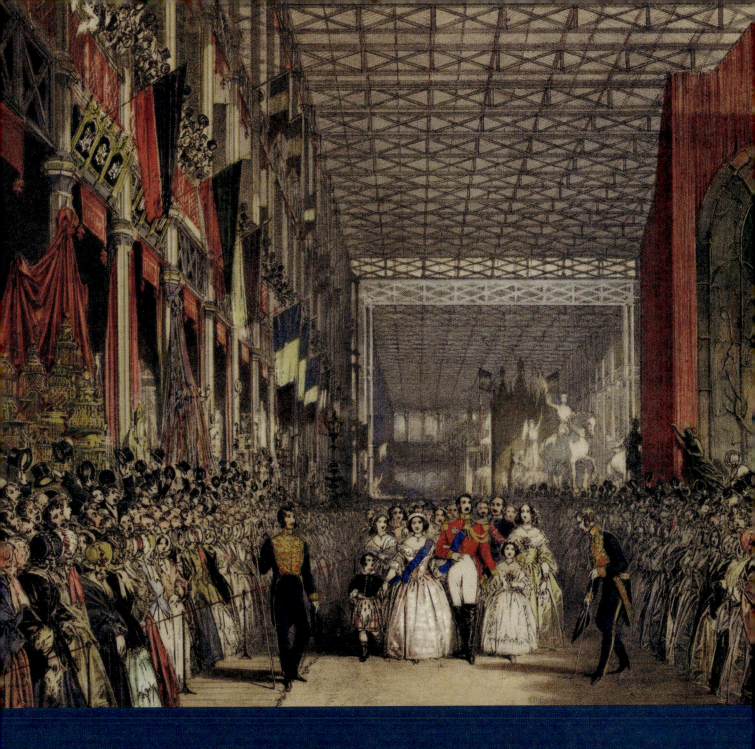

26 The Victorian Era

Queen Victoria and Prince Albert lead a royal procession into the Great Exhibition in London in 1851.

Lessons
126 - World Biography: Queen Victoria
127 - Our World Story: The Crimean War
128 - Daily Life: Japan's Open Door
129 - World Landmark: The Eiffel Tower
130 - God's Wonder: God Created Gold

Literature
In *The Chestry Oak* by Kate Seredy, Prince Michael of Chestry loses everything he knows in World War II, then finds love and hope with a family in America. (See "Notes to Parents on the Literature" in the back of the Answer Key.)

1851-1900

The sun never set on the British Empire when Queen Victoria was on the throne. However, the British fought war after war to hold on to their empire, including the Crimean War when Florence Nightingale brought comfort and better medical care to British troops. In 1853 American Commodore Matthew Perry sailed to Japan to convince that country to end its isolation from the rest of the world and become a trading partner with other nations. The late 1800s were a time of grand exhibitions in large cities, including Paris, where Alexandre Gustave Eiffel constructed the Eiffel Tower on the grounds of the Universal Exposition of 1889. Individuals in various parts of the world discovered gold in the second half of the 1800s, and people scrambled to these faraway places in search of it.

Queen Victoria

Lesson 126   World Biography

Great Britain's first successful overseas colony was Jamestown in North America, established in 1607. The nation continued to establish colonies around the world and became a large empire. Even after losing its thirteen American colonies during the American Revolutionary War, Great Britain continued to gain new territories.

The British Empire grew to its greatest size and greatest international power in the 1800s. At its height, this small island nation governed one-fourth of the world's land area and one-fourth of the world's population.

Queen Victoria reigned over the British Empire from 1837 until 1901. Her reign of almost sixty-four years was the longest in British history at that time. Because of the length of her reign and the power of the empire, the last two-thirds of the 1800s are known as the Victorian Era.

Ancestors of Queen Victoria

As we learned in Lesson 110, after Catholic James II became ruler of Great Britain, Parliament invited James II's Protestant daughter Mary and her husband, William of Orange of the Netherlands, to invade England and depose James II. James left the country and William and Mary ruled in his place. This change in power is known as the Glorious Revolution. Mary died in 1694 and William in 1702. William and Mary left no heirs, so the throne passed to Anne, another daughter of James II.

Queen Anne served as the queen of Great Britain until her death in 1714. Anne's closest Protestant relative was Prince George of the German city of Hanover. He became King George I of Great Britain, even though he spoke little English. George began the House of Hanover in Britain. This same royal family, now called the House of Windsor, rules in Britain today. George I reigned until his death in 1727. His son George II reigned in his place until 1760. When George II died in 1760, his grandson George III became king.

George III reigned for sixty years, from 1760 to 1820, which included the period of the American Revolutionary War. King George became unpopular in Britain when the country lost its American colonies. In his last few years on the throne, George III became mentally ill.

his son, George IV, became regent in 1811, ruling on behalf of his father, and served in that position until his father died in 1820.

George IV ruled as king from 1820 until his death in 1830. He was followed by his brother, William IV, who was king from 1830 until his death in 1837. George IV and William IV were unpopular kings because of their immoral lifestyles. When William died, the next in line for the throne was his niece, Victoria. Victoria's grandfather George III and uncles George IV and William IV are shown below.

George III

George IV

William IV

Family Life

Victoria was born in 1819. Her father was Edward, another son of George III. Her mother was a German princess who was also named Victoria. Edward died shortly after Victoria was born. A governess educated her at home. Victoria became queen when she was eighteen years old. She took the throne when the monarchy was unpopular, but her character and leadership restored honor and **dignity** to the monarchy in the eyes of the British people.

Just three weeks after becoming queen in 1837, Victoria moved into Buckingham Palace, pictured at top right. The home had belonged to the royal family since 1761 when her grandfather George III purchased it, but Queen Victoria was the first British monarch to make Buckingham Palace her London home. Victoria left from Buckingham Palace for her **coronation** at Westminster Abbey in June 1838. Victoria is taking Communion at her coronation below.

In 1840 Queen Victoria married her first cousin, Prince Albert of the German state of Saxe-Coburg and Gotha.

The photo of Buckingham Palace at left includes the Queen Victoria Memorial with its 82-foot-tall marble monument and the memorial gardens where over 22,000 plants are planted each summer. The aerial photo at right shows the fourth wing added by Victoria and Albert, which made the palace a quadrangle. This photo also shows the Queen Victoria Memorial.

Victoria and Albert were devoted to each other and had a strong marriage. Albert, who kept the title of Prince Albert throughout his life, helped Victoria know how to carry out her role as queen effectively. They had nine children, many of whom married into the royal families of other countries in Europe. Their first daughter, Princess Victoria Adelaide Mary Louise, pictured below, married a Prussian prince. Their son Wilhelm, discussed in Lesson 134, grew up to become Kaiser Wilhelm II, King of Prussia and Emperor of Germany.

Albert served as advisor and personal secretary to the queen. He encouraged science, trade, industry, and the arts. Albert died in 1861 at the age of 42 after **contracting** typhoid fever. Victoria plunged into deep grief and was rarely seen in public for many years. She did carry out a number of public functions later in her reign, but she dressed in black for the rest of her life. See the portrait of Victoria in mourning clothes above.

Photograph of Queen Victoria in Mourning Clothes, 1866

Princess Victoria

Prince Albert had been involved in planning the Central Hall to be built in London to promote art and science. When Queen Victoria dedicated the hall in 1871, it was renamed Royal Albert Hall of the Arts and Sciences. Albert also supported the Museum of Manufactures, later renamed the Victoria and Albert Museum. Queen Victoria commissioned several monuments in her husband's honor, including the Albert Memorial. See the photos on the next page.

Above: Royal Albert Hall; Top Right: Statue of Albert on the Exterior of the Victoria and Albert Museum; Right: Albert Memorial

Literature Classics

During the reign of Queen Victoria, people all over the world began to admire British culture. Among the many classics of British literature written in the Victorian Era are *A Christmas Carol* by Charles Dickens, *Treasure Island* by Robert Louis Stevenson, and *At the Back of the North Wind* by George MacDonald.

British Hymns

During this period, many British **hymnists** wrote songs Christians still sing. Frances Havergal learned to read at age four, wrote poetry at age seven, and memorized Psalms, Isaiah, and most of the New Testament. The daughter of a hymnist, she wrote dozens of songs including "I Bring My Sins to Thee," "Take My Life and Let It Be," and "I Gave My Life for Thee." Cecil Frances Alexander wrote "All Things Bright and Beautiful," "Once in Royal David's City," and "Jesus Calls Us." Alexander started a school for the deaf. See plaque from the music room dedicated to her honor at left. One estimate is that some 400,000 hymns were published while Victoria was on the throne.

Alexander's husband served as a bishop at St. Columb Cathedral in Londonderry, Northern Ireland. The music room plaque and church yard are pictured at left.

Lesson 126 - Queen Victoria

The Great Exhibition of the Works of Industry of All Nations

Queen Victoria ruled Britain during a time of great expansion in industry. In 1842 she became the first British monarch to ride on a railroad. Great Britain celebrated industry in 1851 with the Great Exhibition of the Works of Industry of All Nations. Prince Albert headed the planning for this event.

Greenhouse builder Joseph Paxton designed a huge iron and glass building called the Crystal Palace, pictured below and on page 855, to house the displays. The building itself was an architectural wonder. The exhibition included displays from many countries but highlighted the scientific, technological, artistic, and craft accomplishments of the British Empire. The exhibition welcomed some six million visitors from around the world.

Left: Crystal Palace Exhibit Hall; Right: Victoria Memorial, Calcutta, India

The Power of the British Empire

The British Empire was the largest collection of lands and people under one government in the world. A popular Victorian Era saying was true: "The sun never sets on the British Empire." Britain gained control of the Chinese port city of Hong Kong in 1842. It strengthened its control in India in 1858 when the British East India Company gave up its control there. Parliament declared Victoria to be Empress of India in 1877. See her memorial above.

British colonies north of the United States united to form the self-governing country of Canada in 1867. British colonies in Australia united to form the country of Australia in 1901. Canada and Australia maintained close ties with the United Kingdom.

Britain fought several wars during Victoria's reign in order to defend or expand its territory. We will discuss the Crimean War in the next lesson. Great Britain fought for and gained control of

Egypt. They fought the Boer Wars (1880-1881 and 1899-1902) in an effort to take control of South Africa. The Boers in South Africa, now called Afrikaners, were primarily of Dutch ancestry. One chief motivation for the British to fight the Boers was to gain control over the gold mines that had been discovered in South Africa. Great Britain won the wars, but they were costly for the British. No nation challenged Britain's naval power during the Victorian Era, and it was rightly said that the British navy "ruled the waves" of the world's oceans.

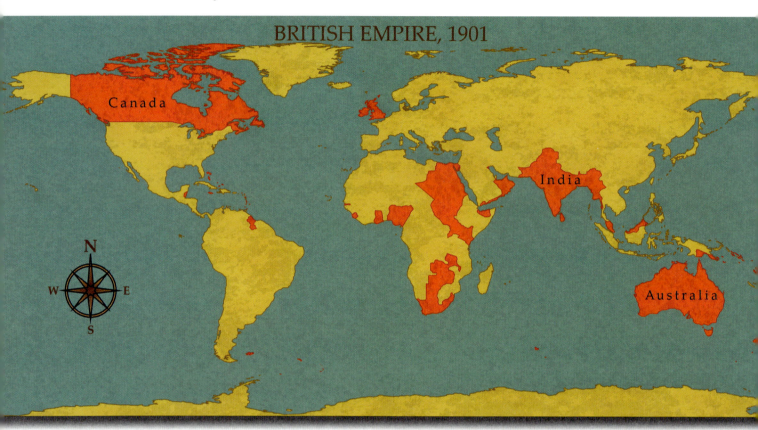

The Irish Potato Famine

Great Britain continued to treat Ireland with cruel **neglect**. English kings had claimed authority over Ireland since the 1100s. The main crop grown in Ireland in the early 1800s was potatoes. A severe blight ruined the potato crop in the 1840s. The British government did little to provide relief for the Irish people. British citizens owned much of the land in Ireland. These landlords did not help the Irish when the crop failures made

1846 Illustration of the Irish Potato Famine

them unable to pay their rent. About one million Irish died of starvation. Almost four million emigrated from Ireland in the 1800s, mostly to America. While the population on the island of Great Britain doubled during Victoria's reign, the population of Ireland was roughly cut in half.

Left: Landlords evict Irish tenants. Right: A Catholic priest blesses Irish who are emigrating to America.

Victoria's Role in the Government of Great Britain

Disraeli

Victoria took an active role in deciding government policies. She lost some of the public's admiration when she withdrew in her grief after the death of her husband Albert. Later in her reign, British Prime Minister Benjamin Disraeli, pictured at left, encouraged Victoria to become a strong leader again. She followed his advice. The Golden Jubilee in 1887 marked her fiftieth year on the throne. See the presentation cup below. The photo below was taken in honor of her Diamond Jubilee in 1897, observing sixty years on the throne. Both jubilees were great celebrations during which her subjects poured out love and appreciation for their queen. Victoria remained active in her role as queen, even making an official visit to Dublin, Ireland, in 1900, the year before she died.

However, the 1800s were a time when monarchs were losing power. More and more countries began to elect representatives to operate their governments. The number of British citizens who could vote in elections increased greatly, especially later in Victoria's reign. She accepted the change in her role and by the end of her reign was content to be the symbolic leader of Britain and the empire.

This presentation cup from India commemorates Queen Victoria's Golden Jubilee.

Queen Victoria

Victoria's reign continued into the twentieth century. She died on January 22, 1901, a few months short of the sixty-fourth anniversary of her ascension to the throne.

British Colonies Honor Their Queen

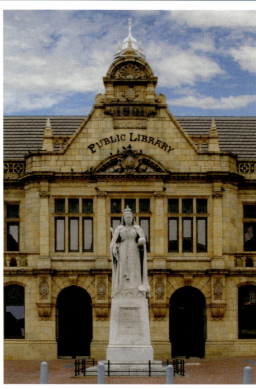

Clockwise from Top Left: Republic Square, Malta; Public Library in Port Elizabeth, South Africa; Stamps from Hong Kong (1991) and Canada (1897); Town Hall, Ballarat, Victoria, Australia; Town Hall, Sydney, Australia; Montreal, Québec, Canada

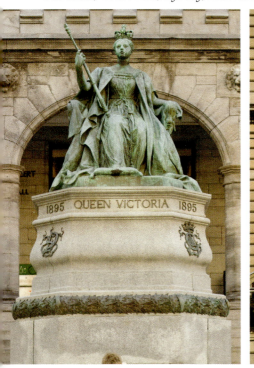

Lesson 126 - Queen Victoria

During the Victorian Era, British missionaries carried the gospel to many places as they obeyed the Lord's call to take the gospel to the world:

And He said to them,
"Go into all the world and preach the gospel to all creation.
He who has believed and has been baptized shall be saved;
but he who has disbelieved shall be condemned."
Mark 16:15-16

Assignments for Lesson 126

Our Creative World — Read the excerpts from the "Journals of David Livingstone" on pages 113-114.

Timeline Book — In the box for Lesson 126 on page 28, write "London hosts the Great Exhibition."

Student Workbook or Lesson Review — If you are using one of these optional books, complete the assignment for Lesson 126.

Queen Victoria Coin, India, 1862

Thinking Biblically — Ask a parent to help you look up the words to one of the hymns mentioned on page 860. Read the words.

Vocabulary — Find each of these words in a dictionary, then find the definition that corresponds to the way the word is used in this lesson: dignity (858), coronation (858), contract (859), hymnist (860), neglect (862). Copy the words and definitions.

Literature — Read chapter 1 in *The Chestry Oak*.

The Crimean War

Lesson 127   Our World Story

T he British fought wars again and again to hold onto the territory they controlled. The Crimean War was the scene of great tragedies, but it also provided one person with the opportunity to introduce changes that helped many people.

Russians Want to Extend Their Territory

Crimea (also called the Crimean Peninsula) extends from the coast of what is now Ukraine south into the Sea of Azov and the Black Sea. In the mid-1800s, Russia controlled Crimea with a naval fleet and an army stationed there. Russia wanted to control more of the Black Sea region, and also more of the Balkan Peninsula, the Middle East, and the Mediterranean, but the Ottoman Empire was in their way. The Ottomans controlled Constantinople, the Bosphorus and Dardanelles (also known collectively as the Straits), the Anatolian Peninsula, and the Balkan Peninsula

except for Greece. However, the Ottoman Empire was becoming weaker in its ability to defend its territory. Russia decided to make this a conflict about religion. Russia was a Slavic nation. Since most of its citizens were members of the Orthodox Church, Russia claimed that it had the right to protect the Orthodox Slavs who lived in the Balkans.

The British Want to Keep the Ottoman Empire Strong

The British saw Russia's desires as a threat. They did not want the Russians to control Constantinople or the Straits. The British wanted the Ottoman Empire to remain strong. They believed this would help the British Empire remain powerful in the Mediterranean, in the Middle East, and along trade routes to India. The British began to call their conflict with Russia the Eastern Question. British leaders wondered what they should do about areas that had historically been controlled by the now-weakening Ottoman Empire. Britain was afraid that other countries would get ahead of them and take control of lands the Ottomans had once ruled.

The French Want Access to the Holy Land

The Roman Catholic Church wanted to maintain churches in the Holy Land and allow Christians access to historical religious sites there. The Catholic nation of France supported the Church in this. The Ottomans controlled the Holy Land at this time. The old conflict between the Orthodox and Catholic Churches caused Orthodox Russia to see Catholic France as a threat.

War in the Crimea

In July 1853 Russia invaded and occupied Moldavia and Wallachia in the Balkans, saying that their purpose was to defend the Orthodox Slavs there. The Ottomans, who controlled the area, protested. Britain and France ordered their fleets to move to the Dardanelles to prepare for an attack against Russia if the Russian army invaded that area. Russia and the Ottoman Empire began fighting each other. In 1854 Great Britain and France declared war on Russia.

Austria demanded that Russia withdraw from Moldavia and Wallachia. Russia withdrew because it did not want to bring Austria into the conflict and it did not want to fight the armies of several other nations. When that happened, the allies (Britain, France, and the Ottomans) responded by invading the Crimean Peninsula in order to defeat the Russians there and keep Russia from becoming a threat in the region.

The allies chose the important Russian military base of Sevastopol as their main target. British photographer Roger Fenton took the photograph at right of an allied camp on the plateau near Sevastopol. After a siege, Sevastopol fell to the allies. Because the Russians faced difficulties in getting additional supplies and troops to the area, they agreed to a peace conference. In the Treaty of Paris, signed in 1856, Russia said that it would remove its military fleet from

Allied Tents and Huts on the Plateau of Sevastopol

the Black Sea, give up its desire for influence in the Balkans, and accept British dominance in the eastern Mediterranean.

Changes in the Way Armies Fight Wars

The Crimean War was the last war fought without modern military technology. It was the last time that British ambassadors had to meet with foreign governments without at least being able to send a telegram to their own government headquarters in London.

Roger Fenton Photographs

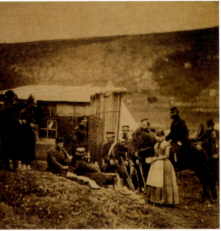

Left Column: Fenton's Wagon; French and English Soldiers; British Supplies at Cossack Bay; Right Column: "Cooking House"; William Russell, Reporter for The Times of London *Newspaper; Officers of the British 4th Light Dragoons*

During the Crimean War, for the first time photographers were able to send home pictures of battle scenes. Reporters, including William Russell at left, sent news reports from the front lines of the battles.

Although Britain was victorious, the Crimean War showed the British government that its military was weak. The British army suffered from poor planning and poor communication. Military leaders tend to fight new wars the way they fought previous wars. For British soldiers in the Crimean War, this meant fighting the way they did at Waterloo in 1815, forty years earlier. Military strategy and technology had progressed since then. In addition, several of the British field commanders were older men who were not prepared for the rigors of war.

One British mistake illustrates the weakness of the British army. Two British officers who had a personal rivalry participated in the Battle of Balaklava. Somehow this rivalry caused a British unit of 673 men, which was called the Light Brigade, to receive incorrect orders to attack Russian soldiers who held a strong military position. Almost 250 of these 673 British soldiers were killed or wounded in the twenty-minute attack. Though it was a misguided attack, the bravery of the British troops impressed the Russians. This mistake inspired English poet Alfred, Lord Tennyson to write his famous poem "The Charge of the Light Brigade."

Florence Nightingale

The suffering that soldiers endured during the Crimean War was horrible. Tens of thousands of men died in battles, but even more died from disease. The Russians lost at least twice as many men as the British, French, and Ottomans combined.

Many soldiers contracted dysentery and cholera. At the military hospital set up at Scutari on the east side of the Bosphorus, sick and wounded soldiers lived in unsanitary conditions and suffered bitterly cold winter weather. Doctors performed operations without anesthesia.

The British government asked Florence Nightingale to go to Scutari and oversee the nursing operations there. She took

"The Lady with the Lamp"

thirty-eight other nurses with her. Nightingale worked tirelessly with limited funds at a cost to her own health, but she did improve conditions at the hospital. She established strict standards for cleanliness and for nursing care. The illustration below shows a ward of the hospital after her arrival. The illustration above depicts her as "The Lady with the Lamp," which is what soldiers came to call Nightingale because of her visits to the sick and wounded at night.

Florence Nightingale said she could never forget what she experienced in the Crimean War. For the rest of her life, she worked to improve health care provided to British soldiers. Because of her weakened health she seldom left her home, but heads of government, military experts, politicians, and reformers came to talk with her and get her advice. She made a revolutionary impact on health care for soldiers in Britain and India. The U.S. government asked for her advice about providing medical care for soldiers during the American Civil War.

Florence Nightingale was born in 1820 in Florence, Italy (for which she was named), to wealthy English parents who were living there at the time. Her parents educated her at home. When she was sixteen, she believed that God had called her to a special mission to

This illustration shows one of the wards of the hospital at Scutari after Florence Nightingale arrived.

Unit 26 - The Victorian Era

Statue of Florence Nightingale, Derby, England

This 1970 United Kingdom stamp celebrates the 150th anniversary of Florence Nightingale's birth.

help people. She received nursing training in the early 1850s, not long before the Crimean War began. When she was thirty-three, she became superintendent of a women's hospital in London.

Florence Nightingale transformed army medical care. In 1860 she established a school to train nurses. She wrote several books that taught others what she learned about nursing. In 1907, three years before her death, she was the first woman to receive the British Order of Merit, an honor given to individuals who make great achievements in the arts, learning, literature, and science. Nightingale was the pioneer of the modern nursing profession.

Florence Nightingale brought much good out of the terrible suffering of war. Her work blessed millions of soldiers, and in a real sense, all who have received medical care since her groundbreaking efforts during the Crimean War.

*Do not be overcome by evil,
but overcome evil with good.
Romans 12:21*

Assignments for Lesson 127

Our Creative World — Read Florence Nightingale's "Letter to W. J. P. Burton" on page 115.

Map Book — Complete the activities for Lesson 127 on Map 38 "The Crimean War."

Timeline Book — In the box for Lesson 127 on page 28, write "Florence Nightingale goes to the Crimea."

Student Workbook or Lesson Review — If you are using one of these optional books, complete the assignment for Lesson 127.

Creative Writing — Imagine that you are a wounded soldier in a British hospital during the Crimean War. Write a letter to your family telling about the changes brought by Florence Nightingale to the hospital.

Literature — Read chapter 2 in *The Chestry Oak*.

Japan's Open Door

Lesson 128   Daily Life

On July 8, 1853, Japanese life and culture began a dramatic change. On that date, Commodore Matthew Perry led a naval expedition of four ships of the U.S. Navy to the Japanese port of Uraga. Two ships were steam-powered, and they towed two sailing ships behind them. The American crew totaled 560 men. Perry was respectful but firm as he insisted that Japan open its ports to American vessels and begin trading with Americans. The print below illustrates Japan in the same year that Perry arrived. The process of arranging a treaty between Japan and the United States took five years, but in the end Japan did open up to foreigners.

Japan Before Perry

As we learned in Lesson 105, in 1639 the Japanese closed their country to foreign influence except from China and a few Dutch traders. The imaginary wall that Japan erected between itself and the rest of the world was practically complete. The shogun enacted strict laws against any citizen of Japan having any contact with foreigners. The Japanese could not receive gifts or even speak to people from other countries. If a Japanese sailor was

Men and women cross bridges from island to island to reach a shrine in this 1853 print by Japanese artist Hiroshige Andō.

lost at sea and a foreign vessel rescued him, the sailor could be executed for having contact with a foreigner. Because of this lack of interaction, by the mid-1800s most Japanese knew little about the rest of the world. Most did not know the United States existed or about the Industrial Revolution, steam engines, railroads, telegraphs, or modern rifles (the Portuguese had brought firearms to Japan centuries before).

Even the few Dutch whom the Japanese permitted to stay on a small island near Nagasaki had to observe strict rules about their contact with Japan. A high wall surrounded the island.

Once a year, one of the Dutch could come to the shogun's palace to bring gifts, crawl on all fours into his presence to present the gifts, then crawl backwards out of the room to avoid turning his back on the shogun, all to express gratitude for the shogun allowing the Dutch to be there.

The shogunate strictly controlled Japanese society. The Japanese people had few freedoms. Laws restricted what people of the different classes could buy and own, the size of house that people in each class could live in, to whom those in each class had to bow, how each class was to dress, and how their clothes were to be made, even down to the size and kind of stitches used in the clothes. All of the *daimyos* (or lords) spent part of every other year at the shogun's palace in Edo, but when the daimyos left the shogun required their families to remain in Edo. In general, Japanese laws, customs, and fashions had not changed in 250 years.

However, the Japanese had an active culture. They had local grade schools as well as universities for lords and samurai. An estimated half of the adult male population could read and write, which was a large percentage for that time. The Japanese produced novels, plays, poetry, paintings, and woodblock printing.

Perry's Military Record

Matthew Perry was fifty-nine years old when he led his first expedition to Japan. He had given a lifetime of service to the United States Navy. Matthew's older brother, Oliver Perry, had led U.S. Navy forces to victory against a British fleet on the Great Lakes during the War of 1812. Matthew Perry served on his brother's ship and was wounded.

Perry was later the commanding officer of the first U.S. steamship, the *Fulton*. He led a naval squadron to help stop the African slave trade in 1843, long after the United States had outlawed it in 1808. Perry had commanded American naval forces when the United States fought against Mexico during the Mexican War (1846-1848).

Photograph of Commodore Perry by American Photographer Matthew Brady

Attempts to Bring Japan into the "Family of Civilized Nations"

U.S. President Millard Fillmore chose Matthew Perry to lead the expedition to Japan. Perry studied hard and prepared himself well so that he could make a successful entry into Japan and bring the country into what he called the "family of civilized nations."

Americans had attempted to open Japan to foreign contact on previous occasions. In 1837 Americans tried to return Japanese sailors who had been shipwrecked. The Japanese fired on their ship, and the Americans left. In 1846 commander James Biddle brought a letter from President James K. Polk to Japan asking for trade relations. However, the Japanese **insulted** the Americans and demanded that they leave, which they did. The Russians and British had also attempted to establish contact with Japan and had been turned away.

Lesson 128 - Japan's Open Door

The Japanese Meet Perry

The Japanese who saw Perry's four huge black ships approaching their coast were terrified at what they thought were giant dragons puffing smoke. They were sure that the crew of "devils

"First landing of Americans in Japan, under Commodore M. C. Perry at Gore-Hama July 14th 1853," by Wilhelm Hein (Gore-Hama was near Uraga.)

with white faces" were dangerous **barbarians**. Men on shore hid their valuables and their families. The shogun ordered 17,000 soldiers to prepare for war.

The low-ranking Japanese officials who approached the ships told the Americans to leave, but Perry refused. He said that he wanted to give the Japanese emperor a letter from President Millard Fillmore. Perry did not understand that the emperor had no contact with other people and that the shogun actually ran the country.

The letter made two specific requests. One was that the Japanese treat shipwrecked American sailors kindly until they could be rescued, instead of **abusing** them and putting them in prison. The other request was that American ships be allowed to purchase coal and other supplies from Japanese ports. American whaling ships worked in the Pacific near Japan, and American steamships needed places where they could purchase additional fuel and supplies. Americans used whale oil for lighting and for lubricating machinery. They knew about petroleum, but it did not become available in large amounts until 1859. Americans had come to understand that Japan had a large coal reserve that could help American vessels. The letter expressed the hope that Japan and the United States could reach a trade agreement.

Perry did not insist on an answer immediately. He said that he would return in the spring of the next year—with more ships—and would expect an answer then. Perry's **strategy** was to be respectful of Japanese ways but to show a willingness to use force if the Japanese rejected the President's letter. Perry sailed to the British port of Hong Kong for the winter. He had been the first Western ambassador to receive an official welcome in Japan in over two hundred years.

The Japanese Decide How to Respond to the Americans

The Japanese didn't know what to make of the Americans, who to them were large (the average height for Japanese men at the time was 5'1"), white-skinned creatures with big noses and hairy faces who wore strange clothes. Some Japanese saw Americans looking at them through telescopes and ducked, thinking the objects were a new kind of weapon. Eventually, however, the Japanese realized that the sailors were not a threat. Japanese artists began to paint pictures of the huge black ships on banners, scrolls, fans, and towels as souvenirs of the event for the Japanese people.

Japanese officials faced what they believed was a monumental decision. Should they defend their traditional ways, even if their refusal of the American request led to war? They had pride in their culture, but they realized that the American ships could destroy Japanese ports. Was there a way to maintain Japanese culture and values but accept modern technology and contact with other peoples?

Most Japanese officials wanted to refuse the Americans. A few believed that ending the pattern of **isolation** would be better for their country. The shogun took the unusual step of asking the daimyos what they thought. He also sought the advice of a man named Manjiro.

In 1841 Manjiro had been a fourteen-year-old Japanese fisherman who was shipwrecked on a deserted island. An American whaling vessel picked him up, and the ship's captain adopted him and enrolled him in school in Massachusetts. Manjiro later worked on a whaling ship, took part in the California gold rush (discussed in Lesson 130), and acquired a small amount of wealth. Manjiro loved the United States but he wanted to go home to Japan. He got a ship to drop him off at Nagasaki, even though he knew he might be executed for having contact with foreigners. Manjiro was imprisoned and endured numerous trials, but Japanese officials decided that his knowledge was too valuable for them to put him to death.

Japanese Painting of Perry

Manjiro told the shogun that the Americans had no desire to take the lands of others and that he hoped the two countries could establish peaceful relations. Manjiro described some of the Americans' strange customs, such as the fact that American men take off their hats when visiting, that they sit on chairs instead of the floor, and that American women make holes in their earlobes and put gold or silver rings through them as ornaments. Manjiro said that the Americans were sturdy and warmhearted people. Many historians believe that his influence made a major difference in the Japanese decision to negotiate with the Americans.

Perry Visits Japan a Second Time

The shogun died soon after Perry and his four ships visited Japan. After Perry heard this news, he learned that the Japanese would need a suitable period of mourning before they could answer the President's letter, perhaps as long as three years. In early 1854 Perry heard that the Russians and the French were planning to approach Japan about beginning trade negotiations. Perry decided that he could not delay.

Lesson 128 - Japan's Open Door

On February 13, 1854, Commodore Matthew Perry arrived in Japan a second time, this time with nine ships so the Americans could present an even more intimidating presence. The Americans and the Japanese carried on a slow, elaborate diplomatic encounter, showing respect for each other while maintaining their individual national dignity. The Americans brought gifts to the Japanese, including modern farm equipment and a small model railroad that the samurai rode around on a 350-foot track. The Japanese gave the Americans gifts of lacquerware, porcelain tea sets, silks, swords, and hundreds of unusual seashells. Sumo wrestlers demonstrated matches and easily carried huge bales of rice to the dock for Americans to load (with difficulty) onto their ships.

After weeks of talks, the Japanese and the Americans concluded a treaty on March 31, 1854. The Japanese agreed to open two small ports where Americans could purchase supplies. The Japanese also agreed to treat shipwrecked sailors kindly. The agreement allowed the Americans to have a consul office at one of the ports. A consul is an official representative who helps people from his own country while they are in a foreign land. The negotiators did not make a trade agreement, but the treaty said that when the two countries reached a trade agreement in the future, the United States would have the most favorable terms that Japan gave to any nation. This is called most favored nation status and is considered the best trading arrangement that one country can give to another. The Japanese were astonished when Americans took photographs of them. Some were afraid that the camera took a person's spirit out of him.

The Results of the Treaty

Fifteen days after the treaty was signed, an American ship landed in Japan in order to return a Japanese sailor who had been lost at sea. The Americans were not mistreated. Townshend Harris arrived in 1856 as the first U.S. consul. The Japanese told him he would have to wait a year before they would begin to negotiate a trade agreement, and it took another year after that before talks produced the Harris Treaty of 1858, the first commercial trade treaty between the U.S. and Japan.

Matthew Perry became the American expert on the Far East. In the photo at right, a color guard from the U.S. Naval War College in Perry's hometown of Newport, Rhode Island, parade the colors in front of his statue.

Statue of Perry, Newport, Rhode Island

Perry recommended that the United States acquire bases in the Pacific to guarantee American military and commercial strength there, but this did not happen until the 1890s. Perry died in 1858.

Japanese leaders were sharply divided over the new policy of openness toward foreigners, but the tide had turned to the future. The shogunate had been weakening in its authority for many years. The last shogun resigned in 1867, and in 1868 the fifteen-year-old Emperor Meiji began his reign and asserted himself as the real authority in Japan. During his reign, Japanese scholars went abroad to study other cultures and the knowledge that the outside world had acquired. The Japanese abolished their caste system, including the samurai.

Foreigners were now welcome. Both the Japanese and the foreigners had been curious and suspicious about each other, but they overcame their suspicions and developed positive relationships. The Japanese people showed that they were willing to adapt to new ways when their leaders allowed them to do so. By 1872 even the emperor wore Western-style clothing. The contact between the Americans and the Japanese, the fear of which had filled each side with such dread and uncertainty, led to a relatively quick, easy, and thorough transition in Japan. As usually happens when two different cultures come in contact, the Americans were changed as well.

U.S. stamp commemorates the 100th anniversary of Perry's visit to Japan.

Commodore Matthew Perry carried out a mission that replaced suspicion and ignorance with a relationship that offered peace and benefit. When Paul wrote to the Christians in Rome, he told them:

> *If possible, so far as it depends on you, be at peace with all men.*
> Romans 12:18

Assignments for Lesson 128

Our Creative World — Look at the examples of Japanese art on pages 116-118.

Timeline Book — In the box for Lesson 128 on page 28, write "Emperor Meiji takes control in Japan."

Student Workbook or Lesson Review — If you are using one of these optional books, complete the assignment for Lesson 128.

Vocabulary — Make a drawing for each of these words that illustrates what it means: insult (872), barbarian (873), abuse (873), strategy (873), isolation (874). Write the word under the drawing. Check in a dictionary if you need help with their definitions.

Creative Writing — Make a list of at least ten questions that Japanese people who first saw Perry's ships might have asked each other.

Literature — Read chapter 3 in *The Chestry Oak*.

The Eiffel Tower

Lesson 129   World Landmark

London's 1851 Great Exhibition in the Crystal Palace was the first of many similar international events held in cities around the world. Paris, France, hosted the next international exhibition in 1855. London was the site again in 1862, followed by Paris again in 1867. Vienna hosted a fair in 1873. Philadelphia planned a fair in 1876 in honor of the 100th anniversary (or centennial) of the founding of the United States. Paris was again the host city in 1878. The fairs moved to Australia next, to Sydney in 1879-1880 and Melbourne in 1880-1881. Barcelona, Spain, was the locale in 1888.

Gustave Eiffel

A committee in each of these cities took responsibility for preparing what became known as a world's fair. A world's fair requires years of planning and a tremendous investment of time, money, land, and other resources.

Plans for the 1889 Paris Exposition

In the mid-1880s, officials in Paris began making plans to host another Universal **Exposition** in 1889, this time in honor of the centennial of the French Revolution.

Fair organizers invited artists, inventors, builders, and companies to submit proposals for displays. One proposal came from the company owned by French structural engineer Alexandre Gustave Eiffel. Eiffel had worked on structures for the 1867 and 1878 Paris fairs. He had developed an international reputation for planning and building iron bridges. The arch bridge he designed to cross the Dours River in Portugal spanned 525 feet. Eiffel also designed the interior framework that supported the copper-clad Statue of Liberty in New York Harbor.

Eiffel wanted to build an impressive structure to demonstrate how people could use iron and steel to erect tall buildings. He also hoped to make money with the tower by having restaurants and **observation** decks in it which fair attendees could visit. Fair organizers were so impressed with Eiffel's plans that they decided to locate his proposed structure at the main entrance to the grounds of the exposition and make it the centerpiece of the event.

Eiffel planned for four iron lattice towers that would slope upward from the ground before meeting in the center and continuing upward as a single column. As with any engineering project, Eiffel had to do much more than simply design an attractive building. He had to determine the best location, since the ground in many places would not support a structure that weighed fifteen million pounds. Eiffel also had to determine the effect of heat and winds on such a large surface area.

April 1888   *July 1888*   *December 1888*   *May 1889*

Work on the project began in January of 1887, over two years before the fair was to open. Forty **draftsmen** produced over 500 engineering drawings for the project. Over 300 workers built the tower at the site. The 18,000 parts for the tower arrived at the construction site with seven million predrilled holes!

The fair organizers awarded Eiffel some money toward the project, but he had to come up with over $1 million himself. Before the fair officially opened, Eiffel took a group of officials into the tower. Only a few dared to climb all the way to the top.

Not everyone appreciated the tower. Some people criticized it as useless and **monstrous**. Others expressed fears that it would obscure other Paris landmarks such as the Cathedral of Notre Dame.

The Tower During the Fair

When finished, the Eiffel Tower stood 984 feet high and was the world's tallest structure. The Washington Monument is 555 feet tall. The Great Pyramid is 455 feet tall, the dome of St. Paul's Cathedral reaches 365 feet, and the Statue of Liberty rises 305 feet. The Eiffel Tower offered people a new experience in many ways. A few people had seen the Earth while riding in hot-air

Lesson 129 - The Eiffel Tower

balloons, but no one had been this high above the ground on a man-made structure before. Among the images below is a photograph taken from a balloon in 1889 of the Eiffel Tower and the exhibition. Also below is a view of balloons inside a pavilion during the exposition.

The tower opened a few days after the official opening of the Universal Exposition. Even then, the elevators were not completed, so those wanting to go to the top had to climb the 1,710 steps. Within the first ten days, the tower had over 30,000 visitors. Over the six months of the fair, almost 1.9 million paid a visit, including Queen Victoria's eldest son (the Prince of Wales, who was the future Edward VII), Buffalo Bill Cody (whose Wild West Show performed at the fair), and American inventor Thomas Edison. Admission fees to the Eiffel Tower paid during the fair covered the construction costs.

Book Published in Barcelona, Spain, About the 1889 Paris Exposition

Scenes from the 1889 Paris Exposition

Top Left: View of Eiffel Tower and the Exposition from a Hot Air Balloon; Top Center: Eiffel Tower Illuminated at Night; Top Right: Tower with Exposition Attendees; Bottom Left: The Procession of All Nations; Bottom Center: Hot Air Balloons On Display In a Fair Pavilion; Bottom Right: A ticket vendor offers tickets to an attendee and her son.

Scenes from the 1889 Paris Exposition

Top Row: Pavilion of Siam (Modern Thailand); Eiffel Tower; Vietnamese Soldier; Second Row: Argentina Pavilion; the Central Dome of the Exposition; Palace of Mexico; Third Row: Pavilion of the Pastel Artists; Central Pavilion; The Village Javanais, Depicting the Lives of Malays and Chinese in a Southeast Asian Village; Fourth Row: Palace of India; Pagoda of Angkor; Anthropology Section, Showing a Sami Tent with Reindeer

Lesson 129 - The Eiffel Tower

Swiss Girls and Vietnamese Actors at the 1889 Paris Exposition

After the Fair

Eiffel owned the rights to make money from the tower in the years after the fair, and he became a wealthy man from admission fees and restaurant sales. In 1909 the city of Paris took over ownership of the tower. Within a few years, a radio tower was added that broadcast signals to help ships at sea navigate correctly.

Following the 1889 Paris Exposition, cities around the world continued to host expositions. Chicago hosted the 1893 World's Columbian Exposition to celebrate the 400th anniversary of Columbus coming to the New World. Brussels, Belgium, was the site in 1897, and Paris again played host in 1900. The Eiffel Tower was refurbished for that event.

The 1851 Great Exhibition in London had one building, 14,000 exhibitors, and six million visitors. The 1900 Paris fair had hundreds of structures, 80,000 exhibitors, and 48 million visitors. Cities around the world have continued to host world's fairs since then. The Bureau of International Expositions, based in Paris, oversees these fairs and gives them its official approval in order to maintain standards regarding size and themes.

Behold, to the Lord your God belong heaven and the highest heavens, the earth and all that is in it.
Deuteronomy 10:14

Assignments for Lesson 129

Timeline Book — In the box for Lesson 129 on page 28, write "The Eiffel Tower is built in Paris."

Student Workbook or Lesson Review — If you are using one of these optional books, complete the assignment for Lesson 129.

Vocabulary — Copy the list of vocabulary words, then write the correct definition beside each word: exposition (877), observation (877), lattice (878), draftsman (878), monstrous (878).

   a. the act of watching

   b. a public show with displays

   c. extraordinarily large, like a monster in appearance

   d. a wall or structure with crossed wood or metal strips

   e. one who draws plans or sketches for engineering projects

Literature — Read chapter 4 in *The Chestry Oak*.

Family Activity — Create an "Eiffel Tower Collage." Instructions begin on page FA-51.

God Created Gold

Lesson 130 — God's Wonder

It is a metal, one of the elements God placed in the earth. It is shiny and attractive. This metal is relatively soft and can be molded into various shapes or hammered into thin sheets. People make jewelry and coins with it and use it in many artistic ways. It has a very high melting point, about 1,948°.

This metal does not form a compound with other elements easily. It does not tarnish the way silver does. It conducts electricity well. Not much of it has ever been found in the history of the world.

People have valued diamonds, rubies, emeralds, and other jewels. They have treasured silver and other metals. But above all these, people have wanted this metal. For thousands of years people in many cultures around the world have placed a high value on it.

Many people have worked hard to obtain it. They have sold all their possessions, made difficult journeys, and even risked their lives in order to get it. The few who have owned much of it have been rich and powerful in the eyes of others. For many years it was the standard on which the money system of the entire world rested.

This highly valued metal is gold.

Gold Mined in Philipsburg, Montana

All of the gold that has ever been found in the history of the world is estimated to weigh between 180,000 and 190,000 tons. It would fit on about 75 tractor trailer trucks but it would be too heavy for the trucks to carry it.

People Value Gold

People throughout history have made statues of gold. Many golden statues have been worshiped as gods. One reason the Spanish explored the New World so eagerly was because they believed that vast treasures of gold waited to be discovered there. Throughout much of history, a country that owned a great deal of gold was considered wealthy; a country that did not own much gold, whatever else it possessed, was not considered wealthy.

For many centuries people carried on trade by using gold and silver coins. They did not use paper money. When people began using paper money or currency for the sake of convenience in buying and selling goods, they understood that the paper bills represented gold. A person who possessed paper money could present it to a bank and receive the actual gold for which it stood.

Gold Mine, Kalgoorlie, Western Australia

Mining for Gold

People have generally mined gold in two ways.

Lode or Vein Mining. People dig into the earth to find a deposit of gold ore. This method is called lode or vein mining. Miners remove the gold and then separate it from the dirt and other minerals that surround it. The mine at left is a lode mine.

Placer Mining. People find loose gold nuggets and flakes that have washed down mountainsides and are concentrated in streams and river bottoms. This is called placer mining. People generally find loose gold by panning for it. Panning involves putting a small amount of earth or rocks into a pan with water, then slowly rotating the pan to let the water and lighter earth slosh out, leaving the heavier gold in the bottom of the pan. Less than one percent of gold has been found by panning.

Gold in Pan, Alaska, 1916

A Gold Rush

Many times the discovery of gold has caused what history calls a "gold rush." When a person found gold, word spread quickly. Many people rushed to cash in on such a valuable discovery. Thousands of people converged on a small area in hopes of finding gold. Usually only a small fraction would "strike it rich" by finding the precious metal.

When people rushed to an area to find gold, they usually began with placer mining because it required only a small investment in equipment. If panners found much gold, large mining companies then moved in with the machinery to do lode mining.

During a gold rush, some people who didn't strike it rich by finding gold took jobs working for other miners. Some opened stores to sell things that gold prospectors needed. Some people gave up on finding gold, but they decided to purchase land near where the gold was found and stay there. Many prospectors gave up and went back home or moved on to another area that seemed promising. Many of these lost all they had invested in the effort to find gold.

When thousands of people wanting to get rich moved into a sparsely-populated area without a strong government presence, maintaining law and order was difficult.

As seen in the map below, gold rushes occurred in several places during the 1800s.

Dahlonega, Georgia

In the summer of 1829 a Georgia newspaper reported that someone had discovered gold in the mountains of the state. Thousands of people converged on the area, hoping to find some of it. Four thousand converged onto one creek in about one year. The community at the center of the find had been called Licklog, but its name was changed to Dahlonega, which is from the Cherokee word meaning golden.

Because of the importance of converting gold into coins, the U.S. Treasury established a mint in Dahlonega to stamp coins from the gold. The major gold find there ended in the early 1840s. Between 1838 and 1861 the Dahlonega mint made 1.5 million gold coins with a face value of about six million dollars.

Sometimes the desire for gold has led to cruelty. Much of the gold discovered in Georgia was found on land where Native Americans of the Cherokee Nation lived. The desire for gold was a major reason why Americans demanded that the government force the Cherokee to give up their land. This demand resulted in the Trail of Tears of 1838-1839, when the U.S. government forced thousands of Cherokee to leave their homes and move to reservations in Oklahoma. About four thousand Cherokee, some twenty percent of the Cherokee population, died because of this harsh treatment.

Sutter's Mill, California

John Sutter, a Swiss who was born in Germany and later emigrated to the United States, owned a large land grant in northern California, which at the time belonged to Mexico. In January of 1848, Sutter and his business partner James Marshall were building a mill on Sutter's property. Marshall discovered gold in a stream. Word of the find gradually leaked out. In December of 1848 President James K. Polk mentioned this discovery of gold in his annual message to Congress. The U.S. had acquired California as a territory from Mexico as a result of the Mexican War. The next year, 1849, thousands of "Forty-Niners" headed for California.

Gold and Roscoelite Mined near Sutter's Mill

While Americans rushed to California, so did gold seekers from China, Germany, Chile, Mexico, Ireland, the Ottoman Empire, and France. Some came overland from the eastern United States, while others sailed around South America to San Francisco and traveled to Sutter's Mill from there. San Francisco's population grew from 812 in 1848 to 25,000 in 1849. Eager prospectors found gold at other nearby sites as well. The population of the California territory ballooned from 15,000 in early 1848 to 100,000 by the end of 1849.

The California gold rush lasted until 1859, when prospectors discovered gold and silver in the Comstock Lode in western Nevada. This gold rush lasted until 1865. Another rush took place there from 1873 until 1882.

Australia

In early 1851 Edward Hammond Hargraves, who had just come to Australia from California, found a grain of gold in a water hole near Bathurst in New South Wales colony in Australia. Hargraves called the place Ophir after the town associated with gold in the Bible (see 1 Kings 9:28, 10:11, and 22:48). See Hargraves at left.

One thousand prospectors came in four months. A few months later, prospectors discovered gold in the Victoria colony of Australia. Over the next few years prospectors found gold in several other places on the continent.

This 1951 Australian Stamp commemorates the 100th anniversary of Hargraves' discovery.

Gold seekers came from North America, the British Isles, New Zealand, and other countries. Australia produced one-third of the world's output of gold during the 1850s. This gold rush resulted in long-term growth for Australia throughout the last half of the 1800s as people settled down, bought land, and engaged in business.

Colorado

Some Cherokee discovered gold in the Colorado region in 1848, but they did not spread the word about it widely. Ten years later William Green Russell, a Georgian who was married to a Cherokee, learned about the find and organized a group to go prospecting for gold in Colorado. They discovered gold in 1858, and by 1859 the rush was on.

Some of the mining camps that prospectors established disappeared in a short time, while others became towns such as Golden and Denver. Prospectors discovered more gold in the 1860s and silver in the 1870s.

Gold Mined at Quartz Hill in Colorado

Lesson 130 - God Created Gold

Transvaal, South Africa

The Transvaal is the northernmost province of South Africa. It contains deposits of several valuable minerals as well as jewels. The Witwatersrand (often called simply the Rand) is a ridge in the Transvaal. Prospectors discovered a large deposit of gold in the Rand in 1886. They found other deposits in later years. Hopeful miners flocked to the region. The Rand is still the world's richest gold field. The rand is also the name of South Africa's currency.

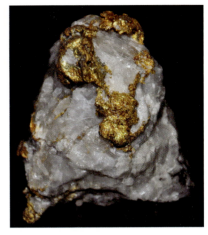

Gold and Quartz Mined at Witwatersrand, South Africa

Klondike, Canada

The Klondike is the region surrounding the Klondike River in the Yukon Territory of Canada near the border it shares with Alaska. Prospectors discovered gold in the Klondike in 1896. A rush of some 30,000 prospectors began the next year. Many men left Seattle and other ports in the northwestern United States on ships, landed in Alaska towns such as Skagway and Dyea, and then made the difficult 600-mile trek to the Klondike on foot while leading pack animals.

Because the Klondike region was so far away from towns and cities, men were advised to take a year's worth of supplies with them. This was difficult because they had to cross steep mountains and deep valleys, which in winter were covered in snow. The photograph below shows a line of gold seekers climbing the Chilkoot Trail on their way to the Klondike. Prospectors who arrived early staked all of the best claims, so most of those who came found no place to prospect for gold. The rush was largely over after a couple of years, and most of the men who came moved on to other places.

Almost immediately after the rush ended, enterprising businessmen in Skagway realized they could develop a tourism industry to serve people who wanted to come there and find out what the gold rush was all about. Skagway continues to attract tourists, while Dyea quickly disappeared.

Gold seekers walk single file up the Chilkoot Trail, heading for the Klondike.

Almost as soon as the Klondike craze ended, others discovered gold at Nome, Alaska, in 1899. By the next year about 10,000 people had come to Alaska, many of whom had been in the Klondike. Prospectors found gold deposits in several other places in Alaska over the next decade.

People still value gold and prize it in its different forms. As much as people desire gold, God's Word teaches us to seek wisdom even more.

Panning for Gold in Nome

*But where can wisdom be found?
And where is the place of understanding?
Man does not know its value,
Nor is it found in the land of the living.
The deep says, "It is not in me";
And the sea says, "It is not with me."
Pure gold cannot be given in exchange for it,
Nor can silver be weighed as its price.
It cannot be valued in the gold of Ophir,
In precious onyx, or sapphire.
Job 28:12-16*

Assignments for Lesson 130

Our Creative World — Read about the Australian gold rush on page 119.

Timeline Book — In the box for Lesson 130 on page 29, write "The Klondike Gold Rush begins in Canada."

Student Workbook or Lesson Review — If you are using one of these optional books, complete the assignment for Lesson 130 and take the test for Unit 26.

Thinking Biblically — Read Job 28.

Creative Writing — Write a poem of at least twelve lines about gold.

Literature — Read chapter 5 in *The Chestry Oak*.

27   The Early 1900s

Poppy Parade Commemorating 100 Years After the Great War, Ypres, Belgium, November 11, 2014

Lessons
- 131 - World Biography: Sun Yat-sen
- 132 - God's Wonder: God Created the North and South Poles
- 133 - Daily Life: Inventions Around the World
- 134 - Our World Story: The Great War
- 135 - World Landmark: Christ the Redeemer, Rio de Janeiro

Literature *The Chestry Oak*

1901-1928

This time period extends from the beginning of the twentieth century until just before the Great Depression. Dynasties had ruled China for almost 4,000 years when Sun Yat-sen worked to establish a republic there in the early 1900s. Americans Robert Peary, his assistant Matthew Henson, and four Inuit assistants, became the first people to reach the North Pole in 1909; Norwegian Roald Amundsen led a team to the South Pole in 1911. In the late 1800s and early 1900s, many individuals used their creative genius to develop products that changed life for people in many ways, including medicine, communication, transportation, and everyday living. The Great War of 1914-1918 was the most devastating war people had experienced until that time. In 1931 Brazilians in the world's fifth largest country dedicated the Christ the Redeemer statue.

The inventions described in Lesson 133 are from around the world.

Sun Yat-sen

Lesson 131　　　　　　　　　　　　　　　　　　　　　　　　　　World Biography

When the twentieth century began, China was divided and in turmoil. To begin to understand this ancient nation around 1900, we must go back to 1644. In that year rebels overthrew the Ming Dynasty. Later that year the Manchus from the region of Manchuria in northeastern China took control of the capital city of Beijing and conquered the rebels. The new leaders called themselves the Qing. Qing is the Chinese word for pure.

The Manchus, like the Mongols, were from north of the Great Wall. Thus, the majority of Chinese, who were of the Han ethnic group, thought of the Manchus as foreigners even though the Manchus accepted the philosophy of Confucius and continued many Chinese customs. The chess set at right dates from the Qing Dynasty.

Chess Set from Qing Dynasty, c. 1800-1900

Trouble Inside China

In the late 1700s, the Chinese population grew faster than the ability of Chinese farmers to grow food. Many Chinese began to go hungry, and they fell into deep poverty. The Qing government was corrupt. Some Chinese attempted to rebel from 1796 to 1804. The Qing defeated the rebels, but this civil war made the Qing government weaker.

Trouble Between China and Other Nations

China also had troubled relations with other nations. During the 1700s, the Qing Dynasty limited most contact with foreigners. Foreigners could only trade at the port of Guangzhou (also called Canton). China exported a great deal of tea and silk but imported very little from other countries. To try to get back some of the money that they spent in China, foreign nations sold a strong, addictive, illegal drug called opium to Chinese citizens. This was harmful to China and took a great deal of Chinese money out of the country.

In 1839 Chinese government officials seized 20,000 chests of opium from British traders in Guangzhou. The British responded by attacking the Chinese. In 1842 the Opium War ended with the British defeating the Chinese. The treaty that ended the war:

- gave Great Britain the port city of Hong Kong.

- required the Chinese to open four more ports to British traders.

- required the Qing government to treat Great Britain as an equal nation and not as subservient barbarians.

- required British citizens living in China to obey British law instead of Chinese law.

The United States and France signed similar treaties with China. Foreign countries came to have greater power within China. These countries wanted to influence China which was becoming a weaker nation.

Between 1856 and 1860, China fought another war against Great Britain. This time France also fought against China. China lost the war. France, Great Britain, Russia, and the United States forced China to sign more treaties which gave the foreigners more trade opportunities and made the Qing Dynasty still weaker.

Chinese Rebellions

Many Chinese understandably resented this loss of power in their own country. They blamed both the Manchus and the foreigners. China suffered from a series of rebellions in the mid-1800s. The most serious one was the Taiping Rebellion, illustrated at left. From 1850 to 1864, the Taiping rebels tried to defeat the Qing government. One of their goals was to distribute land more equally among the people. Some foreign governments helped the Qing Dynasty defeat the Taiping. Millions of people died in the fighting.

Top: This print created in the 1800s illustrates Taiping rebels at Shanghai, China, 1853-54. Bottom: This 1951 Chinese stamp depicts the Taiping Rebellion.

More Trouble with Other Countries

During the 1890s, Japan fought and won a war against China. Japan took the Korean Peninsula and the island of Taiwan away from China. France, Germany, Italy, Japan, Russia, and Great Britain demanded that China treat them even more favorably. The Chinese were afraid that these countries would divide up China into colonies if they did not obey. However, the changes that the foreigners demanded did not happen because these foreign countries didn't trust each other, and the Chinese had a strong national pride and were not willing to become colonies. The United States persuaded the other nations to agree to an open-door policy, which meant that all nations could trade with China as equals.

The Boxer Rebellion

Some Chinese deeply resented the influence Westerners had in China. Westerners is a term used for the people of Europe and also for descendants of Europeans living in other parts of the world. Some Chinese resented the presence of Christian missionaries who worked among the Chinese.

Chinese people formed several secret societies to oppose these influences. The best-known of these was the group called the Fists of Righteous Harmony. This group is called the Boxers because of their gymnastic exercises that looked like shadowboxing.

In 1900 the Boxers began to attack Westerners and Chinese Christians. They killed hundreds of people and destroyed much property. See photos at right of suffering Chinese Christians during this time.

Chinese Christian refugees gather in a mission during a bombardment in Tientsin, China.

Chinese Christians escape from Beijing during the Boxer Rebellion.

The China Inland Mission lost several missionaries. Two well-known missionaries who worked with the China Inland Mission were its English founder, Hudson Taylor, and Scottish missionary Eric Liddell (born in 1902), who became famous for winning a gold medal in track during the 1924 Olympic Games.

The Qing government was on the side of the Boxers, but an army of troops mainly from Japan and Russia crushed the rebellion. Great Britain, the United States, France, Austria-Hungary, and Italy also sent smaller numbers of troops. The Manchus tried to reform their government, but it was too late to save their dynasty.

Sun Yat-sen

A movement had been growing to make China a republic. In a republic, citizens elect representatives who run the government rather than all governmental power being in the hands of a monarch or a certain family.

In 1905 several Chinese groups that were trying to help China change to a republican form of government joined together to create the Revolutionary Alliance. This group chose Sun Yat-sen as their leader.

Emperor's Robe, Qing Dynasty

Sun had become a physician after being educated in Christian missionary schools in Hong Kong and Hawaii. Between 1895 and 1911, Sun Yat-sen traveled in the United States, Europe, and Japan trying to gain support for the republican movement in China and to collect donations from Chinese people living in those places.

In 1911 forces loosely connected with the Revolutionary Alliance attacked the Qing Dynasty and defeated it. On January 1, 1912, leaders who wanted a republican government set up a new capital in Nanjing and named Sun temporary president. The last Manchu emperor, six-year-old Pu Yi, gave up his throne on February 12. See an emperor's robe from the Qing Dynasty above.

The end of dynastic rule was a significant change for China. The first Chinese dynasty had been founded many centuries before Christ. As illustrated in the chart at right, one dynasty after another had ruled almost continuously since that time. You have studied many of them (see Lessons 17, 31, 37, 75, 81, 82, and 90).

Sun wanted to bring unity among the various groups in China, but he was unable to do so. Sun Yat-sen resigned, and Yuan Shikai, another prominent leader, replaced him as president. However, Yuan quickly showed that he did not want a republic. He wanted personal power instead.

Republican leaders organized the Kuomintang Party (meaning Nationalist Party) to try to stop Yuan. A party is a group of people who join together to try to influence a government to do things the way people in that group believe they should be done. The Nationalist Party was unable to stop Yuan and he became a dictator.

After Yuan died in 1916, China had a weak government without good leadership. The country suffered years of civil war among various local warlords who fought each other for power. In 1917 Sun Yat-sen tried to help China by setting up a government in Guangzhou. He worked to unify a badly divided China.

Russia established a Communist government that year. Communism is a form of government where the government owns everything and everyone is supposed to be treated equally. However, countries that have tried this type of government always end up being ruled by dictators. China suffered again when Communists came from the Soviet Union. The Communists convinced the Kuomintang Party to let them join. The Communists began working not for republican principles or the Nationalist Party but for their own power. Sun's government fell apart completely by 1922. He died in 1925.

Chinese Dynasties

Xia
2100 - 1600 BC

Shang
1600 - 1050 BC

Zhou
1046 - 256 BC

Qin
221-206 BC

Han
206 BC - 220 AD

Six Dynasties Period
220 - 589 AD

Sui
581 - 618

Tang
618 - 906

Five Dynasties Period
907 - 960

Song
960 - 1279

Yuan
1279 - 1368

Ming
1368 - 1644

Qing
1644 - 1912

Republic
1912 -1949

1949 - Present
People's Republic of China

Honoring Sun Yat-sen

Left: Statue of a young Sun Yat-sen by Chu Tat-shing, Hong Kong; Center: Sun Yat-sen Statue, Sacramento, California; Right: Statue in Sun Yat-sen Memorial Hall, Taipei City, Taiwan

The Long March

Chiang Kai-shek (see photos below) became the military leader of the Nationalist Party. He drove the Communists out of the party and they fled to rural areas of China. In 1928 the Nationalists set up a government with Chiang as leader.

Chiang only allowed one political party, and he ruled China as a dictator. The Nationalists and the Communists fought a civil war. In 1934 Chiang forced the Communists to withdraw to the northern province of Shaanxi. Communist leader Mao Zedong led the Communists to Shaanxi in what was called the Long March, a

Chiang Kai-shek and His Bride, 1927; Chiang in Uniform in 1945

winding route of over 6,000 miles. Mao Zedong worked to reorganize the Communists and prepared to make another attempt to take control of China.

War with Japan

Meanwhile, Japanese forces invaded China in 1931 and seized Manchuria. Chiang at first gave in to Japanese demands, but when many Chinese opposed this policy, Chiang agreed to fight. Japan began a major attack against China in 1937 and gained control of most of the country. The Nationalists withdrew to Sichuan province. Once again, foreigners ruled China and the Chinese themselves were badly divided.

Sun Yat-sen was an idealist who wanted to create a unified and workable Chinese republic out of a chaotic situation. He was not able to provide the leadership needed to resolve the serious issues that China faced. Sun allowed Communists to be more of an influence in China than he should have. This mistake eventually brought terrible hardship on his beloved homeland.

Many negative influences caused problems with the government of China over many years. As Solomon wrote:

> *Take away the dross from the silver,*
> *And there comes out a vessel for the smith;*
> *Take away the wicked before the king,*
> *And his throne will be established in righteousness.*
> *Proverbs 25:4-5*

Assignments for Lesson 131

Our Creative World — Read about Chinese games on pages 120-121.

Timeline Book — In the box for Lesson 131 on page 29, write "Sun Yat-sen helps found the Kuomintang."

Student Workbook or Lesson Review — If you are using one of these optional books, complete the assignment for Lesson 131.

Thinking Biblically — Copy Proverbs 25:4-5 along the bottom of a piece of paper. Above it, illustrate the verse.

Creative Writing — List these years in a single column on a piece of paper: 1644, 1839, 1842, 1900, 1905, 1912, 1925, 1937. Next to the year, write a sentence in your own words summarizing the event that happened in that year as discussed in this lesson. You can find these events as follows: 1644 - page 891; 1839 - page 892; 1842 - page 892; 1900 - page 893; 1905 - page 894; 1911 - page 894; 1925 - page 895; 1937 - page 897.

Literature — Read chapter 6 in *The Chestry Oak*.

God Created the North and South Poles

Lesson 132   God's Wonder

Midnight Sun near the Antarctic Peninsula

Midnight Sun in Ilulissat, Greenland

God created extremely cold places at the top and bottom of the world: the North Pole and the South Pole. Both the North and South Poles have six months of daytime and six months of nighttime. When the North Pole is experiencing daytime, the South Pole is experiencing nighttime, and vice versa. Both Poles are in constant daylight during their six daytime months. During these months, the sun is always above the horizon.

During their six months of nighttime, the sun never rises above the horizon. Each Pole experiences several weeks of total darkness, but during some of those weeks the sun is close enough to the horizon to give the Poles some light.

Though the poles have many similarities, they also have major differences. There is no land at the North Pole. The North Pole lies in the Arctic Ocean, while the South Pole is on the continent of Antarctica. The North Pole is warmer than the South Pole. The water below the surface of the polar ice at the North Pole raises the air temperature. Another reason that the North Pole is warmer is that lower elevations are warmer than higher ones. The elevation of the North Pole is near sea level, but the South Pole is at about 9,000 feet.

The North Pole

The North Pole lies at 90° north latitude at the center of the Arctic region. At the North Pole, to move in any direction is to go south. The name Arctic comes from the Greek word

THE ARCTIC

arktor meaning bear. The region is named for the Bear constellation in the northern sky. The Arctic region is north of the Arctic Circle, which is at 66°33′ latitude north of the equator. Find the North Pole and the Arctic Circle at right.

The Arctic Ocean is the smallest of the Earth's oceans. The average January water temperature is 28°. The Arctic Ocean is covered with thick chunks of shifting, floating ice that are sometimes frozen together. Most of this is sea ice, which is frozen seawater, while the rest is ice chunks that have broken off of glaciers from land surrounding the ocean.

The Arctic Ocean meets the shorelines of Asia, Europe, and North America. While no one lives at the North Pole, people do live inside the Arctic Circle. Portions of Canada, Greenland, Finland, Iceland, Norway, Russia, Sweden, and the United States (a portion of the state of Alaska) lie inside the Arctic Circle. However, the number of people living within the Arctic Circle is a tiny percentage of the Earth's population.

Inside the Arctic Circle

Clockwise from Top Left: Bearded Seal, Russia; Walruses, Russia; Polar Bear, Canada; Young Reindeer, Norway; Musk Ox, Norway

Exploring the North Pole

Many explorers tried to sail through the Arctic Ocean above North America while searching for a northwest passage to Asia. A few searched for a passage north of Asia. Only a small number actually tried to reach the North Pole.

American Robert Peary, a lieutenant in the U.S. Navy Corps of Civil Engineers, and his assistant Matthew Henson spent several years exploring the Arctic and made several attempts to reach the North Pole. On April 6, 1909, Peary, Henson, and Inuits Ooqueh, Ootah, Egingwah, and Seeglo achieved their goal. The team used dogsleds to cross the ice in late winter, when temperatures were somewhat warmer and the ice was relatively solid.

Richard Byrd and Floyd Bennett were the first to fly a plane over the North Pole,

Ooqueh, Ootah, Henson, Egingwah, and Seeglo at the North Pole, April 1909

Polar bear mother and two cubs walk on the Arctic Ocean near Kaktovik, Alaska.

accomplishing the feat in 1926. In 1958 the nuclear-powered USS *Nautilus* was the first submarine to pass under the North Pole and the first seacraft to reach it. The U.S. stamps below honor Peary, Henson, Byrd, and the success of the *Nautilus*. In 1978 Naomi Uemura of Japan drove a dog sled to become the first man to reach the North Pole alone.

These U.S. stamps honoring polar explorers were issued in 1986, 1988, and 1959.

The South Pole

The South Pole lies in the Antarctic region, which is the bottom one-third of the Southern Hemisphere. The Antarctic region is the area inside the Antarctic Circle which is at approximately 66°33′ latitude south of the equator. The South Pole lies at 90° south latitude. At the South Pole, to move in any direction is to go north. The South Pole is on the continent of Antarctica. Antarctica means *anti* or opposite of the Arctic. Most of Antarctica lies inside the Antarctic Circle.

Antarctica is a landmass with peaks, valleys, and rocky areas. The South Pole itself is on a plateau. Antarctica is larger than either Europe or Australia.

A layer of ice covers about 98 percent of the Antarctic. The frozen water in this ice cap is the largest body of freshwater in the world. It makes up 70 percent of the Earth's freshwater. The Southern Ocean surrounds Antarctica. Find the South Pole, the Antarctic Circle, the Southern Ocean, and the continent of Antarctica at right.

The Antarctic Peninsula extends outside the Antarctic Circle toward South America. Scientists consider it to be an extension of the Andes Mountain range in South America. Mt. Erebus, pictured above, is an active volcano on Ross Island, just off the Antarctic coast.

The temperatures in Antarctica rarely rise above freezing. July temperatures (when it is winter there) range from -94° to -40° inland and -22° to -5° on the coast. January temperatures during the Antarctic summer vary between -31° to -5° inland. The coldest temperature ever recorded on Earth, -128.6°, occurred on Antarctica in 1983. Antarctica has strong winds which average 44 miles per hour. Gusts can reach 120 miles per hour.

Antarctic Scene Near Vernadsky, a Ukrainian Research Base

Mount Erebus on Ross Island

THE ANTARCTIC

Mosses, algae, lichens, and a few small insects can live in coastal areas of Antarctica. Two small flowering plants, Antarctic hair grass and Antarctic pearlwort, grow on the Antarctic Peninsula. About forty different kinds of birds migrate to Antarctica during the summer. Millions of penguins live all or part of the year along its coasts, including the species pictured below.

Penguins of Antarctica

Clockwise from Top Left: Chinstrap, Emperor, Adélie, Macaroni, Gentoo, King (Notice that the Gentoo are sitting on chicks.)

Exploring Antarctica and the South Pole

Ancient Greek philosophers Aristotle and Ptolemy believed that a southern continent existed to balance the continents they knew. Three separate explorers might have sighted Antarctica in 1820: Fabian von Bellinghausen of the Russian navy, Edward Bransfield of the British navy, and Nathaniel Brown Palmer, an American sealer. American sealer John Davis in 1821 was the first person known to set foot on the Antarctic Peninsula. More explorers ventured to the Antarctic region in the mid-1800s.

Several people attempted to reach the South Pole in the early 1900s. Robert F. Scott of Great Britain led a team from 1901 to 1904 but did not reach the pole. Ernest Shackleton, also of Great Britain, led a team that got within about 112 miles of the South Pole in 1909, but they ran short of food and had to turn back.

Lesson 132 - God Created the North and South Poles

Left: Roald Amundsen, Helmer Hanssen, Sverre Hassel, and Oscar Wisting at the South Pole, December 17, 1911; Right: These statues in Oslo, Norway, honor Amundsen and his crew, which included Olav Bjaaland, in addition to those in the photo.

Norwegian Roald Amundsen led the first expedition that reached the South Pole. He had previously explored both the Arctic and the Antarctic regions. Amundsen was preparing to go to the North Pole in 1909 when he learned that Peary had accomplished this feat, so he reorganized and headed for the South Pole the next year. Robert Scott led a team that was attempting to reach the pole at the same time. Amundsen's team arrived on December 14, 1911. He left a note for Scott, who reached the pole about a month later and found the note. However, Scott and his team died of starvation and the extreme cold on their way back to their base camp.

Amundsen died in a 1928 plane crash while flying over the Arctic trying to rescue Italian explorer Umberto Nobile. U.S. Navy officer Richard Byrd, who had flown over the North Pole in 1926, led the first flight over the South Pole in 1929.

> *He stretches out the north over empty space*
> *And hangs the earth on nothing.*
> Job 26:7

Assignments for Lesson 132

Our Creative World — Read the excerpt from *South!* by Ernest Shackleton on pages 122-123.

Map Book — Complete the assignments for Lesson 132 on Map 39 "The Arctic and Antarctic."

Timeline Book — In the box for Lesson 132 on page 29, write "Amundsen's team reaches the South Pole."

Student Workbook or Lesson Review — If you are using one of these optional books, complete the assignment for Lesson 132.

Thinking Biblically — List at least fifteen of God's creations in the Arctic and Antarctic regions.

Literature — Read chapter 7 in *The Chestry Oak*.

Inventions
Around the World

Lesson 133 — Daily Life

In the late 1800s and early 1900s, many individuals used their creative genius to develop products that changed life for people in many ways. This lesson focuses on just a few inventions in medicine, communication, transportation, and everyday living.

This 1965 German stamp honors Wilhelm Röntgen.

Sphygmomanometer, 1900

Medicine

X-rays. Wilhelm Röntgen, at left, was a **physics** professor at the University of Wurzburg in Germany. In 1895 he was experimenting with a vacuum tube (a glass tube from which all the air had been withdrawn). He passed an electric current through it and noticed that a darkened area appeared on photographic paper lying near it. He assumed that the tube was giving off electromagnetic **radiation** of some kind. He didn't know what these rays were, so he called them X-rays.

Upon further experimentation, he discovered that the rays passed through some materials, such as skin, but didn't pass through other materials, such as bone. He realized that using X-rays, he could produce a photographic image of a person's skeleton. Physicians began using X-rays to see the nature of broken bones and other problems inside the body. Röntgen received the first Nobel Prize in Physics in 1901.

Blood Pressure Cuff. Blood pressure is the pressure that blood exerts against blood vessel walls when the heart pumps blood. In 1896 Italian physician Scipione Riva-Rocci, who was thirty-three years old at the time, developed a device to take accurate blood pressure readings. He called it a sphygmomanometer or "pulse pressure meter." It is also called a blood pressure cuff. When medical personnel write down a person's blood pressure, they use the letters "RR" in honor of Riva-Rocci.

Penicillin. Dr. Alexander Fleming was a Scottish physician working at a hospital in London. When he returned from a vacation in 1928, he noticed that a mold, *Penicillin notatum*, had grown among his lab equipment. This mold inhibited the growth of bacteria. It was several more years before other scientists identified how the mold worked and manufacturers found a way to produce penicillin in large quantities. Penicillin helped prevent wounded soldiers from getting infections during World War II. This revolutionized the way doctors treat infection. Three of the scientists who **refined** penicillin received the 1945 Nobel Prize in Medicine. See plaque above.

Communication

Telephone. Alexander Graham Bell, pictured at right, was a Scotsman who had emigrated to Canada and later moved to Boston. His grandfather was an actor, and his father developed a way for the deaf to communicate with others. In 1876 Bell was working on a way to send telegraph messages over multiple lines at once when he invented the telephone. He demonstrated his invention at the Centennial Exposition in Philadelphia that year. The device was an immediate success, and Bell spent the next several years overseeing the development of the Bell Telephone Company.

Linotype. For four hundred years after Gutenberg, printers set type by placing metal letters in frames by hand. Ottmar Mergenthaler was born in Germany and came to live in the United States. In 1884 he developed a machine that set a line of metal letters when the operator pressed the appropriate keys on a keyboard. When the line of letters was finished, the machine created a mold of the line that could then be put into a frame for a page. Since the machine set one "line o' type" at a time, its brand name was the Linotype. The Linotype, pictured at right, made typesetting faster and less expensive.

Radio. The Italian Guglielmo Marconi, at right, was twenty years old in 1895 when he developed a way to broadcast radio signals through the air without using wires between the sender and receiver. The signals he sent at first were Morse

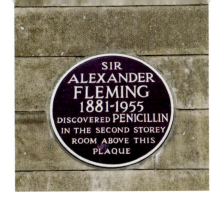

The plaque at St. Mary's Hospital in London, England, identifies the place where Fleming discovered penicillin.

Alexander Graham Bell and his wife Mabel look out to sea from Sable Island, Canada, 1898.

Wesley Notgrass, father of author Ray Notgrass, works at a linotype machine.

Guglielmo Marconi

This 1987 Canadian stamp honors Reginald Fessenden.

code. In 1901 Marconi sent a signal across the Atlantic Ocean. He received the 1909 Nobel Prize in Physics.

Canadian Reginald Fessenden, at left, is credited with making the first public AM radio voice-and-music broadcast on Christmas Eve 1906. From Massachusetts, he broadcast himself playing "O Holy Night" on the violin and his wife reading the story of Jesus' birth from the Bible. Ships at sea reported hearing this broadcast.

Motion Pictures. Inventors developed photography around 1840. In the late 1800s inventors in the United States, Great Britain, and France worked on different kinds of systems to record pictures of moving action ("movies") on celluloid film. American inventor Thomas Edison developed a single device to record pictures on long film and demonstrated his motion picture machine at the 1893 World's Columbian Exposition in Chicago. It showed unenlarged ninety-second moving pictures that one person could watch in a small box. Soon Edison, building on an invention by Charles Jenkins and Thomas J. Armat, developed a projection system by which many people could watch a movie on a large screen. Edison's first demonstration of this system took place in New York City on April 23, 1896.

The first movies did not have sound. Pianists often accompanied movies when they were shown in theaters to convey emotions in various scenes. Filmmakers began **interspersing** printed words on the screen that explained the action or reproduced dialogue. The first movie that told a story was *The Great Train Robbery*. Filmmakers produced this eleven-minute film in 1903. Hollywood, California, became a popular place for movie producers to work.

The Jazz Singer (1927) was the first movie with sound. During a few of the scenes in the movie, the audience heard from a **synchronized** disc the sound of the actors speaking and singing. Walt Disney's 1928 cartoon "Steamboat Willie" featuring Mickey Mouse was the first animated short film to use synchronized sound. Soon moviemakers developed a way to record the sound directly on the film.

Transportation

Bicycle. People began making early forms of two-wheel (bi-cycle) devices in the mid-1800s. The high-wheeler bicycle, invented about 1870, had a large front wheel (about five feet high) which advanced the bicycle a long distance with each push of the pedals. See example at right. Around 1885 J. K. Starley, an English bicycle maker, produced a safety bicycle, so called because both wheels were the same height and it was safer to ride than the high-wheeler.

High-Wheeler Bicycle Race

Lesson 133 - Inventions Around the World

Early Movies

Top Row: Poster advertises an Edison film, c. 1896. Technicians set up the turntable and amplifiers to play The Jazz Singer *in Australia, c. 1927-1928. Inventors George Eastman and Thomas Edison pose with a motion picture camera, c. 1925. Right: 1998 U.S. stamp commemorates* The Great Train Robbery. *1994 U.S. stamp honors Al Jolson, singer and star of* The Jazz Singer.

Motorcycle. Etienne Lenoir, a Belgian living in France, developed the internal combustion engine in 1860. Nikolaus Otto of Germany produced a better model in 1876, and fellow Germans Gottlieb Daimler and Wilhelm Maybach improved it even further in 1885. That year Daimler attached an engine to a bicycle and produced the motorcycle. See stamp at left.

Automobile. Early development of automobiles (the word means self-moving) took place in the 1800s in Europe. Attempts at steam-powered and later electric-powered versions did not prove to be practical. Steam-powered autos had to be large and were therefore dangerous, while electric models could not go very far. Greater success came when inventors used the internal combustion engine. In 1885 German Karl Benz unveiled a motorized tricycle. See stamp at left. Then he introduced a four-wheel auto in 1893 that proved to be more stable and could carry more people.

Automobiles became a large industry in the United States. In 1893 brothers Charles and Frank Duryea produced an automobile powered by an internal combustion engine. See stamp at left. In 1901 Ransom Olds developed methods of

Top to Bottom: 1985 North Korean stamp commemorates Daimler's motorcycle. 1984 Cuban stamp commemorates Benz' motorized tricycle. 1962 San Marino stamp commemorates the Duryea automobile.

The Library of Congress titles this photograph, "The First Oldsmobile."

mass production, meaning ways to make a large number of automobiles faster. Before that, makers produced cars in limited quantities largely by hand. At this point, automobiles were still primarily toys for the wealthy. See an early Oldsmobile at left.

Henry Ford of the United States had the vision of mass-producing inexpensive cars for the general public. He started using improved mass production techniques to make Model Ts in 1908. Ford developed a moving assembly line in 1913. Auto frames moved along the assembly line past workers, who put on parts that other people brought to their stations. By 1930 Americans had bought over twenty million Model Ts.

German Rudolph Diesel patented the engine named for him in 1892. The diesel engine does not use a spark plug, as the internal combustion engine does, but instead compresses and heats air in a cylinder, which causes the injected fuel to ignite.

Better Tires and Starters. The interest in bicycles and automobiles encouraged people to invent better products to use on them. The first wheels were made of solid wood or rubber, which were not easy or comfortable to use. Scottish veterinarian John Dunlop developed an air-filled tire for bicycles in 1888. The Michelin brothers of France devised an inflatable tire in 1895 that they could easily mount on and remove from wheels. These air-filled tires provided a more comfortable ride. The Michelin company modified them for use on automobiles. American engineer Charles Kettering developed an electric starter for cars in 1911. Before that, a person had to use a heavy crank to start the engine, which was difficult and could be dangerous.

Airplane. People had dreamed of flying for centuries. In 1783 French brothers Jacques and Joseph Montgolfier demonstrated the first successful hot air balloons, such as the one at right. In the late 1800s several people in Europe, especially France, tinkered with designs for a heavier-than-air flying machine. Most people believed that powered human flight was impossible. Brothers Orville and Wilbur Wright, bicycle makers in Ohio, believed that it was possible. Their father and sister gave special

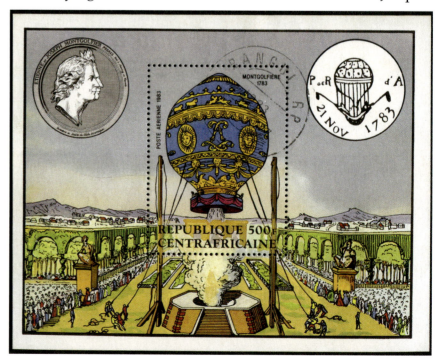

This 1983 stamp from the Central African Republic shows a Montgolfier balloon.

encouragement to them throughout their studies and experiments. Orville and Wilbur conducted test flights with gliders. They worked at Kitty Hawk on the Outer Banks of North Carolina, because of its flat landscape and strong winds.

The Wright Brothers understood that they had to overcome three basic problems: lift, power, and control. They had to get an airplane off the ground, with enough power to make a sustained flight, and with sufficient control to keep the plane from crashing. They worked on ideas for years to develop the best design. On December 17, 1903, Orville flew their engine-powered Flyer for twelve seconds a distance of 120 feet. Their longest flight that day lasted 59 seconds and covered 852 feet. The Wrights continued to experiment and improve their designs. They formed a company that built airplanes for military and commercial use. Wilbur died in 1912 and Orville continued the work alone. He died in 1948.

This 1978 U.S. stamp commemorates the Wright Brothers flight on December 17, 1903.

Everyday Products

Carpet Sweeper. In the late 1800s, American couple Melville and Anna Bissell sold crockery and china. Goods arriving at their store packed in sawdust left a mess on the floor. To solve the problem, Melville developed a carpet sweeper, which he patented in 1876. Within just a few years, the Bissells had a five-story factory to house their new business—manufacturing carpet sweepers. By the late 1890s, Bissell carpet sweepers had even reached Buckingham Palace in England. Queen Victoria required her palace attendants to "Bissell" the floors once a week.

Bakelite Plastic. Leo Hendrick Baekeland was born in Belgium but moved to the United States and became a chemist. During the 1800s, people had developed some artificial materials to make products, but they all had limitations. One popular material was celluloid, mentioned on page 906 as material for film, but celluloid caught on fire easily. In 1909 Baekeland developed a material he called Bakelite plastic. Bakelite did not conduct heat or electricity, and it did not break easily. Bakelite was produced as a powder, so it could be molded into different shapes. See Bakelite objects below.

French Bakelite Telephone, Bakelite Domino, Bakelite Billiard Balls

Nylon. Wallace Carothers was an American chemist who worked for the DuPont chemical company. He led a research team that tried to develop an artificial thread to replace silk. In 1935 they discovered how to produce a strong plastic thread using chemicals from coal, petroleum, agricultural by-products, and natural gas, as well as water and air. They called this thread nylon. Inventors could make it into fibers, bristles, sheets, rods, tubes, or a powder for molding. The first product made with it was a toothbrush. Within a few years, manufacturers were making clothing, fishing line, tires, and other products from nylon.

We live in an amazing time in which we have access to many wonderful inventions. Our responsibility is to use these inventions for the good of others.

And do not neglect doing good and sharing,
for with such sacrifices God is pleased.
Hebrews 13:16

Assignments for Lesson 133

Timeline Book — In the box for Lesson 133 on page 29, write "Marconi sends a radio signal across the Atlantic."

Student Workbook or Lesson Review — If you are using one of these optional books, complete the assignment for Lesson 133.

Vocabulary — Look up each of these words in a dictionary and read their definitions: physics (904), radiation (904), refine (905), intersperse (906), synchronize (906).

Creative Writing — Write a paragraph about how one of the inventions discussed in this lesson is a part of your everyday life.

Literature — Read chapter 8 in *The Chestry Oak*.

Family Activity — Play the "Should Have Called It" Game. Instructions begin on page FA-53.

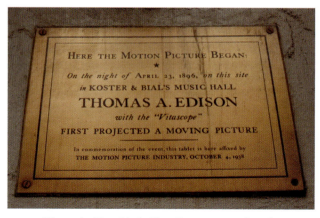

Plaque in New York City Commemorating the
First Projection with a Vitascope in 1896

The Great War

Lesson 134 — Our World Story

The Great War, later known as World War I, took place between 1914 and 1918. It was the most devastating war people had experienced to that time. An estimated nine million soldiers and an additional twenty-one million civilians died from combat, disease, and other causes. The loss of property could not be calculated. The war and associated events changed the way nations of the world related to each other, and it changed the way many people looked at the world. The picture on page 889 was taken during a parade commemorating the start of the Great War.

Causes of the Great War

During the last half of the 1800s, several people groups felt a sense of national pride and a desire for a national homeland. At the same time, some political leaders wanted to expand their control. These factors were in conflict and contributed to the start of the Great War.

A Unified Italy. Italy had long been a collection of small kingdoms and city-states. Some Italians worked to make the peninsula a single, unified country. Advocates of unity believed Italy needed to be a stronger and more democratic nation to succeed in the modern world.

Otto von Bismarck

Some people opposed unity because they were afraid they would lose power in their own localities. Foreign rulers who controlled parts of Italy did not want to lose the areas they ruled. In addition, rural southern Italy and the growing industrial north were quite different. Nevertheless, several strong leaders worked to bring about unity. When the city of Rome agreed to join with the rest of the Italian regions in 1870, Italy became unified.

A Unified Germany. In 1861 King Wilhelm I of Prussia named Otto von Bismarck, pictured at left, as both prime minister and foreign minister. The German states had been divided in a way similar to Italy. The Prussian Kingdom was

Kaiser Wilhem II and His Wife Augusta Victoria

the most powerful German state. Prussia built up a strong military. Prussian leaders worked to unify German states into a single nation, which they expected Prussians to lead.

France, on the other hand, believed that a stronger, unified Germany was a threat to France. France and Prussia had fought each other during the Napoleonic Wars. In 1870, when France and Prussia disagreed about who should become king of Spain, France declared war on Prussia. The Franco-Prussian War lasted only a few months. Prussia defeated France, which lost valuable territory. At the conclusion of that war, on January 18, 1871, at the Palace of Versailles, the Germans proclaimed Prussian king Wilhelm I *Kaiser* (the German form of caesar) of all Germany. It was a final insult to France. Germany was united, and France had become its bitter enemy. Because of a personal conflict, the next German kaiser, Wilhelm II, forced Bismarck to resign in 1890. Kaiser Wilhelm II and his wife are pictured above.

Colonialism. Many nations wanted to gain control of other lands as a way to obtain wealth and gain greater national pride and honor. The British Empire included colonies all over the globe. British leaders wanted to keep the empire strong and to continue to rule the seas with their navy. Other countries, including Belgium, France, Germany, Italy, Portugal, and Spain, wanted to gain more colonies. In the 1800s European nations had taken many portions of Africa as colonies. France took control of much of Southeast Asia. The United States acquired overseas territories as a result of its victory in the Spanish-American War in 1898. As we discussed in Lesson 131, Europeans exerted power in China. Japan became aggressive in attacking China.

Trouble in the Balkans. Austria wanted to keep control of its empire and expand it. It had become Austria-Hungary after Austria took over Hungary in 1867. It had also taken over Bosnia and Herzegovina in the Balkans. At the same time, the Ottoman Empire controlled other parts of the Balkan Peninsula. Millions of Slavic people lived under Austria-Hungary's rule. Many Slavs, especially in the Balkan country of Serbia, resented both Austria and the Ottomans. They wanted the entire region to be independent. Serbian activists wanted a single government for all Slavs, including those who lived in Bosnia and Herzegovina. Several terrorist groups in the Balkans tried to bring this about. Russia, Great Britain, and France encouraged the Serbs in their desire for independence. The conflict between Austria's desire for a colonial empire and the Serbs' desire for national freedom was about to erupt into war. The desire of powerful nations to have colonies conflicted with the desire of people to govern themselves.

International Alliances. As countries increased their military strength, they also made alliances with other countries. Working together made countries even stronger and discouraged their enemies from fighting against them. Germans were afraid that a stronger France might attack them out of revenge for losing the Franco-Prussian War, so Germany formed the Dual

Lesson 134 - The Great War

Alliance with Austria-Hungary in 1879. The Dual Alliance was also called the Central Powers. Italy later joined them, creating the Triple Alliance. France responded by establishing an alliance with Russia, hoping they could keep Germany contained between the two of them. Britain felt threatened by the buildup of the German navy, so it entered into an informal alliance with France and Russia. These countries were called the Allied Powers or the Triple Entente (French for "understanding"). In the photo at right, Russian Czar Nicholas II meets a French general while the two armies are on joint maneuvers (maneuvers is a term used for practicing for war on a large scale).

Czar Nicholas II and French General Joffre, August 1913

In 1839 Great Britain, Austria, France, Prussia, Russia, and the Netherlands had signed a treaty stating that Belgium would remain neutral. In 1870 Great Britain promised to fight any country that tried to take over Belgium.

War Begins

On June 28, 1914, Austrian Archduke Franz Ferdinand, the heir to the Austro-Hungarian throne, was with his wife in Sarajevo, in Bosnia, to remind the Bosnians that Austria-Hungary ruled over them. Ferdinand and his children are pictured below. A Serbian rebel who lived in Bosnia, Gavrilo Princip, assassinated the archduke and his wife. In response, Austria-Hungary made a long list of demands on his home country of Serbia. Austria-Hungary required Serbia to stop all anti-Austrian activities, dismiss all officials who wanted Serbians living in Austria-Hungary to be part of a separate Slavic nation, and allow Austrian officials to enter Serbia in order to investigate the assassination. This last requirement meant that the nation of Serbia would be giving up their national independence. The Serbians agreed to all but the last demand. Not satisfied with this response, Austria-Hungary declared war on Serbia.

Then the dominoes began to fall. Russia began getting its troops ready for war. Germany supported Austria-Hungary by declaring war on Russia and France. Germany attacked first. German troops headed for France, hoping to defeat them quickly and then attack Russia. To invade France, Germany moved across neutral Belgium. Great Britain declared war on Germany to honor its commitment to defend Belgium. The Ottoman Empire announced that it would support Germany and Austria-Hungary. Italy left the Triple Alliance and declared that they would support the Allied Powers, as did Japan. More than twenty nations became directly involved in the fighting. See the Central, Allied, and neutral areas in and around Europe on the map on page 914.

Franz Ferdinand and His Children

THE GREAT WAR

- Central Powers
- Allied Powers
- Neutral Powers

Trench Warfare on the Western Front

British and French forces stopped the German advance in northern France. The two sides lined up against one another in what became **ghastly** trench warfare for almost four years, until the end of the war in late 1918. Soldiers in the trenches endured miserable conditions through rain, cold, and heat. New weapons such as tanks, airplanes, and poison gas caused great devastation. The front battle line hardly moved at all during the rest of the war, even though attack followed attack and the combatants on both sides fought hard. To the east, Russia fought German and Austro-Hungarian armies. These two sides also experienced a stalemate. Some fighting took place in other parts of the world, but by far the most fighting took place in Europe.

Top to Bottom: British soldiers stand in a trench. German soldiers are inside a trench. A German takes photographs from an airplane.

Lesson 134 - The Great War

Trouble in Russia

The war added to the troubles already taking place in Russia. The Russian Empire had long been unraveling. Czar Alexander II had freed the serfs in 1861 and put many reforms in place. However, he still kept a tight control on the country, and many people were ready for major changes. Despite Alexander's reforms, revolutionaries assassinated him in 1881.

Czar Nicholas II and his Family

Some Russians wanted a republican government, but the country also had a growing number of people who demanded Communism, the authoritarian form of government Mao Zedong would soon fight for in China.

As a result of troubles inside Russia and the hardships of war, Czar Nicholas II abdicated in March of 1917. See Nicholas and his family above. Russian leaders formed a republican government. Vladimir Lenin led a Communist revolt in October and gained control of the government. This is called the October Revolution. Lenin's government asked for peace from Germany and withdrew from the war. The Communists executed the czar and his family.

The United States Declares War

When the war began in 1914, President Woodrow Wilson declared that the United States would be neutral, not entering the war on either side. Many Americans saw no purpose in becoming involved in a European war. The Wilson government faced a difficult situation. The U.S. had strong ties to Great Britain as well as a long-standing sense of loyalty to France for their help in the American Revolution. On the other hand, the U.S. also had a large population of German immigrants who quietly supported the Alliance.

Wilson also had to balance his desire for neutrality against continuing German aggression against the United States. In 1915 Germany sank the British ship *Lusitania*, with many Americans on board. Despite repeated warnings from the United States, Germany became more aggressive about attacking any ships in the Atlantic that the Germans thought might help the Allies, whether the ship came from a **neutral** country or one already involved in the war.

In addition, Americans found out that Germany had tried to recruit Mexico to enter the war against the United States, with the promise that Germany might help Mexico recover territory in Texas, New Mexico, and Arizona. This discovery **infuriated** many Americans.

The U.S. Congress declared war on Germany in April of 1917. A large number of American soldiers arrived in Europe in late 1917 and early 1918. Their presence helped the Allies defeat their enemies. Germany asked for an armistice, which went into effect at the eleventh hour of the eleventh day of the eleventh month (11:00 a.m., November 11), 1918.

Seeking Peace

The leaders of the victorious Allied nations met at the Palace of Versailles to write a peace treaty. European leaders said they wanted to "make Germany pay." The treaty they created required Germany to reduce its armed forces to a minimum and to give up its colonies and the lands it had captured in the war. The Allies forced Germany to take the blame for starting the war and to pay heavy reparations (payments) to the victorious nations. Many Germans deeply resented the treaty ending World War I, known as the Treaty of Versailles.

Negotiators at Versailles tried to follow the principle of letting national groups rule themselves. They separated Austria and Hungary into two countries. Poland became a sovereign nation again. The treaty allowed the Slavs living on the Balkan Peninsula to create the all-Slavic nation of Yugoslavia.

The war resulted in the end of the Ottoman Empire, which had ruled from Istanbul since 1453. Because the Ottomans had sided with Germany, the Allies forced them to give up almost all of their territories. Turkey experienced civil war until 1922. Turkish nationalists established the republic of Turkey the next year. Kemal Ataturk served as the first president.

President Wilson had led the United States into the war to achieve what he called peace without victory. He opposed harsh consequences for Germany. Even more, however, he wanted world leaders to form an international organization, which would be called the League of Nations. The League would resolve conflicts between nations by negotiating before they resorted to war. Wilson compromised on his ideals about how to handle Germany so that the other Allied leaders would support him in the formation of the League of Nations. The other leaders agreed to include the League in the treaty (although they were not strongly in favor of it) so that Wilson would agree to their desire to punish Germany harshly.

The majority of American people did not favor joining an international organization. Being involved in a foreign dispute had caused many American soldiers to die. Woodrow Wilson was a member of the Democratic Party, but Republicans led the U.S. Senate, which had to vote on whether to accept the treaty or not. These Republicans did not support Wilson's goals either. The Senate voted against the Treaty of Versailles. The United States never became a member of the League of Nations, and the U.S. made separate treaties with the nations of the Alliance.

Results of the War

Europeans were weary of war. During the 1920s, several nations agreed to **idealistic** treaties. They agreed to cut back on their military strength and decided that war was a poor means for resolving conflict. The British and French especially did not want to prepare for the possibility of another war.

After decades during the late 1800s and early 1900s, when many people had come to believe in what they called social and scientific "progress," a large number of people realized that the world was not on a path of constant improvement after all. The war showed the horrible ways

Lesson 134 - The Great War

that people could treat others. Many people became deeply **disillusioned** about the world after such a large part of the younger generation lost their lives in the war.

Germans struggled economically after the war. They never fully paid the reparations required in the Treaty of Versailles. Italians suffered under poor government leadership. As a result, strong dictators came to power in those two countries. These dictators talked about national pride and strong, authoritarian government. Meanwhile, Japan became increasingly aggressive in the Pacific region.

Woodrow Wilson had hoped that the Great War would be "the war to end all wars." It wasn't. Because of the way that nations handled the outcome of the war, countries experienced new conflicts and old conflicts simmered. We will continue this story when we discuss the Second World War in the next unit.

U.S. President Woodrow Wilson and President Raymond Poincare of France ride together while Wilson visits France for the Versailles Peace Conference.

May mercy and peace and love be multiplied to you.
Jude 2

Assignments for Lesson 134

Our Creative World — Read the "Fragments of Serbian National Wisdom" and "The Garden in Winter" on pages 124-125.

Map Book — Complete the assignments for Lesson 134 on Map 40 "The Great War."

Timeline Book — In the box for Lesson 134 on page 29, write "Ataturk becomes the first President of Turkey."

Student Workbook or Lesson Review — If you are using one of these optional books, complete the assignment for Lesson 134.

Vocabulary — Copy the following sentences, placing the correct vocabulary word in the blank: ghastly (914), neutral (915), infuriate (915), idealistic (916), disillusioned (917).

1. You know it will _____ Mr. Thompson if you use his tools without permission!
2. Do you think the Founding Fathers were _____ or practical in the way they organized our government?
3. James tried to remain _____ but each of his sisters kept trying to win him to her side of the argument.
4. Emily was rather _____ when she joined the dance troupe that had always seemed happy and harmonious, but was full of jealousies and petty disagreements.
5. Granddad said that he hopes we never know for ourselves how _____ war really is.

Literature — Read chapter 9 in *The Chestry Oak*.

Christ the Redeemer
Rio de Janeiro

Lesson 135 — World Landmark

After the difficult times of the Great War, the statue of Christ the Redeemer in Rio de Janeiro, Brazil, stood as a beacon of hope to South America and the world.

A Brief History of Brazil

Portuguese explorer Pedro Cabral landed on the eastern coast of South America in 1500 and claimed the land for Portugal. The Portuguese began settling Brazil in the 1530s. They called a species of tree there brazilwood because the trees were the color of glowing **embers**, which is *brasa* in Portuguese. Thus the land was called Brazil. See brazilwood at top right.

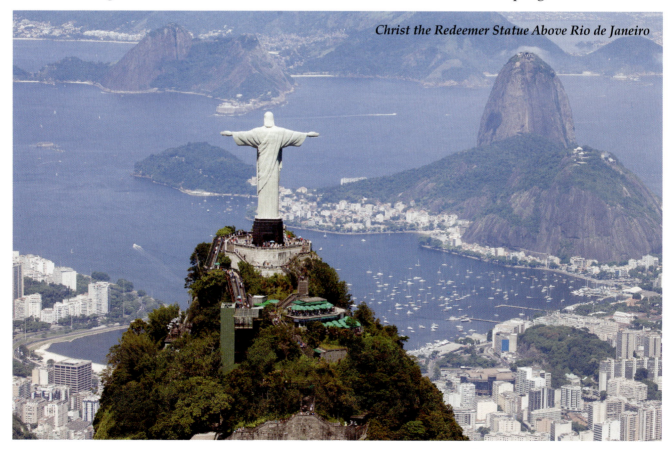

Christ the Redeemer Statue Above Rio de Janeiro

Lesson 135 - Christ the Redeemer, Rio de Janeiro

People from other nations sometimes challenged Portugal and tried to take land in Brazil. In the 1630s, some Dutch settled in northeastern Brazil, but the Portuguese drove them out in 1654. Prospectors discovered gold in Brazil in the 1690s. This brought many new people to the country. Over the years Portuguese settlers established settlements that crossed over into areas which Spain claimed. However, a 1750 treaty between Spain and Portugal confirmed that Portugal could keep the land on which its settlers lived.

Brazilwood

Portuguese settlers forced indigenous Americans and then Africans to work as slaves. As we learned in Lesson 123, Brazil became independent of Portugal in 1822; and slavery ended there in 1888. Brazil sided with the Allies during the Great War. Following the war, Brazil endured many years of political **unrest** as various individuals and groups competed for power.

The Land of Brazil

Brazil is the largest country in South America in terms of land area. The country covers about half of the continent. It is the fifth largest country in the world. Its land area is slightly smaller than that of the United States (3.3 million square miles compared to 3.8 million square miles in the U.S.). Brazil contains dense jungles, rich farmlands, and mountain ranges. The country is home to the Amazon Rainforest, the largest rainforest in the world. The Amazon River and about 1,000 other rivers are found there. See photos at right.

Amazon River

Toucan in Rainforest

Rio de Janeiro

In January 1502 explorer Goncalo Coelho entered what came to be known as Guanabara Bay on the southeastern coast of Brazil. The bay is circled by tall mountains. See photo on page 918. Coelho thought the bay was the mouth of a large river, so he named the unseen river for the month he discovered it: Rio de Janeiro (River of January). However, Coelho was mistaken; there is no Rio de Janeiro. The name stuck, however, and became the name of the settlement that grew there.

The Tupi people were living in the region when the Portuguese came. The French **encroached** on the territory that Portugal claimed and built a settlement there in 1555, but Portuguese soldiers built a fort at the site of the city in 1565 and drove out the French in 1567.

Rio became the capital of the Brazil colony in 1763. When King John of Portugal fled Europe during the Napoleonic Wars in the early 1800s, he made Rio the capital of the Portuguese Empire until he returned home in 1821. When Brazil declared its independence from Portugal in 1822, Rio became the capital of the new country. It remained the capital until the city of Brasilia was founded as the new capital in 1960.

Looking up at the statue from the base of Corcovado Mountain.

Building the Statue

Rising 2,300 feet above sea level, Corcovado Mountain is the tallest mountain around Guanabara Bay. The mountain is pictured at left. In the 1850s, Catholic priest Pedro Maria Boss suggested erecting a Christian monument on the mountain in honor of Isabel, princess regent of Brazil and daughter of Emperor Pedro II (see Lesson 123). However, it was not built.

In 1921 the Catholic archdiocese of Rio proposed that a statue of Christ be built on the mountain. The president of Brazil gave his approval and the Church began a fundraising campaign. The first stone of the foundation was laid on April 4, 1922, the 100th anniversary of Brazilian independence, even though the final design of the statue had not yet been chosen.

Lesson 135 - Christ the Redeemer, Rio de Janeiro

In a competition that year, Brazilian engineer Heitor da Silva Costa, Brazilian artist Carlos Oswald, and French sculptor Paul Landowski were selected to develop the final plans and oversee construction. Work began in 1926 and lasted five years. A railway carried men and materials to the construction site.

The statue was dedicated on October 12, 1931. The inventor of the radio, Guglielmo Marconi, was scheduled to switch on the lights by using a radio signal from Rome. However, the weather was so bad that the signal could not reach Rio. The lights were turned on at the site.

The statue is made of reinforced concrete with an outer layer that is a mosaic of triangular soapstone tiles.

It is ninety-eight feet tall, and the span of the figure's arms is ninety-two feet. The statue stands on top of a base that is twenty-six feet tall. This base stands on top of a platform. People worship in a small chapel located in the pedestal. People also have weddings and christenings there. The statue has stairs inside it, but the general public is not allowed inside.

Tourists can ascend the mountain by road or tram car. They can reach the base by escalators or elevators, or they can climb 222 stairs. Standing at the base of the statue, a visitor has a breathtaking view of the city, the bay, and the surrounding mountains.

The design of the Christ the Redeemer statue is in a style called art deco. This style was popular in architecture, furniture, and sculpture in the 1920s and 1930s. The statue has modern, rounded, **streamlined** forms and sleek elegance. The statue is the largest art deco sculpture in the world. It is also one of the largest statues of Jesus in the world.

Christ the Redeemer of Rio de Janeiro is a powerful **symbolic** illustration of the words of Jesus Himself:

And I, if I am lifted up from the earth, will draw all men to Myself.
John 12:32

Assignments for Lesson 135

Our Creative World — Read the newspaper article "Rio de Janeiro and the Raising of a Statue" on page 126.

Timeline Book — In the box for Lesson 135 on page 29, write "The Christ the Redeemer statue is dedicated."

Student Workbook or Lesson Review — If you are using one of these optional books, complete the assignment for Lesson 135 and take the test for Unit 27.

Thinking Biblically — Imagine that you were asked to write the words for a plaque that explains who Jesus is that would be mounted on the pedestal of the Christ the Redeemer statue. Write one paragraph.

Vocabulary — Copy these words, each on a separate line: ember (918), unrest (919), encroach (920), streamlined (921), symbolic (922). Look up each word in the dictionary. Next to each word, write what part of speech it is according to the way the word is used in the lesson.

Creative Writing — Make a list of ten adjectives that describe the Christ the Redeemer statue.

Literature — Read chapter 10 in *The Chestry Oak*.

28 The Mid-Twentieth Century

A Checkpoint in West Berlin, October 1961

Lessons
- 136 - Our World Story: World War II
- 137 - World Landmark: Berlin and the Cold War
- 138 - God's Wonder: God Created the Land of India
- 139 - Daily Life: Television Around the World
- 140 - World Biography: C. S. Lewis

Literature *The Chestry Oak*

1929-1968

Just over twenty years after the Great War, another war, even more terrible, erupted. Over fifty Allied nations joined together against the Axis powers led by Germany, Italy, and Japan. After the war, a Cold War continued, which was illustrated profoundly in the city of Berlin, Germany. The large nation of India, with its variety of beauties created by the hand of God, won its independence from the British Empire. Television became a source of news and entertainment around the world. C. S. Lewis brought a message of faith to millions through his many books for children and adults. The time period of this unit extends from the beginning of the Great Depression to the Vietnam War.

Lesson 139 talks about television in many countries.

World War II

Lesson 136 — Our World Story

The Great War caused the greatest loss of human life and the greatest destruction of property that people had ever inflicted on one another to that point in history. The Second World War, which followed the first by just over twenty years, was even worse. It ended in a different kind of war, a "cold war," that lasted for decades.

The United States entered this second worldwide conflict and helped bring it to an end. After the war, America provided help, hope, and freedom to people around the world. However, leaders of the Communist Party promoted godlessness and caused the loss of freedom for many. Our world situation today is in great measure the result of events that followed World War II.

Adolf Hitler Comes to Power in Germany

In the Treaty of Versailles, which ended World War I, the Allied nations "made Germany pay" for the Great War. Many Germans felt bitterness and resentment at the Allies' demands for heavy reparations. A few angry Germans formed the National Socialist Party, nicknamed Nazis. This party emphasized German pride and promised to make Germany a powerful nation again. Nazis blamed Jews for the hardships Germans suffered.

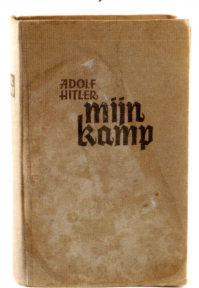

Adolf Hitler was born in Austria. He moved to Germany when he was twenty-four years old. He entered the German army and fought in World War I. Hitler became a leader in the Nazi Party. The German people hated the fact that the Allies had defeated them in World War I. Hitler gave harsh speeches that increased Germans' anger and made them believe that the Nazis could make their country strong again.

In 1923 Hitler led an unsuccessful revolt against the German government. He was sentenced to five years in prison, but was released after nine months. While in prison Hitler wrote *Mein Kampf* (meaning *My Struggle*). A Dutch edition is pictured at left. He wrote that Germany should take back land lost in

World War I; that they should take land from Poland, Russia, and other places in Eastern Europe; and that the country should have a dictator. The book sold over five million copies by 1939.

Poster for Hitler Youth

After the unsuccessful Nazi revolt, the German government made the Nazi Party illegal. However, Hitler continued to lead the party and recruit new members. Slowly he convinced the German government that the party would not do anything illegal, and the government allowed it to exist.

In the early 1930s, the German government was deciding about a plan to make their reparation payments to the Allies. Hitler opposed the plan. He led protest marches, organized large meetings, and gave speeches throughout Germany. When Germany held elections in 1932, the Nazis received the largest number of votes. Hitler insisted that the existing government make him chancellor. Finally, Germany's eighty-five-year-old president agreed. Adolf Hitler became chancellor of Germany on January 30, 1933.

Hitler saw himself as the leader of the Third Reich (meaning regime or empire). He called the Holy Roman Empire the First Reich (see Lesson 78 and the map on page 787). He called the unified Germany under Kaiser Wilhelm I the Second Reich (see page 917).

Though many opposed Hitler when he came to power, he and the Nazis set about trying to brainwash all Germans to his way of thinking. Since the early 1920s, the Nazis had trained boys ages fourteen to eighteen to be loyal Nazis. In 1926 they named the training organization Hitler Youth. The Nazis later formed clubs for girls and for younger boys. In the late 1930s, all German children were required by law to join a Nazi youth organization. Among their activities were singing, sports, hiking, camping, and collecting materials for the Nazi cause. Boys learned military skills. The youths were encouraged to spy on their own families and to report anti-Nazi activity. See Hitler youth poster above.

Hitler rebuilt Germany's military. He then threatened to send German troops to seize portions of other countries to expand the *lebensraum* (living space) that Hitler said the German people needed. In 1936 he sent troops into the Rhineland in western Germany, an area next to France. See picture at right. The Treaty of Versailles had forbidden Germany to have troops in the Rhineland so that Germany could not attack France from there.

Germany took over Austria in 1938. Neither the League of Nations nor other

German troops enter the city of Cologne in the Rhineland.

countries dared to stop Hitler. Europeans did not want to become involved in another war. While Hitler was modernizing and building up the German military, other countries were cutting back on theirs. European leaders gave in to what Hitler wanted. They hoped that doing so would satisfy him and cause him to stop being aggressive. This approach is called appeasement. Appeasement did not satisfy Hitler. It only made him lose respect for those leaders and increased his appetite for more territory. Winston Churchill, a member of the British Parliament, understood the Nazi threat for what it was and spoke out about it. However, most people dismissed Churchill's warnings as unrealistic.

2014 United Kingdom Stamp

Italy and Japan

1941 Italian Stamp with Profiles of Hitler and Mussolini

Italy and Japan also felt that the Treaty of Versailles treated them unfairly. While Hitler was coming to power in Germany, Benito Mussolini founded the Fascist Party in Italy and then took over the country as dictator. His methods were similar to Hitler's. Italian forces invaded and took control of Ethiopia in 1935 and 1936. Hitler and Mussolini signed an agreement in 1936 that made them allies in case of war. They are pictured together on the Italian stamp above. Mussolini arrogantly declared that Rome and Berlin formed the new axis around which the world now turned. Germany and Italy came to be known as the Axis Powers. The Italian Fascists took over Albania in the Balkans in 1939.

Meanwhile, aggressive military leaders gained control of the government of Japan. They built up the Japanese military. A Japanese army unit is pictured below. Japan began invading and taking over countries in Asia, including large areas of China. They said that they needed the natural resources in those countries to supply Japanese industries. The Japanese leaders also claimed that they needed more room for their people. When other nations and the League of Nations criticized what they were doing, the Japanese government ignored them.

The world economic situation added to the crisis. In 1929 an economic depression began in America and spread around the world. Millions of people all over the world were out of work. Since it happened when so many countries were still trying to recover from the Great War, the Great Depression increased the frustrations that many people felt.

Japanese Army Unit, 1933

Attacks on the Jews

For centuries some Europeans had blamed Jews for their troubles. Whether it was the Black Plague or financial difficulties or some other problem, people used the Jews as a scapegoat. Hitler believed that the Germans were a superior race. He especially hated Jews and blamed them for Germany's financial problems. Hitler believed that Jewish bankers conspired together to keep Germany poor and that the only way to solve Germany's problems was to get rid of the Jews. This idea appealed to the prejudices that many people held against Jews. Hitler also felt strong prejudice against the Slavic peoples and Communists. The Soviet Union, a Slavic Communist country, was a special target of his anger.

At first the Nazis limited the Jews' rights. Then they forced Jews to wear yellow Stars of David, such as the one at right, on their clothing so everyone would know who was Jewish. Finally the Nazis began rounding up Jews and sending them to concentration camps. Germans forced Jews to work in those camps, but the main purpose of the camps was to exterminate the Jewish race. Hitler's government called this killing of Jews the "final solution." When people in other countries heard about what the Germans were doing, most of them did not believe that it was really happening.

Jews were required to wear a Star of David such as this one.

The War Begins

In 1917 Russia had become the world's first Communist nation. In 1922 Russia, along with other regions of Eastern Europe, including Ukraine and Belarus, established the Union of Soviet Socialist Republics (usually called simply the U.S.S.R. or the Soviet Union). Most world leaders believed that at some point Germany would fight the Soviet Union, then led by Josef Stalin. The two countries appeared to be great rivals. Thus the world was shocked in August of 1939 when Germany and the U.S.S.R. announced that they had signed a nonaggression treaty. This meant that they had agreed not to attack each other.

On September 1, 1939, Germany launched a fierce invasion of Poland from the west and quickly controlled most of the country. Historians generally see this date as the start of World War II. A few weeks later, the Soviet Union invaded Poland from the east and gained control of the eastern third of the country. The nonaggression treaty had actually been an agreement between Germany and the Soviet Union to carve up Poland and not attack each other.

Having conquered Poland, Germany then took over Denmark, Norway, Luxembourg, Belgium, and the Netherlands. Because of its commitment to defend Belgium, Great Britain declared war on Germany. Germany attacked France just as they had in the Great War, by moving through Belgium. France surrendered within weeks. This left only Britain fighting against German aggression. German planes started bombing London and other major cities in England in what was called the Battle of Britain. Most people assumed that Germany was

Lesson 136 - World War II

about to invade Britain with soldiers on the ground. Royal Air Force planes and anti-aircraft guns brought down many of the attackers, but the Germans destroyed many buildings in London and in other cities and killed many civilians. The British responded by bombing Berlin. See photos of German war activities on this page.

Some Britons wanted their government to ask for peace; in other words, to surrender to Germany in order to survive. Churchill, who had recently become prime minister, refused to do so. Instead, he stirred his countrymen with eloquent speeches, encouraging Britons to resist and continue the fight. Throughout 1940 the British remained defiant toward Germany despite terrible casualties and damage from the bombing. Winston Churchill appealed to the United States for help in defending Great Britain and resisting Germany. See photos of Churchill on pages 927 and 930. See a map showing the greatest extent of Third Reich control on page 930.

Nazis invade Poland, 1939.

Nazi Headquarters in Copenhagen, Denmark, 1940.

Left: German Photo of German Plane Over River Thames in London, 1940. Center: Women stand in the rubble that was once the almshouse where they lived in Newbury, England, 1943. Right: An American newspaper reports on German attacks on British warships which were attempting to defend Norway against invasion.

Left: Nazi Leader Heinrich Himmler in Luxembourg; Center: Tearful Belgian women wave as their men leave to fight the Nazis, May, 1940. Right: The Nazis established the Kamp Vught concentration camp in the Netherlands.

Unit 28 - The Mid-Twentieth Century

Churchill strolls on the deck of the HMS Prince of Wales, *where he and U.S. President Roosevelt met to discuss America helping the Allies.*

The United States began to provide a limited amount of weapons and supplies to Britain. Meanwhile, Japan signed an agreement with Germany and Italy which said the three nations would work together if any one of them were attacked.

Britain's determined and successful resistance to German air attacks caused Hitler to cancel plans to invade the island. Germany and the Soviet Union remained enemies in reality in spite of their previous agreement. As the war continued, Hitler sent millions of troops to attack the Soviet Union. Although Germany inflicted heavy losses on the Russians, ultimately the exhausted Germans suffered defeat in the bitter Russian

Soviet Tank and Soldiers in the Winter of 1942

winter and withdrew, just as Napoleon had. See Soviet forces in winter at left. The Soviet Union became an ally with Great Britain. Meanwhile British forces in northern Africa defeated an Italian army. This showed that Mussolini's talk about Italy being a fearsome fighting force was just that: talk. With the Italian military showing weakness in northern Africa, Germany took control there, too.

Then on December 7, 1941, Japan attacked Pearl Harbor, a U.S. military base in the American territory of the Hawaiian Islands in the Pacific Ocean. Over 2,000 Americans died in this surprise attack on a neutral country. Japanese leaders hoped to knock out the American navy in the Pacific with a first strike so they could continue their aggression. The United States declared war against the Axis powers. Isoroku Yamamoto, the Japanese admiral who planned the attack, reportedly wrote in his diary: "I fear all we have done is to awaken a sleeping giant and fill him with a terrible resolve."

Japan continued its aggression in the Pacific. The map below shows areas they conquered, including two of America's Aleutian Islands, which are part of Alaska. Throughout the fighting in the Pacific, the Japanese inflicted horrible torture on Allied soldiers in prisoner-of-war camps.

Japanese planes damage the USS West Virginia *and the USS* Tennessee *and sink the USS* Arizona *at Pearl Harbor, December 7, 1941.*

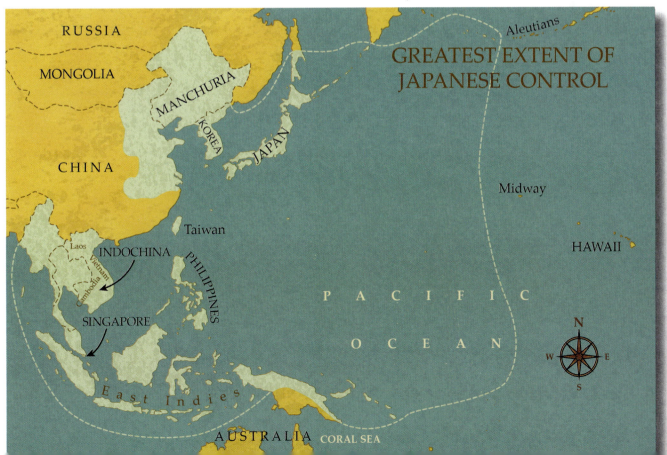

The Tide Turns

America brought more fighting men and more resources to the growing list of Allied nations (see chart on page 935). In the spring of 1942, Allied forces stopped the Japanese advance and slowly began pushing them back toward their home country. The Allies also defeated German forces in northern Africa and began to bomb Germany heavily.

Allied troops land on the beaches of Normandy, France, 1944.

U.S. military officers took over the leadership of the Allied forces. They planned two major invasions of Europe. In 1943 the Allies landed in Italy and pushed north toward Germany amid fierce fighting. In mid-1944, the Allies defeated Italy. Italians who opposed Mussolini captured and executed him and announced their support for the Allies.

An Allied force, made up largely of Americans, landed in northern France on D-Day, June 6, 1944. They also carried out bombing raids on Germany. These forces liberated Paris and the entire country of France from the Germans, then turned east toward Germany. By the end of the year, the Allies were close to victory. The Germans pushed back briefly in the Battle of the Bulge in late December 1944, but the Allies regrouped and continued their advance. The Japanese suffered additional losses during 1944 in the Pacific.

In the spring of 1945, the Allies entered Germany from both east and west. The Americans and the British moved into western Germany, and the Soviets entered eastern Germany. The cowardly Hitler took his own life, and his commanding officers asked the Allies for peace and surrendered. The war in Europe officially ended with V-E Day (Victory in Europe), May 8, 1945.

The Holocaust

When the Allies gained complete access to Germany, they learned the full horror of the Holocaust. The Nazis had rounded up Jews from Germany, Poland, Czechoslovakia, the Netherlands, and other countries, along with many Christians, Gypsies, Communists, people with disabilities, and people who helped the Jews. They placed them in concentration camps. These places also came to be called death camps, because that was what happened to the victims. In gas chambers, through mass executions, and by creating inhuman conditions, the Nazis killed about six million Jews plus perhaps as many non-Jewish civilians. It is estimated that Germany put to death about sixty percent of the Jews in Europe.

Many brave individuals helped the Jews. Several officials used their positions and influence in society to protect Jews secretly and to transport thousands to safety. Among these were Oskar Schindler in Poland and Czechoslovakia; Raoul Wallenberg in Sweden; Ho Feng-Shan, a Chinese diplomat in Austria; Chiune Sugihara, a Japanese diplomat in Lithuania; and Sir Nicholas Winton from Great Britain. Winton died in 2015 at the age of 106. After the war, Otto Frank, a German Jew, published *The Diary of Anne Frank,* which his daughter had kept during the family's time in hiding before they were captured in the Netherlands. Anne died in a concentration camp.

Lesson 136 - World War II

Remembering Holocaust Victims and Heroes

Above: Male Prisoners at a Concentration Camp in Sachsenhausen, Germany, 1938; Right: Sir Nicholas Winton at a Ceremony in his Honor in Prague, Czech Republic, 2014; Below: A 1983 stamp from Israel remembers women who died in the Holocaust.

The End of the War

Most people expected a difficult time in the Pacific as the Allies prepared to invade Japan. However, the United States unveiled a secret weapon: an atomic bomb with much more destructive power than any other weapon ever used. The U.S. dropped two atomic bombs on Hiroshima and Nagasaki, important cities in Japan, on August 6 and 9, 1945. The damage and loss of life in both cities were enormous. Faced with this destruction and the possibility of more, the Japanese government surrendered. V-J Day (Victory over Japan) was September 2, 1945. The photo at left shows the surrender ceremony. Finally the terrible war was over.

General Douglas MacArthur signs the Japanese surrender aboard the USS Missouri, *on September 2, 1945.*

Fighting had raged in North Africa, China, Southeast Asia, islands of the Pacific, the Soviet Union, and the cities and countryside of Europe. Experts estimate that about twenty million soldiers died during the war. Another thirty or forty million civilians died from fighting, bombing, disease, starvation, and executions. The property damage was enormous. The war left millions hungry and without homes.

America's Role in World War II

America had first become a world power during World War I. During World War II, the military might of the United States made the difference on the battle front, but the American home front contributed to the victory as well, producing weapons, planes, ships, and ammunition for the Allies. Many factories switched from making peacetime goods to making wartime goods. Automobile plants produced jeeps and tanks. Nylon producers stopped making women's hose and made parachutes. Scrap metal and rubber drives recycled those materials for war production.

A sad aspect of the American home front was the U.S. government's decision to move over 100,000 persons of Japanese ancestry from the West Coast into relocation camps further inland. About two-thirds of those relocated were American citizens. Though their basic needs were met and they were eventually freed, they lost their homes and jobs as a result of this relocation. There was no evidence that these Americans were going to become disloyal; the relocation effort was the result of anger about the attack at Pearl Harbor and of fear on the part of other Americans.

Results of the War

The United States, the United Kingdom, the Soviet Union, and China led the Allied powers. On January 1, 1942, they and twenty-seven other countries committed their military and economic resources to stop "Hitlerism" by signing a "Declaration by the United Nations" in Washington, D.C. By the end of the war, twenty-one other countries had joined with them. See chart at right.

The Cold War. Almost immediately after the war, the Allies divided into two camps. The Americans, British, and French controlled western Germany and oversaw the recovery of western Europe. These Allies helped leaders in those countries form democratic governments. The Soviet Union, by contrast, controlled eastern Germany and also took charge of Poland and the other countries in eastern Europe. The U.S.S.R. set up Soviet-style Communist dictatorships in these countries, all of which answered to the Soviet government in Moscow.

The Allies and the Soviets viewed each other with suspicion, which replaced the cooperation that they had shown during the war against their common enemy of Germany.

The Marshall Plan. Instead of demanding that Germany make reparation payments as they had after World War I, the Allies took a different approach this time. U.S. Secretary of State George Marshall designed a plan that came to be called the Marshall Plan. In this plan, the victorious nations provided loans and other assistance to help nations devastated by the war, including Germany, get back on their feet. This enabled nations to rebuild their economies, which helped everyday people return to a normal life more quickly. The U.S. took a similar approach in Japan. U.S. General Douglas MacArthur and the American forces which occupied Japan developed a new government for the country and transformed Japanese society into one that was more open and democratic. This assistance helped these countries not be influenced by Communists. In 1997 Germany issued the stamp above to commemorate the fiftieth anniversary of the Marshall Plan.

1960 and 1997 German stamps commemorate the Marshall Plan.

The Allies
(and the Year They Signed the "Declaration by the United Nations")

United States*
United Kingdom*
U.S.S.R.*
China*
Australia*
Belgium*
Canada*
Costa Rica*
Cuba*
Czechoslovakia*
Dominican Republic*
El Salvador*
Greece*
Guatemala*
Haiti*
Honduras*
India*
Luxembourg*
Netherlands*
New Zealand*
Nicaragua*
Norway*
Panama*
Poland*
South Africa*
Yugoslavia*
Mexico 1942
Philippines 1942
Ethiopia 1942
Iraq 1943
Brazil 1943
Bolivia 1943
Iran 1943
Colombia 1943
Liberia 1944
France 1944
Ecuador 1945
Peru 1945
Chile 1945
Paraguay 1945
Venezuela 1945
Uruguay 1945
Turkey 1945
Egypt 1945
Saudi Arabia 1945
Lebanon 1945
Syria 1945

*Original Signers

Unit 28 - The Mid-Twentieth Century

The Canadian delegation meets during the San Francisco Conference which organized the United Nations.

The United Nations. During the war, the United States and Great Britain discussed the possibility of forming a stronger organization of nations to keep peace and to encourage international cooperation. The League of Nations had largely been a failure at maintaining peace, but diplomats hoped that a new international organization would be more effective because the United States would be a member of it. Representatives from many nations met at the San Francisco Conference in April, May, and June of 1945 to work on plans for an international organization.

The United Nations (UN) was formally organized in San Francisco that fall. From 1947 to 1952, the UN operated the International Refugee Organization. In the photo at left, a Belgian refugee family stands in front of the Brandenburg Gate before going to Canada as refugees.

A Belgian refugee family at the Brandenburg Gate before they emigrate to Canada, c. 1950.

Dead Sea Scrolls

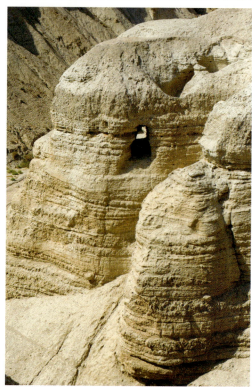

As mentioned in Lesson 42, in 1947, just two years after the end of World War II, a Bedouin goatherd discovered ancient scrolls containing portions of all of the books of the Old Testament except Esther in the caves of Qumran, near the Dead Sea. These scrolls are known as the Dead Sea Scrolls. See map on page 279. Above: Scroll Fragment; Right: View of the Caves of Qumran

Simon Trampatter, an 83-year-old Dutch Jew, cuts the star off the coat of his friend, Joseph Keller, in January 1945.

The history of World War II reveals the need the people of the world have for our Savior. All people sin. The sins of some people, such as Adolf Hitler and the Nazis, hurt and destroy millions. People created in the image of God also do wonderful things, people like Ho, Schindler, Sugihara, Wallenberg, and Winton who rescued Jews. After World War II, many former American soldiers went back to Germany and Japan as missionaries to teach the gospel. The people in war-ravaged countries needed so much, but more than anything else they needed Jesus—the answer God provided to the whole world almost 2,000 years before.

But now apart from the Law the righteousness of God has been manifested ... through faith in Jesus Christ for all those who believe; for there is no distinction; for all have sinned and fall short of the glory of God, being justified as a gift by His grace through the redemption which is in Christ Jesus.
Romans 3:21-24

Assignments for Lesson 136

Our Creative World — Look at the Holocaust memorials on pages 127-129.

Map Book — Complete the assignments for Lesson 136 on Map 41 "World War II in Europe."

Timeline Book — In the box for Lesson 136 on page 29, write "The first Nazi concentration camps open."

Student Workbook or Lesson Review — If you are using one of these optional books, complete the assignment for Lesson 136.

Thinking Biblically — Write at least one paragraph to answer this question: Why do you think people engage in war?

Literature — Read chapter 11 in *The Chestry Oak*.

Berlin
and the Cold War

Lesson 137 — World Landmark

> From Stettin in the Baltic to Trieste in the Adriatic an Iron Curtain has descended across the Continent [of Europe]. Behind that line lie all the capitals of the ancient states of Central and Eastern Europe. Warsaw, Berlin, Prague, Vienna, Budapest, Belgrade, Bucharest and Sofia; all these famous cities and the populations around them lie in what I must call the Soviet sphere, and all are subject, in one form or another, not only to Soviet influence but to a very high and in some cases increasing measure of control from Moscow.

United States President Franklin Roosevelt died shortly before the end of World War II and Vice President Harry Truman became President in his place. Truman and Winston Churchill, who was by then the former prime minister of the United Kingdom, traveled to Fulton, Missouri, in March of 1946. The quote above was part of a speech Churchill gave at Westminster College in Fulton. In the speech Churchill described the growing menace of Communism. He said the people in Eastern Europe whose countries had been taken over by Communists lived behind an "Iron Curtain." The Communist governments behind this Iron Curtain robbed the people of their personal freedom, including freedom to interact with other countries. Churchill warned the United States and other democracies of the threat that Communism posed because the Communists wanted to spread their philosophy around the world.

Churchill's speech described the tense standoff between the forces of freedom and the forces of Communism that existed in the world after World War II. This standoff is called the Cold War since the most powerful countries on each side—the democratic United States and the Communist Soviet Union—opposed each other but never came to an actual, shooting war.

Churchill (left) and Truman (center) stand on the rear platform of a special Baltimore & Ohio train.

Lesson 137 - Berlin and the Cold War

One vivid example of this standoff was the city of Berlin, the capital and largest city in Germany. After World War II, it was divided into a free zone and a Communist zone. This happened in Vienna, Austria, too, but it only lasted a short time and Vienna became a free city.

History of Berlin

About 1200 AD, Germanic people founded the trading village of Berlin where the Spree and Havel Rivers flow together. This small village grew into one of the most important cultural, economic, and political cities of Europe. However, it had its share of sadness also. During the Thirty Years War, for instance, fighting and disease cut the population of the city by half.

Frederick Wilhelm, Duke of Prussia and Elector of Brandenburg from 1640 to 1688, ordered the first canal dug between the Spree and the Oder River, which lay just east of Berlin. This helped the city grow economically. Berliners dug many other canals in later years. Napoleon occupied Berlin between 1806 and 1808. When Germany became unified in 1861, as described in Lesson 134, Berlin became the capital. The city suffered greatly as a result of World War I.

The center of Berlin's social and cultural life is the Unter der Linden ("Under the Linden") Boulevard, which is almost a mile long. The street is named for the linden trees that line it. The street originally led to the emperor's palace. The western end of the boulevard is the most famous landmark in Berlin, the Brandenburg Gate. Frederick Wilhelm II had the gate built between 1788 and 1791. Originally only royalty could use the central portal of the gate.

Allied bombing during World War II, destroyed about one-third of Berlin and about 112,000 civilians died. Before we tell the story of Berlin after the war, let us first step back and learn more about Communism.

Brandenburg Gate, c. 1965

Communism

In the mid-1800s, two German writers, Karl Marx and Friedrich Engels, pictured at right, developed a political and economic theory they called Communism. Marx and Engels strongly opposed capitalism, the economic system in which a few people own the businesses and others work for them. Marx and Engels believed that factory owners and investors around the world oppressed the workers and kept them poor on purpose. Marx and Engels wanted to destroy the

Left: 1980 Czechoslovakian Stamp of Engels;
Right: 1953 Chinese Stamp of Marx

system of capitalism. Their goal was for workers to take over governments and to run factories themselves. They imagined a society without social classes, run by the intellectuals (people like Marx and Engels themselves). They believed that government would eventually fade away and that everyone would work the amount he was able to work, that everyone would receive the pay that he needed, and that all people would own everything in common. Marx and Engels were **atheists** and believed that people used religion like a drug to avoid reality. They did not believe in individual freedom.

Marx and Engels believed that the changes they proposed would happen naturally in the course of history, but they also believed that Communists could help these things happen by starting revolutions.

Some people in various countries became Communists. Not all of them started revolutions and overthrew their governments, but some of them did. However, the leaders then became dictators. In reality, no society has ever existed like the one Marx and Engels envisioned. Moreover, Communists were not content simply to create a Communist government. They wanted to make the whole world Communist.

Headquarters of the Communist Party in Barcelona, Spain, with Banners of Lenin and Stalin, 1936

Communism in Russia

As mentioned in Lesson 136, Russia was the first Communist country and formed the U.S.S.R. Vladimir Lenin, its first leader, was a brutal dictator. After he died in 1924, Josef Stalin, from Lenin's small inner circle of leaders, gained control. Stalin was even more brutal than Lenin. Stalin ordered the deaths of millions of people inside the U.S.S.R. as part of what he called a "people's revolution." He probably oversaw the deaths of more people than Hitler did.

The U.S.S.R. had a totalitarian government, which means that the government had total control of every aspect of life. Secret police spied on what everyone was doing, and anyone who dared oppose or criticize the government would likely be put in prison or executed. The government was officially atheist and only allowed churches to operate under strict regulation. Most people lived in fear. Only a small percentage of people were actually members of the Communist Party. Communist theory said that everyone would have enough, but in reality most people suffered from a lack of food and other daily necessities because Communism does not encourage people to work hard and show initiative. The very highest-ranking officials had what they wanted because they could use their positions to obtain goods.

The U.S.S.R. entered World War II on the side of the Allies and fought Germany in the area between Germany and the U.S.S.R., known during the war as the Eastern Front. The Soviets wanted to defeat Hitler, but Stalin had another agenda as well. He wanted to gain control of as many countries as he could, especially in Eastern Europe, so that he could impose Communism in those countries. That is why the Soviets invaded Poland from the east when Hitler invaded from the west. In addition to Poland, the Soviets invaded and controlled Estonia, Latvia, Lithuania, Czechoslovakia, Hungary, Bulgaria, Romania, Yugoslavia, and Albania. The Allies decided that the Americans and British would stop in western Germany while the Soviets would take over eastern Germany, which included Berlin.

Postwar Berlin

After World War II, most countries became allies either of the U.S. (these were called the free world) or the Soviet Union (these were called the Communist world). Some countries did not align themselves with either great power. These were called third-world countries.

The contrast and confrontation between the free world and the Communist world after World War II was especially stark and divisive in Germany. The Communists controlled the eastern third of the country, while the western portion was made up of three zones overseen by American, British, and French troops. The city of Berlin was entirely within Communist-controlled East Germany, about one hundred miles from West Germany, but the city was likewise divided into four zones: Communist East Berlin and the American, British, and French zones of West Berlin. See photos on page 923 and at right. West Berlin was an island of freedom in the Communist ocean of East Germany. The government Stalin led in the Soviet Union controlled everything the East German and East Berlin governments did.

British, French, and American Commandants Sir Geoffrey Bourne, Jean Ganeval, and Frank Howley, 1949

The Berlin Blockade and Airlift

The Communists tried to force West Berliners to accept Communist control by making their lives miserable. In 1948 the Communists cut water lines to the city and blocked roads and railroads, refusing to let any supplies through. U.S. President Harry Truman arranged for Allied planes to fly supplies into West Berlin. Beginning in June of 1948, the Berlin Airlift provided everything West Berlin needed, including food, water, clothes, and coal. This act of kindness and charity was also called "Operation Vittles." At the height of the airlift, planes landed in Berlin every one to two minutes. The Communists did not try to shoot down any planes, since doing so would have caused a major confrontation that could have resulted in a new war.

Scenes from the Berlin Airlift

Top Row: A woman and children wait while a plane is unloaded. German boys play with toy American airplanes. Germans watch a British Royal Air Force plane land. Second Row: A German woman receives her ration of coal. A German boy eats soup supplied by the airlift. U.S. Air Force Lieutenant Gail Halvorsen ties candy to toy parachutes. Halvorsen became famous as the "candy bomber," because he dropped these "candy bombs" for Berlin's children in an effort airmen called "Little Vittles." Right: The airlift supplied milk. "Candy bombs" fall from an American plane.

The Soviets finally lifted the **blockade** in May of 1949, but planes continued to bring supplies to West Berlin until September. In that year, the three Allied zones of West Germany and West Berlin were combined under a single authority. East Germany allowed a narrow corridor for road and train transportation between West Germany and West Berlin. The West German government moved from Berlin to the city of Bonn. West Berlin was a special district all its own but in practical terms was part of West Germany.

The Berlin Wall

During the 1950s, entry into West Berlin from East Berlin and travel from West Berlin to West Germany were relatively easy, as illustrated at right. Thousands of East Germans

Passengers from Berlin Land in the British Sector of Germany, 1949

escaped Communism and moved to freedom. By 1961 about one thousand people per day were leaving East Germany.

All this changed overnight on August 13, 1961, when East Germany put up a fence to separate the Communist and free parts of the city. The photograph of Berlin's Brandenburg Gate at right was taken that day. Gradually the Communists replaced the fence with a permanent concrete wall.

Barbed wire topped the Berlin Wall, and East German soldiers guarded a wide zone beside the wall. Many families were separated by the wall. If a person lived in West Berlin and his parents lived in East Berlin, he simply was not able to see them. If someone lived on one side of the wall and was visiting the other side of the city on August 13, 1961, he was not able to return home. The photos at right show the wall under construction and a woman waving from behind the barbed wire.

After East Germany built the wall, guards killed many people who tried to escape from East Berlin to West Berlin. It is a sad statement about Communism that its leaders had to build a wall to keep in the people they ruled.

West Germany and East Germany existed as separate countries for forty-four years. West Germany was a democracy and an ally with other democracies, including France, the United Kingdom, and the United States. Residents of East Germany lived under Communism without personal or political freedoms. The East German capital was in East Berlin.

U.S. President John F. Kennedy visited West Berlin on June 26, 1963. He gave a speech to express America's commitment to freedom in Germany. To show his unity with the people of Berlin, Kennedy said in German, *"Ich bin ein Berliner"* ("I am a Berliner," meaning a resident of Berlin). The Berlin Wall became a symbol of the standoff between Communism and freedom.

Border guards stand in front of the Brandenburg Gate on August 13, 1961, the day officials separated East and West Berlin.

Berlin Wall Under Construction, 1961

Woman waves over the wall, 1961.

U.S. President John F. Kennedy speaks in Berlin on June 26, 1963.

Cold War Standoffs in Other Parts of the World

During the Cold War, Russians and Americans suspected each other of doing things secretly that would cause the other country's government to fall. Each side used spies within the two countries and in other parts of the world to obtain information about the other side. The Soviet Union spread propaganda among its people. Like Hitler had done in Germany, the U.S.S.R. formed youth organizations (called Young Pioneers) so that children would grow up believing in Communism. At right is a 1959 U.S.S.R. stamp of a boy in one of these organizations.

The U.S. and the U.S.S.R. built up their military forces and weapons so they would be ready for any confrontation. They also hoped to intimidate the other side into backing down. The dramatic confrontation between the two sides became even more tense in 1949 when the Soviet Union gained the ability to make atomic bombs. Each side produced so many nuclear weapons that they could have destroyed the world many times over. Even though the United States and the Soviet Union did not go to war against each other, several shooting wars in different parts of the world did occur between Communist armies and the armies of democratic countries.

China. Mao Zedong had helped start the Communist Party in China in 1921. The Communist Party in the U.S.S.R. supported the Communist Party in China. Mao and Nationalist Chinese leader Chiang Kai-shek had worked together to fight traditional Chinese warlords for a few years.

Mao (left) and Chiang (right) toast to celebrate the Allied victory at the end of World War II.

In 1927 Chiang ousted the Communists from his Nationalist group. This is when Mao led the Long March (mentioned on page 896). During World War II, China was allied with the U.S.S.R., the United States, and the United Kingdom. Chiang Kai-shek and members of the Nationalist Party had worked alongside Communists in their fight against Japan. See photo at left. After World War II, however, Chinese Communists and Nationalists fought a civil war. The United States went to the aid of the Nationalists, but the Communists won this war.

On October 1, 1949, Mao proclaimed the (Communist) People's Republic of China. Chiang and his followers fled to the island of Taiwan off the coast of China. China had taken Taiwan back from Japan after World War II. Chiang Kai-shek continued to lead a Nationalist government on Taiwan for the next twenty-five years. The Nationalists stated their desire to invade the Chinese mainland and take back control of China, but they never tried to do so.

The Communists expanded the territory of China, taking over Manchuria in 1949 and Tibet in 1950. The Communist governments of China and the Soviet Union had disagreements later and ended diplomatic relations in 1962.

Mao Poster, 1960s

Lesson 137 - Berlin and the Cold War

This was the Cold War standoff in China. The Communists controlled mainland China and Mao ordered the deaths of millions of Chinese who opposed him. The Nationalists controlled the island of Taiwan. Many countries recognized Chiang's government on Taiwan as the legitimate Chinese government. The Nationalist government on Taiwan was a part of the United Nations until 1971, when the UN voted to replace Taiwan with the People's Republic of China.

Korea. Following World War II, Korea was divided at the 38th parallel of latitude into a free southern part and a Communist-controlled northern part. Communist China and the Soviet Union supported North Korea; the United States supported South Korea. On June 25, 1950, soldiers from the Communist north invaded South Korea for the purpose of taking it over for the Communists. The United Nations condemned the invasion and voted to send a military force to oppose it. U.S. Army General Douglas MacArthur led the UN forces, which consisted mainly of U.S. troops with some soldiers from other UN countries. See British and U.S. ships below.

Communist forces pushed the UN troops to the extreme southern portion of the Korean Peninsula. Then MacArthur ordered a daring landing of troops from the sea at the port of Inchon, far to the north of where the North Korean troops had advanced. The Communist troops retreated into North Korea, and the UN force pushed them almost to the border with China.

British ship HMS Belfast *comes alongside the USS* Bataan *near the coast of Korea.*

At this point, thousands of Chinese troops poured over the border and pushed the UN forces back south of the 38th parallel. The two sides signed a ceasefire agreement on July 27, 1953. They agreed that the 38th parallel would continue to be the dividing line between North and South Korea and that no weapons or offensive actions would be allowed in a small area to the north and south of that line. This area is called the Demilitarized Zone or DMZ. See map at right.

Communist and democratic forces continue to have a Cold War standoff on the Korean Peninsula. North Korea has continually had a Communist **totalitarian** government that

Left: U.S. Marines land at the port of Inchon.
Right: The U.S. Navy rescues North Korean refugees.

has built up its military while keeping its people in poverty. South Korea has a democratic government and has developed a strong economy that has helped its people become prosperous. About thirty percent of South Koreans identify themselves as Christian.

Cuba. In 1959 Cuban Fidel Castro seized control of the island nation of Cuba, ninety miles from Florida. The Soviet Union provided assistance to Castro's government, and Castro aligned himself with the Communists. Thousands of Cubans fled their country and came to the United States.

In 1961 a group of Cubans whom the U.S. government had trained within the United States invaded the Bay of Pigs on the southern coast of Cuba in an effort to overthrow Castro. The Cuban army defeated this group. This failure embarrassed the U.S. government and Castro's power became even stronger in Cuba. The relationship between Cuba and the Soviet Union grew stronger.

In October 1962, an American spy plane photographed missile launch sites the U.S.S.R. was building on Cuba. U.S. officials showed the left photo below to President Kennedy on October 16. The U.S. and the U.S.S.R. came very close to war. In the photo at right below, Kennedy is ordering that a ring of U.S. Navy ships surround Cuba to prevent the Soviets from bringing in any more military supplies. He demanded that the Russians remove the missiles. The Soviets agreed to do this, and in return the United States government pledged not to be involved in another invasion of the island as it had been in the Bay of Pigs **incident**.

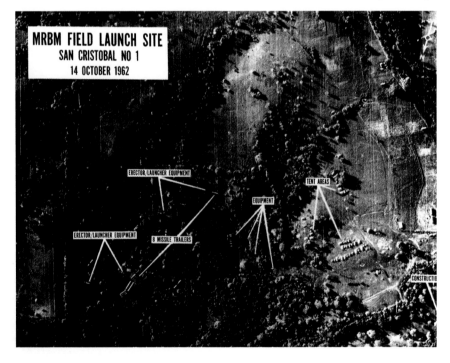

Left: Spy photograph reveals missile launch sites on Cuba. Above: U.S. President John F. Kennedy orders a blockade of Cuba.

Vietnam. After World War II, France continued to control Vietnam as it had since 1874. In 1954 Vietnamese Communists under the leadership of Ho Chi Minh defeated the French at Dien Bien Phu and took control of the northern half of the country. Vietnamese military officers established a free government in South Vietnam, but many of its officials were poor leaders.

Both China and the U.S.S.R. helped North Vietnam try to invade and defeat the South. South Vietnamese Communists called the Viet Cong carried on guerrilla warfare (*guerrilla* is Spanish for "little war") against the South Vietnamese government. In guerrilla warfare, small groups of combatants engage in small battles and surprise attacks. The United States supported South Vietnam and sent military advisers and equipment to help it fight Communism. American officials feared that if one country in Southeast Asia fell to the Communists, other countries would follow just as a line of dominoes falls when one falls against another. This idea came to be called the domino theory.

In August of 1964, North Vietnam reportedly attacked an American navy vessel in international waters in the Gulf of Tonkin off of North Vietnam. The U.S. Congress responded by authorizing the President to use whatever force was necessary to help any country in Southeast Asia with which the U.S. had a treaty obligation to defend its freedom. This included South Vietnam.

Ho Chi Minh Trail

The United States eventually sent over 500,000 troops to South Vietnam. The U.S. military also bombed North Vietnam. American officials never wanted to invade North Vietnam and defeat the Communist government there. They simply wanted to defend and protect the freedom of South Vietnam from Communist attacks. At times the war spread into the neighboring countries of Laos and Cambodia, when North Vietnam used supply routes in those countries to send men and material to the South. American bombers attacked the supply routes which came to be called the Ho Chi Minh Trail.

While Americans tried to help South Vietnam, its government continued to be weak and corrupt. The South Vietnamese army did a poor job fighting the Communists. With thousands of American soldiers dying and hundreds of Americans suffering in North Vietnamese prison camps, many Americans wondered if helping South Vietnam was worth the sacrifice. Some began to protest the war.

In 1969 U.S. President Richard Nixon began withdrawing American troops from Vietnam. The U.S. turned over more of the fighting to the South Vietnamese army and negotiated with North Vietnam on how to end the war. The American goal became to withdraw with honor, while the North Vietnamese goal was to wait as long as necessary to accomplish its goal of taking over South Vietnam. All parties in the war signed a cease-fire in January 1973, and the last American troops left in March. An estimated two to three million people from Vietnam and neighboring countries died during the conflict. The death toll of American troops was about 58,000.

Once the Americans left, the Communists resumed their attack on the South, and the South Vietnamese army proved **incapable** of resisting them. In April of 1975, the last American officials left Saigon, the capital of South Vietnam, as the city and South Vietnam fell to the Communists.

The long-divided country became the unified country of Vietnam with a Communist government based in Hanoi, which had been the capital of North Vietnam. The map shows how Communism spread to country after country. In Unit 29 we will see what happened in the Cold War a few years later.

Blessed are the peacemakers, for they shall be called sons of God.
Matthew 5:9

Assignments for Lesson 137

Our Creative World — Read "From Boat Person to Bishop" on pages 130-131.

Timeline Book — In the first box for Lesson 137 on page 30 (1948), write "The Berlin Airlift begins." In the second box for Lesson 137 on page 30 (1961), write "Construction begins on the Berlin Wall."

Student Workbook or Lesson Review — If you are using one of these optional books, complete the assignment for Lesson 137.

Vocabulary — Copy the list of vocabulary words, then write the correct definition beside each word: atheist (940), blockade (942), totalitarian (945), incident (946), incapable (947).

a. using the military to prevent people or supplies from entering or leaving an area
b. an event, often with negative consequences
c. lacking ability
d. one who does not believe there is a God
e. a form of government in which the leader or leaders have complete control over the lives of citizens

Literature — Read chapter 12 in *The Chestry Oak*.

God Created the Land of India

Lesson 138   God's Wonder

India has had a powerful influence on world history. Early in *From Adam to Us*, we explored the ancient Indus Valley civilization. Later we learned that Alexander the Great spread his empire all the way to India. Many spices that traders carried on the Spice Road originated in India. Early in the history of the church, the apostle Thomas probably took the gospel to India.

Buddhism began in India and spread to China on the Silk Road. The Arabic numerals we use today had their origin in India. When Zheng He sailed his massive ships into the Indian Ocean, he visited India. When Columbus and his crew sailed west and came upon the New World, they were actually searching for India. One purpose of sailing around the Cape of Good Hope was to get to India. We have learned about the influence India had in Southeast Asia, about the Hindu religion in India, and about the Muslim Mughal Empire there. The British East India Company established a post in India in 1639. India later became one of the most important colonies in the British Empire.

India is a subcontinent of Asia. The Himalayan Mountains separate it from the rest of Asia to the north. The Indian Ocean lies to the south of India, the Bay of Bengal to the southeast, and the Arabian Sea to the west.

Above: Kuari Pass through the Himalayan Mountains of India. Below Left: Bull and cows lie beside the Arabian Sea in southern India. Below Right: Fishermen participate in a local festival along the Bay of Bengal.

Unit 28 - The Mid-Twentieth Century

Women pick tea in the rain at Darjeeling, India.

Lotus, National Flower of India

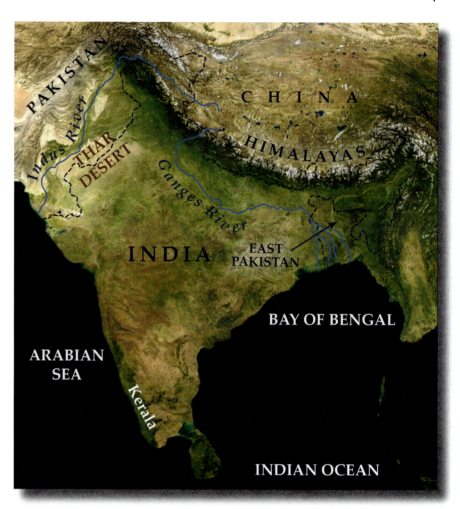

India has a tropical monsoon climate. People often associate monsoons with large amounts of rain, but a monsoon is actually a major seasonal change in the way the wind blows. Monsoons always blow from cold places to warm ones. Most places that experience monsoons are around the Indian Ocean. The results of monsoon winds vary from place to place, but in India monsoons cause winters to be dry and summers to be wet. India's monsoon summer is ideal for growing tea and rice.

God created varied terrain in the land of India, such as the beaches by the Arabian Sea and the Bay of Bengal, the mountains of the Himalayas, the sand dunes of the Great Indian Desert called the Thar, the valleys of the Ganges River, and the hills of tea plantations in Kerala.

The Thar

Ganges River

Kerala Tea Plantation

Lesson 138 - God Created the Land of India

God filled India with diverse wildlife. It is home to more than 47,000 species of plants. Much of India is covered in dense forests. India is also home to many species of wild animals. The national bird is the Indian peacock, and the national animal is the Royal Bengal tiger.

Wildlife of India

Top Row: Asiatic Elephants, Indian Guar Bison, Indian Peacock; Left: Indian Rhinoceros; Right: Gharial Crocodile, Asiatic Lion; Bottom Row: Bonnet Macaque, Sloth Bear, Royal Bengal Tigers

The British in India

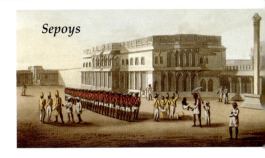

Sepoys

The British East India Company (see page 676 and Lesson 122) was a private company based in London. In 1600 the English government gave it complete control over English trading in Asia. By the end of the 1600s, the company was most interested in India. Indian workers grew cotton and made cotton fabric. Shippers carried the cloth to England, where workers there made it into clothing and home furnishings. Silk, sugar, and indigo dye were other major exports from India. By the mid-1700s, French traders had begun to compete with the British in India. The Mughal Empire had lost much of its power, and independent kings controlled smaller territories. To keep its power, the British East India Company began to control cities and regions in India. Its officials created their own armies made up of Indian soldiers, called sepoys, and smaller numbers of British soldiers.

The Indian Mutiny

In the early 1800s, British leaders in India wanted to control even more of India. They also wanted the courts, economy, and schools of India to be British. The British recruited local Indian leaders to be their allies and used them to gain control of other areas. Soldiers of the British East India Company fought native Indians in several battles in the 1800s. The two sides fought a major war in 1857 called the Indian Mutiny or Rebellion. The British and the Indians who sided with them defeated the rebellion about eighteen months after it began.

After this war, the British government decided to take control away from the East India Company. British India became an official colony of the British Empire rather than the territory of a private company.

This picture from L'Illustration Journal Universel, *published in Paris in 1857, illustrates a battle near Delhi.*

An Indian Citizen of the Empire

Mohandas Gandhi was born in India in 1869. He was the youngest child of his family and had two brothers, one sister, and two half-sisters. Gandhi's family followed the Hindu religion, though Gandhi did not show much interest in it as a boy. His mother was an especially devoted Hindu, while his father encouraged his children to respect people who followed other religions. Gandhi started school at age ten, studying arithmetic, history, geography, the local Gujarati language, and English. He was an average student who remembered later having trouble with his multiplication tables.

Gandhi's parents chose a wife for him when he was thirteen. Her name was Kasturba, and she was fourteen. Mohandas and Kasturba continued to live in their parents' homes, sometimes together and sometimes separately. Gandhi's father died in 1885. Kasturba gave birth to their first child shortly after, and the child also died. Over the next several years Mohandas and Kasturba had four sons.

In 1888 at age nineteen, Gandhi left India and went to England to study law. The bright lights and elegance of London impressed him. When he first went to a hotel, he entered a small room. He was surprised when the room started moving up and took him to another floor. That was his first elevator ride. Gandhi tried to fit into English society by wearing English clothes, taking dancing lessons, and playing the violin; but he felt out of place. Gandhi started reading books about religion, including the Bible. The Sermon on the Mount especially attracted his attention.

After becoming a lawyer, Gandhi returned to India in 1891. He learned that his mother had died during his absence. Gandhi began working as a lawyer in India, but in 1893 he accepted a job working for a company in South Africa run by Muslims from India.

The Dutch and British in South Africa treated the native South Africans as less important members of society. Because he had brown skin, Gandhi faced discrimination, too. Once he had a first-class train ticket for a business trip. While on the train, someone complained that he was riding in the first-class car. When he refused to give up his seat, a guard forced him to get off. Some hotel managers wouldn't let him stay in their hotels. Even though he was treated this way, Gandhi had his own prejudice toward the native Zulus.

Gandhi's family came from India to join him, and they lived in South Africa until 1915. Gandhi began developing ideas about nonviolent resistance to unjust laws and encouraged Indians in South Africa to work together to resist discrimination.

During the Boer War of 1899-1902 (see page 862), Gandhi worked in the British medical corps and recruited 1,100 Indian volunteers to do the same. Though Gandhi did not think war was a solution to problems, he taught Indians to show loyalty to the British. The Indians bravely faced danger on the battlefield to pick up wounded soldiers and carry them to receive treatment.

Medical Corps Staff Members: Gandhi is fifth from the left in the center row.

After the war, Gandhi led a nonviolent movement among Indians in South Africa. For seven years, the Indians protested against discrimination. After Gandhi and many other Indians were beaten and jailed, the South African government finally agreed to a compromise with them. Gandhi had made a pair of sandals while in prison. He sent them as a gift to Jan Smuts, the South African leader who had opposed him. After wearing the sandals for twenty-five years when working on his farm, Smuts returned them to Gandhi. He expressed respect for Gandhi's principles and stated, "I may feel that I am not worthy to stand in the shoes of so great a man."

Indian Bicycle Troops in France

Indians Seek Independence

While Gandhi was in South Africa, Indian leaders were thinking about how to gain independence from the British. Gandhi's success in South Africa brought him attention when he returned to India in 1915. World War I had just begun. The British recruited over one million Indians to serve in the British military in Europe, Africa, and Asia. Some are pictured at left. India played a major role in the eventual Allied victory. Gandhi again supported the British cause in the war.

Many Indians felt that their service during the war earned them the right to run their own country. Some British officials were nervous about the growing movement for independence. At a peaceful gathering in 1919, a British army officer ordered his troops to fire into the crowd. They killed several hundred people and wounded many others.

During the 1920s, Gandhi sought to live a simple life with his family and a few others in a small community he established called the Sabarmati Ashram. Gandhi wanted all Indians, including Hindus, Muslims, Christians, Jews, Buddhists, Sikhs, and others, to live together in peace. He opposed the Hindu caste system, explained on page 723. The people in the lowest segment of society were called "untouchables" and were treated with contempt. Gandhi showed kindness toward untouchables and encouraged other Indians to do the same.

Gandhi helped to inspire a widespread movement among the everyday people of India. It became known as the non-cooperation movement. Indians encouraged each other to use local products instead of British imports, to avoid British schools and courts, to resign from government jobs, and to refuse to pay taxes. The Indian National Congress Party, one of the leading groups seeking independence from Britain, worked with Gandhi in this movement.

During a protest in 1922, protesters provoked police, who responded by firing into the crowd. The crowd became violent and attacked the police station, killing the twenty-two officers inside. Gandhi felt that he had failed to teach the principles of nonviolence adequately. The Congress Party called an end to the non-cooperation movement to avoid further violence. Because of Gandhi's leadership in the non-cooperation movement, the British arrested him and sentenced him to six years in prison. He served two years and was released for health reasons.

In 1930 the Congress Party declared the independence of India from British control, but the British rejected this. That year Gandhi led a march to the ocean to collect salt as a protest against a British tax on salt. This action inspired many Indians to obtain salt without paying the British tax. The British arrested Gandhi and thousands of others.

Gandhi visited England in 1931. He met with King George VI at Buckingham Palace. Gandhi talked to English workers about why he did not want Indians to buy the English products they made. Gandhi continued to protest English rule in India when he returned home. British officials in India arrested him again. Gandhi spent a total of almost six years in prison in India. Gandhi's wife Kasturba was a strong supporter of her husband's efforts. She also worked for civil rights and independence and also spent time in prison.

When World War II began in 1939, the Congress Party offered to support the British in exchange for independence. British Prime Minister Winston Churchill opposed this idea, but India again provided men and materials for the British war effort. Kasturba Gandhi died during the war.

Gandhi at a spinning wheel in the late 1920s.

Independence for the Former British Colony of India

After the war, the British government finally acknowledged that they could no longer rule India. However, the people of India could not agree on how to set up their own government. The major division was between Muslims, more of whom lived in the northern part of India, and Hindus, more of whom lived in the southern part. In 1947 the former British colony of India became two countries:

- India, which included most of the land area of the former British colony of India. Most of its citizens were Hindu.

- Pakistan, which included its main section to the northwest of India, and another province then called East Pakistan, which is about one thousand miles to the east of Pakistan. See map on page 950. Most of the people living in both sections were Muslim. East Pakistan is no longer a part of Pakistan. Since 1971, it has been the independent country of Bangladesh.

Calcutta, India, in 1947, the Year of India's Independence

Many Hindus who lived in East Pakistan moved to India. Many Muslims who were living in India moved to Pakistan. India and Pakistan have had an unsettled relationship ever since.

Gandhi's Legacy

A few months after independence, on January 30, 1948, Gandhi was walking to a religious gathering at the house of a friend. A young man suddenly came up to him and shot him. The man who killed Gandhi was a Hindu who did not like Gandhi's tolerance for Muslims. Jawaharlal Nehru, who had worked with Gandhi for independence, had become the first Prime Minister of India. The day Gandhi died, Nehru said, "The light has gone out of our lives."

The life and message of Gandhi inspired Nelson Mandela and others who struggled for civil rights in South Africa, and Martin Luther King Jr. and others who worked for civil rights in the United States. Albert Einstein had corresponded with Gandhi and wrote this about him:

> Gandhi's life achievement stands unique in political history. He has invented a completely new and humane means for the liberation war of an oppressed country, and practised it with greatest energy and devotion. The moral influence he had on the consciously thinking human being of the entire civilized world will probably be much more lasting than it seems in our time with its overestimation of brutal violent forces. Because lasting will only be the work of such statesmen who wake up and strengthen the moral power of their people through their example and educational works.

One principle that Jesus taught was a non-violent response to those who mistreat us.

You have heard that it was said,
"An eye for an eye, and a tooth for a tooth."
But I say to you, do not resist an evil person;
but whoever slaps you on your right cheek, turn the other to him also.
If anyone wants to sue you and take your shirt, let him have your coat also.
Whoever forces you to go one mile, go with him two.
Give to him who asks of you,
and do not turn away from him who wants to borrow from you.
Matthew 5:38-42

Assignments for Lesson 138

Our Creative World — Read the excerpt from *Indian Home Rule* by Gandhi on pages 132-133.

Timeline Book — In the box for Lesson 138 on page 30, write "India gains independence from the British."

Student Workbook or Lesson Review — If you are using one of these optional books, complete the assignment for Lesson 138.

Thinking Biblically — Copy Matthew 5:38-42

Creative Writing — Write a poem of at least eight lines about the life of Gandhi.

Literature — Read chapter 13 in *The Chestry Oak*.

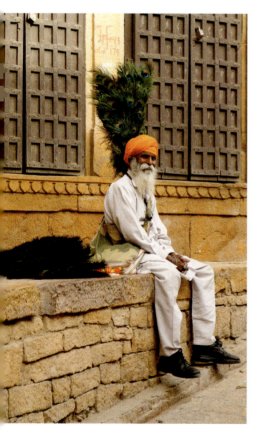

Peacock feather vendor rests in Jaisamler, India

Television
Around the World

Lesson 139 — Daily Life

After Reginald Fessenden made the first public broadcast of voice and music by radio in 1906, he and other inventors continued to make improvements in radio technology. By the 1920s, millions of people around the world received information and entertainment in their homes by means of radio (see pages 905-906). People listened to news on the radio and sat **spellbound** as they heard entertaining stories portrayed with voices, music, and sound effects. At this same time, movies became popular entertainment outside the home.

As early as the 1850s, inventors had begun working on ways to transmit sound and pictures over long distances. Scientists from many countries worked on developing a system of television broadcasting. Many people have been called the inventor of television. As with many inventions, including radio, the work of several people developed this means of communication that is now known around the world.

Russia

Constantin Perskyi (1854-1906), a science professor in St. Petersburg, Russia, invented the word *television* in 1900. The word means "to see far." Perskyi shared his paper on research into

Farm family in Michigan listens to the radio, 1930.

Yemenite rabbi listens to the radio, c. 1937.

Woman listens to the radio, 1930s.

"Television by Means of Electricity" at the First International Congress of Electricity, held in Paris that year. Boris Rosing (1869-1933) was another early Russian television inventor.

France

Édouard Belin (1876-1963) began working on television in 1903. He introduced a device in 1907 that could **transmit** photographs over telephone and telegraph wires. In 1928 Rene Barthelemy (1889-1954) began to oversee television research at a French business, Compagnie des Compteurs. Barthelemy's team made a public demonstration in 1931 and made the first official television broadcast in France in 1935.

Japan

Kenjiro Takayanagi (1899-1990) read about television research in a French magazine in 1925. He developed and demonstrated an electronic television set in 1926. Takayanagi continued to be involved in television research and development for many years.

This display at the NHK Broadcasting Museum in Tokyo, Japan, recreates an early television transmission experiment. Notice the image projected on the wall at the left.

Germany

Early Cathode-Ray Tube

Paul Nipkow (1860-1940) created a mechanical device in 1884 that came to be called the Nipkow Disc. The disc had holes in it. As light passed through the disc in a camera, the captured image was sent to a receiver, which had another disc to display the image. German Karl Braun (1850-1918) invented the cathode-ray tube (also called a CRT) in 1897. The CRT was crucial for the development of electronic television. August Karolus (1893-1972) worked in the 1920s on improving ways to capture and reproduce images.

Dénes Mihály (1894-1953) was born in Hungary and studied mechanical engineering in Budapest. He moved to Berlin and pursued research on transmitting still pictures and then moving pictures. In 1935 he introduced a television set that he created with physicist E. H. Traub.

The first regular electronic television service began in Berlin in 1935. It was called the *Fernsehsender Paul Nipkow* (*fernsehsender* is German for television station). Three times a week, the station broadcast ninety minutes of programming. See Germans watching TV at left. Few people owned their own receivers, so Berliners went to television parlors to watch shows. The 1936 Summer Olympic Games in Berlin were broadcast on television in Berlin and Hamburg.

Wounded German soldiers watch TV.

German woman watches television.

United Kingdom

Alan Archibald Campbell-Swinton (1863-1930) was a Scottish electrical engineer. He wrote a letter about television in 1908 that the science journal *Nature* published. Campbell-Swinton thought that mechanical television would not prove effective in the long run and proposed a system using a CRT both to transmit and receive images.

John Logie Baird (1888-1946), also from Scotland, demonstrated a working mechanical television system in 1925. His invention used bright lightbulbs and a mechanical system with thirty lenses. In his first demonstration, his television was not sensitive enough to show a human face, because a face is mainly one shade of color. Instead he used two painted ventriloquist dummy heads named James and Stooky Bill. Baird made his first television broadcast in 1929 using the transmitter of the British Broadcasting Corporation (BBC). The BBC started its own television broadcasts in 1932. Notice the BBC television transmitting tower at right. Television engineers transmitted sound and pictures from tall broadcast antennas which sent television signals out using radio waves. This is similar to the way sound is transmitted to a car radio today.

Baird demonstrated a color electronic television in 1944, but color TV did not become widespread until the 1960s.

British Broadcasting Corporation Television Transmitting Tower, 1936

United States

Charles Jenkins (1867-1934) worked on developing a movie projector in the 1890s (see Lesson 133). Jenkins then moved on to developing television technology. He demonstrated his mechanical system in 1925 and started the first television broadcast in the United States in 1928.

Philo Farnsworth (1906-1971) developed an electronic television system using a camera called an image dissector. He demonstrated his system in 1927 in San Francisco. Farnsworth's system had features that were similar to later successful televisions.

David Sarnoff was born into a Jewish family in 1891 in a part of the Russian Empire now in Belarus. He immigrated to the United States with his family in 1900. At age fifteen, he began working at the Marconi Wireless Telegraph Company of America, which later became the Radio Corporation of America (RCA). As a business leader, Sarnoff helped to develop radio and then television as ways to broadcast information to large audiences.

Sarnoff oversaw the work of another Russian immigrant, Vladimir Zworykin. Zworykin, who had worked with Boris Rosing, developed several important **components** of television in the 1930s. RCA had a commercial television system ready to debut at the 1939 World's Fair in New York. Franklin Roosevelt was the first U.S. President to appear on television when he made a speech at the fair. An estimated 1,000 people in and around New York City were able to see

FCC commissioners inspect a new "lightweight" television, 1939.

Boy with Television in Eugene, Oregon, c. 1953

First Czech Television, 1953

Cleaning a Television in the Netherlands

the broadcast. The United States government established the Federal Communications Commission (FCC) to oversee radio and television. The television pictured at left was described at the time as "portable and can be carried in a taxicab as compared to the huge **cumbersome** truck which has been used until now."

Television Becomes a Part of Everyday Life

World War II slowed down the development of television as researchers and factories focused on military needs. After the war, television grew in popularity around the world, as seen in the photos at left.

At first many television shows were broadcast live. Stations could also broadcast movies, which were recorded on film. In the 1950s and 1960s, companies produced a wide variety of live and filmed programs for television audiences in addition to news broadcasts and political coverage.

TV Antennas

During the 1950s and 1960s, most people continued to receive television signals by way of antennae, which converted radio waves back into picture and sound. A small **antenna** which sat on top of the television received the radio waves for people who lived near a television station. Many of these antennae were nicknamed "rabbit ears." People who lived farther away had roof-mounted versions. See examples of these on the next page.

The tallest television broadcast antenna in the world was completed in 1963 in Blanchard, North Dakota. It is 2,063 feet tall. Technically called a mast, this antenna was also the tallest structure in the world for many years. See this mast at top right. The Warsaw Radio Mast in Poland, completed in 1974, was slightly taller at 2,121 feet. That mast collapsed in 1991 and was not reconstructed.

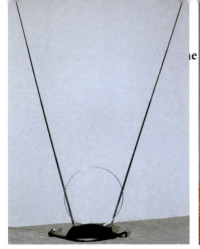  

Left to Right: "Rabbit Ears"; Roof Antenna; Mast, Blanchard, North Dakota

Popular Programs Around the World

Television stations broadcast comedy shows, dramatic shows, sporting events, game shows, and variety shows, which included music plus other forms of entertainment such as comedy, dancing, acrobatics, or skits. Here are a few examples of popular programs.

Australia. *Bandstand* was a musical/variety program that ran from 1958 to 1972. *World of Sport* featured sports commentary and humor from 1959 to 1987.

Canada. *La Famillie Plouffe* (*The Plouffe Family*), a dramatic series about a middle-class family in Montreal, debuted in 1953 and ran until 1959. Originally made in French, an English version was also popular. *Front Page Challenge* was a game show about current events and history that ran from 1957 to 1995. Panelists asked a hidden guest questions in order to solve the mystery. *The Friendly Giant* was a children's program that aired from 1958 to 1985. A human played a giant named Friendly. Friendly had puppet friends Rusty (a rooster) and Jerome (a giraffe). See photograph at right.

Canada: Set of The Friendly Giant

Colombia. *Yo y tú* (*Me and You*) was a sitcom (short for situation comedy) in Colombia that began in 1956 and ran until 1976. A sitcom is a television series about a group of people who experience humorous situations. Dozens of Colombian actors made guest appearances on it.

France. *Les Cinq Dernières Minutes* (*The Last Five Minutes*) was broadcast periodically from 1958 to 1996. In each episode, the audience followed police detectives looking for clues to solve a crime.

Germany. *Unser Sandmännchen* (*Our Little Sandman*) is a children's program that began in 1959 and continues broadcasting today. Stop-motion animation portrays everyday life and fanciful adventures. The show has also been broadcast in Scandinavian countries. See photos on page 962.

Germany: Unser Sandmännchen

Stahlnetz was another police drama. It ran from 1958 to 1968. It was similar to a U.S. show called *Dragnet*, which began in 1951. The stories were based on real incidents. Like many TV series, *Dragnet* was first a series on radio and later made the switch to television.

Italy. *Canzonissima* (*Song Contest*) ran from 1958 to 1963 and from 1967 to 1974. It included competitions between musical performers plus dance and comedy routines with special guests. *Carosello* (*Carousel*), which ran from 1957 to 1977, was a comedy show featuring live action, animation, and puppetry.

Japan. *Kōhaku Uta Gassen* (*Red and White Song Battle*) is an annual musical competition between two teams: the red team, with female vocalists, and the white team, with male vocalists. Producers of the show choose Japanese artists who are popular that year. First broadcast on radio in 1951, the show appeared on television in 1953 and continues today. *Okaasan to Issho* (*With Mother*) is a show for children that debuted in 1959 and also continues today. It features songs and animation.

Italy: Canzonissima

United Kingdom. *This Is Your Life* started in the United States in 1948. A British version launched in 1955. It ran until 1964 and then again from 1969 to 2003. On this show, friends and family members made surprise appearances and told the story of the life of a special guest. The program featured television pioneer John Logie Baird in 1957. Baird was the only person honored on the show who was no longer living. He had died in 1946, and his wife, Margaret, appeared on the show in his place.

In Scotland, *Scotsport* was a popular and long-running sports program. From 1957 to 2008, it provided coverage primarily of Scottish football (soccer). In Wales, a monthly musical program called *Gwlad y Gan* (*Land of Song*) ran from 1958 to 1964. It was broadcast in the Welsh language with captions in English.

Venezuela. *El Observador* (*The Observer*) was a news program that ran from 1953 to 2012. *El Show de las Doce* (*The Noon Show*), a musical and comedy variety show, ran from 1954 to 1964.

International Broadcasting

The coronation of Queen Elizabeth II of the United Kingdom on June 2, 1953, was a major event in television history. It was broadcast live across the United Kingdom to millions of viewers. The transmission was also distributed live to stations in France, Belgium, the Netherlands, and West Germany. Viewers in Canada and the United States could not watch the program live, but they were able to see it a few hours later. Film of the coronation was flown across the Atlantic and rebroadcast the same day.

Europeans founded Eurovision in 1954 to facilitate sharing television broadcasts between European countries. It spread to include countries in North Africa and the Middle East. The first official broadcast, of a festival in Switzerland, was on June 6, 1954 (exactly ten years after the D-Day landing in France during World War II). When the 1956 Winter Olympic Games took place in Cortina d'Ampezzo, Italy, Eurovision broadcast portions of the Games live to several countries in Western Europe.

In July, 1962, the U.S. National Aeronautics and Space Administration (NASA) launched Telstar 1, developed by the American Telephone and Telegraph (AT&T) company. This satellite made it possible for the first live television signals to be sent across the Atlantic Ocean. See photo below. Television viewers in France and England saw President Kennedy conduct a live news conference. Viewers in the U.S. watched the changing of the guard at Buckingham Palace in London and a performance by French singer Yves Montand.

The Relay 1 satellite launched in December 1962. On November 23, 1963, it provided the first satellite television transmission across the Pacific. Viewers in Japan watched news coverage of the assassination of U.S. President John F. Kennedy, which had taken place the previous day.

The Impact of Television

Television became so popular that just about every home in the United States had at least one TV set. The percentage was not as high in other countries; but in industrialized nations, the vast majority of homes had a television. Television actors became celebrities the way movie and radio stars had.

American Telephone and Telegraph (AT&T) personnel watch a test of a broadcast transmitted by Telstar 1, July 10, 1962.

As with most other inventions, people can use television to accomplish good, and they can use it to do harm. Television greatly expanded access to entertainment and information for millions of people around the world. The Vietnam War was the first time television networks broadcast film reports from battlefields into people's homes. This harsh reality influenced people's attitudes about the war.

Television is a powerful influence. Early in the history of television, Christians began to use it as a means to share the gospel. American Christians produced television programs for viewing in the United States and in other countries. In 1957 evangelist Billy Graham held a crusade in Madison Square Garden in New York City. The ABC television network broadcast his messages live on national television. More people watched these programs than any program ABC had televised up until that time.

Not all television entertainment has encouraged truth and righteousness; and more information is not always helpful, especially when that information is false or biased. As Christians, we must not simply follow the culture. We must use good judgment in determining what we let into our minds and hearts.

I will set no worthless thing before my eyes . . .
Psalm 101:3

Assignments for Lesson 139

Timeline Book — In the box for Lesson 139 on page 29, write "Regular TV broadcasts begin in Germany."

Student Workbook or Lesson Review — If you are using one of these optional books, complete the assignment for Lesson 139.

Vocabulary — Write five sentences, using one of these words in each: spellbound (957), transmit (958), component (959), cumbersome (960), antenna (960). Check in a dictionary if you need help with their definitions.

Creative Writing — Write a puppet script of at least one page for a children's television program.

Literature — Read chapter 14 in *The Chestry Oak*.

C. S. Lewis

Lesson 140 World Biography

The most influential Christian writer of the twentieth century was C. S. Lewis. His more than thirty books have sold over 100 million copies. Lewis wrote works of theology, which explained God and His works; apologetics, which explained and defended the Christian faith to unbelievers; and **fiction**, which taught Christian truths in the form of stories. Lewis, pictured at right, was a popular speaker on spiritual topics, and he wrote many articles for religious publications. Lewis was not formally trained or educated in Christian theology. He was a scholar in English Literature and Language, first at Oxford University and later at Cambridge University, both in England.

Early Life

Clive Staples Lewis was born on November 29, 1898, in Belfast, Ireland (now Northern Ireland). His parents were Albert Lewis, an attorney, and Florence Hamilton Lewis, a college-educated daughter of a minister. Albert's father had migrated to Ireland from Wales. Clive's brother Warren had been born in 1895. The family attended the Anglican Church (Church of Ireland). The Lewis home was filled with books, and the parents encouraged the boys to read widely.

Before Clive was four years old, he announced to his mother that he wanted to be called Jack. He used that name for the rest of his life. Jack and Warren (whom Jack called Warnie) loved playing together. They created an imaginary world called Boxen, filled with talking animals. They wrote stories about the adventures of the animals in Boxen.

In 1905 the Lewis family moved to the outskirts of Belfast to a house called Little Lea. The Lewises sent Warnie to Wynyard School in England that year. Jack's mother and a governess taught Jack at home. Mrs. Lewis died on August 23, 1908, a loss that devastated the boys. Less than a month later, Mr. Lewis sent Jack to join Warnie at Wynyard. The school was absolutely terrible, and Warnie begged his father to let them leave. Mr. Lewis sent Warnie to Malvern College in western England. He sent Jack to Cherbourg House, a school near the college. During this time, Jack decided to leave the Christian faith of his early childhood. Jack later attended Malvern, as well.

Warnie decided to become an officer in the British army, so his father sent him to a tutor who helped him prepare for military school. In 1914 Jack began studying under Warnie's tutor to prepare for admission to Oxford. The **tutor** was W. T. Kirkpatrick, who had by then retired as headmaster of the college the boys' father had attended.

In 1916 Lewis read *Phantastes* by George MacDonald, a Scottish minister and writer from the 1800s. This book helped Jack to think again about things that were holy. Jack loved fantasy stories and liked the way MacDonald helped him to imagine **realms** that were different from the physical world around him.

To Oxford, to War, and Back to Oxford

In 1917 Jack Lewis began his studies at Oxford University. However, the Great War was raging in Europe. Not long after beginning at Oxford, Lewis enlisted in the British army. While he was in officer training, his roommate was Paddy Moore. Before they left for the front, Lewis and Moore pledged to each other that, if one of them should not return home, the other would take care of his friend's parent (Lewis' father or Moore's mother).

Lewis arrived at the battlefront in Europe on his nineteenth birthday in November 1917. Longing to be a poet, Jack worked on his poetry every chance he had, including writing in a small notebook in the trenches during the war.

In April of 1918, Lewis was wounded in action and returned to England to recover. He learned that his friend Paddy Moore had been killed in action. After the war, Lewis returned to Oxford to continue his studies. When he was able to do so, he set up a household in which he provided for Mrs. Moore and her twelve-year-old daughter, Maureen. Lewis kept his commitment to Paddy by caring for Mrs. Moore until she died in 1951. Maureen married and moved away in 1940.

Lewis accomplished an excellent academic record at Oxford. While studying there, he read more books that encouraged him to have faith in God. G. K. Chesterton was one author who influenced Lewis. Chesterton had also left the Christian faith in which he had been reared, but he had returned to it. He wrote powerfully in favor of Christianity. The message of *The Everlasting Man* was particularly helpful to Jack.

Lesson 140 - C. S. Lewis

Teaching at Oxford

Magdalen College, Oxford University

In May of 1925, Lewis became a fellow at Magdalen College in Oxford and a tutor in English language and Tudor literature. Lewis held this position for twenty-nine years.

Albert Lewis died in 1929. The two brothers and Mrs. Moore purchased a home in Headington, just outside of Oxford in 1930. The home was called The Kilns for the brick kilns in the backyard. Jack and the Moores moved there, and Warnie joined them in 1932 when he retired from military service. Warnie became an expert in French history and published several works on that subject.

At Oxford Jack became friends with a group that had great professional and spiritual influence on him. The group called themselves the Inklings and met regularly to discuss various topics and to hear each other read portions of books they were writing. For Lewis one of the most influential of the Inklings was J. R. R. Tolkien, a Catholic who also taught at Oxford and who was the author of *The Hobbit* and other books. A pub called The Eagle and Child, pictured below, was a favorite meeting place for the Inklings.

Later in life, Lewis recorded that in 1929, he began to believe in God again. In 1931 he came to faith in Jesus Christ as Savior and Lord. Lewis said that a long conversation with Tolkien and another of the Inklings, Hugo Dyson, convinced Lewis that the gospel is true. Lewis wrote that a few days after the conversation, he traveled with Warnie to the Whipsnade Zoo, not far from Oxford. Warnie drove a motorcycle and Jack sat in the sidecar. In Lewis' words, "When we set out I did not believe that Jesus Christ is the Son of God, and when we reached the zoo I did." Warnie returned to the Christian faith in 1931 as well.

Lewis' first book on Christianity was *The Pilgrim's Regress*, published in 1933. The book was an **allegory** based on *The Pilgrim's Progress* written by John Bunyan in 1678. *The Pilgrim's Regress* described Lewis' journey of faith to that point in his life.

The Eagle and Child, Oxford

Scholar and Christian Writer

Lewis developed a reputation as an excellent scholar in medieval English Literature and was a popular lecturer on the subject. In 1936 he published *The Allegory of Love*, which examined the theme of love in medieval writing. Also during this time Lewis began writing articles for religious journals and speaking at church services and religious meetings. He also wrote many book reviews. In 1940 Lewis published *The Problem of Pain*. He wrote about how God is good and why we can believe in Him even though there is pain and suffering in the world.

Unit 28 - The Mid-Twentieth Century

C. S. Lewis in His Study

C. S. Lewis had several opportunities to share his faith during World War II. The British Broadcasting Corporation (BBC) asked him to present several series of talks on the radio explaining the basics of the Christian faith. These talks were published in 1952 as *Mere Christianity*, which has become one of Lewis' best-known books about the Christian faith. He also gave addresses to assemblies of Royal Air Force personnel during the war. Lewis served in the Home Guard, which helped defend England against possible German invasion and fulfilled other wartime duties while so many young men were away in the army. Lewis walked the streets of Oxford at night, staying on the lookout for German agents. Warnie served briefly in active duty and then also in the Home Guard.

In 1941 Lewis published a series of letters in a Christian magazine. He wrote them as if he were a senior devil giving advice to a less experienced devil about how to tempt people. The "letters" taught Christian truths in an unusual way. The series was published as *The Screwtape Letters* in 1942 and became a best seller. The book helped Lewis become well-known in the United States as a Christian author. *Time* magazine, a weekly newsmagazine published in the United States, put his picture on the cover of its September 8, 1947, issue and included a feature article about him. Lewis published other books about Christianity that became popular.

The Chronicles of Narnia

Lewis said that he once had a mental picture of a faun carrying packages through the snow. That image became an early scene in *The Lion, the Witch, and the Wardrobe*, which he published in 1950 as the first of seven books in The Chronicles of Narnia. Lewis wrote the series about the imaginary land of Narnia in order to teach Christian truths to children. The most important character in the series is Aslan the Lion, who

The Kilns

sacrifices his life for a child who had committed a sin that hurt other people. A new book in the series appeared every year until 1956. One scene Lewis described in *The Lion, the Witch, and the Wardrobe* inspired the sculpture on the opposite page.

The Narnia books increased the number of people who wrote letters to Jack Lewis, including many children. Nearly every morning Lewis, with Warnie's help, responded personally to every letter. Lewis never learned how to type, so he wrote every letter and every book he produced by hand. A number of Lewis' replies to children are collected in the book *Letters to Children*.

Lesson 140 - C. S. Lewis

Cambridge

In 1954 Lewis was passed over for a promotion at Magdalen College. Many believe those making the decision disapproved of his popular Christian writings. Magdalene College at Cambridge University offered him a professorship in Medieval and Renaissance English, which was a higher-ranking position than the one he had at Oxford. When Cambridge arranged his schedule so that he could live in Oxford on weekends and stay in Cambridge only a few days during the week, Lewis accepted. He began teaching in Cambridge in 1955. That same year Lewis met Billy Graham while Graham was on an evangelistic campaign in England.

The Wardrobe, *a Sculpture Inspired by the Chronicles of Narnia, East Belfast, Northern Ireland*

Lewis published an autobiography, *Surprised by Joy: The Shape of My Early Life*, in 1955. He wrote about the deep inner joy that he longed for early in his life and that he found when he put his faith in Jesus Christ.

Joy Gresham

One of the many people who wrote to Lewis during 1950 was Joy Davidman Gresham, an American writer from a Jewish family who at one time had abandoned her faith in God. Lewis' books had helped her come to believe in Jesus, and she began a correspondence with him as a result. Joy's husband was unfaithful to her and they divorced. Joy and her two sons eventually moved to England, first to London and then to Oxford.

In 1956 the British government refused to let Joy stay in the country any longer, which meant that she would have to go back to the U.S. Lewis married Joy on April 23, 1956, in a civil ceremony. He did this to enable her to stay in the country as the wife of a British citizen. They continued to live in their own homes.

Later that year, Joy was diagnosed with advanced cancer and was expected to die soon. By then Jack and Joy had developed a deep love for each other. On March 21, 1957, they were married in an Anglican ceremony while Joy was a patient in the hospital. However, she made a remarkable recovery and regained much of her health. She and her sons moved into The Kilns. Jack and Joy had a happy married life. They took a trip to Greece and Italy in the spring of 1960, the only time that Lewis left the British Isles except for his service in the Great War. Then Joy's cancer returned with a vengeance, and she died at The Kilns on July 13, 1960. The home is pictured at left.

In 1961 Lewis published *A Grief Observed*, a short book made up of entries he wrote in his journal after Joy died. He wrote about the deep struggle and grief he endured after losing her and about his renewed faith in God. Lewis published the book under a **pseudonym**. Someone who did not know that he wrote it sent him a copy thinking it would help him in his own recent loss!

Lewis gave much of the money he earned from his books to charity or to people he knew who needed help.

His Final Years

In the 1960s Lewis' health declined. He died on November 22, 1963, a week before his 65th birthday and the same day that U.S. President John F. Kennedy was assassinated in Dallas, Texas. Lewis was buried in the churchyard of Holy Trinity Church in Headington where he attended. Warnie died on April 9, 1973, and was buried next to his brother.

A few more of Lewis' writings were published after his death. Literature scholars continue to respect the scholarly works of C. S. Lewis, and his Christian books have influenced many people. They continue to teach, encourage, challenge, and evangelize their many readers. Lewis' life was not perfect, as is true about anyone. However, his devotion to helping people understand the reality of God and the Lordship of Jesus, truths that he once rejected but then believed again with all his heart, has blessed millions. The apostle Paul set the pattern for someone using his life in this way:

*It is a trustworthy statement, deserving full acceptance,
that Christ Jesus came into the world to save sinners,
among whom I am foremost of all.
Yet for this reason I found mercy, so that in me as the foremost,
Jesus Christ might demonstrate His perfect patience
as an example for those who would believe in Him for eternal life.
1 Timothy 1:15-16*

Assignments for Lesson 140

Our Creative World — Read C. S. Lewis' "Letter to Sarah" on page 134.

Timeline Book — In the box for Lesson 140 on page 30, write "C. S. Lewis publishes *The Lion, the Witch, and the Wardrobe*."

Student Workbook or Lesson Review — If you are using one of these optional books, complete the assignment for Lesson 140 and take the test for Unit 28.

Thinking Biblically — Copy 1 Timothy 1:15.

Vocabulary — Write a paragraph that uses all of these words: fiction (965), tutor (966), realm (966), allegory (967), pseudonym (969). Consult a dictionary if you need help with their definitions.

Literature — Read the Afterword in *The Chestry Oak*. If you are using the Student Workbook or Lesson Review, answer the literature review questions on *The Chestry Oak*.

Family Activity — Complete the "Share Narnia" activity. See page FA-55 for instructions.

29 The End of the Twentieth Century

Buzz Aldrin walks on the moon, 1969.

Lessons
141 - World Biography: Douglas Nicholls, an Aboriginal Australian
142 - God's Wonder: God Created Space
143 - Our World Story: Nikolaikirche and the End of Communism in Europe
144 - World Landmark: Building Up
145 - Daily Life: People Groups Around the World

Literature
In *Children of the Storm*, Natasha Vins tells how her family held fast to their faith in Jesus amidst persecution in the U.S.S.R. (See "Notes to Parents on the Literature" in the back of the Answer Key.)

1969 - 2000

Douglas Nicholls was an Aboriginal Australian who improved the lives of his people. In 1969 the first event in history occurred in which humans stood somewhere other than Earth—people walked on the moon. After decades of Communist rule in Russia and Eastern Europe, the Iron Curtain the Communists had built between the free world and the Communist world came down in a quiet revolution. As man reached for the moon, he also built taller and taller buildings on Earth. Though technology has advanced rapidly in the last years of the twentieth century, ethnic groups around the world continue to hold on to traditions passed down by their ancestors.

The pin for Lesson 144 points to the tallest building in the world in 2016. Lesson 145 talks about people groups around the world.

Douglas Nicholls
An Aboriginal Australian

Lesson 141 — World Biography

Australia is the world's smallest continent. It is the lowest and flattest continent and the second driest after Antarctica. Almost one-fifth of the continent is desert. Most Australians live along the coast, particularly the south and east where the climate is pleasant and the land is better suited for farming. Australia is the world's only continent entirely made up of one country.

A giant rock, taller than the Eiffel Tower and almost six miles in circumference, stands in the middle of the desert in central Australia. Aboriginal Australians call the rock Uluru. British colonists later called it Ayers Rock. Uluru is one of the largest rocks on Earth. Australia, its

island state of Tasmania, and the nearby island of New Guinea are home to many animals found nowhere else on Earth. These include the bilby, quoll, wombat, numbat, echidna, platypus, koala, and kangaroo.

Endemic Animals of Australia

Top Row: Bilby, Quoll, Wombat; Center Row: Numbat, Echidna, Platypus; Right: Koala; Kangaroos hop on Emerald Beach in New South Wales on the eastern coast of Australia.

Thousands of islands encircle Australia. Fraser Island is the world's largest sand island. It is home to tall rainforests, beautiful sand cliffs, and many freshwater lakes. In northeast Australia is Cape York Peninsula, a wilderness with tropical rainforests, mangrove forests, and melaleuca swamps. Off the coast of the peninsula is the Great Barrier Reef.

Left to Right: Tropical Rain Forest on Fraser Island; Daintree National Park on Cape York Peninsula; Great Barrier Reef

Lesson 141 - Douglas Nicholls, An Aboriginal Australian

The First Australians

The first people believed to have lived in Australia are known today as Aboriginal Australians (or Aborigines). Sometime after the Tower of Babel, their ancestors traveled across southern Asia and made their way to Australia. Over the centuries, Aboriginal Australians spread out and lived in many different clans. The various clans eventually spoke about 250 different languages and had different traditions.

Aborigines hunted animals using clubs, spears, and boomerangs. They also gathered fruit, nuts, seeds, and insects for food. Music and dancing are important parts of Aboriginal culture. One common instrument is the didgeridoo, a wooden pipe that makes a single sound. Aborigines also use clapsticks to produce **rhythm**.

Uluru and the surrounding area has special religious significance for Aboriginal Australians.

Above: Uluru (Ayers Rock); Right Column: Clapsticks; A Yugambeh Aboriginal man sings and holds boomerangs during an Aboriginal culture show in Queensland, Australia. An Aboriginal man plays the didgeridoo.

The Arrival of Europeans

European ships explored the coast of Australia in the early 1600s. In 1606 Dutch captain Willem Janszoon became the first known European to meet Aboriginal Australians. The Dutch began calling the western part of Australia New Holland. Other Dutch expeditions visited over the next several decades.

In 1770 Captain James Cook claimed the east coast of Australia for Britain and named it New South Wales. On January 26, 1788, a fleet of eleven British ships landed in Australia to establish the first European settlement. Out of 1,350 people on the ships, about half were convicts sent to Australia as punishment. The colony struggled for many years to grow enough food to survive.

The British had friendly relations with the Aboriginal Australians at first. The new settlers depended on the Aborigines for food, which they obtained through trade. Some of the colonists made formal agreements with the Aborigines to use their land. However, in 1835 the governor of New South Wales declared that the Aborigines had no legal claims to the land they lived on. Therefore, in his view, the British could simply take and divide the land. As the British settlers spread, the way of life of the Aborigines was **endangered**.

Britain sent many thousands more prisoners to Australia. Free settlers arrived, too. The British government established five more colonies: Western Australia (1832), South Australia (1836), Victoria (1851), Tasmania (1856), and Queensland (1859). Eventually a majority of British colonists in Australia decided to separate from Great Britain. On January 1, 1901, the six separate colonies joined together to become the Commonwealth of Australia.

Treatment of Aboriginal Australians

During the 1800s and early 1900s, the government of Australia set up reserves or stations for Aboriginal Australians. These were similar to the reservations that the U.S. government created for Native Americans. The government provided food and sometimes housing and education. Churches also established missions that provided similar help. However, a majority of Aborigines continued to live outside of the reserves.

Some government leaders wanted Aborigines to **assimilate** into white society. One way they attempted to do this was by taking Aboriginal children, particularly girls, away from their families. These children grew up in institutions or with white families so they could learn the English language and way of life. Since many white Australians looked down on all Aborigines, even those who had been "assimilated" often were not welcome in the larger society.

Douglas Nicholls was born on December 9, 1906, at the Cummeragunja mission in New South Wales, the fifth child in his family. His parents were Herbert and Florence. Officials forced his sixteen-year-old sister Hilda to leave the family when Douglas was eight years old. Douglas remembered in particular the pain it brought his mother, who is pictured with him at left. Douglas received limited formal education, but his parents and community gave him a good foundation for life.

Nicholls started working at age fourteen. He also began competing in sports. He was relatively short (5 feet, 2 inches), but he was strong and fast. Nicholls won running competitions but became best known as an Australian football player. He competed for several years as the only Aboriginal player in the Victorian Football Association. He was twice recognized as the "best and fairest" player.

Douglas Nicholls and His Mother

Nicholls grew up attending church, but he drifted away as a young man. After his mother died in 1932, he returned

Lesson 141 - Douglas Nicholls, An Aboriginal Australian

to his spiritual roots and committed his life to Christ. He remained open about his faith while he was an athlete and throughout his life.

Day of Mourning

People around Sydney had been celebrating January 26 as the anniversary of the founding of New South Wales since the early 1800s. Other Australian states celebrated their founding on other dates. By 1935, however, the entire country recognized January 26 as a special day of celebration. The year 1938 marked 150 years since the British arrived in 1788. Citizens planned great celebrations for January 26 of that year. That date had become known as Australia Day.

Left: Nicholls (at top right) Sings at Church; Right: Nicholls as a Football Player
In Australian rules football, two opposing teams each have eighteen players on the field. Current rules allow players to move the ball by kicking it, running with it, or hitting it with one hand like a volleyball serve. Players score points by kicking the ball between two tall goal posts.

William Cooper was a prominent Aboriginal leader who sought equal rights for Aborigines. Douglas Nicholls was one of his great-nephews. William Cooper led an organization called the Australian Aborigines League. Nicholls joined this movement to change the way the Australian government treated Aborigines.

The Australian Aborigines League joined with another organization called the Aborigines Progressive Association to hold their own event on January 26, 1938. Instead of a day of celebration, however, the Aboriginal Australians called it a Day of Mourning. They wanted to protest 150 years of mistreatment by the British settlers.

The Day of Mourning began with a march through Sydney. Some non-Aborigines supported their efforts. About 100 Aboriginal Australians met at the Australian Hall to make a public appeal for equal treatment. Several people, including Douglas Nicholls, made speeches at the event. The tradition of holding a Day of Mourning on Australia Day has continued every year since then. See photo at right.

The Leadership of Douglas Nicholls

Douglas Nicholls became a prominent figure in Australia through his humble and determined leadership. He was a spiritual leader, serving as a preacher and pastor. He was a cultural leader who encouraged Aborigines to pursue excellence in sports and the arts. Nicholls was also a political leader who encouraged Australians to work together, regardless of their skin color. This is an excerpt from one of his sermons:

Douglas Nicholls speaks at a later Day of Mourning.

And I want to suggest three things why you should bother about the Aborigines. Firstly, we belong to the great family of God and He had made out of one blood all nations of men. Secondly, why you should bother about the Aborigines, we're a part of the great British Commonwealth of nations. And thirdly, we want to walk with you, we don't wish to walk alone.

Nicholls joined the military in 1941 and served as the batman (personal assistant) of Major Frank Corr. Nicholls was discharged in 1942 to continue his service in the Aboriginal community. He helped those struggling with alcohol and gambling, and he mentored those who were in trouble with the law.

Douglas married Gladys Nicholls in 1942. She was the widow of Douglas' brother Howard and already had three children. Douglas and Gladys had two more children together.

Many Aboriginal young people lacked support and **guidance**. The Nicholls family helped many of them. They welcomed young people into their own home, and they worked to set up **hostels** as safe places for young people to live in community with others.

Gladys Nicholls organized the Aboriginal Children's Christmas Tree Appeal in the 1940s. It operated for thirty years. In the photo at right, an Aboriginal Santa Claus gives a present to a happy child.

Nicholls became a Member of the Order of the British Empire (OBE) in 1957 and then an Officer of the OBE in 1968. The British government established these honors during World War I to recognize people who made positive contributions to the British Empire.

Aboriginal Santa Claus and Child

In 1972 Nicholls traveled to London with his wife to receive knighthood for his "distinguished services to the advancement of the Aboriginal people." They received the titles of Sir Douglas and Lady Gladys.

On December 1, 1976, Sir Douglas was inaugurated as the appointed Governor of South Australia. He was the first Aboriginal Australian to hold such a position. Nicholls welcomed Queen Elizabeth II on her royal tour in March. Poor health forced him to resign his position soon after.

Lady Gladys died in 1981, and Sir Douglas died in 1988. They were survived by children and grandchildren who cherished their memory and by thousands of Australians who appreciated their service over many decades. All of the Douglas Nicholls photographs in this lesson are from the Nicholls Family Collection, provided by his descendants.

Lesson 141 - Douglas Nicholls, An Aboriginal Australian

Australia Today

The forced removal of children from Aboriginal families continued into the 1960s. The Australian Parliament passed a Motion of Reconciliation in 1999 that admitted the mistreatment of Aboriginal Australians, but it did not include a formal apology. In 2008 Australian Prime Minister Kevin Rudd proposed another motion, which Parliament passed. It included these words:

Gladys and Douglas Nicholls

> For the pain, suffering, and hurt of these Stolen Generations, their descendants and for their families left behind, we say sorry. To the mothers and the fathers, the brothers and the sisters, for the breaking up of families and communities, we say sorry.

In a world of sinners, there is much to forgive. Jesus provides the way to receive God's forgiveness and reconciles us to Him. This can lead to reconciliation with our fellow human beings.

> *Will they not go astray who devise evil?*
> *But kindness and truth will be to those who devise good.*
> *Proverbs 14:22*

Assignments for Lesson 141

Our Creative World — Read the "Day of Mourning Statement" and the "Speech on Investiture as Governor of South Australia" by Douglas Nicholls on pages 135-136.

Map Book — Complete the assignments for Lesson 141 on Map 42, "Australia and Surrounding Islands."

Timeline Book — In the box for Lesson 141 on page 30, write "Nicholls becomes Governor of South Australia."

Student Workbook or Lesson Review — If you are using one of these optional books, complete the assignment for Lesson 141.

Vocabulary — Copy the list of vocabulary words, then write the correct definition beside each word: rhythm (975), endangered (976), assimilate (976), guidance (978), hostel (978).
  a. to become fully a part of another culture or society
  b. wisdom, help, or advice
  c. a beat; a regular pattern of sounds and/or movements
  d. a place to stay overnight (for travel); or a supervised place to live for a longer period
  e. in danger of being hurt or killed; vulnerable

Literature — Read the Preface and chapters 1-2 in *Children of the Storm*.

God Created Space

Lesson 142 — **God's Wonder**

*The heavens are telling of the glory of God;
And their expanse is declaring the work of His hands.
Psalm 19:1*

As the psalmist expressed, people have long looked at the heavens with wonder and amazement. During the Middle Ages and the Renaissance, people ventured in ships across the oceans to explore lands that were new to them. Beginning in the mid-1900s, mankind ventured into space, calling it the "final frontier."

Space is the vast realm in which objects in the physical universe move. The Earth is surrounded by a layer of atmosphere. The air in the atmosphere gets thinner as one moves away from Earth. There is no distinct boundary between the atmosphere and space, but scientists generally think of space as beginning about sixty miles above the Earth's surface. Space contains a few molecules of air and particles called space dust. It also contains magnetic fields and radiation from the sun and other stars. Large objects in space include meteors, comets, stars, the planets and moons in our solar system, and apparently other planets that orbit distant stars.

*He counts the number of the stars;
He gives names to all of them.
Psalm 147:4*

Mankind developed the ability to explore outer space with astonishing speed. It took from the Garden of Eden until 1903 for people to learn to fly above the Earth in a plane that was heavier than air. Less than sixty years later, men had orbited the Earth in space.

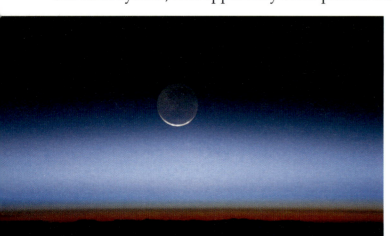

Above: The Hubble telescope took this image of part of the Sagittarius constellation in 2015. Left: This NASA photo shows the moon and the layers of Earth's atmosphere.

Lesson 142 - God Created Space

Early Ideas About Space Travel

Before the 1900s, people had written theories and speculations in books and articles about space travel. One example is the 1865 novel *From the Earth to the Moon* by French writer Jules Verne. The characters in the book build a huge gun to shoot a projectile containing three men to the moon. *The First Men in the Moon* by British author H. G. Wells, published in 1901, is another example. In this story people invent a material that defies gravity and enables them to fly to the moon. In the *Space Trilogy* (a series of three books) by C. S. Lewis, published between 1938 and 1945, people travel to Mars and Venus.

Rockets

The first requirement for a spacecraft to orbit the Earth or travel into space is to create the thrust needed to overcome Earth's gravity. A few scientists saw the possibility of doing this by using rockets. The Chinese were the first people known to build rockets. They used them to shoot weapons at their enemies rather than for flying, except perhaps for one Chinese official, named Wan-Hu. According to Chinese legend, he assembled a flying chair with two large kites and forty-seven rockets. He died making the attempt to fly.

This U.S.S.R. stamp from 1957 honors Konstantin Tsiolkovsky.

This 1982 Romanian stamp honors Hermann Oberth.

After the Chinese used rocket-powered weapons against the Mongols in 1232, the Mongols began building rockets, too. Many Europeans experimented with rockets during the 1200s to 1400s, perhaps after learning about them from the Mongols.

Three men are considered the founders of modern rocketry. In 1903 a Russian high school teacher, Konstantin Tsiolkovsky, published a paper that discussed the possibility of using rockets for space travel. Tsiolkovsky, who was deaf, continued to research rocket travel throughout his life, from the period of the czars into the Communist era. See the stamp above.

Hermann Oberth was born in Austria-Hungary (in an area that is now in Romania) in 1894. He studied rocketry while serving in the medical corps in Austria-Hungary during the Great War, but the German army rejected his ideas as unworkable. After the war he studied physics at the University of Heidelberg in Germany. He wrote a thesis about rocketry to earn his degree, but the university rejected the thesis as unrealistic.

Oberth published his thesis in 1923 as a book, *The Rocket to Interplanetary Space*. He also wrote *Ways to Space Travel* in 1929. Oberth became a popular speaker throughout Europe during the 1920s. In World War II, the German army worked on a rocket program and Oberth served as an advisor. The Germans developed the V-1 rocket, using it as a missile to carry a bomb. When the missile's fuel ran out, the bomb fell and exploded. The V-2, developed near the end of the war, was more like a modern guided missile. It flew high into the atmosphere and came down faster than the speed of sound. These weapons did a great deal of damage to Britain. Oberth's 1954 book, *Men in Outer Space,* proposed a reusable space shuttle. Oberth died in 1989.

Robert Goddard was born in 1882 in Massachusetts. He received a doctoral degree in physics from Clark University in Worcester, Massachusetts, in 1911, and then taught there. In 1919 he published an article, "A Method of Reaching Extreme Altitudes," which described the use of rockets to reach the moon. Many were skeptical of his ideas, so he continued his studies in secret. In 1926 Goddard launched the first successful rocket that used liquid fuel. During World War II, he did research for the U.S. Navy on rocket motors. He died in 1945.

First Rocket Launched at Cape Canaveral, Florida, 1950

This 1964 U.S. stamp honors Robert Goddard.

Following World War II, the Russians forced some German rocket scientists to come to the Soviet Union. The leading German rocket scientist, Wernher Von Braun, as well as many others, came to the United States where they helped the U.S. Army develop its rocket program and later worked in the U.S. space program.

The Space Age Begins

In the mid-1950s, the United States and the Soviet Union were the two countries with the experts and the technology that gave them the best chance for making space travel a reality. Both countries had conducted rocket tests to determine whether they could launch a satellite into orbit around the Earth. The United States conducted their experiments, such as the one above, in public, which meant that American citizens and the rest of the world knew when scientists had a setback, such as a rocket blowing up on launch or a test being delayed. The Soviet Union, on the other hand, conducted their tests in complete secrecy so that neither the Russian public nor the rest of the world knew what was happening. Most people assumed that U.S. technology was ahead of what the Soviets had. The world was shocked when on October 4, 1957, the Soviet Union launched a 194-pound unmanned artificial satellite, called *Sputnik,* into orbit around the Earth. *Sputnik's* simple radio transmitter sent beep-beep signals back to receivers on Earth.

After this U.S. scientists worked harder to put their own satellite into space, but before they succeeded, the Russians launched *Sputnik 2* into orbit on November 3, 1957. A small dog named Laika was on board *Sputnik 2* so the Russians could test the effects of space travel on a living creature. When the Americans finally put *Explorer 1* into Earth orbit on January 31, 1958, the space race between the U.S. and the U.S.S.R. was on.

1972 Soviet stamp commemorates Sputnik. *1982 Mongolian stamp commemorates* Sputnik 2 *and Laika.*

Lesson 142 - God Created Space

The Space Race Continues

The competition in space travel between the Soviet Union and the United States was of great importance to the leaders of both countries. The space race was part of the Cold War, and both sides wanted to be ahead. Both countries wanted to show that their system of government and society was superior to the other. They saw accomplishments in space as proving superiority.

Each side also saw advances in space as giving their own country greater security against possible military aggression by the other. If a country could launch a satellite into space, the satellite could conceivably obtain vital information about the other country. In addition, each country could conceivably launch a missile armed with a nuclear bomb toward the other country. Each country built systems using missiles as defensive weapons. In the United States, Congress authorized increased Federal spending for science education in high schools and colleges, to help close the gap between Russian and American preparedness. The Federal government formed the National Aeronautics and Space Administration (NASA) to coordinate efforts at space travel.

For a time the Soviets were ahead in the space race. Their space program accomplished many firsts. On January 2, 1959, the Russians sent a spacecraft called the *Luna* past the moon. It came within 3,700 miles of the moon's surface. Two months later the American *Pioneer 4* flew past the moon. In September, the Russian *Luna 2* hit the moon. A month later *Luna 3* orbited the moon and took photographs of the backside of the moon, which never faces the Earth.

The First People in Space

On April 12, 1961, Soviet cosmonaut Yuri Gagarin launched into space in the *Vostok* spacecraft and completed one orbit of the Earth before returning. The trip took just over 100 minutes. Whereas it had taken Magellan's crew and Sir Francis Drake years to circle the globe in the 1500s, now the feat could be accomplished in a little more than an hour and a half.

April 13, 1961, Soviet newspaper Komsomolskaya Pravda *reports about Yuri Gagarin's flight.*

America began sending men into space on May 5, 1961, when astronaut Alan Shepard Jr. took a fifteen-minute flight from Cape Canaveral, Florida. As seen in the drawing on page 984, Shepard entered the upper realms of the atmosphere only briefly and then splashed down in the Atlantic Ocean. Americans celebrated this great accomplishment. Less than three weeks later, President John F. Kennedy gave a speech to Congress in which he challenged the U.S. to send a man to the moon and return him safely to Earth before the end of the 1960s.

Kennedy's challenge was especially bold given that the U.S. had made only one brief manned flight, but the government and the people took on the challenge. On February 20, 1962, John Glenn became the first American to orbit the Earth, when he made three orbits in less than

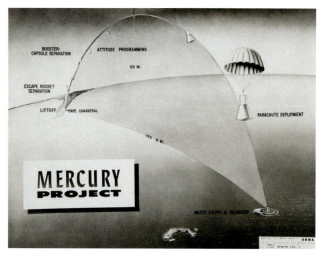
Diagram of Shepard's Flight

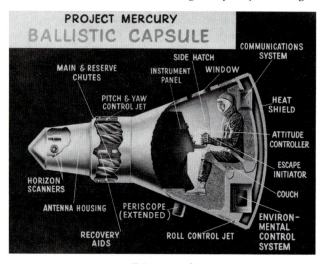
Diagram of Mercury Space Capsule

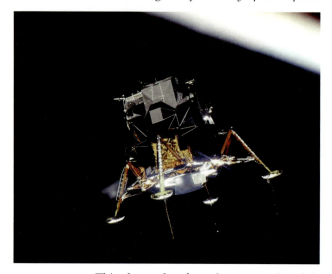
This photo taken from the command module shows the Eagle *about to land, 1969.*

five hours. Both Shepard and Glenn were part of NASA's Mercury space program. See diagram of Mercury space capsule at left.

Soviet space mission successes continued, and in June of 1963 Russian cosmonaut Valentina Tereshkova became the first woman in space. The Americans and the Soviets made many trips into space during the 1960s. In October of 1964 the Russians sent a two-man crew into space for twenty-four hours.

Americans began a two-man program, called Gemini, in 1965. Then NASA began to launch three-man space capsules in a program named Apollo. The goal of this series was to meet Kennedy's challenge of landing a man on the moon. Early Apollo flights stayed in Earth orbit for extended periods. Later missions circled the moon but did not land.

"One Small Step for Man, One Giant Leap for Mankind"

On July 16, 1969, American Apollo astronauts Neil Armstrong, Buzz Aldrin, and Michael Collins left Earth on the Apollo 11 mission. Four days later, Armstrong and Aldrin separated the lunar module, seen at left and called the *Eagle*, from the command module, which was piloted by Michael Collins. At 4:17 and 43 seconds p.m. Eastern Daylight Time, on July 20, 1969, the lunar module landed on the surface of the moon while Collins orbited the moon.

Neil Armstrong became the first human being to put his foot on the moon. An estimated 530 million people watched and listened on television as pictures and his first words were broadcast around the world. He said, "That's one small step for man; one giant leap for mankind." Armstrong looked down at his left boot and then stepped down with his right foot. Then, he said, "Yes, the surface is fine and powdery. I can kick it up loosely with my toe . . . .

Lesson 142 - God Created Space

I can see the footprints of my boots and the treads in the fine, sandy particles."

A short while later Aldrin, still in the *Eagle*, said, "That looks beautiful from here, Neil."

Armstrong replied, "It has a stark beauty all its own. It's like much of the high desert of the United States. It's different, but it's very pretty out here."

Soon Aldrin, too, stepped out on the moon. His first words were, "Beautiful view."

"Isn't that something! Magnificent sight out here," Armstrong replied.

"Magnificent desolation," said Aldrin.

While on the moon, Armstrong and Aldrin gathered rock and soil samples and conducted other experiments. They also left a plaque on the moon. During the broadcast, Armstrong read the message from the plaque to the world: "Here Men from the planet Earth first set foot upon the Moon, July 1969 A.D. We came in peace for all mankind." Beneath those words were the signatures of the three crew members and of Richard Nixon, President of the United States. Armstrong and Aldrin also set up a flag pole and left an American flag on the moon.

When their mission was completed, Armstrong and Aldrin went back into the lunar module and fired small rockets that took it out of the moon's gravity. They rejoined Collins in the command ship. The crew returned to Earth safely and became heroes around the world.

Over the next three years, five other Apollo missions accomplished moon landings. To date the twelve Americans who went to the moon on those missions are the only people who have walked on the moon. At right is a photo from the last U.S. space flight to the moon. The Soviets tried to develop their own manned moon program secretly but failed to do so.

In 1975 an American Apollo spacecraft and a Soviet Soyuz spacecraft linked together on a mission while in Earth orbit. The two crews performed experiments together. Scientists and historians see this event as the end of the space race.

Buzz Aldrin carries experiment packs on the surface of the moon.

Plaque Left on the Moon

Astronaut and scientist Harrison Schmitt stands by an American flag on the Apollo 17 mission in December 1972. Schmitt and Gene Cernan were the last people to stand on the moon. See Earth in the distance.

Space Stations and Space Shuttles

After the U.S. moon landing, the Russian space program began to emphasize long-term missions in Earth orbit, aboard space stations that flew 200 to 300 miles above the Earth's surface. The first *Salyut* space station launched on April 19, 1971. A three-man crew spent twenty-three days on it, but sadly they were killed in an accident while returning to Earth. The Soviets built several *Salyut* stations in the 1970s and 1980s, and missions generally lasted up to eight months. In 1987 and 1988, two Russian cosmonauts were in space for a mission that lasted 366 days. The Soviet *Mir* space station began operation in 1986 and continued to function until 2001. In 1994 and 1995, cosmonaut Valeri Polyakov remained aloft on the *Mir* for 438 days, the record for space endurance.

First Space Shuttle Launch, April 1981

The first American space station, *Skylab*, began service in 1973 and continued until it fell from orbit and broke up without a crew onboard in 1979. The space programs of several nations combined efforts to construct the International Space Station (ISS) beginning in 1998. The first crew, consisting of one American and two Russians, worked on the ISS in 2000. Astronauts from several countries continue to engage in missions aboard the ISS.

The United States developed reusable space vehicles called shuttles that could return to Earth and then be launched into space again. The first Space Shuttle mission took place in 1981. NASA built several shuttles, and each flight carried as many as eight members. In 1998 John Glenn, who had made the first American orbital flight in 1962, returned to space as a shuttle crew member on a nine-day mission. At the time Glenn was seventy-seven years old and a U.S. Senator from Ohio. Glenn is the oldest person ever to make a space flight.

Space Stations

Left: Skylab; Center: American astronaut Shannon Lucid works inside the Mir *Space Station, 1996. Right: International Space Station*

Lesson 142 - God Created Space

Other Countries Go into Space

Only the United States and the Soviet Union participated in the first decades of space travel. Other nations began space programs later. The European Space Agency combines the resources of several European countries and has launched satellites into space. Germany, Japan, China (which sent a *taikonaut* or Chinese astronaut into space), India, Canada, Israel, Australia, Italy, Brazil, Sweden, South Africa, and Iran have launched spacecraft. In addition, NASA has worked with a few private companies to launch satellites for business uses. Hundreds of satellites are in orbit around the Earth. They provide weather or other scientific data, military information, and television and communication links.

Space travel and exploration have occurred in only a tiny portion of the universe. The immense size of the universe speaks profoundly of the amazing power of our Creator God.

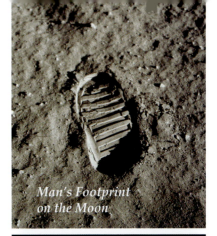

Man's Footprint on the Moon

For since the creation of the world His invisible attributes,
His eternal power and divine nature, have been clearly seen,
being understood through what has been made,
so that they are without excuse.
Romans 1:20

Assignments for Lesson 142

Our Creative World — Read the excerpts from the International Space Station blog on pages 137-139.

Timeline Book — In the first box for Lesson 142 on page 30 (1957), write "*Sputnik* is the first artificial satellite." In the second box for Lesson 142 on page 30 (1969), write "Humans land on the moon."

Student Workbook or Lesson Review — If you are using one of these optional books, complete the assignment for Lesson 142.

Thinking Biblically — Read Psalm 19:1-6.

Creative Writing — Write a poem of at least twelve lines about space.

Literature — Read chapters 3-5 in *Children of the Storm*.

Nikolaikirche and the End of Communism in Europe

Lesson 143 — Our World Story

Communism promised to give people a worker's paradise, in which everyone would have plenty and all people would share in the responsibility and authority of government. In practice, however, Communist governments were controlled by a small group that allowed no freedom of speech and limited freedom of worship, created an economy in which no one could have his own business, and ruled a society in which the police spied on the citizens. In addition, people who lived under Communism always struggled to have basic necessities, because an economy led by government workers instead of one based on free enterprise does not produce enough for everyone.

Communists Control Eastern Europe

We have seen how Communists took control of Russia in 1917 and formed the Union of Soviet Socialist Republics in 1922. We have also seen how, after World War II, the Soviet Union seized East Germany, Czechoslovakia, Hungary, Romania, Bulgaria, Yugoslavia, and Poland. Because of the power the Soviets held over these countries, they came to be called satellites of the U.S.S.R. The Communist countries of Eastern Europe had programs similar to the Young Pioneers of the U.S.S.R. The stamps below show an idealized view of Communism for children.

Young Pioneer Orchestra, East Germany, 1973; Young Pioneer Girl with Doll, Czechoslovakia, 1959; Young Pioneers, Hungary, 1951; Young Pioneer Red Cross Nurses, Bulgaria, 1974; Children receive Young Pioneer scarves, Romania, 1968.

Lesson 143 - Nikolaikirche and the End of Communism in Europe

The Soviet government controlled everything that went on in its satellite countries. The few people who spoke out against Soviet control risked going to prison or even being killed. Communist governments tried to indoctrinate people through education, media, and art into thinking life under Communism was ideal. The wall mosaic at right is an example of this propaganda. However, the idealized view of Communism was in stark contrast to the reality of life in Communist countries. When Hungarians tried to break free of Communism in 1956, Soviet military forces violently crushed them.

Propaganda Mosaic in Hungarian Train Station

The Soviet government also crushed an anti-Communist protest in Czechoslovakia in 1968. Workers in Poland formed a labor union called Solidarity. Its members began working for a free Poland with a democratic government. The Communist government of Poland (with Soviet approval) attempted to wipe out Solidarity, but the group continued to operate secretly.

Even though Communism appeared to be strong, it had serious weaknesses. What is more, it could not crush the longing people had for freedom.

For decades the U.S.S.R. built up its military strength at the expense of the well-being of its people. The government kept the people poor but justified it to them with propaganda that claimed the United States was threatening their country so fiercely that they had to defend themselves. The Soviet government tried to keep accurate information about the rest of the world out of Russia and Eastern Europe, but people there knew enough to know that Western Europeans were much better off economically than they were.

Mikhail Gorbachev, Leader of the Soviet Union

Mikhail Gorbachev became the head of the Communist Party in the Soviet Union in 1985. While he was in power, Gorbachev changed the way the government operated in the Soviet Union. He announced new policies of *perestroika*, which means reform, and of *glasnost*, which means openness. He tried to improve the Soviet Union's relationships with free countries.

In 1987 U.S. President Ronald Reagan traveled to West Berlin and gave a speech at the Berlin Wall, just as Kennedy had done in 1963. During the speech, Reagan challenged Gorbachev, telling him, "Mr. Gorbachev, tear down this wall!"

Leipzig and Nikolaikirche

In Lesson 113, we learned of Johann Sebastian Bach's work as the *kapellmeister* in Leipzig, Germany. Leipzig was in eastern Germany, so when the Iron Curtain fell on Europe, Leipzig became part of Communist East Germany.

Mikhail Gorbachev, 2011

Unit 29 - The End of the Twentieth Century

Entrance to Nikolaikirche

Invitation to Monday Meetings

Catholics in Leipzig had founded St. Nicholas Church (*Nikolaikirche* in German) in 1165. Following the Protestant Reformation in the early 1500s, Nikolaikirche became a Lutheran congregation. The premier performance of Bach's *St. John Passion* was performed in Nikolaikirche. After the Communists took control of East Germany, atheism became the official government position. Authorities allowed Nikolaikirche and other churches to continue meeting, but spies closely watched what happened.

Christian Fuehrer became pastor of Nikolaikirche in 1980. In 1982 he began weekly prayer meetings on Monday evenings. People would pray, read passages of Scripture, and sometimes discuss social and political issues. In 1988 Fuehrer invited fifty people to a Monday evening discussion. He specifically wanted to discuss the desire of East German citizens to gain the right to travel freely outside of their country. Six hundred people showed up.

The banner above is an invitation to the Monday meetings. The German is translated, "Prayer for Peace in St. Nikolai, Every Monday at 5:00 p.m." The words in the center say, "Swords to Plowshares," referring to this verse from the Old Testament:

And He will judge between many peoples
And render decisions for mighty, distant nations.
Then they will hammer their swords into plowshares
And their spears into pruning hooks;
Nation will not lift up sword against nation,
And never again will they train for war. Micah 4:3

More and more people began to attend. The state police sent spies to the meetings. The spies had two purposes. First, they wanted to check on what was being said (they heard prayers and Scripture in the process!). Second, they wanted to fill the church building so fewer genuinely interested people could take part. Sometimes those who attended were arrested, beaten, and put in jail; but the people kept coming. As word about the Monday meetings in Leipzig spread, people in other East German cities began meeting in city centers on Monday evenings. In May of 1989, police tried to close off Nikolaikirche by setting up barricades around it; but people still came. The movement based on faith and prayer was growing.

Tension Builds

The Soviet Union and Eastern Europe were not the only countries where citizens tried to change the conditions in which they lived. When Chinese citizens in favor of democracy demonstrated against their government in Tiananmen Square in Beijing in early June of 1989, the Communist government of China attacked them brutally. East German leaders praised what the Chinese Communists did. However, during that same summer the Soviet Union began to change its policy toward the countries it had controlled. Gorbachev announced that the Soviet Union would no longer interfere with what happened in other countries. Poland held a free election in June of 1989, and the Polish people voted the Communist Party out of power. New hope for freedom blossomed in countries that had suffered for decades under Soviet domination.

Police arrested Pastor Christian Fuehrer and an associate pastor in late September and told them to discontinue the Monday meetings, but they refused to do so. Authorities beat protesters marching in Leipzig on Monday, October 2.

Saturday, October 7, was the fortieth anniversary of the official founding of East Germany. About 4,000 people gathered outside Nikolaikirche and tried to march peacefully along the city's ring road. The police violently broke up the march and arrested several participants. Leipzig police warned that any demonstration on the following Monday, October 9, would be stopped with whatever means they thought necessary. Hospital staffs prepared to treat what they feared might be a large number of injured persons.

The Wall Comes Tumbling Down

On Monday, October 9, eight thousand people gathered at Nikolaikirche, completely filling the building and spilling outside. Four other churches in Leipzig opened their doors to receive demonstrators. The crowd at Nikolaikirche joined others to walk around the ring road. Between 70,000 and 100,000 people took part in the peaceful march. They carried lighted candles, chanted "We are the people," and prayed. Some policemen who were dressed in regular clothes moved in among the demonstrators and tried to stir up trouble, but other people surrounded them and called out "No violence!" A few people were arrested, but in general the police merely stood by and watched.

Interior of Nikolaikirche

Leipzig officials tried to contact the national government in Berlin to find out what they should do, but they were not able to do so. The Leipzig authorities were not prepared for the huge number of marchers and did not expect the crowd to remain peaceful. The authorities decided not to try to break up the quiet demonstration, especially since the marchers were their friends, neighbors, and family members. As one East German official said later, "We were ready for anything, except candles and prayer."

When it became clear that neither local, East German, nor Soviet officials would try to stop the Monday demonstrations, the marches grew quickly. On Monday, October 16, 1989, some 120,000 people walked peacefully through Leipzig.

Monday Marches in Leipzig, October and November 1989

October 16, 1989

October 23, 1989

October 30, 1989

November 6, 1989

On October 23, an estimated 320,000 people took part in another peaceful demonstration in Leipzig. On November 4, one million people marched in East Berlin on behalf of freedom.

Realizing that the Soviet Union would not stand behind them, East German officials announced on November 9, 1989, that people were free to pass through the Berlin Wall to West Berlin without hindrance. Thousands did so. With free movement between East and West Berlin now permitted, the wall was no longer needed to keep East Berliners in. Hundreds stood on the wall and cheered; others began tearing it down. Some chipped at it with hammers while others used machinery to remove huge sections. Freedom had come to East Germany!

Communism Falls in Europe

This time it was Communist "dominoes" that began to fall. By the middle of 1990, all of the Communist governments in Eastern Europe had been replaced by freely elected governments. Violence occurred in a few places, but overall the revolution was peaceful. East and West Germany officially reunified into one country on October 3, 1990. The Soviet Union itself was dissolved on December 26, 1991.

Communism remains the form of government in China, Laos, Cuba, North Korea, and Vietnam. Though China has made movements toward a capitalist economy, all of the Communist governments still practice censorship and totalitarian control of their people.

The Monday meetings at Nikolaikirche in Leipzig played a vital part in the fall of Communism in Europe. Following reunification, Christian Fuehrer started programs to help people in financial trouble as the German economy struggled to adapt to the new arrangement. Fuehrer, who retired in 2008, said in a 2009 interview:

> What I saw that evening [of October 9, 1989] still gives me shivers today. And if anything deserves the word 'miracle' at all, then this was a miracle of Biblical proportions. We succeeded in bringing about a revolution which achieved Germany's unity . . . . It was a peaceful revolution after so much violence and so many wars that we, the Germans, so often started. I will never forget that day.

The world watched in awe as the Berlin Wall came down and Communist governments in Russia and Eastern Europe collapsed—not through a military confrontation, but through quiet protests and the prayers of God's people.

Years after he left office, Mikhail Gorbachev, a believer, said that he had become convinced while in college that God had raised him up to free his people from Communism when the right man—a leader who would not attack or invade his country—became President of the United States. In the 1980s, with Ronald Reagan serving as the U.S. President, Gorbachev believed the time had come.

In 1990 Germany celebrated the first anniversary of the fall of the Berlin Wall with this stamp.

On October 9, 2009, citizens of Leipzig reenacted their peaceful candlelit march twenty years before.

God guided the events of the 1900s as He does in every century. Compare this photo of the Brandenberg Gate with the one on page 943. Faith really does move mountains, prayer really does change things, and God really does work in our lives and in the world.

Brandenburg Gate

And Jesus answered saying to them, "Have faith in God.
Truly I say to you, whoever says to this mountain,
'Be taken up and cast into the sea,' and does not doubt in his heart,
but believes that what he says is going to happen, it will be granted him.
Therefore I say to you, all things for which you pray and ask,
believe that you have received them, and they will be granted you."
Mark 11:22-24

Assignments for Lesson 143

Our Creative World — Read the excerpts from Mikhail Gorbachev's "Address to the 43rd UN General Assembly Session" on page 140.

Timeline Book — In the box for Lesson 143 on page 31, write "The Soviet Union is dissolved."

Student Workbook or Lesson Review — If you are using one of these optional books, complete the assignment for Lesson 143.

Thinking Biblically — Copy Mark 11:22-24.

Creative Writing — Write a news report of one or two paragraphs about the demonstration in Leipzig on October 9, 1989, as if you were a reporter on the scene.

Literature — Read chapters 6-8 in *Children of the Storm*.

Building Up

Lesson 144 World Landmark

Ever since the Tower of Babel, humans have been fascinated with the idea of building up. Throughout history, people around the world have constructed tall monuments and other structures. Some of these have had a religious purpose, symbolically reaching toward the skies. Some have had a political purpose, honoring a prominent leader. Some have had an economic purpose, to show the prestige of a business and provide room for it to operate.

Please note the technical difference between the words *building* and *structure* in this lesson. A building has a roof and walls and is designed as a place for humans to live, shop, work, or worship. A building is one type of structure. Structures not designed for continuous human occupation, such as arenas, bridges, dams, or monuments, are technically known as nonbuilding structures.

From Ancient to Modern Times

For over 3,000 years the Great Pyramid of Giza, Egypt, was the tallest known structure in the world. It now measures 455 feet tall, but it was probably about 481 feet tall when the Egyptians built it. The Lighthouse of Alexandria was approximately 350 feet tall. The original height of the Jetavanaramaya was about the same. It is a Buddhist memorial built in the 300s on the island of Sri Lanka.

No manmade structure was taller than the Great Pyramid until the construction of Lincoln Cathedral in England. Completed in 1311, this cathedral had a central **spire** that rose over 500 feet. A storm destroyed the spire in 1549, and it was not rebuilt.

Ulm Minster, Ulm, Germany

People in Europe built other cathedrals successively higher over the next few centuries. The tallest church in the world is Ulm Minster in Ulm, Germany. Ground-breaking took place in 1377, but the steeple of the building was not finally completed until 1890. It is 530 feet tall.

Washington Monument, Washington, D.C.

When the Washington Monument, at left, was completed in 1884, it became the world's tallest structure. At 555 feet, the monument remains the tallest all-stone structure. The Eiffel Tower **surpassed** the Washington Monument in 1889. Rising 986 feet, it was the world's tallest structure for 41 years.

The First Skyscrapers

In the 1900s, new technology and construction techniques made it possible for people to build buildings ever higher. These new tall buildings were called skyscrapers. The Chrysler Building, completed in New York City in 1930, was the first structure to rise over 1,000 feet. The Empire State Building, also in New York, surpassed it the next year, rising to 1,250 feet. It was the first building to have more than 100 floors. See photo below. The Empire State Building remained the world's tallest building until the completion of the World Trade Center towers in New York City in the early 1970s. These will be discussed in Lesson 147.

Building a Skyscraper

A man works on the Empire State Building with the Chrysler Building in the background, 1930.

The process of building a skyscraper takes years from the initial planning to the public opening. The architects and engineers who design the building must take into consideration how the building will be used, how much the people building it want to spend, the laws of the city where it is built, and the appearance of the building in relation to surrounding buildings. Planners must do research on ground conditions and weather conditions to make sure the completed building is stable and safe. They must make plans for how people will park cars in or under the building, how people will get up and down in the building, how water and sewer systems will work, how security will be provided, and how the windows will be washed.

The materials and equipment in a skyscraper come from around the world. Depending on the location of the skyscraper and the budget of the owner, the construction company will obtain products from different locations. For example, steel may come from Luxembourg. Stone may come from Portugal. Aluminum may come from Australia. Elevator motors may come from Japan. Glass may come from Great Britain. Wood may come from Mozambique or Hungary or the United States. Carpet may come from India. Deliveries of these products must be planned and timed so that construction can proceed on schedule.

Lesson 144 - Building Up

Because a skyscraper is so heavy, it needs a strong foundation. Workers must dig out tons of dirt to reach **bedrock**. Workers attach footers or piers to the bedrock, and then they can begin building the steel frame of the building. Huge cranes raise steel beams into place, and workers fasten them together. As the frame of the building rises, workers move the cranes to reach higher levels. In the center of the frame is a core that makes the building stable and a location for elevators and stairways.

Skyscrapers cannot be completely rigid. They are designed to sway up to a foot in the wind. If they moved more than that, people on the higher floors would feel seasick. Heavy objects on upper floors, such as water tanks or large concrete or steel blocks, help provide balance and decrease **vibrations** that people and machines cause in the building.

As workers complete the frame, they install windows and design elements to the outside of the building. They thread pipes, ducts, wires, and cables for miles through the frame of the building to provide **ventilation** and air conditioning, water and sanitation, electricity, and Internet access.

Tall Buildings Around the World

Most of the world's skyscrapers over 1,000 feet tall are in the United States, the Middle East, and East Asia. The tallest building in Europe and Russia is the Lakhta Center in St. Petersburg, Russia, which reaches 1,516 feet high.

People have built relatively few skyscrapers in the Southern Hemisphere. The tallest building in Australia is called Q1. It was completed in 2005. Located in Surfers Paradise, it rises 1,058 feet. The tallest building in South America was completed in 2013. The Costanera Center Torre 2 is located in Santiago, Chile, and rises 984 feet. The tallest building in Africa is the Carlton Centre in Johannesburg, South Africa. Built in 1973, it rises 730 feet. Construction of what is expected to become the tallest building in Africa began in 2015 in Casablanca, Morocco.

The Willis Tower in Chicago (formerly called the Sears Tower) became the world's tallest building in 1973. It held this title until 1998 when the Petronas Towers were completed in Malaysia. The Petronas Towers have lower top floors than the Willis Tower but taller architectural tops. Since then, the race to build the tallest skyscraper has intensified. The following illustration compares tall buildings in the early twenty-first century and those built earlier in world history.

Skyscrapers of the Southern Hemisphere

Among the skyscrapers in this photo of Surfers Paradise, Australia, Q1 is the second from the left.

The Constanera Center Torre 2 is located at right in this photograph of Santiago, Chile.

Carlton Centre stands just to the left of center in this photograph of Johannesburg, South Africa.

Tall Structures of the World

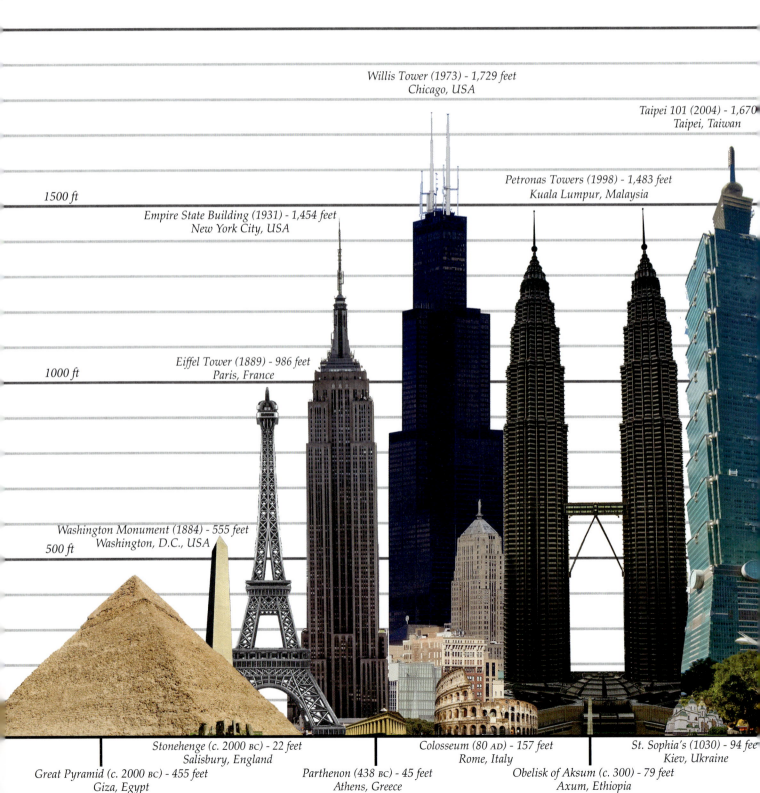

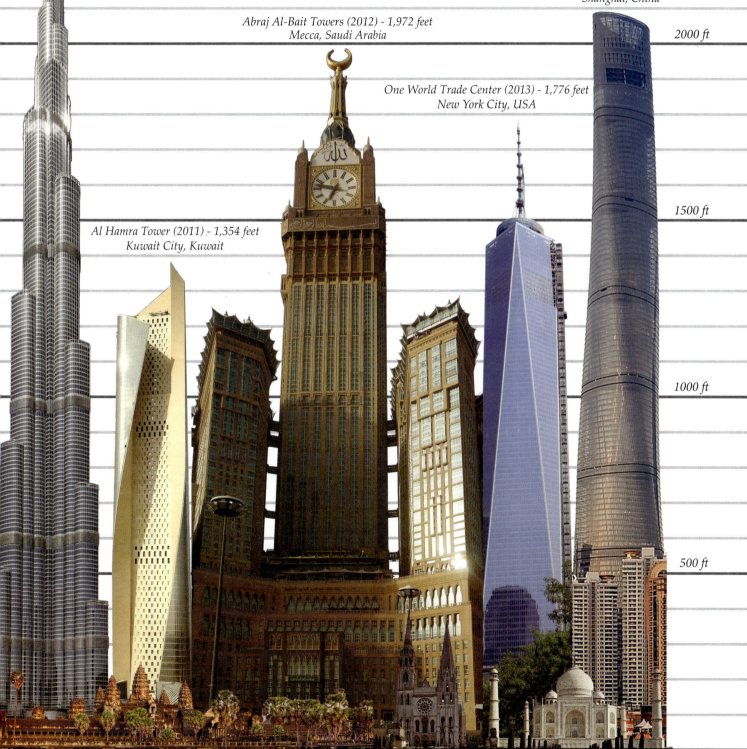

The Council on Tall Buildings and Urban Habitat (CTBUH) formed in 1969. It is a nonprofit organization that studies the planning, design, and construction of tall buildings. It also makes declarations of which building is the tallest in various categories. Because tall buildings can be measured in different ways, the CTBUH compares them in different ways. One way is to measure the height of the structural or architectural top of the building, which can include spires that are part of the building design but does not include antennas. This measurement is commonly used to define which building is the tallest.

Every few years, a new building takes the lead. As of this writing, China has six of the ten tallest skyscrapers completed or nearly completed in the world (five on the mainland and one in Hong Kong). As seen in the illustration on pages 998-999, in early 2016, the tallest building in the world was Burj Khalifa in Dubai, United Arab Emirates, completed in 2010 and standing 2,717 feet tall. It is pictured at left.

Burj Khalifa rises above the early morning fog in Dubai, United Arab Emirates, 2013.

Tall buildings are great accomplishments of man's intelligence and skill. We must always remember, though, that God stands higher than anything man can build.

The Lord is high above all nations;
His glory is above the heavens.
Psalm 113:4

Assignments for Lesson 144

Timeline Book — In the box for Lesson 144 on page 31, write "The Burj Khalifa is the world's tallest building."

Student Workbook or Lesson Review — If you are using one of these optional books, complete the assignment for Lesson 144.

Vocabulary — Make a drawing for each of these words that illustrates what it means: spire (995), surpass (996), bedrock (997), vibration (997), ventilation (997). Write the word under the drawing. Check in a dictionary if you need help with their definitions.

Creative Writing — Write a short story of at least one page that takes place in or around a tall structure (real or imagined).

Literature — Read chapters 9-10 in *Children of the Storm*.

Family Activity — Conduct a "Twentieth-Century Interview." See page FA-56 for instructions.

People Groups Around the World

Lesson 145   Daily Life

Though the world has fewer than 200 countries, it has thousands of people groups. In Lesson 136, we learned about the United Nations. In the year 2016, 193 countries were members of the UN. Vatican City has chosen not to be a part of the UN. The UN rejected Taiwan as a member in 1971 when it allowed the People's Republic of China to join in its place. Kosovo fought a war for independence from Serbia in the late 1990s, but not all countries of the world recognize it as an independent country and it has not joined.

The terms *ethnic group* and *nation* can be used interchangeably with the term *people group*. One Christian mission organization has identified 16,324 such groups.

The population of Canada, for example, includes people who identify themselves as members of 200 ethnic groups. Most citizens of Canada call themselves Canadian, but the ancestors of these Canadians came from many people groups, mainly from the United Kingdom and other European countries, but also from Africa and other continents. People groups with more than one million residents in Canada include English, French, Scots, Irish, German, Italian, Chinese, First Nations, Ukrainian, Indian (from India), Dutch, and Polish.

Indigenous Peoples

Thousands of nations and **tribes** around the world are called **indigenous** peoples. An indigenous people is a distinct group, who lived in a place before others from outside the area established a colony there. Indigenous people living today are

A Woman of the Mohawk People in Montreal, Quebec, Canada

People dressed as a Chinese lion entertain in a parade in Edmonton, Alberta, Canada.

the descendants of those who lived in a place before another group arrived. Indigenous groups often carry on their **traditional** ways of life. Most indigenous groups are in the **minority** in their country, although indigenous people in Bolivia make up about 50 to 70 percent of the population. Most of these are Quechua and Aymara.

Scholars who study indigenous people groups estimate there are a total of 350 to 400 million persons in about 5,000 distinct indigenous people groups living in dozens of countries. Therefore, indigenous groups comprise about 5 percent of the world's population. Indigenous people groups live in every climate and on every continent except Antarctica. An estimated 70 percent of them live in Asia and the islands of the Pacific. There are about one thousand indigenous languages in Papua New Guinea alone. The indigenous groups in Asia and the Pacific use an estimated 4,000 languages.

Indigenous People of Today

King of Ashanti People, Ghana; Maori Woman, New Zealand; Kurdish Woman, Turkey; Dhimba Boys, Namibia; Kosovar Albanian Refugee in Albania

Macua Woman, Mozambique; Togolese Man, Togo; Sami Woman, Norway; Ji-Paiya-Kutumb Woman, Papua New Guinea; Fulani Woman—The Fulani live mainly in Nigeria, Mali, Guinea, Cameroon, Senegal, and Niger.

Left: Ndebele Man, Zimbabwe; Bushmen, Botswana; Right: The Aymara people live in Peru, Bolivia, Argentina, and Chile.

Lesson 145 - People Groups Around the World

Ethnic Identity

People in a certain ethnic group often look similar to one another because of skin color, hair color, and facial features. Sometimes members of an ethnic group are of a similar height and have a similar body build. People in some ethnic groups wear distinctive clothing, especially at times of ceremonies and celebrations; but their identity is much deeper than their appearance. Many of these groups have strong traditions about courtship and wedding customs, family life, young persons coming of age, religion, and relationships with one another within their society.

Traditional Ethnic Costumes

*Top Row: Kazakhstani, Two Croatians, Two Ecuadorians;
Second Row: Bulgarian, Albanian, Cameroonian, People of Trinidad and Tobago, Scot;
Left: Uganda, Philippines;
Right: Georgian; Djibouti*

Traditional Weddings

Villagers in a Romanian village gather for a wedding. The bride and groom are holding hands above.

Hungarians participate in a wedding. The bride is at far right.

Hungarian dancers, singers, and musicians participate in a Hungarian wedding.

Left: A festival in Russia demonstrates the wedding ceremony of people living above the Arctic Circle. Above: A Welsh Love Spoon—Traditionally a Welsh man gave a love spoon to a woman he wanted to court. Right: Turkmen Bride and Groom, Turkmenistan

Lesson 145 - People Groups Around the World

Though many members of a people group may use modern ways to travel, some continue to use methods their ancestors used, at least part of the time. All people groups have a history of traditional crafts that their ancestors created. Some continue to use these items and others make them for the sake of tradition or to sell to collectors and tourists.

Traditional Ways to Travel, Transport, and Carry

Top Row: Man crosses Niger River in Mali. Camels carry firewood in Eritrea. Women ford stream while carrying sand on their heads in Madagascar. Bottom Row: Girl travels by boat in Benin. Man leads camel in Niger. Donkey carries man and goods in Sudan. Woman carries container of goods to sell on the beach in Mozambique.

Traditional Crafts

Top Row: Stamps honor Mapuche weaving in Argentina, embroidered quilts in Bangladesh, wood carving in Burundi, and traditional crafts of Cabo Verde. A man in the Solomon Islands carves wooden spoons. Left: Traditional Foods and Pottery of Moldova; Hammocks of El Salvador, Carved Coconuts of Bali in Indonesia; Right: Wood Carving of Gabon.

Members of an ethnic group often pass down traditional stories to children. Some of these stories are true oral histories and others, like the European fairy tales of the Brothers Grimm, are fables that teach valuable lessons. Ethnic groups also have traditions of music and dance.

Traditional Music and Dance

Dancers from Swaziland; Instruments from Bangladesh and Chad; Dancers from the Bahamas and Poland

Armenian, Azerbaijani, and Kosovar Dancers

Lithuanian, Serbian, and Batwa Pygmy (from Uganda) Dancers

Below: Serbian and Udmurt (from Russia) Dancers; A man performs a fire dance in the Hina cave in Tongo.

A Lahu woman from Thailand plays a Chinese flute; Drums from Angola and Dominica; Seashell Horn from Fiji

Singing by Yakut People Group of Russia; Candombe Drummers from Uruguay; Wooden Horns from Lithuania

Longing for a Homeland

Throughout history some ethnic groups have lived peacefully side by side while others have had conflict, sometimes leading to war. Many ethnic groups are content to live as a minority within the country where they reside, but others long for a homeland of their own.

About 2.5 million Basque people live in northern Spain and a half-million in southern France. The Basque have lived in the region for centuries. Experts believe that their language, Euskara, is one of the oldest European languages still in common use today. One fourth of modern Basque speak Euskara. See Basque dancers at right.

Basque Dancers

France and Spain have ruled the Basque for centuries. During the 1800s, some Basque began working to preserve their culture and to become independent of Spain. In 1937 Spanish dictator Francisco Franco crushed these efforts, abolished most of their rights, and forbade the use of Euskara. The language came back into more common use after Franco's death in 1975. In the 1960s, the Basque again tried to form a separate government. Some Basque used violence against the Spanish government. In 1980 Spain made three Basque provinces a self-governing region within Spain. In 2011 the group most responsible for the violence promised to end that practice.

What every person in the world needs, regardless of his or her ethnic background, is Jesus. Jesus is the Savior who can change people's hearts and bring the diverse peoples of the world to God and to each other in mutual love.

Traditional Homes

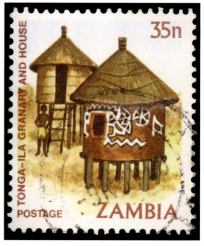

*After these things I looked, and behold,
a great multitude which no one could count,
from every nation and all tribes
and peoples and tongues,
standing before the throne and before the Lamb,
clothed in white robes,
and palm branches were in their hands;
and they cry out with a loud voice, saying,
"Salvation to our God who sits on the throne,
and to the Lamb."
Revelation 7:9-10*

Assignments for Lesson 145

Our Creative World — Read the excerpt from *The Dayuma Story* on pages 141-143.

Timeline Book — In the box for Lesson 145 on page 30, write "Spain makes three Basque provinces self-governing."

Student Workbook or Lesson Review — If you are using one of these optional books, complete the assignment for Lesson 145 and take the test for Unit 29.

Thinking Biblically — If someone were going to be a missionary to an indigenous people group, what should he or she learn about them to be able to minister well? Make a list of at least five things.

Vocabulary — Write five sentences, using one of these words in each: ethnic (1001), indigenous (1001), tribe (1001), traditional (1002), minority (1002). Check in a dictionary if you need help with their definitions.

Literature — Read chapters 11-12 in *Children of the Storm*.

Zambia, Lesotho, Niger, Samoa, Palau

30 Us

Grand Folk Dance Concert of the Latvian Youth Song and Dance Festival, Riga, Latvia, 2015

Lessons
- 146 - World Biography: Queen Elizabeth II
- 147 - Our World Story: Turmoil in the Middle East
- 148 - World Landmark: Sports Bring Us Together
- 149 - God's Wonder: God's World Still Supports Human Life
- 150 - Daily Life: Our Interconnected World

Literature *Children of the Storm*

Twenty-First Century

We began *From Adam to Us* learning about what God did at the dawn of the history of the world. The Earth that He created so wonderfully in the Creation week continues to provide for the now seven billion people of the world. On September 9, 2015, Queen Elizabeth II became the longest-reigning monarch of the United Kingdom. The tragic story of conflict in the Middle East that began in ancient times continues. The Olympic Games, other sporting events, and technological advancements of the last several decades bring the nations of the world together.

The pin for Lesson 148 points to Uruguay, host of the first World Cup. Lessons 149 and 150 talk about many places around the world.

Queen Elizabeth II

Lesson 146   World Biography

Queen Elizabeth II of the United Kingdom is the longest-reigning monarch in British history. She became queen after a period of national turmoil and world war, and she has represented her nation faithfully and well. The Queen is greatly loved in the United Kingdom and has been one of the most admired women in the world for decades.

House of Windsor

The family name of Queen Victoria was Hanover. The family name of her husband, Prince Albert, was Saxe-Coberg-Gotha. Albert's family was German. After Victoria died in 1901, her son, Edward VII, became king when he was fifty-nine years old. His family name was Saxe-Coberg-Gotha. He reigned as the monarch of the United Kingdom from 1901 until 1910.

Edward's son, George V, ruled from 1910 until his death in January of 1936. During the Great War, George V dropped the family's German Saxe-Coberg-Gotha name and changed it to House of Windsor. This change was meant to show loyalty to Britain during the fight against Germany.

Edward VIII, son of George V, became king in 1936. Edward's reign was **controversial** because of his relationship with Wallis Simpson, an American woman who had been divorced. King Edward chose Mrs. Simpson over being king. He abdicated (or gave up) the throne in December of that same year and later married Mrs. Simpson.

Since Edward VIII did not have any children, the throne passed to his brother, who became George VI. As the younger brother, George had not expected to become king. However, he was humble and hardworking in his new role; and the British people loved him. George VI, who is pictured at right, had a severe speech **impediment** which he worked to overcome so that he could make speeches in person and on the radio. His wife, Elizabeth, also won the hearts of the British people.

During World War II, the royal couple remained in London and endured many of the German bombing raids. They visited

In 1939 King George VI and Elizabeth visited President and Mrs. Franklin Roosevelt in Washington, D.C. From left to right in the photo at left are King George, President Roosevelt, a U.S. military officer, Mrs. Roosevelt, and Elizabeth.

places that had suffered severe damage from the bombings so that they could encourage the people who had lost so much. The stamp at right pictures the royal couple during the war.

Birth and Childhood of Elizabeth

George VI and Elizabeth had two daughters: Elizabeth, born in 1926, and Margaret, born in 1930. They are pictured with their parents in the stamp at lower left. The girls received their education at home. When their father became king, Elizabeth became next in line for the throne. Knowing that she would one day become Queen,

This 2012 stamp pictures George VI and Elizabeth during World War II.

This 1943 stamp from St. Kitts and Nevis pictures King George VI.

Elizabeth began studying constitutional history and law. The Archbishop of Canterbury gave the princess religious instruction. Elizabeth learned to speak French, a skill she has used often during her reign. She joined the Girl Guides, a British organization similar to the Girl Scouts, when she was eleven. Elizabeth became a champion swimmer, winning the children's medal at the London Bath Club when she was thirteen. She has long loved horses and horsemanship.

In March of 1945, near the end of World War II, Elizabeth joined the Auxiliary Territorial Service, which carried out needed functions within the country while the men in the military served overseas. Elizabeth began training as a mechanic to work on military vehicles, but the war in Europe ended in May and she was released from service.

This 1946 stamp from New Zealand pictures the royal family.

Lesson 146 - Queen Elizabeth II

Elizabeth Marries and Later Becomes Queen

Elizabeth married Lieutenant Philip Mountbatten, the son of Prince Andrew of the royal family of Greece. Both Elizabeth and Philip are great-great-grandchildren of Queen Victoria.

1997 United Kingdom stamp shows Elizabeth and Philip on the day they married, November 20, 1947.

Since Britain was still recovering from World War II, the government still rationed many items. British citizens were only allowed to receive a certain number of coupons for rationed items each month. People could collect extra coupons from friends and family. Like any bride at the time, Elizabeth had to collect extra ration coupons to be able to purchase fabric for her wedding dress. When they married, Philip received the title of Prince Philip, Duke of Edinburgh.

Elizabeth's father's health declined shortly after her marriage. King George VI died on February 6, 1952. Elizabeth was traveling in a remote part of Kenya. She became Queen Elizabeth II when she was not quite twenty-six years old.

Winston Churchill, who had become prime minister once again, welcomed home the new, mourning Queen at the London airport. The formal crowning ceremony for a monarch is called a coronation. This ceremony requires a great deal of planning and preparation. The coronation of Queen Elizabeth II took place in Westminster Abbey in London over a year later, on June 2, 1953. At the Queen's request, the ceremony was broadcast around the world on radio. It was also broadcast on television in Great Britain and portions of Europe.

This teacup and program are souvenirs of the coronation. These statues of King George VI and his wife Elizabeth are in London. George's wife was also called Queen Elizabeth because although the husband of a reigning queen in the United Kingdom is called a prince, the wife of a reigning king is usually called a queen.

The Role of the Monarch of the United Kingdom

Today, the powers of the British monarch are greatly reduced from what they once were. The modern queen or king does not plan military strategy, declare new laws, or work with advisers on new policies. The elected officials of Parliament have the real power in the United Kingdom's constitutional monarchy. The monarch serves as a symbol of national pride and heritage. Queen Elizabeth is head of state, which means she carries out ceremonial duties on behalf of the country. She is not head of government; that role is filled by the prime minister.

Queen Elizabeth is the head of the British Commonwealth. The British Empire no longer exists. Instead, the Commonwealth is made up of fifty-three independent countries most of which were once part of the British Empire. Fifteen of these countries still recognize the British monarch as their head of state. It also includes a few smaller territories which Britain still claims. See chart at right.

This Royal Mail postbox has the ER insignia and the 1977 stamp from Brunei includes the Queen's coat of arms.

The Queen's coat of arms, pictured at left, or a picture of her crown **adorns** every official document. The Queen's profile, portrait, or photograph is printed on every UK postage stamp and on many in the Commonwealth. The Queen's profile or crown with the letters "ER" on either side of the image is placed on official uniforms; on Royal Mail postboxes, such as the one pictured above; and in other government locations. "ER" stands for "Elizabeth Regina"; *Regina* is Latin for Queen. The letters for Queen Elizabeth's father were GR, which stood for "George Rex." *Rex* is Latin for king. The names of ships in the Royal Navy begin with "HMS," which means either His Majesty's Ship or Her Majesty's Ship, depending on who is on the throne.

The monarch opens the annual session of Parliament. She gives a speech that outlines the government's plans and policies, but the prime minister writes the speech for her. After Parliament passes new laws, the Queen signs them to give her royal **assent**. She appoints the prime minister after an election, but she has no choice in the matter. In the United Kingdom, the head of the political party that wins a majority of the seats in the House of Commons becomes prime minister. The prime minister meets with the Queen every week to keep her up to date about what is happening in the government and the country. The Foreign Office informs her about international matters. She meets all new ambassadors who come to Great Britain to represent their home countries. She has also made many official visits to countries around the world, including the one she made to Jamestown to celebrate the 400th anniversary of its founding. See page 684. By the time she celebrated her Diamond Jubilee (sixty years on the throne) in 2012, Queen Elizabeth had made 261 official visits overseas.

Lesson 146 - Queen Elizabeth II

The British Commonwealth

Africa
Botswana
Cameroon
Ghana
Kenya
Lesotho
Malawi
Mauritius
Mozambique
Namibia
Nigeria
Rwanda
Seychelles
Sierra Leone
South Africa
Swaziland
Uganda
United Republic of Tanzania
Zambia

Asia
Bangladesh
Brunei Darussalam
India
Malaysia
Maldives
Pakistan
Singapore
Sri Lanka

Caribbean and Americas
Antigua and Barbuda
The Bahamas
Barbados
Belize
Canada
Dominica
Grenada
Guyana
Jamaica
St. Lucia
St. Kitts and Nevis
St. Vincent and The Grenadines
Trinidad and Tobago

Europe
Cyprus
Malta
United Kingdom

Pacific
Australia
Fiji
Kiribati
Nauru
New Zealand
Papua New Guinea
Samoa
Solomon Islands
Tonga
Tuvalu
Vanuatu

These stamps from Commonwealth nations honor Queen Elizabeth II. Some specifically honor a birthday, a visit to a Commonwealth country, the silver anniversary of her coronation, or the fiftieth anniversary of her marriage to Prince Philip.

Left: Queen Elizabeth visits Toronto, Canada, 2006. Right: Queen Elizabeth and Prince Philip wave from the balcony of the town hall in Frankfurt, Germany, 2015.

Twice each year the Queen announces a list of people who will receive honors. She will make some of these individuals a knight or a dame. Others will receive the Order of the British Empire. Some individuals receive other medals and honors. In the last unit, we learned about the honors Douglas and Gladys Nicholls received.

Queen Elizabeth and Prince Philip host occasional public receptions attended by thousands of invited guests from all walks of life. Members of the royal family sponsor hundreds of charities. The Queen herself is patron to over 600. Queen Elizabeth and Prince Philip write many letters practically every day.

The Queen makes many public appearances, as do other members of the royal family. She visits new facilities such as hospitals and ships, attends opening ceremonies, and goes places to honor people who are doing good for others. For instance, on October 24, 2014, Elizabeth opened an exhibition about the Information Age at the Science Museum in London and sent her first Twitter message. She occasionally gives speeches, but she never grants interviews.

Left Column: Queen Elizabeth II visits Liverpool during her Diamond Jubilee tour of Great Britain, 2012. Queen Elizabeth II visits Nottingham, 2012. Right Column: The Queen attends the opening of Royal Open Air Theatre in Scarborough, 2010. Queen Elizabeth II and Prince Philip ride in the royal coach in the Queen's birthday parade, also called Trooping the Colours in London, 2014.

Lesson 146 - Queen Elizabeth II

The British monarch is head of the Church of England. On Christmas Day, Queen Elizabeth broadcasts an annual message. In her 2014 message she included these words of faith:

> For me, the life of Jesus Christ, the Prince of Peace, whose birth we celebrate today, is an inspiration and an anchor in my life. A role-model of reconciliation and forgiveness, he stretched out his hands in love, acceptance, and healing.

The Queen's Family

Elizabeth and Philip have four children. Prince Charles, born in 1948, is the oldest, pictured as a baby at right. The other children are Princess Anne, born in 1950 and now titled the Princess Royal; Prince Andrew, born in 1960; and Prince Edward, born in 1964. When Andrew and Edward were born, they were the first children in over one hundred years to be born to a British monarch during his or her reign. Elizabeth and Philip have eight grandchildren and five great-grandchildren. The stamp at right celebrates their sixtieth wedding anniversary.

Queen Elizabeth II and Charles

This 2006 UK stamp honors the royal couple's sixtieth anniversary.

The family has seven royal residences, six of which are in or near London: Buckingham Palace, St. James Palace, Kensington Palace, Kew Palace, Hampton Court, and Windsor Castle. The seventh is the Palace of Holyrood House in Edinburgh, Scotland. The family only uses Buckingham Palace, Windsor Palace, and Holyrood House regularly. The family also owns two private residences: Sandringham House in Norfolk in northern England and Balmoral Castle in Aberdeenshire, Scotland. The government of the United Kingdom provides millions of British pounds in financial support each year to the royal family for travel, maintenance on their homes, salaries for staff, and other expenses.

The Queen's sister, Princess Margaret, died of a stroke in 2002. Queen Elizabeth's mother Elizabeth, the wife of George VI, lived to be 101. The Queen Mother (or "Queen Mum" as she was called) was born August 4, 1900, and died March 30, 2002, just a few weeks after the death of Princess Margaret. Since the twentieth century officially began on January 1, 1901, the Queen Mum lived in three centuries! Stamps honoring the Queen Mother are pictured at right.

This Tuvalu stamp honored the Queen Mother on her 80th birthday, and Seychelles honored her on her 100th birthday.

As the heir to the throne, Prince Charles' title is Prince of Wales. He was once married to Diana Spencer, whose title became the Princess of Wales. After their divorce, she died in a car accident in 1997. Their oldest son is Prince William, the Duke of Cambridge, who is heir to the throne after his father Prince Charles. William is married to Princess Catherine, the Duchess of Cambridge. Their oldest son is George, who is the next heir to the throne. The Queen and the next three heirs to the throne are pictured above.

From left on the front row are Prince Charles, Prince George, Prince William, the Queen, and other members of the royal family on the occasion of Prince George's first appearance on the balcony at Buckingham Palace, 2015.

On September 9, 2015, Elizabeth passed her great-great-grandmother Queen Victoria to become the longest reigning monarch in British history. She is leaving a positive **legacy** for her family and her nation.

Honor all people, love the brotherhood, fear God, honor the king.
1 Peter 2:17

Assignments for Lesson 146

Timeline Book — In the box for Lesson 146 on page 31, write "Elizabeth II celebrates 60 years as queen."

Student Workbook or Lesson Review — If you are using one of these optional books, complete the assignment for Lesson 146.

Vocabulary — Write your own definition for each of these words: controversial (1011), impediment (1011), adorn (1014), assent (1014), legacy (1018). Look in the lesson for clues for the meaning of the words. When you are finished writing your definitions, look in a dictionary for comparison.

Creative Writing — Write down five questions you would like to ask Queen Elizabeth II.

Literature — Read chapters 13-14 in *Children of the Storm*.

Turmoil in the Middle East

Lesson 147   Our World Story

The earliest human history involved people, places, and events in Mesopotamia, Canaan, Egypt, and surrounding areas. Today, thousands of years later, some of the most **urgent** stories we hear about in the news involve people and events in those very same places.

The Middle East has a complicated story which is difficult to convey. The issues there involve race, religion, culture, tradition, and politics, thus touching the core of the hearts and beliefs of people there and around the world.

Historical events and decisions made long ago impact what happens there today. It is hard to find any two people who completely agree about what has happened, what is happening, or what should happen. Jews have differing opinions among themselves, and the same is true for Muslims and Christians. The story does not involve only nations within the region. Nations far away have interests in what goes on there and attempt to influence what happens. Within this region live millions of people who endure trial, prejudice, heartache, and loss, but who continue to hope for better days.

The Middle East

Geographers define the Middle East as stretching from the former Soviet republic of Georgia on the Black Sea in the north to Yemen on the southern tip of the Arabian Peninsula to the south, and from Turkey in the west to Iran in the east.

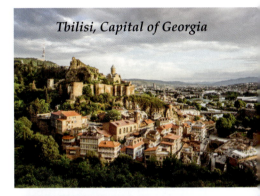
Tbilisi, Capital of Georgia

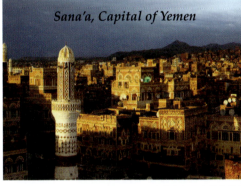
Sana'a, Capital of Yemen

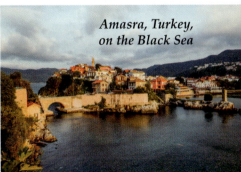
Amasra, Turkey, on the Black Sea

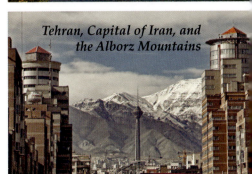
Tehran, Capital of Iran, and the Alborz Mountains

Israel

Many people groups have moved into the Middle East, lived in the Middle East, and left the Middle East. In ancient times, God chose Abraham to be the father of His special, chosen people and set them in the land that has been called at different times Canaan, Israel, and Palestine. Even the name of the region is controversial. God promised to give this land to His people forever (Genesis 17:8), but this promise was conditional on Israel's faithfulness to Him (Deuteronomy 28:58-67).

Islam

In the 600s AD, Muslims spread the religion of Islam from Arabia into the rest of the Middle East and on into northern Africa and the Balkans. Islam became the dominant religious faith in the Middle East. In the centuries that followed, Muslims spread their faith into Afghanistan, India, Malaysia, and the East Indies. While Islam began in the Middle East, today Indonesia off the coast of Southeast Asia has the largest number of Muslims of any country in the world.

As Islam spread, Muslims took control of Palestine and the city of Jerusalem. Christians recaptured Jerusalem and the area around it for a time during the Crusades, but Muslims took over Palestine again and continued to hold it during the period of the Ottoman Empire. A small number of Jews continued to live in Palestine, as did some Christians. The Muslims, Jews, and Christians who lived there got along relatively well.

Zionism

In the late 1800s and early 1900s, widespread persecution of Jews in Russia and Eastern Europe caused many Jews to want a separate country where they could live securely. This movement was called Zionism. The term Zion for the Jewish homeland refers to the Old Testament name

Left: A long wagon train of Jewish refugees from the Russian countryside travels through a town in Ukraine as they flee persecution. Right: A 1960 stamp from Israel honors Theodor Herzl.

of the location of the temple on Mount Zion in Jerusalem. Theodor Herzl, pictured above at right, was leader of the Zionist movement. A small number of European Jews purchased land in what was then called Palestine. They hoped that a homeland for Jews would be created there. Some Jews began to move onto this land. During World War I, Great Britain stated their approval of establishing a Jewish country. After the war, more Jews moved to Palestine.

Lesson 147 - Turmoil in the Middle East

Left: A Fenced-Off Jewish Immigration Camp in Tel Aviv in the 1920s. Center: Jews gather almonds at a farming cooperative called a kibbutz, c. 1936. Right: Jewish immigrants gather after harvesting hay on a kibbutz by the Sea of Galilee, c. 1938.

The Founding of Modern Israel

During World War I, Britain and France divided up much of the Middle East and planned to oversee it after the war. Britain took Palestine and Iraq while France took Syria and Lebanon. After the war, the League of Nations gave Britain and France the responsibility to oversee the sections they claimed. The way world leaders drew the map of the Middle East at that time has caused problems there. For example, they drew **boundary** lines that divided the homeland of the Kurdish people, who do not now have a country of their own.

The Holocaust during World War II **intensified** the desire of many Jews to establish a homeland. One of the first major actions that the United Nations took after World War II was to pass a resolution that a Jewish state and an Arab state should be founded side by side in Palestine. This resolution passed in 1947. Jews declared the establishment of Israel in 1948, as seen in the photo at right. The United States was the first country to recognize the new nation. Many Palestinians left Israel and became refugees in Muslim countries nearby. See photo below.

David Ben-Gurion, first prime minister of Israel, declares the state of Israel, May 14, 1948. Large poster depicts Theodor Herzl.

Left: Palestinian Refugees; Above: Jews arriving in Israel c. 1950 used tents as temporary housing.

Egypt, Jordan, Iraq, and Syria immediately combined forces to attack Israel. Various Middle Eastern countries have attacked Israel at different times since its founding. Israel has fought back and it has taken land in the West Bank, the Golan Heights, and the Gaza Strip.

The map at left shows the countries of the Middle East as they exist today. Within lands claimed by the government of Israel are small areas where Palestinians live, collectively known as the Palestinian National Authority.

Jews, Israelis, Muslims, and Arabs

The term *Jew* has both an ethnic and a religious meaning. Ethnically, Jews are a people group who are descended from Abraham through Isaac. Modern Jews are primarily descendants of Isaac's grandson Judah because Assyria took the tribes of Northern Israel into captivity and they largely ceased to be a distinct ethnic group. Religiously, Jews follow the religion that is based on the Law of Moses in the Old Testament. There are several sects or groups of Jews that disagree with each other about what it means to follow the Law faithfully. Some people who are not Jews ethnically have converted to Judaism. Some people who are Jews ethnically do not practice the religion of Judaism. Some ethnic Jews have come to believe in Jesus as the Messiah and are called Messianic Jews. Many people who are Jewish both ethnically and religiously live in Israel. Citizens of modern Israel are called Israelis.

Arabs are an ethnic group who **originated** on the Arabian Peninsula. They speak Arabic and follow Arab traditions. Today Arabs live in many different countries. Arab culture is a major influence in the Middle East. Most Arabs are Muslim, but not all. There are Christian Arabs and Jewish Arabs.

Muslims are followers of Islam, the religion founded by Muhammad. Most Muslims who live outside of the Middle East, such as those in northern Africa, Pakistan, Indonesia, and Afghanistan, are not Arabs. Iran is a Muslim country in the Middle East, but most Iranians are Persian.

Lesson 147 - Turmoil in the Middle East

Sunnis and Shiites

The two main factions of Muslims continue to be the Sunnis and Shiites. As we learned in Lesson 63, they differ on who is the rightful leader of Islam since the death of Muhammad and on whether traditional Muslim practices are authoritative in addition to the teachings of the Qur'an. About 80 to 90 percent of Muslims are Sunnis. Shiites are a majority of Muslims in Iran and Iraq and make up a large number (though not the majority) in Saudi Arabia, Lebanon, and some other Arab countries.

Shiite Muslims walk toward a Muslim site in Najaf, Iraq.

Continuing Issues

Terrorism. Throughout history, some individuals and groups have used surprise acts of violence called terrorism to try to achieve certain goals. Some radical Muslims have formed terrorist groups to try to change the situation in the Middle East. These terrorists have carried out attacks in several places around the world. The most devastating terrorist attacks occurring on a single day took place on September 11, 2001, when nineteen terrorists hijacked four U.S. passenger jets. They flew two into the World Trade Center towers in New York City and destroyed them. One struck the Pentagon building outside of Washington, D.C. A fourth was probably headed for another target in Washington, but passengers forced it to crash in Pennsylvania in order to prevent it from reaching its target. Over 2,000 people died in these attacks. See photos of memorials for people who have died in terrorist attacks below.

Left: This memorial in Hyde Park, London, honors people who died in terrorist attacks in London in 2005. Center: Visitors view a portion of the National September 11 Memorial in New York City. Right: This memorial to victims of a bombing in Bali has three linked figures which represent family, friends, and community who are bowed in sorrow and remembrance as they comfort, support, and protect each other.

The Wailing Wall holds special significance for Jews.

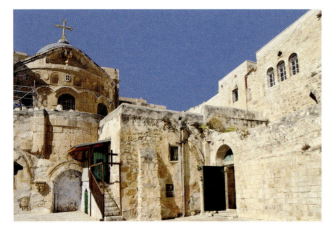

The Church of the Holy Sepulchre holds special significance for Christians.

The Dome of the Rock holds special significance for Muslims.

Jerusalem. The basic issue in Israel involves who owns what land. Part of the land issue is the question of who should control Jerusalem. Jews want it and Muslims want it. Jews, Muslims, and Christians have strong religious reasons to want access to Jerusalem. Sites that have special significance to each group are pictured at left.

Oil. The Middle East is home to much of the world's known oil reserves. Many countries in other parts of the world want to buy that oil. Because of this, the relations between oil-buying nations and Middle Eastern nations are important. Oil facilities in Bahrain are pictured below.

Instability. Beginning in 2010, Egypt and several other Muslim countries experienced uprisings by citizens who called for more freedom and democracy. These protests were called the Arab Spring and resulted in both political changes and increased unrest.

Persecution. Some people in the Middle East have persecuted others who believe differently than they do. Many Middle Easterners have died in religiously-motivated violence, including people from Christian minorities.

Refugees. For decades, tensions in the Middle East have caused people to seek refuge in other places. This has created a crisis as people in those other places work to provide **adequate** food, shelter, and services such as schools, medical care, and sanitation.

Oil and Gas Pipes, Bahrain

Hope for Peace

From time to time, the tension in the Middle East lessens. For instance, Egypt and Jordan have at different times signed separate peace treaties with Israel. Many Muslims and Jews desire a peaceful solution to the conflicts in the Middle East.

Lesson 147 - Turmoil in the Middle East

Turmoil in the Middle East has caused great anguish for many people. Though the situation is complicated, we know for certain that God loves every person who lives there and everywhere and that He wants each of us to love one another.

Beloved, let us love one another, for love is from God;
and everyone who loves is born of God and knows God.
The one who does not love does not know God, for God is love.
1 John 4:7-8

Assignments for Lesson 147

Our Creative World — Read about the re-opening of a church in Turkey on pages 144-145.

Map Book — Complete the assignments for Lesson 147 on Map 43 "The Middle East."

Timeline Book — In the box for Lesson 147 on page 31, write "Protests in Egypt lead to political changes."

Student Workbook or Lesson Review — If you are using one of these optional books, complete the assignment for Lesson 147.

Vocabulary — Write a paragraph that uses all of these words: urgent (1019), boundary (1021), intensify (1021), originate (1022), adequate (1024). Consult a dictionary if you need help with their definitions.

Literature — Read chapters 15-16 in *Children of the Storm*.

Sunrise Over Jerusalem

Sports
Bring Us Together

Lesson 148 — World Landmark

Since ancient times, children and adults have played sports. Sometimes people play for fun with family and friends. Other times people have formal competitions with elaborate rules and rituals associated with the games. In recent decades, several sports have become popular in multiple countries, with large numbers of fans and both professional players and players who play for recreation.

Nippon Professional Baseball Game, Hiroshima, Japan, 2011

Baseball

Baseball originated in the United States in the 1800s, where it still enjoys great popularity. It has also become extremely popular in Japan and has spread to Canada, Mexico, and Korea. Because teams play many games per year, total attendance at baseball games is particularly high compared with other sports. Many professional players in the United States come from Latin America.

Cricket

The game of cricket has an obscure origin that goes back hundreds of years. People across western Europe played various games using a ball and club. By the 1500s, people in England were playing a game similar to modern cricket. It increased in popularity and in the 1800s spread to other parts of the British Empire. Fans in the UK, Australia, and South Africa follow the game closely; and it is especially popular in India and Pakistan.

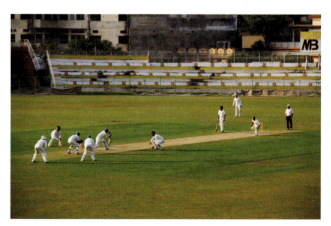

Quaid-e-Azam Trophy Cricket Match, Sialkot, Pakistan, 2011

Spanish player Rafael Nadal returns a ball to Dutch player Robin Haase at the 2010 Wimbledon Championships in England.

Tennis

In the Middle Ages French monks played *jeu de paume*, which involved hitting a ball back and forth with the palm of the hand. The game spread among royal courts of Europe. Louis X of France and Henry VIII of England were avid players. Players began using rackets in the 1500s. Shakespeare makes reference to tennis in his play *Henry V*. The modern game changed in the 1800s with the invention of bouncy rubber balls.

Tennis is not the most popular sport in any one country, but it enjoys wide popularity around the world. Major televised matches have large audiences. The top professional players come from a wide variety of countries. The four major annual tournaments take place in Australia, France, England, and the United States.

Basketball

James Naismith was born and grew up in Canada. He moved to Springfield, Massachusetts, in 1891 and developed the game of basketball for students at the YMCA School for Christian Workers. The YMCA introduced the game in other countries over the next few years. Today basketball is extremely popular in the United States, China, and Turkey, with devoted fans and players in other countries around the world as well.

Turkish Basketball League Game, Izmir, Turkey, 2015

Association Football

When you look at the number of professional teams, the number of attendees per game, the number of television viewers, and the number of amateur and recreational players, association football is by far the world's most popular competitive sport. Known as soccer in the United States and Canada, the game is called football in most other English-speaking nations. It is *fútbol* in Spanish, *futebol* in Portuguese, and *voetbal* in Dutch. In many other languages, the word for football is pronounced in a similar way to the English or is translated into the native words for "foot" and "ball."

Children enjoy football in Suratthani, Thailand, 2014.

Association football officially began in England in 1863. Over the next few decades, the British spread the game around the world. The Fédération Internationale de Football Association (FIFA) formed in Switzerland in 1904. It currently has 209 member associations, representing nearly every populated part of the planet.

Uruguay hosted the first FIFA World Cup in 1930, the same year that country celebrated 100 years of independence. Uruguay defeated Argentina in the final game to win the tournament.

Honduran fans cheer their team in the 2010 World Cup.

The Italian team won the 1934 World Cup in Italy and the 1938 World Cup in France. World War II delayed plans to hold another World Cup in the 1940s.

The World Cup **resumed** in 1950 and has been held every four years since. While countries around the world have hosted the event, the winning team has always been from Europe or South America. Brazil has won the title five times. Germany and Italy have each won four times.

The first FIFA Women's World Championship was held in China in 1991. Held every four years since, the tournament is now known as the FIFA Women's World Cup. The United States team won the first title and has won twice more, making it the winningest national women's team in association football. Two women—Formiga of Brazil and Homare Sawa of Japan—have competed in six World Cup competitions, more than any other male or female player.

Fans in Angola celebrate the first time their national team qualified for the World Cup in 2006.

The Olympic Games

The Olympic Games bring together countries from around the world. We learned about the ancient Olympics in Greece in Lesson 25. The idea of athletes coming together from different places inspired Pierre de Coubertin of France. In 1894 he founded the International Olympic Committee (IOC).

1987 Djibouti Stamp with Coubertin

Coubertin wanted to promote peace and education through sports. He served as President of the IOC from 1896, when the first modern Olympic Games were held in Athens, Greece, until 1925. He said, "The important thing in life is not the **triumph** but the fight; the essential thing is not to have won, but to have fought well."

World Cup Finals

Year	Host Country	Winning Team
1930	Uruguay	Uruguay
1934	Italy	Italy
1938	France	Italy
1950	Brazil	Uruguay
1954	Switzerland	West Germany
1958	Sweden	Brazil
1962	Chile	Brazil
1966	England	England
1970	Mexico	Brazil
1974	West Germany	West Germany
1978	Argentina	Argentina
1982	Spain	Italy
1986	Mexico	Argentina
1990	Italy	West Germany
1994	United States	Brazil
1998	France	France
2002	South Korea / Japan	Brazil
2006	Germany	Italy
2010	South Africa	Spain
2014	Brazil	Germany
2018	Russia	
2022	Qatar	

Stamps celebrate the World Cup. Liberia, 1978; Cabo Verde, 1982; Niger, 1986; and Somalia, 1998

Joan Verdu Sanchez of Andorra skis in a slalom competition in the Winter Games in Austria in 2012.

2000 Olympic Stamp from Malawi

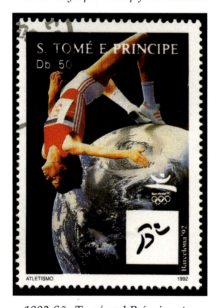

1992 São Tomé and Príncipe stamp illustrates the high jump.

Except for the war years of 1916, 1940, and 1944, the Summer Olympic Games have been held every four years since 1896. The Winter Olympic Games have been held every four years since 1924, except for 1940 and 1944. Originally held in the same year, the Summer and Winter Games now alternate every two years. After the 1992 Winter Games in France, the next Winter Games were held two years later in Norway.

The 2008 Summer Games in Beijing, China, were the biggest ever. A total of 10,942 athletes from 204 countries and territories participated. Since fewer countries have the weather necessary for winter sports, the Winter Games are not as large. However, 2,873 athletes from eighty-eight countries participated in the 2014 Winter Games in Sochi, Russia.

Cities compete with each other for the opportunity to host the Olympic Games. The IOC examines the proposals from each city that wants to host the games and announces its choice several years in advance. Hosting a modern Olympic Games is extremely expensive. The host city must build or renovate arenas and other competition areas. They must also prepare for thousands of athletes and many thousands more trainers, journalists, and spectators who will need accommodations and transportation. Ticket sales for events and money from sponsors offset only a portion of the costs.

London is the only city to have hosted the Olympic Games three times (1908, 1948, and 2012). The United States has hosted the Games more than any other country. It has hosted four Summer Games (1904, 1932, 1984, and 1996) and four Winter Games (1932, 1960, 1980, and 2002). France has hosted two Summer Olympics and three Winter Olympics. The 2016 Summer Games in Rio de Janeiro, Brazil, are the first Olympics held in South America. Beijing is scheduled to host the 2022 Winter Games, which will make it the first city to host both the Summer and Winter Games.

Usain Bolt

The winner of the men's 100-meter dash at the Summer Olympics earns the title of the World's Fastest Man. The earliest official record for this race was set by Donald Lippincott of the United States at the 1912 Olympics in Stockholm, Sweden. Lippincott ran the distance in 10.6 seconds in a **preliminary** heat. He lost the final race.

Lesson 148 - Sports Bring Us Together

One of the most successful Summer Olympic athletes in recent Games is Usain Bolt. Born in Jamaica in 1986, Bolt enjoyed playing cricket as a boy before turning to **sprinting**. At age 17, he was chosen to represent Jamaica at the 2004 Games in Athens but did not earn a medal.

In 2008, at a race before the Olympics, Bolt broke the world record for the 100-meter dash with a time of 9.72 seconds. Later that year, he broke his own record with a time of 9.69 seconds and won the Olympic gold medal in Beijing. See picture above. Bolt also broke the world record for the 200-meter dash, and then he and three other Jamaicans broke the world record in the 4x100 meter relay race.

Bolt sets a world record in the 100 meters at the 2008 Olympics.

At the 2009 Berlin World Championships, Bolt broke his 100-meter world record again with a time of 9.58 seconds and also broke his previous world record in the 200-meter race. At the 2011 World Championships, Bolt and his teammates again broke the world record in the 4x100 meter relay. Returning to the Olympics in 2012, Bolt again won gold medals in the 100-meter and 200-meter races and joined teammates to win gold in the 4x100 meter relay, in which they again broke the world record.

Bolt is Catholic and has used his success to give children in Jamaica opportunities to pursue their dreams through education and cultural development.

Some Remarkable Olympic Medalists

Ole Einar Bjørndalen of Norway has competed in six Winter Games and won thirteen medals, more than any other winter athlete. He competes in the biathlon, which includes cross-country skiing and rifle shooting. During the 2014 Sochi Games, when Bjørndalen was forty years of age, he became the oldest athlete to win a gold medal in an individual event.

Sylke Otto of Germany is the oldest woman to win an individual gold medal. She was champion in the luge at the 2006 Turin Games, when she was thirty-six.

Two female athletes have won gold medals at age thirteen. Marjorie Gestring of the United States was a diver at the 1936 Berlin Games. Kim Yunmi of South Korea was a speed skater at the 1994 Lillehammer Games.

Swimmer Michael Phelps of the United States has won more Olympic medals than any other athlete. He has won a total of twenty-two, including eighteen gold, two silver, and two bronze.

Larisa Latynina, a gymnast from the former Soviet Union, won eighteen medals, including nine gold, five silver, and four bronze. She has the highest medal count among female athletes and the most medals in individual events (fourteen) of any athlete.

Christa Luding-Rothenburger of Germany and Clara Hughes of Canada both won medals in cycling (Summer) and in speed skating (Winter).

Ian Millar of Canada has competed in more Olympic Games than any other athlete. He has ridden horses in equestrian events at ten Olympic Games, starting in 1972. He could have participated in eleven Olympic Games, but Canada boycotted the 1980 Moscow Games. The Canadian equestrian team won silver in 2008, giving Millar his first Olympic medal.

Paea Wolfgramm won a silver medal in boxing at the 1996 Atlanta Games. He is from Tonga, an independent country in the Pacific Ocean. It has about 100,000 people who live on fifty-two islands. Tonga is the smallest independent country to have a medalist in the Summer Olympics.

Even smaller than Tonga is Liechtenstein, a tiny nation between Austria and Switzerland. With nine total medals and a population of less than 40,000, this country has won more medals in comparison to its population than any other. Hanni Wenzel won four of those medals and her brother Andreas won two; both were alpine skiers.

The Olympic Games bring the world together every two years, as thousands of athletes compete before tens of thousands in person and a world television audience of hundreds of millions. To compete in the Olympics is a dream come true for the athletes, who have trained for years. To win a gold medal is the ultimate in athletic accomplishment.

The writer of Hebrews used the image of a race before a large audience to **portray** the Christian life, with Jesus who has run the race before us as our example:

> *Therefore, since we have so great a cloud of witnesses surrounding us,*
> *let us also lay aside every encumbrance and the sin which so easily*
> *entangles us, and let us run with endurance the race that is set before us,*
> *fixing our eyes on Jesus, the author and perfecter of faith,*
> *who for the joy set before Him endured the cross, despising the shame,*
> *and has sat down at the right hand of the throne of God.*
> *Hebrews 12:1-2*

Assignments for Lesson 148

Our Creative World — Read about two Olympic athletes on pages 146-148.

Timeline Book — In the box for Lesson 148 on page 31, write "Olympics are first held in South America."

Student Workbook or Lesson Review — If you are using one of these optional books, complete the assignment for Lesson 148.

Thinking Biblically — Copy Hebrews 12:1-2.

Vocabulary — Copy these words, each on a separate line: resume (1028), triumph (1028), preliminary (1030), sprinting (1031), portray (1032). Look up each word in a dictionary. Next to each word, write what part of speech it is according to the way the word is used in the lesson.

Literature — Read chapters 17-18 in *Children of the Storm*.

Family Activity — Host a "Sillympics." Instructions begin on page FA-57.

God's World
Still Supports Human Life

Lesson 149 — God's Wonders

Our planet originally had two people. It now has over seven billion people. Having more people is good for the world because we have more people to think new thoughts, more people to create opportunities, more people to love and to be loved by.

God Takes Care of the World

After the catastrophic climate change of the flood, when rain fell for the first time and the whole Earth was covered with deep water, God gave Noah and his family this assurance about the climate on Earth:

> *"While the earth remains,*
> *Seedtime and harvest,*
> *And cold and heat,*
> *And summer and winter,*
> *And day and night*
> *Shall not cease."*
> *Genesis 8:22*

People will always have a time of year to plant seeds and a time to harvest them. The Earth will always have cold weather and hot weather. It will always have seasons and daytime and nighttime. We can be confident that God continues to care for the world and the people He made to live on it, for:

> *. . . in Him we live and move and exist . . .*
> *for we also are His children. Acts 17:28*

Tea Harvest in Bangladesh and Winter in the Swiss Alps

Unit 30 - Us

Buada Lagoon in Nauru

St. Kitts

Piton Mountains, St. Lucia

Liechtenstein

Islands of Palau

Good Stewards of Creation

God has the whole world in His hands, from Afghanistan to Zimbabwe. God called the planet He created good, and He wants people to be good managers of what He has provided for us. We should use God's gifts wisely to glorify our Creator and to benefit our families and the people who come after us. We do this out of gratitude to the One who placed it in our care.

God put Adam in the Garden of Eden "to cultivate it and keep it" (Genesis 2:15). Every gardener and farmer knows that raising healthy plants requires attention and care.

The laws God gave to Moses taught conservation. In Deuteronomy 20:19-20, we read, "When you besiege a city a long time, to make war against it in order to capture it, you shall not destroy its trees by swinging an axe against them; for you may eat from them, and you shall not cut them down. For is the tree of the field a man, that it should be besieged by you? Only the trees which you know are not fruit trees you shall destroy and cut down, that you may construct siegeworks against the city that is making war with you until it falls."

In this law, God told his people not to practice careless destruction, even during war. As Christians, our goal is to live at peace with all men. How much more should this apply in time of peace?

Another law instructed the Israelites to let their land rest every seven years as a kindness to the poor and to the animals (Exodus 23:10-11). The Israelites failed to keep this law along with many others. We read in 2 Chronicles 36:15-21 that one of the reasons the Israelites were taken into captivity in Babylon was so that the land could enjoy its sabbath rest.

Market in Honduras

Family Store in Grenada

Lobstering in Wales

Lesson 149 - God's World Still Supports Human Life

In the Book of Jonah, we read that Jonah was angry about his shade plant that withered. Jonah was also disappointed that God allowed the people of Nineveh to repent instead of being destroyed. God challenged Jonah by saying, "You had compassion on the plant for which you did not work and which you did not cause to grow, which came up overnight and perished overnight. Should I not have compassion on Nineveh, the great city in which there are more than 120,000 persons who do not know the difference between their right and left hand, as well as many animals?" (Jonah 4:10-11). God cared about the people of Nineveh, but He also cared about the animals He had created.

We read in Deuteronomy 22:6-7, "If you happen to come upon a bird's nest along the way, in any tree or on the ground, with young ones or eggs, and the mother sitting on the young or on the eggs, you shall not take the mother with the young; you shall certainly let the mother go, but the young you may take for yourself, in order that it may be well with you and that you may prolong your days."

If a person took a wild bird and her eggs to eat, then the mother would not be able to lay more eggs. If we are wasteful of the resources God provides for us, we may make it harder for other people to obtain what they need.

Proverbs 12:10 says, "A righteous man has regard for the life of his animal, but even the compassion of the wicked is cruel." God has given us permission to use animals to work for us and to use them for food, but we must not mistreat them.

As Christians, we can learn conservation principles in the Old Covenant laws God gave to Moses. Ultimately, we should take care of the plants, animals, water, and land around us to honor God. We should also do this to bless other people.

Fishing in Kiribati

Bananas in Barbados

Vegetable Stand in Belize

Rose Harvest in Zambia

Cattle in Liechtenstein

Fruit Market in Vanuatu

Raising Cattle in Andorra

A Bountiful Harvest

People are learning that if they use the natural resources God has provided, the Earth has the capacity to nourish more and more people. The good stewardship God commands works in a practical way. For instance, many companies that harvest lumber now plant more trees than they cut down. These changes have enabled many countries, including Russia, the United States, China, India, Spain, Italy, Vietnam, the Philippines, Turkey, Uruguay, Chile, Cuba, Tunisia, and Morocco, to see their forests grow instead of shrink.

The chart at right and the photos in this lesson illustrate the bounty God has provided, as does this passage King David wrote many centuries ago.

You visit the earth and cause it to overflow;
You greatly enrich it;
The stream of God is full of water;
You prepare their grain,
for thus You prepare the earth.
You water its furrows abundantly,
You settle its ridges,
You soften it with showers,
You bless its growth.
You have crowned the year with Your bounty,
And Your paths drip with fatness.
The pastures of the wilderness drip,
And the hills gird themselves with rejoicing.
The meadows are clothed with flocks
And the valleys are covered with grain;
They shout for joy, yes, they sing.
Psalm 65:9-13

Lentil Harvest in Saskatchewan, Canada

Fig Harvest in Turkey

Date Harvest in Egypt

Quinoa Harvest in Bolivia

Orange Harvest in Brazil

Cranberry Harvest in Massachusetts

Greatest Producers

These countries grow more of these foods than any other country.

Country	Foods
Bolivia	brazil nuts, quinoa
Brazil	coffee, oranges, sugarcane
Canada	lentils, mustard seeds
China	apples, cabbages, carrots, cauliflower, chestnuts, cucumbers, eggs, garlic, grapefruit, grapes, green beans, honey, kiwi, mushrooms, onions, peaches, pears, pork, potatoes, spinach, strawberries, sweet potatoes, tea, tomatoes, watermelons, wheat
Costa Rica	pineapples
Côte d'Ivoire	cocoa beans
Egypt	dates
Germany	gooseberries, rye
India	bananas, buffalo meat, butter and ghee, chickpeas, dry chilies and peppers, ginger, lemons, millet, okra, papayas, sesame seeds
Indonesia	cinnamon, cloves, coconuts, palm oil, vanilla
Iran	pistachios
Mexico	avocados
Nigeria	yams
Russia	barley, oats, raspberries
Saudi Arabia	yogurt
Somalia	camel milk
Spain	olives
Sudan	camel meat
Turkey	apricots, cherries, figs, hazelnuts, poppy seeds
Ukraine	sunflower seeds
United States	beef, blueberries, cheese, corn (maize), cranberries, sorghum, soybeans
Vietnam	cashews

A pineapple grows in Costa Rica.

Vegetable Market in Malawi

Basket of Vegetables in Vanuatu

Lychees in a Fruit Market in Guatemala

Onion Harvest in Zambia

For sale in this market in Tehran, Iran, are sour plums, sour cherries, and forest fruits, along with strips of traditionally dried and processed forest fruits.

For hundreds of years, some people have warned that our planet cannot support large increases in the human population. However, the human population has nearly tripled since 1950, and their dire predictions have not come to pass. Our planet has plenty of space and plenty of resources to support over seven billion people and many more.

Some people do not have reliable and affordable access to enough food, but this is not because the Earth cannot produce enough food for everyone. It is largely caused by poor government and economic systems that disrupt the free trade of food and other resources and by people now and in the past failing to care for the resources God provided. This is not a new problem. As Proverbs says:

Abundant food is in the fallow ground of the poor, But it is swept away by injustice.
Proverbs 13:23

One way that Christians around the world love others is by sharing food and other resources with their neighbors. Christians also look for creative ways to help people make long-term improvements in their lives. Christians help by teaching better farming methods, digging wells, and providing animals such as chickens and goats to help the poor be able to provide for their families.

Lesson 149 - God's World Still Supports Human Life

God created this planet to be inhabited by people made in His image. We should not worship the Earth or treat the environment as more important than people; but since God cares about the birds and animals and plants, we should care about them, too. God invites us to join Him in taking care of the world He gave us. As we do this, we can help other people see the beauty of Creation and learn about the Creator.

Tortilla Factory in Belize

> *For thus says the Lord,*
> *who created the heavens*
> *(He is the God who formed*
> *the earth and made it,*
> *He established it and*
> *did not create it a waste place,*
> *but formed it to be inhabited),*
> *"I am the Lord, and there is none else."*
> *Isaiah 45:18*

Assignments for Lesson 149

Timeline Book — In the box for Lesson 149 on page 31, write "Estimated world population passes 7 billion."

Student Workbook or Lesson Review — If you are using one of these optional books, complete the assignment for Lesson 149.

Thinking Biblically — Copy Genesis 8:22 (found on page 1033) and illustrate the verse.

Creative Writing — Make a list of five things that we can learn about God by observing the world He created.

Literature — Read chapters 19-20 in *Children of the Storm*.

Woman with Fruit in India

Paddy Crop in Bangladesh

Our Interconnected World

Lesson 150 — Daily Life

Your neighbor awakes in the morning to the alarm sounding from his watch made in Switzerland. He reads from a Bible printed in the United States. He makes the bed he purchased from a company based in Sweden. He gets ready for the day with toiletries from Israel that he purchased at a kiosk in the mall. His shirt was made in Honduras, and his trousers were sewn in Vietnam. His shoes were made in Italy. He eats breakfast from a handmade bowl he bought in Peru while on a mission trip. He drinks coffee grown in Brazil.

Vietnamese Clothing Factory

While he eats, he reads the headlines on his smartphone that was designed in the U.S. and assembled in South Korea. The lead story of the day involves news from the Middle East and reminds him to pray for his brother-in-law, who is in the army and serving a tour of duty in Kuwait.

He drives to work in his car, which was made by an American company at its factory in Canada with some parts made in Mexico. As he drives, he listens to music recorded by a group from England.

At work, he has a teleconference meeting with his company's office in Singapore, despite a fourteen-hour time difference. He drinks a cup of tea that was grown in India. He meets a friend for lunch at his favorite Japanese restaurant.

On the way home, he decides to go to the drive-thru window at a Mexican restaurant and pick up some food for supper. After supper, he watches a YouTube video about a missionary in Mozambique whom he knows. Then he emails the missionary to set up a time they can talk face-to-face over the Internet on Saturday afternoon. Before he goes to bed, he reads a chapter from a classic novel written by a French author in a copy printed in China.

We live in an interconnected world. Computer technology is one huge development that has given human beings new opportunities to calculate, create, communicate, and collaborate with each other. The term that is often used to describe the increasing interdependency of people around the world is *globalization*.

No Person Knows How to Make a Pencil

In 1958 businessman Leonard Read wrote an essay entitled, "I, Pencil." He described the different people involved in the manufacture of a plain, ordinary, wooden pencil.

The cedar wood used in the pencil grew in northern California or Oregon. People had to make the tools the lumbermen used to cut it down and transport it. The graphite used in the pencil came from Sri Lanka, the clay from Mississippi, and the wax from Mexico. The eraser was made using rapeseed oil from Indonesia and pumice from Italy. People had to manufacture the containers that carried all these items to the factory. The pencil was made at a factory in Pennsylvania. People designed and built the factory, as well as the power plant that provided its electricity.

Leonard Read explained that no one involved in this complicated process did what he did because he personally wanted a pencil. They each earned a living by performing one small step in the process. Although each person played a part, Read explained, no one person could perform every step involved in making a pencil. We could write an essay like Read's about almost every other product we use.

Top: Pumice Quarry in Italy
Bottom: Oregon Cedar

Getting There and Getting Here

People have traveled for thousands of years, but today more people can travel to more places with less expense and more ease than ever before. A trip across the Atlantic in wind-powered ships took the early English colonists coming to America two months. Today someone can board a plane at an American airport in the evening and have lunch in Paris the next day. See Paris airport at right.

An event in one place has an impact in other places. A flight delay due to a snowstorm in one city causes delays in other cities because many flights are continuous between several cities. Flights cannot leave if they have nowhere to land, and they cannot land if they are "stacked up" in the air above a snow-covered runway.

People from all over the world travel all over the world. Visit a popular tourist site, and you are likely to hear languages from many lands.

Top: Planes wait to be loaded with shipping containers at Charles de Gaulle Airport, Paris. Bottom: Tourists explore a flower garden in Japan.

Getting the Goods

People in one place have traded with people from other places for thousands of years. Much of this trade involved traveling over land, but sea trade was important also. Today 90 percent of the world's trade is carried on the oceans.

A trade caravan once took months or years to travel from Europe to China. The Silk Road and the Spice Road connected different parts of the world, but it took a long time to complete the connection. Today goods can move from China to Europe or the U.S. in a matter of days. Manufacturers can ship raw materials to China, Chinese workers can turn those raw materials into products, and then merchants can ship the products back to the location that sent the raw materials in the first place, all more quickly than a wind-powered trading ship could travel in just one direction. Indian and Chinese clothing factory workers are pictured at right.

Top: Men work in a clothing factory in Delhi, India. Bottom: Women work in a clothing factory in China.

Modern ships carry cargo in sea containers like those at the ports of Hong Kong (left), Rotterdam, The Netherlands (center), and San Pedro, California (right). These sea containers are approximately the size of a semi trailer.

Rapid Communication

Satellite communication has brought people in the world closer to each other. In the twentieth century, a phone call outside your local area was a "long-distance call." Long-distance calls were expensive. Today communication satellites circle the Earth, allowing people to call long distances, talk as long as they like, and not pay anything extra beyond regular monthly phone charges.

Once upon a time events took place in distant parts of the globe that people elsewhere never heard about. Today people hear and see details about events all over the world on television and the Internet just moments after they happen.

In earlier centuries kings and other national leaders had to wait weeks between urgent messages they sent to each other. In January of 1815 British and American soldiers fought against each other in the last battle of the War of 1812. Neither side knew yet that the two sides had signed a peace treaty in Paris weeks earlier. Today a nation's leader can see satellite

Lesson 150 - Our Interconnected World

An ice cream vendor in Malaysia talks on a phone on his motorcycle. Center: A woman in the country of Georgia sells a traditional sausage-shaped candy, called churchkhela, while drinking tea and talking on her phone. Right: A rickshaw driver in Beijing, China, uses his phone, as does another man nearby.

images of any spot on the planet and discuss urgent matters immediately through electronic communication.

During World War II, Allied troops fought in places in the Pacific they had not known of before and their families back home waited weeks to hear from them. Today military personnel can have video calls with the folks back home.

With electronic communication and the easy availability of shipping, people make purchases from all over the world every day without ever leaving home or actually seeing or hearing another human being.

Our world has many networks. We have trade networks, travel networks, voice networks, and data networks. Only a few centuries ago, many people lived and died without ever touching a book. Now, in the Information Age, more information is available to more people more easily than ever before. In fact, information is so valuable to our world that more of the world's economy is in digital networks than in actual products you can touch.

God wants us to be careful what information we allow into our minds. Access to much information requires great discernment as we decide what we read, what we look at, and who we listen to. God teaches us:

> *Finally, brethren, whatever is true, whatever is honorable, whatever is right, whatever is pure, whatever is lovely, whatever is of good repute, if there is any excellence and if anything worthy of praise, dwell on these things. Philippians 4:8*

Important Connections

Our interconnected world means much more than faster travel, easier communication, and increased ways to make purchases. It means that we can know and understand more about the people with whom we share our planet. It means that new inventions and new technologies discovered in one place can help people elsewhere in a relatively short time.

Top: A man in Jodhpur, India, talks on a phone in an outdoor market. Bottom: A woman in Kenya uses a phone at a flower market.

Sea of Galilee

The Son of God, who walked beside the Sea of Galilee 2,000 years ago, called His disciples the light of the world. Living in an interconnected world means that we have an opportunity to shine that light to people in many places. On the night before Jesus died on the cross, He prayed to His Father for His disciples. The prayer He prayed for them is what He desires for all people of the world:

> *The glory which You have given Me I have given to them,*
> *that they may be one, just as We are one;*
> *I in them and You in Me, that they may be perfected in unity,*
> *so that the world may know that You sent Me,*
> *and loved them, even as You have loved Me.*
> *Father, I desire that they also, whom You have given Me,*
> *be with Me where I am, so that they may see My glory*
> *which You have given Me,*
> *for You loved Me before the foundation of the world.*
> *John 17:22-24*

Assignments for Lesson 150

Timeline Book — In the box for Lesson 150 on page 31, write "The world has more mobile devices than people."

Student Workbook or Lesson Review — If you are using one of these optional books, complete the assignment for Lesson 150 and take the test for Unit 30.

Thinking Biblically — Write down five things you have learned about in *From Adam to Us* that show you God is at work in history.

Creative Writing — Who is one person from world history that you would like to meet? Why? Write one paragraph answering these questions.

Literature — Read chapter 21 and the Epilogue in *Children of the Storm*. If you are using the Student Workbook or Lesson Review, answer the literature review questions on *Children of the Storm*.

Family Activity   Unit 16

Mansa Musa's Caravan

This activity will give you a taste of the scale of Mansa Musa's caravan, which displayed his mind-boggling wealth and influence.

Instructions

1. Printable pages for this activity are available here: notgrass.com/a2ulinks

   - Page 1 represents the 500 servants that walked in front of Mansa Musa. There are 100 per page; print five copies.

   - Page 2 represents the horse that Mansa Musa rode. Print one copy.

   - Page 3 represents the 80 camels in Mansa Musa's baggage train. There are 10 per page; print eight copies.

   - Page 4 represents the 60,000 people that traveled in Mansa Musa's caravan. There are 4,000 per page; print fifteen copies. If possible, print on jewel-toned paper (purple, blue, turquoise, magenta) to represent the "brocade and Persian silk" worn by his retinue.

2. Draw three yellow circles on each of the camel pictures to represent the 300 pounds of gold carried by each.

3. Draw Mansa Musa sitting on the horse. What might he have looked like? How would he be dressed? Also draw finery on his horse befitting the wealth of his owner.

4. Cut out the camels. If desired, cut the pages of servants with staffs into strips of 10. If desired, cut the pages of faces into groupings of 1,000.

5. Line up the caravan on the floor, with the servants first, the horse second, the camels single-file next, and lastly the groupings of 1,000. You will need to let the caravan snake around the floor in your house.

Unit 17　　　　　　　　　　　　　　　　　　　　　　　　　　Family Activity

Coral Reef Art

Coral reefs are beautiful underwater cities full of living creatures. See examples of coral reefs in the South China Sea and Indian Ocean in Lesson 81. In this activity, you will create a coral reef using your imagination, dry pasta, and a lot of glue!

Supplies

- large piece of cardboard
- styrofoam pieces (we used cones and spheres)
- pasta in various shapes
- glue (white glue, craft glue, and hot glue are possibilities)
- pipe cleaners (also known as chenille stems or fuzzy sticks)

Please Note: **If you choose to use a hot glue gun for this activity, make sure your children are safe! The hot glue and the glue gun can cause serious burns.**

Instructions

1. Cut cardboard into desired shape. Cover your work surface.

Family Activities

2. Arrange styrofoam pieces and glue to cardboard. We cut our spherical pieces in two to make four flat-bottomed rounded shapes. We also cut the bottom from one of the cones and used both pieces. (You can get creative and use items out of your recycling bin instead of styrofoam pieces. Coral comes in all shapes and sizes!)

3. Go crazy gluing pasta on every surface! We used lasagna, rotini, penne, rigatoni, and shell pasta. To make it look more like coral, group one kind of pasta in an area rather than mixing them up. You can use simple white glue for the flat areas. A stronger glue will be helpful for upright surfaces and 3-D shapes. Craft glue or hot glue (**adult use only!**) would be good choices. For some areas, you might need an extra pair of hands to hold the pasta in place for a moment for the glue to take hold. You can create 3-D shapes on the table and then glue them in place.

4. Make some cute fishies from colorful pipe cleaners. Glue in place.

Enjoy your lively coral reef!

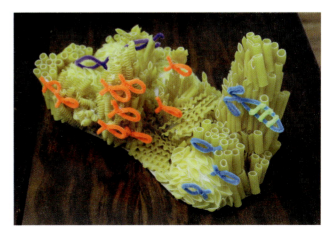

Unit 18　　　　　　　　　　　　　　　　　　　　　　　Family Activity

Making Paper

In the essentials, the process for making paper hasn't changed since it was invented centuries ago. New paper is made from plant fibers, but you can make paper at home using recycled paper and a few simple tools.

Supplies

- paper torn into small pieces, none larger than one-inch square
- blender
- large plastic embroidery hoop (ours is 10 inches in diameter)
- tulle (a fine mesh fabric)
- old towels

Instructions

1. Start with 4 cups of torn paper. Cover with water.

2. Blend water and paper in the blender until it reaches a mushy, pulpy consistency. The more you blend, the smoother your paper will be. Add a little more water if it does not blend well. (If papermaking becomes your new hobby, you might want to buy a cheap blender dedicated to papermaking, as it can be hard on your blender.)

Family Activities

3. Place a double layer of tulle between the two circles of the embroidery hoop and tighten. (3/8 yard of tulle was wide enough for our hoop.)

4. Place hoop on top of a folded towel. Transfer pulp to a bowl. Scoop handfuls of the pulp into the hoop, pressing to make a thin, even layer. You don't want any holes and you want the thickness to be consistent. Fill the circle and press well with your hand.

5. Fold the towel over and press firmly to squeeze out as much water as possible. Be careful not to disturb the paper layer. Slowly and carefully peel back the towel.

6. Place paper on rack to dry. You can remove the embroidery hoop and insert more tulle to make another sheet of paper. Four cups of torn paper plus water should be enough for two 10-inch paper circles. Drying time will depend on the thickness of your paper.

Papermaking is experimental. Try different kinds of recycled paper. You can stir in accents like glitter or tiny bits of yarn, grass, leaves, and/or flower petals after blending. What will you create?

Unit 19 — Family Activity

Creation Collage

This activity for all ages and levels lets everyone work together to celebrate God's Creation!

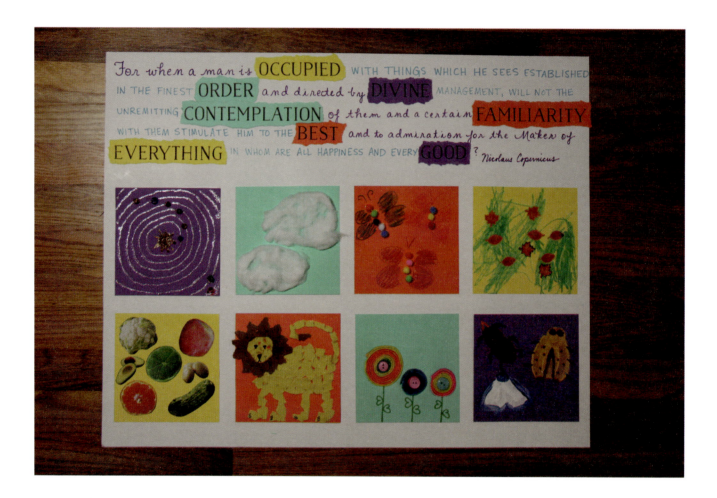

Supplies

- white posterboard
- colored paper
- various art media of your choice

Instructions

Write the following quote on the posterboard:

> For when a man is occupied with things which he sees established in the finest order and directed by divine management, will not the unremitting contemplation of them and a certain familiarity with them stimulate him to the best and to admiration for the Maker of everything, in whom are all happiness and every good? — Nicolaus Copernicus

Give each participant a piece of paper. We used 6-inch squares. Let each person decide his or her subject and medium to feature one of God's creations. Glue to posterboard.

See our collage for inspiration. We used markers, glue, paper, glitter glue, cotton balls, pompons, crayons, stickers, magazine photos, yarn, buttons, and paint.

Unit 20   Family Activity

Silver Coins of Potosi

Your kitchen will be a silver mine in this activity where you make coins that you can eat!

Please Note: **Adult supervision and involvement is required for this activity. Recipe requires the use of a knife and heat. Please make sure your children are safe!**

Supplies

- 30-35 small paper cups
- 12-oz bag chocolate chips
- saucepan and metal mixing bowl OR microwave-safe bowl
- aluminum foil
- pencil

FA-40

Instructions

1. Cut about 30 paper cups down to about one inch tall.

2. Melt chocolate. On the stove, set a metal bowl on top of simmering water. Be careful of steam burns if you lift the bowl! Or in the microwave, heat the chips on medium for 10 seconds at a time, stirring in between, until they are melted.

3. Stir melted chocolate until it is smooth.

4. Use a spoon to drop a small amount of chocolate into each mold. Gently spread to the edges. Aim for an even thickness for all coins. Ours were about 4 mm thick. Shake cup gently from side to side to help smooth the surface. You'll get the hang of it! Cut a few more cups if needed. (We made 33 two-inch coins with 12 ounces of chocolate.)

5. Avoid getting chocolate on the side of the mold, as this will make the coins hard to remove and look ugly!

6. Arrange on tray and allow to cool until hard.

7. You can cool your coins in the refrigerator to speed the process, but it may cause your chocolate to "bloom" as seen here, a result of sudden changes in temperature. This does not harm the quality or taste but does not look pretty.

   Unmold the hardened chocolate by gently squeezing the top edge of the cup to release and turning the cup upside down.

8. Cut small pieces of aluminum foil about four inches square. With the dull side of the foil up, place the bumpy side of the coin down.

9. Leaving the coin on your work surface, fold corners in to wrap coin. Press back side down firmly. Contact with your hands will cause the chocolate to begin to melt, so touch it as little as possible.

10. Neaten the rim of the coin by pressing with your fingers from the side.

11. With a not-too-sharp pencil, gently draw Spanish and Inca-inspired designs on the front of the coins. See the examples on page FA-40.

Enjoy sharing and eating your coins!

Family Activity   Unit 21

Old World New World Cookbook

This activity celebrates some of the many foods that traveled between the Old World and the New World in the age of exploration, enriching life for people in many places: rice, corn, wheat, sorghum, potatoes, cassava (tapioca), sweet potatoes, chocolate, coffee, sugarcane, and tea.

Supplies

- card stock
- paper
- pens, markers, colored pencils, etc.
- binding for pages (suggestions follow)
- ingredients to prepare one or more recipes

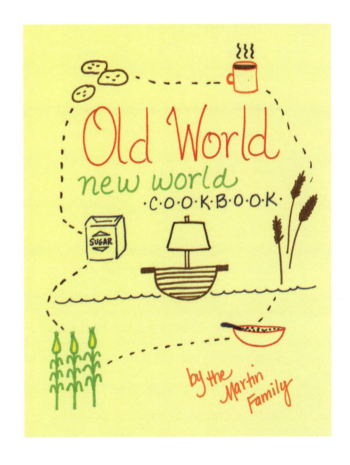

Instructions

1. Choose one recipe for each food listed above. First, choose recipes from your family's favorites. For foods you have not prepared before, find a new recipe you would like to try. It is not necessary to test every recipe that you have not tried before, but it would be fun to try one or more new ones.

2. Make a colorful cover for the cookbook on card stock with the title "Old World New World Cookbook."

3. Title each page with the featured food. Include a fact from Lesson 103 for each food. Then copy the recipe and illustrate the page.

4. Bind the cookbook with your preferred method, such as:
   - 3-hole punch the pages and insert in a 3-prong folder or narrow 3-ring binder.
   - 3-hole punch the pages and tie the holes with yarn or string (use another piece of card stock for a back cover).
   - Place pages in a file folder and staple near the fold.
   - Have the pages spiral-bound at a print shop.

5. Enjoy making and eating one or more of your new recipes together!

Recipe Ideas

- rice: fried rice, stir fry with rice, Spanish rice, rice pudding
- corn: cornbread, grits, corn casserole, corn on the cob, popcorn
- wheat: bread, cookies, muffins, pancakes, waffles, cake, pie
- sorghum: syrup on pancakes or waffles, sorghum flour used in many gluten-free recipes
- potatoes: baked potatoes, mashed potatoes, roasted potatoes, potato soup
- cassava (tapioca): tapioca pudding, tapioca flour used in many gluten-free recipes
- sweet potatoes: baked sweet potatoes, sweet potato casserole, roasted sweet potatoes, sweet potato soup, sweet potato pie
- chocolate: cake, cupcakes, cookies, hot chocolate, chocolate milk, fudge, frosting
- coffee: coffee, coffee-flavored desserts
- sugar: candy, many desserts
- tea: iced tea, hot tea, chai

Family Activity   Unit 22

Let's Go to London Game

Make this memory match game of London landmarks and icons. Then challenge your family members to play with you!

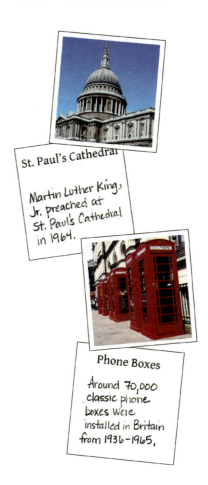

Instructions

1. Print the "Let's Go to London" game cards found at notgrass.com/a2ulinks on white card stock. You can also make your own cards. Print a set of cards on paper to serve as a matching guide when you play the game.

2. Research to discover one interesting fact about each location or icon. You can research in books, encyclopedias, or the Internet (with adult supervision).

3. Neatly write the fact on the card that corresponds to each location and icon. Use a pencil so the words cannot be seen through the back of the card.

4. Cut out the cards.

How to Play

Shuffle cards. Lay them facedown in rows. In turn, players turn over two cards. If the cards do not match, turn them back over, and the next player takes a turn. If the cards match, the player keeps those two cards and continues turning over cards two at a time until he does not get a match. Game is over when all matches are located. Player with the most matches is the winner.

Unit 23   Family Activity

A Musical Evening

This 1985 stamp from India commemorates the 300th anniversary of the birth of Handel and Bach. Though they were born in the same year less than 100 miles apart, these two great composers never met.

In Lesson 113 you learned about Bach and the way people enjoyed music in his day. This activity guides you in celebrating music with your family (and friends, if you wish) in your home.

As you share a musical evening with your family, you will learn more about music and about each other. Have each family member prepare ahead of time to share one of their favorite songs or pieces of music. It can be from any musical genre. Here are some suggestions of ways people can share about music:

- Share a favorite hymn or praise song. Lead the others in singing. Share the background story of the song and its writer. Tell about any other special historical connections. Tell why the song is important to you.

- Share a favorite folk song. Lead the others in singing. Share the background story of the song and its writer. Tell about any other special historical connections. Tell why the song is important to you.

- Share a favorite classical piece. Play a recording of it. Share about the composer and any historical information about the piece. Share about the musicians who recorded the piece.

- Perform a piece of music on an instrument or with singing. Tell about the song/piece you share.

Domenico Scarlatti was also born in 1685, in the Italian Kingdom of Naples. He worked as a composer in Italy, Portugal, and Spain.

- Share a song by a contemporary performing artist. Tell the background of the song and something about the artist.

If you wish, invite friends to join the evening. Let them know to prepare ahead of time to share a song or piece of music that is important to them. Serve refreshments and enjoy sharing the gift of music!

Two prominent English hymnwriters lived at the same time as Johann Sebastian Bach. Isaac Watts (1674-1748) wrote at least 600 hymns, including "Joy to the World," "O God, Our Help in Ages Past," and "When I Survey the Wondrous Cross." Charles Wesley (1707-1788) wrote at least 6,000 hymns, including "Christ the Lord is Risen Today," "Hark! the Herald Angels Sing," and "And Can It Be That I Should Gain?"

Unit 24 — Family Activity

"The Industrial Revolution: Before and After" Book

The Industrial Revolution brought enormous changes in everyday life. This activity explores specific ways of life before and after these changes.

Instructions

1. Think about the needs and luxuries of everyday life. How are these parts of life different since the Industrial Revolution? List these on a piece of paper: food, shelter, transportation, clothing, toys, tools, and education. Think of at least three other aspects of life to add to the list.

2. Think about how you could photographically represent before and after the Industrial Revolution for each of these aspects of life. See examples at right. Make notes of your ideas for photographs on your list.

3. Take the photographs. Take your time to create interesting, quality photographs. Take a few different shots of each subject so that you have a selection to choose from for your book.

4. Each opening in your book will have one pair of before and after pictures. Look at the samples at right. Write or print the category at the top of the left page and attach your photos to the pages, labeling them "before" and "after." Arrange all pairs of photos in your book. (You may have your photos printed or print them from your computer.)

5. Make a cover for the book with the title "The Industrial Revolution: Before and After" and a title page that includes the names of all those who worked on the book. Give credit to any people who posed for your photographs.

Family Activities   FA-49

Transportation

before

after

Food

before

after

Toys

before

after

6. Bind the pages together with your preferred method, such as:

- 3-hole punch the pages and insert in a 3-prong folder or narrow 3-ring binder.

- 3-hole punch the pages and tie the holes with yarn or string (use another piece of card stock for a back cover).

- Place pages in a file folder and staple near the fold.

- Have the pages spiral-bound at a print shop.

Stories by Hans Christian Andersen

Unit 25 — Family Activity

Choose at least three stories by Hans Christian Andersen to read aloud as a family. Below is a list of some of his most popular stories. The titles are sometimes translated differently:

- The Brave Tin Soldier
- The Emperor's New Clothes (or Suit)
- The Little Match-Seller
- Little Tiny or Thumbelina
- The Princess and the Pea
- The Ugly Duckling

You can find a link at notgrass.com/a2ulinks to free online versions of his works with illustrations from the 1800s, such as the one at right of Thumbelina.

Please Note: **The original versions of Andersen's fairy tales are often quite different from modern retellings of them. Some of the stories include violent and otherwise disturbing content. Be aware that you may want to preview Andersen's stories before reading them to or giving them to your child.**

Eiffel Tower Collage

In this activity, you will create five different images of the Eiffel Tower using different media, then combine the images to create a series of collages. You can do this activity by yourself or with other family members. Depending on the number of people involved, one person can create multiple images or people can work as a team on a single image.

Supplies

- 5 copies of an 8"x10" Eiffel Tower image (we have one here: notgrass.com/a2ulinks)
- 5 pieces of white paper cut to 8"x10"
- choice of 5 of these media: paint, chalk, colored pencil, ink, crayons, pencil, pastels, markers
- construction paper in 5 different colors 9"x12"
- magazines, catalogs, newspaper, junk mail, etc. (to cut out letters and numbers)
- glue stick

Instructions

1. Have each person choose a medium for his or her image. Give each person a piece of white paper and an image of the Eiffel Tower.

2. Have each person go to a different location in the house to work. Each person: Trace the basic outline of the Eiffel Tower on 8"x10" white paper (holding paper on a window during daylight helps make tracing easy). Using the media of choice, draw the Eiffel Tower and other parts of the image on the paper. Each person may choose how much detail to include in his or her image and what colors to use, if applicable to media. People can add their own artistic flourishes as desired. Take time to create an interesting, quality image.

3. Back together as a group, cut each image into five strips, 8 inches by 2 inches each (as shown in example and on Eiffel Tower image).

4. Place one strip from each image onto the 5 pieces of construction paper, creating five different complete pictures for each piece of construction paper. Glue in place with a small gap between each strip.

5. Working as a group, look through magazines, catalogs, newspaper, junk mail, etc. to find and cut out a variety of interesting letters and numbers to spell out:

   EIFFEL TOWER 1889

6. Glue the letters and numbers evenly spaced along the bottom of the 5 pieces of construction paper divided as follows: E I F / F E L / T O W / E R 1 / 8 8 9

7. Display your beautiful collages!

Family Activity   Unit 27

"Should Have Called It" Game

Telephone? Why not a "Talky-talky," "Sleepwrecker," or "Buzzing Box"? This game will inspire creativity and laughter. The more players the better, so invite some extended family or friends to join you.

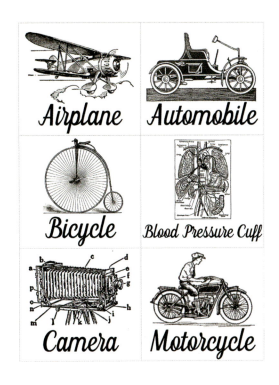

Supplies

- Game cards and slips available for printing at notgrass.com/a2ulinks (or use index cards and paper of one color, not white)
- pencils

Instructions

1. Print and cut apart the printed game cards if using these. If you are not using the printed game cards, write these words on separate index cards. Illustrate them if desired.

Airplane	Camera	Plastic
Automobile	Carpet Sweeper	Radio
Bicycle	Motorcycle	Telephone
Blood Pressure Cuff	Movie	X-Ray

2. Print the provided blank paper slips on colored paper (all on one color, not white), if using them. Print one page of slips per person playing. If making your own strips, cut slips of paper (all of one color, not white) of equal size (2.5" square is a good size).

FA-53

Game Play

1. Seat all players around a table. Place cards with names of inventions in a stack face down in the center of the table. Provide each player with slips of paper and a pencil. Assign a scorekeeper.

2. Each round proceeds as follows:

   - Player 1 turns over an invention card and shows it to all other players.
   - All players except Player 1 make up an alternate name for the invention and secretly write it on a slip of paper.
   - Players hand in their slips face down to the player seated at Player 1's right (Player 2).
   - After all slips are collected, Player 2 mixes them and reads all the alternate names aloud, but does not reveal who wrote them.
   - Player 2 reads each slip again. After each slip is read, Player 1 tells the name of the person whom he thinks wrote it. Player 2 places the slip face down in front of that person.
   - When all slips have been placed in front of players (there will be one slip in front of each player except Player 1), players turn over the slip in front of them.
   - Players raise their hand if Player 1 guessed their alternate name correctly. Player 1 gets 1 point for each correct guess. All players whose alternate name was not guessed correctly get 1 point.

3. Play then shifts to Player 2, who turns over another card and shows it to all other players. All other players (including Player 1), secretly write an alternate name for the invention on a slip of paper. Players hand in their slips face down to the player seated on Player 2's right (Player 3). The round proceeds as described above. Continue the rounds, giving each player at least one chance to guess the answers. The player with the most points accumulated at the end is the winner.

For continued play, you can make your own cards featuring other inventions!

Family Activity — Unit 28

Share Narnia

During World War II, C. S. Lewis took in three girls from London, who came to live at The Kilns to get away from German bombing. This was one of many experiences that influenced the creation of The Chronicles of Naria.

Lewis completed writing *The Lion, the Witch, and the Wardrobe* in 1949. By the time it was published in 1950, Lewis was already writing other books in the series. *The Lion, the Witch, and the Wardrobe* has sold many millions of copies around the world, having been translated into 47 languages.

Gather together as a family, put all electronic devices in another room, and read aloud the first five chapters of *The Lion, the Witch, and the Wardrobe*. If you enjoy it, read the rest of the book together!

C. S. Lewis Mural in Belfast, Northern Ireland

Unit 29 — Family Activity

Twentieth-Century Interview

In this activity, you will learn about the twentieth century from a person who was there.

1. Select a person to interview who was born early enough to remember the twentieth century. You can select one of your parents, grandparents, aunts, uncles, friends, etc.

2. Here are some possible interview questions. Add two or three questions of your own to the list.

   - What was your life like when you were a child?
   - What are some historic events of the twentieth century that you remember?
   - Who were some of the most notable people of the twentieth century in your opinion?
   - Did you travel outside of your own country during the twentieth century? If so, please tell me about it.
   - What is something from the twentieth century that you miss?

3. Schedule the interview at a convenient time and place for the interviewee.

4. Practice reading your questions ahead of time.

5. Make a video or audio recording of your interview. Ask a family member to help you with the recording if needed. Share the recording with your family afterward.

6. During the interview, ask a few appropriate follow-up questions. For example, suppose you asked your interviewee, "Who were some of the most notable people of the twentieth century in your opinion?" and he or she answers, "I admire Mother Teresa, Martin Luther King, Jr., and my grandparents." You could follow-up with, "Would you tell me more about your grandparents?"

7. Be attentive, polite, and respectful during your interview.

8. Send a thank you note to your interviewee following the interview.

Family Activity • Unit 30

Sillympics

Host a fun and zany family Sillympics at ideal local sports venues: your living room and backyard! Invite friends and family!

Instructions

1. Choose an appropriate number of events, based on the number of people participating. Here are some ideas. Add your own!

    How many marbles can you pick up and drop in a bucket with your toes in one minute?
    How many T-shirts can you put on in one minute?
    How many cookies or crackers or blocks can you stack before they fall?
    How long can you go without smiling (while people try to make you!)?
    How many pieces of torn paper can you make out of one piece of paper in one minute?
    How long can you keep two balloons in the air?
    How many pens or pencils can you hold in one hand before one falls?
    How many beans are in the jar?
    Throw a ball or bean bag in a bucket several feet away
    High jump
    Long jump
    Shoe kick
    Staring contest
    Relay race
    Three-legged race
    Sack race
    Wheelbarrow race (one participant holds a partner's ankles while he walks on his hands)
    Carry a (hard-boiled) egg on a spoon race
    Hop on one foot race
    Crabwalk race
    Spelling Bee

2. Make a program listing the order of your events.

3. Make paper medals in gold, silver, and bronze (the closest colors you can find). Trace a circle with the top of a glass. Cut out circles. Punch a hole near the edge and string a piece of yarn through the hole long enough to place easily over a person's head. Decorate as you wish. Make one of each medal for each event on your program and include the name of the event. (You can also use small paper plates for medals.)

4. Provide a stick-on name tag for each participant. Write the names of lesser-known countries on the tags ahead of time. Before you start your events, let each participant choose what country he or she will represent.

5. Prepare snacks and cool drinks for the participants to enjoy at the "closing ceremonies."

6. Designate someone to take pictures at each event, keep time if needed, and keep records of winners.

7. Provide platforms of successive heights for bronze, silver, and gold medalists (such as step-stools and foot-stools).

8. Have a zany good time at your Sillympics! Have a medal ceremony for all events at the end.

Credits

Historical maps by Nate McCurdy. The push pins on the unit intro world maps are © Angela Jones/Shutterstock.com. Images marked with one of these codes are used with the permission of a Creative Commons Attribution or Attribution-Share Alike License. See the websites listed for details.

CC-BY-2.0	creativecommons.org/licenses/by/2.0/
CC-BY-SA-2.0	creativecommons.org/licenses/by-sa/2.0/
CC-BY-SA-2.0-DE	creativecommons.org/licenses/by-sa/2.0/de/
CC-BY-3.0-DE	creativecommons.org/licenses/by/3.0/de/
CC-BY-SA-3.0	creativecommons.org/licenses/by-sa/3.0/
CC-BY-SA-3.0-DE	creativecommons.org/licenses/by-sa/3.0/de/
CC-BY-SA-4.0	creativecommons.org/licenses/by-sa/4.0/

509	David Herraez Calzada/Shutterstock.com
511	Quick Shot/Shutterstock.com
512t/m	Quick Shot/Shutterstock.com
512b	James Michael Dorsey/Shutterstock.com
513	Watchtheworld/Shutterstock.com
514	Walters Art Museum / CC-BY-SA-3.0
515l	Quick Shot/Shutterstock.com
515r	Vixit/Shutterstock.com
516	Sue Smith/Shutterstock.com
517t	Valery Egorov/Shutterstock.com
517bl	Bildagentur Zoonar GmbH/Shutterstock.com
517br	Marcin-linfernum/Shutterstock.com
518t	Samot/Shutterstock.com
518m	Sergio Gutierrez Getino/Shutterstock.com
518bl	David Hughes/Shutterstock.com
518br	Viacheslav Lopatin/Shutterstock.com
519t	RossHelen/Shutterstock.com
519bl	AVN Photo Lab/Shutterstock.com
519bm	Aleksei Lazukov/Shutterstock.com
519br	Jan Mastnik/Shutterstock.com
520tl	Ancher/Shutterstock.com
520tr	GTS Productions/Shutterstock.com
520bl	Dawid Lech/Shutterstock.com
520br	dtopal/Shutterstock.com
521	Gareth Kirkland/Shutterstock.com
522	Filimages/Shutterstock.com
523	Nancy Bauer/Shutterstock.com
524	Kletr/Shutterstock.com
526	NASA image courtesy Jeff Schmaltz, MODIS Rapid Response Team at NASA GSFC.
527	Clockwise from Top Left: Stockr/Shutterstock.com;OlenaTur/Shutterstock.com;canadastock/Shutterstock.com; Brian Burk / Flickr / CC-BY-2.0; Tatiana Popova/Shutterstock.com; Tatiana Popova Shutterstock.com; Kevin Poh / Flickr / CC-BY-2.0; Kārlis Dambrāns / Flickr / CC-BY-2.0; Tatiana Popova Shutterstock.com; cesc_assawin/Shutterstock.com
528t	canadastock/Shutterstock.com
528b	Zvonimir Atletic/Shutterstock.com
529	Anibal Trejo/Shutterstock.com
530	karnizz/Shutterstock.com
531t	katatonia82/Shutterstock.com
531bl	Henner Damke/Shutterstock.com
531br	Marc Venema/Shutterstock.com
532t	Mariusz Strawinski / Flickr / CC-BY-2.0
532ml	Alexander A.Trofimov/Shutterstock.com
532m	Niar/Shutterstock.com
532mr	Niar/Shutterstock.com
532bl	kosmos111/Shutterstock.com
532br	Jules & Jenny / Flickr / CC-BY-2.0
533tl	chrisdorney/Shutterstock.com
533tm	Renata Sedmakova/Shutterstock.com
533tr	Renata Sedmakova/Shutterstock.com
533b	Chamille White/Shutterstock.com
535	Top to Bottom: Bildagentur Zoonar GmbH/Shutterstock.com; Roni Ben Ishay/Shutterstock.com; jorisvo/Shutterstock.com; InavanHateren/Shutterstock.com
536	Luke Jones / Flickr / CC-BY-2.0
538	Malcolm Chapman/Shutterstock.com
538	Ron Ellis/Shutterstock.com

539	Randy OHC / Flickr / CC-BY-2.0	561tr	rook76/Shutterstock.com
540	Peter Probst/Shutterstock.com	561b	LianeM/Shutterstock.com
541	Sergey Novikov/Shutterstock.com	562t	OPIS Zagreb/Shutterstock.com
543	Dung Pham Hoang Tuan/Shutterstock.com	562b	Danield/Shutterstock.com
544tl	A Cotton Photo/Shutterstock.com	563	muharremz/Shutterstock.com
544tr	Mike Veitch/Shutterstock.com	564	Lefteris Papaulakis/Shutterstock.com
544ml	designbydx/Shutterstock.com	565	the lost gallery / Flickr / CC-BY-2.0
544mr	Sergey Novikov/Shutterstock.com	566	Koraysa/Shutterstock.com
544b	Filip Fuxa/Shutterstock.com	568	Renata Sedmakova/Shutterstock.com
545tl	Mark Atkins/Shutterstock.com	569	Tomasz Bidermann/Shutterstock.com
545tr	Andrey Armyagov/Shutterstock.com	570t	Viacheslav Lopatin/Shutterstock.com
545b	cbpix/Shutterstock.com	570b	Olga Popova/Shutterstock.com
546t	Los Angeles County Museum of Art (www.lacma.org)	571t	Wikimedia Commons
546b	Attila JANDI/Shutterstock.com	571b	Aleks49/Shutterstock.com
547t	feiyuezhangjie/Shutterstock.com	572	Nattee Chalermtiragool/Shutterstock.com
547b	Joinmepic/Shutterstock.com	573	Raxenne / Flickr / CC-BY-2.0
548	PerseoMedusa/Shutterstock.com	574	Neftali/Shutterstock.com
549	NASA Goddard Space Flight Center Image by Reto Stöckli (land surface, shallow water, clouds). Enhancements by Robert Simmon (ocean color, compositing, 3D globes, animation). Data and technical support: MODIS Land Group; MODIS Science Data Support Team; MODIS Atmosphere Group; MODIS Ocean Group Additional data: USGS EROS Data Center (topography); USGS Terrestrial Remote Sensing Flagstaff Field Center (Antarctica); Defense Meteorological Satellite Program (city lights).	575	Pat Hawks / Flickr / CC-BY-2.0
		577t	ueuaphoto/Shutterstock.com
		577b	francesco de marco/Shutterstock.com
		578	photosmatic/Shutterstock.com
		579tl/tr	Walters Art Museum / CC-BY-SA-3.0
		579b	Valeri Potapova/Shutterstock.com
		580t	Mariia Golovianko/Shutterstock.com
		580b	Umberto Shtanzman/Shutterstock.com
		581t	canadastock/Shutterstock.com
		581bl	canadastock/Shutterstock.com
		581mr	Maciej Czekajewski/Shutterstock.com
		581br	S.Borisov/Shutterstock.com
		582	Paolo Costa/Shutterstock.com
550	Joinmepic/Shutterstock.com	583tl	Los Angeles County Museum of Art (www.lacma.org)
551	Sean Pavone/Shutterstock.com	583bl	Phant/Shutterstock.com 89044615
552t	aphotostory/Shutterstock.com	583tr/mr	Evgeniya Karpova/Shutterstock.com
552m	chungking/Shutterstock.com	583br	Jean-Michel Moullec / Flickr / CC-BY-2.0
552b	pan demin/Shutterstock.com	584	Ivan Varyukhin/Shutterstock.com
553t	gary718/Shutterstock.com	585t	Ivan Varyukhin/Shutterstock.com
553m	Brian Kinney/Shutterstock.com	585b	NikAlex/Shutterstock.com
553b	Brian Kinney/Shutterstock.com	586	BestPhotoPlus/Shutterstock.com
554	Nate McCurdy	587	Top Left: BestPhotoPlus/Shutterstock.com; All Others: ID1974/Shutterstock.com
555	Brian Kinney/Shutterstock.com	588t	Vladimir Wrangel/Shutterstock.com
556	Gilles Paire/Shutterstock.com	588b	BestPhotoPlus/Shutterstock.com
557	StockPhotosArt/Shutterstock.com	589	Walters Art Museum / CC-BY-SA-3.0
558	Francisco Javier Gil/Shutterstock.com	590	Los Angeles County Museum of Art (www.lacma.org)
559	Morocco: Maciej Czekajewski/Shutterstock.com; Western Sahara: David Stanley / Flickr / CC-BY-2.0; Mauritania: Oksana Ph/Shutterstock.com; Gambia: Anton_Ivanov/Shutterstock.com; Senegal: Sean 2013/Shutterstock.com; Guinea: Jeff Attaway / Flickr / CC-BY-2.0; Guinea-Bissau: gaborbasch/Shutterstock.com	591t	Everett Historical/Shutterstock.com
		591b	Walters Art Museum / CC-BY-SA-3.0
		592tl	Patrik Tschudin / Flickr / CC-BY-2.0
		592tr	Richard Rutter / Flickr / CC-BY-2.0
		592mr	Biblioteca General Antonio Machado (Fondo Antiguo) / Flickr / CC-BY-2.0
560	marzolino/Shutterstock.com		
561tl	rook76/Shutterstock.com		
561tm	nadi555/Shutterstock.com	592bl	Library of Congress

Credits and Sources

592bm	Jorg Hackemann/Shutterstock.com
592br	Kiev.Victor/Shutterstock.com
593	Everett Historical/Shutterstock.com
594l	Francisk Skarina/Shutterstock.com
594tr	IgorGolovniov/Shutterstock.com
594br	chrisdorney/Shutterstock.com
595	Top to Bottom: Lefteris Papaulakis/Shutterstock.com; Boris15/Shutterstock.com; Sergey Kohl/Shutterstock.com; YANGCHAO/Shutterstock.com
597	Los Angeles County Museum of Art (www.lacma.org)
598t	Elzbieta Sekowska/Shutterstock.com
598	Animals, Clockwise from Top Left: ostill/Shutterstock.com; bobistraveling / Flickr / CC-BY-2.0; David / Flickr / CC-BY-2.0; Eduardo Rivero/Shutterstock.com; Cameris/Shutterstock.com; Alexey Stiop/Shutterstock.com; Andy Poole/Shutterstock.com; Lighttraveler/Shutterstock.com; Niall Corbet / Flickr / CC-BY-2.0
599t	KBF Media/Shutterstock.com
599b	Gail Johnson/Shutterstock.com
600	Clockwise from Top Left: Narongsak Nagadhana/Shutterstock.com; Jorg Hackemann/Shutterstock.com; Gail Johnson/Shutterstock.com; Alex.Polo/Shutterstock.com; Jorg Hackemann/Shutterstock.com; Linda Hilberdink Photography/Shutterstock.com; Steve Allen/Shutterstock.com; Armando Frazao/Shutterstock.com;
602	Danor Aharon/Shutterstock.com
603	Charlesimage/Shutterstock.com
604	Top to Bottom: Jean-Michel Moullec / Flickr / CC-BY-2.0; www.sandatlas.org/Shutterstock.com; Los Angeles County Museum of Art (www.lacma.org)
605l	Jun Mu/Shutterstock.com
605tr	chungking/Shutterstock.com
605br	chungking/Shutterstock.com
606tl	François Philipp / Flickr / CC-BY-2.0
606tr	Jun Mu/Shutterstock.com
606b	Dishes: Los Angeles County Museum of Art (www.lacma.org)
607t	Los Angeles County Museum of Art (www.lacma.org)
607b	Xuan Che / Flickr / CC-BY-2.0
608	Joinmepic/Shutterstock.com
609	funkyfrogstock/Shutterstock.com
611	Dutourdumonde Photography/Shutterstock.com
612t	Roberto Binetti/Shutterstock.com
612b	gnoparus/Shutterstock.com
613tl/tr	catwalker/Shutterstock.com
613b	ndphoto/Shutterstock.com
614	Aleks49/Shutterstock.com
615	digitalmama824 / Flickr / CC-BY-2.0
616t	MCAD Library / Flickr / CC-BY-2.0
616b	Tramont_ana/Shutterstock.com
617tl	afitz/Shutterstock.com
617tr	Nathan Hughes Hamilton / Flickr / CC-BY-2.0
617b	Gabriele Maltinti/Shutterstock.com
618	Pecold/Shutterstock.com
619t	BlueOrange Studio/Shutterstock.com
619b	Vilainecrevette/Shutterstock.com
621	Claudio Divizia/Shutterstock.com
622t	Neftali/Shutterstock.com
622b	Henner Damke/Shutterstock.com
623t	shtanzman © 123RF.com
623b	tuulijumala/Shutterstock.com
624	Joseph Sohm/Shutterstock.com
625	Montserrat: MarkauMark/Shutterstock.com; USA: Charlesimage/Shutterstock.com; Brazil: Neftali/Shutterstock.com; Dominican Republic: Sergey Kohl/Shutterstock.com; Nicaragua: tristan tan/Shutterstock.com; Paraguay: Boris15/Shutterstock.com; Guatemala: Neftali/Shutterstock.com; Guyana: Lefteris Papaulakis/Shutterstock.com; Colombia: Sergey Kohl/Shutterstock.com; Chile: IgorGolovniov/Shutterstock.com; Peru: Neftali/Shutterstock.com; Cuba: catwalker/Shutterstock.com; USA: Neftali/Shutterstock.com; St. Vincent: neftali/Shutterstock.com; USA: Sergey Kohl/Shutterstock.com
627	Shesternina Polina/Shutterstock.com
628	ermejoncqc/Shutterstock.com
629	irisphoto1/Shutterstock.com
630t	Lefteris Papaulakis/Shutterstock.com
630b	BokehStock/Shutterstock.com
631tl	Nickolay Stanev/Shutterstock.com
631tr	Bob Cheung/Shutterstock.com
631bl	Lefteris Papaulakis/Shutterstock.com
631br	CHeitz / Flickr / CC-BY-2.0
632t	nbnserge/Shutterstock.com
632b	Kattigara / Wikimedia Commons / CC-BY-SA-3.0
633	Ake13bk/Shutterstock.com
634	Neirfy/Shutterstock.com
635	Everett Historical/Shutterstock.com
636	Stavrida/Shutterstock.com
637	jolly/Shutterstock.com
638	Krylova Ksenia/Shutterstock.com
639	gary yim/Shutterstock.com
640	360b/Shutterstock.com
641t	photogearch/Shutterstock.com
641m	Vladimir Sazonov/Shutterstock.com
641b	Elenarts/Shutterstock.com
642	Iakov Kalinin/Shutterstock.com
643	Bucchi Francesco/Shutterstock.com

645	i4lcoc12/Shutterstock.com
646tl/tr	i4lcocl2/Shutterstock.com
646	Mirek Hejnicki/Shutterstock.com
647t	Peter Allen / Flickr / CC-BY-2.0
647b	Fondo Antiguo de la Universidad de Sevilla / Flickr / CC-BY-2.0
648	Neftali/Shutterstock.com
649t	Georgios Kollidas/Shutterstock.com
649m	gutaper/Shutterstock.com
649b	Sergey Goryachev/Shutterstock.com
650tl	Andrew West/Shutterstock.com
650tr	McCarthy's PhotoWorks/Shutterstock.com
650bl	chrisdorney/Shutterstock.com
650br	McCarthy's PhotoWorks/Shutterstock.com
651	Wikimedia Commons
653t	Walters Art Museum / CC-BY-SA-3.0
653bl	Nanisimova/Shutterstock.com
653br	RnDmS/Shutterstock.com
654	Arkady Mazor/Shutterstock.com
655tr	Leonid S. Shtandel/Shutterstock.com
655bl	Trevor Butcher / Flickr / CC-BY-2.0
655bm	Emmanuel DYAN / Flickr / CC-BY-2.0
655br	Mariusz S. Jurgielewicz/Shutterstock.com
656	Leszek Kozlowski / Flickr / CC-BY-2.0
657	iev.Victor/Shutterstock.com
658tl	rook76/Shutterstock.com
658tr	Songquan Deng/Shutterstock.com
658bl	Alfonso de Tomas/Shutterstock.com
658br	Neftali/Shutterstock.com
659	Mirror: Los Angeles County Museum of Art (www.lacma.org); Stone Sculptures: Walters Art Museum / CC-BY-SA-3.0; Bust: ChameleonsEye/Shutterstock.com
661tl	Free Wind 2014/Shutterstock.com
661bl	hecke61/Shutterstock.com
661r	Pyty/Shutterstock.com
662tl	flocu/Shutterstock.com
662tr	flocu/Shutterstock.com
662ml	chiakto/Shutterstock.com
662mr	Free Wind 2014/Shutterstock.com
662bl	Free Wind 2014/Shutterstock.com
662br	Shutterstock.com
663	Matyas Rehak/Shutterstock.com
664	Curto/Shutterstock.com
665	ihsan Gercelman/Shutterstock.com
666t	BasPhoto/Shutterstock.com
666b	Mikhail Markovskiy/Shutterstock.com
667tl/tr	Photo © Museum Associates / Los Angeles County Museum of Art (www.lacma.org)
667b	ihsan Gercelman/Shutterstock.com
669tl	OlegD/Shutterstock.com
669bl	Sharif Putra Sharif Ubong/Shutterstock.com
669r	anandoart/Shutterstock.com
670	Simon Dannhauer/Shutterstock.com
672	Clockwise from Top Left: non15/Shutterstock.com; reptiles4all/Shutterstock.com; Mawardi Bahar/Shutterstock.com; doctorneab/Shutterstock.com; Pixel Homunculus STOCK/Shutterstock.com; sergette/Shutterstock.com; Don Mammoser/Shutterstock.com; Rueangrit Srisuk/Shutterstock.com; Frolova_Elena/Shutterstock.com
673t	DC_Aperture/Shutterstock.com
673m	PIMPUN TAWAKOON/Shutterstock.com
673bl	Faiz Zaki/Shutterstock.com
673br	Valery Shanin/Shutterstock.com
674t	suphanat/Shutterstock.com
674b	alphonsusjimos/Shutterstock.com
675t	GParker/Shutterstock.com
675b	Lena Serditova/Shutterstock.com
676t	varandah/Shutterstock.com
676b	tristan tan/Shutterstock.com
677tl	Lano Lan/Shutterstock.com
677bl	Art Phaneuf Photography/Shutterstock.com
677r	OlegD/Shutterstock.com
678	JM Travel Photography/Shutterstock.com
679	Anibal Trejo/Shutterstock.com
681	Zoran Karapancev/Shutterstock.com
682l	V. J. Matthew/Shutterstock.com
682r	Kenneth Summers/Shutterstock.com
683	Barry Lewis / Flickr / CC-BY-2.0
684l	Zack Frank/Shutterstock.com
684m	Joseph Sohm/Shutterstock.com
684r	Joseph Sohm/Shutterstock.com
685	Andreas Juergensmeier/Shutterstock.com
685	Stephen Bonk/Shutterstock.com
688	Atosan/Shutterstock.com
689t	Kwiatek7/Shutterstock.com
689b	Patryk Kosmider/Shutterstock.com
690t	gary718/Shutterstock.com
690b	David Steele/Shutterstock.com
691	Neftali/Shutterstock.com
692t	Claudio Divizia/Shutterstock.com
692b	Padmayogini/Shutterstock.com
693t	Claudio Divizia/Shutterstock.com
693b	chrisdorney/Shutterstock.com
694	Earl McGehee / Flickr / CC-BY-2.0
695	Dmitry Chulov/Shutterstock.com
696t	Mark Skalny/Shutterstock.com
696m	Antoshananarivo / Wikimedia Commons / CC-BY-SA-4.0 (cropped)
696b	Jeff Attaway / Flickr / CC-BY-2.0
697l	KalypsoWorldPhotography/Shutterstock.com
697r	pichitchai/Shutterstock.com
698	Top Row: IgorGolovniov/Shutterstock.com; YANGCHAO/Shutterstock.com

Credits and Sources

	Middle Row: irisphoto1/Shutterstock.com; Lefteris Papaulakis/Shutterstock.com; Sergey Kohl/Shutterstock.com; rook76/Shutterstock.com; IgorGolovniov/Shutterstock.com
	Bottom Row: Lefteris Papaulakis/Shutterstock.com; Lefteris Papaulakis/Shutterstock.com; rook76/Shutterstock.com
699t	Joseph Sohm/Shutterstock.com; Magdalena Paluchowska/Shutterstock.com
700	Clockwise from left: Juhku/Shutterstock.com; GUDKOV ANDREY/Shutterstock.com; Zhao jian kang/Shutterstock.com; Alf Ribeiro/Shutterstock.com; bonga1965/Shutterstock.com
701	Top to bottom: joeborg/Shutterstock.com; Milind Arvind Ketkar/Shutterstock.com; Deatonphotos/Shutterstock.com; Kamira/Shutterstock.com
702tl	Vlad Karavaev/Shutterstock.com
702tm	Neftali/Shutterstock.com
702tr	JuRitt/Shutterstock.com
702bl	Matt Ragen/Shutterstock.com
702br	Andrew Bassett/Shutterstock.com
703	Valentyn Volkov/Shutterstock.com
704	Scandphoto/Shutterstock.com
705tl	Adrian Lindley/Shutterstock.com
705tm	rook76/Shutterstock.com
705tr	V. Belov/Shutterstock.com
705bl	Inger Anne Hulbækdal/Shutterstock.com
705br	Erkki & Hanna/Shutterstock.com
706t	Bildagentur Zoonar GmbH/Shutterstock.com
706b	Tommy Alven/Shutterstock.com
708t	rook76/Shutterstock.com
708bl	Boris15/Shutterstock.com
708br	rook76/Shutterstock.com
709	Stavrida/Shutterstock.com
710	Attila JANDI/Shutterstock.com
711	Top Four: Los Angeles County Museum of Art (www.lacma.org); Bottom: mihalec/Shutterstock.com
712	Walters Art Museum / CC-BY-SA-3.0
713	Kasia Soszka/Shutterstock.com
715	Patricia Hofmeester/Shutterstock.com
717	CreativeNature R.Zwerver/Shutterstock.com
718t	Cloud Mine Amsterdam/Shutterstock.com
718b	J. Marijs/Shutterstock.com
719tl	Dennis van de Water/Shutterstock.com
719tr	elroyspelbos/Shutterstock.com
719ml	TonyV3112/Shutterstock.com
719mr	Giancarlo Liguori/Shutterstock.com
719br	Lisa-Lisa/Shutterstock.com
720	Patricia Hofmeester/Shutterstock.com
721tl	brandonht/Shutterstock.com
721tr	Neftali/Shutterstock.com
721bl	Oleg Golovnev/Shutterstock.com
721bm	Elena11/Shutterstock.com
721br	Lana Veshta/Shutterstock.com
722	rook76/Shutterstock.com
724t	Walters Art Museum / CC-BY-SA-3.0
724bl	Elena Ermakova/Shutterstock.com
724br	fayska/Shutterstock.com
725t	Walters Art Museum / CC-BY-SA-3.0
725b	Los Angeles County Museum of Art (www.lacma.org)
726tl	Walters Art Museum / CC-BY-SA-3.0
726tr	Walters Art Museum / CC-BY-SA-3.0
726bl	Walters Art Museum / CC-BY-SA-3.0
726br	Los Angeles County Museum of Art (www.lacma.org)
727	All except top middle: Los Angeles County Museum of Art (www.lacma.org); Top middle: Walters Art Museum / CC-BY-SA-3.0
728	Byelikova Oksana/Shutterstock.com
729	Los Angeles County Museum of Art (www.lacma.org)
730l	Neftali/Shutterstock.com
730r	Lefteris Papaulakis/Shutterstock.com
732t	rook76/Shutterstock.com
732m	Olga Popova/Shutterstock.com
732b	mrHanson/Shutterstock.com
733tl	Jose Ignacio Soto/Shutterstock.com
733tr	pedrosala/Shutterstock.com
733ml	Pecold/Shutterstock.com
733mr	Netfalls - Remy Musser/Shutterstock.com
733bl	Kiev.Victor/Shutterstock.com
733br	Frederic Legrand - COMEO/Shutterstock.com
734	Jorg Hackemann/Shutterstock.com
735	HUANG Zheng/Shutterstock.com
736	Kiev.Victor/Shutterstock.com
737	Top to bottom: orin/Shutterstock.com; Daniel Prudek/Shutterstock.com; kunl/Shutterstock.com; Hung Chung Chih/Shutterstock.com
738	Top to bottom, left to right: Meiqianbao/Shutterstock.com; df028/Shutterstock.com; Meiqianbao/Shutterstock.com; Jimmy Tran/Shutterstock.com; Göran Höglund (Kartläsarn) / Flickr / CC-BY-2.0; Adriena Vyzulova/Shutterstock.com; Anton Jankovoy/Shutterstock.com
739	Clockwise from top left: aleksandr hunta/Shutterstock.com; LIUSHENGFILM/Shutterstock.com; rweisswald/Shutterstock.com; Hung Chung Chih/Shutterstock.com; Zzvet/Shutterstock.com; cnyy/Shutterstock.com; Philip Yuan/Shutterstock.com; Hung Chung Chih/Shutterstock.com; Hung Chung Chih/Shutterstock.com
740	Clockwise from top left: Vladimir Wrangel/Shutterstock.com; Wang LiQiang/Shutterstock.

	com; Bahadir Yeniceri/Shutterstock.com; Vladimir Melnik/Shutterstock.com; Alexandr Junek Imaging s.r.o./Shutterstock.com; sevenke/Shutterstock.com; vonne Wierink/Shutterstock.com; jeep2499/Shutterstock.com; SIHASAKPRACHUM/Shutterstock.com; PeterVrabel/Shutterstock.com; Dmitri Gomon/Shutterstock.com; Vladimir Wrangel/Shutterstock.com; SJ Allen/Shutterstock.com
741t	Göran Höglund (Kartläsarn) / Flickr / CC-BY-2.0
741m	qian/Shutterstock.com
741b	Hung Chung Chih/Shutterstock.com
742	Belozorova Elena/Shutterstock.com
743	Claudio Divizia/Shutterstock.com
744tl	littlesam/Shutterstock.com
744tr	Wikimedia Commons
744b	Pavel L Photo and Video/Shutterstock.com
745t	tristan tan/Shutterstock.com
745	Reenactors: david muscroft/Shutterstock.com
746	Claudio Divizia/Shutterstock.com
747t	Norbert1986/Shutterstock.com
747b	Sergey Goryachev/Shutterstock.com
748	Coinman62 at English Wikipedia
749	Alberto Loyo/Shutterstock.com
751t	Renata Apanaviciene/Shutterstock.com
751b	Axel Rouvin / Flickr / CC-BY-2.0
752tl	KKulikov/Shutterstock.com
752tr	Adamina / Flickr / CC-BY-2.0
752m	Jaideep Khemani / Flickr / CC-BY-2.0
752bl	myroslava/Shutterstock.com
752br	Adamina / Flickr / CC-BY-2.0
753t	gailhampshire / Flickr / CC-BY-2.0
753b	AlexanderZam/Shutterstock.com
754	Parakeet: colin houston / Flickr / CC-BY-2.0; Flying Fox: Luis Correia / Wikimedia Commons / CC-BY-SA-3.0; All others: gailhampshire / Flickr / CC-BY-2.0
755t	Kletr/Shutterstock.com
755b	Dennis Albert Richardson/Shutterstock.com
757	Everett Historical/Shutterstock.com
758	Mikhail Markovskiy/Shutterstock.com
759tl	Popova Valeriya/Shutterstock.com
759bl	mar_chm1982/Shutterstock.com
759r	Olga Popova/Shutterstock.com
760tl	S.Borisov/Shutterstock.com
760tr	volkova natalia/Shutterstock.com
760ml	volkova natalia/Shutterstock.com
760mr	Tereshenok Olga/Shutterstock.com
760b	Leonid Andronov/Shutterstock.com
762	Rostislav Ageev/Shutterstock.com
763t	rook76/Shutterstock.com
763b	Marzolino/Shutterstock.com
764t	eisenach germany/Shutterstock.com
764b	Everett Historical/Shutterstock.com
765tl	Claudio Divizia/Shutterstock.com
765tm	Christian Draghici/Shutterstock.com
765tr	Claudio Divizia/Shutterstock.com
765bl	pixy/Shutterstock.com
765bm	Bildagentur Zoonar GmbH/Shutterstock.com
765br	Claudio Divizia/Shutterstock.com
766l	Claudio Divizia/Shutterstock.com
766r	anyaivanova/Shutterstock.com
767	Igor Bulgarin/Shutterstock.com
768	Marcel Mooij/Shutterstock.com
769	Alberto Loyo/Shutterstock.com
770t	David Berkowitz / Flickr / CC-BY-2.0
770b	Anton_Ivanov/Shutterstock.com
771t	Agustin Esmoris/Shutterstock.com
771b	Tero Hakala/Shutterstock.com
771m	Adwo/Shutterstock.com
772	Top to bottom: hecke61/Shutterstock.com; Wikimedia Commons; Alberto Loyo/Shutterstock.com; Ashley Whitworth/Shutterstock.com
773t	Vladimir Korostyshevskiy/Shutterstock.com
773b	Wikimedia Commons
774	Alberto Loyo/Shutterstock.com
775	Renata Sedmakova/Shutterstock.com
776t	Wikimedia Commons
776m	Bettenberg / Wikimedia Commons / CC-BY-SA-2.0-DE
776b	Timo Pilgram / Wikimedia Commons / CC-BY-SA-3.0-DE
777tl	Skara kommun / Flickr / CC-BY-2.0
777tr	Andreas Praefcke / Wikimedia Commons
777b	David Cranz / Wikimedia Commons
778t	Fernando Garcia Esteban/Shutterstock.com
778b	rook76/Shutterstock.com
779	LEE SNIDER PHOTO IMAGES/Shutterstock.com
781	Everett Historical/Shutterstock.com
783	ER_09/Shutterstock.com
784	Top to bottom: karnizz/Shutterstock.com; Sergey Kelin/Shutterstock.com; posztos/Shutterstock.com; Lemonpink Images/Shutterstock.com
785	Wikimedia Commons
786t	Wikimedia Commons
786b	Walters Art Museum / CC-BY-SA-3.0
787	Hein Nouwens/Shutterstock.com
788t	ArTono/Shutterstock.com
788b	Marten_House/Shutterstock.com
789	Wikimedia Commons
790	Everett Historical/Shutterstock.com
791t	Ralph Malan / Flickr / CC-BY-2.0
791bl	Georgios Kollidas/Shutterstock.com
791bm	Alex Lilvet / Flickr / CC-BY-2.0

Credits and Sources

791br	Alex Lilvet / Flickr / CC-BY-2.0
792	Everett Historical/Shutterstock.com
793	Everett Historical/Shutterstock.com
794	Paul Matthew Photography/Shutterstock.com
795	IgorGolovniov/Shutterstock.com
796t	H.C. Williams / Flickr / CC-BY-2.0
796m	H.C. Williams / Flickr / CC-BY-2.0
796b	scott conner/Shutterstock.com
797	Everett Historical/Shutterstock.com
798	Neftali/Shutterstock.com
799	Kiev.Victor/Shutterstock.com
800	Zvonimir Atletic/Shutterstock.com
801	Zvonimir Atletic/Shutterstock.com
801	Verkhovynets Taras/Shutterstock.com
802	Zvonimir Atletic/Shutterstock.com
803	Kiev.Victor/Shutterstock.com
804	Tema_Kud/Shutterstock.com
805	Pigprox/Shutterstock.com
806	Wikimedia Commons
807	catwalker/Shutterstock.com
808tl	Joseph Sohm/Shutterstock.com
808tr	Kevin M. McCarthy/Shutterstock.com
808bl	Kevin M. McCarthy/Shutterstock.com
808br	holbox/Shutterstock.com
809t	Joseph Sohm/Shutterstock.com
809bl	Everett Historical/Shutterstock.com
809bm	irisphoto1/Shutterstock.com
809br	Walters Art Museum / CC-BY-SA-3.0
810	Olga Popova/Shutterstock.com
811	Library of Congress
813	Jacques Descloitres, MODIS Rapid Response Team, NASA/GSFC
814	Clockwise from top left: NeydtStock/Shutterstock.com; Michel Piccaya/Shutterstock.com; Felix Lipov/Shutterstock.com; Nathan Chor/Shutterstock.com; orangecrush/Shutterstock.com; Allen.G/Shutterstock.com; SRTM Team NASA/JPL/NIMA
815	Clockwise from top left: David Steele/Shutterstock.com; Grobler du Preez/Shutterstock.com; Ivonne Wierink/Shutterstock.com; dirkr/Shutterstock.com; David Steele/Shutterstock.com; BPpix/Shutterstock.com; Dominique de La Croix/Shutterstock.com; David Steele/Shutterstock.com
816	Following order of captions: Sergey Uryadnikov/Shutterstock.com; Chris Fielding/Shutterstock.com; kbremote/Shutterstock.com; Sergey Uryadnikov/Shutterstock.com; Stacey Ann Alberts/Shutterstock.com; EcoPrint/Shutterstock.com; Ehrman Photographic/Shutterstock.com; Andrew M. Allport/Shutterstock.com; chris kolaczan/Shutterstock.com; john michael evan potter/Shutterstock.com; EcoPrint/Shutterstock.com; Erni/Shutterstock.com; MartinMaritz/Shutterstock.com; Terry Straehley/Shutterstock.com; David Steele/Shutterstock.com
817	Following order of captions: Dominique de La Croix/Shutterstock.com; JMx Images/Shutterstock.com; Bildagentur Zoonar GmbH/Shutterstock.com; Jan-Nor Photography/Shutterstock.com; EcoPrint/Shutterstock.com; EcoPrint/Shutterstock.com; Grobler du Preez/Shutterstock.com; Grobler du Preez/Shutterstock.com
818tl	john michael evan potter/Shutterstock.com
818tr	feathercollector/Shutterstock.com
818m	john michael evan potter/Shutterstock.com
818b	EcoPrint/Shutterstock.com
819	Library of Congress
821	Morphart Creation/Shutterstock.com
822t	Eugene Sergeev/Shutterstock.com
822b	T.W. van Urk/Shutterstock.com
823tl	chrisdorney/Shutterstock.com
823bl	Ekaterina Bykova/Shutterstock.com
823bm	Ekaterina Bykova/Shutterstock.com
823br	Ekaterina Bykova/Shutterstock.com
824	Stamp: Lefteris Papaulakis/Shutterstock.com
824	Waterloo: Colette3/Shutterstock.com
825t	Everett Historical/Shutterstock.com
825b	Milosz_M/Shutterstock.com
828	Frog: kurt_G/Shutterstock.com
828	Agamid: kurt_G/Shutterstock.com
828	Butterfly: Doug Schnurr/Shutterstock.com
828	Parrot: Lovely Bird/Shutterstock.com
828	Squirrel: Sainam51/Shutterstock.com
828	Orchid: Michael Maes/Shutterstock.com
828	Lizard: clearviewstock/Shutterstock.com
828	Rainforest: Tom Fawls/Shutterstock.com
829t	antoni halim/Shutterstock.com
829b	Wibowo Djatmiko / Wikimedia Commons / CC-BY-SA-3.0
830	lancelee/Shutterstock.com
831tr	tristan tan/Shutterstock.com
831ml	joyfull/Shutterstock.com
831m	Trong Nguyen/Shutterstock.com
831mr	gracethang2/Shutterstock.com
831bl	t.natchai/Shutterstock.com
831br	t.natchai/Shutterstock.com
832	EQRoy/Shutterstock.com
835	Wikimedia Commons
836tl	Everett Historical/Shutterstock.com
836tm	Everett Historical/Shutterstock.com
836tr	Boris15/Shutterstock.com
836b	Wikimedia Commons

837tl	Wikimedia Commons
837tr	Wikimedia Commons
837bl	Danilo Prudêncio Silva / Wikimedia Commons CC-BY-SA-3.0
837br	Wikimedia Commons
839t	Wikimedia Commons
839bl	Adwo/Shutterstock.com
839bm	Leonard Zhukovsky/Shutterstock.com
839br	Library of Congress
840	Architect of the Capitol
842	mountainpix/Shutterstock.com
844t	Shanker Pur / Wikimedia Commons / CC-BY-SA-3.0
844b	Tropenmuseum, part of the National Museum of World Culture / Wikimedia Commons / CC-BY-SA-3.0
845	Wikimedia Commons
846	Stephencdickson / Wikimedia Commons / CC-BY-SA-4.0
847	Nikonboy/Shutterstock.com
848	Andy Lidstone/Shutterstock.com
849t	mary416/Shutterstock.com
849m	Kåre Thor Olsen / Wikimedia Commons / CC-BY-SA-3.0
849b	Ron Zmiri/Shutterstock.com
850	Clockwise from top: YANGCHAO/Shutterstock.com; Olga Popova/Shutterstock.com; IgorGolovniov/Shutterstock.com; Lefteris Papaulakis/Shutterstock.com; Neftali/Shutterstock.com
851l	Wikimedia Commons
851m	Kiev.Victor/Shutterstock.com
851r	© 2005 by Tomasz Sienicki / Wikimedia Commons / CC-BY-SA-3.0
852	Following order of captions: Christian Mueller/Shutterstock.com; Mikhail Markovskiy/Shutterstock.com; Paolo Bona/Shutterstock.com; Wikimedia Commons; Paolo Bona/Shutterstock.com; Wikimedia Commons; Leonard Zhukovsky/Shutterstock.com; Wikimedia Commons; Neftali/Shutterstock.com
854	Wikimedia Commons
855	Everett Historical/Shutterstock.com
858tl	Everett Historical/Shutterstock.com
858ml	Kiev.Victor/Shutterstock.com
858bl	Georgios Kollidas/Shutterstock.com
858br	Everett Historical/Shutterstock.com
859tl	Norbert1986/Shutterstock.com
859tr	Neil Mitchell/Shutterstock.com
859m	Wikimedia Commons
859bl	Everett Historical/Shutterstock.com
859br	Wikimedia Commons
860tl	Marco Rubino/Shutterstock.com
860tr	chrisdorney/Shutterstock.com
860mr	Marco Rubino/Shutterstock.com
860ml	horslips5 / Flickr / CC-BY-2.0
860bl	horslips5 / Flickr / CC-BY-2.0
861l	Library of Congress
861r	flocu/Shutterstock.com
862	Everett Historical/Shutterstock.com
863tl	Everett Historical/Shutterstock.com
863tr	Everett Historical/Shutterstock.com
863ml	chrisdorney/Shutterstock.com
863bl	Los Angeles County Museum of Art (www.lacma.org)
863br	Wikimedia Commons
864	Clockwise from top left: AnneMS/Shutterstock.com; Charmaine A Harvey/Shutterstock.com; tristan tan/Shutterstock.com; IgorGolovniov/Shutterstock.com; K.A.Willis/Shutterstock.com; JM Travel Photography/Shutterstock.com; doma Shutterstock.com
865	Swapan Photography/Shutterstock.com
866	map of crimea unit 26.eps
867	Roger Fenton / Library of Congress
868tl	Everett Historical/Shutterstock.com
868ml	Roger Fenton / Library of Congress
868bl	Everett Historical/Shutterstock.com
868tr	Roger Fenton / Library of Congress
868mr	Roger Fenton / Library of Congress
868br	Los Angeles County Museum of Art (www.lacma.org)
869t	Everett Historical/Shutterstock.com
869b	William Simpson / Library of Congress
870t	Guy Erwood/Shutterstock.com
870b	chrisdorney/Shutterstock.com
871	Library of Congress
872	Library of Congress
873	Wilhelm Heine / Library of Congress
874	Library of Congress
875	Ezra Bolender / U.S. Naval War College
876	CTR Photos/Shutterstock.com
877	Library of Congress
878	Amio Cajander / Flickr / CC-BY-2.0
879tr	Fondo Antiguo de la Universidad de Sevilla / Flickr / CC-BY-2.0
879ml	Alphonse Liébert / Library of Congress
879m	USMC Archives / Flickr / CC-BY-2.0
879mr	Library of Congress
879bl	USMC Archives / Flickr / CC-BY-2.0
879bm	Library of Congress
879br	USMC Archives / Flickr / CC-BY-2.0
880	USMC Archives / Flickr / CC-BY-2.0
881tl	USMC Archives / Flickr / CC-BY-2.0
881tr	manhhai / Flickr / CC-BY-2.0
881bl	xlibber / Flickr / CC-BY-2.0

Credits and Sources

881br	Alexander Kachkaev / Flickr / CC-BY-2.0
883	James St. John / Flickr / CC-BY-2.0
884t	Chris Fithall / Flickr / CC-BY-2.0
884b	Library of Congress
885	James St. John / Flickr / CC-BY-2.0
886t	tristan tan/Shutterstock.com 333809198
886b	James St. John / Flickr / CC-BY-2.0
887t	James St. John / Flickr / CC-BY-2.0
887b	Library of Congress
888	Library of Congress
889	skyfish/Shutterstock.com
891	Los Angeles County Museum of Art (www.lacma.org)
892	Everett Historical/Shutterstock.com
892	IgorGolovniov/Shutterstock.com
893	Library of Congress
894	Los Angeles County Museum of Art (www.lacma.org)
896tl	Hong Kong by Dennis Wong / Flickr / CC-BY-2.0
896tm	A Yee / Flickr / CC-BY-2.0
896tr	edwin.11 / Flickr / CC-BY-2.0
896bl	Wikimedia Commons
896br	Wikimedia Commons
898t	Steve Allen/Shutterstock.com
898b	Female Traveller/Shutterstock.com
899t	NASA/Goddard Space Flight Center Scientific Visualization Studio
899b	Clockwise from top left: Ondrej Prosicky/Shutterstock.com; Christopher Michel / Flickr / CC-BY-2.0; City Escapes Nature Photo/Shutterstock.com; Aleksandra Suzi/Shutterstock.com; Nicram Sabod/Shutterstock.com 256819084
900t	Wikimedia Commons
900m	Anita Ritenour / Flickr / CC-BY-2.0
900bl	IgorGolovniov/Shutterstock.com
900bm	Neftali/Shutterstock.com
900br	Boris15/Shutterstock.com
901t	Volodymyr Goinyk/Shutterstock.com
901m	Sergey Tarasenko/Shutterstock.com
901b	NASA/Goddard Space Flight Center Scientific Visualization Studio
902	Clockwise from top left: Amelie Koch/Shutterstock.com; vladsilver/Shutterstock.com; Volt Collection/Shutterstock.com; Anton_Ivanov/Shutterstock.com; Angela N Perryman/Shutterstock.com; jo Crebbin/Shutterstock.com
903l	Wikimedia Commons
903r	Nanisimova /Shutterstock.com
904t	rook76/Shutterstock.com
904b	Collezione Rocchini Dumas - Gianfranco Rocchini / Wikimedia Commons / Free Art License (http://artlibre.org/licence/lal/en/)
905	Top to bottom: chrisdorney/Shutterstock.com; Everett Historical/Shutterstock.com; Notgrass Family Collection; Library of Congress
906t	rook76/Shutterstock.com
906b	Library of Congress
907	Vitascope: Library of Congress
907	Jazz Singer: State Library of New South Wales / Flickr
907	Eastman and Edison: Everett Historical/Shutterstock.com
907	USA Stamps: catwalker/Shutterstock.com
907	North Korea: Irina Rogova/Shutterstock.com
907	Cuba: EtiAmmos/Shutterstock.com
907	San Marion: duryea/Shutterstock.com
908t	Library of Congress
908b	Olga Popova/Shutterstock.com
909t	Yuriy Boyko/Shutterstock.com
909bl	PROFrédéric BISSON / Flickr / CC-BY-2.0
909bm	Calsidyrose / Flickr / CC-BY-2.0
909br	Chemical Heritage Foundation / Flickr / CC-BY-2.0
910	Charlene Notgrass
911	Everett Historical/Shutterstock.com
912	jorisvo/Shutterstock.com
913t	Everett Historical/Shutterstock.com
913b	Library of Congress
914	Everett Historical/Shutterstock.com
915	Everett Historical/Shutterstock.com
917	Everett Historical/Shutterstock.com
918	dmitry_islentev/Shutterstock.com
919t	visicou/Shutterstock.com
919m	Dan From Indiana / Flickr / CC-BY-2.0
919b	Det-anan/Shutterstock.com
920	kovgabor/Shutterstock.com
921	lazyllama/Shutterstock.com
922	Leandro Neumann Ciuffo / Flickr / CC-BY-2.0
923	Library of Congress
925	Micimakin/Shutterstock.com
926	Everett Historical/Shutterstock.com
927t	Olga Popova /Shutterstock.com
927m	Neftali/Shutterstock.com
927b	born1945 / Flickr / CC-BY-2.0
928	zeevveez / Flickr / CC-BY-2.0
929	All images by Everett Historical/Shutterstock.com except Kamp Vught by FaceMePLS / Flickr / CC-BY-2.0 and Heinrich Himmler by Bundesarchiv, Bild 101III-Weill-061-25 / Weill / CC-BY-SA 3.0
930	Library of Congress
931	Everett Historical/Shutterstock.com

932	Everett Historical/Shutterstock.com
933	Clockwise from top left: catwalker/Shutterstock.com; Everett Historical/Shutterstock.com; yakub88/Shutterstock.com; Arkady Mazor/Shutterstock.com; catwalker/Shutterstock.com; catwalker/Shutterstock.com; Olga Popova/Shutterstock.com; Jennifer Boyer / Flickr / CC-BY-2.0
934	U.S. Army
935l	Neftali/Shutterstock.com
935r	Solodov Alexey/Shutterstock.com
936t	Wikimedia Commons
936m	Australian National Maritime Museum / Flickr
936bl	Library of Congress
936br	Robert Hoetink/Shutterstock.com
937	Everett Historical/Shutterstock.com
938	National Archives and Records Administration
939t	Duane Tate / Flickr / CC-BY-2.0
939bl	Lena Lir/Shutterstock.com
939br	Dmitro2009 /Shutterstock.com
940	Everett Historical/Shutterstock.com
941	Der Telegraf / Wikimedia Commons / CC-BY-SA-3.0
942	Top row: U.S. Department of Agriculture / Flickr / CC-BY-2.0 (first two photos); Wikimedia Commons
942	Second row: U.S. Air Force except second image by U.S. Department of Agriculture / Flickr / CC-BY-2.0
942	Milk: Wikimedia Commons
942	Passengers: The National Archives UK / Flickr / CC-BY-2.0
943	Top to bottom: Steffen Rehm / Wikimedia Commons; Wikimedia Commons (two photos); Bundesarchiv, B 145 Bild-P085282 / CC-BY-SA 3.0
944t	artnana/Shutterstock.com
944m	Wikimedia Commons
944b	Thomas Fisher Rare Book Library, University of Toronto, Toronto, Ontario Canada / Flickr / CC-BY-2.0
945t	U.S. Navy
945bl	U.S. Marines Corps
945br	U.S. Navy
946	John F. Kennedy Presidential Library and Museum, Boston
947	Wikimedia Commons
949t	Michal Knitl/Shutterstock.com
949bl	sergeisimonov/Shutterstock.com
949br	Zzvet/Shutterstock.com
950tl	T photography/Shutterstock.com
950ml	areeya_ann/Shutterstock.com
950mr	Matyas Rehak/Shutterstock.com
950bl	Mivr/Shutterstock.com
950br	f9photos/Shutterstock.com
951	First Row: SasinT/Shutterstock.com; Martin P/Shutterstock.com; Alexandra Giese/Shutterstock.com
951	Second Row: jessadapong promjuntuk/Shutterstock.com; Vladimir Wrangel/Shutterstock.com; Skorpionik00/Shutterstock.com
951	Third Row: Humming Bird Art/Shutterstock.com; Nagel Photography/Shutterstock.com; Shivang Mehta/Shutterstock.com
951	Sepoys: Wikimedia Commons
952	Marzolino/Shutterstock.com
953	Wikimedia Commons
954	Wikimedia Commons
955	Everett Historical/Shutterstock.com
956	Rafal Cichawa/Shutterstock.com
957	Everett Historical/Shutterstock.com
958tr	User:Sphl at ja.wikipedia.org / CC-BY-SA-3.0
958mr	ajt/Shutterstock.com
958ml	Bundesarchiv, Bild 146-2006-0196 Orbis / CC-BY-SA 3.0
958bl	Everett Historical/Shutterstock.com
959	Everett Historical/Shutterstock.com
960	Top to bottom: Library of Congress; John Atherton / Flickr / CC-BY-SA-2.0; Wolfgang Sauber / Wikimedia Commons / CC-BY-SA-3.0; Nationaal Archief / Flickr / CC-BY-2.0
961tl	Mark Wagoner / Wikimedia Commons / CC-BY-2.5
961tm	High Contrast / Wikimeica Commons / CC-BY-3.0-DE
961tr	Ratsbew / Wikimedia Commons / CC-BY-SA-3.0
961b	Keith Schengili-Roberts / Wikimedia Commons
962tl	Bundesarchiv, Bild 183-1984-1126-312 / CC-BY-SA 3.0
962tr	Bundesarchiv, Bild 183-1984-1126-313 / CC-BY-SA 3.0
962b	Wikimedia Commons
963	Library of Congress
965	Used by permission of The Marion E. Wade Center, Wheaton College, Wheaton, IL.
967t	Oliver Woodward / Wikimedia Commons / CC-BY-SA-2.0
967b	oxeye / Wikimedia Commons / CC-BY-SA-3.0
968t	Used by permission of The Marion E. Wade Center, Wheaton College, Wheaton, IL.
968b	jschroe / Wikimedia Commons / CC-BY-2.0
969	kindonnelly / Flickr / CC-BY-2.0
971	NASA
972	Moon: Gregory H. Revera / Wikimedia Commons / CC-BY-SA-3.0

Credits and Sources

974	**First row:** Susan Flashman/Shutterstock.com; deb talan/Shutterstock.com; Marco Tomasini/Shutterstock.com **Second row:** Julian W/Shutterstock.com; Kristian Bell/Shutterstock.com; worldswildlifewonders/Shutterstock.com **Third row:** PeterMooij/Shutterstock.com; Chris Howey/Shutterstock.com **Fourth row:** Janelle Lugge/Shutterstock.com; AustralianCamera /Shutterstock.com; Benedikt Juerges/Shutterstock.com
975l	Stanislav Fosenbauer/Shutterstock.com
975tr	Joan Gomez Pons/Shutterstock.com
975mr	ChameleonsEye/Shutterstock.com
975br	fritz16/Shutterstock.com
976	Nicholls Family Collection
977	Nicholls Family Collection
978	Nicholls Family Collection
979	Nicholls Family Collection
980t	NASA / ESA
980b	NASA
981t	rook76/Shutterstock.com
981b	Brendan Howard/Shutterstock.com
982t	Everett Historical/Shutterstock.com
982m	chrisdorney/Shutterstock.com
982bl	Boris15/Shutterstock.com
982br	rook76/Shutterstock.com
983	FedotovAnatoly/Shutterstock.com
984t	Everett Historical/Shutterstock.com
984m	Everett Historical/Shutterstock.com
984b	NASA
985	NASA
986t	Everett Historical/Shutterstock.com
986b	NASA
987	Everett Historical/Shutterstock.com
987	chrisdorney/Shutterstock.com
988	Following order of captions: sokolenok/Shutterstock.com; Solodov Alexey/Shutterstock.com; mrHanson/Shutterstock.com; artnana/Shutterstock.com; Brendan Howard/Shutterstock.com
989t	Viktor Konya/Shutterstock.com
989b	Peter Scholz/Shutterstock.com
990t	Bethany Poore
990b	Mev McCurdy
991	Bundesarchiv, Bild 183-1990-0921-309 / Grubitzsch (geb. Raphael), Waltraud / CC-BY-SA 3.0
992tl	Bundesarchiv, Bild 183-1990-0922-002 / CC-BY-SA 3.0
992tr	Bundesarchiv, Bild 183-1989-1023-022 / Friedrich Gahlbeck / CC-BY-SA 3.0
992bl	Bundesarchiv, Bild 183-1989-1030-033 / CC-BY-SA 3.0
992br	Bundesarchiv, Bild 183-1989-1106-023 / Friedrich Gahlbeck / CC-BY-SA 3.0
993t	catwalker/Shutterstock.com
993b	Mev McCurdy
994	S-F/Shutterstock.com
995	Mikhail Markovskiy/Shutterstock.com
996t	mandritoiu/Shutterstock.com
996b	Lewis Hine / Wikimedia Commons
997t	Taras Vyshnya/Shutterstock.com
997m	Tifonimages/Shutterstock.com
997b	Felix Lipov/Shutterstock.com
998	Pyramid: Merydolla/Shutterstock.com; Stonehenge: aslysun/Shutterstock.com; Parthenon (Nashville, TN): f11photo/Shutterstock.com; Colosseum: 1989studio/Shutterstock.com; Obelisk of Aksum: Ondřej Žváček / Wikimedia Commons / CC-BY-SA-3.0; St. Sophia's: Dmitrydesign/Shutterstock.com; Angkor Wat: Lena Serditova/Shutterstock.com; Chartres Cathedral: Tony Hisgett / Flickr / CC-BY-2.0; Moai: Bjørn Christian Tørrissen / Wikimedia Commons / CC-BY-SA-3.0; Taj Mahal: saiko3p/Shutterstock.com; Washington Monument: SurangaSL/Shutterstock.com; Eiffel Tower (model): Denis Rozhnovsky/Shutterstock.com; Empire State Building: IVY PHOTOS/Shutterstock.com; Willis Tower: Songquan Deng/Shutterstock.com; Petronas Towers: Shanti Hesse/Shutterstock.com; Taipei 101: ronan chen/Shutterstock.com; Burj Khalifa: Donaldytong / Wikimedia Commons / CC-BY-SA-3.0; Al Hamra Tower: Mohdalg / Wikimedia Commons / CC-BY-3.0; Abraj Al-Bait Towers: artpixelgraphy Studio/Shutterstock.com; One World Trade Center: Leonard Zhukovsky/Shutterstock.com; Shanghai Tower: atiger/Shutterstock.com
1000	Naufal MQ/Shutterstock.com
1001t	meunierd/Shutterstock.com
1001b	Tyler McKay/Shutterstock.com
1002	**First row:** Paul D Smith/Shutterstock.com; Stanislav Fosenbauer/Shutterstock.com; thomas koch/Shutterstock.com; erichon/Shutterstock.com; Northfoto/Shutterstock.com **Second row:** gaborbasch/Shutterstock.com; Anton_Ivanov/Shutterstock.com; V. Belov/Shutterstock.com; Amy Nichole Harris/Shutterstock.com; Attila JANDI/Shutterstock.com **Third row:** meunierd/Shutterstock.com; Dietmar Temps/Shutterstock.com; Ruslana Iurchenko/Shutterstock.com 298336394
1003	**First row:** Pikoso.kz/Shutterstock.com; Zvonimir Atletic/Shutterstock.com; Renato

Pejkovic/Shutterstock.com; Fotos593/Shutterstock.com (two photos)
Second row: nikolay100/Shutterstock.com; Brilliant Eye/Shutterstock.com; Sergey Goryachev/Shutterstock.com; Salim October/Shutterstock.com; Route66/Shutterstock.com
Third row: Palenque/Shutterstock.com; Art Phaneuf Photography/Shutterstock.com; kaetana/Shutterstock.com; mountainpix/Shutterstock.com

1004 **First row:** salajean/Shutterstock.com
Second row: salajean/Shutterstock.com
Third row: salajean/Shutterstock.com
Fourth row: Sergey Velikanov/Shutterstock.com; John C Evans/Shutterstock.com; velirina/Shutterstock.com

1005 **First row:** Hector Conesa/Shutterstock.com; David Stanley / Flickr / CC-BY-2.0; Anton_Ivanov/Shutterstock.com 175302686
Second row: Anton_Ivanov/Shutterstock.com; Jean Rebiffé / Flickr / CC-BY-2.0; Mark52/Shutterstock.com; erichon/Shutterstock.com 287746538
Third row: rook76/Shutterstock.com; =Soft=/Shutterstock.com; IgorGolovniov/Shutterstock.com; AdrianNunez/Shutterstock.com; Oliver Foerstner/Shutterstock.com
Fourth row: Chumash Maxim/Shutterstock.com; Milosz_M/Shutterstock.com; asawin klabma/Shutterstock.com; debra millet/Shutterstock.com

1006 **First row:** Gil.K/Shutterstock.com; Boris15/Shutterstock.com; risphoto1/Shutterstock.com; Crebbin/Shutterstock.com; Zvonimir Atletic/Shutterstock.com
Second row: Emena/Shutterstock.com; Faraways/Shutterstock.com; Zvonimir Atletic/Shutterstock.com
Third row: skyfish/Shutterstock.com; nikolay100/Shutterstock.com; Palenque/Shutterstock.com
Fourth row: Florin Cnejevici/Shutterstock.com; AdrianNunez/Shutterstock.com; Don Mammoser/Shutterstock.com

1007 **First row:** Stephane Bidouze/Shutterstock.com; testing/Shutterstock.com; alfotokunst/Shutterstock.com; Angelo Giampiccolo/Shutterstock.com 330241205
Second row: ermess/Shutterstock.com; Kobby Dagan/Shutterstock.com; skyfish/Shutterstock.com
Bottom: Zvonimir Atletic/Shutterstock.com 154005305

1008 **Top to bottom:** Stephen B. Goodwin/Shutterstock.com; Earle Klosterman / Flickr / CC-BY-2.0; Jean Rebiffé / Flickr / CC-BY-2.0; Valery Shanin/Shutterstock.com; Department of Foreign Affairs and Trade (Australia) / Flickr / CC-BY-2.0

1009 Ints Vikmanis/Shutterstock.com
1011 Sergey Goryachev/Shutterstock.com
1012t FDR Presidential Library and Museum / Flickr / CC-BY-2.0
1012mr Sergey Goryachev/Shutterstock.com
1012ml Solodov Alexey/Shutterstock.com
1012b CTR Photos/Shutterstock.com
1013t Andrey Lobachev/Shutterstock.com
1013bl essie / Flickr / CC-BY-2.0
1013bm Karen Roe / Flickr / CC-BY-2.0
1013br Kiev.Victor/Shutterstock.com
1014l marcyano/Shutterstock.com
1014r chrisdorney/Shutterstock.com

1015 **First column:** Australia: Neftali/Shutterstock.com; Grenada: YANGCHAO/Shutterstock.com; Singapore: Gwoeii/Shutterstock.com; New Zealand: Boris15/Shutterstock.com; Australia: Dariush M/Shutterstock.com; Australia: CTR Photos/Shutterstock.com
Second column: Australia: catwalker/Shutterstock.com; Canada: Lefteris Papaulakis/Shutterstock.com; Cyprus: IgorGolovniov/Shutterstock.com; Jamaica: Sergey Kohl/Shutterstock.com; Fiji: IgorGolovniov/Shutterstock.com; Malta: Sari ONeal/Shutterstock.com; Papua New Guinea: Neftali/Shutterstock.com
Third column: Tuvalu: Neftali/Shutterstock.com; St. Lucia: Lefteris Papaulakis/Shutterstock.com; Barbados: Patricia Hofmeester/Shutterstock.com; Belize: brandonht/Shutterstock.com; Belize: brandonht/Shutterstock.com; Seychelles: Solodov Alexey/Shutterstock.com; Kiribati: Neftali/Shutterstock.com

1016tl Zoran Karapancev/Shutterstock.com
1016tr Jorg Hackemann/Shutterstock.com
1016ml Shaun Jeffers/Shutterstock.com
1016mr Atlaspix/Shutterstock.com
1016bl Featureflash/Shutterstock.com
1016br ImageFlow/Shutterstock.com
1017t Lefteris Papaulakis/Shutterstock.com
1017m LiliGraphie/Shutterstock.com
1017bl Neftali/Shutterstock.com
1017br Solodov Alexey/Shutterstock.com
1018t Lorna Roberts/Shutterstock.com
1018b catwalker/Shutterstock.com
1019 **Top to bottom:** Magdalena Paluchowska / Shutterstock.com; sunsinger Shutterstock.com; Borna_Mirahmadian/Shutterstock.com; muratart/Shutterstock.com
1020l Everett Historical/Shutterstock.com

Credits and Sources

1020r	Arkady Mazor/Shutterstock.com
1021t	Everett Historical/Shutterstock.com (three photos)
1021mr	Wikimedia Commons
1021bl	Wikimedia Commons
1021br	Everett Historical Shutterstock.com
1023t	thomas koch/Shutterstock.com
1023bl	chrisdorney/Shutterstock.com
1023bm	Kamira/Shutterstock.com
1023br	Leah-Anne Thompson/Shutterstock.com
1024	**Top to bottom:** Robert Hoetink/Shutterstock.com; Tasha2030 Shutterstock.com; Eunika Sopotnicka/Shutterstock.com; Philip Lange / Shutterstock.com
1025	Suprun Vitaly Shutterstock.com
1026t	Sean Pavone/Shutterstock.com
1026b	Naiyyer/Shutterstock.com
1027t	Alison Young/Shutterstock.com
1027m	Nadir Keklik/Shutterstock.com
1027b	somsak suwanput/Shutterstock.com
1028t	fstockfoto/Shutterstock.com
1028m	Nathan Holland/Shutterstock.com
1028b	rook76/Shutterstock.com
1029	**Top to bottom:** Olga Popova/Shutterstock.com; paulinux/Shutterstock.com; Lestertair/Shutterstock.com; Papaulakis/Shutterstock.com
1030t	Herbert Kratky/Shutterstock.com
1030m	rook76/Shutterstock.com
1030b	tristan tan/Shutterstock.com
1031	PhotoBobil / Flickr / CC-BY-2.0
1033t	Dana Ward/Shutterstock.com
1033b	Natali Glado/Shutterstock.com
1034	Nauru: Department of Foreign Affairs and Trade (Australia) photo by Lorrie Graham / Flickr / CC-BY-2.0; St. Kitts: Darryl Brooks Shutterstock.com; St. Lucia: Darryl Brooks Shutterstock.com; Liechtenstein: Jordan Tan/Shutterstock.com; Palau: BlueOrange Studio Shutterstock.com; Honduras: by milosk50/Shutterstock.com; Grenada: rj lerich/Shutterstock.com; Wales: DJTaylor/Shutterstock.com
1035	Kiribati: Department of Foreign Affairs and Trade(Australia)/Flickr/CC-BY-2.0; Barbados: Allen Brewer / Flickr / CC-BY-2.0; Belize: Charlene Notgrass; Nauru: anfo/Shutterstock.com; Zambia: africa924/Shutterstock.com; Andorra: duchy/Shutterstock.com; Vanuatu: GTS Productions/Shutterstock.com; Liechtenstein: InavanHateren/Shutterstock.com
1036	Canada: Roger de Montfort/Shutterstock.com; Turkey: asliuzunoglu/Shutterstock.com; Bolivia: T photography/Shutterstock.com; Brazil: Alf Ribeiro/Shutterstock.com; Egypt: maudanros/Shutterstock.com; Massachusetts: John Kropewnicki / Shutterstock.com
1037	Roger de Montfort/Shutterstock.com
1038	Malawi: Dennis Albert Richardson/Shutterstock.com; Iran: Borna_Mirahmadian /Shutterstock.com; Vanuatu: livcool / Shutterstock.com; Guatemala: Kobby Dagan /Shutterstock.com; Zambia: africa924/ Shutterstock.com
1039t	Charlene Notgrass
1039m	Katoosha/Shutterstock.com
1039b	Mark52/Shutterstock.com
1040	MACHIKO/Shutterstock.com
1041	Top to bottom: luigi nifosi/Shutterstock.com; M. Niebuhr/Shutterstock.com; Frederic Legrand - COMEO/Shutterstock.com; Chayatorn Laorattanavech/Shutterstock.com
1042tr	paul prescott/Shutterstock.com
1042mr	Luisa Fernanda Gonzalez/Shutterstock.com
1042bl	nui7711/Shutterstock.com
1042bm	hans engbers/Shutterstock.com
1042br	Philip Pilosian/Shutterstock.com
1043tl	DoublePHOTO studio/Shutterstock.com
1043tm	vicspacewalker/Shutterstock.com
1043tr	DoublePHOTO studio/Shutterstock.com
1043mr	paul prescott/Shutterstock.com
1043br	Aleksandar Todorovic/Shutterstock.com
1044	Suprun Vitaly/Shutterstock.com
FA-34	Bethany Poore
FA-35	Bethany Poore
FA-36	Bethany Poore
FA-37	Bethany Poore
FA-38	Bethany Poore
FA-39	Bethany Poore
FA-40	Bethany Poore
FA-41	Bethany Poore
FA-42	Bethany Poore
FA-43	Bethany Poore
FA-44	Bethany Poore
FA-45	Bethany Poore/JupiterImages
FA-46t	IgorGolovniov/Shutterstock.com
FA-46b	Wikimedia Commons
FA-47	Wikimedia Commons
FA-49	Bethany Poore/JupiterImages
FA-50	hca.gilead.org.il
FA-52	Bethany Poore
FA-53	Bethany Poore/JupiterImages
FA-55	Keresaspa / Wikimedia Commons / CC-BY-3.0
FA-58	Bethany Poore

Sources

Articles

"Bloodlines: The Nicholls Family." http://www.abc.net.au/tv/messagestick/stories/s3014566.htm

"A Brief History of Chocolate" by Amanda Fiegl. March 1, 2008. http://www.smithsonianmag.com/arts-culture/a-brief-history-of-chocolate-21860917/

"Brief History of the Moravian Church." Moravian Theological Seminary. http://www.moravianseminary.edu/moravian-studies/about-the-moravians/brief-history-of-the-moravian-church.html

"Cassava" http://www.cgiar.org/our-strategy/crop-factsheets/cassava/

"Christian Führer Obituary." *The Telegraph.* http://www.telegraph.co.uk/news/obituaries/10938435/Christian-Fuhrer-obituary.html

"The Fall of Constantinople" by Judith Herrin. *History Today* Volume 53, Issue 6, July 2003. http://www.historytoday.com/judith-herrin/fall-constantinople

"Gold Rush" by David Williams. *New Georgia Encyclopedia.* http://www.georgiaencyclopedia.org/articles/history-archaeology/gold-rush

"Growing Cocoa" by Queensland Government, Department of Agriculture and Fisheries. https://www.daf.qld.gov.au/plants/fruit-and-vegetables/fruit-and-nuts/other-fruit-crops/growing-cocoa

"He Still Tumbles Walls" by Billy Ray Cox. *Church and Family Magazine,* Spring 2005, pp. 17-19.

"History of AT&T and Television." http://www.corp.att.com/history/television/

"History of Coffee" by National Coffee Association, USA. http://www.ncausa.org/About-Coffee/History-of-Coffee

"How the Potato Changed the World" by Charles C. Mann. *Smithsonian Magazine*, November 2011.

"Immigration and Ethnocultural Diversity in Canada," https://www12.statcan.gc.ca/nhs-enm/2011/as-sa/99-010-x/99-010-x2011001-eng.cfm

"The Introduction of the Horse into the Western Hemisphere." *The Hispanic American Historical Review,* Vol. XXIII, November, 1943, No. 4.

"Meet Mansa Musa I of Mali--the richest human being in all history" by John Hall. *The Independent.* October 17, 2012. http://www.independent.co.uk/news/world/world-history/meet-mansa-musa-i-of-mali-the-richest-human-being-in-all-history-8213453.html

"Meeting the 'Christian' Hans Christian Andersen" by Jeanne Conte. *The Lutheran.* October 2005. http://www.thelutheran.org/article/article.cfm?article_id=5523

"New Crop Fact Sheet: Cassava" by Stephen K. O'Hair, Tropical Research and Education Center, University of Florida. Purdue University Center for New Crops and Plant Products. https://www.hort.purdue.edu/newcrop/CropFactSheets/cassava.html

"Nicholls, Sir Douglas Ralph (Doug) (1906–1988)" by Richard Broome. Australian Dictionary of Biography. http://adb.anu.edu.au/biography/nicholls-sir-douglas-ralph-doug-14920

"NICHOLLS, Douglas Ralph (1906-1988)" by Mavis Thorpe Clark. Australian Dictionary of Evangelical Biography. http://webjournals.ac.edu.au/ojs/index.php/ADEB/article/view/944/941

"On Six Legs" by Tom Turpin, Professor Entomology Purdue University, Purdue Extension, November 1999. https://www.agriculture.purdue.edu/agcomm/newscolumns/archives/OSL/1999/November/111199OSL.html

"One Small Step" by Eric M. Jones. https://www.hq.nasa.gov/alsj/a11/a11.step.html

"Origin, History, and Uses of Corn (Zea mays)" by Lance Gibson and Garren Benson, Iowa State University, Department of Agronomy. http://agron-www.agron.iastate.edu/Courses/agron212/readings/corn_history.htm

"Origin, History, and Uses of Oats (Avena sativa) and Wheat (Triticum aestivum)" by Lance Gibson and Garren Benson, Iowa State University, Department of Agronomy, Revised January 2002. http://agron-www.agron.iastate.edu/Courses/agron212/Readings/Oat_wheat_history.htm

"Potatoes," United States Department of Agriculture, Economic Research Service, http://www.ers.usda.gov/topics/crops/vegetables-pulses/potatoes.aspx

"The Rise of the Turks and the Ottoman Empire," edited by Paul M. Pitman. *Turkey: A Country Study*. Washington, DC: Federal Research Division of the Library of Congress, 1987.

"Sorghum—Forage," Alternative Field Crops Manual. University of Wisconsin Extension, Cooperative

Extension and Univeristy of Minnesota: Center for Alternative Plant and Animal Products and the Minnesota Extension Service. https://www.hort.purdue.edu/newcrop/afcm/forage.html

"A Sweet Potato History" by Jennifer Harbster. Inside Adams Science, Tehnology & Business, Library of Congress, November 24, 2010. http://blogs.loc.gov/inside_adams/2010/11/a-sweet-potato-history/

"Tea—A Brief History of the Nation's Favourite Beverage" by UK Tea and Infusions Association. http://www.tea.co.uk/tea-a-brief-history

"The United States and the Opening to Japan, 1853." U.S. Department of State, Office of the Historian. http://www.history.state.gov/milestones/1830-1860/opening-to-japan

"What happened in the Great Fire of London?" Museum of London. www.museumoflondon.org.uk/explore-online/pocket-histories/what-happened-great-fire-london/

"What Was the Klondike Gold Rush?" National Park Service. http://www.nps.gov/klgo/learn/goldrush.htm

Books

Academic American Encyclopedia. Danbury: Grolier, 1989.

Barlett, John. *Bartlett's Familiar Quotations*. Fourteenth Edition. Boston: Little, Brown, and Company, 1855, 1968.

Blumberg, Rhoda. *Commodore Perry in the Land of the Shogun*. New York: Lothrop, Lee & Shepard, 1985.

Board on Science and Technology for International Development, National Research Council. *Lost Crops of Africa: Volume 1: Grains*. National Academy Press, Washington, D.C., 1996. Borrero, Mauricio. *Russia: A Reference Guide from the Renaissance to the Present*. New York: Facts On File, Inc., 2004.

Carlyle, Thomas. *History of the Frederick the Second called Frederick the Great, Vol. 1*, New York: Lovell, Coryell & Company.

Copernicus, Nicholas. *On the Revolutions*, 1543. Translated by Edward Rosen.

Cumo, Christopher. *Foods that Changed History: How Foods Shaped Civilization from the Ancient World to the Present*. ABC-CLIO, LLC. Santa Barbara, California, 2015.

Davis, John. *Venice*. New York: Newsweek Book Division, 1973.

Deagan, Katheleen A. and José María Cruxent. *Archaeology at La Isabela: America's First European Town*. New Haven: Yale University Press

Dowley, Tim, Organizing Editor. *Eerdmans' Handbook to the History of Christianity*. Grand Rapids: Eerdmans, 1977.

Gilbert, Felix, General Editor. *The Norton History of Modern Europe*. New York: W. W. Norton and Company, 1971.

Goodman, Susan E. and Michael J. Doolittle. *Skyscraper*. Alfred A. Knopf / Random House: New York, 2004.

Graham, Gerald. *A Concise History of the British Empire*. London: Thames and Hudson, 1970.

Greer, Thomas H. and Gavin Lewis. *A Brief History of the Western World, Sixth Edition*. Fort Worth: Harcourt Brace Jovanovich College Publishers, 1992.

Hooper, Walter. *C. S. Lewis: A Companion and Guide*. San Francisco: Harper Collins, 1996.

Hutton, Joseph E. *A History of the Moravian Church, 2nd edition*. London: Moravian Publication Office, 1909.

Latourette, Kenneth Scott. *Japan from Ancient Times to 1918*. Lecturable, 2012.

Lepoer, Barbara Leitch, editor. *Singapore: A Country Study*. Washington: Library of Congress, 1989

Macaulay, David. *Castle*. Boston: Houghton Mifflin, 1977

Massie, Robert. *Peter the Great: His Life and World*. New York: Random House, 1980.

Max Planck Institute. *Encyclopedia of Public International Law*. Amsterdam: Elsevier Science Publishers, 1984.

Mitchell, Pratima. *Gandhi: The Father of Modern India*. New York: Oxford University Press, 1997.

Myers, Philip Van Ness. *Mediaeval and Modern History*. Boston: Ginn and Company, 1905.

Okey, Thomas. *The Story of Paris*. London: J. M. Dent and Company, 1911.

Osborne, Milton. *Southeast Asia: An Introductory History, 11th Edition*. Sydney, Australia: Allen & Unwin, 2013

Paszkiewicz, Piotr and Hanna Faryna-Paszkiewicz. *DK Eyewitness Travel Guide: Canary Islands*. London: Dorling Kindersley Limited, 2013.

Reynolds, Carol. *Discovering Music*. Bowie, Texas: Silver Age Music, 2009.

Routledge, Katherine. *The Mystery of Easter Island*. Privately printed, 1919.

Severance, John B., *Gandhi: Great Soul*. New York: Clarion Books, 1997.

Teitelbaum, Michael. *Television*. Ann Arbor, MI: Cherry Lake Publishing, 2009.

Thomson, David. *England in the Nineteenth Century*. Baltimore: Penguin, 1950.

Tuchman, Barbara W. *A Distant Mirror: The Calamitous 14th Century*. New York: Alfred A. Knopf, 1978.

Wood, Anthony. *Nineteenth Century Britain, 1815-1914*. New York: David McKay Company, 1960.

Worsford, W. Basil. *A Visit to Java with an Account of the Founding of Singapore*. London: Richard Bentley and Sons, 1893.

Websites

Art and Life in Africa. https://africa.uima.uiowa.edu/
Asia for Educators. http://afe.easia.columbia.edu/
Austria National Tourist Office. http://www.austria.info/au
Avalon Project. Yale Law School. Lillian Goldman Law Library. http://avalon.law.yale.edu/
BBC - Religions. http://www.bbc.co.uk/religion/religions/
BBC - History. http://www.bbc.co.uk/history
Biggest Global Sports. http://www.biggestglobalsports.com
British Monarchy. http://www.royal.gov.uk/
British Museum. http://www.britishmuseum.org
Catholic Encyclopedia. http://www.newadvent.org/cathen/
Christianity Today. http://www.christianitytoday.com
Encyclopædia Britanica. http://www.britannica.com
FIFA. http://www.fifa.com
Food and Agriculture Organization of the United Nations. http://www.fao.org
Foundation for The Protection of Lublin Jewish Cemeteries. http://www.kirkuty-lublin.pl/
Heilbrunn Timeline of Art History. http://www.metmuseum.org/toah/
International Olympic Committee. http://www.olympic.org
Jewish Community of Warsaw – Lublin Branch. http://lublin.jewish.org.pl/index_en.html
Jewish Virtual Library. http://www.jewishvirtuallibrary.org
John F. Kennedy Presidential Library and Museum. http://www.jfklibrary.org/
Land Salzburg. http://www.salzburg.gv.at/en/en-index
Latin American History. http://latinamericanhistory.oxfordre.com/
Music History 102: a Guide to Western Composers and their music by Robert Sherrane. http://www.ipl.org/div/mushist/bar/bach.html
National Geographic. http://www.nationalgeographic.com/
National Museums of Kenya. http://www.museums.or.ke/
National Portal of India. http://india.gov.in/
NOVA. http://www.pbs.org/wgbh/nova/
The Palace Museum. http://www.dpm.org.cn
Potosi Documents. http://www.lasalle.edu/~mcinneshin/356/wk06/potosi.htm
Robert C. Williams Museum of Papermaking. http://www.ipst.gatech.edu/amp/index.html
Royal Museums Greenwich. http://www.rmg.co.uk
Russiapedia. http://russiapedia.rt.com/
Salt Institute. http://www.saltinstitute.org
Smithsonian National Museum of African Art. http://africa.si.edu/
Smithsonian National Postal Museum. http://arago.si.edu/
The Story of Africa. http://www.bbc.co.uk/worldservice/africa/features/storyofafrica/index.shtml
Travel China Guide. http://www.travelchinaguide.com
UNESCO. http://en.unesco.org/
World Book Online. http://worldbookonline.com

Index

Aboriginal Australians, 973-979
Abraham, 75-82, 86, 118-119, 137, 141, 145, 188, 271-273, 286, 292, 297, 420
Afghanistan, 233, 376-377, 724, 1020, 1022, 1034
Aksum, 363-370, 998
Albania, 155, 927, 941, 1002-1003
Alexander the Great, 229-234, 237-238, 377, 701
Alexandria (Egypt), 232-233, 237-242, 267, 316, 324, 326, 359, 376-377, 578, 621, 633, 652
Algeria, 154, 381, 512, 666
Andersen, Hans Christian, 849-854
Andorra, 1030, 1035
Angola, 1007, 1028
Antarctica, 32, 35-36, 452, 544, 814-815, 898, 900-903
Antigua & Barbuda, 686, 701, 1015
Arabian Peninsula, 119, 147, 198-199, 263-265, 365, 367-368, 419-423, 502, 544, 548-549, 666, 699, 1019-1022, *see also* Saudi Arabia
Arabian Sea, 89, 198-199, 264, 546, 949-950
Arabs, 263-264, 266, 310, 366, 419-423, 478, 590, 700, 755, 831, 843, 1021-1023
Argentina, 698-699, 838-839, 880, 1002, 1005, 1028-1029
Aristotle, 224-228, 232, 633-634, 902
Armenia/Armenian, 45, 47, 143, 361, 499, 508, 1006
Arms and armor, 257, 287-289, 468, 520, 646, 684, 797, 808-809, 823-824, 836-837, 867-868, 873, 892, 913-914, 926-927, 929, 931-932, 945, 952-953
Assyria, 169-178, 180, 183-184, 187, 190-191, 194, 249, 652, 701, 842, 1022
Augustine (of Hippo), 380-385, 401-402, 516, 573
Augustus Caesar, 258-259, 272, 274, 324-325, 334, 346
Australia, 16, 36, 544, 815, 861, 864, 877, 884-886, 907, 935, 961, 973-979, 987, 996-997, 1015, 1026-1027
Austria (including Austria-Hungary), 289, 382-383, 406, 477, 526-529, 666-667, 699, 707-708, 718, 784, 786-787, 823-826, 867, 912-913, 916, 925-926, 932, 939, 981, 1030
Azerbaijan, 1006

Babylon/Babylonians, 172-175, 178, 180-181, 183-192, 194, 233, 240, 275, 293
Bach, Johann Sebastian, 763-768, 788, 990
Bahamas, 623, 685-686, 1006, 1015
Bahrain, 199, 201, 1024
Bangladesh, 547, 724, 955, 1005-1006, 1015, 1033, 1039
Barbados, 686, 1015, 1035
Belarus, 17, 460, 594, 852, 928, 959
Belgium, 380, 385, 440, 474, 532-533, 647, 717-718, 735, 796-797, 824, 881, 889, 909, 912-913, 928-929, 935, 963
Belize, 427, 1015, 1035, 1039
Benin, 1005
Bermuda, 685-686
Bhutan, 724, 737
Bolivia, 660-664, 838, 935, 1002, 1036-1037
Bosnia and Herzegovina, 155, 912-913
Botswana, 1002, 1015
Brazil, 38, 625, 631, 682, 698, 700, 702, 835-838, 844-845, 847, 918-922, 935, 987, 1028-1029, 1036-1037, 1040
Britain/British, 38, 90, 103, 106, 334-338, 357, 392-393, 398, 429-431, 435, 446, 450, 462, 464, 466-467, 523, 641, 649, 676, 681-689, 701, 712, 735, 743, 748, 759, 773, 784, 786-787, 790-797, 805-809, 817, 823-824, 826, 830-833, 836, 840, 844-847, 857-870, 872-873, 886, 892, 894, 902, 906, 912-916, 927-932, 935-936, 941-942, 945, 949, 951-955, 959, 962, 965-970, 975-978, 981-982, 996, 1011-1018, 1020-1021, 1026, 1028, 1042, *see also* United Kingdom
Brunei Darussalam, 670-672, 676, 1014-1015
Buddhism, 377, 417-418, 503-505, 603, 674-676, 713, 741, 949, 954, 995
Bulgaria (including Bulgars), 232, 460, 519, 564, 941, 988, 1003
Burkina Faso, 556
Burma, *see* Myanmar
Burundi, 1005
Byzantine Empire, 390, 401, 405-411, 441, 444, 453-455, 459, 473-474, 478, 481-482, 562-566, 584-585, 706

Cabo Verde, 1005, 1029
Cambodia, 595, 670-675, 947, 999
Cameroon, 1002-1003, 1015
Canada, 10, 22-23, 38, 394, 451, 539, 631, 636, 682-683, 688-689, 698, 732, 808, 861, 864, 887-888, 899, 905-906, 935-936, 961, 963, 987, 1001, 1015-1016, 1026-1027, 1031-1032, 1036-1037, 1040
Canary Islands, 622-623, 696
Cape of Good Hope, 629-630, 720, 813-818
Caribbean Sea, 394, 446, 619-626, 682-689, 696-699, 701-702, 707, 719, 778, 835, 844, 1015

I-1

Carthage, 135, 159-162, 256, 259, 381, 406
Cell phones/smartphones, 1040, 1043
Central African Republic, 908
Ceylon, *see* Sri Lanka
Chad, 1006
Charlemagne, 439-445, 528, 717
Chartres Cathedral, 487-493, 999
Chile, 597, 625, 699, 749, 769, 838-839, 935, 997, 1002, 1029, 1036
China, 38-39, 111-116, 205-211, 243-248, 263-264, 373-379, 387, 407, 416-417, 494-508, 543-555, 589-590, 603-608, 621, 627, 662, 671, 674-676, 682, 697, 699-701, 714, 724, 741, 755, 829-832, 842, 861, 871, 880, 891-897, 912, 915, 927, 932, 934-935, 939, 944-945, 947, 949, 981, 987, 990-991, 993, 999-1001, 1007, 1027-1028, 1030, 1036-1037, 1040, 1042-1043
Christ the Redeemer (statue), 918-922
Coins, 203, 251, 260, 297, 354, 402, 406, 423, 583, 604, 664, 727, 745, 748, 865
Cold War, 935, 938-948, 983
Colombia, 20-21, 38, 597, 619, 625, 838-839, 935, 961
Columbus, Christopher, 609, 619-627, 658, 695-701, 835, 881
Communism, 895-897, 915, 928, 932, 935, 938-948, 988-994
Comoros, 850
Confucius, 205-211, 245, 416-417, 891
Congo, Democratic Republic of the, 561, 697
Constantine, 339, 357-362, 398, 400, 409-410, 487
Constantinople, 350, 359-361, 369, 376-377, 390-391, 398, 400-402, 405-409, 430, 444, 455, 458-459, 473-475, 478, 562-566, 570, 578, 866
Copernicus, Nicolaus, 633-637
Corsica, 150-151, 154, 821-822
Costa Rica, 702, 935, 1037
Côte d'Ivoire (Ivory Coast), 1037
Crete, 98-102, 131-132, 150-151, 155-156, 212-214, 217, 316, 336, 578
Crimean War, 866-870
Croatia, 39, 152, 155, 351-356, 459-460, 477, 1003
Crusades, 469, 471-481, 485, 488, 578, 653
Cuba, 561, 619-620, 624-625, 701, 753, 844, 847, 907, 935, 946, 993, 1036
Cyprus, 150-151, 155, 238, 313, 469, 477, 578, 613, 698, 1015
Cyril, 458-461, 585
Czech Republic (and Czechoslovakia), 382, 458-461, 486, 524, 540, 706, 932-933, 935, 939, 941, 960, 988-989

David, 16, 141, 143-146, 149, 179-180, 272, 274, 291-292, 295-297, 319, 613, 928
Dead Sea, 278-281, 330, 936
Denmark/Danes, 429, 450, 464-466, 534, 704-707, 823, 849-854, 928-929
Djibouti, 1003, 1028
Dominica, 624, 686, 1007, 1015

Dominican Republic, 620, 625, 681, 695, 702, 935
Dutch, *see* Netherlands/Dutch

East Germany (German Democratic Republic), 763, 941-943, 988-994
East Timor (*see* Timor-Leste)
Easter Island, 749, 769-774, 999
Ecuador, 36-37, 697, 702, 838-839, 935, 1003
Egypt, 6, 50, 56-61, 64-65, 70-71, 76-79, 86, 100, 117-122, 125-129, 138, 144, 146, 150-151, 154, 156, 173-174, 180-181, 190-191, 193, 215, 226, 232-233, 237-242, 250, 258-259, 264, 267, 271, 276, 288, 293, 298, 310, 325-326, 359, 363, 367-369, 422, 430, 476-478, 480, 485, 513, 578, 621, 652, 699, 802, 821, 842, 861-862, 935, 998, 1022, 1024, 1036-1037
Eiffel Tower, 877-882, 996, 998
El Salvador, 427, 935, 1005
Elizabeth I (England), 647-650, 683-684, 688, 691, 744
Elizabeth II (United Kingdom), 684, 692, 963, 978, 1011-1018
England/English, 1, 8, 29, 38-39, 47, 103, 105-110, 145-146, 310, 312, 315, 320, 329, 334-339, 357-358, 361, 398, 430-436, 442, 462-468, 472, 477, 480, 506, 517-518, 520-523, 532-533, 538-539, 593, 631, 643, 645-651, 653, 681-694, 696-702, 713, 721, 734-735, 743-748, 773, 778, 790-798, 802-803, 806-808, 814, 819, 823, 830, 835, 844-848, 851, 857, 862, 868-870, 894, 905-906, 909, 928-929, 951-952, 954, 963, 966-970, 995, 998, 1017, 1026-1029, 1040, *see also* United Kingdom of Great Britain and Northern Ireland
English Channel, 357, 393, 521, 799
Equatorial Guinea, 824
Eritrea, 1005
Estonia, 487, 509, 532, 708, 941
Ethiopia, 39, 53, 55, 196, 312, 316, 363-370, 430, 514, 557, 699, 702, 927, 935, 998
Exodus, 120-124, 129, 140, 145

Fiji, 1007, 1015
Finland, 13, 34, 584, 705, 708, 778, 899
Fishing, 17, 27, 97, 152, 200, 282-283, 317-318, 669, 719, 910, 1035
Flood, 43-49, 141
Forbidden City, 551-555, 607
France/French, 20-21, 122, 151-152, 154, 258, 307, 357, 391, 422, 440-442, 450, 463, 466-467, 471, 473-478, 481, 483, 485, 487-493, 498, 506, 518, 520-523, 530, 536, 557, 569, 571, 590, 593, 612, 631-632, 641-642, 649, 653, 666, 676, 681-683, 688, 696, 698-700, 702, 704-705, 707, 709, 721, 730-736, 745, 751, 755, 758, 773, 786-787, 790, 796-797, 799-812, 817, 821-826, 830, 835-837, 844, 847, 867-869, 874, 877-882, 892, 894, 906-909, 912-917, 920-921, 926, 928, 932, 935, 941, 943, 946, 951, 953, 958, 961, 963, 967, 981, 998-999, 1007, 1021, 1027-1030, 1040
Francis Drake, 649, 683, 696, 814, 983

Francis of Assisi, 480-486
Frederick the Great (Prussia), 783-789, 806

G
Gabon, 1005
Gambia, The, 559
Garden of Eden, 18-25, 27, 349, 980, 1034
Georgia (country), 499, 1003, 1019, 1043
Germany, 84, 133, 184, 187, 222, 273, 401, 406, 429, 441, 444-445, 471, 474, 477-478, 528, 530-537, 573, 590-595, 631, 638-642, 647, 653-654, 679, 696, 698-699, 704-709, 717, 719, 734, 763-768, 776-778, 783-789, 796-797, 803, 823, 826, 850, 857-859, 885, 892, 904-905, 907-908, 911-917, 923-944, 958, 961-963, 981-982, 987-993, 995, 1011, 1016, 1028-1029, 1031, 1037, *see also* Prussia
Ghana, 38, 629, 1002, 1015
Gibraltar, 150-151
Gobi Desert, 245, 494-501, 503, 508
Gold rushes, 874, 883-888
Great Britain, *see* Britain/British
Great Wall of China, 243-248, 376, 387, 499, 891
Great War, *see* World War I
Greece/Greeks, 39, 60, 98-99, 102, 130-134, 150, 153, 155, 157-158, 163-166, 198, 212-234, 238-241, 249-250, 256, 258-259, 263-264, 314-315, 323-326, 334, 336-337, 351, 363, 367, 376-377, 387, 390-391, 409, 422, 430, 450, 456, 459-460, 462, 564, 568, 570-571, 634, 666, 746, 803, 842, 902, 930, 935, 969, 998, 1013, 1028
Greenland, 3, 35, 446, 451, 670, 778, 898-899
Grenada, 685, 702, 1015, 1034
Guatemala, 12, 424-425, 427, 625, 935, 1038
Guinea, 559, 1002
Guinea-Bissau, 385, 559
Gulf of Mexico, 4, 424-425, 619-620, 732
Gutenberg, Johann, 575, 590-595, 803, 905
Guyana, 625, 778, 1015

H
Haiti, 620, 835-836, 838, 844, 847, 953
Hanseatic League, 530-535, 543, 706, 731
Henry the Navigator, 556-561, 621, 665
Henry VIII, 646-650, 691, 1027
Himalayan Mountains, 88-89, 111737-742, 949-950
Hinduism, 674-675, 723-725, 728, 949, 952, 954-955
Hittites, 79, 81, 83-87, 126-127, 183, 187, 336
Holland, *see* Netherlands/Dutch
Holocaust, 928, 932-933, 1021
Holy Roman Empire, 443-444, 478, 481-482, 590, 639, 706, 708-709, 735, 784-787, 926
Honduras, 427, 935, 1028, 1034, 1040
Hong Kong, 861, 864, 873, 892, 894, 896, 1000, 1042
Hungary, 346-350, 390, 499, 519, 595, 641, 666-667, 850-851, 912, 916, 941, 958, 988, 996
Huns, 386-391, 398, 577

I
Iceland, 14, 26, 39-40, 446-452, 899
Inca, 596-602, 660, 663-664, 696, 699
India/Indians, 13, 20-21, 64, 88-89, 196, 198-199, 233, 263-264, 314, 368, 377, 422, 546-548, 621, 629-630, 662, 674-676, 682, 697, 700-701, 707, 713, 723-729, 737, 755-756, 829-832, 842, 861, 863, 865, 867, 869, 880, 935, 949-956, 987, 996, 999, 1001, 1015, 1020, 1026, 1036-1037, 1039-1040, 1042-1043
Indian Ocean, 363, 375, 544-546, 549, 578, 751, 755
Indigenous Americans, 93-97, 424-428, 596-602, 623-626, 658-664, 682, 696-697, 699, 702, 732, 778, 842, 885, 900, 919-920, 976
Indochina, *see* Southeast Asia
Indonesia, 669, 672, 676, 698
Industrial Revolution, 790-798, 871
Iran, 49, 167, 190-198, 200-202, *see also* Persia
Iraq, 68, 184-185
Ireland, 371, 392-397, 689, 698, 790, 792, 862
Isaac, 78-82, 86-87, 118-119, 141, 292, 297, 420
Islam/Muslims, 419-423, 440-441, 454-455, 473-482, 485, 499, 505-506, 511-515, 548, 556-558, 562-566, 570, 583, 607, 621, 630, 652, 665-667, 676, 682, 697, 723-728, 802, 843, 949, 952, 954-955, 1019-1025
Israel, 14, 76-79, 81, 137-149, 153-154, 249-253, 272, 275-286, 289, 291-322, 329-333, 422, 475, 477, 479, 568, 698, 933, 936-937, *see also* Jerusalem
Italy, 20-21, 141, 143, 147, 152, 154, 235, 254-256, 331, 341, 358-359, 381, 444, 478, 507, 517, 541, 569-572, 577-582, 611-618, 621, 631, 653, 927, 962
Ivan the Great, 583-588

J
Jacob, 80-82, 86-87, 117-123, 129, 137, 141, 181, 262, 272, 297, 698, 701
Jamaica, 14, 620, 624-625, 686, 702, 844, 1015, 1031
Japan/Japanese, 13, 207, 209, 345, 412-418, 621, 676, 682, 700, 710-714, 720, 871-876, 892, 894, 897, 900, 912-913, 917, 927, 930-932, 934-935, 937, 944, 958, 962-963, 987, 996, 1026, 1028-1029, 1040-1041
Jerusalem, 15, 47, 144-146, 148, 156, 173, 176-181, 185, 188-189, 196-197, 250-253, 262, 264, 273-276, 279, 283, 285, 291-306, 309-316, 321-322, 329-330, 356, 360, 365, 390, 420-423. 444, 471, 473-478, 488, 506, 568, 656, 666, 1020, 1024-1025
Jesus, 11-16, 22, 24, 27, 44, 49, 67, 82, 124, 149, 182, 211, 223, 228, 252, 271-277, 281-286, 289-290, 293-306, 309-310, 313, 317-322, 338, 349, 410, 420, 471, 478, 488, 515, 535, 613-614, 678, 709, 853-854, 918-922, 994, 1017, 1044
Jewelry, 22, 160, 367, 407, 416, 503, 532, 725, 727, 791, 883
Jews, 178, 188, 196, 240-242, 249-253, 271-277, 282, 285-286, 289, 291-322, 325-333, 341, 348, 353, 420, 422-423, 474, 505, 522, 640, 652-657, 714, 788, 925, 928, 932-933, 937, 954, 959, 969, 1019-1022, 1024
Jordan (country), 6, 28, 257, 263-268, 479, 1022, 1024
Jordan River, 56, 77, 138, 249, 277-283, 311, 360
Julius Caesar, 242, 257-258, 325, 334, 491, 611, 693, 800
Justinian I, 403, 405-411, 481

Kazakhstan, 386, 388, 1003
Kenya, 548, 1013, 1015, 1043
Kiribati, 1015, 1035
Korea, 207, 245, 412-413, 604, 892, see also North Korea and South Korea
Kosovo/Kosovar, 1001-1002, 1006
Kurds, 1002, 1021
Kuwait, 199, 999, 1040
Kyrgyzstan, 20-21, 376, 386

Laos, 670-673, 700, 947, 993
Latvia, 532-533, 708, 941, 1008
Lebanon, 126, 146, 152, 154, 156-158, 259, 935, 1021, 1023
Lesotho, 1008, 1015
Lewis, C. S., 965-970, 981
Liberia, 935, 1029
Libya, 127, 154, 240, 310
Liechtenstein, 1032, 1034-1035
Lindisfarne, 429-436
Lithuania, 122, 584, 655-657, 708, 932, 941, 1006-1007
Louis XIV (France), 730-736, 803, 700
Luther, Martin, 638-642, 646, 706
Lutheran Church, 638-642, 645, 647, 649, 706, 708, 763-768, 776-780, 849, 990
Luxembourg, 717, 928-929, 935, 996

Maccabeans, 249-253, 293, 331
Macedonia, 203, 227, 229-234, 238, 316, 343, 405, 411, 459-461
Machu Picchu, 8, 596-602,
Madagascar, 7, 38, 756, 1005
Malawi, 987, 1015, 1030, 1038
Malaysia/Malays, 546-549, 669-674, 677, 829, 831-832, 880, 997-998, 1015, 1020, 1043
Maldives, 545, 548-549, 1015
Mali, 511-515, 1002, 1005
Malta, 5, 316, 650, 666, 864, 1015
Mansa Musa, 511-515, 525
Marco Polo, 494, 502-508, 578, 621-622
Masada, 279, 281, 329-333
Mauritania, 512, 559
Mauritius, 751-756, 1015
Maya, 424-428, 625, 699, 702
Mediterranean Sea, 50-51, 64-65, 83, 98-100, 130, 150-162, 173, 191, 215, 237-238, 259, 475-476, 481, 562, 666
Methodius, 458-461, 585
Mexico, 16, 20-21, 38, 424-428, 658-659, 661, 677, 698-699, 872, 880, 885, 915, 935, 1026, 1029, 1037, 1040-1041
Micronesia, Federated States of, 7
Ming Dynasty, 244, 545-555, 603-608, 895
Minoans, 98-102, 132
Mogul Empire, see Mughal Empire
Moldova, 1005

Monaco, 154
Mongolia/Mongols, 48, 244, 386-388, 494-501, 504-507, 511, 543, 545, 562-563, 583, 603-604, 674, 724, 741, 981-982
Montenegro, 152, 155, 578
Moravians, 775-780
Morocco, 18, 154, 480, 506, 519, 558-559, 997, 1036
Mozambique, 548-549, 630, 996, 1002, 1005, 1015, 1040
Mughal Empire, 723-729, 951
Muhammad, 419-423, 511, 564, 1022-1023
Music (including instruments and singing), 16, 29, 72, 75, 97, 114, 121, 146, 177, 189, 208, 292, 430, 443, 462, 502, 505, 511, 629, 645, 666, 725-726, 732, 763-768, 786, 788-789, 849, 860, 906, 926, 957, 961-962, 975, 1004, 1006-1007, 1009, 1040
Muslims, see Islam/Muslims
Myanmar, 669, 670-673, 724, 737

Namibia, 1002, 1015
Napoleon Bonaparte, 811, 821-826, 835-836, 838-839, 939
Native Americans, see Indigenous Americans
Nauru, 1015, 1034
Nepal, 27, 377, 724, 737
Netherlands/Dutch, 119, 534, 539, 570, 589, 642, 649-650, 676, 681-682, 688, 696, 698-700, 702, 709, 712, 714-715, 717-722, 734-735, 747, 755, 759, 773, 776, 817, 824, 826, 830-831, 834, 844, 857, 862, 871-872, 919, 925, 928-929, 932, 935, 937, 953, 960, 963, 975, 1001, 1027, 1042
New Guinea (island), 670-671, 974, see also Papua New Guinea
New Zealand, 41, 722, 815, 886, 935, 1002, 1012, 1015
Nicaragua, 625, 698, 935
Nicholls, Douglas, 976-979
Niger, 1002, 1005, 1008, 1029
Nigeria, 696, 1002, 1015, 1037
Nile River, 50-56, 58, 73, 118-119, 127, 150-151, 237, 370, 478
Noah, 43-49, 67, 141, 348, 420, 508, 1033
Normans, 466-468, 478, 482
North Korea (Democratic People's Republic of Korea), 245, 649, 907, 945-946, 993, see also Korea
North Pole, 34-35, 898-903
Northern Ireland, 393-394, 462, 860, 965-968
Norway, 446, 450-451, 467, 490, 704-707, 823, 899, 903, 928-929, 935, 1002, 1030

Olympic Games, 163-166, 325, 894, 958, 963, 1028, 1030-1032
Oman, 199, 201-202
Orthodox Church, 138, 430, 439, 455-457, 458-461, 471-473, 478, 564-566, 585-586, 761, 866-867
Ottoman Empire, 562-566, 570, 665-668, 758-759, 866-869, 912-913, 916, 1020

Index

Pakistan, 22, 88-91, 377, 422, 701, 724, 728, 832, 955, 1015, 1022, 1026
Palau, 1008, 1034
Palenque, 424-428
Palestinians, 1021-1022
Panama, 619, 625, 658, 838, 935
Papua New Guinea, 1002, 1015
Paraguay, 625, 838, 935
Patrick, 392-397
Persia/Persians, 187-188, 190-198, 219, 229-233, 238. 264, 323, 376-377, 406-407, 409, 487, 499, 502, 507, 512, 699, 723, 725, 759, 842, 1022, *see also* Iran
Persian Gulf, 68, 198-202, 252, 263-264, 363, 419, 548-549, 666, 682
Peru, 8, 38, 93-97, 596-602, 625, 660, 696, 838-839, 935, 1002, 1040
Peter (Apostle), 283-284, 300-301, 304-305, 309-322, 349, 423, 429, 524, 571, 608, 709, 714, 722, 762, 775, 780, 834, 1018
Peter the Great (Russia), 759-762
Petra (Jordan), 261-268
Philippines, The, 345, 631, 670-672, 676-677, 931, 935, 1003, 1036
Plato, 224-228, 361, 382-383, 569
Poland, 499, 517, 531-532, 584, 634-637, 652-657, 707-708, 757-758, 786-787, 795, 916, 926, 928-929, 932, 935, 941, 960, 988-989, 991, 1006
Polycarp, 341-345
Porcelain, 504-505, 546, 548, 603-608, 831, 875
Portugal/Portuguese, 130, 476, 518, 557-561, 621-623, 627-631, 653-654, 660, 665, 676-677, 681-682, 697-698, 700, 712, 755, 764, 813-814, 817, 823, 826, 829-830, 836-837, 844, 871, 877, 912, 918-920, 996, 1027
Protestant Reformation, 539-540, 638-642, 646-651, 718, 730, 775-776, 784, 990
Prussia, 783-789, 806, 808, 823-824, 859, 911-912, 939
Pyramids (Americas), 94, 424-427, 659
Pyramids (Egypt), 56-61, 245, 347, 998

Qatar, 199, 201, 1029

Ramses II, 125-129
Reformation, *see* Protestant Reformation
Renaissance (European), 526, 566, 568-574, 579, 586, 611-618, 627, 633, 641, 803
Roman Catholic Church, 345, 429-436, 439, 442-444, 450, 455, 460, 464, 471-493, 520, 528, 536-540, 556, 564, 568-574, 611-618, 624, 634-642, 646-651, 654, 677, 681, 685, 705-708, 713, 720, 730-731, 734, 747-748, 776, 788, 800-801, 822, 863, 867, 920-922, 967, 990, 1031
Roman Empire, 254-260, 272, 274, 286-303, 314-316, 323-362, 398-402, 429, 462, 487, 491, 528, 530, 533, 743-744, 800
Romania, 46, 519, 941, 981, 988, 1004

Russia/U.S.S.R., 5, 23, 314, 319, 361, 386-388, 412, 453-456, 459-461, 499-500, 532, 583-588, 594, 657, 683, 705-707, 721, 757-762, 786-787, 823, 843, 866-870, 872, 874, 892, 894-895, 899, 902, 912-915, 926, 928, 930-932, 934-935, 938, 940-947, 957-959, 981-993, 997, 1004, 1006-1007, 1019-1020, 1029, 1031, 1036
Rwanda, 561, 1015

Sahara Desert, 18, 53, 494, 511-515, 556, 558
Samoa, 1008, 1015
San Marino, 907
São Tomé & Príncipe, 1030
Sardinia, 154, 156
Saudi Arabia, 199, 420-421, 935, 999, 1023, 1037, *see also* Arabian Peninsula
Scotland, 357, 392-393, 431, 446, 462-463, 642, 649-650, 684, 791, 959, 962, 1017
Sea of Galilee, 278-286, 305-306, 317-319, 1021, 1044
Senegal, 27, 559, 1002
Serbia/Serbs, 460, 912-913, 1001, 1006
Seychelles, 544, 1015, 1017
Shakespeare, William, 690-694, 696, 1027
Shang Dynasty, 111-116, 210, 895
Siam, *see* Thailand
Sicily, 150-151, 154, 156, 159, 230, 240, 256, 259, 482
Sierra Leone, 1015
Silk Road, 247, 373-379, 496, 500, 503, 621, 949, 1042
Singapore, 670-671, 675, 827-833, 931, 1015, 1040
Skyscrapers, 995-1000
Slovakia, 461, 852
Slovenia, 155, 577
Socrates, 224-228
Solomon, King, 141, 146-149, 156, 170, 262-264, 284, 292, 365, 369, 420, 665, 897
Solomon Islands, 1005, 1015
Somalia, 548, 1029, 1037
South Africa, 48, 629, 702, 719-720, 778, 813-818, 862, 864, 887, 935, 952-953, 955, 987, 997, 1015, 1026, 1029
South Korea (Republic of Korea), 945-946, 1026, 1029, 1031, 1040, *see also* Korea
South Pole, 35, 898-903
South Sudan, 53, 364
Southeast Asia (Indochina),
Soviet Union, *see* Russia/U.S.S.R.
Space exploration, 245, 980-987
Spain/Spanish, 6, 19-21, 130, 152, 154, 160, 256, 258-259, 400-401, 407, 422, 425, 441, 476, 485, 557, 609, 621-627, 631, 646, 648-651, 653-654, 658-664, 666, 677, 681, 683-684, 686-688, 696-698, 701-702, 704, 707, 709, 712, 718, 734-735, 773, 775, 823, 826, 835, 837-840, 844, 847, 877, 879, 883-884, 912, 919, 940, 947, 1007, 1027, 1029, 1036-1037
Spice Road, 261-268, 419, 949, 1042
Sri Lanka (Ceylon), 263, 367, 546, 719, 723, 995, 1015, 1041
St. Kitts & Nevis, 686, 1012, 1015

St. Lucia, 685, 702, 1015, 1034

St. Vincent & The Grenadines, 625, 1015

Stained Glass, 47, 146, 271, 307, 310, 312, 315, 320-321, 343, 380, 385, 440, 442, 485, 492, 523, 539, 800, 802

Stamps (postage), 187, 385, 431, 444, 461, 500, 507, 547, 550, 561, 570, 574, 588, 594-595, 603, 608, 613, 622, 625, 629-631, 638, 648-649, 657-658, 676, 691, 698, 702, 705, 708, 721-722, 730, 732, 745, 747, 753, 763, 778, 795, 798, 807, 809-810, 824, 831, 836, 848, 850-852, 864, 876, 886, 892, 900, 904, 906-909, 939, 944, 981-982, 987-988, 993, 1003, 1005-1006, 1008, 1011-1015, 1017-1018, 1020, 1028-1030

Stonehenge, 103, 105-110, 998

Sudan, 53, 364-365, 511, 1005, 1037

Sumer/Sumerians, 49, 62, 64-65, 67-70, 75, 86, 90, 842

Sun Yat-sen, 891-897

Suriname, 688, 778, 844

Swaziland, 1006, 1015

Sweden, 450, 532, 698, 704-709, 758-759, 899, 932, 987, 1029-1030, 1040

Switzerland/Swiss, 48, 267, 641, 730, 826, 881, 885, 963, 1028-1029, 1033, 1040

Syria, 64, 85, 100, 126, 155-156, 173, 178, 232-233, 238, 250-252, 264, 313, 322, 376-377, 386, 421-422, 430, 473-475, 478, 487, 699, 802, 935, 1021-1022

Taiwan, 206, 892, 896-897, 944-945, 998, 1001

Tajikistan, 376, 724

Tanzania, 8, 699, 1015

Telephone, 905, 909, 958, 1042, *see also* Cell phones

Television, 957-964, 984, 987

Terra-cotta, 91, 171, 178, 208, 247-248, 260, 428, 809

Thailand/Siam, 546, 633, 670-672, 674, 676, 697, 880, 1007, 1027

Tibet, 31, 111, 671, 737-742, 944

Tibetan Plateau, 88, 111-112, 494

Timor-Leste, 670-671, 678

Togo, 613, 1002

Tonga, 1015, 1032

Tower of Babel, 49-50, 63, 83, 184, 975, 995

Trinidad & Tobago, 624, 1003, 1015

Tunisia, 135, 154, 159-162, 666, 802, 1036

Turkey, 12, 45, 62, 64, 76, 80, 83-87, 143, 150, 155, 173, 323-328, 342, 344, 357, 359, 362, 409-410, 506, 562-566, 607, 665-668, 719, 916, 935, 1002, 1019, 1027, 1036-1037, *see also* Ottoman Empire

Turkmenistan, 1004

Tuvalu, 1015, 1017

U.S.S.R./Soviets, *see* Russia/U.S.S.R.

Uganda, 52, 1003, 1006, 1015

Ukraine, 386-387, 437, 453-457, 460, 583, 594, 767, 866, 928, 998, 1020, 1037

United Arab Emirates, 199, 201, 574, 999-1000

United Kingdom, 1, 8, 39, 462, 648-649, 691, 745, 747, 848, 870, 927, 934-935, 938, 943-944, 959, 962-963, 1001, 1011-1018, 1026, *see also* England, Northern Ireland, Scotland, and Wales

United States, 11, 12, 15, 19, 20-21, 35, 38, 48, 185, 221-222, 245, 262, 405, 594-595, 619, 624-625, 660, 682, 684-685, 689, 696, 698-699, 701, 732, 734, 778-779, 795-798, 805-812, 822, 834-835, 838-840, 844-847, 852, 857, 861, 869, 871-877, 879, 884-888, 892-894, 896, 899-900, 902-903, 905-910, 912, 915-917, 929-932, 934-937, 938, 941-947, 955, 957-960, 962-964, 968-970, 982-987, 989, 993, 996-999, 1012, 1021, 1023, 1026-1031, 1036-1037, 1040-1042

Uruguay, 838, 935, 1007, 1028-1029, 1036

Uzbekistan, 376-377

Vanuatu, 1015, 1035, 1038

Vatican City, 257, 259, 612, 614, 642, 1001

Venezuela, 619-620, 624, 837-839, 935, 962

Victoria (United Kingdom), 855, 857-865, 909, 1011, 1013

Vietnam, 207, 543, 546, 548, 622, 670-671, 673-674, 880-881, 946-948, 964, 993, 1036-1037, 1040

Waldensians, 536-537

Wales, 38, 108, 335, 392, 462-463, 518, 962, 965, 1034

West Germany (Federal Republic of Germany), 941-943, 963, 992, 1029

Western Sahara, 558-559

Wilberforce, William, 819, 845-848

World Cup, 1028-1029

World War I, 911-917, 939, 953, 978, 1020-1021

World War II, 345, 788, 905, 925-939, 944, 954, 960, 968, 978, 981-982, 1011-1012, 1021, 1028, 1043

Yemen, 263-264, 957, 1019

Yiddish, 654

Zambia, 1008, 1015, 1035, 1038

Zheng He, 543-550, 603, 627, 630, 674, 949

Zimbabwe, 38, 1002

Visit our website for more exciting homeschool curriculum that helps you teach the heart, soul, and mind.

www.notgrass.com